ON LINE

Daily Life in
Medieval Times

Daily Life in
Medieval Times

A Vivid, Detailed Account of Birth, Marriage and Death; Food, Clothing and Housing; Love and Labor in the Middle Ages

BY FRANCES AND JOSEPH GIES

BLACK DOG
& LEVENTHAL
PUBLISHERS
NEW YORK

PUBLISHED BY

Black Dog & Leventhal Publishers, Inc.
151 W 19th St.
New York, NY 10011

DISTRIBUTED BY

Workman Publishing Company
708 Broadway
New York, NY 10003

Photo direction and captions by Ted Goodman
Photo research by Diana Gongora
Design by Martin Lubin Graphic Design

h g f e d c b a

Library of Congress Cataloging-in-Publication Data

Gies, Frances.
    Daily life in medieval times / by Frances & Joseph Gies.
        p. c.m.
    Includes bibliographical references (p.   ) and index.
    ISBN 1-57912-069-5
    1. Civilization, Medieval. 2. Social history--Medieval,
500-1500. 3. Europe--Social life and customs. 4. City and town
life--Europe--History--To 1500. 5.Villages--Europe--History--To
1500. 6. Castles--Europe--History--To 1500. 7. Chepstow Castle.
I. Gies, Joseph. II. Title.
CB353.G477 1999
940. 1--dc21   98-56015

Manufactured in Hong Kong

ALSO BY FRANCES GIES:

The Knight in History (1984)

Joan of Arc (1981)

ALSO BY FRANCES AND JOSEPH GIES:

Marriage and the Family in the Middle Ages (1987)

Women in the Middle Ages (1978)

The Ingenious Yankees (1976)

Merchants and Moneymen: The Commercial Revolution, 1000–1500

Leonard of Pisa and the New Mathematics of the Middle Ages

ACKNOWLEDGMENTS

This book was researched at the Harlan Hatcher Graduate Library of the University of Michigan.

The authors gratefully acknowledge the assistance of Professor J. A. Raftis of the Pontifical Institute of Mediaeval Studies in Toronto, Mr. Alan Clark of Elton, Miss Kate Chantry of the Cambridgeshire Public Record Office in Huntingdon, Dr. Sylvia L. Thrupp, Alice Freeman Palmer professor of history at the University of Michigan; Dr. John F. Benton, professor of history at the California Institute of Technology; Dr. J. Lee Shneidman, assistant professor of history at Adelphi College; and Dr. Peter Riesenberg, professor of history at Washington University, St. Louis, John Benton, Professor C. Warren Hollister of the University of California at Santa Barbara, the Northwestern University Library, the British Museum, the British Department of the Environment, the Sterling Library of Yale University, and the Newberry Library of Chicago.

Special acknowledgment is due to four people who helped make the construction of a Gothic cathedral come to life: Rowan and Irene Le Compte, stained-glass artists and creators of windows for the Washington Cathedral; and R. T. Feller and John Fanfani, Clerk of the Works and Assistant Clerk of the Works at the Washington Cathedral.

Finally, mention should be made of the numerous French citizens, from archivists to First World War widows in charge of national monuments, who helped us during our research in France.

CONTENTS

SECTION I
LIFE IN A MEDIEVAL CASTLE

PROLOGUE
CHEPSTOW CASTLE

North of the Severn suspension bridge, on the Welsh border in Monmouthshire, Chepstow Castle rises from a narrow ridge commanding the River Wye, a broad, shallow stream that fluxes daily with the tidal Severn from a navigable river to a nearly dry mud flat.

From the opposite bank of the Wye, the castle presents the image of a rugged and almost intact stone fortress, of immense length (nearly seven hundred feet), oriented east-west, its battlemented walls buttressed by several powerful towers, both square and cylindrical. The stone, varying from gray limestone to yellow and dark red sandstone, reinforces the towers' suggestion of more than one period of construction.

Entry to the castle is through the Great Gate-house at the eastern end, leading to a large grassy court-yard some two hundred feet square. South from the gatehouse extends a forty-foot-high wall that ends at the castle's southeast corner in an enormous tower, flat on the inner side, semicircular on the outer, known as Marten's Tower, a designation it acquired late in its history when Henry Marten, a seventeenth-century political prisoner, was confined in it for the last twenty years of his life. On the north side, facing Marten's Tower, an array of thirteenth-century buildings known as the domestic range hugs the wall overlooking the river. Examined more closely, the domestic range resolves into two large stone halls, with chambers, cellars, store-rooms, and—positioned directly over the river latrines.

This easternmost court is known as the Lower

Bailey. Beyond it to the west, with access through a tower-guarded inner gate, lies the Middle Bailey, another walled enclosure. At its farther end, oriented like the entire castle east and west and almost completely occupying the narrowest part of the ridge, rises the Great Tower. Now a floorless, roofless shell with half its upper story destroyed, the Great Tower is the oldest part of Chepstow, originally built in the eleventh century, and until the construction of the domestic range the center of the castle's life. Twice remodeled, with a third story added to its initial two, Chepstow Castle in its earliest form can here be identified by masonry and architectural detail: huge yellow stone blocks in the base supporting walls of smaller, rougher yellow stone, pierced by small roundheaded (Romanesque) windows and doorways with similar arches, or with square lintels. The first remodeling, in the second quarter of the thirteenth century, marked by rough limestone masonry, added a third story to the western third of the tower and enlarged the openings of the second story, converting them into pointed-arch (Gothic) windows and doors, with elaborate carved decoration. The final addition late in the thirteenth century of the eastern two-thirds of the upper story is indicated by the use of roughly-squared rubble and red sandstone.

On the northern side of the Great Tower runs a passageway known as the Gallery, once timber-covered, squeezed between the Great Tower and the wall fronting the river. Another fortified gate (now gone) once guarded the entrance from the Gallery into the third and westernmost courtyard, the Upper Bailey, at the end of which stands a rectangular tower built to command the western gateway of the castle. This entry was further strengthened by the addition of an outer walled enclosure, or barbican, with its own gatehouse, marking the western extremity of the castle.

Despite the disappearance of timber roofs, floors, and outbuildings, and the dilapidation of the upper part of some walls and towers, Chepstow Castle is exceptionally well preserved. In size, strength, and setting, it is one of the most imposing of the great medieval castles of Europe, the more impressive for the fact that it is unmarred by modern restoration. Its assemblage represents three centuries of castle-building; its lords were four powerful Anglo-Norman families. The weathered stones speak in unmistakable accents of an age of hardihood, few comforts, and much danger, an age dominated by Chepstow and all the other castles from Scandinavia to Italy. Everywhere in Europe in the High Middle Ages the castle played a crucial role: military, political, social, economic, cultural. In England an extraordinary historical context made its career especially dramatic, and England today has one of the richest collections of medieval castle ruins of all the lands where castles appeared—one authority asserts there are remnants of at least fifteen hundred.

How such castles came to be built, their function in history, and especially the life that filled them during their thirteenth-century day of glory, is the subject of this book. Because Chepstow illustrates many of the features of castle architecture and living arrangements, and because its lords were among the foremost barons of their time, the story will center around Chepstow. Other castles, in England and on the Continent, will also be freely drawn on, since the exploration of one castle, even a Chepstow, does not suffice to illustrate all the many facets of the life within and surrounding the medieval castle.

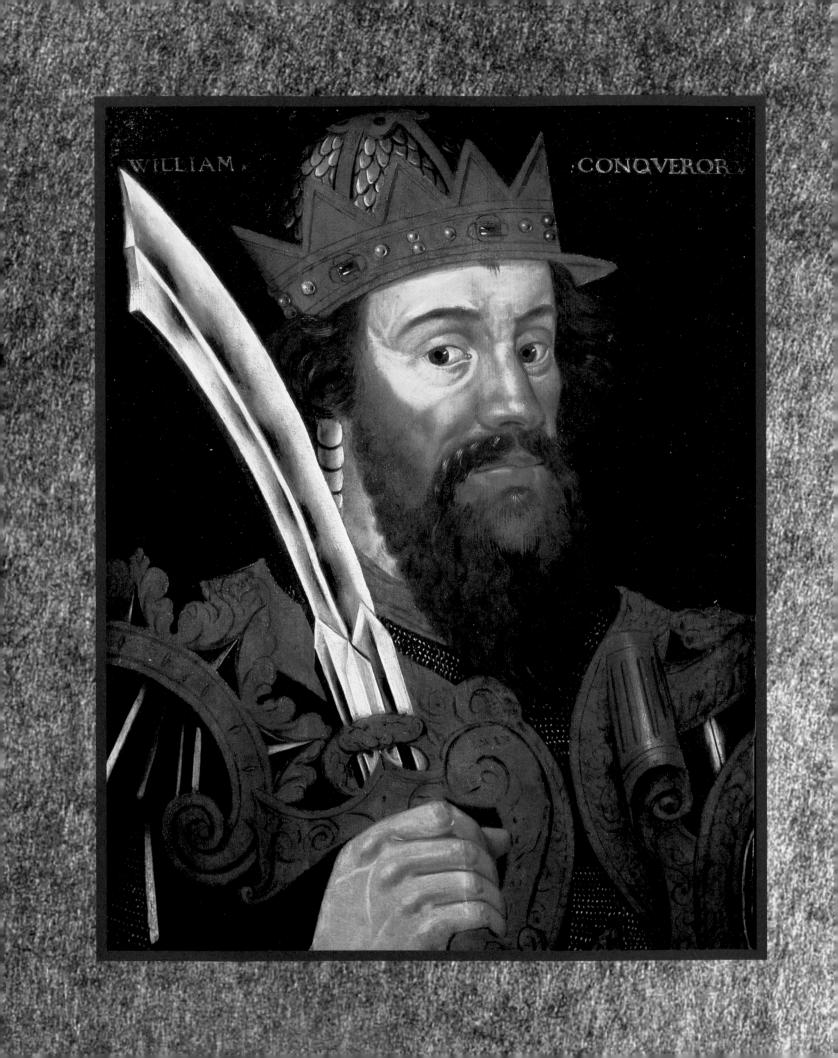

WILLIAM · CONQVEROR ·

I

THE CASTLE COMES TO ENGLAND

O n the morning of September 28, 1066, nearly a thousand double-ended, open longboats, each mounting a single square sail, suddenly appeared off the coast of England at Pevensey, about forty miles southwest of Dover. As the boats ran up on the beach, some seven thousand armed men leaped from them and waded ashore. The army of Duke William of Normandy, after waiting weeks for a favorable wind, had crossed seventy miles of water in a single night to enforce their leader's claim to the English throne. Recruited not only from his own vassals in Normandy, but from mercenaries and adventurers throughout northern France and even farther away, it was for the eleventh century not only a very large but an exceptionally well disciplined force, a tribute to the authority as well as the financial resources of Duke William.

England had seen many seaborne invading forces,

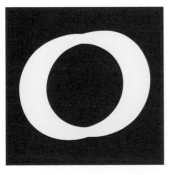

Portrait of William I, The Conqueror (1027–87) English School (16th c.).

but probably never one this large. A novel feature of Duke William's amphibious army was its horses, no fewer than three thousand of which had been successfully ferried across the Channel by means of a technique—probably some kind of sling-harness—that Norman soldiers of fortune apparently learned from the Byzantine Greeks. Carried in the flotilla was a prefabricated fort, the timbers cut, shaped, framed, and pinned together in France, dismantled, packed in great barrels, and loaded on the ships. Disembarking at Pevensey, the Normans had the reassembled fort complete by evening.

The timber fort at Pevensey was an omen. Norman chronicler Ordericus Vitalis made the highly significant observation that in Saxon England there were "but few of the fortresses which the Normans call castles." The whole of England in 1066 had perhaps half a dozen: one in Essex, near the east coast; three in Hereford, near the Welsh border; one at Arundel, in Sussex, near the Channel (all built by Norman knights in the service of Edward the Confessor); and finally, one at Dover, built by Edward's successor and William's rival, King Harold Godwinson. Most if not all of these were of timber and earthwork, like nearly all the castles on the Continent.

Jean de Colmieu described the typical "motte-

and-bailey" castle of northern France:

> It is the custom of the nobles of the neighborhood to make a mound of earth as high as they can and then encircle it with a ditch as wide and deep as possible. They enclose the space on top of the mound with a palisade of very strong hewn logs firmly fixed together, strengthened at intervals by as many towers as they have means for. Within the enclosure is a house, a central citadel or keep which commands the whole circuit of the defense. The entrance to the fortress is across a bridge . . . supported on pairs of posts . . . crossing the ditch and reaching the upper level of the mound at the level of the entrance gate [to the enclosure].

Requiring no skilled labor, such motte-and-bailey castles were quick and cheap to construct. They had a further advantage in that they were basically independent of considerations of terrain, and could be built anywhere that a fortification was needed. The motte, or mound, was steep-sided, sometimes partly natural, sometimes wholly artificial, formed in part by soil from the encircling ditch. Flat-topped, roughly circular, usually one hundred to three hundred feet in diameter at the base and anywhere from ten to one hundred feet high, the motte was crowned by a wall of timber palisades. The "central citadel or keep" was hardly more than a blockhouse or tower, usually of wood, though occasionally, where stone was plentiful, of masonry. The tower was too small to house more than the lord or the commander (castellan) of the castle and his immediate family, and the entire space of the motte was too restricted to accommodate the garrison with its animals

and supplies except on an emergency basis.

Therefore a much larger space was cleared below the motte, given its own ditch and palisade, and connected to the upper fort by an inclined trestle with a drawbridge. This lower court, or bailey, was roughly circular or oval, its exact shape depending on the contours of the land. Sometimes there were two baileys, or even three, in front of the mound or on either side of it. The sense of the arrangement was that the garrison could use the whole interior of motte and bailey for everyday living, secure against minor attacks. In case of a serious threat, the garrison crowded up into the steep-walled motte.

Despite their scarcity in England, such motte-and-bailey castles were numerous on the Continent. Fortification was, of course, an ancient art, widely practiced even in pre-Roman Europe. The castle built by King Harold at Dover occupied the site of (and made use of) a Roman fort that had itself taken over the site of a much earlier Iron Age stronghold. The Roman legions were famed for their skill at fortification, building ditched and walled ramparts in a matter of hours at whatever point they encamped. If a legion remained long in one place, it habitually turned the temporary castrum into a permanent stone fortress. At least eight other Roman fortresses besides Dover dotted the old "Saxon shore" of eastern England to fend off third- and fourth-century pirates. Elsewhere, too, the Romans built large stone fortresses, often taking advantage, as at Dover, of Iron Age ruins. The immense fortified village of Old Sarum was another such Roman renewal of older works.

Nevertheless, the Roman constructions were not really castles in the sense of a later day. They were forts built to be manned by large professional garrisons, and consequently they were not required to have great intrinsic defensive strength. Essentially they were all, like the largest Roman fortification in England, Hadrian's Wall, of value only as long as they were fully manned.

The burghs built by the Romans' Saxon successors were similarly fortifications but not castles—communally owned, walled enclosures protecting towns, each encompassing a much larger area than that of a castle, and defended by a large garrison. The ancestor of the true castle, capable of defense by a small garrison,

Exterior of Dover Castle, Dover, Kent, built in the 1180s for Henry II.

Detail from the Bayeux Tapestry showing William the Conqueror and preparations for the Battle of Hastings (11th c.).

was pioneered by the "Eastern Romans," the Byzantine Greeks, especially during the sixth-century campaigns of Belisarius in North Africa. Ain Tounga, built in Tunisia, consisted of a polygonal wall of thick masonry, with high towers at the corners and a gate tower to protect the entrance. One of the corner towers was elaborated to serve as the garrison's ultimate refuge, or as the Europeans who adopted the Byzantine model a few centuries later called it, the "keep" or "donjon." The Muslims adopted the Byzantine art of masonry fortification, using it in Spain in the eighth and ninth centuries to build hundreds of hilltop castles strengthened by square towers, a form later imitated by the Christians in the Reconquest.

The true castle—the private fortress—first appeared in northwest Europe in the ninth century, by no coincidence the period of the devastating raids by Vikings and Saracens. By 863, when Charles the Bald, Charlemagne's grandson, ordered castles to be built against the invaders, castle-building was probably already under way. The decentralized character of the Carolingian state dictated that the new strongholds should be for the most part in the hands of dukes, counts, and barons who lived in them with their families, servants, and armed retainers. Technology and economics determined that they be constructed of earth and wood. Rough-and-ready motte-and-bailey castles sprang up all over France, Germany, Italy, and the Low Countries.

Castle construction had a profound effect on the European political scene. Not only could a castle block invasion of a region, but it could also provide effective control over the local population. Both aspects of the castle were well understood in Continental Europe, where the owners of castles were soon unchallenged owners of power.

Yet when William invaded England, King Harold, whose castles were few and scattered, had to put his kingdom at hazard on the result of a single pitched battle. His army fought well at Hastings through the long bloody day of October 14, but in the end it was overcome, apparently after a ruse by the Norman horsemen, who pretended to flee and drew some of the defenders down from their hillside position. King Harold was slain along with his two brothers and most of his best troops.

The intensity of the battle and its decisive character were typical of eleventh-century fighting. Two battles just fought in the north, Harold Hardraada's victory over the earls of Mercia and Northumberland at Gate Fulford, and Harold Godwinson's victory over Hardraada at Stamford Bridge, had been very similar. Evidently the relative ineffectiveness of missile weapons forced eleventh-century armies to engage at close quarters. It is not surprising, therefore, that despite his own severe losses William found himself on October 15 in command of the only serious fighting force in England.

In addition, the death of Harold and his brothers left William with a virtually uncontested claim to the throne. Yet the ease with which he now completed the conquest of England is astonishing, and was certainly due in no small measure to the scarcity of English castles. Of those that did exist, only Dover was situated to embarrass William, and Dover surrendered at his approach, probably because its garrison had fought and been destroyed at Hastings.

His coastal base secure, William turned west, and after a tentative raid on London by some of the cavalry, moved in a wide arc to cut the capital off from the interior. With no castle to obstruct his movements, he swung his army completely around London from southeast to northwest, and the isolated city submitted. On Christmas Day William was crowned, and had himself presented to his new subjects by the archbishop of York, speaking English, and the bishop of Coutances, speaking French. Londoners were promptly set to work

Exterior of Chepstow Castle, South Wales (1070–1300) with the River Wye in foreground.

to build a castle. Inside the Roman city walls, on the Thames shore between the city and the sea, this original Tower of London was apparently of earth and timber. It was replaced a dozen years later by the square stone bulk of the White Tower.

When early in 1067 William left England for a stay in Normandy, he took additional precautions, completing another castle, at Winchester, the most important city in

southwest England, and entrusting it to William Fitz Osbern, described by Ordericus Vitalis as "the best officer in his army" and "the bravest of all the Normans." The king gave Dover Castle—much strengthened—and the Kent countryside into the hands of his own half-brother, Odo, bishop of Bayeux, and made the two men co-justiciars, or regents, with the task of extending the castle complex outward from the Dover–London–Winchester triangle. The native population was ruthlessly conscripted for labor service. Fitz Osbern and Odo "wrought castles widely throughout the land and oppressed the poor people," soberly recorded *The Anglo-Saxon Chronicle*.

During William's absence, an insurrection broke out in the southeast that gained support from Count Eustace of Boulogne, a disaffected French baron, revealing an unforeseen potential danger to the regime. The rebellion failed in its objective of capturing Dover Castle, and the castle garrison, by a surprise sortie, routed the rebels. On Christmas of 1067 William was back in England, but the next three years saw several fresh insurrections, sometimes abetted by foreign aid from Denmark, Scotland, and Wales. William's response was unvarying: to suppress the rebels and to build a new castle on the spot. "He gave the custody of castles to some of his bravest Normans," wrote Ordericus, "distributing among them vast possessions as inducements to undergo cheerfully the tolls and perils of defending them."

After Hastings, William had seized the estates of Anglo-Saxon landowners killed in the battle to reward his chief lieutenants, but had left most of the lands of the English nobility untouched. Now he confiscated English lands right and left, "raising the lowliest of his Norman followers to wealth and power," as Ordericus noted. Several thousand separate English holdings were combined into fewer than two hundred great estates called honors, nearly all in the hands of Normans. Where an original English landholder retained possession, he was dropped one level in the feudal hierarchy, becoming subject to a Norman lord who held his honor as a tenant-in-chief of the king. The entire county of Hereford, on the border of Wales, fell to

Tower of London (White Tower) with Charles, Duke of Orleans seated in the foreground writing (c.1500).

William Fitz Osbern, the duke's faithful right hand. Fitz Osbern transferred his headquarters from Dover to Chepstow, or Strigull, as it was sometimes called, from a Welsh word meaning "the bend" (in the River Wye).

Either because of the rocky site or the strategic location, or both, Fitz Osbern determined to build his castle of stone. The rectangular keep that rose on the narrow ridge above the Wye was consequently one of the strongest in Norman England, its menacing bulk suggesting not merely a barrier to contain the Welsh but a base for aggression against them.

Chepstow was one of the few Anglo-Norman castles not sited to command an important town. Sometimes instead of a city causing a castle to be built, the reverse was true, as craftsmen and merchants settled close by for protection and to serve the castle household. One English example of such a castle-originated city is Newcastle-on-Tyne, which grew up around the stronghold built by William the Conqueror's son Robert to command the Tyne crossing. Several of the chief cities of Flanders were castle-derived: Ghent, Bruges, Ypres.

By 1086, when at William's orders the elaborate survey of his conquered territory known as *The Domesday Book* was compiled, the iron grip of the invading elite was beyond shaking. Only two native Englishmen held baronies as tenants-in-chief of the king in the whole of England from Yorkshire south. English chronicler William of Malmesbury commented, "Perhaps the king's behavior can be excused if he was at times quite severe with the English, for he found scarcely any of them faithful. This fact so irritated his fierce mind that he took from the greater of them first their wealth,

The Domesday Book (1085–86), the general survey of Britain ordered by William the Conqueror.

then their land, and finally, in some instances, their lives."

William died the following year, 1087, bequeathing to his elder son, Robert, the rich old domain of Normandy, and to his younger son, William Rufus, the family's new realm of England. But though the English were now docile under their immense bridle of castles, the castles were now showing another aspect. Unchallenged centers of local power, they corrupted the loyalty of their Norman owners, who threw off their feudal obligations to assert the rights of petty sovereigns. In 1071 loyal William Fitz Osbern had been killed fighting in Flanders and his estates divided between his sons, the younger, Roger de Breteuil, inheriting his father's English lands, including Chepstow Castle. In 1074 Roger and his brother-in-law, the Breton Ralph de Guader, earl of Norfolk, had organized a rebellion, "fortifying their castles, preparing arms and mustering soldiers." King William crushed this rebellion of his Norman followers like so many previous English outbreaks, and made an effort to conciliate its leaders. To the captive lord of Chepstow he sent an Easter box of valuable garments, but sulky Roger threw the royal gifts into the fire. Roger was then locked up for life and Chepstow Castle confiscated.

By the turn of the twelfth century the half dozen English castles of 1066 had grown to the astounding number of more than five hundred. Most were of timber, but over the next century nearly all were converted to masonry as a revolution in engineering construction swept Europe. New techniques of warfare and the increasing affluence of the resurgent West, giving kings

The First Crusade sets sail from *Li Romans de Godefroy de Buillon et de Salehadin* (14th c.).

Ruins of Crusader Castle of Krak des Chevaliers in Syria built by the Knights Hospitalers (1131).

and nobles augmented revenues from taxes, tolls, markets, rents, and licenses, brought a proliferation of stone fortresses from the Adriatic to the Irish Sea.

A major contributor to the sophistication of the new castles was the extraordinary event known to the late eleventh century as the Crusade, and to subsequent generations as the First Crusade. Of the peasants and knights who tramped or sailed to the Holy Land and survived the fighting, most soon returned home. The defense of the conquered territory was therefore left to a handful of knights—primarily the new military brotherhoods, the Templars and the Hospitallers. Inevitably their solution was the same as that of William the Conqueror, but the castles they built were from the start large, of complex design, and of stone. The Crusaders made use of the building skills of their sometime Greek allies and their Turkish enemies, improved by their own experience. The results were an astonishing leap forward to massive, intricately designed fortresses of solid masonry. The new model of castle spread at once to western Europe, including England.

On the Continent, even before the Crusade, where conditions were favorable, powerful keeps were sometimes built of stone, like that constructed by Fulk Nerra at Langeais on the Loire about A.D. 1000 or Brionne Castle in Normandy (early eleventh century), or like the keeps built by the Normans after their conquest of

southern Italy and in the eleventh century. The baileys that accompanied such stone keeps were probably defended by timber stockades. Between the Conquest and the Crusade a few stone castles appeared in England.

Some of the new structures were conversions of motte-and-bailey castles to "shell keeps" by the erection of a stone wall to replace the timber stockade atop the motte. Within this new stone wall, living quarters were built, usually of timber, either against the wall to face a central courtyard or as a free-standing tower or hall.

In many cases the mound was too soft to support a heavy stone wall, and the new stronghold had to be erected on the lower, firmer ground of the barley. These new keeps were usually rectangular in plan. Sometimes they were built on high or rocky ground, but site was still not a significant factor. All over northern France in the eleventh century new rectangular stone keeps rose on low or high ground, while in England William Fitz Osbern's castle at Chepstow was joined by the White Tower of London and the keeps at Canterbury and Colchester. The old wooden palisades of the barley were now replaced by a heavy stone "curtain wall," made up of cut stone courses enclosing a rubble core and "crenelated," that is, crowned with battlements of alternating solid parts (merlons) and spaces (crenels), creating a characteristic square-toothed pattern. The curtain wall was further strengthened with towers.

In the twelfth century rectangular stone keeps continued to multiply—in England at Dover, Kenilworth, Sherborne, Rochester, Hedingham, Norwich, Richmond, and elsewhere, with thick walls rising sixty feet or more. Usually entrance was on the second story,

Interior view of the Great Hall, Castle Hedingham, Essex, Great Britain (c.1130).

reached by a stairway built against the side of the keep and often contained in and protected by a forebuilding. The principal room, the great hall, was on the entrance floor, with chambers opening off it; the ground floor, windowless or with narrow window slits, was used for storage. A postern or alternate gate, protected by towers, frequently opened on another side of the curtain. A well, often descending to a great depth, was an indispensable element of a keep, its water pipe carried up through two or three floors, with drawing places at each floor.

Gradually experience revealed a disadvantage in the rectangular keep. Its corners were vulnerable to the sapper, or miner, and the battering ram, and afforded shelter to attackers in the form of "dead ground" that defensive fire could not reach. The Byzantines and Saracens were the first to build circular or multiangular towers, presenting no screen to the enemy at any point. But the rectangular plan remained more convenient for organizing interior space, and the European transition was gradual. For a while engineers experimented with keeps that were circular on the outside and square on the inside. Or keeps were built closely encircled by a high wall called a chemise. Entry was by a gateway in the chemise, from which one climbed a flight of steps against its interior face, and the steps led to a wall walk, which was connected to the keep by a bridge or causeway with a draw section. The drawbridge might be pulled back on a platform in front of the gate, or it might be hinged on the inner side and raised by chains on the outer so that when closed it stood vertically against the face of the gate, forming an additional barrier. Or it might turn on a horizontal pivot, dropping the inner section into the pit while the outer rose to block the gateway. An attacking enemy had to force the gate, climb the stairs, follow the wall walk, and defile across the causeway, exposed to attack from all directions.

The Tour de César in Provins, east of Paris, built in the middle of the twelfth century on the mound of an earlier motte-and-bailey, had a keep that was square below and circular above, the two elements joined by an octagonal second floor. Four semicircular turrets rose from the corners of the base, while a battlemented chemise ran around the edge of the mound and down into the bailey. Entrance was by a vaulted stairway up the mound leading to the chemise, whence a causeway and drawbridge connected with the tower itself.

Other elaborations appeared. Vertical sliding doors, or portcullises, oak-plated and shod with iron, and operated from a chamber above with ropes or chains and pulleys, enhanced the security of gateways. Machi-

Exterior view of the eighteen-sided Keep with three square turrets built for Henry II, Orford Castle, Suffolk, Great Britain (1165–72).

colations—overhanging projections built out from the battlements, with openings through which missiles and boiling liquids could be dropped—were added, at first in wood, later in stone. The curtain walls were protected by towers built close enough together to command the intervening panels. Arrow loops, or *meurtrières* ("murderesses"), narrow vertical slots, pierced the curtains at a level below the battlements. Splayed, or flared to the inside, these gave the defending archer room to move laterally and so cover a broad field of fire while presenting only the narrow exterior slit as a target. A recess on the inner side sometimes provided the defender with a seat.

By the later twelfth century, older castles were being renovated in the light of the new military technology. Henry II gave Dover a great rectangular inner keep with walls eighty-three feet high and seventeen to twenty-one feet thick, with elaborate new outworks. At Chepstow the castle's most famous owner, William Marshal, built a new curtain wall, with gateway and towers, around the eastern bailey, one of the earliest defenses in England to use round wall towers and true arrow loops. In the second quarter of the thirteenth century William's sons added the barbican on the west, defended by its own ditch and guarded by a tower. On the east they built a large new outer bailey, with a double-towered gatehouse closed by two portcullises

Exterior view of the Keep, Colchester Castle, Essex, Great Britain (11th c.), that was built on the site of the Roman temple to Claudius.

and defended by two lines of machicolations. A successor, Roger Bigod III, completed the fortifications by building the western gatehouse, finished about 1272, to protect the barbican, and constructing the great Marten's Tower at the southeast corner of the curtain walls, begun about 1283 and completed in the 1290s. Increased security permitted the building of the new range of stone domestic buildings along the north wall, including a spacious great hall, completed in time for a visit by Edward I in December 1285.

New castles built in the thirteenth century showed even more clearly the impact of Crusader experience. They were sited wherever possible on the summit of a hill, with the inner bailey backed against the more precipitous side, and the main defense was constructed to face the easier slope. Two or three lines of powerful fortifications might front the approach side, making it possible, as at Chepstow, to abandon the keep as a residence for more comfortable quarters in the secure bailey. These quarters were often built of timber, while the stone keep, now usually round, and smaller but stronger, became the last line of defense and served during a siege as the lord's or castellan's command post. Stairways and passages, sometimes concealed, facilitated the movement of defense forces. Occasionally the keep

was isolated within its own moat, spanned by a drawbridge, and encircled by a chemise.

In a final period, from about 1280 to 1320, some of the most powerful castles of any age or country were built in Great Britain—mainly in Wales by Edward I. From his cousin Count Philip of Savoy, Edward borrowed an engineering genius named James of St. George, who directed a staff of engineers from all over Europe and a work force that at times mirrored up to fifteen hundred. James received an excellent salary, plus life pensions for himself and his wife.

James kept the outworks of his castles strong, but concentrated the main defense on a square castle enclosed by two concentric lines of walls with a stout tower at each corner of the inner line. The keep now disappeared, rendered superfluous by the elaborate towers and gatehouses which could hold out independently even if the enemy won the inner bailey. Multiple postern gates, protected by outworks, increased flexibility. At Conway, James followed the contour of a high rock on the shore of an estuary with a wall and eight towers, and a gateway at either end protected by a bar-

Exterior view of Conway Castle, Caernarvon, Wales (begun 13th c.).

bican. Within, a crosswall divided the castle into two baileys, the outer containing the great hall and domestic offices of the garrison, the inner the royal apartments and private offices. Access was by a steep stairway over a drawbridge and through three fortified gateways under direct fire from towers and walls on every side. Caernarvon, Harlech, Flint, Beaumaris, and Denbigh likewise had defenses skillfully adapted to their sites. All were built along the coast of North Wales, the wild country where the stubborn Welsh put up their stoutest resistance. In South Wales the magnificent castle of Caerphilly was built (1267–77) by Richard de Clare, earl of Gloucester, whose family had once owned Chepstow. Caerphilly's site, as picturesque as it was defensible, was on an island in a lake, surmounted by a double line of walls equipped with four powerful gatehouses, and protected by a moat and barbican with a fifth gatehouse.

Thus the castle, born in tenth-century continental Europe as a private fortress of timber and earthwork, brought to England by the Normans, converted to stone in the shell keeps and rectangular keeps of the eleventh and twelfth centuries, refined and improved by engineering knowledge from Crusading Syria, achieved its ultimate development at the end of the thirteenth century in the western wilds of the island of Britain.

Exterior view of Caerphilly Castle, Glamorgan, Great Britain.

II

THE LORD

OF THE CASTLE

Saxon England, nearly devoid of castles, was also devoid of most of the social and economic apparatus that typically produced the castle. "Feudalism," the term given by a later age to the dominant form of society of the Middle Ages, had in 1066 hardly made its appearance on the island of Britain. In the homeland of the Norman invaders, on the contrary, feudalism was well developed in all its aspects. These consisted of the sworn reciprocal obligations of two men, a lord and a vassal, backed economically by their control of the principal form of wealth: land. The lord—the king or great baron—technically owned the land, which he gave to the vassal for his use in return for the vassal's performance of certain services, primarily military. The vassal did not work the land himself, but gave it over to peasants to work for him under conditions that by the High Middle Ages had become institutionalized.

William and the Normans brought feudalism to England, not only because it was the social and political form they were accustomed to, but because it suited their needs in the conquered territory. William in effect laid hold of all the land in England held by secular lords-arable, forest, and swamp; took a generous share (about a fifth) for his own royal demesne and parceled out the rest to his lay vassal followers in return for stated quotas ("fees") of knights owed him in service. The Church, which had backed the Conquest, was left in undisturbed possession of its lands, though prelates owed knights' service the same as lay lords. William's eleven chief barons received nearly a quarter of all England. Such immense grants, running to hundreds of square miles of domain, implied "subinfeudation," again the term of a later age, in which the great vassal of the king became in turn the lord of lesser vassals. In order to produce the military quota he owed the king, the lord gave his vassals "knights' fees" (fiefs) in return for their service. By the accession of Henry I in 1100 this process was far advanced, and England had become, if anything, more feudal than Normandy.

Splendidly representative of the great Norman barons of the twelfth century were the lords of Chepstow Castle. After the disgrace and imprisonment of William Fitz Osbern's son Roger, the royal power had retained possession of Chepstow, but sometime prior to 1119 Henry I granted it, with all its vast dependencies, to Walter de Clare, a kinsman and royal stalwart of the

Master, carpenter and stonemason from *Des Proprietez des Choses* (1482).

21

Exterior view of Tintern Abbey founded by Walter de Clare (1131). Altered 13th–14th c. Painting by George F. Watts (1817–1904).

lucrative for Gilbert defend it against rival claimants by judicial duel, and for his son John, William's father, to go a step farther and successfully assert by judicial combat that the job was hereditary. Following his victory John assumed the aristocratic-sounding name of John Fitz Gilbert le Maréchal.

In the chronicle of the civil war between Stephen of Blois (nephew of Henry I) and Matilda of Anjou (Henry I's daughter) over the English throne, John le Maréchal, or John Marshal, won mention as "a limb of hell and the root of all evil." Two instances of his hardihood especially drew the notice of the chroniclers. Choosing Matilda's side in the war, John at one moment found himself in a desperate case: to cover Matilda's retreat from a pursuing army he barricaded himself in a church with a handful of followers. Stephen's men set fire to the church, and John, with one companion, climbed to the bell tower. Though the lead on the tower roof melted and a drop splashed on John Marshal's face, putting out an eye, he refused to surrender, and when his enemies concluded that he must be dead in the smoking ruins, made good his escape.

A few years and many escapades later John was prevailed upon to hand over his young son William to the now King Stephen as a hostage against a possible act of treachery during a truce. John then went ahead and committed the treachery, reinforcing a castle the king was besieging. King Stephen threatened to hang young William unless the castle surrendered. The threat had no effect on John, who coolly answered that he did not care if his son were hanged, since he had "the anvils and hammer with which to forge still better sons."

The lad was accordingly led out next morning toward an oak tree, but his cheerful innocence won the heart of King Stephen, a man of softer mold than John Marshal. Picking the boy up, the king rode back to

king. Walter, remembered for founding Tintern Abbey, one of the greatest of the great English medieval monasteries, was succeeded at Chepstow by his nephew Gilbert Fitz Gilbert de Clare, who aggressively extended the family's Welsh holdings and in 1138 was made earl of Pembroke. Gilbert, surnamed Strongbow, plotted and took arms against the royal power, but turned around and came to terms with it, marrying the king's mistress, Isabel of Leicester. Their son, Richard Fitz Gilbert, also surnamed Strongbow, became one of the most renowned of all the famous Norman soldier-adventurers of his age. In 1170 this second Strongbow conquered the greater part of Ireland, taking Waterford and Dublin and restoring to power King Dermot MacMurrough of Leinster, in return for Dermot's daughter Eve and the bequest of his kingdom. On Dermot's death Strongbow made good his conquest by defending Dublin against a two-month siege by a rival Irish king, and demonstrated his loyalty (and political sagacity) by arranging to do homage for his conquest to the new king of England, Henry II (Plantagenet).

Strongbow's only son dying in childhood, his daughter Isabel became heiress for the immense holdings of the Clare family in western England, Wales, and Ireland. The choice of Isabel's husband, the new lord of Chepstow, was of obvious moment to the royal power. Henry II exercised his feudal right as lord with his habitual prudence, and Isabel was betrothed to a landless but illustrious supporter of the crown, Guillaume le Maréchal, or William Marshal, the most admired knight of his day, and a prime example of the upward mobility that characterized the age of the castle. William Marshal's grandfather had been art official at the court of Henry I. His name was simply Gilbert; *maréchal* ("head groom") was the name of his post. The office was sufficiently

Painting of the Royal Effigies of the Plantagenet Kings at Fontevrault, France: Henry II (1133–89) (both center and far left), his wife Eleanor of Aquitaine (c.1122–1204), their son Richard I, The Lionhearted (1157–99) and Isabella of Angouleme (wife of their son King John).

camp, refusing to allow him to be hanged, or—an alternative proposal from the entourage—to be catapulted over the castle wall. The king and the boy were later found playing "knights" with plantain weeds and laughing uproariously when William knocked the head off the king's plantain. Such tender-heartedness in a monarch was almost as little admired as John Marshal's brutality, *The Anglo-Saxon Chronicle* succinctly observing of Stephen that "He was a mild man, soft and good, and did no justice."

Thanks to Stephen's lack of justice, William Marshal was permitted to grow up to become the most distinguished of all the lords of Chepstow Castle and the most renowned knight of his time. Gifted with his father's soldierly prowess but free of his rascally character, William first served King Stephen and afterward his Plantagenet successor, Henry II (son of the defeated Matilda of Anjou), from whom he received Chepstow along with Isabel de Clare, the "*pucelle* [damsel] of Estriguil, good, beautiful, courteous and wise," according to William's biographer. The gift was confirmed by

Henry's successor, Richard the Lionhearted, who generously (or sensibly) overlooked a past episode when William had fought Richard during the latter's rebellion against his father. As a member of the royal council, William served Richard and Richard's brother John for many years and played a leading—perhaps the leading—role in negotiating Magna Carta. On John's death he efficiently put down the rebel barons supporting Prince Louis of France and during a reluctant but statesmanlike term as regent established the boy Henry III securely on the throne.

William was succeeded as lord of Chepstow and earl of Pembroke by each of his five sons, one after the other. William Marshal II died in 1231, and was succeeded by his brother Richard, who was murdered in Ireland in 1234, possibly at the instigation of Henry III. The third son, Gilbert, died in 1241 from an accident in a tournament at Hertford. Four years later Walter Marshal succumbed, and was outlived by the fifth brother, Anselm, by only eight days. Thus was fulfilled a curse pronounced at the time of their father's death by

the bishop of Ferries in Ireland. William had seized two manors belonging to the bishop's church, and the bishop had pronounced excommunication. The sentence had no effect on William Marshal, but it troubled the young king Henry III, who promised to restore the manors if the bishop would visit William's tomb and absolve his soul. The bishop went to the Temple, where William was buried, and in the presence of the king and his court addressed the dead man, as Matthew Paris commented, "as if addressing a living [person]. 'William, if the possessions which you wrongfully deprived my church of be restored . . . I absolve you; if otherwise, I confirm the said sentence that, being enmeshed in your sins, you may remain in hell a condemned man for ever.'" The king, though annoyed by the bishop's response, asked William Marshal II to return the manors. William refused, his brothers upheld his position, the young king abandoned his attempt at reconciliation, and the bishop pronounced his curse: "'In one generation his name shall be destroyed' [in the words of the psalm] and his sons shall be without share in that benediction of the Lord, 'Increase and multiply!' Some of them will die a lamentable death, and their inheritance will be scattered." Chepstow passed out of the family by way of William's daughter Maud, who inherited after the death of Anselm in 1245.

On Maud's death in 1248, the royal power had no hand in settling the ownership of Chepstow because Maud had been a widow with grown sons. Her husband had been a Bigod, a Norman family that had risen to prominence after the Conquest. The new lord of Chepstow was Maud's oldest son, Roger Bigod, who also had the title of earl of Norfolk, and who now acquired the unique one of "earl marshal of England," an honor won by William Marshal and now officially made hereditary. The name "marshal" thus completed a cycle from designation of a job to surname to title of nobility.

Had the king been able to choose Maud's husband, he might well have passed over the Bigods, one of the most unruly families in the kingdom. Roger Bigod proved true to the tradition of his own forebears rather than to that of loyalist William Marshal. Roger joined Simon de Montfort's rebellion that wrested control of the government from Henry III, then changed sides and fought against Montfort at the battle of Lewes in 1264. Roger was succeeded by his nephew, also named Roger, who turned once more against the royal power, which he battled for many years.

Although one of their characteristics worth noting is individuality—William Marshal contrasted with the Bigods—the lords of Chepstow share a number of traits that may be taken as those of the great English lord of the High Middle Ages, and to a considerable degree, those of European lords in general. One, relatively superficial, is their Frenchness. The Clares, Marshals, and Bigods, French in origin, continued to speak French, the language of the elite, for several generations. They were French in other ways, as were the Flemish, Spanish, and German barons of the same period, France supplying not only the language of the nobility but the style—the Crusade, *the chanson de geste,* the trouvère and troubadour poetry, the tournament, the castle, the cathedral architecture.

A more deeply ingrained trait of the lords of the castles was their love of land. Even more than their much-advertised love of fighting, their dedication to getting, keeping, and enlarging their estates dominated their lives. Estate management itself, even on a smaller scale than Chepstow, was extremely demanding. No lord, however fond of fighting, could afford to neglect his estates. Many twelfth- and thirteenth-century lords passed up perfectly good wars and even stubbornly resisted participating in them because it meant leaving their lands. Few English lords, and by the thirteenth century few Continental lords, participated in the distant Crusades; they left the Holy Land to be defended mainly by Knights Templars and mercenaries. English barons even objected strenuously to fighting in defense of their king's French territories. Roger Bigod, future lord of Chepstow, and others accompanied Henry III to France only reluctantly in 1242, seizing the earliest opportunity to protest that the king had "unadvisedly dragged them from their own homes," whither they at once returned.

Land was the basis of lordship, and living on, by, and for the land had an undoubted influence on the lord's personality. He drew his revenues from it, and used his nonfarming lands for hunting.

Politics certainly interested the lord, but nearly always because of its relation to land economics. If the sovereign's demands grew excessive, or if self-interest dictated, the baron seldom hesitated to take up arms in rebellion, his feudal oath notwithstanding. He sat on the king's council and attended what in the thirteenth century was beginning to be called parliament, partly to help the king make decisions, but mainly to look out for his own interests.

Between politics and estate management, the lord's days were typically crowded. Far from loafing in his castle during the intervals between wars, he scarcely found time to execute his many functions. At Chepstow, where the Fitz Osberns and Clares were "marcher" earls, enjoying the power that went with guarding the frontier, and where the later Marshals and Bigods had the distinction of the title of earl marshal, they exercised major functions: police, judicial, and fiscal. Such powers, delegated to the marcher earls by the king, gave them much of the independent status enjoyed by the great Continental dukes, counts, and bishops, who paid only nominal allegiance to their sovereigns and even possessed such regalian rights as that of coinage.

Most Norman barons of England were much more tightly circumscribed by the authority of the Crown. In 1086, in the setting of Roman-walled Old Sarum, William the Conqueror accepted homage and fealty from "all the landholding men of any account," that is, not only the barely two hundred tenants-in-chief but the barons' vassals. William's successors continued to encroach on baronial prerogatives. The criminal jurisdiction that traditionally belonged to large landholders was gradually usurped by the Crown. Under Henry II the Curia Regis, the royal council, assumed the role of an appeals court, as did the king's eyre (itinerant justices), whose visits to the shires to settle property suits were regularized by the later years of Henry II.

Henry II also gave decisive impetus to the jury system, which after 1166 was regularly employed to investigate crimes and to settle important civil cases. The law dispensed was a mixture of the old codes of the Saxon kings, feudal custom brought over from Normandy, and new decrees. Judgments were severe: Thieves were hanged, traitors blinded, other offenders mutilated. Sometimes a criminal was drawn and quartered. Prisoners might be confined in a castle tower or basement to await ransom or sentencing, but rarely as punishment, prison as punishment being little known in the Middle Ages. The term "dungeon" (from donjon) as a synonym for prison dates from a later era when many castles were so employed.

Though justice was summary, it was not unenlightened. Torture was not often employed even to extract confessions from thieves, confession hardly being needed if the man was caught with the goods. The records of many court cases, both civil and criminal, reveal considerable effort to determine the truth, and not infrequently a degree of lenience. By the thirteenth century the worst of the ancient barbarian legal practices were being abandoned. In 1215 the Lateran Council condemned trial by ordeal, in which a defendant strove to prove his veracity by grasping a red-hot iron without seriously burning his hand or by sinking when thrown

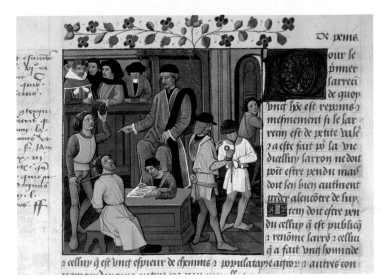

A judge interrogating prisoners (15th c.).

into water, and in 1219 the custom was outlawed in England. Judicial combat, by which the defendant or his champion fought the accuser, survived longer.

On the Continent, justice was divided into high and low, with administration of high justice, comprising crimes of violence, arson, rape, kidnapping, theft, treason, counterfeiting, and false measure, generally held by the largest feudatories—kings, dukes, counts, bishops, abbots, and other great lords. The complications of the feudal system led to many special arrangements by which a lord might retain low justice, give it up to another lord, or keep only the money fines and give up the confiscations of property. Great lords, of course, did not preside over their own courts either in England or on the Continent, but were represented by provosts and seneschals.

Robbed of much of their judicial power, and thus of important revenues from the fines and confiscations, the English barons sought to compensate by acquiring posts in the royal government. The most important was that of justiciar of the realm, created by Henry I, made permanent as a kind of prime minister by Henry II, and disappearing in the thirteenth century. Other great officers of state included the chancellor, the chamberlain, the treasurer, the marshal, and the constable, backed by lesser or assistant justiciars and a throng of subordinate officials. On the local level, William the Conqueror had found an ideal policing instrument in the old Anglo-Saxon post of sheriff, chief officer of the shire (county), and had entrusted it throughout the country to his Normans.

William began by choosing his officials from among his greatest barons, such as Chepstow's William Fitz Osbern. But the tendency of many of these men, made doubly powerful by possessions and official posts, to assume independent power, induced a change of policy. Young Henry III had as his chief justiciar Hubert de Burgh, a member of a knightly family of moderate means, who acquired nearly dictatorial powers and immense wealth that apparently led to his downfall in 1232. The office of justiciar was then left vacant, and its powers passed to the chancellor.

The sheriffdom, or shrievalty, was even more a focus of conflict as the fractious barons strove to occupy it themselves or place it in friendly local hands. By the thirteenth century the office had become one of the most embattled prizes of the baronial-royal conflict. Loyal William Marshal served the king ably and faithfully as sheriff (as well as marshal, assistant justiciar, and regent), but he was an exception. More typical was ambitious, rebellious Falkes de Bréauté, who at one time held the sheriffdom in several different counties but was ultimately stripped of all office. After the baronial victory at Lewes in 1264, the barons replaced royal sheriffs wholesale, but following the royal Victory at Evesham the next year, the barons' men were all turned out again. Thus the sheriff's office, which embraced important police, fiscal, and judicial functions on the county level, kept the English barons occupied in one way or another, either exercising the office or battling to control it.

On the Continent in the eighth century, the time of Charlemagne, the local government was administered in a unit much like the English one: the *pagus* or *comitatus,* counterpart of the English shire, and like the shire divided into hundreds *(centenae),* with local judicial and police powers. The court of the *pagus* was presided over either by the emperor's official, the count, or by his deputy, the viscount, the French equivalent of the sheriff. But development on the Continent followed a very different course. By the twelfth century, the *pagi* and their courts had almost disappeared, their territory and jurisdiction taken over by local feudal lords, often descendants of the old local officials, whose offices had become hereditary. In the courts of these lords most of the judicial business of the land was conducted, and they exercised most of the police and military power. In the thirteenth century the French monarchy was steadily encroaching on the great feudatories by increasing the royal domain at their expense, but the process was far from complete. Lesser barons and knights found employment in both the royal and the feudal administrations, as viscounts, bailiffs, seneschals, provosts of a town, keepers of trade fairs, and many other offices.

The great lord, even with no official post, had more than enough to occupy him in overseeing his estates and manors and making sure his household staff did not rob him.

Underlying the social, economic, and political position of the great lord, English or Continental, were always the two pillars of feudalism: vassalage and the fief. By the thirteenth century both were hallowed, even decadent institutions, their roots in a past so far distant that few lords could give an account of them.

Vassalage was the relationship to the lord, who for all the great English barons was the king. The fief was the land granted by the lord in return for the vassal's service, or more technically, a complex of rights over the land which theoretically remained the legal possession of the lord.

The feudal relationship, which by the thirteenth century had accumulated a large train of embellishments, had originated as a simple economic arrangement designed to meet a military problem in an age when money was scarce. In late Roman times a custom had grown up whereby a man attached himself to a superior by an act of "commendation," a promise of military service in return for support, often in the form of a grant of land known as a benefice. The Frankish Carolingian rulers of the eighth century expanded this custom to meet their need for heavily armed, mounted warriors, a need that arose from the new technique of war—mounted shock combat. The enhanced military value of the mounted warrior brought a corresponding rise in his social status, symbolized by a more personal relationship between lord and vassal. This more personal relationship was in turn symbolized by a new commendation ritual reinforced by an oath of fealty. In the commendation, the vassal placed his hands within the hands of the lord. The oath was sworn on a relic— a saint's bone, hair, or scrap of garment—or on a copy of a Gospel. The contract entered into could not be lightly broken.

Charlemagne laid down precise and exceptional cases in which the vassal might justifiably foreswear his oath: if the lord tried to kill or wound him, to rape or seduce his wife or daughter, to rob him of part of his land, or to make him a serf, or, finally, if he failed to defend him when he should. The lord had no absolute power over his vassal; if he accused the vassal of wrongdoing, he had to accord him trial in the public court, with the "jury of his peers."

In Charlemagne's time a vassal who owed military service, on horseback, with full equipment, needed a benefice amounting to from three hundred to six hundred acres, requiring about a hundred villeins to plow, plant, and harvest it. Although the land continued to belong formally to the lord, custom more and more favored the permanent retention of the land by the vassal's family. The new vassal performed the commendation and oath as had his father. William Longsword, ancestor of William the Conqueror, on succeeding his father as duke of Normandy in 927, "committed himself into the king's hands," according to the chronicler Richer, and "promised him fealty and confirmed it with an oath." An example of the renewal of vassalage following the death of the lord, as practiced in the twelfth century, is recorded by Galbert of Bruges at the time of the succession of William Clito as count of Flanders in 1127, when a number of knights and barons did homage to the new count:

"The count demanded of the future vassal if he wished without reserve to become his man, and he replied, 'I so wish'; then, with his hands clasped and enclosed between those of the count, their alliance was sealed by a kiss." The vassal then said: "I promise by my faith that from this time forward I will be faithful to Count William and will maintain toward him my homage entirely against every man, in good faith and without any deception." Galbert concluded: "All this was sworn on the relics of saints. Finally, with a little stick which he held in his hand, the count gave investiture."

In England the oath of homage always contained a reservation of allegiance toward the king. A thirteenth-century English legal manual cites this formula:

> With joined hands [the vassal] shall offer himself, and with his hands under his lord's mantle he shall say thus I become thy man of such a tenement to be holden of thee, to bear to thee faith of life and member and earthly worship against all men who live and can die, saving the faith of my lord Henry king of England and his heirs, and of my other lords—if other lords he hath. And he shall kiss his lord.

The ceremonial kiss was widely used, though it was less significant than the ritual of homage and the oath of fealty.

The vassal's obligations fell into two large classes, passive and active. His passive obligations were to refrain from doing the lord any injury, such as giving up one of his castles to an enemy, or damaging his land or other property. The active duties consisted of "aid and counsel." Under the "aid" heading came not only the prescribed military duty, *ost* or host, commonly forty days

with complete equipment, either alone or with a certain number of knights, but a less onerous duty, *chevauchée* or cavalcade, which might mean a minor expedition, or simply escort duty, for example when the lord moved from one castle to another. In addition there was often the important duty of castle guard, and the further duty of the vassal to hold his own castle open to the lord's visit. Highly specialized services also appeared, ranging from the obligation of the chief vassals of the bishop of Paris to carry on their shoulders the newly consecrated bishop on his formal entry into Notre Dame, to that of a minor English landholder of Kent of "holding the king's head in the boat" when he crossed the choppy Channel.

In the twelfth century a wholly new kind of service had developed that gave the vassal-lord relationship a fresh significance. This was scutage (from the Latin *scutum,* "shield"), a money payment that took the place of military service. Its appearance showed how far Europe had come since Charlemagne's time in economic sophistication. The new custom was especially conspicuous in England, where William the Conqueror had laid direct hold of the land, something quite impossible for the king of France or the emperor of Germany, whose domains were entangled in a mass of ancient feudal relationships. Richard the Lionhearted, calling on his barons for a war in France, proposed that they each send just seven knights and fulfill the remainder of their obligations with money. The barons, averse to leaving their castles, preferred the arrangement. So did Richard. In place of self-willed vassals whose terms of service might run out the day before a battle, he got mercenary soldiers who did as they were told and stayed as long as they were paid.

Included in the "aid" part of vassalage were financial obligations entirely apart from the money substituted for military service. "Relief" was a payment made by a new tenant at the beginning of his tenancy. A new knight paid his lord one hundred shillings for his knight's fee (fief). The great lord paid a relief to the king proportionate to his holdings, sometimes running to a thousand pounds or more.

The term "aid" itself came to be used to designate certain money obligations exacted by all great lords on special occasions, three of which were widely recognized: ransom of the lord's person, marriage of his eldest daughter, and knighting of his eldest son. These three were specified in the Magna Carta as all that the king of England could require of his barons. Sixty years later the Statute of Westminster (1275) fixed rates: twenty shillings of aid per each twenty pounds' worth of land held at a rent, that is, a levy of five per cent, usually twice in the lord's lifetime. A fourth aid, for going on Crusade, was widely accepted on the Continent. Aids were not restricted to baronial vassals, but were charged to many others, including the wealthy burghers of the towns, often a surer source of revenue than even the large barons.

The "counsel" part of the vassal's obligation required him to come to his lord's (i.e., in the case of a tenant-in-chief, the king's) castle when summoned, and the word counsel, or council, was soon attached to the gathering itself. A lord was expected to consult his vassals on major questions of policy, such as negotiating an important marriage or going to war. But often the purpose was to try judicial cases. Occasionally the sovereign might prefer to have someone else take the blame for offending one party or another in a dispute, and so welcomed his vassals' help, but more often the contrary was the case—that is, the sovereign's interest was served by trying his barons himself, finding them guilty, and extracting fines or expropriations. King John's abuse of this power was a prime cause of the baronial revolt that led to Magna Carta, with the specification of the already time-honored "jury of his peers" for the accused baron.

An important reciprocal obligation of every lord toward his vassals, whether the king toward his barons or a baron toward his knights, was that of defending them when they were accused in other courts—for example, in those of the Church. Self-interest dictated honoring the obligation, since any danger to a vassal's fief arising from such litigation threatened financial harm to the lord.

Vassalage was thus a many-faceted arrangement. Its economic basis, the second component of the feudal relationship, was the fief. In the eleventh century the term, from the Latin *feodum,* had gradually supplanted the older "benefice" to designate the property a lord conferred on a vassal for his maintenance. A fief might be anything that brought in revenue—a mill, a rented house, a market with its fees, a toll bridge, or even a saleable chattel (movable property). Abbeys and churches often belonged as fiefs to lay vassals who pocketed the tithes and endowments and even sometimes the offerings of the faithful. Land, however, was by far the commonest form of fief. In the twelfth and thirteenth centuries western Europe, including Britain, was covered with fiefs of sizes ranging from thousands of acres and

embracing farm, pasture, woodland, and village, down to fiefs of a mere half dozen acres.

By the thirteenth century the feudal relationship had become so complex through inheritances and grants that a baron might hold his castle as a fief from one lord and much of his land from another, and several other revenue-producing fiefs from still others. In England, because of the Conqueror's seizure of all land, a tidy pyramid of fiefs originally existed, with the king the sole landowner and the great lords—the tenants-in-chief, of Chepstow and other vast estates—the only direct fief-holders. The tenants-in-chief sub-granted some of their lands to lesser lords and knights, who in turn often further subdivided them. The lords seized the opportunity to exact relief from inheriting vassals, and by the end of the twelfth century this payment had been widely fixed at a year's revenue of the fief. Magna Carta set a barony's relief at one hundred pounds, and that of a knight's fee (fief) at a maximum of five pounds.

In case of a minor succeeding to a fief, the lord in England (and Normandy) enjoyed the revenues of the fief until the heir was of age, with only the obligation of protecting him. Elsewhere an older relative was commonly assigned as protector.

"Alienation," or sale, of a fief ran counter to the whole sense of the feudal system, with its hereditary relationships, its emphasis on military-style loyalty, and its religious sanctions. Yet inevitably a commerce in fiefs developed. Inheritance might lead to holdings that could be consolidated by judicious trading. Or a poor knight might simply be desperate for money. By the twelfth century, transactions in fiefs were a recognized part of the system, with the lord merely taking care to be formally included in the document to protect his own rights against erosion. In 1159 Thierry of Alsace, the count of Flanders, issued a charter respecting the trade of a piece of land by one of his vassals for a larger tract, presumably of equal value, belonging to the church of St. Nicholas of Furnes:

> It is my wish that the following facts be known, that 45½ measures of land held of me in fief by Leonius and of the latter by his brother Guy were resigned by Guy to Leonius and by the latter to me, and that I have now given them to the church of St. Nicholas of Furnes to possess freely and for ever. And in exchange for them I have received from the church 91 measures of land which I have given to the said Leonius to be held in fief of me, and he has handed

them over to his brother to hold them in fief of him.

Concern over the growing transformation of the feudal relationship was expressed by Holy Roman Emperor Frederick Barbarossa in 1158:

> We have heard bitter complaints from the princes of Italy... that the fiefs which their vassals hold from them are either used as security for loans or sold without the permission of their lords... whereby they lose the service owed, and the honor of the Empire and the strength of our army is diminished.
>
> Having taken the advice of bishops, dukes, margraves, counts... and other leading men, we decree, God willing, this permanent law: No one may sell or pledge the whole or part of a fief or alienate it in any way without the consent of his lord from whom he is known to hold the fief....
>
> We also forbid those clever tricks by which fiefs are sold and money is received... under color of a pretended enfeoffment [granting of a fief].... In such illegal contracts, both seller and buyer shall lose the fief, which then will revert to the lord. The notary who knowingly draws up such a contract shall lose his office... and have his hand cut off.

But the trend was too deeply embedded in the resurgent European economy to be checked. By the thirteenth century, with commerce flourishing, money abundant, and a new-rich class constantly growing, fiefs were bought and sold, except in form, like any other property. A baron whose family had held land for hundreds of years might, coming on hard times, sell some or all to a city burgher who, having made a fortune in banking or the cloth trade, wished to invest in land to protect his capital and gain entry to the aristocracy.

Another problem developing for the feudal system in the later Middle Ages was that of multiple fiefs, automatically demanding multiple homage and so destroying the ideological foundation of the system, the sworn loyalty of a subordinate to a chief. When Henry I, son of William the Conqueror, succeeded in purchasing the vassalage of Count Robert of Flanders, Count Robert spelled out the disingenuous means by which he would fulfill the agreement at the expense of his true feudal lord, the king of France:

> If King Philip plans to attack King Henry in England, Count Robert, if he can, will persuade King Philip to stay at home.... And if King Philip invades England and brings Count Robert with him, the count shall bring as few men with him as he can without forfeiting his fief to the king of France.
>
> ... After Count Robert is summoned by the king of England, he shall get a thousand knights together as quickly as possible in his ports, ready to cross to England. And the king shall find... enough ships for these knights, each knight having three horses.... And if King Henry wishes Count Robert to help him in Normandy or in Maine... the Count shall go there with a thousand knights and shall aid King Henry faithfully, as his ally and lord from whom he holds a fief.
>
> ... And if at this time, King Philip shall attack King Henry in Normandy, Count Robert shall go with King Philip with only twenty knights, and all his other knights shall remain with King Henry.
>
> The king promises to protect Count Robert in life and limb... and give as a fief to Count Robert 500 pounds of English money every year.

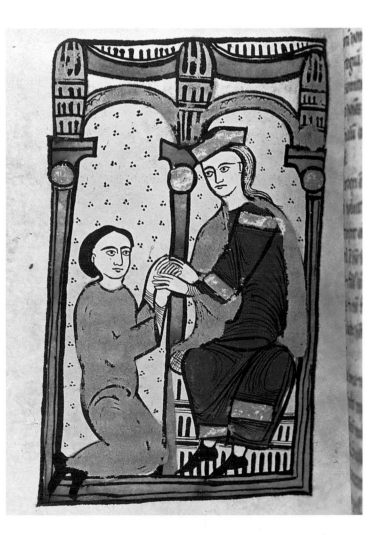

Lord and vassal, from a decorated vellum page (7th c.).

In other words, Count Robert was to receive a of 500 pounds a year to fight on King Henry's side with 1,000 knights, or, if he was simultaneously summoned by King Philip, to fight on both sides at once, taking the field in person for Philip, but with only 20 knights, while sending 980 knights to fight for Henry.

The Count of Flanders was deliberately placing himself in an awkward position in order to profit from a handsome money payment, but many lords found themselves in similar situations merely through their inheritances. In the thirteenth century John of Toul had four lords, and foresaw a variety of complications of loyalty that he tried to meet:

> If it should happen that the Count of Grandpré should be at War with the Countess and Count of Champagne for his own personal grievances, I will personally go to the assistance of the Count of Grandpré and will send to the Countess and Count of Champagne, if they summon me, the knights I owe for the fief which I hold of them. But if the Count of Grandpré shall make war on the Countess and Count of Champagne on behalf of his friends and not for his own personal grievances, I shall serve in person with the Countess and Count of Champagne and I will send one knight to the Count of Grandpré . . .

The significance of such dilemmas as those of Count Robert and John of Toul was not the problems created for the vassals by multiple loyalty but the freedom of choice conferred. A baron with multiple loyalties could always find a solution that met with his own self-interest. Basically, the baron enjoying a fief consisting of a strong castle and broad manors had a powerful position for bargaining with anyone. With his revenues from fines, tolls, taxes, and fees, he could maintain a high degree of independence, regardless of how lawyers described his situation.

The most powerful barons, holders of castles and fiefs from a number of lords, were the strong men of the thirteenth century, able to resist kings and emperors. Even the powerful king of England had to acknowledge their rights in Magna Carta.

William Marshal was universally praised by contemporaries for his "loyalty," that is, his unwavering fidelity to the obligations between vassal and lord, even when it came into conflict with his relations with the king. William stuck to his lord, young Henry, eldest son of Henry II, when the young man rebelled against his father; he refused to do homage to Richard the Lionhearted for the Irish lands that he held of Richard's brother John; and in 1205 he declined to fight for John against Philip Augustus, to whom he had done homage for his Norman lands. Marshal's old-fashioned feudal code, however, was beginning to come into conflict with the new stirrings of nationalism. In 1217, when as regent for Henry III he concluded a lenient peace with the invading forces of Prince Louis of France and the rebel English barons, he had to resist strong pressures from those who wanted to fight on in hopes of recovering Normandy for the English crown. While William would doubtless have been happy to recover Normandy for his sovereign, he regarded the question as academic as far as his own baronial interests were concerned, because he saw no reason why a man should not hold lands simultaneously of the king of England and the king of France. Despite his famous loyalty, "sovereignty" was to him a feebler, less material concept than "lordship." A new day was dawning, however, and emphasis shifting. After William's death, Henry criticized his moderation, and much later, in 1241, even went so far as to condemn it to one of William's sons as treachery.

In the long, drawn-out struggle of the English barons with the king, economic disputes played a major role. The barons succeeded rather better in this area than in others, while profiting from the slow but fairly steady rise in their own manorial incomes through the twelfth and thirteenth centuries. Although agricultural technology and acreage yields virtually stood still through the High Middle Ages, most lords were able to increase their revenues by improving their landholdings in various ways, usually at the expense of their peasants. The growth of towns also helped many lords to find a market for crop surpluses and even to practice regular cash-crop farming. Yet even in the High Middle Ages, the market was too weak to provide an adequate incentive for dramatic agricultural improvement, which had to await a later age.

In fact, the real enemy of the castle barons and their privileges was not the royal power but the slow, irresistible surge of economic change. The cloth merchants and other businessmen who exploited their workers, not perhaps more brutally, but more effectively than the barons did their villeins, were moving ahead in the economic race, while the lords of the countryside, in their arrogant but economically torpid castles, were standing still.

Some were not even able to do that. What happened to a baron who neglected his estates in favor of politics was demonstrated by the fate of the younger Roger Bigod, who inherited Chepstow from his uncle in 1270. An unreconstructed rebel after the baronial defeat at Evesham in 1265, Roger spent his whole substance, English, Welsh, and Irish, tilting at the monarchic power, to such effect that in the end he had to make an ignominious fiscal surrender. In return for the liquidation of his mountain of debts, improvident Roger signed over all his estates to the king, receiving them back for life only. By this arrangement Chepstow Castle passed into the royal demesne with Roger Bigod's death in 1302.

Thus came to an end for the mighty fortress on the Wye more than two centuries of history as a baronial castle, during which it sheltered through the long noontime of the feudal age some of the most powerful of the aristocracy of Norman England.

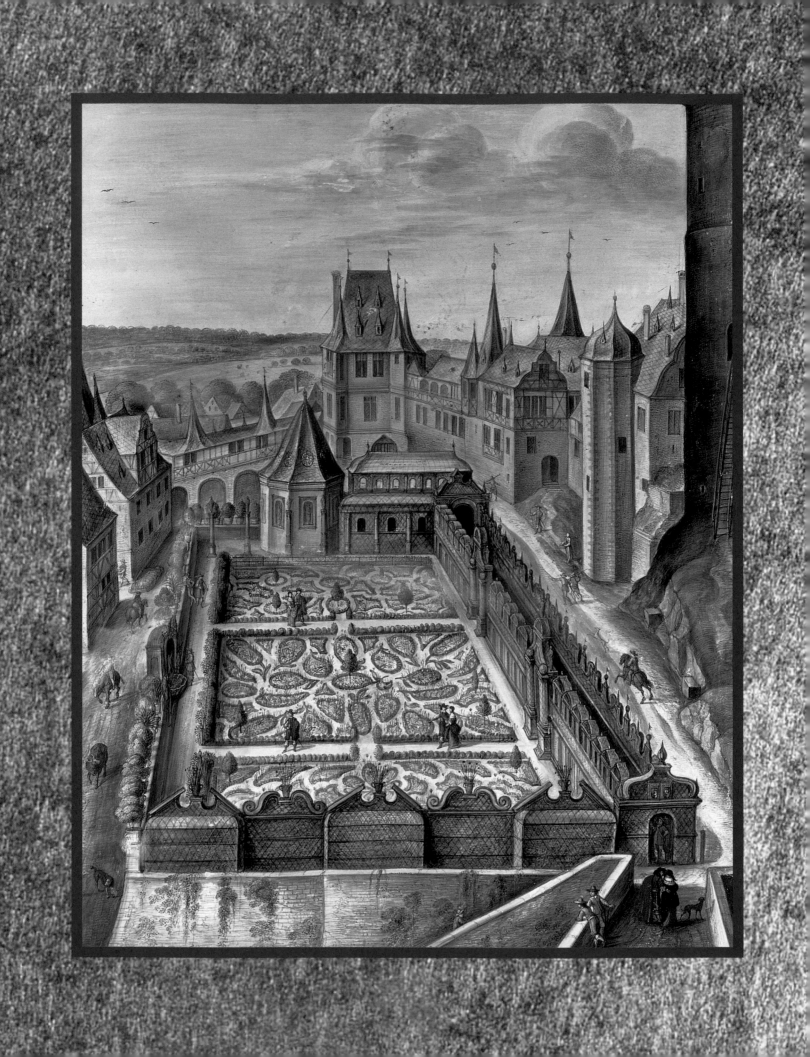

III
THE CASTLE AS HOUSE

While military engineering was elaborating the castle's system of earthworks, palisades, walls, towers, gatehouses, barbicans, and battlements, the castle's domestic aspect was undergoing a parallel advance in the direction of comfort and privacy.

Few descriptions survive of the old motte-and-bailey castle, and only one gives information about living arrangements. Chronicler Lambert of Ardres described a timber castle hall built on a motte at Ardres, in Flanders, early in the twelfth century:

> The first story was on the ground level, where there were cellars and granaries and great boxes, barrels, casks, and other household utensils. In the story above were the dwelling and common rooms of the residents, including the larders, pantry and buttery and the great chamber in which the lord and lady slept. Adjoining this was...the dormitory of the ladies-in-waiting and children...

A Garden, by Johann Walter (French, 1660).

In the upper story of the house were attic rooms in which on the one side the sons of the lord of the house, when they so desired, and on the other side the daughters, because they were obliged, were accustomed to sleep. In this story also the watchmen and the servants appointed to keep the house slept at various times. High up on the east side of the house, in a convenient place, was the chapel, decorated like the tabernacle of Solomon.... There were stairs and passages from story to story, from the house into the [separate] kitchen, from room to room, and from the house into the gallery, where they used to entertain themselves with conversation, and again from the gallery into the chapel.

So elaborate an architecture was exceptional in the motte-and-bailey castle, which rarely had room for accommodations on such a scale. The usual arrangement must have been for the lord's family to eat and sleep in a building on top of the motte, while the kitchen, servants' quarters, barracks, smithy, stables, barns, and storehouses occupied the bailey. Alternatively the lord's family may have lived in a hall in the bailey, with the motte serving solely as watchtower and refuge.

Whether on the motte, in the bailey, inside the walls of the shell keep, or as a separate building within

The main Hall of a medieval chateau (c.1150).

the great curtain walls of the thirteenth century, the living quarters of a castle invariably had one basic element: the hall. A large one-room structure with a lofty ceiling, the hall was sometimes on the ground floor, but often, as in Fitz Osbern's Great Tower at Chepstow, it was raised to the second story for greater security. Early halls were aisled like a church, with rows of wooden posts or stone pillars supporting the timber roof. Medieval carpenters soon developed a method of truss (triangular support) roof construction that made it possible to eliminate the aisles, leaving a broad open space. Windows were equipped with wooden shutters secured by an iron bar, but in the eleventh and twelfth centuries were rarely glazed. By the thirteenth century a king or great baron might have "white [greenish] glass" in some of his windows, and by the fourteenth glazed windows were common.

In a ground-floor hall the floor was beaten earth, stone, or plaster; when the hall was elevated to the upper story the floor was nearly always timber, supported either by a row of wooden pillars in the basement below, as in Chepstow's Great Tower, or by stone vaulting. Carpets, although used on walls, tables, and benches, were not employed as floor coverings in

England and northwest Europe until the fourteenth century. Chronicler Matthew Paris reported the reaction of Londoners in 1255 when Eleanor of Castile, wife of the future Edward I, was housed in an apartment "hung with palls of silk and tapestry, like a temple, and even the floor was covered with tapestry. This was done by the Spaniards, it being in accordance with the custom of their country; but this excessive pride excited the laughter and derision of the people." Floors were strewn with rushes and in the later Middle Ages sometimes with herbs, including basil, balm, chamomile, costmary, cowslip, daisies, sweet fennel, germander, hyssop, lavender, marjoram, pennyroyal, roses, mints, tansy, violets, and winter savory. The rushes were replaced at intervals and the floor swept, but Erasmus, noting a condition that must have been true in earlier times, observed that often under them lay "an ancient collection of beer, grease, fragments, bones, spittle, excrement of dogs and cats and everything that is nasty."

Medieval cooking, East Anglia, from a margin illustration from the *Latin/Luttrell Psalter* (14th c.).

Entrance to the hall was usually in a side wall near the lower end. When the hall was on an upper story, this entrance was commonly reached by an outside staircase next to the wall of the keep. In some castles, as at Dover and Rochester, this staircase was enclosed in and protected by a building which guarded the entry to the keep—a "forebuilding"; in others it was merely roofed over. In Fitz Osbern's keep the entrance stairway was constructed in the thickness of the wall, leading from a doorway on the ground floor to the upper hall.

The castle family sat on a raised dais of wood or stone at the upper end of the hall, opposite to the entrance, away from drafts and intrusion. The lord (and perhaps the lady) occupied a massive chair, sometimes with a canopy by way of emphasizing status. Everyone else sat on benches. Most dining tables were set on temporary trestles that were dismantled between meals; a permanent, or "dormant," table was another sign of prestige, limited to the greatest lords. But all tables were covered with white cloths, clean and ample.

Lighting was by rushlights or candles, of wax or tallow (melted animal fat), impaled on vertical spikes on an iron candlestick with a tripod base, or held in a loop, or supported on wall brackets or iron candelabra. Oil lamps in bowl form on a stand, or suspended in a ring, provided better illumination, and flares sometimes hung from iron rings in the walls.

If the later Middle Ages had made only slight improvements in lighting over earlier centuries, a major technical advance had come in heating: the fireplace, an invention of deceptive simplicity. The fireplace provided heat both directly and by radiation from the stones at the back, from the hearth, and finally, from the opposite wall, which was given extra thickness to absorb the heat and warm the room after the fire had burned low. The ancestor of the fireplace was the central open hearth, used in ground-level halls in Saxon times and often on into later centuries. Such a hearth may have heated one of the two halls of Chepstow's thirteenth-century domestic range, where there are no traces of a fireplace. If so, it was probably situated below the high table and the dais, but away from the traffic of servants at the

A couple in bed: a medieval portrait of Tobias and Sarah (German, 16th c.).

lower end of the hall. Square, circular, or octagonal, the central hearth was bordered by stone or tile and sometimes had a backing (reredos) of tile, brick, or stone. Smoke rose through a louver, a lantern-like structure in the roof with side openings that were covered with sloping boards to exclude rain and snow, and that could be closed by pulling strings, like venetian blinds. In the fourteenth century, louvers were built to revolve according to the direction of the wind. There were also roof ventilators of pottery representing knights, kings, or priests, with smoke coming out of their eyes and mouths and the tops of their heads. A *couvre-feu* ("fire cover") made of tile or china was placed over the hearth at night to reduce the fire hazard.

When the hall was raised to the second story, a fireplace in one wall took the place of the central hearth, dangerous on an upper level, especially with a timber floor. The hearth was moved to a location against a wall with a funnel or hood to collect and control the smoke, and finally, funnel and all, was incorporated into the wall. This early type of fireplace was arched, and set into the wall at a point where it was thickened by an external buttress, with the smoke vent-

ing through the buttress. Toward the end of the twelfth century, the fireplace began to be protected by a projecting hood of stone or plaster which controlled the smoke more effectively and allowed for a shallower recess. Flues ascended vertically through the walls to a chimney, cylindrical with an open top, or with side vents and a conical cap.

At Chepstow, where the two halls of the thirteenth century domestic range were built at ground level, the slope of the land was utilized to place the service rooms of the larger Great Hall above those of the Lesser Hall. The lower part of the Great Hall, containing the entranceway, was partitioned off to form a "screens passage." Such screens consisted at first of low wooden partitions projecting from side walls, with a curtain or movable screen covering the central opening. Later the central barrier became a permanent partition, with openings on either side. Above the screens commonly rose a musicians' gallery overlooking the hall.

On the lower side of the screens passage of the Great Hall at Chepstow, three doorways opened side by side. Two led to the two rooms with a passageway between them that comprised the service area. A buttery, for serving beverages, stood on one side; a pantry, for bread, on the other. In early days of castle building, these service rooms had been rough huts or lean-tos, but by the twelfth century they were usually, as here, integral parts of the hall. They were equipped with shelves and benches on which food brought from the kitchen could be arranged for serving. The buttery of Chepstow's Great Hall contained a drain opening over the river, where a sink was doubtless situated. The third of the three doors opened between the buttery and pantry on a flight of stairs leading to the passage between the two halls. In one direction this passage led to a double latrine, cupboards and steps down to a vaulted storage basement under the Great Hall, with an opening through which supplies could be drawn up from boats on the river below. In the other direction it led to the kitchen, located in a separate building in the Lower Bailey.

In the thirteenth century the castle kitchen was still generally of timber, with a central hearth or several fireplaces where meat could be spitted or stewed in a cauldron. Utensils were washed in a scullery outside. Poultry and animals for slaughter were trussed and tethered nearby. Temporary extra kitchens were set up for feasts, as for the coronation of Edward I in 1273 when a contemporary described the "innumerable kitchens . . . built" at Westminster Palace, "and number-less leaden cauldrons placed outside them, for the cooking of meats." The kitchen did not normally become part of the domestic hall until the fifteenth century.

In the bailey near the kitchen the castle garden was usually planted, with fruit trees and vines at one end, and plots for herbs, and flowers—roses, lilies, heliotropes, violets, poppies, daffodils, iris, gladioli. There might also be a fishpond, stocked with trout and pike.

Both the interior and exterior stonework of medieval castles were often whitewashed. Interiors were also plastered, paneled, or ornamented with paintings or hangings. Usually these interior decorations, like most of the comforts of the castle, began with the dais area of the hall, often the only part to be wainscoted and painted. A favorite embellishment was to paint a whitewashed or plastered wall with lines, usually red, to represent large masonry blocks, each block decorated with a flower. The queen's chamber at the Tower of London in 1240 was wainscoted, whitewashed, given such sham "pointing" or "masoning," and painted with roses. Wainscoting was of the simplest kind, vertical paneling painted white or in colors. In England the wood was commonly fir imported from Norway. In the halls of Henry III's castles, the color scheme was frequently green and gold, or green spangled with gold and silver, and many of the chambers were decorated with murals: the hall at Winchester with a map of the world, a lower chamber at Clarendon with a border of heads of kings and queens, an upper chamber with paintings of St. Margaret and the Four Evangelists and, as described in the king's building instructions, "heads of men and women in good and exquisite colors." Wall hangings of painted wool or linen that were the forerunners of the fourteenth-century tapestries were not merely adornments, but served the important purpose of checking drafts.

In the earliest castles the family slept at the extreme upper end of the hall, beyond the dais, from which the sleeping quarters were typically separated only by a curtain or screen. Fitz Osbern's hall at Chepstow, however, substituted for this temporary division a permanent wooden partition. In the thirteenth century William Marshal's sons removed the partition, making the old chamber part of the hall. They constructed a masonry arcade to support a new chamber above, with access by a wooden stair. In the last decade of the thirteenth century the new third-story chamber was extended over the entire hall.

The Great Hall of the domestic range at Chepstow had its own chamber on the floor above, while the Lesser Hall was equipped with a block of chambers at the upper end, on three levels. Sometimes castles with ground-floor halls had their great chamber, where the lord and lady slept, in a separate wing at the dais end of the hall, over a storeroom, matched at the other end, over the buttery and pantry, by a chamber for the eldest son and his family, for guests, or for the castle steward. These second-floor chambers were sometimes equipped with "squints," peepholes concealed in wall decorations by which the owner or steward could keep an eye on what went on below.

The lord and lady's chamber, when situated on an upper floor, was called the solar. By association, any private chamber, whatever its location, came to be called a solar. Its principal item of furniture was a great bed with a heavy wooden frame and springs made of interlaced ropes or strips of leather, overlaid with a feather mattress, sheets, quilts, fur coverlets, and pillows. Such beds could be dismantled and taken along on the frequent trips a great lord made to his other castles and manors. The bed was curtained, with linen hangings that pulled back in the daytime and closed at night to give privacy as well as protection from drafts. Personal servants might sleep in the lord's chamber on a pallet or trundle bed, or on a bench. Chests for garments, a few "perches" or wooden pegs for clothes, and a stool or two made up the remainder of the furnishings.

The greatest lords and ladies might occupy separate bedrooms, the lady in company with her attendants. One night in 1238, Henry III of England had a narrow escape, reported by Matthew Paris, when an assassin climbed into his bedchamber by the window, knife in hand, but found him not there. "The king was, by God's providence, then sleeping with the queen." One of the queen's maids, who was awake and "singing psalms by the light of a candle," saw the man and alerted the household.

Sometimes a small anteroom called the wardrobe adjoined the chamber—a storeroom where cloth, jewels, spices, and plates were stored in chests, and where dressmaking was done.

In the thirteenth century, affluence and an increasing desire for privacy led to the building of small projecting "oriel" rooms to serve as a secluded corner for the lord and his family, off the upper end of the hall and accessible from the great chamber. Often of timber, the oriel might be a landing at the top of external stairs, built over a small room on the ground floor. It usually had a window, and sometimes a fireplace. In the fourteenth century, oriels expanded into great upper-floor bay windows. An example for an extraordinary purpose was added to Stirling Castle during the siege by Edward I in 1304 in order to provide the queen of Scotland and her ladies with a comfortable observation post.

In the early Middle Ages, when few castles had large permanent garrisons, not only servants but military and administrative personnel slept in towers or in basements, or in the hall, or in lean-to structures; knights performing castle guard slept near their assigned posts. Later, when castles were manned by larger garrisons, often of mercenaries, separate barracks, mess halls, and kitchens were built.

An indispensable feature of the castle of a great lord was the chapel where the lord and his family heard morning mass. In rectangular hall-keeps this was often in the forebuilding, sometimes at basement level, sometimes on the second floor. By the thirteenth century, the chapel was usually close to the hall, convenient to the high table and bed chamber, forming an L with the main building or sometimes projecting opposite the chamber. A popular arrangement was to build the chapel two stories high, with the nave divided horizontally; the family sat in the upper part, reached from their chamber, while the servants occupied the lower part.

Except for the screens and kitchen passages, the domestic quarters of medieval castles contained no internal corridors. Rooms opened into each other, or were joined by spiral staircases which required minimal space and could serve pairs of rooms on several floors. Covered external passageways called pentices joined a chamber to a chapel or to a wardrobe and might have windows, paneling, and even fireplaces.

Water for washing and drinking was available at a central drawing point on each floor. Besides the well, inside or near the keep, there might be a cistern or reservoir on an upper level whose pipes carried water to the floors below. Hand washing was sometimes done at a laver or built-in basin in a recess in the hall entrance, with a projecting trough. Servants filled a tank above, and waste water was carried away by a lead pipe below, inflow and outflow controlled by valves with bronze or copper taps and spouts.

Baths were taken in a wooden tub, protected by a tent or canopy and padded with cloth. In warm weather, the tub was often placed in the garden; in cold weather, in the chamber near the fire. When the lord traveled, the tub accompanied him, along with a bathman who prepared the baths. In some important thirteenth-century castles and palaces there were permanent bathrooms, and in Henry III's palace at Westminster there was even hot and cold running water in the bath house, the hot water supplied by tanks filled from pots heated in a special furnace. Edward II had a tiled floor in his bathroom, with mats to protect his feet from the cold.

The latrine, or "garderobe," an odd euphemism not to be confused with wardrobe, was situated as close to the bed chamber as possible (and was supplemented by the universally used chamber pot). Ideally, the garderobe was sited at the end of a short, right-angled passage in the thickness of the wall, often in a buttress. When the chamber walls were not thick enough for this arrangement, a latrine was corbeled out from the wall over either a moat or river, as in the domestic range at Chepstow, or with a long shaft reaching nearly to the ground. This latter arrangement sometimes proved dangerous in siege, as at Château Gaillard, Richard the Lionhearted's castle on the Seine, where attackers obtained access by climbing up the latrine shaft. As a precaution, the end of the shaft was later protected by a masonry wall. Often several latrines were grouped together into a tower, sometimes in tiers, with a pit below, at the angle of the hall or solar, making them easier to clean. In some castles rainwater from gutters above or from a cistern or diverted kitchen drainage flushed the shaft.

Henry III, traveling from one of his residences to another, sent orders ahead:

> Since the privy chamber . . . in London is situated in an undue and improper place, wherefore it smells badly, we command you on the faith and love by which you are bounden to us that you in no wise omit to cause another privy chamber to be made . . . in such more fitting and proper place that you may select there, even though it should cost a hundred pounds, so that it may be made before the feast of the Translation of St. Edward, before we come thither.

Before a visit to York in 1251 for the marriage of his daughter Margaret to Alexander III of Scotland, the king specified a privy chamber twenty feet long "with a deep pit" to be constructed next to his room in the archbishop's palace.

Hay often served as toilet paper; Jocelin of Brakelond tells how Abbot Samson of Bury St. Edmunds one night dreamed he heard a voice telling him to rise, and woke to find a candle carelessly left by another monk in the privy about to fall into the hay.

By the later thirteenth century, the castle had achieved a considerable degree of comfort, convenience, and privacy. The lord and lady, who had begun by eating and sleeping in the great hall with their household, had gradually withdrawn to their own apartments. Bishop Robert Grosseteste thought the tendency toward privacy had gone too far and advised the countess of Lincoln: "When not prevented by sickness or fatigue, constrain yourself to eat in the hall before your people, for this shall bring great benefit and honour to you. . . . Forbid dinners and suppers out of the hall and in private rooms, for from this arises waste and no honour to the lord and lady."

A century later, in *Piers Plowman,* William Langland echoed the bishop's warning. Langland blamed the change on technology: the wall fireplace, with its draft chimney, which freed the household from huddling around the central hearth of the old days:

> Woe is in the hall each day in the week.
> There the lord and lady like not to sit.
> Now every rich man eats by himself
> In a private parlor to be rid of poor men,
> Or in a chamber with a chimney
> And leaves the great hall.

IV
THE LADY

[The lady of Faiel] entered, a golden circlet on her blonde hair. The castellan saluted her, sighing: "Lady, God give you health, honor and joy." She replied: "And God give you pleasure, peace and health." Then he took her hand and made her sit down near him. . . . He looked at her without saying anything, too moved to speak, and grew pale. The lady saw this and apologized for the absence of her husband. The castellan replied that he loved her and that if she did not have mercy on him, nothing mattered to him. The lady reminded him that she was married and that he must ask her for nothing which would soil the honor of herself or her lord. He replied that nothing would keep him from serving her all his life.
—THE CASTELLAN OF COUCY

Her hair was golden, with little love-locks; her eyes blue and laughing; her face most dainty to see, with lips more vermeil than ever was rose or cherry in the time of summer heat; her teeth white and small; her breasts so firm that they showed beneath her vesture like two rounded nuts; so frail was she about the girdle that your hands could have spanned her, and the daisies that she broke with her feet in passing showed altogether black against her instep and her flesh, so white was the fair young maiden.
—AUCASSIN AND NICOLETTE

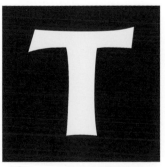 he lady of Faiel and Nicolette were heroines of two popular thirteenth-century romances. Renaut de Coucy's lady, "best, noblest and most intelligent of the land," was worshipped by her lover, who wore her sleeve as a token in battle, composed songs to her, and endured a series of painful trials before at last winning her favor. Beautiful, accomplished, adored, she devoted her life to love—outside the marriage bond.

Nicolette, for her part, physically exemplified the medieval feminine ideal—blonde, delicate, fair-skinned, boyish of figure.

Scores of similar ladies dazzled lovers in the outpouring of fiction of the twelfth and thirteenth centuries, but how much they reflect the flesh-and-blood lady of the castle is difficult to say. Little information is available on the personalities and private lives of the women who presided over Chepstow and other castles. One fact, however, is well substantiated: The castle lady customarily was a pawn in the game of politics and economics as played by men.

A woman playing a viol, from 'Des Cleres et Nobles Femmes' (15th c.).

Although a woman could hold land, inherit it, sell it, or give it away, and plead for it in the law courts, most of a woman's life was spent under the guardianship of a man—of her father until she married, of her husband until she was widowed. If her father died before she married, she was placed under the wardship of her father's lord, who was felt to be legitimately concerned in her marriage because her husband would be his vassal. In the case of an heiress, marriage was a highly profitable transaction—a suitor might pay a large sum for the privilege. But wardship itself was a sought-after prize, because the guardian pocketed the income from the estate until the ward's marriage. Many medieval legal battles were fought over rich wards, and even those not so rich attracted greedy notice. In 1185 Henry II ordered an inventory of all the widows and heirs in the realm with a view to possible royal claims. The age, children, lands, livestock, rents, tools, and other possessions of widows were painstakingly enumerated. A typical entry read:

> Alice de Beaufow, widow of Thomas de Beaufow, is in the gift of the lord king [i.e., in his wardship]. She is twenty and has one son as heir, who is two. Her land in Seaton is worth £5 6s. 8d. with this stock, namely two plows, a hundred sheep, two draught animals, five sows, one boar, and four cows. In the first year in which the land has been in her hand she has received in rent 36s. and 10d. and two pounds of pepper, and apart from the rent her tenants have given her 4s. and three loads of oats.

The wardship of a wealthy three-month-old orphan provoked a spirited resistance by Abbot Samson of Bury St. Edmunds against Henry's son Richard the Lionhearted. In the end the king surrendered to the prelate in return for the gift of some hunting dogs and horses. But the abbot was foiled by the infant's grandfather, who successfully kidnapped her, and Samson finally sold his claim to the wardship to the archbishop of Canterbury for 100 pounds. The little girl survived and appreciated in value, the archbishop in his turn selling the wardship to Thomas de Burgh, brother of the king's chamberlain and future justiciar, for 500 marks (333 pounds).

The daughter of a great lord was typically brought up away from home, in the castle of another noble family, or in a convent, where she might spend her life if she did not marry. Education of girls evidently compared favorably with that of their brothers. The differences in the training of the two sexes were given a jocular exag-geration by the writers of romances, who pictured boys as learning "to feed a bird, to hawk, to know hunting dogs, to shoot bow and arrow, to play chess and backgammon," or "fencing, horsemanship and jousting," whereas girls learned "to work with needle and shuttle . . . read, write and speak Latin," or to "sing songs, tell stories and embroider." Ladies of rank were patrons of poets and wrote poetry themselves, and some devoted themselves to learning. Yet, like their husbands, ladies enjoyed hunting and hawking (on their seals they were often portrayed holding a falcon) and chess.

Girlhood was brief. Women were marriageable at twelve and usually married by fourteen. Heiresses might be married in form as young as five and betrothed even younger, though such unions could be annulled before consummation. By twenty a woman had a number of children, and by thirty, if she survived the hazards of childbirth, she might be widowed and remarried, or a grandmother.

Whereas personal choice and attraction played a part in the marriages of peasant girls on the manors (where marriage commonly followed pregnancy), the marriages of ladies were too important to be left to predilection. There were exceptions. King Henry III's sister Eleanor, married to Chepstow's Earl William Marshal II at the age of nine and widowed at sixteen, married Simon de Montfort, earl of Leicester, in 1238 in the king's private chapel at Westminster, with the king giving the bride away. The following year the king quarreled with De Montfort, who, he revealed, had "basely and clandestinely defiled" Eleanor during courtship. "You seduced my sister before marriage, and when I found it out I gave her to you in marriage, though against my will, in order to avoid scandal," were the king's words, reported by Matthew Paris.

There is evidence that many marriages were happy. The fourteenth-century noble author Geoffrey de la Tour touchingly described his late wife as

> both fair and good, who had knowledge of all honor . . . and of fair behavior, and of all good she was the bell and flower; and I delighted so much in her that I made for her love songs, ballads, rounders, virelays, and diverse things in the best wise I could. But death, that on all makes war, took her from me, which has made me many a sorrowful thought and great heaviness. And so it is more than twenty years that I have been for her full of great sorrow. For a true lover's heart never forgets the woman he has truly loved.

Although there was no legal divorce, the taboo against consanguineous unions provided general grounds for annulment suits, especially since it extended to distant cousins, and even relationship by marriage could be invoked. The Church did not always admit such claims. When in 1253 Earl Roger Bigod, lord of Chepstow and grandson of the first William Marshal, repudiated his wife, the daughter of the king of Scotland, because he was allegedly related to her, the Church ruled that he should take her back, and Roger gave in: "Since such is the judgment of the Church, I safely and willingly accede to the marriage, of which I was formerly doubtful and suspicious."

The bride brought a marriage portion and received in return a dower amounting to a third part of her husband's estate, sometimes specific lands named at the church door on her wedding day, which became hers on her husband's death. Even without this formal assignment, a third of his lands was legally hers, and if the heir was slow to turn it over to tier, she could bring an action in the royal courts to secure it. The dower was accepted as a fixed charge throughout the feudal age, but was gradually replaced by a settlement made at the time of the marriage.

Once married, a woman was "under the rod" or "under the power" of her husband. She could not "gainsay" him even if he sold land which she had inherited, could not plead in court without him, or make a will without his consent.

Women recovered some of these rights when they became widows. Sometimes a widow even successfully sued to recover land sold by her husband "whom in his lifetime she could riot gainsay." But in England before Magna Carta the king could force the widows of his tenants-in-chief to remarry, and if they wished to remain unmarried or to choose their own husbands they had to pay him large fines. Magna Carta limited the king's power in this respect while reiterating that a widow must not marry without the consent of her lord, whether he was the king or one of the king's vassals. Another article of Magna Carta provided that the king's wards, whether widows or maidens, should not be "disparaged"—married to someone of lower rank.

Consent was one of the legal conditions for marriage, and marriages could be annulled on the grounds that they had been contracted against the will of one of the parties. In 1215 King John gave young Lady Margaret, daughter of his chamberlain and widow of the earl of Devon's heir, as a reward to the mercenary captain Falkes de Bréauté. When Falkes was exiled in 1224, Margaret presented herself before the king and the archbishop and asked for an annulment, declaring that she had never consented to the marriage. On her death in 1252, Matthew Paris, characterizing the marriage as "nobility united to meanness, piety to impiety, beauty to dishonor," quoted a Latin verse someone had written about the marriage:

> Law joined them, love and concord of the bed.
> But what kind of law? What kind of love? What kind of concord?
> Law out of law, love that was hate, concord that was discord.

The chronicler did not mention the fact that Margaret, who had been married to Falkes for nine

A margin illustration showing a wife beating her husband from the *Latin/Luttrell Psalter* (14th c.).

years and had had at least one child by him, had waited for his downfall to seek legal redress. Falkes died in Rome in 1226 while petitioning the Pope to restore his wife and her patrimony to him.

For all her legal disabilities, the lady played a serious, sometimes leading role in the life of the castle. When the lord was away at court, war, Crusade, or pilgrimage, she ran the estate, directing the staff and making the financial and legal decisions. The ease with which castle ladies took over such functions indicates a familiarity implying at least a degree of partnership when the lord was at home. Besides helping to supervise the household staff and the ladies who acted as nurses for her children, the lord's wife took charge of the reception and entertainment of officials, knights, prelates, and other castle visitors. Bishop Robert Grosseteste advised the countess of Lincoln to deal with her guests "quickly, courteously and with good cheer," and to see that they were "courteously addressed, lodged and served."

Inferior legal status did not reduce women to voiceless shadows. Contemporary satirists in fact pictured women as quarrelsome and pugnacious. In one of his sermons, the famous Paris preacher Jacques de Vitry told the story of the man with a wife

> so contrary that she always did the reverse of what he commanded, and received in a surly manner the guests whom he often asked to dinner. One day he

invited several to dine with him, and had the tables set in the garden near a stream. His wife sat with her back to the water, at some distance from the table, and regarded the guests with an unfriendly face. Her husband said: "Be cheerful to our guests, and draw nearer the table." She on the contrary pushed her chair farther from the table and nearer the edge of the stream at her back. Her husband, noticing this, said angrily: "Draw near the table." She pushed her chair violently back and fell into the river and was drowned. Her husband jumped in a boat and began to seek his wife with a long pole, but up the stream. When his neighbors asked him why he looked for his wife up the stream instead of below as he should, he answered: "Do you not know that my wife always did what was contrary and never walked in the straight way? I verily believe that she has gone up against the current and not down with it like other people."

An incident of 1252 described by Matthew Paris furnishes a picture of the medieval lady as a person capable of self-assertion even against so daunting an opponent as the king. Isabella, countess of Arundel, visited King Henry III to protest his claim of a wardship of which he owned a small portion, but which belonged mainly to her. The countess, "although a woman" (in Matthew Paris' aside), demanded, "Why, my lord king, do you avert your face from justice? One cannot now obtain what is right and just at your court. You are appointed a mediator between the Lord and us, but you do not govern well either yourself or us . . . moreover, without fear or shame, you oppress the nobles of the kingdom in divers ways." The king replied ironically, "What is this, my lady countess? Have the nobles of England . . . given you a charter to be their spokeswoman and advocate, as you are so eloquent?" The countess answered, "By no means, my lord, have the nobles of your kingdom given me a charter, but you have given me that charter [Magna Carta], which your father granted to me, and which you agreed and swore to observe faithfully and to keep inviolate. . . . I, although a woman, and all of us, your natural and faithful subjects, appeal against you before the tribunal of the awful judge of all; and heaven and earth will be our witnesses, since you treat us with injustice, though we are innocent of crime against you—and may the Lord, the God of vengeance, avenge me." The king, according to Matthew, was silenced by this speech, and the countess,

Roman de la Rose: **Garden Scene, the Lover and the Dame Oyeuse (c.1230–80).**

without obtaining, or even asking for permission, returned home."

Notwithstanding feudal law, a woman occasionally even arranged her own marriage. Isabelle of Angoulême, widow of King John, found an opportunity to make an advantageous (or at any rate congenial) second marriage, and seized it, in the process displacing her own ten-year-old daughter Joan, who had been betrothed to the man in question for six years. Isabelle wrote home to her "dearest son," King Henry III, from Angoulême, whither she had gone to take up the reins of government of the county:

> We hereby notify you that, the Count of La Marche [the bridegroom's father, who had died on Crusade] . . . having departed this life, the lord Hugh de Lusignan is left, as it were, alone and without heir . . . and his friends would not allow our daughter to be united with him in lawful marriage because of her tender age, but advise him to seek an heir speedily, and it is proposed that he should take a wife in France. If that were to happen, all your lands in Poitou and Gascony and ours too would be lost. Seeing the great danger that might result if such a union took place, and getting no advice from your councillors . . . we have therefore taken the said Hugh, Count of La Marche, as our lord and husband; and let God be our witness that we have done this more for your welfare than our own. Wherefore we ask you, as our dear son . . . since this may yield greatest benefit to you and yours, that you restore to us what is ours by right, namely Niort, Exeter, and Rockingham, and the 3,500 marks which your father, our late husband, bequeathed us.

Isabelle's dowry and inheritance were not forthcoming, however, Henry refusing to relinquish them until Joan, in custody in La Marche, was back in England, and Isabelle refusing to give up Joan until she had the lands and money. Under pressure from the Pope, Isabelle and Hugh at last yielded up Joan, who then married King Alexander of Scotland. But Henry, Isabelle, and Hugh continued to bicker over the dowry for many years.

Another spirited lady was described by the chronicler Ordericus Vitalis.

> The faculties of [William] count of Évreux [d. 1118] were naturally somewhat feeble as well as being reduced by old age, and trusting perhaps more than was proper to his wife's abilities, he left the administration of his county [of Évreux] completely in her hands. The Countess [Helvise] was notable for her wit and beauty. She was one of the tallest women in all Évreux and of very high birth. . . . Ignoring the counsels of her husband's barons, she chose instead to follow her own ideas and ambition. Often inspiring audacious measures in political affairs, she readily engaged in rash enterprises.

Many medieval ladies showed political capacity of a high order. Countess Matilda of Tuscany presided over one of the most important feudal states in eleventh-century Italy, decisively intervened on the side of the Pope against Emperor Henry IV in the greatest political struggle of her day, and made her castle of Canossa a byword in Western languages. Blanche of Castile ruled France for a quarter of the thirteenth century. In England the wives of William the Conqueror, Henry I, and Henry II all served as regents during their husbands' absences.

Although at a disadvantage in a military society, women not only defended their castles in sieges but actually led armies in battles. Long before Joan of Arc, women put on armor and rode to war. William the Conqueror's granddaughter Matilda, called the Empress Matilda because of her earlier marriage to the German emperor Henry V, led her army in person against her cousin Stephen of Blois in England's twelfth-century civil war. Momentarily victorious, Matilda, according to the hostile chronicler of the *Gesta Stephani* ("Deeds of Stephen"), "at once put on an extremely arrogant demeanor, instead of the modest gait and bearing proper to a gentle woman, and began to walk and speak and do all things more stiffly and more haughtily than she had been wont, . . . began to be arbitrary, or rather headstrong, in all that she did." The *Gesta Stephani* went on to describe Matilda's behavior at Winchester when the king of Scotland, the bishop of Winchester, and her brother, the earl of Gloucester, "the chief men of the whole kingdom" and part of her permanent retinue, came before her with bended knee to make a request. Instead of rising respectfully to greet them and agreeing to what they asked, she brusquely dismissed them and refused to listen to their advice. Later she advanced upon London with a large army, and when the citizens welcomed her, according to the chronicler, replied by sending for the richest men and demanding "a huge sum of money, not with unassuming gentleness, but with a voice of authority." Upon their protesting, she lost her temper.

Later, her fortune changing, Matilda was besieged in Oxford Castle. She again showed mettle, [leaving] the castle by night, with three knights of ripe judgment to accompany her, and went about six miles on foot, by very great exertions on the part of herself and her companions, through the snow and ice (for all the ground was white with an extremely heavy fall of snow, and there was a very thick crust of ice on the water). What was the evident sign of a miracle, she crossed dry-footed, without wetting her clothes at all, the very waters that had risen above the heads of the king [Stephen] and his men when they were going over to storm the town, and through the king's pickets, which everywhere were breaking the silence of the night with the blaring of trumpeters or the cries of men shooting loudly, without anyone at all knowing except her companions.

At one point in the struggle, the Empress Matilda found herself pitted against another Matilda, Stephen's wife, "a woman of subtlety and a man's resolution," who led troops in an attack on London, ordering them to "rage most furiously around the city with plunder and arson, violence and the sword."

A thirteenth-century lady who played a military role was Dame Nicolaa de la Haye, widow of the sheriff of Lincoln, a "vigorous old lady," in the words of a chronicler, who commanded the royalist stronghold of Lincoln Castle against the forces of Prince Louis of France and the rebel English barons at the time of King John's death, holding out against every assault until William Marshal arrived with relief forces.

One of the greatest of all examples of hardihood and independence was the Empress Matilda's daughter-in-law, Eleanor, heiress to the vast province of Aquitaine in southwestern France. Eleanor's first marriage, to Louis VII of France, was terminated by her affair with Raymond of Antioch in the Holy Land, but far from retiring to a convent after the scandal, Eleanor married Matilda's son, who two years later gained the English throne as Henry II. Eleanor meddled actively in politics, encouraging her sons in rebellions against their father until exasperated Henry imprisoned her in Salisbury Castle. (Chepstow's William Marshal was sent in 1183 to tell her that Henry had released her.) After Henry's death she traveled from city to city and castle to castle in England and France, holding court, and at the age of eighty she played a decisive role in the struggle for the English throne between her grandson Arthur and her son John.

Eleanor's native French province, Aquitaine, was the birthplace of the poetry of the troubadours, founders of the Western poetic tradition. Eleanor's

A widow at the collection box, detail from a Byzantine mosaic (6th c.)

grandfather, Count William IX of Aquitaine, was the earliest troubadour whose work has survived, and Eleanor is sometimes credited with the introduction of troubadour verse into northern France and England. Eleanor's daughter by her first marriage, Marie de Champagne, was also a patroness of poets, notably the celebrated Chrétien de Troyes, creator of the Lancelot-Guinevere romance. At Marie's court in Troyes (or at the court of France) a work was formulated that had immense influence in aristocratic circles: De Amore ("On Love"), written by Andreas Capellanus ("André the Chaplain"), borrowing freely from Ovid. The treatise supplies an insight into the manners, morals, conversation, and thought of the noble ladies of the High Middle Ages, revealing a sophistication and wit at variance both with the image of pampered sex object of the romances and with the disenfranchised pawn of the legal system.

The thesis of De Amore is summed up in a letter purported to be written by Countess Marie to Andreas in response to the question of whether true love could have any place in marriage:

We declare and we hold as firmly established that love cannot exert its powers between two people who are married to each other. For lovers give each other everything freely, under no compulsion or necessity, but married people are in duty bound to give in to each other's desires and deny themselves to each other in nothing.

Besides, how does it increase a husband's honor if after the manner of lovers he enjoys the embraces of his wife, since the worth of character of neither can be increased thereby, and they seem to have nothing more than they already had a right to?

And we say the same thing for still another reason, which is that a precept of love tells us that no woman, even if she is married, can be crowned with the reward of the King of Love unless she is seen to be enlisted in the service of Love himself outside the bonds of wedlock. But another rule of Love teaches that no one can be in love with two men. Rightly, therefore, Love cannot acknowledge any rights of his between husband and wife.

But there is still another argument that seems to stand in the way of this, which is that between them there can be no true jealousy, and without it true love may not exist, according to the rule of Love himself, which says, "He who is not jealous cannot love."

A chapter of *De Amore* cited "love cases" which were supposed to have been tried in "courts of love" before ladies of Eleanor's and Marie's courts and those of other noble ladies assemblages—now believed to be no more than an elegant fiction:

A certain lady had a proper enough lover, but was afterward, through no fault of her own, married to an honorable man, and she avoided her lover and denied him his usual solaces. But Lady Ermengarde of Narbonne demonstrated the lady's bad character in these words: "The later contracting of a marital union does not properly exclude an early love except in cases where the woman gives up love entirely and is determined by no means to love any more. . . ."

A certain woman had been married, but was now separated from her husband by a divorce, and her former husband sought eagerly for her love. In this case the lady replied: "If any two people have been married and afterward separate in any way, we consider love between them wholly wicked. . . ."

A certain knight was in love with a woman who had given her love to another man, but he got from her this much hope of her love—that if it should ever happen that she lost the love of her beloved, then without a doubt her love would go to this man. A little while after this the woman married her lover. The other knight then demanded that she give him the fruit of the hope she had granted him, but this she absolutely refused to do, saying that she had not lost the love of her lover. In this affair the Queen gave her decision as follows: "We dare not oppose the opinion of the Countess of Champagne, who ruled that love can exert no power between husband and wife. Therefore we recommend that the lady should grant the love she has promised. . . ."

The Countess of Champagne was also asked what gifts it was proper for ladies to accept from their lovers. To the man who asked this the Countess replied, "A woman who loves may freely accept from her lover the following: a handkerchief, a fillet for the hair, a wreath of gold or silver, a breastpin, a mirror, a girdle, a purse, a tassel, a comb, sleeves, gloves, a ring, a compact, a picture, a wash basin, little dishes, trays, a flag as a souvenir . . . any little gift which may be useful for the care of the person or pleasing to look at or which may call the lover to her mind, if it is clear that in accepting the gift she is free from all avarice.

"But . . . if a woman receives a ring from her lover as a pledge of love, she ought to put it on her left hand and on her little finger, and she should always keep the stone hidden on the inside of her hand; this is because the left hand is usually kept freer from dishonesty and shameful contacts, and a man's life and death are said to reside more in his little finger than in the others, and because all lovers are bound to keep their lover secret. Likewise, if they correspond with each other by letter they should refrain from signing their own names. Furthermore, if the lovers should for any reason come before a court of ladies, the identity of the lovers should never be revealed to the judges, but the case should be presented anonymously. And they ought not to seal their letters to each other with their own seals unless they happen to have secret seals known only to themselves and their confidants. In this way their love will always be retained unimpaired."

If "courtly love" (a phrase coined in much later times) was the medieval literary ideal, in practice a firmly masculine double standard prevailed toward adultery. The Church condemned it in both sexes, but commonly kings, earls, barons, and knights had mistresses, and illegitimate children abounded (Henry I had twenty-odd, John five known bastards). Adultery in women was a different matter, and an erring wife was often disgraced and repudiated, her lover mutilated or killed. The issue was not morality but masculine honor. Adultery with the lord's wife was regarded as treason. In the reign of Philip the Fair of France two nobles accused of adultery with the wives of the king's sons were castrated, dragged behind horses to the gallows, and hanged as "not only adulterers, but the vilest traitors to their lords."

The fine points of matters of honor (as well as the fact that the honor in question was exclusively masculine) are illustrated by two cases recorded by Matthew Paris. A knight named Godfrey de Millers entered the house of another knight "for the purpose of lying with his daughter" but was seized, with the connivance of the girl herself, "who was afraid of being thought a married man's mistress," and was beaten and castrated. The perpetrators of this deed, including the girl's father, were punished by exile and the seizure of their property. Ambiguous though the evidence was the girl may well have simply been defending herself against attack—Matthew Paris unhesitatingly pronounced her a "harlot" and "adultress" and the punishment of the knight "a deed of enormous cruelty. . . an inhuman and merciless crime." At about the same time "a certain handsome clerk, the rector of a rich church," who distinguished himself by surpassing all the neighboring knights by the lavishness of his hospitality and entertainments—a universally admired trait in aristocratic circles—was similarly treated for a similar malfeasance. The king, like Matthew Paris, deeply grieved at the cleric's misfortune, ordered it to be proclaimed as law that no one should be castrated for adultery except by a cuckolded husband, whose honor, unlike that of the lady's father, her family, or the lady herself, was sacred.

The man who made a conquest, on the other hand, might boast of it—as did Eleanor of Aquitaine's grandfather William IX when he versified about disguising himself as a deaf-mute and visiting the wives of "Lords Guarin and Bernard" (whether these were the names of real personages is not known). After testing him and assuring themselves that he in truth was "dumb as a stone,"

> Then Ann to Lady Eleanor said:
> "He *is* mute, plain as eyes in your head;
> Sister, get ready for bath and bed
>   And dalliance gay."
> Eight days thereafter in that furnace
>   I had to stay.
> How much I tupped them you shall hear:
> A hundred eighty-eight times or near,
> So that I almost stripped my gear
>   And broke my equipment;
> I never could list the ills I got—
>   Too big a shipment.

Medieval ideas were far from the Victorian notion that nice women did not enjoy sex. Physiologically, men and women were considered sexual equals—in fact, as in William IX's verses, women were commonly credited with stronger sexual feelings than men. In the fabliaux and in the satiric writings of medieval moralists women were constantly portrayed as lusty and even insatiable. The author of the thirteenth-century *Lamentations of Matthew* complained that his wife claimed her conjugal rights with energy, and "if I don't give them to her because I don't have my old vigor, she pulls my hair."

An excerpt from a commentary on Aristotle by the thirteenth-century German scholar Albertus Magnus, widely circulated under the title *On the Secrets of Women,* asked the question, Was pleasure in intercourse greater in men than in women? The answer was no. In the first place, according to the sages, since matter desires to take on form, a woman, an imperfect human being, desires to come together with a man, because the imperfect naturally desires to be perfected. Therefore the greater pleasure and appetite belonged to the woman. In the second place, orgasm was the indication of the emission of the female seed in intercourse. Double pleasure was better than single pleasure, and while in men pleasure came from the emission of seed, in women pleasure came from both emission and reception. Consequently, any woman who conceived was believed to have taken pleasure in intercourse, and judges denied suit for rape if a woman became pregnant from the assault. Another theory of Albertus, also taken from Aristotle, stated that the female seed, or *menstruum,* gradually collected in the womb, increasing sexual desire as it accumulated. Menstruation, seen as the equivalent of a man's ejaculation, provided periodic relief. Therefore, though men's pleasure might be more intensive, women's was more extensive. During pregnancy, when the *menstruum* was retained to form and nourish the fetus, a woman was thought to be at the peak of her sexual desire. The sexual attitudes set forth by Albertus were also an expression of a cleric's contempt for women; the woman's desire was greater not merely physiologically, but because of the weakness of her judgment, and because of her imperfection, the inferior's desire for the superior.

The conventions of chivalry directed that, in the words of the thirteenth-century *Roman de la Rose,* men should "do honor to ladies. . . . Serve ladies and maidens if you would be honored by all." Men were to be courteous, witty, accomplished, to speak gently, to "do nothing to displease" a lady—yet in practice a lord might strike or beat his wife. Geoffrey de La Tour tells of a man breaking his wife's nose because she talked back to him before strangers, "and all her life she had her nose crooked, which spoiled and disfigured her visage so that she could not for shame show it, it was so foully blemished."

Courtesy, in any case, did not mean an improvement in women's status; on the contrary, it emphasized woman's role as an object. A dialogue between a knight and lady in De Amore told of a lady, loved by two suitors, who "divided the solaces of love" into two parts and let them choose either the upper or the lower half of her; the question to be debated was which suitor had chosen the better part. The knight contended that the solaces of the upper part were superior, since they were not those of the brute beasts, and since one never tired of practicing them, whereas "the delight of the lower part quickly palls upon those who practice it, and it makes them repent of what they have done." The lady disagreed: "Whatever lovers do has as its only object the obtaining of the solaces of the lower part, for there is fulfilled the whole effect of love, at which all lovers chiefly aim and without which they think they have nothing more than certain preludes to love." In De Amore the question was resolved in favor of the knight, but it was adjudged differently in another work, the French *Lai du Lecheoir* ("Lay of the Lecher"): Eight ladies in a Breton court, "wise and learned," discussed the question of knights' motives for their tournaments, jousts, and adventures:

> Why are they good knights?
> Why do they love tournaments? . . .
> Why do they dress in new clothes?
> Why do they send us their jewels,
> Their treasures and their rings?
> Why are they frank and debonair?
> Why do they refrain from doing evil?
> Why do they like gallantry. . . ?

The answer is given by the poet in a series of plays on the French word *con,* the earthy designation for the center of the "solaces of the lower part."

Whatever the effect on the lady of the castle, the ideas of chivalry and courtly love had their influence for good or ill on a later age, in much of modern etiquette, and above all in the concept of romantic love.

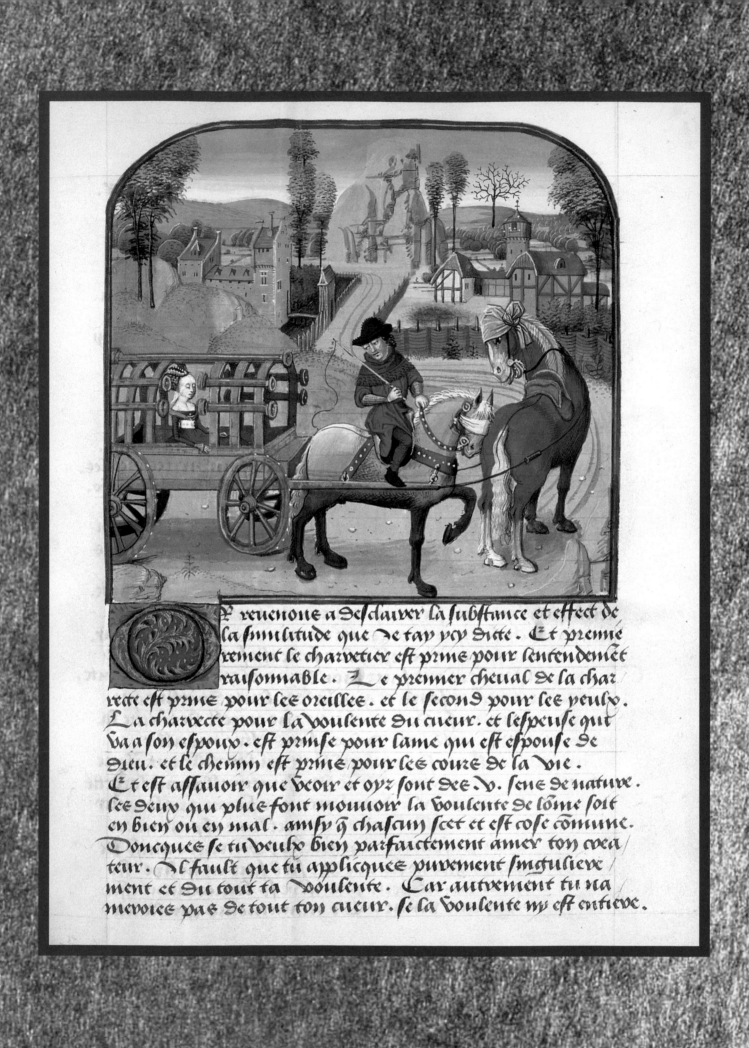

Et reuenons a desclairer la substance et effect de
la similitude que de tay ycy dicte. Et premie
rement le charretier est prins pour lentendemet
raisonnable. Le premier cheual de la char
rette est prins pour les oreilles. et le second pour les yeulx.
La charrette pour la voulente du cueur. et lespeuse qui
va a son espoux. est prinse pour lame qui est espouse de
dieu. et le chemin est prins pour le cours de la vie.
Et est assauoir que veoir et oyz sont des .v. sens de nature.
les deux qui plus font mouuoir la voulente de lôme soit
en bien ou en mal. ainsy q chascun scet et est cose comune.
Donecques se tu veulx bien parfaictement amer ton crea/
teur. Il fault que tu appliques purement singuliere/
ment et du tout ta voulente. Car autrement tu na
meroies pas de tout ton cueur. se la voulente ny est entiere.

V
THE HOUSEHOLD

**B**esides the lord, his lady, and their children, the household of a castle consisted of a staff that varied in size with the wealth of the lord, but that usually comprehended two main divisions. The military personnel, or *mesnie,* included household knights and knights from outside performing castle-guard duty, squires, men-at-arms, a porter who kept the outer door of the castle, and watchmen. The ministerial and domestic staff, headed by the steward, or seneschal, administered the estate, handled routine financial and legal matters, and directed the servants.

Out of a natural division of duties by departments of the house grew the principal offices of the castle. The steward was at first the servant in charge of the great hall; the chaplain or chancellor was in charge of the chapel or chancel (the altar area of a church); the chamberlain was responsible for the great chamber; the keeper of the wardrobe, for clothing; the but-

Manor with a thatched roof behind a lady in a covered cart from *L'Instruction Dung Josne Prince* by Rene of Anjou (c.1470–80).

ler (or bottler), for the buttery, where beverages were kept, in butts or bottles; the usher, for the door of the hall; the cook, for the kitchen, and the marshal, for the stables. Some of these offices expanded in the course of time to entail larger duties: The steward became the manager of the estate; sometimes the chamberlain, sometimes the wardrobe keeper became the treasurer; the chaplain and his assistants became a secretarial department.

In royal households, the duties gradually decayed into honorific rituals. The biographer of William Marshal tells how on Christmas Day in Caen, just before the feast, a servant prepared to pour water for Henry II and his sons to wash their hands when William Marshal's sponsor, the Norman baron William of Tancarville, burst into the room, seized basins and executed the function which was his by right as hereditary chamberlain of Normandy. Matthew Paris described the ceremonies at the wedding of Henry III, in which the king's great barons performed the menial tasks prescribed by their offices:

> The grand marshal of England, the earl of Pembroke [William Marshal's son Gilbert] carried a wand before the king and cleared the way before him both in the church and in the banquet hall, and arranged the banquet and the guests at table. . . .

"Les Evangiles des Quenouilles. Les Advineaux amoreaux", miniature depicting women spinning (French, 15th c.)

The earl of Leicester supplied the king with water in basins to wash before his meal, the Earl Warenne performed the duty of king's cupbearer, supplying the place of the earl of Arundel because the latter was a youth and not as yet made a belted knight.... The justiciar of the forests arranged the drinking cups on the table at the king's right hand....

Under the household officials a large staff of servants operated. In 1265 the king's sister Eleanor de Montfort, countess of Leicester, had more than sixty, while in the 1270s the household of Bogo de Clare, an ecclesiastical kinsman of the Chepstow lords whose accounts have survived, included two knights, "numer-

ous" squires, thirteen grooms, two pages, a cook, a doctor, and many clerks and lesser servants.

The most important member of the castle staff was the steward. In the twelfth century the steward commonly supervised both the lord's estates and his household, but by the thirteenth century there were often two stewards, one in charge of the estates, the other in charge of the domestic routine. The estates steward, frequently a knight, held the lord's courts, headed the council of knights and officials that advised the lord, supervised local officials, and sometimes represented the lord at the king's court or acted as his deputy. He was highly paid, furnished with fine robes trimmed with fur, and sometimes had a house of his own. Simon de Montfort's steward, Richard of Havering, held one-fourth of a knight's fee from his lord, together with other lands and rents, including a parcel for which the annual rent was a symbolic single rose. During the great baronial rebellion led by Simon in 1265 his trusted steward was given charge of Wallingford Castle.

With the aid of auditors, the steward kept the accounts of the lord's lands and fiefs, listing the revenues, acreage, produce, and livestock on each manor, the taxes and other charges paid, the money rents, and the profits from his law courts.

A thirteenth-century manual on estate administration called *Seneschaucie* ("Stewardship") described the requirements for the steward, or seneschal:

> The seneschal of lands ought to be prudent and faithful and profitable, and he ought to know the law of the realm, to protect his lord's business and to instruct and give assurance to the bailiffs who are beneath him in their difficulties. He ought two or three times a year to make his rounds and visit the manors of his stewardship, and then he ought to inquire about the rents, services, and customs . . . and about franchises of courts, lands, woods, meadows, pastures, waters, and other things which belong to the manor. . . .
>
> The seneschal ought at first coming to the manors to cause all the demesne lands of each to be measured by true men . . . to see and inquire how they are tilled, and in what crops they are, and how the cart-horses and cattle, oxen, cows, sheep and swine are kept and improved. . . . The seneschal ought to see that each manor is properly stocked, and if there be overcharge on any manor more than the pasture can bear, let the overcharge be moved to another manor where there is less stock. And if the lord be in want of money to pay the debts due, or to make a purchase at a particular term, the seneschal ought before the term, and before the time that need arises, to look to the manors from which he can have money at the greatest advantage and smallest loss. . . .
>
> The seneschal ought, on coming to the manors, to inquire how the bailiff bears himself within and without, what care he takes, what improvement he makes, and what increase and profit there is in the manor in his office, because of his being there. And also of . . . all other offices. . . . He ought to remove all those that are not necessary for the lord, and all the servants who do nothing. . . .
>
> The seneschal ought, on his coming to the manors, to inquire about wrongdoings and trespasses done in parks, ponds, warrens, rabbit runs, and dovehouses, and of all other things which are done to the loss of the lord in his office.

A picture of a steward at work is given by the letters of Simon of Senlis, steward of the bishop of Chichester, who reported to his lord in 1226:

> Know, my lord, that William de St. John is not in Sussex, wherefore I cannot at present carry through the business which you enjoined upon me, but as soon as he comes into Sussex, I will work as hard as I can to dispatch and complete it in accordance with your honor. I sent to you 85 ells of cloth bought for distribution for the use of the poor. As regards the old wine which is in your cellar at Chichester, I cannot sell to your advantage because of the over-great abundance of new wine in the town of Chichester. Further, my lord, know that a certain burgess of Chichester holds one croft which belongs to the garden given to you by our lord the king, for which he pays two shillings a year, which the sheriff of Sussex demands from him. Wherefore, since the land belongs to the said garden, and was removed from it in ancient times, please give me your advice about the said rent. I am having marling [fertilizing with clay containing carbonate of lime] properly done in your manor of Selsey, and by this time five acres have been marled. . . .

Later he wrote:

> To Richard, whom Thomas of Chichester sent to you, I have committed the keeping of the manor of Preston, since, as I think, he understands the care of sheep, and I will see that your woods at Chichester are meanwhile well treated, by the grace of God, and are brought to their proper state; also I wish your excellency to know that Master R., your official, and I shall be at Aldingbourne on the Sunday after St. Faith's day, there to make the division between my lord of Canterbury and you. And if it please you, your long-cart can easily come to Aldingbourne on that day, so that I can send to you in London, should you so wish, the game taken in your parks and other things, and also the cloth bought for the use of the poor, as much as you wish, and of which I bought 300 ells at Winchester Fair. For at present I cannot send these by your little carts on the manors because sowing time is at hand. Among other things, know that the crops in your manors have been harvested safely and profitably and to your advantage and placed in your barns.

And again:

> Know, dearest lord, that I have been to London, where I labored with all my might and took care that you should there have . . . wood for burning,

brewing and repairs. Thanks be to God, all your affairs, both at West Mulne and elsewhere, go duly and prosperously. Also I have taken care that you should have what I judge to be a sufficient quantity of lambs' wool for your household against the winter.... Speak also with Robert of Lexington about having beef for your larder in London.... If you think it wise, my lord, I beg that part of the old corn from West Mulne shall be ground and sent to London against your coming....

In other letters Simon arranged for the purchase of iron and its transport to Gloucester and then to Winchester; advised his lord to think of getting his sheep from the abbey of Vaudey in Yorkshire and sending them down to his Sussex manors; reported on the vicar of Mundeham's two wives, on a dilatory agent, on the servant of one of the manors whom he wished to promote.

The household steward kept the accounts of the daily expenditures of the castle—sometimes, in a great household, separate accounts for the lord and the lady, and in the royal household even one for the children. Every night, either in person or through a deputy appointed by the lord, the steward went over expenses with the cook, the butler, the pantler (the servant in charge of the pantry, i.e., "breadery"), and the marshal, and listed supplies received—meat, fish, grain. The meat was cut up in his presence and enumerated as it was delivered to the cook; the steward had to know how many loaves could be made from a quarter of wheat, and see that the baker delivered that number to the pantler.

Household accounts were kept from Michaelmas (September 29) to Michaelmas, and they listed, usually in the same order, the amount of grain or bread, the wine and beer, the kitchen supplies, the stable supplies, the number of horses, the amount of hay and oats, and the manor which furnished them. Guests were also listed. They were not always welcome to the household staff. The accounts of Prince Edward (later Edward II) in June 1293 recorded: "There came to dinner John of Brabant [Prince Edward's brother-in-law], with 30 horses and 24 valets, and the two sons of the Lord Edmund [younger brother of King Edward I], and they stay at our expenses in all things in hay, oats and wages." For four days afterward the accounts laconically reported: "Morantur [They remain]." Finally the entry: "They remain until now, and this is the onerous day"— the guests, with some foreigners, went to the jousts at

Fulham, and the household had to provide a sumptuous entertainment.

A rare insight into the domestic economy of the thirteenth-century castle is provided by the accounts of Eleanor de Montfort, the earliest such accounts preserved. For a typical week (in May 1265), they give minute particulars of the household's subsistence. (To give an idea of monetary values, the usual daily wage of a skilled craftsman in the thirteenth century was about 4½ pence—there were 12 pence in a shilling, 20 shillings in a pound.)

> On Sunday, for the Countess and lord Simon de Montfort, and the aforesaid persons of her household: bread, 1½ quarters; wine, 4 sextaries; beer, already reckoned. *Kitchen.* Sheep from Everley, 6, also for 1 ox and 3 calves and 8 lbs. of fat, 12s. 2d.; 6 dozen fowls 3s.; also eggs 2od. flour 6d. Bread for the kitchen 3d. Geese 10, already reckoned. *Marshalcy* [stable]. Hay for 50 horses. Oats, 3 quarters and a half.
>
> Sum 17s. 7d.
>
> For the poor, for 15 days, 1 quarter 1 bushel [of bread]. Beer, 34 gallons. Also for the hounds for 15 days, 5 quarters 5 bushels [of bread]. Also for the poor, on Sunday 120 herrings. Paid for preparing 27 quarters of malt wheat from grain at Odiham [Castle], 2s. 3d. Also for the laundry from Christmas, 15d. Also for yeast, 6½d. For the carriage of 3 pipes of wine from Staines to Odiharn by Seman, 13s. 6d.; and that wine came from the Earl's household at London.
>
> Sum 17s. 6½d.
>
> On the following Monday, for the Countess and the aforesaid persons, dining at Odiharn and leaving late for Portchester [Castle], bread, 1 quarter, 2 bushels of grain; wine, 4½ sextaries; beer already reckoned. *Kitchen.* Meat, already reckoned, eggs, 15d., fowls already reckoned. *Marshalcy.* Smithy, 2d. For one horse placed at the disposal of Dobbe the Parker to guide the Countess, 10d.
>
> Sum 27d.
>
> Tuesday and Wednesday, the household was paid for by lord Simon de Montfort at Portchester.
>
> On the Thursday following, for the Countess, at Portchester, R. de Bruce and A. de Montfort being present, with their household, and lord Simon's servants, and the garrison of the castle; bread bought, 8s., and also ½ a quarter received from a servant from Chawton; wine, from stock. *Kitchen.* Meat bought, 2s. 5d., 6 sheep from a servant from Chawton, and 1 cured hog from the stock of the castle. Eggs, 400, 18d. Salt, 3½,d. *Marshalcy.* Hay for 45 horses, of which the Countess had 24, the lord Simon and his household 9, Amaury 8, the parson of

Kemsing 3, from the castle stock. Oats, 1 quarter received from the servant from Chawton and 2 quarters bought, 5s. Food for the fowls, 14d.

Sum 18s. 4½d.

On the Friday following, for the Countess and the aforesaid persons, bread 6s. 2d., bought, and also 1 quarter from Chawton. Wine from stock, 9 sextaries good and 10½ sextaries of another sort. *Kitchen.* Mackerel, 21d. Fat, 8d. Mullet and bar, 15d. Flounders, 7d. Eggs, 9d. Meal, 13d. Earthen Pots, 3d. Salt, 3½,d. Capers, 3½d. *Marshalcy.* Hay for 48 horses, of which the lord Simon had 12, 12d. Oats, 3 qrs., 1 bushel, of which 1 quarter was bought, and cost 2s. 6d. For gathering grass for 3 nights, 2d.

Sum 16s. 9d.

On the Saturday following, for the Countess and the aforesaid persons, J. de Katerington and others; bread 1½ quarters, from the servant from Chawton; wine, 16 sextaries, of which 9 were of good wine. Pots and cups, 6½,d. *Kitchen.* Fish, 4s. 7d., eggs, 2s. 4d., cheese for tarts, 10d. For 4 mortars bought, 17d. For vinegar and mustard, 5d. Porterage, 5d. *Marshalcy.* Grass, bought in bulk, 13s. 1d. Oats for 52 horses, of which the lord Simon had 12, 2½, quarters, from the servant from Chawton. For carrying two cartloads of grass, 7½d.

Sum 24s. 3½ d.

Administration of an estate required specialized training—in letter-writing, legal procedure, the preparation of documents, and accounting. Beginning in the reign of Henry III, a regular course in estate management was taught by masters in the town of Oxford. The course, which seems to have taken from six months to a year, prepared the young man who had the opportunity of entering the employ of a lord for his practical apprenticeship.

It was a career worth entering. The steward's legitimate perquisites were excellent and were reputed to be frequently augmented by less legitimate ones. A fourteenth-century book of manners declared of stewards, "Few are true, but many are false," and the moralist Robert Mannyng commented that dishonest stewards and other servants

> . . . do much wrong in many things;
> Therefore shall they and their counsel
> Go to hell, both top and tail.

Henry III's butler, a knight named Poyntz Piper, enriched himself as a member of the king's household "by unlawful as well as lawful means," according to Matthew Paris, progressing from the ownership of a few acres of land to "having the wealth of an earl." Poyntz's manors included one at Tedington, where he built a palace, chapel, and other fine stone buildings with lead roofs and established orchards and warrens. Matthew recorded with satisfaction in 1251 that Poyntz had "gone the way of all flesh," and that his widow had married "a brave and handsome knight," who fell heir to all of the estates acquired by the deceased.

The pantry, larder, buttery, and kitchen had their own staffs, including dispensers, cupbearers, fruiterers, a slaughterer, a baker, a brewer, a man to look after the tablecloths, a wafer maker, a candle maker, a sauce cook, and a poulterer, each with boy helpers. The chamberlain employed a cofferer, who was responsible for the chests that contained money and plate—silver cups, saucers, spoons. The keeper of the wardrobe employed tailors to make the robes of the lord and the livery of his retainers. A laundress washed the clothes, sheets, tablecloths, and towels (Bogo de Clare's laundress also washed his hair).

The marshal's stable staff included grooms, smiths, carters, and clerks. Their duties included transporting household goods, delivering purchases made at the fairs or from London merchants, and arranging for the supply of bran, oats, and hay for the horses, and sometimes procuring horseshoes and nails. The marshal and his clerks bought other supplies (carts, sacks, and trunks for the pack horses), paid the grooms, and checked the state of horses and carts. Horses too old for service were given to the poor. Carts were repaired, their iron fittings replaced, axles greased, harness renewed.

Full-time messengers were indispensable to a great lord whose holdings were scattered over a large area. They transported receipts and commodities as well as letters, and ranked in status and pay between the grooms below them and the squires and men-at-arms above them. Besides pay they were provided with robes and shoes every year. Messengers encountered an unusual occupational hazard; Matthew Paris reported that Walter de Clifford, a Welsh baron, was convicted in 1250 of having "in contempt of the king violently and improperly treated his messenger, who bore his royal letters, and of having forced him to eat the same, with the seal." Walter was fined the large sum of 1,000 marks (£667). Later Bogo de Clare's officials similarly treated an emissary of the archbishop of Canterbury, who arrived at Bogo's London house with a citation to serve on the noble prelate. They "by force and against his will made him eat the letters and the appended seals, imprisoned him there, beat and maltreated him." Injury to the messenger was assessed at £20, and damages for contempt of the Church and the king at £1,000, but Bogo succeeded in evading payment.

Another essential department of the lord's household was the office of the chaplain (or chancellor in a very large household). Besides presiding at Mass, the chaplain kept the lord's seal and wrote his business and personal letters in Latin or French. His clerk took charge of the vessels and vestments for Mass, and when the household traveled was responsible for the transport of the portable altar, a wooden table with a stone center to hold relics. Other clerks assisted with the accounts, ran errands, and made purchases.

An important member of the chaplain's department was the almoner, who had charge of offerings to the poor. The almoner gathered the leftovers from the table and saw that they were distributed among the poor and not pilfered by the servants and grooms. A thirteenth-century manual was emphatic that the king's almoner ought to

> visit for charity's sake the sick, the lepers, the captive, the poor, the widows and others in want and the wanderers in the countryside, and to receive discarded horses, clothing, money and other gifts, bestowed in alms, and to distribute them faithfully. He ought also by frequent exhortations to spur the king to liberal almsgiving, especially on saints' days, and to implore him not to bestow his robes, which are of great price, upon players, flatterers, fawners, talebearers, or minstrels, but to command them to be used to augment his almsgiving.

Countess Eleanor de Montfort's almoner, John Scot, was provided with an average of four pence a day for the poor in her accounts of 1265, in addition to table scraps and an occasional full dinner. Not all the nobility were as generous. Bogo de Clare, an avid collector of rich benefices, was notoriously stingy. Bogo gave a banquet in 1285 for which the food-and-drink bill was a sizeable eight pounds six shillings, with additional payments of six shillings eight pence to one wafer maker (the king's, incidentally), four shillings to another, and five shillings to a harpist. At the end of the list of the day's expenses came the item: "On the same day in alms, one penny."

Besides the official departments of the household, there were personal attendants: the ladies-in-waiting, who were not servants but companions, of slightly lower rank than the lady of the castle; the chambermaids; the barber, who also functioned as a surgeon, bloodletter, and dentist; and the doctor.

A large retinue moved with the lord from one of his castles to another. Pack horses carried household goods—one horse loaded with the lord's dismantled bed, sheets, rugs, furs, and mattress, another with the wardrobe, another with the buttery, others with kitchen furniture, candles, portable altar, and chapel furnishings. Two-wheeled carts and less maneuverable but more capacious four-wheeled wagons, built of timber with wooden wheels rimmed with iron strakes, studded with nails with projecting heads that aided traction, carried the heaviest goods, such as wine, cloth, and armor. Sometimes they carried window glass from castle to castle. Lord, lady, children, and guests rode chargers and palfreys with embroidered and gilded saddles. Matthew Paris described the traveling household of Earl Richard of Gloucester on a trip to France in 1250 as including "forty knights, equipped in new accoutrements, all alike, mounted on beautiful horses, bearing new harness, glittering with gold, and with five wagons and fifty sumpter-horses."

By the late thirteenth century, the usual horseback travel was supplemented for noble ladies by the covered chariot. Devoid of springs, the new vehicle represented little technological advance over the baggage carts. Not until the late fourteenth century did the "rocking chariot" *(chariot branlant)* appear, with strap or chain suspension. What the thirteenth-century chariot lacked in comfort it sought to make up in elegance, often being painted or gilded and covered with leather or fine wool cloth in bright colors.

If travel was uncomfortable for lords and ladies, it was rougher for the staff. When night fell on the road, the best, or only, available lodgings went to the lord's family and chief officials. Peter of Blois, a member of the household of Henry II, found that traveling even with the king was an ordeal. He and his fellow courtiers, wandering around in the dark at the place of bivouac, were fortunate if they came upon "some vile and sordid hovel," which they sometimes fought over with drawn swords.

Though most of the permanent staff, comprising the chief servants, journeyed with the lord and lady, many casual servants hired locally—grooms, huntsmen, kitchen boys, tenders of mews and kennels—were dismissed to be rehired on the lord's return. It was an opportunity to weed out bad servants, a chronic problem for every lord of a castle. Bishop Robert Grosseteste advised the countess of Lincoln to observe servants' behavior to see that porters, ushers, and marshals were courteous to guests, and to see that her liveried knights and gentlemen were carefully dressed and did not wear "old tunics, dirty cloaks and shoddy jackets." Servants should be kept on a tight leash and seldom allowed to go home for a holiday. He concluded: "No one should be kept in your household if you have not reasonable belief that he is faithful, discreet, painstaking, and honest, and of good manners."

VI

A DAY IN THE CASTLE

The castle household was astir at daybreak. Roused from their pallets in the attics and cellars, servants lighted fires in kitchen and great hall. Knights and men-at-arms clambered to the walls and towers to relieve the night watch. In the great chamber, the lord and lady awakened in their curtained bed.

They slept naked, and before rising put on linen undergarments—drawers for the lord, a long chemise for the lady. After washing in a basin of cold water, they donned outer garments, essentially the same for both: a long-sleeved tunic, slipped over the head and fastened at the neck with a brooch; a second tunic, or surcoat, over it, shorter, and either sleeveless or with wide, loose sleeves, and often fur-lined; finally a mantle, made from an almost circular piece of material, lined with fur and fastened at the neck either with another brooch or with a chain. The lord's garments were shorter than the lady's,

Bedroom scene: a lady listens to her servant from *Recueil de miniatures* **(French, 15th c.).**

with looser sleeves. Both wore belts tied at the waist or fastened with a metal buckle. The man's costume was completed by long hose attached to the belt that held up his drawers, while the woman's hose, shorter, were suspended from garters below the knee. Both wore shoes—slippers for the house, low boots for outdoors.

The colors of tunics, mantles, hose, and shoes were bright—blues, yellows, crimsons, purples, greens—and the fabric of the garments was usually wool, though fine silks such as samite, sendal (taffeta), and damask (a kind of brocade) were occasionally worn. Camlet, imported from Cyprus, was sometimes used for winter robes, woven from camel's or goat's hair. The fur trimmings and linings were of squirrel, lambskin, rabbit, miniver, otter, marten, beaver, fox, ermine, and sable. Tunics and mantles were decorated with embroidery, tassels, feathers, or pearls. For festive occasions belts might be of silk with gold or silver thread, or adorned with jewels. Both men and women wore head coverings indoors and outdoors. The lord usually wore a linen coif tied by strings under the chin, sometimes elaborately embroidered, or decorated with feathers and buttons; the lady wore a linen wimple, either white or colored, that covered hair and neck. Outdoors, hoods and caps were worn over the colts and wimples. Elegant gloves, sometimes fur-

Manuscript detail, showing Sir Geoffrey Luttrell dining with his family from the *Latin/Luttrell Psalter* (14th c.).

lined, and jewelry—gold rings with stones, pins, necklaces, hairbands, shoebuckles, and bracelets—completed the costume.

The lady might arrange her hair with the aid of a mirror—an expensive article, usually small and circular, mounted in a wooden or metal case, and made either of polished steel or of glass over a metal surface. Despite the disapproval of preachers and moralist writers, ladies wore cosmetics—sheep fat, and rouge and skin whiteners with which they tinted themselves pink and white—and used depilatory pastes.

After mass in the chapel, the household breakfasted on bread washed down with wine or ale. The morning was spent in routine tasks or amusements, depending on whether the castle had guests. The lord had his round of conferences with stewards and bailiffs, or with members of his council; the lady conversed with her guests or busied herself with embroidery and other domestic projects. Knights and squires practiced fencing and tilting, while children did their lessons under the guidance of a tutor, commonly the chaplain or one of his clerks. Lessons over, the children were free to play— girls with dolls, boys with tops and balls, horseshoes, bows and arrows.

Archery was a favorite pastime with boys of all ages. In the twelfth century the son of the lord of Haverford Castle in Wales, and two other boys sent there for their education, made friends with an outlaw confined in the castle who fashioned arrows for their bows. One day the robber took advantage of the negligence of the guards to seize the boys and barricade himself in his prison. "A great clamor instantly arose," recorded the chronicler Gerald of Wales, "as well from the boys within as from the people without; nor did he cease, with an uplifted axe, to threaten the lives of the children, until indemnity and security were assured to him."

In the castle courtyard the grooms swept out the stables and fed the horses; the smith worked at his forge on horseshoes, nails, and wagon fittings; and domestic servants emptied basins and chamber pots and brought in rushes for the freshly swept floors. The laundress soaked sheets, tablecloths, and towels in a wooden trough containing a solution of wood ashes and caustic soda; then she pounded them, rinsed them, and hung them to dry. In the kitchen the cook and his staff turned the meat—pork, beef, mutton, poultry, game—on a spit and prepared stews and soups in great iron cauldrons hung over the fire on a hook and chain that could be raised and lowered to regulate the temperature. Boiled meat was lifted out of the pot with an iron meat hook, a long fork with a wooden handle and prongs attached to the side. Soup was stirred with a long-handled slotted spoon.

Meat preservation was by salting or smoking, or, most commonly and simply, by keeping the meat alive till needed. Salting was done by two methods. Dry-salting meant burying the meat in a bed of salt pounded to a powder with mortar and pestle. Brine-curing consisted of immersing the meat in a strong salt solution. Before cooking, the salted meat had to be soaked and rinsed.

In addition to roasting and stewing, meat might be pounded to a paste, mixed with other ingredients, and served as a kind of custard. A dish of this kind was *blank-manger,* consisting of a paste of chicken blended with rice boiled in almond milk, seasoned with sugar, cooked until very thick, and garnished with fried almonds and anise. Another was a *mortrews,* of fish or meat that was pounded, mixed with bread crumbs, stock, and eggs, and poached, producing a kind of *quenelle,* or dumpling. Both meat and fish were also made into pies, pasties, and fritters.

Sauces were made from herbs from the castle garden that were ground to a paste, mixed with wine, *verjuice* (the juice of unripe grapes), vinegar, onions, ginger, pepper, saffron, cloves, and cinnamon. Mustard, a favorite ingredient, was used by the gallon.

In Lent or on fast days fish was served fresh from the castle's own pond, from a nearby river, or from the sea, nearly always with a highly seasoned sauce. Salt or

Musicians floating down a river from a Flemish Book of Hours (c.1500).

smoked herring was a staple, as were salted or dried cod and stockfish. Fresh herring, flavored with ginger, pepper, and cinnamon, might be made into a pie. Other popular fish included mullet, shad, sole, flounder, plaice, ray, mackerel, salmon, and trout. Sturgeon, whale, and porpoise were rare seafood delicacies, the first two "royal fish," fit for kings and queens. Pike, crab, crayfish, oysters, and eels were also favorites. A royal order to the sheriff of Gloucester in the 1230s stated that

> since after lampreys all fish seem insipid to both the king and the queen, the sheriff shall procure by purchase or otherwise as many lampreys as possible in his bailiwick, place them in bread and jelly, and send them to the king while he is at a distance from those parts by John of Sandon, the king's cook, who is being sent to him. When the king comes nearer, he shall send them to him fresh.

The most common vegetables, besides onions and garlic, were peas and beans. Staples of the diet of the poor, for the rich they might be served with onions and saffron. Honey, commonly used for sweetening, came from castle or manor bees; fruit from the castle orchard—apples, pears, plums, and peaches—was supplemented by wild fruits and nuts from the lord's wood. In addition to these local products, there were imported luxuries such as sugar (including a special kind made with roses and violets), rice, almonds, figs, dates, raisins, oranges, and pomegranates, purchased in town or at the fairs. Ordinary sugar was bought by the loaf and had to be pounded; powdered white sugar was more expensive.

At mealtimes, servants set up the trestle tables and spread the cloths, setting steel knives, silver spoons, dishes for salt, silver cups, and *mazers*—shallow silver-rimmed wooden bowls. At each place was a trencher or *manchet*, a thick slice of day-old bread serving as a plate for the roast meat. Meals were announced by a horn blown to signal time for washing hands. Servants with ewers, basins, and towels attended the guests.

At the table, seating followed status: The most important guests were at the high table, with the loftiest place reserved for an ecclesiastical dignitary, the second for the ranking layman. After grace, the procession of servants bearing food began. First came the pantler with the bread and butter, followed by the butler and his assistants with the wine and beer. Wine, in thirteenth-century England mostly imported from English-ruled Bordeaux, was drunk young in the absence of an effective technique for stoppering containers. Wine kept a year became undrinkable. No attention was paid to vintage, and often what was served even at rich tables was of poor quality. Peter of Blois described in a letter wine served at Henry II's court: "The wine is turned sour or mouldy—thick, greasy, stale, flat and smacking of pitch, I have sometimes seen even great lords served with wine so muddy that a man must needs close his eyes and clench his teeth, wry-mouthed and shuddering, and filtering the stuff rather than drinking."

A Jester, detail from Betley stained glass window (c.1621).

The solid parts of soups and stews were eaten with a spoon, the broth sipped. Meat was cut up with the knife and eaten with the fingers. Two persons shared a dish, the lesser helping the more important, the younger the older, the man the woman. The former in each case broke the bread, cut the meat, and passed the cup.

Etiquette books admonished diners not to leave the spoon in the dish or put elbows on the table, not to belch, not to drink or eat with their mouths full, not to stuff their mouths or take overly large helpings. Not surprisingly, in the light of the finger-eating and dish-sharing, stress was laid on keeping hands and nails scrupulously clean, wiping spoon and knife after use, wiping the mouth before drinking, and not dipping meat in the salt dish.

The lord and lady were at pains to see their guests amply served. Bishop Robert Grosseteste advised the countess of Lincoln to make sure that her servants were judiciously distributed during dinner, that they entered the room in an orderly way and avoided quarreling. "Especially do you yourself keep watch over the service until the meats are placed in the hall, and then . . . command that your dish be so refilled and heaped up, and especially with the light dishes, that you may courteously give from your dish to all the high table on the right and on the left." At his own house, he reminded the countess, guests were served at dinner with two meats and two lighter dishes. Between courses, the steward should send the servers into the kitchen and see to it that they brought in the meats quietly and without confusion.

An everyday dinner, served between 10:00 AM and noon, comprised two or three courses, each of several separate dishes, all repeating the same kinds of food except the last course, which consisted of fruits, nuts, cheese, wafers, and spiced wine.

On such festive occasions as holidays and weddings, fantastic quantities of food were consumed. When Henry III's daughter married the king of Scotland on Christmas Day 1252 at York, Matthew Paris reported that "more than sixty pasture cattle formed the first and principal course at table . . . the gift of the archbishop. The guests feasted by turns with one king at one time, at another time with the other, who vied with one another in preparing costly meals." As for the entertainment, the number and apparel of the guests, the variety of foods: "If I were more fully to describe [them] . . . the

The castle bought wine by the barrel and decanted it into jugs. Some was spiced and sweetened by the butlers to go with the final course. Ale, made from barley, wheat, or oats, or all three, was drunk mainly by the servants. A castle household brewed its own, hiring an ale-wife for the task and using grain from its own stores. At the royal court, according to Peter of Blois, the ale was not much better than the wine—it was "horrid to the taste and abominable to the sight."

Ceremony marked the service at table. There was a correct way to do everything, from the laying of cloths to the cutting of trenchers and carving of meat. Part of a squire's training was learning how to serve his lord at meals: the order in which dishes should be presented, where they should be placed, how many fingers to use in holding the joint for the lord to carve, how to cut the trenchers and place them on the table.

Medieval musicians.

relation would appear hyperbolical in the ears of those not present, and would give rise to ironical remarks." Such feasts included boars' heads, venison, peacocks, swans, suckling pigs, cranes, plovers, and larks.

During dinner, even on ordinary days, the party might be entertained with music or jokes and stories. Many households regularly employed harpers and minstrels. Adam the harper was a member of Bogo de Clare's household, and on occasion Bogo hired *ystriones* ("actors") and at least once a *ioculator* ("jester"), William Pilk of Salisbury. When the meal was over, one of the guests might regale the company with a song; many a knight and baron composed songs in the tradition of the trouvères, the knightly poets who were the troubadours of the North (although in some cases the tunes for their verses seem to have been written by the traveling professional minstrels known as jongleurs). They might be accompanied by the harp, the lute, or the viele, ancestor of the violin. Sometimes the accompanist played chords as a prelude to the song and as background to an occasional phrase; sometimes the singer accompanied himself in unison on the viele and played the tune over once more when he had finished singing, as a coda. The verses—in French—were sophisticated in form and stylized in subject matter, usually falling into established categories: dawn songs, spinning songs, political satires (*sirventes*), laments, debates, love songs. They might be May songs, like the following celebrated poem by Bernard de Ventadour, protégé of Eleanor of Aquitaine (the notation is modern; medieval music was normally recorded without division into measures, the rhythm being supplied by the words—except in part-singing or polyphonic music, where more precise time was necessary for synchronization):

> When the flower appears beside the green leaf, when I see the weather bright and serene and hear in the wood the song of the birds which brings sweetness to my heart and pleases me, the more the birds sing to merit praise, the more joy I have in my heart and I must sing, as all my days are full of joy and song and I think of nothing else.

Or they might be songs of the Crusade, like the following, by the early thirteenth-century trouvère Guiot de Dijon:

> I shall sing to cheer my heart, for fear lest I die of my great grief or go mad, when I see none return from that wild land where he is who brings comfort to my heart when I hear news of him. O God, when they cry "Forward," help the pilgrim for whom I am so fearful, for the Saracens are evil.

Or lively picaresque songs like one by Colin Muset, another thirteenth-century poet:

chric. que uos amcz enprisonez
le meillor chr del monce. fil uos

Men playing cards, manuscript detail.

bluff called hoodman blind, in which a player reversed his hood to cover his face and tried to catch the others. In *The Castellan of Coucy,* "after dinner there were wine, apples, ginger; some played backgammon and chess, others went to snare falcons." Chess, widely popular, was played in two versions, one similar to the modern game, the other a simpler form played with dice. Either was commonly accompanied by gambling—the household accounts of John of Brabant on one occasion recorded two shillings lost at chess. Dice games were played in all ranks of society, and even the clergy indulged. Bogo de Clare's accounts reported three shillings handed to him on Whitsunday 1285 to play at dice. Bowls, a favorite outdoor pastime, also was accompanied by betting.

Recreation included horseplay. Matthew Paris described disapprovingly how Henry III, his half brother Geoffrey de Lusignan, and other nobles, while strolling in an orchard, were pelted with turf, stones, and green apples by one of Geoffrey's chaplains, a man "who served as a fool and buffoon to the king . . . and whose savings, like those of a silly jester . . . excited their laughter." In the course of his buffoonery, the chaplain went so far as

When I see winter return, then would I find lodging, if I could discover a generous host who would charge me nothing, who would have pork and beef and mutton, ducks, pheasants, and venison, fat hens and capons and good cheeses in baskets.

Sometimes songs were sung with refrains to be repeated by a chorus; there were also lays, in which each verse had a different structure and musical setting.

The meal finished, tables were cleared, the company washed hands again, and turned to the afternoon's tasks and amusements. "The ladies and the bachelors danced and sang caroles after dinner," on a festive occasion in *The Castellan of Coucy.* A carole was a kind of round dance in which the dancers joined hands as they sang and circled. Guests could be entertained with parlor games such as hot cockles, in which one player knelt blindfolded and was struck by the other players, whose identity he had to guess, or a variety of blind man's

Couple in bed from the *Chroniques des Rois de France* (15th c.).

to press "the juice of unripe grapes in their eyes, like one devoid of sense."

Supper was served in the late afternoon. Robert Grosseteste recommended "one dish not so substantial, and also light dishes, and then cheese."

There were also late suppers, just before bedtime, drawing suspicion from such moralists as Robert Mannyng, who described midnight "rere suppers" of knights, "when their lords have gone to bed," as giving rise to gluttony and waste, not to mention lechery.

The romance *L'Escoufle* ("The Kite") pictures an evening in a castle, after supper: The count goes to relax in front of the fire in the damsels' chamber, taking off his shirt to have his back scratched and resting his head in the lap of the heroine, Aelis, while the servants stew fruits over the hearth.

The household of the castle retired early. Manuals for household management describe the activities of the chamberlain in preparing his lord for bed:

> Take off his robe and bring him a mantle to keep him from cold, then bring him to the fire and take off his shoes and his hose . . . then comb his head, then spread down his bed, lay the head sheet and the pillows, and when your sovereign is in bed, draw the curtains. . . . Then drive out dog or cat, and see that there be basin and urinal set near your sovereign, then take your leave mannerly that your sovereign may take his rest merrily.

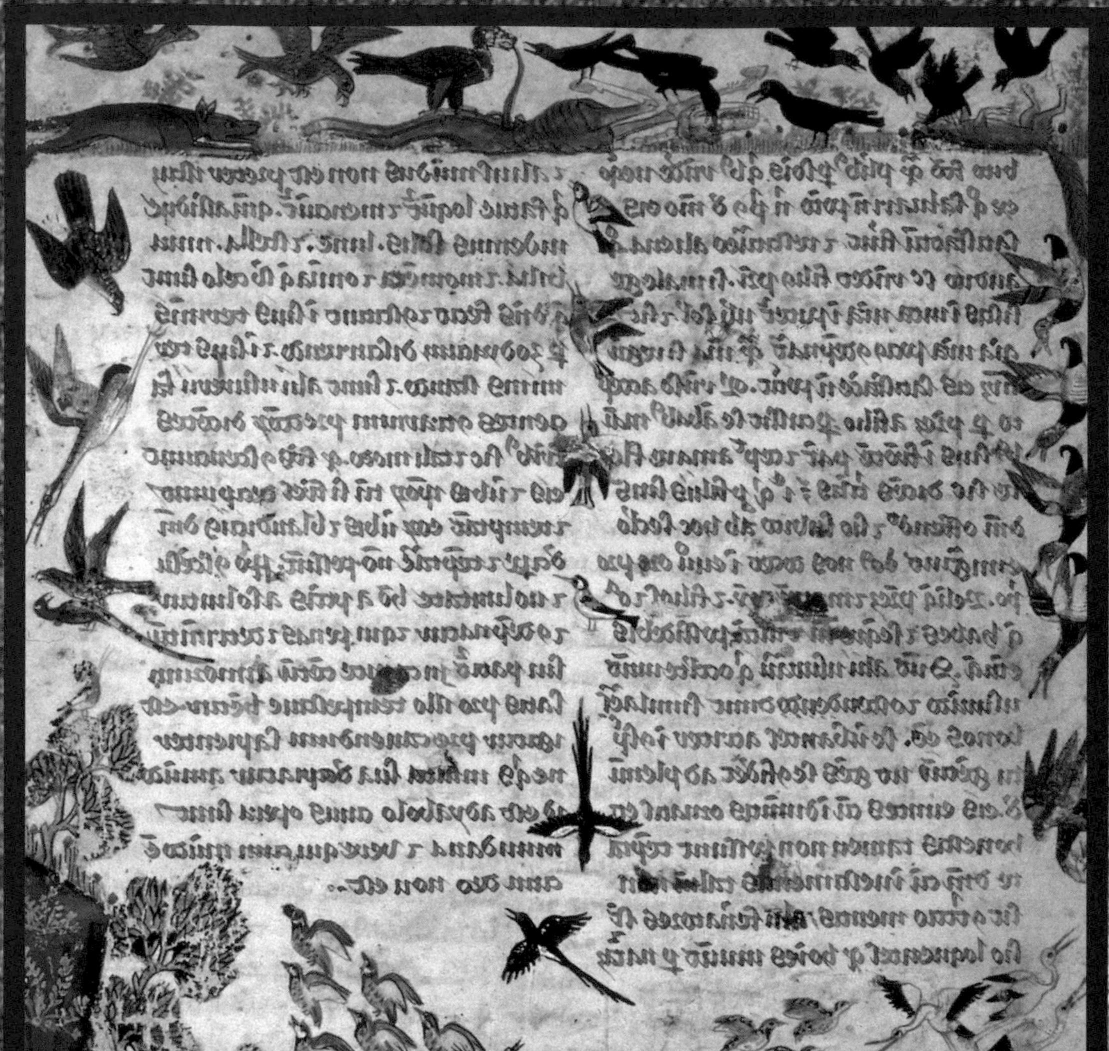

VII
HUNTING AS A WAY OF LIFE

A t dawn on a summer day, when the deer were at their fattest, the lord, his household, and guests loved to set out into the forest. While the huntsman, a professional and often a regular member of the lord's staff, stalked the quarry with the leashed dogs and their handlers, the hunting party breakfasted in a clearing on a picnic meal of meat, wine, and bread.

When the dogs found a deer's spoor, the huntsman estimated the animal's size and age by measuring the tracks with his fingers and by studying the scratches made by the horns on bushes, the height of the rubbed-off velvet of the antlers on trees, and the "fumes" (droppings), some of which he gathered in his hunting horn to show his master. The lord made the decision as to whether it was a quarry worth hunting. Sometimes the huntsman, by silently climbing a tree, could get a sight of the deer.

The dogs were taken by a roundabout route to

Men and boys hawking (late 14th c.).

intercept the deer's line of retreat. They were usually of three kinds: the lymer, a bloodhound that was kept on a leash and used to finish the stag at bay; the brachet, a smaller hound; and the greyhound or levrier, larger than the modern breed and capable of singly killing a deer.

The huntsman advanced on foot with a pair of lymers to drive the deer toward the hunting party. Meanwhile the lord raised his ivory hunting horn, the olifant, and blew a series of one-pitch notes. This was the signal for the greyhounds. Once begun, the chase continued until the hounds brought the stag to bay, when one of the hunters was given the privilege of killing it with a lance thrust. Sometimes the hunters used bows and arrows. The kill was followed by skinning and dividing up the meat, including the hounds' share, laid out on the skin.

Although the hart could be a dangerous quarry, the wild boar, usually hunted in the winter, was more formidable. A wily enemy, he would not venture out of cover without first looking, listening, and sniffing, and once his suspicions were aroused no amount of shouting and horn blowing would lure him from his narrow den. The boar-hunting dog was the alaunt, a powerful breed resembling the later German shepherd. Even when dogs and hunters caught the boar in the open, his

Stag hunting from the *Livre de la Chasse* by Gaston Phebus (begun 1387).

great tusks were a fearful weapon. "I have seen them kill good knights, squires and servants," wrote Gaston de la Foix in his fourteenth-century *Livre de la Chasse* ("Book of the Hunt"). And Edward, duke of York, in the fifteenth century treatise *The Master of Game* wrote, "The boar slayeth a man with one stroke, as with a knife. Some have seen him slit a man from knee up to breast and slay him all stark dead with one stroke." An old boar usually stood his ground and struck desperately about him, but a young boar was capable of rapid maneuvers preceding his deadly slashes.

The huntsman was always well paid, and in a great household might be a knight. Henry I employed no fewer than four, at eight pence a day, at the head of a hunting company that included four horn blowers, twenty sergeants (beaters), several assistant huntsmen, a variety of dog handlers, a troop of mounted wolf hunters, and several archers, one of whom carried the king's own bow. A royal hunting party was a small military expedition.

But the form of hunting that stirred the widest interest throughout medieval Europe was falconry. Hawks were the only means of bringing down birds that flew beyond the range of arrows. Every king, noble, baron, and lord of the manor had his falcons. A favorite bird shared his master's bedroom and accompanied him daily on his wrist. Proud, fierce, and temperamental, the falcon had a mystique and a mythology. Of many treatises and manuals about falconry, the most famous was the exhaustive *De Arte Venandi cum Avibus* ("The Art of Falconry") by the erudite emperor Frederick II (from which most of the following information is drawn).

The birds used in medieval falconry belonged to two main categories. The true falcons, or long-winged hawks, included the gerfalcon, the peregrine, the saker, and the lanner, all used to hunt waterfowl, and the merlin, used for smaller birds. The short-winged hawks included the goshawk and the sparrow hawk, which could be flown in wooded country where long-winged hawks were at a disadvantage. Only the female, larger and more aggressive than the male, was properly called a falcon; the smaller male was called a tiercel, and although sometimes used in hunting was considered inferior.

One of the essential buildings in a castle courtyard was the mews where the hawks roosted and where they took refuge during molting season. It was spacious enough to allow limited flight, had at least one window, and a door large enough for the falconer to pass through with a bird on his wrist. The floor was covered with gravel or coarse sand, changed at regular intervals.

In the semidarkness inside, perches of several sizes were adapted to different kinds of birds, some high and well out from the wall, others just far enough off the floor to keep the bird's tail feathers from touching. Outside stood low wooden or stone blocks, usually in the form of cones, point down, driven into the ground with sharp iron spikes, on which the falcons "weathered," that is, became accustomed to the world outside the mews.

A good falcon was expensive chiefly because her training demanded infinite patience and care. The birds were obtained either as eyases—nestlings taken from a tree or a cliff-top—or as branchers, young birds that had just left the nest and were caught in nets. Branchers were put into a "sock," a close-fitting linen bag open at both ends, so that the bird's head protruded at one end, feet and tail at the other.

Gerald of Wales reported that once when Henry II was staying at the Clares' Pembroke Castle and "amusing himself in the country with the sport of hawking," he saw a falcon perched on a crag, and let loose on it a large high-bred Norway hawk. The falcon, though its flight was at first slower than the Norway hawk's, finally rose above its adversary, became the assailant, and pouncing on it with great fury, laid the royal bird dead at the king's feet. "From that time the king used to send every year in the proper season for the young falcons which are bred in the cliffs on the coast of South Wales; for in all his land he could not find better or more noble hawks."

The falconer's first task was to have the bird prepared for training. The needle points of the talons were trimmed, the eyes usually "seeled"—temporarily sewn closed—and two jesses, strips of leather with rings at the end, were fastened around the legs. Small bells were tied to the feet to alert the falconer to the bird's movements. She was then tied to the perch by a long leather strap called a leash. At the same time, whether seeled or not, she was usually introduced to the hood, a piece of leather that covered her eyes, with an opening for the beak. Now, blinded, she had to be trained through her senses of taste, hearing, and touch.

The falcon's first lesson was learning to stand on a human wrist. To begin with, she was carried gently about in a darkened room for a day and a night, and passed from hand to hand, without being fed. On the second day, the falconer fed her a chicken leg, while talking or singing to her, always using the same phrase or bar of a song, stroking her while she ate. Gradually the bird was unseeled, at night or in a darkened room, with the attendant being careful not to let her see his face, on the theory that the human face was particularly repugnant to the falcon. Again she was carried about for a day and a night and fed in small quantities while being gently stroked, and gradually she was exposed to more light. When she was well accustomed to the new situation, she was taken outdoors before dawn, and brought back while it was still dark. Finally her eyesight was fully restored, and the falconer exposed her to full daylight.

The initial stage of her training was accomplished: The captive was partially tamed and accustomed to handling. But the falconer still had to guard the sensitive, excitable creature closely to prevent her from taking alarm and injuring herself. If she became restless and tried to fly off her perch, or bit at her jesses and bell and scratched at her head, she had to be quieted by gentle speech, stroking, and feeding, or by being sprinkled with drops of water, sometimes from the falconer's mouth (which had first to be scrupulously cleansed). Once the bird felt at home on her master's wrist outdoors, she was taken on horseback.

Now the falcon was ready to be taught to return to her master during the hunt by means of the lure. This device was usually made of the wings of the bird which was to be the falcon's quarry, tied to a piece of meat. If a gerfalcon, a bird distinguished by its size, dignity, speed, and agility, was to be used to hunt cranes, the lure was made of a pair of crane's wings tied together with a leather thong, in the same position as if folded on the crane's back. To the lure was tied a long strap. To keep the falcon from flying away during these first departures from his fist, the falconer fastened a long slender cord, the creance, to the end of her leash.

In the field, as much of the line was unwound as was necessary for the bird's flight, and she was taken on the falconer's fist. An assistant handed him the lure as he removed the falcon's hood, at the same time repeating the familiar notes or words that he always used while feeding her. The falconer held firmly onto her jesses while she tasted the meat fastened to the lure. Then his assistant took the lure and moved away with it, always keeping it in the falcon's vision, finally placing it on the ground and withdrawing, while the falconer released the bird, letting the line run through his free hand. When the falcon landed on the lure, the assistant slowly approached her, holding meat out, repeating her call notes, and finally setting it down before her. While she seized it, he picked her up on the lure, and gathered the jesses and drew them tight.

Once the falcon responded well to the lure, she was taught to come to it when it was whirled in the air by the assistant while he uttered the call notes. Finally the falcon sprang eagerly from the fist when she saw the lure and flew directly to it. The creance was now abandoned and the bird could be allowed to fly free.

Now she was ready to be taught to hunt. A gerfalcon to be used in hunting cranes was often started on hares, because the same method of flight was used for both, and because a hare would be unlikely to distract a falcon when she hunted for cranes, since hares always had to be driven out of cover by dogs. Sometimes a stuffed rabbit pelt baited with meat was dragged in front of the falcon, with the falconer on horseback racing over the fields after the decoy, letting the falcon loose only to jerk her up short before she could strike, teaching her to swoop and pounce suddenly. Then the falconer brought out the hounds, who drove live rabbits out for the falcon.

Next the gerfalcon was exposed to snipe and partridge. Only when she became proficient with these was she ready for her real quarry, and even now her introduction was gradual. At first a live crane was staked in a meadow, its eyes sealed, its claws blunted, and its beak bound so that it could not injure the gerfalcon. Meat was tied to its back. The gerfalcon was unhooded and the crane shown to her. When the falcon killed the crane, the falconer removed its heart and fed it to the falcon. The process was repeated, increasing the distance between the mounted falconer and the crane bait until the gerfalcon began her flight a bowshot away (300 to 400 yards). At the same time the falconer trained the falcon to recognize a crane's call by slitting a crane's larynx and blowing into it.

Dogs, usually greyhounds, were often used in teaching the gerfalcon to capture larger birds. This meant special training for the dogs as well as the falcons, so that the dog did not desert the hunt to chase a rabbit. Dog and falcon were fed together to enhance their comradeship, while the dog was trained to run with the falcon and help her seize her prey.

A different technique was used for "hawking at the brook," that is, hunting ducks on the riverbank. Here the hawk was trained to circle above the falconer's head, "waiting on," while the hounds raised the ducks. She then "stooped" (dived) to strike them in the air.

The good falconer, according to Frederick II, who employed more than fifty in his Apulian castles, had to be of medium size—not too large to be agile and not too small to be strong. Besides the cardinal virtue of patience, the falconer needed acute hearing and vision, a daring spirit, alert mind, and even temper. He could not be a heavy sleeper, lest he fail to hear the falcon's bells in the night. And he had to be well-versed in the ailments of hawks and their remedies—medicines for

A manuscript illustration depicting falconry, from the *Treatise on Hunting* **(1459).**

headaches and colds, salves for injuries: mixtures of spices, vinegar, snakemeat, gristle, and drugs almost as unpleasant as the medicines prescribed for human beings.

Hunting was much more than a sport, and the forest much more than a recreation ground. The deer and other quarry supplied a substantial share of the meat for the castle table, and the forest supplemented game with nuts, berries, mushrooms, and other wild edibles. It also furnished the principal construction material and fuel for all classes. King Henry III granted ten oaks from the Forest of Dean in 1228 to William Marshal II to use in remodeling and heightening Fitz Osbern's Great Tower; later he granted more oaks to Gilbert Marshal to finish the work. Forest land was a natural resource of immense value, and consequently coveted, defended, and fought over. William the Conqueror, a great lover of hunting, brought "forest law" from France to England to preserve the English forests for his own use. Medieval land clearance and sheep grazing had had a major impact on the ecology of Europe (something like that of agricultural expansion on North America in the nineteenth century), and although William and other European princes who enacted regulations were not interested in ecology, their actions had the effect of curbing deforestation.

Stringent prohibitions were promulgated against poaching. *The Anglo-Saxon Chronicle* reported:

> William set aside a vast deer preserve and imposed laws concerning it, so that whoever slew a hart or hind was to be blinded. He forbade the killing of boars, even as the killing of harts, for he loved the tall deer as if he had been their father. . . . The rich complained, and the poor lamented, but he was so stern that he cared not though all might hate him.

William established as royal forest or game preserve large tracts that embraced villages and wasteland as well as woods. On these lands no one but the king and those authorized by him—not even the barons who held the land—could hunt the red deer, the fallow deer, the roe, and the wild boar. Hounds and bows were forbidden. Because foxes, hares, badgers, squirrels, wild cats, martens, and otter were considered harmful to the deer and boar, rights of "warren" were often granted for hunting these smaller quarry. Birds hunted in falconry were generally also included in the "beasts of the warren," although they were not harmful to the deer. Dogs kept within the forest had to be "lawed"—three talons cut from each front foot.

The twelfth-century chronicler Florence of Worcester attributed the death of the Conqueror's son, William Rufus, in a hunting accident in the New Forest (south of Winchester), to his father's strict forest laws.

> Nor can it be wondered that . . . Almighty power and vengeance should have been thus displayed. For in former times . . . this tract of land was thickly planted with churches and with inhabitants who were worshippers of God; but by command of King William the Elder the people were expelled, the houses half ruined, the churches pulled down, and the land made an habitation for wild beasts only; and hence, as it is believed, arose this mischance. For Richard, the brother of William the Younger, had perished long before in the same forest, and a short time previously his cousin Richard, the [natural] son of Robert, earl [duke] of Normandy, was also killed by an arrow by one of his knights, while he was hunting. A church, built in the old times, had stood on the spot where the king fell, but as we have already said, it was destroyed in the time of his father.

William Rufus' death was vividly pictured by Ordericus Vitalis:

> [That morning—August 1, 1100] King William, having dined with his minions, prepared, after the meal was ended, to go forth and hunt in the New Forest. Being in great spirits, he was joking with his attendants while his boots were being laced, when an armorer came and presented to him six arrows. The king immediately took them with great satisfaction, praising the work, and unconscious of what was to happen, kept four of them himself and gave the other two to Walter Tirel [lord of Poix and castellan of Pontoise, fifteen miles northwest of Paris]. "It is but right," he said, "that the sharpest arrows should be given to him who knows best how to inflict mortal wounds with them." . . . [The king] hastily rose, and mounting his horse, rode at full speed to the forest. His brother, Count Henry, with William de Breteuil [son of William Fitz Osbern] and other distinguished persons followed him, and, having penetrated into the woods, the hunters dispersed themselves in various directions according to custom. The king and Walter posted themselves with a few others in one part of the forest, and stood with their weapons in their hands eagerly watching for the coming of the game, when a stag suddenly running between them, the king quitted his station, and Walter shot an arrow. It grazed the beast's horny back, but glancing from it, mortally wounded the king who stood within its range. He immediately fell to the ground, and alas! suddenly expired. . . . Some of the servants wrapped the king's bloody corpse in a mean covering, and brought it, like a wild boar pierced by the hunters, to the city of Winchester.

Henry II, William Rufus' great-nephew, was another enthusiastic hunter. According to Gerald of Wales,

> He was immoderately fond of the chase, and devoted himself to it with excessive ardor. At the first dawn of day he would mount a fleet horse, and indefatigably spend the day in through the woods, penetrating the depths of forests, and crossing the ridges of hills. . . . He was inordinately fond of hawking or hunting, whether his falcons stooped on their prey, or his sagacious hounds, quick of scent and swift of foot, pursued the chase. Would to God he had been as zealous in his devotions as he was in his sports!

By the thirteenth century, forest law was even more strictly enforced in England than on the Continent, where there were fewer royal forests and more grants of hunting rights. William I's successors had persistently striven to extend the area of the royal forest, although Richard I and John, when they needed money, "disafforested" large areas, opening them to local lords in return for cash payments. In 1217, under William Marshal's regency in the early years of Henry III's reign, the Forest Charter was granted as a kind of postscript to Magna Carta, to further satisfy the barons. By it the forest law was codified and a commission directed to make "perambulations" of the royal forest, reviewing additions made under Henry II, Richard, and John, and retaining only those that were in the king's own demesne. Ten years later, when Henry came of age, he summoned the knights who had made the perambulations and forced them to revise their boundaries in the royal favor. The forest then remained essentially unchanged until 1300, when Edward I was forced once more to disafforest large tracts.

The Forest Charter designated the courts to enforce forest law: local courts that met regularly every six weeks, special forest inquisitions called to deal with serious trespasses, and the royal forest eyre (circuit court) that had ultimate jurisdiction. The local attachment courts dealt with minor offenses to the "vert"—the greenwood of the forest: cutting; clearing; gathering dead wood, honey, and nuts; allowing cattle to graze or pigs to feed on acorns and beechnuts. When a graver offense against the vert or a crime against the "venison"—the right to hunt deer—was committed, a special court was called to hear the case before the forest officers, and either send the offender to prison until the next eyre or attach him to appear before it, depending on the seriousness of the crime. Any evidence—

arrows, antlers, skins, poachers' greyhounds—was delivered to forest officials to be produced before the justices (the deer was usually given to the poor, the sick, or lepers). Sentence to imprisonment by the special inquisition was not punishment, but merely insurance that the accused would duly appear before the eyre. If the accused could find pledges to secure his appearance, he was released.

Every seven years the forest eyre, made up of four barons and knights appointed by the king, traveled from county to county hearing the accumulated forest cases. Trespassers were brought from prison or produced by the sheriff, the foresters and other officers presented their exhibits and the record of the special inquisition. The record was usually accepted as proof of the facts without any further hearing of evidence, and the prisoner was sentenced to prison for a year and a day—again not as punishment but against the payment of a ransom or fine. Usually the fine was in proportion to the prisoner's condition, and sometimes trespassers were pardoned because they were poor. If a man had spent much time in jail waiting to be tried, he was released: "And because Roger lay for a long time in prison, so that he is nearly dead, it is judged that he go quit; and let him dwell outside the forest." "Because he was a long time in prison and has no goods, therefore he is quit thereof." On the other hand, if he failed to appear, the trespasser was outlawed.

Every three years an inspection of the forests was made by a body of twelve knights, the "regarders," who were supposed to report any encroachments on the king's demesne—the erection of a mill or a fishpond, the enlargement of a clearing, the enclosure of land without license, or any abuse of the right to cut wood.

Besides the regarders, the forest was administered by a large hierarchy of officials, headed by the justice, who directed the whole forest administration of England. Next in authority were the wardens, also called stewards, bailiffs, or chief foresters, who had custody of single forests or groups of forests; below them were officers called verderers, knights or landed gentry nominally in charge of the vert but actually with a variety of duties; and there were also foresters, who acted as gamekeepers, responsible to the wardens and appointed by them. Usually each forest had four agisters, too, appointed by the wardens to collect money for the pasturing of cattle and pigs in the king's demesne woods and lawns, allowed at certain seasons. The agisters counted the pigs as they entered the forest and collected

Stalking deer in a wood, by Gaston Phebus' *Livre de la Chasse* **(early 15th c.).**

the pennies as they came out. Landowners inside the forest also employed woodwards, their own foresters.

On their estates many barons set up private forests or "chases," either on wooded country not under forest law or by receiving from the king grants of "vert and venison." By the reign of Edward I, the royal forest of Dean, in Gloucestershire, north and east of Chepstow, contained the private chases of thirty-six landowners, mostly the great magnates of the region, including the lord of Chepstow, Earl Roger Bigod; the abbot of St. Peter's, Gloucester; the bishop of Hereford; the earl of Lancaster; the earl of Warwick; and Baron Richard Talbot.

Once the king had granted a forest to a subject, royal forest law was suspended and royal forest justices and courts surrendered jurisdiction to the baron who owned the chase. The baron's foresters could arrest trespassers against the venison, but only when they were caught "with the mainour," in the act and with the evidence. Then they were held in prison until they paid a fine to the lord.

Sometimes districts were enclosed with palings or ditches and became parks. Later such enclosures had to be licensed by the king, but in the time of Henry III a license was not necessary as long as there was no infringement on the royal forest. The baron who created a park, however, was obliged to keep it effectively enclosed so that the king's beasts did not enter it. Some owners of parks neighboring the royal forests evaded the law by building sunken fences called deer leaps so designed that the king's deer could leap them to enter the park, but once in could not get out again. Forest courts often ordered deer leaps removed, and even ruled certain parks close to the forest legal "nuisances" because the owner might be moved to entice the king's deer into the enclosure.

Ecclesiastical as well as lay landlords established their own preserves. In the twelfth century Abbot Samson of Bury St. Edmunds, according to Jocelin of Brakelond, "enclosed many parks, which he replenished with beasts of chase, keeping a huntsman with dogs; and upon the visit of any person of quality, sat with his monks in some walk of the wood, and sometimes saw the coursing of the dogs; but I never saw him take part in the sport." Other prelates joined in the hunt.

An exception to forest law was provided for the earl or baron traveling through a royal forest. Either in the presence of a forester, or while blowing his hunting horn to show that he was not a poacher, he was allowed to take a deer or two for the use of his party. The act was carefully recorded in the rolls of the special forest inquisitions under the title "Venison taken without warrant." A roll of Northamptonshire of 1248 read:

> The lord bishop of Lincoln took a hind and a roe in Bulax on the Tuesday next before Christmas Day in the thirtieth year [of the reign of Henry III]. Sir

Guy de Rochefort took a doe and a doe's brocket [a hind of the second year] in the park of Brigstock in the vigil of the Purification of the Blessed Mary in the same year. . . .

Deer killed with the king's permission were listed as "venison given by the lord king":

The countess of Leicester had seven bucks in the forest of Rockingham of the gift of the lord king on the feast of the apostles Peter and Paul. . . . Aymar de Lusignan had ten bucks in the same forest. . . . . Sir Richard, earl of Cornwall, came into the forest of Rockingham about the time of the feast of the Assumption of the Blessed Mary, and took beasts in the park and outside the park at his pleasure in the thirty-second year. . . . Sir Simon de Montfort had twelve bucks in the bailiwick of Rockingham of the gift of the lord king about the time of the feast of St. Peter's Chains in the thirty-second year.

The records of the forest courts were full of dramatic episodes.

A certain hart entered the bailiwick of the castle of Bridge by the postern; and the castellans of Bridge took it and carried it to the castle. And the verderers on hearing this came there and demanded of Thomas of Ardington, who was then the sheriff, what he had done with the hart. . . . The township of Bridge was attached for the same hart.

Sir Hugh of Goldingham, the steward of the forest, and Roger of Tingewick, the riding forester, perceived a man on horseback and a page following him with a bow and arrows, who forthwith fled. Wherefore he was hailed on account of his flight by the said Hugh and Roger; and he was followed . . . and taken, as he fled, outside the covert, with his surcoat bloody and turned inside out. He was asked whence that blood came, and he confessed that it came from a certain roe, which he had killed. . . .

When Maurice de Meht, who said that he was with Sir Robert Passelewe, passed in the morning with two horses through the town of Sudborough, he saw three men carrying a sack. . . . And when the aforesaid three men saw him following them, they threw away the sack and fled. And the said Maurice de Meht took the sack and found a doe, which had been flayed, and a snare, with which the beast had been taken. . . .

Clerical as well as lay hunters became embroiled with the law or with their neighbors. In 1236 at the coronation of Queen Eleanor, the earl of Arundel was unable to take part in the ceremony because he had been excommunicated by the archbishop of Canterbury for seizing the archbishop's hounds when the archbishop hunted in the earl's forest.

In 1254 a poacher, in the employ of the parson of Easton, was imprisoned for taking a "beast" in the hedge of Rockingham Castle. Freed from prison on pledge, the poacher died, but the parson, Robert Bacon, who had apparently also taken part in the hunt, and Gilbert, the doorkeeper of the castle, were ordered to appear. At the hearing Sir John Lovet, a forest official who may have been bribed by the accused, declared that the "beast" was not a deer but a sheep. The accused men were acquitted, but John Lovet was imprisoned for contradicting his own records, and released only after the payment of a fine of twelve marks.

One night in 1250 foresters found a trap in Rockingham Forest and nearby heard a man cutting wood. Lying in wait, they surprised Robert Le Noble, chaplain of Sudborough, with a branch of green oak and an axe. The next morning they searched his house and found arrows and a trap that bore traces of the hair of a deer. The chaplain was arrested at once and his chattels, wheat, oats, beans, wood, dishes, and a mare were seized as pledges for his appearance before the forest eyre. Another cleric was one of a company that spent a day in 1272 shooting in the forest, killing eight deer. Cutting off the head of a buck, they stuck it on the end of a pole in a clearing and put a spindle in its mouth, and in the words of the court rolls, "they made the mouth gape towards the sun, in great contempt of the lord king and his foresters."

Sometimes malefactors used clerical privilege to obtain release from prison, as when in 1255 one Gervais of Dene, servant of John of Crakehall, archdeacon of Bedford and later the king's treasurer, was arrested for poaching and lodged in the prison of Huntingdon. The vicar of Huntingdon, several chaplains, and a servant of the bishop of Lincoln came to the prison armed with book and candle, claiming that Gervais was a clerk and threatening to excommunicate the foresters. Taking off the prisoner's cap, they exposed a shaven head. Gervais was allowed to escape, though the foresters suspected that he had been shaved that day in prison. But at the forest eyre of Huntingdon in 1255 John of Crakehall was fined ten marks for harboring Gervais, who along with the vicar was turned over to the archdeacon of Huntingdon to deal with.

Usually the sons of knights or freeholders, foresters often abused their powers for gain—felling trees, grazing their own cattle, embezzling, taking bribes, extorting "sheaves, cats, corn, lambs and little pigs" from the people at harvest time (although specifically forbidden to do so by the Forest Charter), and killing the very deer they were supposed to protect. Not only the people who lived within the royal forests, but the nobles suffered. Matthew Paris complained that a knight named Geoffrey Langley, marshal of the king's household, made an inquisition into the royal forests in 1250 and

> forcibly extorted such an immense sum of money, especially from nobles of the northern parts of England, that the amount collected exceeded the belief of all who heard of it...The aforesaid Geoffrey was attended by a large and well-armed retinue, and if any one of the aforesaid nobles made excuses . . . he ordered him to be at once taken and consigned to the king's prison. . . . For a single small beast, a fawn, or hare, although straying in an out-of-the-way place, he impoverished men of noble birth, even to ruin, sparing neither blood nor fortune.

Villagers in forest areas were supposed to raise the "hue and cry" (shouting when a felony was committed and turning out with weapons to pursue the malefactor) when an offense had been committed against the forest law. But their sympathies were often with the poachers. Again and again the rolls of the forest courts record the statements of the neighboring villages that they "knew nothing," "recognized nobody," "suspected no one," "knew of no malefactor."

Forest officers were a hated class. A Northamptonshire inquisition of 1251 recorded an exchange between a verderer and an acquaintance he met in the forest who refused to greet him, declaring, "Richard, I would rather go to my plow than serve in such an office as yours."

Many of the accounts of the forest inquests have the ring of Robin Hood, whose legend, significantly, sprang up in the thirteenth century. In May 1246 foresters in Rockingham Forest heard that there were poachers "in the lawn of Beanfield with greyhounds for the purpose of doing evil to the venison of the lord king." After waiting in ambush, they

> saw five greyhounds, of which one was white, another black, the third fallow, a fourth black spotted, hunting beasts, which greyhounds the said William and Roger [the foresters] seized. But the fifth greyhound, which was tawny, escaped. And when the aforesaid William and Roger returned to the forest after taking the greyhounds, they lay in ambush and saw five poachers in the lord king's demesne of Wydehawe, one with a crossbow and

four with bows and arrows, standing at their trees. And when the foresters perceived them, they hailed and pursued them.

> And the aforesaid malefactors, standing at their trees, turned in defense and shot arrows at the foresters so that they wounded Matthew, the forester of the park of Brigstock, with two Welsh arrows, to wit with one arrow under the left breast, to the depth of one hand slantwise, and with the second arrow in the left arm to the depth of two fingers, so that it was despaired of the life of the said Matthew. And the foresters pursued the aforesaid malefactors so vigorously that they turned and fled into the thickness of the wood. And the foresters on account of the darkness of the night could follow them no more. And thereupon an inquisition was made at Beanfield before William of Northampton, then bailiff [warden] of the forest, and the foresters of the country . . . by four townships neighboring . . . to wit, by Stoke, Carlton, Great Oakley, and Corby.

> Stoke comes and being sworn says that it knows nothing thereof except only that the foresters attacked the malefactors with hue and cry until the darkness of night came, and that one of the foresters was wounded. And it does not know whose were the greyhounds.

> Carlton comes, and being sworn, says the same.

> Corby comes, and being sworn, says the same.

> Great Oakley comes, and being sworn, says that it saw four men and one tawny greyhound following them, to wit one with a crossbow and three with bows and arrows, and it hailed them and followed them with the foresters until the darkness of night came, so that on account of the darkness of night and the thickness of the wood it knew not what became of them. . . .

> The arrows with which Matthew was wounded, were delivered to Sir Robert Basset and John Lovet, verderers.

> The greyhounds were sent to Sir Robert Passelewe, then justice of the forest.

Matthew died of his wounds, and a later inquisition revealed that Matthew's brother and two other foresters had seen the same three greyhounds in April when dining with the abbot of Pipewell, and that they belonged to one Simon of Kivelsworthy, who was thereupon sent to Northampton to be imprisoned. The abbot of Pipewell had to answer before the Justices for harboring Simon and his greyhounds. The case was later brought before the forest eyre in Northampton in 1255, where Simon proved that his greyhounds "were led there by him at another time but not then," and was released after paying a fine of half a mark. The real culprit was never found.

VIII
THE VILLAGERS

Quoth Piers Plowman, "By Saint Peter of Rome!
I have an half acre to plow by the highway;
Once I have plowed this half acre and sown it after,
I will wend with you and show you the way...
I shall give them food if the land does not fail,
Meat and bread both to rich and to poor, as long as I live,
For the love of heaven; and all manner of men
That live through meat and drink, help him to work wightly
Who wins your food..."
And would that... Piers with his plows...
Were emperor of all the world, and then perhaps all men would be Christian!

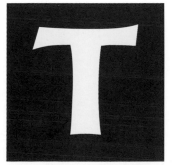 hough many castles were built inside towns for political and strategic reasons, the castle was rooted economically in the countryside. It was connected intimately with the village and the manor, the social and economic units of rural Europe. The village was a community, a collective settlement, with its own ties, rights, and obligations. The manor was an estate held by a lord and farmed by tenants who owed him rents and services, and whose relations with him were governed by his manorial court. A manor might coincide with a village, or it might contain more than one village, or a village might contain parts of manors or several entire manors.

The manor supplied the castle's livelihood. The word "manor" came to England with the Conqueror, but the arrangement was centuries old. On the Continent, it was used to provide a living for the knight and his retainers at a time when money was scarce.

A great castle such as Chepstow commanded a large number of manors, often widely scattered and interspersed with land belonging to other lords. The kind of settlement and cultivation on these manors depended on their location. On most of the plain of northern Europe, and in England in a band running southwest from the North Sea through the Midlands to the English Channel, the land lay in great open stretches of field broken here and there by stands of trees and the clustered houses of villages. This was "champion" ("champagne," open field) country. Contrasting with it was the "woodland" country of Brittany and Normandy and the west, northwest, and southeast of England, where small, compact fields were marked off with hedges and ditches, and the farmhouses were scattered in tiny hamlets.

A man sowing autumn grain from a series of Labors of the Months. English stained glass roundel (15th c.).

A swineherd grazing his pigs (November) from a calendar in an English psalter (c.1250–75).

In champion country, the villages were large, with populations of several hundred. The surrounding fields were divided into either two or three sectors, farmed according to a traditional rotation of crops. In each sector every villager held strips of land, alongside and mixed in with those of his fellows and those of the lord. Land usually descended to the eldest son, but younger brothers and sisters could stay on and work for the heir, as long as they remained unmarried. Many younger sons of champion country left home to seek their fortunes in the cities, or became mercenary soldiers.

In woodland country, on the other hand, each man worked his own separate farm. Land passed to all the surviving sons, who held and worked it together, living in a single large house or in a small group of adjoining houses. Tenants combined to perform labor service for their lord, but the system of inheritance made responsibility for services harder to assign. In consequence, woodland farmers tended to pay money rents instead of performing services, while in champion country the feudal work obligation tended to be the rule.

The village of champion country was typically a straggle of houses and farm buildings that had grown up along an existing road, but sometimes simply developed by itself, the paths between buildings and fields and adjacent villages over the centuries becoming worn and sunken to form the streets. If there was a manor house, this large building, a lesser form of the castle hall, dominated the scene, along with the parish church, which on varying occasions served as storehouse, courthouse, prison, and fort. For the men in the fields, its bell sounded the alarm as well as the celebration of the mass. In its yard the villagers gathered to gossip, dance, and play games, and to hold fairs and markets.

Except in areas where stone was plentiful, houses were built of wattle and daub, that is, of timber framework supporting oak or willow wands covered with a mixture of clay, chopped straw or cow-hair, and cowdung. In England the timber was most commonly oak. Sometimes a trunk and main branch of a tree were first trimmed of branches, then felled, split, and reassembled to form an arched "cruck" truss supporting roof and walls, strengthened with beams. The roofs were thatched. Houses were easily built, and could easily be moved— or destroyed; thieves were known to dig through house walls. The smallest huts consisted of a single room, and even in the largest, most of the household ate and slept together in the main room, still another version of the hall, with an open hearth in the middle and a smoke vent in the roof. The floor, usually of beaten earth, was covered with rushes. Sometimes there was a separate room for the owner, sometimes even one for the old grandparents, or part of the family might sleep in a loft reached by ladder and trapdoor. Typically the cattle were housed at one end of the building, under the same roof. The kitchen was often in a separate building, or in a lean-to.

A peasant's possessions consisted of three or four benches and stools, a trestle table, a chest, one or two iron or brass pots, a little pottery ware, wooden bowls, cups, and spoons, linen towels, wool blankets, iron tools, and, most important, his livestock. A reasonably prosperous villager owned hens and geese, a few skinny half-wild razor-backed hogs, a cow or even two, perhaps a couple of sheep, and his pair of plow oxen.

Outside the house, chickens scratched in the little farmyard (toft or messuage) containing one or two outbuildings, in the rear of which lay a garden plot, or croft, that the householder could farm as he pleased.

Contrary to widespread impression, the villagers of the thirteenth century were not limited to subsistence farming. They grew crops for their own households, for their payments to the lord, and sometimes for cash sales to markets. In England wheat was usually a cash crop, to be sold to pay for the money rents and taxes of the peasant household, while barley, oats, and rye were grown mainly for home consumption. Not all grains were baked into bread; some were brewed into ale. Peas and beans were usually boiled into soup. Other vegetables grew in the garden patches of the tofts and crofts—onions, cabbages, leeks. Staple crops were sown twice a year: wheat and rye in the fall, and barley, vetches, oats, peas, and beans in early spring. Crops matured and were harvested in August and September.

Agricultural technology, if limited and unimaginative by the standards of a later age, was not entirely static despite the lack of scientific knowledge. The thirteenth-century farmer employed three ways to restore and improve the soil: by fallowing, that is, letting a field rest for a year; by marling, spreading a clay containing carbonate of lime; or by using sheep or cattle manure. But marl was scarce, and shortage of feed limited the number of animals and the supply of manure. To feed his cattle, the farmer had only the grass that grew in the commonly-held "water meadows," wetlands left untitled, and the stubble of the harvested fields. The advantages of planting grasses or turnips specifically for cattle feed were not yet perceived. The result was that there was never enough feed to see the livestock through the winter, and some had to be slaughtered every fall, in turn limiting the supply of manure for spring fertilizing. The technique of growing crops of clover and alfalfa to be plowed into the soil as fertilizer also was unknown.

For fallowing, the chief means of restoring the fields' fertility, the villagers used crop rotation in either the ancient two-field or the newer three-field system. In the latter, one field was plowed in the fall and sown with wheat and rye. Each villager planted his own strip of land, all with the same seed. In the spring a second field was plowed and sown to oats, peas, beans, barley, and vetches. A third field was left fallow from harvest to harvest. The next year the field that had been planted with wheat and rye was planted with the oats, barley, and legumes; the fallow field was planted with wheat

and rye; and the field that had grown the spring seed was left fallow.

In the older but still widely used two-field system, one field was left fallow and the other tilled half with winter wheat and rye, half with spring seed. The next year the tilled field lay fallow and the fallow field was tilled, with winter and spring crops alternating in the sections that were planted.

The plowman was the common man of the Middle Ages, Piers Plowman, guiding his heavy iron-shod plow, sometimes mounted on wheels to make it go more evenly, cutting the ground with its coulter, breaking it with its share, and turning it over with its wooden mould-board. The medieval husbandman plowed in long narrow strips of "ridge and furrow," starting just to one side of the center line of his piece of land, plowing the length of the strip, turning at the end and plowing back along the other side, and continuing around. In the wet soil of northern Europe, this ridge-and-furrow plowing helped free the soil from standing water that threatened to drown the grain. Peas and beans were planted in the furrow, grain on the ridge. The ancient pattern of ridge and furrow can still be seen in England in fields long abandoned to grazing.

The husbandman's plow was drawn by a team of oxen whose number has provided a tantalizing mystery

Harvesting grain (August) from a series of Labors of the Months. English stained glass roundel (15th c.).

for scholars. Manorial records in profusion refer to teams of eight oxen, but pictorial representations nearly always show a more credible two, or occasionally four. Two men operated the plow, the plowman proper grasping the plow handles, or stilts, while his partner drove the oxen, walking to their left and shouting commands as he used a whip or goad. Behind followed men and women who broke up the clods with plow-bats or, in planting time, did the sowing.

On occasion villages increased their area under cultivation either by sowing part of the field that would normally have lain fallow or by making *assarts,* bringing wasteland under the plow. Such important measures were executed only with the agreement of all the villagers, and the land thus gained was shared equally.

Equality, in fact, was the guiding principle in the village, within the limits of two basic social classes: the more prosperous peasants, whose land was sufficient to support their families, and the cottars, who had to hire out as day-laborers to their better-off neighbors. The better-off villagers commonly held a "yardland" or a "half-yardland" (thirty or fifteen acres, or, in the terminology of northern England, two *oxgangs* or one *oxgang*). Along with these holdings went a portion of the village meadow, about two acres, the location decided by an annual lottery. At the lower end of the scale, the cottars held five acres of land or less; they had to borrow oxen from their neighbors for plowing, or were even forced to "delve," that is, cultivate with a spade. At least half an average village's holdings were in the cottar class, too small to feed a family and requiring the supplement of income gained by hiring out. In some demesnes the lord's land was cultivated chiefly or even entirely by such hired labor.

A second distinction among the villagers was based on personal rather than economic status: They were either free or non-free. Most of the villagers, whether half-yardlanders or cottars, were non-free, or villeins (the term "serf" was less common in England), which meant mainly that they owed heavy labor service to their lords: "week's work," consisting of two or three days a week throughout the year. A villein had other disabilities—he was not protected by the royal courts, but was subject to the will of his lord in the manorial courts; he could not leave his land or sell his livestock without permission; when his

daughter married, he had to pay a fee; when he succeeded to his father's holding, he paid a "relief," or fine, and also a *heriot,* usually the best beast of the deceased. Most important, however, in an age of limited technology, when every hour's work was precious, was the compulsion to work on the lord's lands, plowing, mowing hay, reaping, shocking and transporting grain, threshing and winnowing, washing and shearing the lord's sheep. By the thirteenth century labor services were often commuted into money payments. But in cash or kind, approximately half of all the villein's efforts ultimately went, in one way or another, to the lord's profit.

The rents and services of a villein were described in the manor custom books, often in elaborate detail: how much land the tenant was to plow with how many oxen, whether he was to use his own horse and harrow, or fetch the seed himself from the lord's granary. Usually there were special rents for special rights—a hen at Christmas (the "woodhen") in return for dead timber from the lord's wood, or the right to pasture cattle on some of the lord's land in return for a plowing. At certain times of crisis during the year the lord could call on all of his tenants—free and unfree—to leave their own farming and work for him, plowing, mowing, or reaping. These movable works, called *boons* or *benes,* were the longest preserved of all work services. In return, the lord gave food, drink, or money, or sometimes all three. Benes were classified accordingly—the *alebidreap* and the *waterbidreap,* when the lord gave ale or water; the *hungerbidreap,* when the villagers were obliged to bring their own food; the *dryreap,* when there was no ale. The food donated by the lord was generally plentiful—meat or fish, pea or bean soup, bread and cheese. In theory these benes were done for the lord out of love—they were "love-boons"—as for any neighbor that needed help, like the community effort of a barn-raising or a town bee. Like these, they were the occasion of social gatherings. A characteristic feature was the "sporting chance"; at the end of the working day the lord gave each hay-maker a bundle of hay as large as he could lift with his scythe, or a sheep was loosed in the field, and if the mowers could catch it they could roast it.

In every village were found at least a few free tenants. Some simply held their land free of most labor services, owing money rents and "suit," meaning attendance at certain courts. Others were the skilled craftsmen: the miller, the smith, the carpenter, the weaver,

Almoner distributing bread to the poor, from *Les Miracles de Notre Dame de Gautier de Colnay* (13th c.).

the tanner, the shoemaker. Most prosperous among these, and least popular, was the miller, who paid the lord for the right to operate the mill, a strictly enforced monopoly. The villagers brought their grain there, contributing in payment the *multure,* a sixteenth to a twenty-fourth part of the grain. Since the millers did the measuring, they naturally fell under suspicion of cheating on weight. They were also accused of substituting bad grain for good. A medieval riddle asked, "What is the boldest thing in the world?" and replied, "A miller's shirt, for it clasps a thief by the throat daily." A few villagers secretly ground their grain with

a hand-mill at home, but ran the risk of seizure and punishment.

The smith had the privileges of using charcoal from the lord's wood and having his land plowed by the lord's plows, in return for which he shod the lord's horses and ground his scythes and sheep shears, along with those of the villagers. The carpenter, with similar privileges, repaired the plows, carts, and harrows, and built and mended houses and furniture.

The poorest people in the village, the cottars, were sometimes free too, although they might hold nothing more than their cottages and the yards that surrounded them. When they were unfree, they owed lesser services than the more substantial villeins—"hand work" rather than plowing: spreading dung, repairing walls and thatches, digging ditches.

Given the choice between freedom and more land, any would have chosen land. Land, in fact, was the real freedom.

Over the majority of villagers, the landholding villeins, the lord in theory had arbitrary power. He could increase a villein's rents and services at will, or seize his holdings. In practice, however, the lord's legal position was modified by an accumulation of traditions that had the force of law. Custom was reinforced by the fact that the lord could not survive without the services of his tenants. The lord rarely pressed them so hard that they ran away, or even resisted him. Unless a tenant failed to perform his services, he remained in possession of his holding and could pass it on to his heir. Even the wood and wasteland, theoretically owned by the lord, could only be exploited within limits imposed by custom.

Lord and tenant rarely met face to face, the manor's affairs being left to the steward or bailiff. Nevertheless, the tenant-lord relationship was as reciprocal as it was real. Furthermore, it was permanent. Villeins were bound to the land, but at the same time custom ruled that they could not be deprived of their holdings. A villein could leave the manor if he paid a fine and a yearly fee while he stayed away, but leaving meant losing his land.

The village community met at intervals in an assembly called a bylaw, a term that applied to the body as well as to the rules it passed. At these bylaws, all matters were decided that were not automatically regulated by custom—the choice of herdsmen, problems of pasture and harvest, the repair of fences, and the clearing of ditches. It was decided who should be hired to glean and reap, when and how the harvesting should take place, in what order animals should be allowed to graze after the harvest. Every villager had a voice. Decisions were made not by vote but by consensus: Everyone expressed his view, but once a general agreement emerged from the discussion, it became unanimous. No lengthy disagreement was tolerated, and the stubborn or rebellious were threatened with fines.

The bylaws of an Oxfordshire manor in 1293 declared: "No one shall in time of autumn receive anyone as a gleaner who is able to do the work of a reaper." In other words, able-bodied men, strong enough to swing a scythe in reaping, were not to do gleaning—gathering the grain after the reapers were finished—a job reserved for elders and women. Second, "No one shall give anyone sheaves in the field." Reapers who received their wages in sheaves were not to carry them off from the fields; to prevent stealing, the sheaves had to be taken to the villagers' own homes and given out by the man from whose lands they came. Third, "No one shall enter the fields with a cart to carry grain after sunset; . . . none shall enter the fields except at the village entrances; . . . all grain . . . gathered in the fields shall be borne out openly through the midst of the town and not secretly by back ways." In this way the villagers could watch everyone who came and went during the harvest.

A bylaw of 1329 read: "No one shall take in outsiders or natives who behave themselves badly in the gleaning or elsewhere. . . . Also, no one may tether horses in the fields amid growing grain or grain that has been reaped where damage can arise. Also, no one may make paths, by walking or driving or carrying grain, over the grain of another to the damage of the neighbors or at any other time." With holdings scattered and intermixed, roadways and paths required strict regulation.

Another early fourteenth-century bylaw read: "Item, that sheep shall not precede the larger animals"—that is, plow oxen were to be pastured on the stubble of harvested fields before the close-cropping sheep.

In the bylaws, the villagers met not as tenants of a lord but as a democratic community. The regulations they agreed on involved not their relationship to the lord but to each other. The lord was affected by the bylaws only as another landholder in the village, with a common interest in the harvest and pasture. In the written records of the bylaws found in the rolls of manorial courts, the lord was seldom mentioned; instead the regulations were enacted by the "community" or the "homage" or the "tenants" or the "neighbors."

A characteristic institution of the manor was its court, known in England as the *hallmote* or *halimote,* a place where the lord dealt justice to his tenants, pocketing the fines. The lowest court in the feudal hierarchy, it was also the chief private court. Except in cases of murder or felony (tried by royal courts), the manorial court had general jurisdiction over all matters concerning the villagers. It took its name from the lord's hall; it was a moot (Anglo-Saxon, "court") that met in the hall, although actually it sometimes met in the open air, under a traditional tree, or in the parish church.

Presiding over the court was the lord's steward, but he did not act as judge. His presence gave weight to the court's decisions, but the verdicts, decided by the custom of the manor, were rendered either by a jury of the court or by the whole body of its suitors. These were the men who owed attendance, or "suit," to the court, that is, the villeins of the manor and freeholders whose ancestors had owed suit, or who held land by a charter stipulating that they owed suit. Failure to attend meant a fine, unless the suitor sent someone with an excuse; the manorial court roll usually began with a list of the jurors, followed by a list of the excuses (essoins). The jurors, usually twelve in number, were chosen from the suitors. If a freeman was to be tried, a special jury of freemen seems to have been formed. In some villages the same men, a kind of aristocracy jurymen, were chosen again and again.

The hallmote was more than a court of law; it handled many of the functions of the manorial government: the election and swearing in of manorial officials; payments for permission to marry, to enter the Church, to inherit a holding. When an heir succeeded to his father's land, a ceremony was enacted in the manorial court similar to that in which a king or baron invested the heir of a vassal with his lands. He received seisin (possession) of his holding "by the verge," which, as in the case of king or baron, dramatized the legal fiction that was the basis of relationship between lord and tenant: that the lord repossessed the holding and then regranted it to the heir, although inheritance was in fact fixed by custom. The steward held out a "verge" (stick) to the heir. When the heir took hold of the end of it, he was understood to have possession, as if the right flowed from steward to tenant along the stick.

Besides these official matters, the courts handled infractions of manorial customs concerning harvest, pasture, the maintaining of fences, and disputes among villagers over slanders, trespasses, boundaries, debts, and contracts. The usual punishment for a misdemeanor was a fine, sometimes in money, sometimes in workdays, which went to the lord.

Lawyers were not allowed in the manorial courts.

Cases were presented by the manorial officers concerned, or by the plaintiffs. In criminal cases, the steward might order the accused to find a certain number of men who would swear with him as a body that he was innocent of the misdeed with which he was charged. In a community where everyone knew his neighbor's business, if a man could find the necessary oath takers, he went free.

In civil cases, the procedure was by complaint. The plaintiff appeared before the court and complained that the defendant had injured him in such-and-such a way. The defendant could delay the case through a certain number of summonses, distraints, and excuses. Sometimes the plaintiff dropped the case. If he did so, however, he had to pay a fine, so that the lord did not have his court's time wasted. If the case did come to trial, the plaintiff opened with a statement of his plea, following traditional formulas, and the defendant replied, answering each item of the plea word for word, great stress being placed on the accuracy of wording. After both parties had been heard, judgment might be given by the jury, or by the whole court. The case was decided according to the facts and the custom: which of the two parties was believed to be telling the truth, and what was the custom of the manor. Sometimes the court decided that the suit was merely an expression of bad feelings and the steward ordered the parties to hold a "love-day" before another hallmote at which they settled their differences and were reconciled.

Twice a year in some of the English counties, courts of the View of Frankpledge were held. In these districts all men twelve years and over were divided into groups of ten or twelve persons called frankpledges or tithings. The head of each tithing, the chief pledge, or tithingman, was usually elected for a year but often served for many years. Frankpledge was a police measure, a system by which a group of men was made responsible for the misdeeds of any of its members. Any malefactors in the group had to be brought to court, and the tithing could be fined for failure to do so. The twice-yearly inspection of the system known as the View of Frankpledge was originally held by the sheriff as a royal officer, but later, in many cases, it was usurped by the lords of manors as a source of income. It was also the occasion for the meeting of the most important manorial courts of the year, the Great Courts, which freeholders exempted from the ordinary hallmotes were compelled to attend, and where matters of local police and lesser cases of the Crown were presented.

The everyday relations of the villagers with the castle were governed by ancient custom and regulated by a group of officials at whose head was the lord's bailiff. The bailiff's duties on the lord's demesne land, as summed up in *Seneschaucie*, were manifold. He must survey the manor every morning—its woods, crops, meadows, and pastures; see that the plows were yoked; order the land marled and manured. He must watch over the threshers, the plowmen, the harrowers, and sowers; over the reaping and shocking, the sheep shearing, and the sale of wool and skins. He must inspect the lord's oxen, cows, heifers, and sheep, and weed out the old and weak, selling those that could not be maintained over the winter.

To the villagers the bailiff was the collector and enforcer—collector of rents and enforcer of labor services. Understandably, he was little loved. A fourteenth-century sermon told of a bailiff who, while riding to a village to collect rents, met the Devil in human form. The Devil asked, "Where are you going?" The bailiff replied, "To the next village, on my master's business." The Devil asked if he would take whatever was freely offered to him. The bailiff said Yes, and asked the questioner who he was and what was his business. The Devil replied that he was the Devil, busy like the bailiff in quest of gain, but willing "not to take *whatever* men would give me; but whatsoever they would gladly bestow with their whole heart and soul, that will I accept." "You do most justly," said the bailiff. As they approached the village, they saw a plowman angrily commending to the Devil his oxen that repeatedly strayed from the course. The bailiff said, "Behold, they are yours!" "No," said the Devil, "they are in no wise given from the heart." As they entered the village they heard a child weeping, and its mother wishing it to the Devil. Said the bailiff, "This is yours indeed!" "Not at all," said the Devil, "for she has no desire to lose her son." At length they reached the end of the village. A poverty-stricken widow whose only cow the bailiff had seized the day before saw him coming, and on her knees with hands outstretched shrieked at him, "To all the devils of hell I commend thee!" Whereupon the Devil exclaimed, "To be sure, this is mine. Because thus cordially you have been bestowed on me, I am willing to have you." And snatching up the bailiff, he bore him away to hell.

Under the bailiff a number of villagers held office both as servants of the lord and as village functionaries. The hayward—in charge of the *haie*, the hedge or fence—made sure that after fields were sowed the gaps in their hedges (usually "dead hedges" made of stakes and brushwood) were closed to keep out animals, and the fields were thus put "in defense." He also sometimes served as an officer of the hall-mote, was part of the management of the lord's demesne farm, and impounded stray cattle. His badge of office was his horn, used to sound a warning that the cattle were in the corn (Little Boy Blue was a hayward). The woodward, who had charge of the lord's woods, was also a villager, elected by his fellows. In some villages there were also shepherds, swineherds, and oxherds, though often families had their own herdsmen. Although illiterate, the shepherds and haywards had no difficulty keeping accurate records of labor services, stock, expenditures of grain, and expenses. Their instrument was a stick, on which they cut notches that the reeve or bailiff translated into parchment records.

The reeve, the most important of the village officers, was commonly elected by the tenants from among their own number—"the best husbandman in the village," according to *Seneschaucie*. His responsibilities embraced every aspect of the manorial economy: overseeing all the activities of the villagers and the manorial servants, hailing them before the manorial court when they failed in their service, seeing to the upkeep of manorial buildings and implements and to the care of the lord's livestock. Himself intimately connected with the village, the reeve had an understanding of his neighbors that an outsider like the steward or bailiff could never have. This close relationship must also have added to the difficulties of his position, in which he belonged to the village while serving the lord. Although the reeve was usually released from all customary services, paid a stipend, and allowed to keep his horse in the lord's pasture and eat at the lord's table during the harvest, men often avoided the office if possible and even paid fines to be released from having to serve in it. When villages sent representatives to the royal courts, the reeve usually headed the delegation of four of the "best men" of the village.

The men of a medieval village were members of a parish which coincided with the village rather than the manor. The church was usually the only stone building of the village. On its altar stood the principal image of the saint to whom the church was dedicated. The rood (cross) over the entrance to the choir was lit by candles endowed by the pious.

The parish priest was supported partly by tithes—every tenth sheaf, or the crop of every tenth acre—partly by offerings on feast days, and partly by the *glebe,* land that belonged to the church and was tilled sometimes by tenants, sometimes by the priest himself. In many parts of England and Europe the "second-best beast" of every villein who died belonged to the priest. According to custom he returned a third of his revenues in alms and hospitality to the poor, to repair the church, and to pay his chaplain or clerk, but abuse of the office was common. Often the holder of the benefice was an absentee who lived at the university or at court and hired a vicar to take his place. Sometimes an abbot or convent held the church and appointed a vicar. Poor vicars were often villeins whose fathers had paid the lord to allow them to enter the church. Such ill-educated clerics were sometimes accused of using their churches as barns, threshing corn in the nave, and pasturing cattle in the churchyard. Late in the thirteenth century Archbishop of Canterbury John Peckham was constrained to order parish priests to preach at least four times a year.

Despite its shortcomings, the parish church played an important part in the life of every villager. He worked in the fields to the sound of its bells, and though its Latin remained a mystery to him, he regularly attended Mass. The church's festivals marked the turning points of the year, and its rites every stage of a man's passage through life: birth, marriage, and death.

The ideal of the village community, where within each class opportunity was rendered equal, where neighbors worked together, where status and blood line were carefully preserved, century after century, endured for a long time. By contrast, the similar ideal of the medieval city dweller, toward which the craft guilds worked and legislated—every man practicing his craft and selling what he made, none very rich, none very poor—was only briefly and partially realized before the revival of commerce brought the rise of the great merchants and an increasing gap between rich and poor.

Much of the explanation for the greater durability of the ideal lay in the slowness with which the money economy penetrated the countryside. Under the manorial system there was little scope for the kind of enterprise and industry that enriched the more successful city dwellers. Not until the sixteenth century did capitalist farmers appear in England, enclosing cultivated land, converting it to pasture, and changing tenants into wage laborers. Then, in the words of historian R. H. Tawney, "Villeinage ceases but the Poor Laws begin."

JACQUES DE MOLAY, chef des Templiers

IX

THE MAKING
OF A KNIGHT

When [Geoffrey of Anjou] entered the inner chamber of the king's hall [at Rouen], surrounded by his knights and those of the king and a crowd of people, the king. . . went to meet him, affectionately embracing and kissing him, and, taking him by the hand, led him to a seat. . . . All that day was spent in joyful celebration. At the first dawn of the next day, a bath was prepared, according to the custom for novice knights. . . . After bathing, Geoffrey donned a linen undergarment, a tunic of cloth of gold, a purple robe, silk stockings, and shoes ornamented with golden lions; his attendants, who were being initiated into knighthood with him, also put on gold and purple. [Geoffrey], with his train of nobles, left the chamber to appear in public. Horses and arms were brought and distributed. A Spanish horse of wonderful beauty was provided for Geoffrey, swifter than the flight of birds. He was then armed with a corselet of double-woven mail which no lance or javelin could pierce, and shod with iron boots of the same double mesh; golden spurs were girded on; a shield with golden lions was hung around his neck; a helmet was placed on his head gleaming with many precious stones, and which no sword could pierce or mar; a spear of ash tipped with iron was provided; and finally from the royal treasury was brought an ancient sword. . . . Thus our novice knight was armed, the future flower of knighthood, who despite his armor leapt with marvelous agility on his horse. What more can be said? That day, dedicated to the honor of the newly made knights, was spent entirely in warlike games and exercises. For seven whole days the celebration in honor of the new knights continued.

Portrait of Jacques de Molay, Master of the Knights Templars (c.1243–1314) French School, engraving. by Ghevauchet (19th c.).

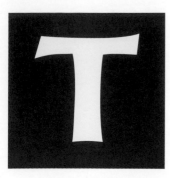

Thus, in the description of chronicler Jean of Tours, was fifteen-year-old Geoffrey of Anjou initiated into knighthood by his future father-in-law, Henry I, in 1128. To the secular ritual the later twelfth century added a religious element. The aspirant kept a nightlong vigil in the castle chapel, purifying his soul as the bath cleansed his body. At daybreak a priest celebrated Mass, after which the youth joined family and friends for breakfast. He then dressed in new clothes made especially for the occasion, usually of pure white rather than the purple-and-gold of Geoffrey of Anjou—white silk shirt, trunks, and tunic, and an ermine robe.

The dubbing ceremony commonly took place in the open air, on a platform or carpet, amid flourishes of trumpets and the music of minstrels. The youth's father and several other knights, often including the father's lord, helped him with his armor and equipment. The sword, blessed the night before by the priest, was brought; the young man reverently kissed its hilt, in the hollow of which holy relics might be encased.

Now came the climax, the *colée,* or buffet, usually executed by the father. Far from being a gently symbolic blow, the *colée* was an open-handed whack that often knocked its recipient, prepared though he was, off his feet. According to the Spanish writer Ramon Lull, the purpose of the *colée* was an aid to memory, so that the young knight would not forget his oath, now administered.

"Go, fair son! Be a true knight, and courageous in the face of your enemies," says the father in one romance. "Be thou brave and upright, that God may love thee—and remember that thou springest from a race that can never be false," says another. The young man replies, "So shall I, with God's help!"

The ceremony over, the new-made knight sometimes entered the church and placed his sword on the altar, in sign of its dedication to the Holy Church.

He was now a knight, a member of the order of chivalry. His war horse, a gift of his father or lord, was led up in full harness. As soon as he was in the saddle, the young man was given his lance and shield, and after a gallop about, attacked the quintain, a dummy fashioned of chain mail covered with a shield and set on a post. Sometimes there was more than one post for the new knight to knock down, to make the test more difficult and more interesting. The show was usually topped off with mock fighting with lance and shield.

On occasion, knights were dubbed on the battlefield. William Marshal was knighted in 1167 by his sponsor and older cousin, William of Tancarville, hereditary chamberlain of Normandy, during the war between Henry II and Louis VII of France. On his way with reinforcements for the count of Eu at Drincourt, the chamberlain summoned the Norman barons under his command for the ceremony. Dressed in a new mantle, William Marshal stood before his cousin, who "girt him with a sword" and gave him the *colée.* Several years later, in 1173, William Marshal similarly knighted young Henry, Henry II's eldest son, as preparation for battle. Henry handed the sword to William, saying, "I wish this honor to come from God and from you," and in the presence of Henry's entourage and assembled barons and knights, William "girt on the sword." Instead of a buffet, William bestowed a kiss on the young man, "and," in the words of William's biographer, "so he was a knight." More than four decades later William knighted another royal personage, nine-year-old Henry III, on the eve of his coronation.

Originally the term *chevalier (caballero, cavaliere, Ritter*—the word in all languages, except the English "knight," means horseman) simply indicated a warrior who fought on horseback, but even in its earliest stage it connoted a superiority of class, since only a man of means could afford a horse. The foundation of the crusading Order of the Temple in the twelfth century contributed both to the formalization of knighthood and to its association with Christianity. A Knight Templar wore a distinctive white-mantled uniform and swore to live by a Rule drawn from the Augustinian and Benedictine monks.

Thus the knight was a member of the noble class socially through the profession of arms, economically through the possession of horse and armor, and officially through a ceremony imbued with a religious sanction.

The origin of the knight's horse (destrier, charger) remains something of a mystery. Apparently bred from partly Arab stock, he was huge and strong, capable of sustaining the shock combat that had revolutionized warfare. Through no coincidence, northwest France, the cradle of feudalism, was noted for its horse breeding. The later Percheron and Belgian draft horses (as well as the Suffolk in England) were descended from the medieval destriers.

As clashes between armed and mounted knights multiplied and as the Italian-introduced crossbow was adopted, improvements in armor became necessary, made possible by the growing affluence of the twelfth century. The conical, open-faced helmet of the First Crusade was replaced by a massive pot helmet that covered head, face, and neck, while the old-fashioned hauberk (shirt of mail), made of small metal discs sewn on linen, turned into chain mail, composed of interlocking iron rings and weighing forty pounds or more. (Plate armor still lay far in the future.)

Through the twelfth century the tendency toward exclusivity grew in the knightly class. Frederick Barbarossa and probably other sovereigns forbade peasants to become knights or to carry sword or lance, and by the thirteenth century the knightly aristocracy was in theory a closed caste, set apart from the rest of society. "Ah, God! how badly is the good warrior rewarded who makes the son of a villein a knight!" warns the romance *Girart de Roussillon*. But the poet's admonition is itself evidence that villeins did indeed become knights in the twelfth century, and in the thirteenth the process was almost commonplace. The chief reason was the growing wealth of the merchant class. A grandfather might found a business, a father expand it, a son inherit a fortune. Such a son might purchase estates in the country from which he could draw an aristocratic name; he could afford expensive entertainment and bribes to great lords, and be knighted if he chose. Thenceforward his descendants were knights. Rather than seeking to suppress the custom, the great lords, in defiance of such edicts as Barbarossa's, took the sensible course of regularizing it by charging a fixed fee for knighthood.

At the other end of the economic scale, again despite all prohibitions to the contrary, many a poor soldier won knighthood through valor in the service of a lord. Despite this double-ended openness of the knightly class, it nevertheless retained a distinct caste rigidity. Its newest members, like parvenus of every age, copied or even excelled the hauteur of their older brothers in aristocracy.

Whatever his father's origin, the son of a knight normally grew up to be knighted. As a squire, or knight-aspirant, he began his apprenticeship, often in the household of his father's lord, cleaning out stables, currying horses, cleaning armor, serving at table, while he learned to ride a horse and wield sword and lance, with plenty of practice at the quintain. William Marshal underwent this training for eight years in the household of William of Tancarville.

The youthful aspirant was thoroughly imbued with the code of chivalry. In the twelfth and thirteenth centuries the chivalric ideal was fostered by the legends that had grown up around Charlemagne and Roland, and in England by the newer King Arthur stories. Arthur, a barely discernible real-life figure in sixth-century Britain (as was Roland in ninth-century France) was first given prominence in the twelfth century by Geoffrey of Monmouth in his highly imaginative *History of the Kings of Britain*. Robert Wace, a Norman poet from the island of Jersey, read Geoffrey's book and made

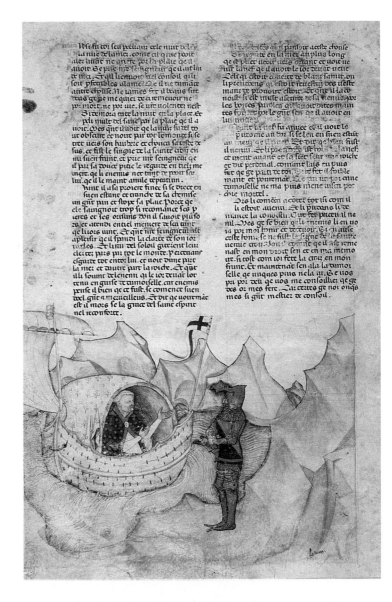

Percival: the White Ship Comes to Rescue Him—His Triumph over Sin from *Quete du Saint Graal et la Mort d'Arthus* (14th c.).

Arthur the hero of a romance he composed for Eleanor of Aquitaine. Wace embellished Arthur's court with a Round Table, and Chrétien de Troyes, a poet at the court of Eleanor's daughter Marie of Champagne, moved Arthur's court from Caerleon, Monmouthshire, to fictitious (or undetermined) Camelot. Chrétien's romances completed an important transition by shifting emphasis from Arthur himself to the knights, especially Lancelot and Percival. Chrétien and other poets, English, French, and German, glorified the code by which knights were supposed to live, stressing honor, generosity, loyalty, and dedication to God and Church.

The castle lord who dubbed Percival, depicted as a naive young savage from Wales, told him:

> With this sword [I have given you] the highest Order
> That God has made and commanded:
> It is the Order of Chivalry
> Which should be without taint [vilenie].

Percival was admonished to spare the vanquished enemy who asked grace, to assist maidens and women in distress, to pray in church regularly, and not to talk too much—this last evidently a reflection on the knightly inclination to boast.

Many thirteenth-century knights, including William Marshal, themselves composed verses. It was a poor knight who could not read and write. One romance credits its noble young hero with learning Latin and astronomy from a tutor who "attended his pupil everywhere, took him to school, prevented him from eating too much, taught him polite language and good manners, and never left him even when he dressed or went to bed."

Despite precepts, codes, and admonitions from the Church, however, the knight's life was normally lived on a lower plane than that embodied by the chivalric ideal. The reason was that the great majority of knights were, horse and armor aside, penniless. The system of primogeniture left younger sons even of great families without fiefs, and so without income. These young men were sent out into the world with the training and equipment for a single profession, that of arms. The normal business of the knight was war, and often as a mercenary. By the twelfth century, the practice of hiring knights was well established, and even if a knight served his liege lord as part of a feudal levy, the thought of gain was in the forefront of his mind. One of young William Marshal's first lessons, immediately following his initiation into battle at Drincourt, was an exercise in economics. That night at dinner, William of Mandeville, earl of Essex, who had shared command with the chamberlain during the battle, ironically asked William for a small present out of his spoils—"just a crupper or an old horse-collar . . . surely you won forty or sixty horses today?" Embarrassed, William had to admit that not only had he failed to seize the opportunity of booty, but he had even lost his own horse. A few days later there was a tournament that William, horseless, could not enter. At the last moment William's tutor provided him with a horse. The young man fought three victorious combats, and took care to exact horses, arms, armor, baggage, and ransom money.

Many years later William Marshal, as regent for young Henry III, defeated Prince Louis of France and rebel English barons at Lincoln. Roger of Wendover, in his chronicle *Flowers of History,* reports that William allowed his men to do much more than seize enemy horses and treasure-laden wagons:

> The whole city was plundered to the last farthing, and then they proceeded to rob all the churches throughout the city, breaking open all the chests and cupboards with hatchets and hammers, and seizing gold and silver, cloth of all colors, women's ornaments, gold rings, goblets, and precious stones. When at last they had carried off all kinds of merchandise so that nothing remained untouched in any corner of the houses, they all returned to their own lords rich men. When the peace of King Henry had been proclaimed throughout the city by all, they feasted and drank and made merry.

The Provençal poet Bertrand de Born wrote lyrically about war—its pageantry, its excitement, and its booty:

> . . . I love to see,
> Amid the meadows, tents and pavilions spread out,
> And it gives me great joy to see
> Drawn up on the field
> Knights and horses in battle array,
> And it delights me when the scouts
> Scatter people and herds in their path. . . .
> Maces, swords, helms of different colors,
> Shields that will be riven and shattered
> When the fight begins;
> Many vassals struck down together,
> And the horses of the dead and wounded
> Roving at random. . . .
> I tell you I find no such savor
> In food, or in wine, or in sleep,
> As in hearing the shout "On! On!"

From both sides, and the neighing of steeds
That have lost their riders,
And the cries of "Help! Help!"
In seeing men great and small go down
On the grass beyond the castle moat;
In seeing at last the dead,
The pennoned stumps of lances
Still in their sides.

Bertrand, who personally stirred up so much strife between great feudal lords that Dante awarded him a special place in Hell, with his head permanently severed from his body, was explicit about the material reasons for "finding no pleasure in peace":

Why do I want
The rich to hate each other?
Because a rich man is much more
Noble, generous and affable
In war than in peace.

And again:

We are going to have some fun.
For the barons will make much of us. . . .

If they want us to remain with them,
They will give us money.
To the soldier's pay will be added loot:
Trumpet, drums, flags and pennons,
Standards of horses white and black—
This is what we shall shortly see.
And it will be a happy day,
For we shall seize the usurers' goods,
And pack animals will no longer pass in safety,
Or the burgher journey without fear,
Or the merchant on his way to France,
But the man full of courage will be rich.

Addressing himself to the count of Poitiers, Bertrand offered his services: "I can help you. I have already a shield at my neck and a helm on my head. . . . Nevertheless, how can I put myself in the field without money?"

A similarly enthusiastic attitude toward war was expressed by a Welsh chronicler describing a campaign of Prince Llewelyn in 1220 in which he stormed and razed two castles, burned the town of Haverford, and "went round Rhos and Deugleddyv in five days, making vast slaughter of the people of the country. And after making a truce he returned home happy and joyful."

Of all sources of knightly enrichment, the ransom of wealthy prisoners was the foremost. Following a battle in the *Chanson* of *Girart de Roussillon,* Girart and his followers casually put to the sword all their penniless prisoners, but spared the "owners of castles." Ransom of an important personage could reach astronomical figures—like the "king's ransom" of Richard I when he was captured by Leopold of Austria and turned over to Emperor Henry VI: 150,000 marks (several million dollars in twentieth-century American currency), which had to be raised by special taxes levied in both England and Normandy, on knights, laymen, clergy, churches, monasteries. The sum could not be raised, and when Richard was freed, he had to give hostages for the remaining debt.

In France the peace established in the thirteenth century under Louis IX left many knights without a field of action. Numbers of them went to the East as members of the two Crusading orders, the Temple and the Hospital; others went to Spain and Portugal. Their

Tomb effigy of Richard I, The Lionhearted (1157–99). Tombs of the Plantagenet Kings, Fontevrault, France (colored stone, 13th c.).

A jousting tournament in London: Duel at the Fence from *Chroniques* by Jean Froissart (14th c.).

intention was, of course, to fight the Saracen infidels, but it did not always work out that way. Even the Cid, epic hero of Spanish chivalry, spent considerable time in the employ of the infidels, leading expeditions for the Moorish king of Saragossa against Christian princes. For poor knights dependent on their swords for their livelihood, one employer was as good as another. *Girart de Roussillon* paints a sad picture of the knight when peace has come—his income cut off, and the moneylender after him. Girart and his wife, roaming the countryside, meet some merchants restored to prosperity by the peace that has ruined Girart. They find it prudent to conceal Girart's identity, and his wife tells the merchants he is dead. "God be praised," says one, "for he was always making war and through him we have suffered many ills." Frustrated, Girart wishes he could cut the fellow down with one blow of his good sword, but he no longer has it.

In the lean times of peace there remained one source of action and possible gain: the tournament. Historically an outgrowth of old pagan games, taken over like so many other pagan institutions by the early Middle Ages and accorded a Christian coloration, the tournament had by the thirteenth century evolved its own rules and formalities. Great lords and princes organized tournaments for their own entertainment and that of their friends, and to show off their wealth. The principal feature was a mock battle between groups of knights from different regions. Heralds were sent around the countryside to proclaim the tournament, and on the appointed day the knights donned their armor, mounted their horses, and lined up at opposite ends of a level meadow. At a flourish from a herald, the two bands of horsemen charged at each other. The field was open-ended, because when one team was defeated and sought to retreat, the other, exactly as in real war, pursued it through wood and dale to capture prisoners. When it was all over, the defeated knights had to arrange with their captors for their ransom, usually the value of horse and armor, redeemed by a money payment. William Marshal and another knight made a two-year tour of France attending tournaments, in one ten-month period capturing 103 knights and doing a profitable business in ransoms.

There were also prizes, sometimes for several categories of prowess. William Marshal once won a fish, a pike of unusual size. The knights who delivered it found William at the blacksmith's, down on his knees, his head on the anvil, while the smith labored to release him from his helmet, which had gotten turned around backwards from a lance's blow.

Until the latter part of the fourteenth century, there was little individual jousting. The tournament was essentially training for war, and the mass melee intentionally resembled a real battle. The combative ardor of the participants was often very akin to the spirit of genuine war, especially if knightly loyalties were enlisted. Serious and even fatal injuries were common. At one tournament William Marshal's son Gilbert was exhibiting his skill at horsemanship when the bridle broke. Gilbert was tumbled from the saddle and, catching one foot in the stirrup, was dragged across the field and fatally injured. After the accident, the tournament degenerated into a brawl in which one of Gilbert's retainers was killed and many knights and squires were badly wounded. A decade later a tournament near Rochester ended with English squires belaboring the defeated French knights with sticks and clubs.

The earliest English tournaments had been licensed by the king, but Henry III consistently opposed them. William Marshal forbade one in Henry's name in 1217, and thereafter the prohibitions multiplied, but they were so ineffectual that according to the monastic chronicler of the *Annals of Dunstable,* "tourneyers, their alders and abettors, and those who carried merchandise or provisions to tournaments were ordered to be excommunicated, all together, regularly every Sunday."

The tournament at which Gilbert Marshal was

killed had been forbidden by the king—a fact which Henry pointed out to Walter Marshal when the latter claimed his brother's inheritance: "And you too, Walter, who against my wish and notwithstanding my prohibition, and in contempt of me, were present at the tournament . . . on what grounds do you demand your inheritance?" Walter's protests that he could not leave his brother did not soften the king's anger, but the intercession of the bishop of Durham finally brought about a reconciliation.

Aside from the fear that the king expressed when he canceled two tournaments in 1247 between knights of his own French province of Poitou and those of his English domain (he was afraid, in the words of Matthew Paris, that "after the spears were shivered, bloody swords might flash forth"), Henry III regarded tournaments as pretexts for conspiracy by the barons. In several cases these mock wars were closely connected with baronial uprisings. On the occasion of an abortive rising at Stamford in 1229 after Henry's coming of age, the barons involved rode off to Chepstow with William Marshal II for a tournament, only to be confronted with a writ by the justiciar, Hubert de Burgh, forbidding the meeting. Seventy-three more prohibitions were recorded in the ensuing three decades. Several times knights holding tournaments had their lands seized. On one occasion the king's brother, William de Valence, urged his knightly companions to defy the king's order and hold a tournament, which was only prevented by a heavy fall of snow. A little later William staged the tournament and succeeded in severely wounding a fellow knight.

The Church joined Henry in its opposition, not only because of the violence of the combats and the danger of sedition. Besides such innocent auxiliary sports as wrestling, dart shooting, lance hurling, and stone throwing, the tournaments were famous for eating, drinking, and lovemaking. Jacques de Vitry, the Paris preacher renowned for the acerbity of his sermons, liked to use the tournament to illustrate all seven of the deadly sins. The Church's strictures were not very effective. Jocelin of Brakelond records how Abbot Samson of Bury St. Edmunds forbade a band of young knights to hold a tournament and went so far as to lock the town gates to keep them from the field. Next day, on the Feast of Peter and Paul, the young men foreswore combat and came to dine with the abbot. But after dinner, sending for more wine, they caroused, sang, ruined the abbot's afternoon nap, and finally marched out, broke open the town gates, and held their tournament. The abbot excommunicated the lot.

In the 1250s a milder form of combat, known in England as a Round Table (named after King Arthur's assemblies), anticipated the tournaments of the fourteenth and fifteenth centuries, replacing the mass melee with adversaries in single combat with blunted weapons. Such meetings were usually preceded by feasting and games. But even the Round Tables could be lethal. In 1252 Matthew Paris recorded the death of Arnold de Montigny in a joust with Roger de Lernburn, which brought suspicion of murder because the iron point of Roger's lance, when drawn from the dead man's throat, was found not to have been blunted as it should have been. Further, Roger had previously wounded Arnold in a tournament. Matthew concluded, "But God only knows the truth of this, who alone searches into the secrets of men's hearts."

At another Round Table in 1256, held at Blyth, the seventeen-year-old Prince Edward fought in armor of linen cloth and with light weapons; but the meeting, like the mass melees, ended in turmoil, with the participants beaten and trampled on. According to Matthew Paris, a number of nobles, including Earl Marshal Roger Bigod of Chepstow, "never afterwards recovered their health." Prince Edward, as Edward I, sought to regulate rather than ban tournaments and Round Tables. His statute of 1267 aimed at preventing riots by limiting the number of squires and specifying the weapons carried by knights, squires, grooms, footmen, heralds, and spectators. At Edward's own royal tourneys, there were no casualties.

In France the melee gave way to the joust even earlier. Tournaments of the later type are depicted by the authors of the romances as brave and colorful pageants. In the *Castellan of Coucy*, the heralds appeared at an early hour to awaken the many guests who had arrived at the castle:

> Mass sung and the ladies installed in the pavilions, the jousts began without delay. The first was between the Duke of Limbourg and a bachelor named Gautier de Soul, who broke three lances apiece without losing the stirrups. . . . The seventh was one of the most powerful shows of arms and the most pleasant to see: the first champion wore a sleeve [a token of his lady] on his right arm, and when he went to his station, the heralds cried, "Coucy, Coucy, the brave man, the valiant bachelor, the Castellan of Coucy!" Against him appeared successively Gaucher of Chatillon and Count Louis of Blois. . . . Two more jousts took place; then night fell and the assembly separated to La Fère and Vendeuil. . . . The next day the jousts continued [until] only three

**King Arthur and Charlemagne by Giacomo Jaquerio.
Castle, Manta, Italy.**

knights were left, the others all being wounded. . . .
At the first pass the Castellan knocked down his
adversary's helmet into the dust, and blood ran from
his mouth and nose. . . . On the third try both men
were disarmed and fell unconscious to the ground.
Valets, sergeants and squires laid them on their shields
and carried them from the field. . . . But it was only,
thank God, a passing unconsciousness; neither man
was dead. Everyone thanked God and the saints.

Then the Sire de Coucy invited the knights and
ladies to dine. . . . More than twenty tents were set
up between the Oise and the forest, in fields full of
flowers. The Sire de Coucy and all the Vermandois
were dressed in green samite studded with golden
eagles; they came to the tents leading by the finger
the ladies of their country. The men of Hainaut and
their ladies were dressed in gold embroidered with
black lions; they arrived singing, two by two. The
Champenois, the Burgundians, the men of Berri,
were also in uniform, scarlet samite decorated with
golden leopards.

The tournament gave an impetus to one of the
best known traditions of feudalism and knighthood—
the art of heraldry, which took its name from the fact
that tournament heralds became experts in the design

of heraldic devices. Symbols on banners and shields to
distinguish leaders in the melee of a feudal battle were
common as early as the eleventh century. The Bayeux
Tapestry shows such devices for both Harold and
William. In the twelfth century the custom grew of
passing on the device from father to son, like the shield
with the golden lions which Geoffrey of Anjou received
at his knighting from his father-in-law, Henry I, an
emblem inherited by Geoffrey's grandson William
Longespée, earl of Salisbury. Another early device was
that of the Clare family, lords of Chepstow; in about
1140 Gilbert de Clare adopted three chevrons, similar to
those later used in military insignia. The Clare arms
appeared on the lord's shield, and probably flew from
Chepstow to signal the owner's presence in his castle.
Crests, in the form of three-dimensional figures—a
boar, a lion, a hawk—were added to the helmet as early
as the end of the twelfth century.

In the thirteenth century, the functional value of
the heraldic device, or coat of arms, as it came to be
called from its use on surcoats, was strongly reinforced as
chivalric ideology became popular and affluence encouraged the decorative arts. Even more important was
its character as a badge of nobility, visually setting its
owner apart from the common people (although wealthy
townsmen continued to acquire knightly status and coats
of arms to authenticate it). From art, heraldry progressed
to become a science, with its own rigid rules and its own
jargon. Shields could be partitioned into segments only in
certain specified ways, such as *tierced in fesse* (divided into
three horizontally) or *in saltire* (cut into four portions by
a diagonal cross). Dragons, lions, leopards, eagles, fish, and
many other animals, including mythological ones, were
used, besides stars, moons, trees, bushes, flowers, and other
objects both natural and man-made. The addition of a
motto came into fashion, like the French kings' *Montjoye,*
the rallying cry and standard of Charlemagne in the
Chanson de Roland. All the elements of the arms—crest,
helmet, shield, and motto—were finally assembled in a
standardized form of heraldic device.

A custom of English nobles that may date to the
thirteenth century, that of hanging their heraldic banners outside inns where they were staying, led to the inn
sign of later times: the White Hart from the badge of
Richard II, the Swan from that of the earls of Hereford,
the Rose and Crown from the badge of England.

In the thirteenth century the institution of knighthood, closely related to the life of the castle, was perhaps
at its zenith. Already, in fact, signs of decadence were
evident in the growing sophistication of attitudes. The

Chanson de Roland, written at about the time of the First Crusade, and in which the word "chivalrous" makes its first appearance, breathes a spirit of rugged Christian naiveté. Roland brings disaster on Charlemagne's rear guard by refusing to sound his horn and let Charlemagne know the Saracens are attacking, because to call for help would be cowardly. "Better death than dishonor," is Roland's view. His strategy is simple: "Strike with your lance," he tells Oliver, "and I will smite with Durendal, my good sword which the emperor gave me. If I die, he who shall inherit it will say: it was the sword of a noble vassal." Durendal contains in its hilt, among other sacred relics, a scrap of the Virgin's garment. After a terrific battle in which Saracens are cut down in windrows while the French knights drop one by one, the dying Roland is left alone on the corpse-strewn field, his last thoughts of his two lords, Charlemagne and God, to whom he holds his glove aloft as he expires.

The chivalric ideal of the *Chanson de Roland,* developed and celebrated by the poets of the twelfth century, embraced generosity, honor, the pursuit of glory, and contempt for hardship, fatigue, pain, and death.

But by the thirteenth century it was possible to write a totally different kind of book on the same theme of crusading against the Saracens. The *Histoire de Saint-Louis,* by the Sieur de Joinville, seneschal of Champagne, presents a striking contrast to *Roland.* The chronicle of the ill-fated crusade of Louis IX to Egypt tells in honest prose a story not dissimilar to that of Roland—Christian French knights fighting bravely against heavy odds and in the end nearly all dying. But the difference in tone is vast: Joinville's knights are real, they suffer from their wounds and disease, and death seems more miserable than glorious. And even though Joinville cherishes and admires the saintly Louis much as Roland loved Charlemagne, his attitude is very different. St. Louis asks Joinville, "Which would you prefer: to be a leper or to have committed some mortal sin?" The honest seneschal reports, "I, who had never lied to him, replied that I would rather have committed thirty mortal sins than become a leper."

Common sense has intruded on chivalry.

X

THE CASTLE AT WAR

Warfare in the Middle Ages centered around castles. The clumsy, disorganized feudal levies, called out for a few weeks' summer service, rarely met in pitched battles. Their most efficient employment was in sieges, a condition that fitted neatly into the capital strategic value of the castle.

Medieval warfare was not as incessant as some of the older historians have pictured it. The motte-and-bailey stronghold of the ninth and tenth centuries was frequently embroiled, either with Viking, Saracen, and Hungarian marauders or with neighboring barons, but by the eleventh century the marauders had been discouraged and private warfare was on the wane. In England it was outlawed by William the Conqueror and effectively suppressed by his successors. To take its place there were the Crusades, including those against Spanish Moors and French Albigensians; international wars, such as those waged by Richard the

Lionhearted, John and Henry III in France, and the wars of conquest in Wales, Scotland, and Ireland, and civil wars, such as that fought by Stephen of Blois and the Empress Matilda over the throne, and the numerous rebellions of barons against royal authority. Despite all these, many twelfth- and thirteenth-century castles were rarely besieged, and Chepstow was unusual but by no means unique in passing entirely through the Middle Ages without ever seeing an enemy at its gates.

Nevertheless, when war broke out, it inevitably revolved around castles. Enemy castles were major political-military objectives in themselves, and many were sited specifically to bar invasion routes. Typically the castle stood on high ground commanding a river crossing, a river confluence, a stretch of navigation, a coastal harbor, a mountain pass, or some other strategically important feature. The castle inside a city could be defended long after the city had been taken, and an unsubdued castle garrison could sally out and reoccupy the town the moment the enemy left. Even a rural castle could not safely be bypassed, because its garrison could cut the invader's supply lines. The mobility of the garrison—nearly always supplied with horses—conferred a large strategic radius for many purposes: raiding across a border, furnishing a supply base for an army on the offensive, interrupting road or river traffic at a distance. For all these reasons, medieval

Battle scene (top), a Stoning (bottom) from the *Maciejowski Bible* illuminated in Paris; presented to Shah Abbas the Great of Persia by the Papal Mission (c.1250) Pierpont Morgan Library, New York, Ms. 638.

Chepstow Castle, South Wales, (built c.1070): Exterior view of the rectangular Great Tower (c) with the towers of the barbican (l).

military science was the science of the attack and defense of castles.

The castle's main line of resistance was the curtain wall with its projecting towers. The ground in front of the curtain was kept free of all cover; if there was a moat, the ground was cleared well beyond it. Where the approach to the castle was limited by the site, and especially where it was limited to one single direction, the defenses on the vulnerable side multiplied, with combinations of walls, moats, and towers masking the main curtain wall. At Chepstow the eastern end was protected by the Great Gatehouse, with its arrow loops, portcullises, and machicolations. The barbican built by the Marshals to protect the western end consisted of a walled enclosure a hundred feet wide by fifty deep, with a powerful cylindrical tower at the southwest corner and a fortified gatehouse on the northwest. The barbican was separated from the west curtain wall by a broad ditch, or dry moat, crossed by a bridge with a draw span and overlooked by a strong rectangular tower on the inner side. The ditch ended at the south wall in an inconspicuous postern which, even if forced, would admit the enemy only to a trap, enfiladed by the towers and the wall parapet. The long sides of the castle had strong natural defenses: the river with its high bluff on the north, and the steep slope of the ridge on the south toward the town.

Such a castle as Chepstow was practically proof against direct assault, while its size provided ample facilities for storing provisions. Some castles kept a year's supply of food or even more on hand, and the relatively small size of a thirteenth-century garrison often meant that in

a prolonged siege the assailants rather than the besieged were confronted with a supply problem. A garrison of sixty men could hold out against an attacking force ten times its number, and feeding sixty men from a well-stocked granary supplemented by cattle, pigs, and chickens brought in at the enemy's approach might be far easier than feeding 600 men from a war-ravaged countryside.

By the late thirteenth century, castle logistics were on a sophisticated basis, with supplies often purchased from general contractors, such as the consignments ordered from one John Hutting in June 1266 to supply the castle of Rochester, used as a base by Henry III's general Roger Leyburn: 251 herrings, 50 sheep, 51 salted pigs, and quantities of figs, rice, and raisins. More commonly a single commodity was bought from an individual merchant or group of merchants; for Rochester, Roger Leyburn bought fish from merchants of Northfleet and Strood; oats from Maidstone, Leeds, and Nessindon; rye from a merchant of Colchester, and wine from Peter of London and Henry the Vintner of Sittingbourne.

A castle's water supply frequently offered a more vulnerable target than its food supply. Although a reliable well, in or near the keep, was one of the basic necessities of a castle, wells sometimes failed, and when they did the results were disastrous. In the First Crusade, when the Turks besieged the Crusaders in the castle of Xerigordo near Nicaea and cut off their water supply, the beleaguered Christians suffered terrific hardships, drinking their horses' blood and each other's urine, and burying themselves in damp earth in hope of absorbing the moisture. After eight days without water the Christians surrendered, and were killed or sold as slaves. Two decades later Count Fulk of Anjou, besieging Henry I's

Exterior of Rochester Castle (1130).

castle of Alençon, managed to locate and destroy an underground conduit from the river Sarthe, and the garrison was forced to surrender. In 1136, when King Stephen was besieging a rebellious baron, Baldwin of Redvers, in the castle of Exeter, the castle's two wells suddenly went dry. The garrison drank wine as long as it lasted, also using it to make bread, to cook, and to put out fires set by the attackers. In the end the rebels yielded, and, in the words of the chronicler of the *Gesta Stephani,* "when they finally came forth you could have seen the body of each individual wasted and enfeebled with parching thirst, and once they were outside they hurried rather to drink a draught of any sort than to discharge any business whatsoever."

Hunger and thirst aside, no defensive fortification was proof against all attack, and even the strongest castles of the twelfth and thirteenth centuries could be, and were, captured. The castle had few vulnerable points, but what few it had were assiduously exploited by its enemies.

A frequent structural weakness of castles lay in their subsoil. Unless a castle was founded wholly on solid rock, some part of its walls could be undermined by digging. The procedure was to drive a tunnel beneath the wall, preferably under a corner or tower, supporting the tunnel roof with heavy timbers as the sappers advanced. When they reached a point directly under the wall, the timbering was set ablaze, collapsing earth and masonry above. The process was not as easy as it sounds. In 1215, when King John laid siege to Rochester Castle, a vast twelfth-century square keep defended by about a hundred rebel knights and a number of foot soldiers and bowmen, he ordered nearby Canterbury to manufacture "by day and night as many picks as you are able." Six weeks later the digging had progressed to the point when John commanded justiciar Hubert de Burgh to "send to us with all speed by day and night forty of the fattest pigs of the sort least good for eating to bring fire beneath the tower." The lard produced a sufficient blaze in the mine to destroy the timbering and bring down a great section of the wall of the keep.

A castle built on a solid rock foundation, such as Chepstow, had to be attacked with two other main devices inherited by medieval military engineers from ancient predecessors: the mobile assault tower and the siege engine or catapult artillery. The assault tower, usually called a cat, but sometimes a bear or other figurative term, was normally assembled from components brought to the site. The aim of all the many designs was to provide the storming party with cover and height, neutralizing the advantages of the defenders. The tower might be employed to seize a section of the rampart or to provide cover for sappers or a battering ram. The immense gates of the powerful castles of the High Middle Ages were rarely forced by ramming, though a small castle might be vulnerable to the heavy beam or tree trunk, fronted with an iron or copper head (sometimes literally a ram's head), either grasped directly by its crew or swung from leather thongs. Before any form of direct assault, the moat defense had first to be dealt with, usually by filling it in with brush and earth. The assault tower, containing both archers and assault troops to engage the defenders hand-to-hand, could then be wheeled forward to the castle wall. A large besieging army could build and man several such towers and by attacking different points of the wall exploit its numerical advantage. Since the towers were wooden, the castle's defenders tried to set them afire by hurling torches or fire-bearing arrows.

Medieval engineers used the ancient tension and torsion engines, in the commonest form of which a tightly wound horizontal skein, its axis parallel to the wall under attack, was wound still tighter by an upright timber arm fixed to its shaft at right angles, and drawn back to ground level. The timber arm, or firing beam, now under great tension, was charged with a missile at its extreme end and released. At the upright position the arm's leap forward was halted by a padded crossbar, causing the missile to fly on. Data on ranges are scarce, but modern experiments have achieved a distance of 200 yards with 50-pound rocks.

Medieval engineers devised another form, the trebuchet, driven by a counterweight, an invention also used for castle drawbridges. The Arabs had used a catapult in which the beam was pulled down by a gang of men and released. European military engineers introduced a decisive improvement. In the trebuchet, the firing beam was pivoted on a crosspole about a quarter of its length from its butt end, which was pointed at the enemy castle. The butt end was weighted with a number of measured weights calibrated for range, and the long end, pulled down by means of a winch, was loaded with the missile. Released, the beam sprang to the upright position, discharging the missile with a power and accuracy said to be superior to that of the tension and torsion engines. First used in Italy at the end of the twelfth century, the trebuchet was widely employed in the Albigensian Crusade of the early 1200s. It made its appearance in England in 1216 during the siege of Dover by Prince Louis of France. The following year a trebuchet was carried on one of Louis's ships when his fleet, attempting to enter the mouth of the Thames, was decisively defeated in the battle of Sandwich; the machine weighed down the ship "so deep in the water that the deck was almost awash," and proved a handicap rather than an advantage in the encounter. The effectiveness of the trebuchet in a siege was formidable, however, because of its capacity to hit the same target repeatedly with precision. In 1244 Bishop Durand of Albi designed a trebuchet for the siege of Montségur that hurled a succession of missiles weighing forty kilograms (eighty-eight pounds) at the same point in the wall day and night, at twenty-minute intervals, until it battered an opening.

Ammunition of the attackers included inflammables for firing the timber buildings of the castle bailey. The effectiveness of stone projectiles depended on the height and thickness of the stone walls against which they were flung. The walls of the early twelfth century could be battered down, and often were. The result was the construction of much heavier walls—in Windsor Castle, for example, reaching a thickness of twenty-four feet.

Defenders of large castles used artillery of their own for counter-battery fire. During Edward I's Welsh wars, an engineer named Reginald added four *springalds* (catapults) to the towers of Chepstow, one mounted on William Fitz Osbern's keep. Trebuchets and mangonels, mounted on the towers or even on the broad walls of castles, hurled rocks, frequently the besiegers' own back at them, with the additional advantage gained from height.

A different principle—that of the crossbow—supplied another form of artillery for both besiegers and besieged. The ancient Roman ballista, easy to mount on castle walls, discharged a giant arrow, or quarrel. The smaller crossbow was the basic hand-missile weapon of besiegers and besieged throughout the Middle Ages. Used but apparently not appreciated by the Romans, the crossbow mysteriously disappeared for several centuries before its reintroduction into Europe, probably in eleventh-century Italy. In the First Crusade it proved a novelty to both Turks and Byzantine Greeks. Apparently a new, stronger trigger mechanism was responsible for the crossbow's resurgence. In the form best known in the twelfth and thirteenth centuries, it was cocked by means of a stirrup at the end of the stock, or crosspiece. Placing the weapon bow down, so that the stock was in a vertical position, the archer engaged the stirrup with his foot while hooking the bowstring to his belt. He pushed down with his foot to cock the bow, which was caught and held by a trigger mechanism. Unhooking the string from his belt, the archer raised the weapon and fired by squeezing a lever under the stock. A range of up to 400 yards was attainable. The crossbow was exceptionally well suited to castle defense, for which the Welsh-English longbow, effective on the open battlefield, was less successful. The longbow had a shorter range and shot a lighter missile, and its greater portability and rapid rate of fire were of less account in castle defense than on the battlefield.

The chronicle *Annals of Dunstable* gave a vivid description of the capture of Bedford Castle, seat of the unruly lord Falkes de Bréauté, by the forces of Henry III in 1224, in an arduous eight-week siege. Falkes' castle consisted principally of two stone towers, an old and a new, separated by an inner bailey and surrounded by a broad outer bailey with a gate defended by a strong barbican.

> On the eastern side was a stone-throwing machine and two mangonels which attacked the [new] tower every day. On the western side were two mangonels which reduced the old tower. A mangonel on the south and one on the north made two breaches in the walls nearest them. Besides these, there were two wooden machines erected . . . overlooking the top of the tower and the castle for the use of the crossbowmen and scouts.
>
> In addition there were very many engines there in which lay hidden both crossbowmen and stingers. Further, there was an engine called a cat, protected

Border detail of an archer from the *Latin/Luttrell Psalter* (14th c.).

by which underground diggers called miners . . . undermined the walls of the tower and castle.

Now the castle was taken by four assaults. In the first the barbican was taken, where four or five of the outer guard were killed. In the second the outer bailey was taken, where more were killed, and in this place our people captured horses and their harness, corselets, crossbows, oxen, bacon, live pigs and other things beyond number. But the buildings with grain and hay in them they burned. In the third assault, thanks to the action of the miners, the wall fell near the old tower, where our men got in through the rubble and amid great danger occupied the inner bailey. Thus employed, many of our men perished, and ten of our men who tried to enter, the tower were shut in and held there by their enemies. At the fourth assault, on the vigil of the Assumption, about vespers, a fire was set under the tower by the miners so that smoke broke through into the room of the tower where the enemy were; and the tower split so that cracks appeared. Then the enemy, despairing of their safety, allowed Falkes' wife and all the women with her, and Henry [de Braybroke], the king's justice [whose capture by Falkes' brother William had caused the siege], with other knights whom they had shut up before, to go out unharmed, and they yielded to the king's command, hoisting the royal flag to the top of the tower. Thus they remained under the king's custody, on the tower for that night.

On the following morning they were brought before the king's tribunal, and when they had been absolved from their excommunication by the bishops, by the command of the king and his justice they were hanged, eighty and more of them, on the gallows.

At the prayers of the leaders the king spared three Templars, so that they might serve Our Lord in the Holy Land in their habit. The chaplain of the castle was set free by the archbishop for trial in an ecclesiastical court. . . .

Falkes himself took the cross and was allowed to leave the country and go to Rome. The castle was dismantled except for the inner bailey, where living quarters were left for the Beauchamp family, earls of Bedford; the stones of the towers and outer bailey were given to local churches (poetic justice, since they had been built with the stones of two churches pulled down for that purpose by Falkes).

Garrisons surrendering at discretion were not usually so harshly dealt with. In ordinary conflict, without the added passion of religious difference or rebellion against authority, the whole garrison might be spared. Or the knights might be ransomed and the footsoldiers massacred or mutilated. Often a rebel castle surrendered before it was absolutely necessary, in return for the garrison's being allowed to depart in freedom.

Even a castle sited on rock, well-provisioned with food and water, and stout-walled against artillery might still be taken by ruse. Usually the ruse was of the Trojan horse variety, that is, designed to effect entry by a small party. A popular trick was the nocturnal "escalade," a silent scaling of the wall at an inadequately guarded point. Another was a diversion designed to draw defenders away from a secondary gate or weak point that might then be suddenly overwhelmed. A third was penetration by means of a special ingress, such as a mine, a disused well, or a latrine, as in the case of Richard the Lionhearted's Château Gaillard in 1204. Occasionally the garrison might be lured into a sortie, so that the attackers could penetrate the gates as the defenders fled back into the castle.

Another form of ruse involved disguise. The attacking army might raise the siege and ostentatiously march away, but remain just out of sight. Some of its soldiers, donning the dress of peasants or merchants, might then gain access to the provision-hungry castle and seize the gatehouse. Knights were sometimes smuggled into a castle concealed in wagonloads of grain. The men of Count Baldwin of Flanders rescued their lord from imprisonment in a Turkish castle in 1123 by disguising themselves as peddlers and daggering the gate guards.

The dominant role of the siege helps explain one of the most characteristic aspects of medieval warfare: its stop-and-go, on-again-off-again pattern. Truces were natural between adversaries who might for long periods remain within ready range of communication but safe from each other's attack. In the war between Prince Louis of France and Henry III, at least five truces were made between October 1216 and February 1217, all related to castle sieges.

A shrewd commander besieging a castle might take advantage of a truce to plant a spy or bribe a member of the garrison. He might obtain valuable information, for example on the castle's supplies, or he might arrange for a postern to be opened at midnight or a rampart to be left unguarded. In 1265, a spy, apparently disguised as a woman, reported to Henry III's son Edward (later Edward I) that the garrison of Simon de Montfort's Kenilworth Castle planned to leave the stronghold for the night in order to enjoy baths in the town. According to the *Chronicle of Melrose*, the king's men surprised Simon's knights asleep and unarmed, and "some of them might be seen running off entirely naked, others wearing nothing but a pair of breeches, and others in shirts and breeches only."

Simon's son (Simon de Montfort III), in command of the party, regained the castle by swimming the Mere, the castle's lake, in his nightshirt. His father was killed three days later in the battle of Evesham, and the following spring young Simon had to defend Kenilworth Castle against the royal army. Despite a terrific pounding by siege engines, the castle held out against every assault, beating off a giant cat carrying 200 bowmen, and destroying another with a well-directed mangonel shot. Even the intervention of the archbishop of Canterbury had no effect; when the prelate appeared outside the castle to pronounce excommunication of the garrison, a defender donned clerical robes and jeered from atop the curtain wall. The king offered lenient terms, but Simon turned them down. It was nearly Christmas when Simon, his provisions exhausted, slipped out of the castle with his brothers to escape abroad, permitting his starving and dysentery-ridden garrison to surrender.

Bohemund d'Hauteville captured the powerful Saracen stronghold of Antioch by a combined bribe and ruse. Corrupting Firuz, an emir who commanded three towers, with promises of wealth, honor, and baptism, he had his own Frankish army feign withdrawal. That night the Franks returned stealthily and a picked band scaled the walls of Firuz' sector, killed resisting guards, and opened the gate. By morning the city was in the hands of Bohemund, who true to knightly tradition, even in a Crusade, had already extracted a promise from his fellow barons that the whole place would be turned over to him.

The chronicler of the *Gesta Stephani* related with relish the story of a ruse that was worked on Robert Fitz

Hubert, one of the barons who rebelled against King Stephen and "a man unequaled in wickedness and crime," at least according to the partisan historian. Fitz Hubert took Stephen's Devizes Castle by a night escalade and then refused to turn it over to the earl of Gloucester, on whose side in the civil war he was supposed to be fighting. But Fitz Hubert came a cropper in negotiating with a neighbor baron, none other than John Fitz Gilbert the Marshal, father of William Marshal, whom the chronicler describes as "a man equally cunning and very ready to set great designs on foot by treachery." John had seized Marlborough, a strong castle belonging to the king. Fitz Hubert sent word to John that he would make a pact of peace and friendship, and that he wanted to parley with him at Marlborough. John agreed, but after admitting him to the castle behaved characteristically; he shut the gates behind him, "put him in a narrow dungeon to suffer hunger and tortures," then handed him over to the earl of Gloucester, who took him back to his own castle of Devizes and hanged him in sight of the garrison. The knights of the garrison then accepted a bribe and turned over the castle to the earl of Gloucester.

The following year, 1141, King Stephen's side scored a decisive victory in the war by another extraordinary tactic, a siege of the besiegers. The Empress Matilda, Stephen's rival for the throne, and her brother, the earl of Gloucester, laid siege to the castle of the bishop of Winchester. The bishop appealed for help to Stephen's supporters—Stephen being at the moment a prisoner—and hired knights himself. Stephen's queen (also named Matilda) brought an army reinforced by troops nearly a thousand strong sent by the city of London. The besieged occupiers of the bishop's castle flung out firebrands, burning down the greater part of the town, including two abbeys, while Stephen's forces guarded the roads into the town to prevent provisions being brought to the townspeople, who were soon suffering from famine. By way of diversion, the earl of Gloucester began to fortify the abbey of Wherwell, six miles distant.

> But the king's forces . . . suddenly and unexpectedly arrived at Wherwell in an irresistible host, and attacking them vigorously on every side they captured and killed a great many, and at length compelled the rest to give way and take refuge in the church. And when they used the church for defense like a castle,

Château Gaillard ruins near Les Andelys, Normandy, France. Built in 1196 by Richard I, The Lionhearted, the Chateau was partially dismantled in 1591.

Kenilworth Castle ruins, Warwickshire, Great Britain. Founded by Geoffrey de Clinton (1120); passed to Simon de Montfort family (13th–14th c.).

the other side threw in torches from every quarter and made them leave the church. . . . It was indeed a dreadful and wretched sight, how impiously and savagely bodies of armed men were ranging about in a church, a house of religion and prayer, especially as in one place mutual slaughter was going on, in another prisoners were being dragged off bound with thongs, here the conflagration was fearfully ravaging the roofs of the church and the houses, there cries and shrieks rang piercingly out from the virgins dedicated to God who had left their cloisters with reluctance under the stress of the fire.

The Empress Matilda and the earl of Gloucester decided to raise the siege and save their army, but as the besiegers were moving out of Winchester, the alert royal army fell upon it from both sides and routed it. The chronicler reports:

> You could have seen chargers finely shaped and goodly to look upon here straying about after throwing their riders, there fainting from weariness and at their last gasp; shields and coats of mail and arms of every kind lying everywhere strewn on the ground; tempting cloaks and vessels of precious metal, with other valuables, flung in heaps, offering themselves to the finders on every side.

Thus the defensive strength of a castle permitted an offensive counterstroke to be launched. Sometimes a castle's siege was tied into an even more complex strategic pattern. In 1203 one of the few successes of King John in his war against Philip Augustus involved such a pattern. The French king was besieging the great castle of Arques, southeast of Dieppe, held by John's garrison, while Philip's ally, Arthur of Brittany, besieged Mirabeau, defended by a force under his own grandmother, John's mother, Eleanor of Aquitaine. William Marshal and two other Anglo-Norman earls were striving to relieve Arques when John struck a successful surprise blow at Arthur's army outside Mirabeau. Arthur's defeat exposed Philip to a combined attack by the armies of King John and William Marshal, compelling Philip to raise the siege of Arques without an arrow being fired. In retreat, Philip aimed a blow at William's small force, but William outdistanced him and escaped to Rouen. The following year John's inability to divert Philip from the long siege of the Château Gaillard brought the fall of that powerful castle, laying open the Seine valley to Philip and eventually leading to the surrender of Rouen and all Normandy.

Some castles underwent many sieges, others few, and some, like Chepstow, none. Unscathed Chepstow's history underlines the castle's other military function, as a springboard for offensive action. Chepstow was deliberately designed as a base for aggression in Wales, and was put to effective use for this purpose by William Fitz Osbern and his Clare successors. On occasion Chepstow also served as a base for operations against the royal power, as in 1074, when William Fitz Osbern's son Roger and the earl of Norfolk rebelled against the Conqueror.

Pembroke Castle, on the southwest tip of Wales, provides an even more striking example than Chepstow of the aggressive role of the castle. In 1093, during the reign of William Rufus, Arnulph de Montgomery, a Norman baron, arrived at Pembroke by water, built a motte-and-bailey castle on a rocky peninsula on the site of an old Roman camp, and set about subduing the countryside. When Arnulph rebelled against Henry I in 1102, the king seized Pembroke Castle; in 1138 King Stephen granted it to Gilbert Strongbow de Clare, who fortified it. Gilbert's son Richard Strongbow used it as a base for the conquest of Ireland. Later William Marshal further strengthened the castle by building the great keep and hall. His son William Marshal II, reversing the procedure of Strongbow, brought a force from Ireland, where he served as justiciar, and employed Pembroke as a base for crushing the rebellious Welsh.

It was often the offensive capabilities of the castle that provoked sieges, but it was its incomparable defensive strength that conferred its military importance. Always ready, requiring little maintenance and repair, demanding scant advance notice of impending attack, the castle remained the basic center of power throughout the Middle Ages.

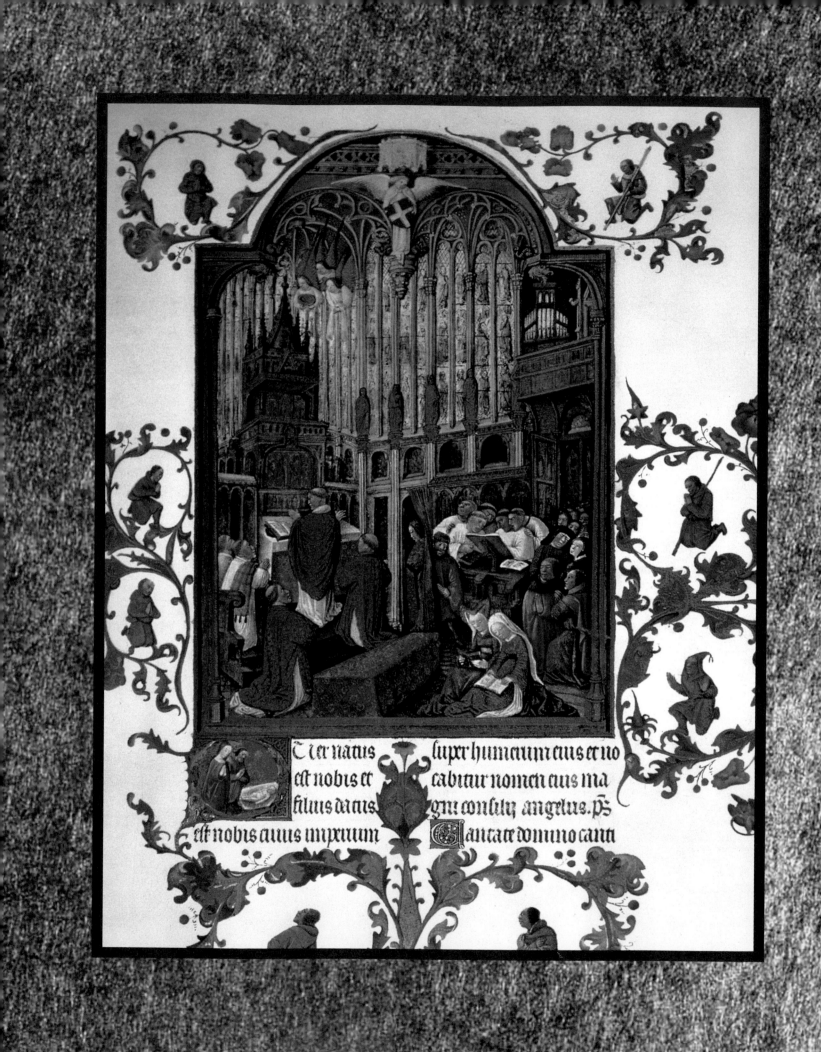

XI

THE CASTLE YEAR

For those who lived in and around the medieval castle, the seasons of the year were marked by a succession of feast days consecrated by the Church but with pagan origins reaching far back in time. Four seasons, somewhat differently distributed from those of the modern calendar, were marked by ancient agricultural festivals in Christian guise.

Winter was the season from Michaelmas (September 29) to Christmas when wheat and rye were sown. From the end of the Christmas holidays to Easter was the season when spring crops were sown: oats, peas, beans, barley, and vetches. From the end of Easter week to Lammas (August 1) was summer, and from Lammas to Michaelmas was harvest, or autumn.

Christmas and Easter were the most important of the season-marking holidays, while Pentecost or Whitsunday, in Maytime (the seventh Sunday after Easter),

was of almost equal moment. Each of these three great festivals was celebrated by a feast of the Church followed by a week or more of vacation, followed by another feast, not of the Church but of the people, to mark the resumption of work. Lesser religious holidays had unmistakable roots in husbandry: Candlemas (February 2), when tillage was resumed; Hocktide, at the end of Easter week, the beginning of summer; the three smaller Maytime feasts, Mayday, the Rogation Days, and Ascension; Midsummer, or St. John's Day, June 24; Lammas, the feast of St. Peter and Vincula; and finally Michaelmas following the harvest.

Michaelmas marked not only the beginning of winter but the beginning of the castle's fiscal year. As the villagers opened the hedges to allow cattle to enter the harvested fields and graze on the stubble, and as plowing and narrowing began on the previously fallow fields, the castle stewards and manorial officers totaled up their accounts.

November was slaughter time, the "blood month" of the Anglo-Saxon calendar. Feed was too scarce to keep most of the animals through the winter, and smoked and salted meat was essential for human survival. The month began with the ancient feast of All Hallows, originally for the propitiation of evil spirits from the

Celebration of Christmas Mass by the Limbourg Brothers from the *Très Riches Heures du Duc de Berry* (early 15th c.).

dead, but adapted by the Church as All Saints, followed next day by All Souls. Martinmas, or St. Martin's Day (November 11), marked another Christianized traditional holiday, the feast of the plowman—celebrated, at least in later days, with cakes, pestles, and *frumenty,* a pudding made of wheat boiled with milk, currants, raisins, and spices.

The dreary fortnight from Christmas Eve to Epiphany, or Twelfth Day (January 6), when the fields were drowned with rain or bound with frost, was transformed into the longest holiday of the year, a fourteen- or fifteen-day vacation. Services required of villeins were suspended, and the manorial servants—the hayward, the lord's plowman, the shepherd, swineherd, and oxherd—received their "perquisites," bonuses such as food, clothing, drink, and firewood, that were their traditional Christmas due.

Besides conviviality, carol singing, and entertainment, the Christmas holidays brought a suspension of everyday standards of behavior and status. On the eve of St. Nicholas' Day (December 6), the cathedrals chose "boy bishops" who presided over services on the Feast of the Holy Innocents (December 28), assisted by schoolboys and choirboys. On January 1, in the Feast of the Fools, priests and clerks wore masks at Mass, sang "wanton songs," censed with smoke from the soles of old shoes, and ate sausages before the altar. During the boisterous Christmas season the lord often appointed a special force of watchmen for the twelve nights in anticipation of rioting. Tenants on a manor belonging to St. Paul's cathedral, London, were bound to watch at the manor house from Christmas to Twelfth Day, their pay "a good fire in the hall, one white loaf, one cooked dish, and a gallon of ale [per day]."

During the Christmas season "every man's house, as also their parish churches, was decked with holme [holly], ivy, bay, and whatsoever the season of the year afforded to be green," wrote William Fitzstephen in his description of London in the twelfth century. On Christmas Eve the Yule log was brought in—a giant section of tree trunk which filled the hearth, and was kept burning throughout the twelve nights.

Christmas brought celebration to the castle population from bottom to top. Tenants on the manors owed special rents but also enjoyed special privileges. Usually they owed the lord bread, hens, and ale, which they brewed themselves, while in return he gave them Christmas dinner, consisting mainly of the food they had provided; the lord thus organized Christmas dinner at little cost to himself, the tenants often even providing their own fuel, dishes, and napkins. A group of three prosperous villeins on a manor belonging to Wells Cathedral in the early fourteenth century received "two white loaves, as much beer as they will drink in the day, a mess of beef and of bacon with mustard, one of browis [stew] of hen, and a cheese, fuel to cook their food . . . and to burn from dinner time till even and afterwards, and two candles." Another villein who held less land was to have Christmas dinner, "but he must bring with him . . . his own cloth, cup and trencher, and take away all that is left on his cloth, and he shall have for himself and his neighbors one wastel [loaf] cut in three for the ancient Christmas game to be played with the said wastel." The "ancient Christmas game" may have been a version of "king of the bean," in which a bean was hidden in a cake or loaf, and the person who found it became king of the feast. Many of the manors of Glastonbury Abbey gave Christmas feasts in the manor hall to which the tenant brought firewood and his own dish, mug, and napkin "if he wanted to eat off a cloth." Bread, broth, and beer were served, and two kinds of meat, and the villeins were entitled to sit drinking after dinner in the manor hall.

At the upper end of the scale, baron and king entertained their knights and household with a feast and with gifts of "robes" (outfits comprising tunic, surcoat, and mantle) and jewels. In 1251 Matthew Paris complained that Henry III not only economized on his Christmas expenditures but exacted gifts from his subjects:

> At this most celebrated feast, the king (being perhaps saving in his anxiety about his pilgrimage) did not distribute any festive dresses to his knights and his household, although all his ancestors had made a practice from times of old of giving away royal garments and costly jewels. The usual richness and hospitality of the royal table was also diminished; and he now, without shame, sought his lodgings and his meals with abbots, priors, clerks, and men of low degree, staying with them and asking for gifts. And those persons were not considered courteous who did not, besides affording hospitality and splendid entertainments to him and his household, honor him and the queen, Prince Edward and the courtiers, separately with great and noble presents; indeed, he did not blush to ask for them, not as a favor, but as though they were his due. . . . Nor did the courtiers and royal household appreciate any presents unless they were rich and expensive; such as handsome palfreys, gold or silver cups, necklaces with choice jewels, imperial girdles, or such-like things.

All over Europe the twelve days of Christmas brought the appearance of the mummers, bands of masked pantomimists who paraded the streets and visited houses to dance and dice. A fourteenth-century mummery in London for the entertainment of Prince Richard (later Richard II), son of Edward the Black Prince, was described by John Stow:

> In the night, one hundred and thirty citizens, disguised and well-horsed, in a mummery, with sounds of trumpets, sackbuts [medieval trombones], cornets, shalmes [reed pipes], and other minstrels and innumerable torchlights of wax, rode to Kennington, near Lambeth, where the young Prince remained with his mother. In the first rank did ride forty-eight in likeness and habit of squires, two and two together, clothed in red coats and gowns of sendal [silk], with comely visors [masks] on their faces. After them came forty-eight knights, in the same livery. Then followed one richly arrayed, like an emperor; and after him some distance, one stately attired, like a pope, whom followed twenty-four cardinals; and after them eight or ten with black visors, not amiable, as if they had been legates from some foreign princes.
>
> These maskers after they had entered the manor of Kennington alighted from their horses and entered the hall on foot; which done, the Prince, his mother, and the lords came out of the chamber into the hall, whom the mummers did salute, showing, by a pair of dice upon the table, their desire to play with the young Prince, which they so handled that the Prince did always win when he cast them.... After which they were feasted and the music sounded, the Prince and lords danced on the one part with the mummers, who did also dance; which jollity being ended, they were again made to drink, and then departed in order as they came.

In England, plays accompanied the mumming. The earliest of these "mummers' plays" now extant apparently date to the sixteenth century, but undoubtedly they had medieval ancestors. Mummers' plays appeared in many variations, and sometimes included a sword dance or a St.-George-and-the-dragon play, but always had a common theme, probably with a ritual origin, symbolizing the death and coming to life of all growing things: a fight in which a champion was killed and brought back to life when a doctor gave him a magic pill. Stock characters in the plays were a fool and a man dressed as a woman.

New Year's, like Christmas, was an occasion for gift giving, and Matthew Paris noted that in 1249 Henry III exacted from London citizens "one by one, the first gifts, which the people are accustomed superstitiously to call New Year's gifts." "First gifts" were omens of success for the coming year. So was the first person who entered the house after midnight, the "first-foot," who determined the fortunes of the family for the year. In some places this portentous visitor had to be a dark-complexioned man or boy, in others light-haired, while elsewhere it was considered desirable for him to be flat-footed.

On the manors, the resumption of work after the Christmas holidays was marked with special ceremonies honoring the plow and the "rock," the distaff. A feature of Plow Monday, the first Monday after Epiphany, was a plow race, beginning at sunrise, among the freemen of the village, who plowed part of the common pasture which was to be cultivated for the coming year, with each man trying to draw a furrow in as many different strips as he could; the ridges that he marked he could sow that year. A custom of later times that probably dated from even before the Middle Ages was that of the "fool-plow," hauled through the village by a group of young plowmen who asked for pennies from door to door. If anyone refused, they plowed up the ground before his door. Their leader was dressed as an old woman called Bessy, with a bullock's tail under his gown; sometimes they were accompanied by a man wearing a fox's skin as a hood and by a fool with a stick and bladder.

Little real plowing was done until Candlemas (February 2), a holiday formally known as the Feast of the Purification of the Virgin. It commemorated Mary's "churching," the ceremony of purification after childbirth in which the new mother donned her wedding gown and entered the church carrying a lighted candle. The village celebrated with a procession carrying candles. Candlemas was followed by Shrove Tuesday, a profane holiday dedicated to games and sports.

Throughout Lent the sanctuaries of the castle chapel as well as of the parish church were hung with veils, the cross and images shrouded. On Palm Sunday the parishioners carried yew or willow twigs in procession, following the Host and the Cross around the churchyard. On Good Friday the Cross was unveiled and set on the steps of the altar, the congregation coming forward to kiss it, kneeling and bowing low— "creeping to the Cross." Then the Cross and Host were buried in a special "Easter sepulchre" in the walls of the church or in a chapel, surrounded with candles. On Easter Eve all the fires and candles were extinguished, a new fire ceremonially kindled, and the great Paschal candle lit during an all-night vigil in the church. On Easter morning the sepulchre was opened and the Cross and Host carried to the altar.

Easter, like Christmas, was a day of exchanges between lord and tenant. Tenants brought the lord eggs; the lord gave his manorial servants dinner. The week that followed was a holiday for the villeins, celebrated with games; Fitzstephen described tilting at the quintain in boats on the Thames in London in the twelfth century during Easter week, while "Upon the bridge, wharfs and houses by the river side stand great numbers to see and laugh thereat."

Easter week ended with Hocktide, the second Monday and Tuesday after Easter, a two-day festival which in some places involved a custom of wives whipping husbands on Monday and husbands wives on Tuesday.

After Hocktide, medieval summer began with the Mayday celebrations, a time for lovemaking, when moral taboos were relaxed. Before daybreak the young people of the village and sometimes their elders, including even the clergy, joined in "bringing in the May," venturing into the woods to cut wildflowers, greenery, and hawthorn boughs. Sometimes they spent the night in the forest. The thirteenth-century romance *Guillaume de Dole* describes a Mayday celebration in Mainz, "a very gay city," in which the citizens passed the night in the woods "according to ancient custom," and in the morning "carried the May" through the city, singing, and hung it from windows and balconies. A young lord and lady of May were elected to preside over dances and games.

The Rogation Days, the Monday, Tuesday, and Wednesday before Ascension (the fortieth day after Easter), were celebrated in the countryside under the name of Gangdays. The people of the villages went "a-ganging" in a procession led by the priest and carrying the cross, banners, bells, and lights around the boundaries of the village, "beating its bounds" with willow wands. Small boys were ducked in brooks and ponds and their buttocks bumped against trees and rocks to help them memorize the village bounds. The procession halted at certain customary points, under a traditional oak or ash, while the priest said prayers and blessed the crops. Next came Whitsunday, the third and last of the Maytime feasts, with another week's holiday when villeins did not have to work for their lords.

In June, after sheep shearing, the feast of the summer solstice was celebrated: Midsummer, the eve of the Feast of the Nativity of St. John the Baptist (June 24). A thirteenth-century book of sermons describes St. John's Eve, when boys collected bones and rubbish and burned them, and carried brands about the fields, to drive away the dragons that were believed to be abroad poisoning the wells. A wheel was set afire and rolled down the hills, to signify that the sun had reached its highest point and was turning back.

St. John's Day was the traditional time to begin the hay harvest; Lammas (August 1) was the end of the harvest. Lammas—from the Anglo-Saxon *hlaf-mass* ("loaf mass") was a feast of first fruits, a day when bread made from new wheat was blessed in church.

After Lammas came harvest time, the season when

May Dance and Game of Small Papers, illustration for month of May, from the *Hours of the Dutchess of Burgundy*.

the villeins worked for the lord in the harvest boons, the *bidreaps.* On the last day of reaping, teams of workers raced each other to see which could first finish a ridge. Sometimes they left the last stand of corn for a ceremony, in which it was cut by the prettiest girl, or the reapers threw their sickles at it till it fell. The last sheaf might be decorated and brought in to the barn with music and merriment. In the evening the harvest-home supper was held, and in some places the villeins were bound to come to the lord's court to "sing harvest home"—to sing at the harvest feast.

With Michaelmas the cycle of the year began again.

One holiday varied locally: Wake Day. Most holidays were celebrated as wakes—eves—with people stay-

ing up late the night before the feast, always a treat for farmers as for children. But Wake Day, the feast of the parish saint, when congregations formed by separation from an older parish went in procession to honor the mother church, was an occasion for brawls and bloodshed, as parishes contended for precedence. In later times, and probably in the thirteenth century, people stayed up all night and in the morning went to a mass in honor of the patron saint, then spent the day in sports, usually in the churchyard. In the course of time some Wake Days became the occasion of important trade fairs.

Such was the course of the year for the thirteenth-century villager and for the castle-dweller whose existence depended on the village and its cycle of planting and harvesting.

An mil iiij
rlviij a la fin
du mois dap
uril aprez
pasques les
anglois pundrent treues po
viij mois et fianchierent la
fille du roy kener roy de sezille
pour estre femme du roy henri
dangleterre en esperance que

paix seroit entre les deux roys
et puis sen ketourneient lesdiz
anglois en angleterre pour
parler a leur roy et auxffre
dangleterre et pour oncsitir
du fait de sa paix En ce
temps conchid le roy de fran
et son conseil que on enuoye
roit les gens darmes de fran
ce tant francoiz come anglois

XII

THE DECLINE

OF THE CASTLE

The decline in military importance of the castle, apparent in the fourteenth century and rapidly accelerated in the fifteenth, is associated, like that of the armored knight, with the introduction of gunpowder. In the closing stage of the Hundred Years' War (1446–53), the old strongholds of western France that had withstood so many sieges fell with astonishing speed to the ponderous iron bombards, firing heavy stone cannonballs, of the French royal army. Yet the new weapons did not automatically and by themselves destroy the value of the castles. Thick masonry walls could stand even against cannonballs, and could furnish platforms for cannon of their own that would even enjoy certain advantages. Neither the castle nor the armored knight was automatically eliminated from war by the new firepower, and in fact both continued to take part in war throughout the sixteenth century and even later.

A Battle from the Hundred Years War (1337–1453) from the *Chronicles of Enguerrand de Monstrelet.*

At Chepstow in the seventeenth century, the battlements of some of the towers were modified for use with guns, and the southern curtain wall was thickened and its parapet loopholed for muskets. Bodiam Castle in Sussex, built in 1386 for coastal defense, had in its gatehouse gunports of keyhole design, of two sizes. In the sixteenth century Henry VIII built an array of castles along the southeast coast to carry cannon.

In the fifteenth-century War of the Roses in England, in the sixteenth-century religious wars in France, and in the seventeenth-century Civil War in England, body armor and castle walls played prominent but steadily diminishing roles. Their true destroyer was not gunpowder but central government. The rapid growth of major political units around monarchies (or dictatorships) was based to a great extent on the rapid growth of European cities with their wealthy merchant classes, whose money taxes provided the wherewithal to hire and supply large mercenary armies equipped with expensive cannon. A single knight might still be more effective on the battlefield than a foot soldier without armor and with a clumsy arquebus, but he was less valuable than ten such, and more expensive. The same sort of economics applied to castle building, with the added factor that the new political geography made obsolete

111

The Castle of Angers, Maine-et-Loire, France, showing the 13th c. wall built by Louis IX and the moat planted with flowers.

many of the old frontier castles, such as those guarding the long-embattled English-Welsh and Norman-Breton-French borders.

Castles destroyed in the gunpowder era were usually razed rather than battle-damaged. Most of the English castles rallied to Charles I in the Civil War of the 1640s, and one after another were taken by the Puritans. Chepstow, never threatened in the Middle Ages, was breached and stormed; a plaque in the restored south curtain wall records the spot where its commandant, Sir Nicholas Kemeys, was killed. Even more seriously damaged by siege was Arundel, on whose barbican walls marks of cannonballs can still be seen, and much of whose extensive latter-day restoration was made necessary by its battering. More typical was the fate of Kenilworth, the rugged old stronghold of Simon de Montfort and his son that had fought the memorable siege of 1266. In 1649 a movement was begun in Parliament to demolish Kenilworth lest it become a center for renewed Royalist resistance, as had Pembroke, which the year before had sustained a violent siege by Oliver Cromwell. Lord Monmouth, whose family had succeeded the Montforts as stewards of Kenilworth for the king, talked the government into merely "slighting" the castle—rendering it militarily useless by making gaps in the curtain and razing one wall of the keep.

A similar slighting of castles was carried out in France by Cardinal Richelieu at about the same time, usually by removing the heads of the towers. In obstinate cases, such as that of the youthful conspirator Cinq-Mars, Richelieu removed the head of the owner along with those of the towers of his castle on the Loire.

To the military obsolescence of the castle was added a domestic obsolescence. The desire for more comfortable and elegant living quarters, which had already modified the castle in the Middle Ages, by the seventeenth century had created a taste for purely residential palaces for the nobility. Sometimes an old castle or part of it was radically altered to turn it into a comfortable residence with light, heat, and other amenities, and it continued to be used, now and then, by the family that had originally built it. In other cases, ancient keeps were allowed to decay into picturesque ruins while next to them or in front of them elegant, many-windowed residences were built. In these new palaces the great hall, the basic living quarters of castles from the first motte-and-bailey strongholds to the domestic buildings of thirteenth-century castles, suffered a change. Expanded and elaborated throughout the Middle Ages, it now shrank and diminished in importance as the desire for privacy multiplied separate dining and "withdrawing" rooms for the castle family. The great hall of the thirteenth century finally dwindled into the servants' hall of the seventeenth.

Many castles no longer suitable for ordinary residential use found a more specialized purpose. Marten's Tower at Chepstow served as a comfortable prison for its single Puritan captive, but many others—the Tower of London, Paris' Bastille, and dozens more—provided grim quarters for generations of prisoners, many political. Enlightenment and prison reform at length did away with this inglorious role, and some castles, especially those situated in capitals and large towns, gained a more respectable one in conversion to government archives, record centers, and bureaus. Some, such as Gisors, in Normandy, furnished sites for handsome public gardens. Many were converted to museums, notably Norwich Castle in England, which houses a fine collection of ancient and prehistoric British archaeological findings; Saumur, on the Loire, which contains both a decorative arts and a horse museum; and the Sforza Castle in Milan, with its rich archaeological and art galleries.

Yet amid such peaceful vocations, castles even in modern times occasionally reverted to their more heroic past. Some, such as Dover, continued to be garrisoned and armed in the nineteenth century and even the twentieth, and in both World Wars castles all over Europe saw combat duty. Many English coastal castles, including ancient Hastings, served as observation posts and antiaircraft-gun emplacements. In 1940 at Pevensey, built by the Normans within the walls of one of the third-century Roman forts of the "Saxon coast," two machine-gun posts and a pillbox were incorporated into the Roman walls, disguised as part of the original enceinte, in preparation against a German invasion. Four years later the ancient fort became a radio direction center for the U.S. Air Corps. In France, Germany, and Italy, castles repeatedly served as strong points and refuges against small-arms and even artillery fire. GIs of the U.S. 42nd Division, for example, found the walls of Wurzburg Castle, Germany, in 1945 very satisfactory

protection against German 88-mm. projectiles from across the Main River, modern thin-shelled high explosives proving much less damaging to masonry than the stone cannonballs of the fifteenth-century bombards.

But the final role of the European medieval castle seems to be that of tourist attraction. In Britain, France, Germany, Spain, Italy, and elsewhere, with the aid of a guide and some imagination, one can stand in the grassy barley and re-people the weathered stone ramparts and towers and the vanished wooden outbuildings with archers and knights, servants, horses, and wagoners, the lord and lady and their guests, falcons and hunting dogs, pigs and poultry—all the unkempt, unsafe, unsavory but appealing life of the thirteenth century.

GREAT MEDIEVAL CASTLES: A GEOGRAPHIC GUIDE

A catalog of even the most important and interesting medieval castles could occupy a volume, and the following list is only a sampling. The many post-medieval castles whose battlements served purely decorative purposes long after military and economic history made them otherwise obsolete are excluded. Even nineteenth-century America built such replicas, in a profusion that justified a recent book on "American castles." Those below all belong to the Middle Ages. Within each region they are listed chronologically, in accordance with the local historical development of the castle.

ENGLAND

English medieval castles embrace the whole history of castle-building, from the eleventh-century motte-and-bailey (of which many earthwork traces remain, some crowned by later shell keeps) to the mighty Edwardian fortresses of the late thirteenth and early fourteenth centuries, whose formidable curtain walls, gatehouses, and towers, built on carefully chosen sites, represent the ultimate in medieval defensive works.

Berkhamsted. 25 miles northwest of London. One of the earliest Anglo-Norman castles, with both motte-and-bailey surrounded by wet moats; the ruins of a shell keep; thirteenth-century outworks.

Warwick. 75 miles northwest of London. A motte-and-bailey fortified by William the Conqueror in 1068, converted to a shell keep late in the eleventh century, with fourteenth- and fifteenth-century walls and towers and residential buildings of the seventeenth century.

York. 250 miles north of London. Two motte-and-bailey castles, built in 1068 and 1069, the former now surmounted by Clifford's Tower (1245).

Windsor. 20 miles west of London. The Round Tower, shell wall built about 1170 on a motte constructed in 1070, previously guarded by a wooden tower; curtain walls built by Henry II late in the twelfth century and by Henry III in the thirteenth; chapel and residential buildings by later kings.

Launceston. Cornwall. Stone shell wall added in the twelfth century to motte of 1080; round inner tower built in the thirteenth century.

Totnes. Devon. Motte of 1080 enclosed by a late twelfth century shell wall; hall built in the bailey below in the thirteenth century; shell wall rebuilt early in the fourteenth century.

Restormel. Cornwall. Twelfth-century shell wall with projecting square tower; domestic quarters, barracks and chapel added in the thirteenth century around the inside of the wall with a central court.

White Tower (Tower of London). Rectangular keep built in 1080, 90 feet high to the battlements, originally of three stories, divided internally by a cross-wall; the topmost story, with the great hall, solar, and chapel, rises the height of two floors; entrance was by a forebuilding, now destroyed; the towers of the inner curtain and parts of the walls themselves date from the late twelfth and the thirteenth centuries, such as the Wakefield Tower, where the Crown jewels are kept, and the Bloody Tower, where the little princes Edward V and his younger brother Richard are believed to have been murdered on the instructions of Richard III, and where Sir Walter Raleigh was imprisoned. Both towers were built in the reign of Henry III.

Colchester. 50 miles northeast of London. Rectangular keep built in 1087, with three stories.

Rochester. 25 miles east of London. Great keep with a parapet 113 feet high and corner towers rising 12 feet higher, built in 1130, with three residential floors above a basement; the entire building is divided internally from top to bottom by a cross-wall; entrance is in a forebuilding.

Dover. Rectangular keep built in the 1180s by Henry II, 83 feet high, with turrets at the corners 12 feet higher, three stories, entrance to the main (third) floor in a forebuilding that also contains two chapels; keep divided internally by a cross-wall into two large halls in each story, with chambers in the walls; curtain walls of the thirteenth century.

Kenilworth. 80 miles northwest of London. Rectangular keep called Caesar's Tower, built 1150–75, of exceptionally powerful construction, walls 14 feet thick, strengthened by buttresses and massive corner turrets; two stories, one large hall in each story, original entrance to the second story by external stairs; curtain walls of the thirteenth century; great hall built by John of Gaunt in the fourteenth century.

Orford. 75 miles northeast of London on the Suffolk coast. Built 1166–70, circular internally, multiangular externally, with three large square turrets; three stories, hall on the second floor, forebuilding containing entrance porch at the second-story level, with chapel above; spiral stairway to the basement and battlements in one turret, chambers in the other turrets.

Conisborough. 145 miles north of London. Built 1180–90, tall cylindrical tower with very thick walls supported by six massive buttresses the height of the building, commanding the whole front of the keep; vaulted basement, three upper floors, original entrance at the second story reached by a drawbridge; sloping base to prevent attackers from approaching close to the keep.

Pembroke. Wales. Round keep built about 1190, 54 feet in diameter, 80 feet high, with four stories; the entrance to the second story is by stairs in a forebuilding leading to a drawbridge before the doorway; a spiral stairway from the entrance floor leads to the basement and the upper floors and battlements; halls and living rooms are in the inner bailey near the keep.

Edwardian Castles of Wales. Most of them are in a good state of preservation: Beaumaris, Caernarvon, Caerphilly, Conway, Denbigh, Flint, Harlech, Kidwelly, Rhuddlan.

FRANCE

Like England, France has extant castles representing all the architectural types.

Langeais. On the Loire. Rectangular keep built by Fulk Nerra about 1010, with three stories: first and second floors for storage, hall on the third story; the rest of the present castle was built by Louis XI in the fifteenth century.

Loches. On the Indre, south of the Loire. Four-story rectangular keep built about 1020, 122 feet high, with a large forebuilding; thirteenth-century curtain walls, fifteenth-century Round Tower and square Martelet Tower.

Gisors. Normandy. Shell keep built early in the twelfth century, four-story tower with irregular octag-

onal plan added by Henry II of England on the motte late in the century; Tour du Prisonnier added in 1206—a round keep incorporated in the curtain wall, with three vaulted stories entered at third-story level from a wall-walk on the curtain on one side, a postern at the same level on the other side, stair-ways to lower floors from the third story, the tower a self-contained residence.

Arques. Near Dieppe. Great rectangular keep built by Henry I of England about 1125, with four stories; entrance on the third story by a stairway built around two sides of the keep and protected by an outer wall; partition wall dividing the lower three floors each into two large halls with no communication between them except by a complicated system of wall passages and stairways; top floor command-post undivided. The castle is now known as Arques-la-Bataille because of Henry IV's victory there in 1589 in the French civil war.

Houdan. 30 miles west of Paris. Built about 1130, square on the inside, circular on the outside, with four projecting semicircular turrets; two very high stories, ground floor storeroom, second-story hall with chambers in three of the turrets, spiral stairs in the fourth leading to battlements and basement, original entrance in this turret twenty feet above ground reached by a drawbridge from a wall-walk on the curtain wall of the castle, now destroyed.

Étampes. 30 miles south of Paris. Built about 1160, large four-lobed three-story keep built around a central pier, vaulted great hall on the second story, chambers on the third story, entrance midway between floors, probably reached by a wall-walk and drawbridge from the curtain, now destroyed.

Châteaudun. 70 miles southwest of Paris on the Loire River. Round keep built early in the twelfth century, one of the earliest and best preserved of its type; 95 feet high, containing three floors, the lower two covered with domes; entrance on the second floor; chapel and block of residential buildings built by Joan of Arc's companion-at-arms, Dunois.

La Roche Guyon. On the Seine 35 miles northwest of Paris. Round keep built in the last half of the twelfth century on a precipitous cliff, with ascent from the riverbank by subterranean stairways and narrow ledges cut through the rock; a central tower is surrounded by a chemise and an outer wall, and all three are prow-shaped, the prow pointing away from the cliff and toward the line of approach from above.

Château Gaillard. Normandy. Built by Richard the Lionhearted in 1198 on a precipitous cliff 300 feet above the Seine, with three baileys arranged in line; the keep, in the inner bailey, on the edge of the precipice, is circular and thickened by a prow at the side toward the bailey; the keep was once protected by machicolations (now destroyed), one of the earliest examples of stone machicolations in Western Europe; the great hall is near the keep in the inner bailey; the curtain of the inner bailey is protected by corrugations on its outer face rather than by wall towers; the curtains of the outer and middle baileys are strengthened by circular wall towers.

Chinon. On the Vienne. Three groups of buildings: the Fort St. Georges, where Henry II of England died in 1189; the Chateau du Milieu, where Joan of Arc met the Dauphin in 1429; and the Chateau du Coudray, with its Tour du Coudray, built by Philip Augustus early in the thirteenth century, a round keep with stairways along the inside of the walls, guarded at each turn by machicolations, leading to the upper stories. The Templars were held for trial in the Tour du Coudray in 1308.

Angers. On the Maine near its juncture with the Loire, on the site of an earlier castle built by Fulk Nerra of Anjou. Great curtain wall built by Louis IX, 1230–40, with seventeen round towers with thickened bases rising almost half the height of the towers, two posterns, a chapel and residential quarters, no keep.

Tour de Constance. Aigues-Mortes, Provence. Built in the mid-thirteenth century, a large circular keep isolated by a moat at one corner of the city's fortifications, originally a castle in itself before the town walls were built; two vaulted stories with large halls over a small basement.

Fougères. Brittany. Represents many periods of castle building, from the foundations of a round keep razed by Henry II of England in 1166 to the thirteenth-century curtain walls, the Melusine and Gobelin Towers of the thirteenth and fourteenth centuries, and the fifteenth-century Surienne and Raoul Towers; the stone columns that supported the second story of the great hall can still be seen in the inner bailey; entrance to the castle is protected by a moat, a barbican, and four towers. Fougères is unusual in that it is built on a plain, with the neighboring town on a hilltop.

Najac. Southern France. Built 1250–60, a three-story vaulted round keep consisting of one of the corner towers of a rectangular curtain wall equipped with an elaborate system of stairways and passages; the entrance to the keep on the ground floor is protected by a moat and drawbridge, and a spiral stairway rises from the entrance to the upper floors and battlements; the great-hall is on the second story; all operations were directed from the keep, and each section of the defensive system was capable of being isolated by barriers.

Vincennes. On the eastern edge of Paris. Early fourteenth century, great 170-foot-high keep containing the king's living quarters, isolated from the rest of the castle by a chemise and a wide moat, and strongly fortified; a first-story basement and kitchen, royal apartments on the second and third stories; the fourth story occupied by attendants, the fifth by servants, the sixth used for defense.

Pierrefonds. 45 miles northeast of Paris. Built by Louis d'Orleans, count of Valois, 1390–1400, on a rocky height; strong double curtain walls, the inner defended by eight round towers; barracks and service quarters built around the inner courtyard; the count's residence in a tall keep near the gate, capable of independent defense; approach route between curtain walls around the whole enclosure, then through a barbican and across a drawbridge; restored in the nineteenth century by Viollet-le-Duc.

ITALY

Italian castles belong to four classes: Dark Age castles; Norman fortresses built after the conquest of southern Italy beginning in the 1040s; castles built in the thirteenth century by Frederick II all over Italy and Sicily, sometimes on the foundations of Norman castles; and castles built by the despots in the fourteenth and fifteenth centuries, many of them in the cities.

Canossa. Emilia. Picturesque ruins of a tenth-century fortress perched on a rock, scene of the famous barefoot-in-the-snow penance of Emperor Henry IV in 1077 during the investiture controversy with Pope Gregory VII.

Bari. Southern Italy. Castle built by the Norman ruler of Sicily, Count Roger I, in 1131, and rebuilt in 1233 by Emperor Frederick II; corner towers and inner court added in the sixteenth

century.

Barletta. Southern Italy. Eleventh-century Norman castle rebuilt by the Hohenstaufens, enlarged by Charles of Anjou late in the thirteenth century.

Capuan Castle. Naples. Built by the Normans in the

eleventh century, remodeled by Emperor Frederick II in the thirteenth century.

Castel Nuovo. Naples. Built by the Angevins in 1282, modeled on the castle of Angers; five round towers added in the fifteenth century by Alfonso I of Aragon.

Castles of Frederick II. Characteristically, these have rectangular enclosures with square corner towers. Lucera, a great square tower with an enclosed court, and a curtain wall added late in the thirteenth century by Charles of Anjou; Gioia del Colle, Apulia; Prato, northwest of Florence; Gravina, Apulia, a hunting castle; Castello Ursino, Catania, a rectangular enclosure with round towers; Castel del Monte, Apulia, octagonal with eight octagonal towers and inner octagonal court.

Gradara. On the Adriatic coast south of Rimini. Square castle with round corner towers built in the thirteenth century by the Grifi family, afterward owned by the Malatestas and the Sforzas; here Giovanni Malatesta is supposed to have murdered his wife, Francesca da Rimini, and her lover, Paolo, in the tragic love story immortalized by Dante.

Castello di Sarzanello. North of Pisa. Built by the Luccan despot Castruccio Castracane in 1322; thick triangular curtain wall with round towers, surrounded by a deep moat, with a square keep commanding a bridge that links the enclosure to a detached bastion.

Scaliger Castle. Verona. Built by Can Grande II della Scala in 1354 on the Adige River, with the square tower of the keep guarding a fortified bridge.

Castello delta Rocca. Cesena (near Rimini). Castle of the Malatestas, built about 1380, with a polygonal inner bailey on top of a hill and an outer bailey running down the slope; the inner bailey is surrounded by powerful walls with towers at the angles, and protected by a strongly defended gatehouse and a small barbican; the approach to the barbican is intercepted by cross-walls forming a winding passage with gateways at the turning points.

Castello d'Este. Ferrara. Built about 1385, on level ground, with a rectangular curtain that has square towers at each corner; guarded by moats and four gatehouses with drawbridges; living quarters are built around an internal courtyard.

Castello Visconteo. Pavia. Built by the Visconti family in the late fourteenth century, surrounded by walls nearly 100 feet high, punctuated by square corner towers.

Castello San Giorgio. Mantua. Built by the Gonzagas in the late fourteenth century; a square enclosure with powerful square corner towers and machicolations; surrounded by a deep moat.

Castello Sforzesco. Milan. A huge square brick castle, the largest castle in Italy, built by Francesco Sforza in 1412 on the site of a Visconti fortress of 1368, with curtain walls 12 feet thick, a gatehouse, and two great round towers at the front corners; the interior is divided into one large and two small courtyards, and the smallest, the rochetta, which comprises the inner fortress, is guarded by a square tower with machicolations.

SPAIN

Spain, like Italy, has some of the oldest castles in Europe. Those of Spain fall into four categories: Muslim castles, before the twelfth century; castles of the Christian military orders, late twelfth and early thirteenth century; castles built during the Reconquest to protect important centers; and castle-palaces of the fifteenth century. The Muslim castles, which were later imitated by the Christian military orders, were typically built of tapia, a combination of pebbles and mortar, and were rectangular, with square wall towers and a square extramural tower; points in the curtain walls needing stronger defense were protected by pentagonal towers. Later Christian castles were often of brick.

Almeria. Province of Granada, on the Mediterranean coast. Built by the Moors in the eighth century on the site of a Phoenician fortress; a great enclosure with square towers on top of a ridge; captured by the Christians in 1147, recaptured by the Muslims in 1157 and held by them until 1489; round towers added by Ferdinand and Isabella.

Baños de la Encina. Near Jaén, south central Spain. Castle built by the Moors in 967 to defend the Guadalquivir River; rectangular enclosure with square towers on a hilltop; captured in 1212 by the Christians, who built an extramural tower for an added defense.

Alcala de Guadaira. Province of Seville. Muslim castle, curtain walls with eight square towers, one defending the gate, and an extramural tower protecting the bridge leading to the gate; cross-walls dividing the attacking forces into separate sectors.

Gormaz. Castile. Built by the Muslims in the tenth century on top of a limestone rock, given to the famous hero-adventurer, the Cid, at the end of the eleventh century by Alfonso VI; two baileys, irregular plan, with square towers, curtain wall 30 feet high and 3,000 feet long.

Almodovar del Rio. Province of Cordoba. Muslim castle high on the banks of the Guadalquivir River, used as a treasure house in the fourteenth century by Peter the Cruel; has high, crenelated walls; an extramural tower 130 feet high is connected to the rest of the castle by a high stone bridge.

Calatrava la Nueva. Castile. Built by the military Order of Calatrava about 1216 on the site of an Arab castle; the main enclosure has an irregular octagonal shape and is surrounded by a moat; there is a second enclosure to protect livestock, an extramural tower, a great church with a rose window.

Zonta de los Canes. Province of Guadalajara. Castle originally built by the Muslims, conquered in 1085 by Alfonso VI, reconquered by the Arabs in the twelfth century, later taken over by the Order of Calatrava, who rebuilt it; on a mound overlooking the Tagus River; an outer curtain has powerful towers, the southern serving as a keep; an extramural tower on the northeast is connected to the castle by a solid Gothic arch; entrance to the castle is through an arched gateway protected by a gatehouse.

Consuegra. Province of Toledo. Built by the Hospitallers in the twelfth century and modeled after the Crusader castles of Syria; double-walled enceinte, central keep with round towers.

La Mota. Medina del Campo, north of Madrid. Built about 1440 on the ruins of a thirteenth-century castle; outer curtain wall with two galleries in thickness, tall rectangular keep with four pairs of turrets at the corners, machicolations between; favorite residence of Columbus' patroness Isabella, who died here in 1504; later her daughter Joanna the Mad was imprisoned here, as was Cesare Borgia (who managed to escape).

Peñafiel. North of Madrid. Built about 1450, following the contours of the top of an eminence above the Duero River; a long narrow enclosure with two lines of curtain walls strengthened by round towers, a square central tower-keep 112 feet high.

Alcazar. Segovia. Built by Alfonso VI late in the eleventh century, rebuilt in the 1350s; on a rocky eminence; the walls are strengthened with semicircular towers; there are two great square towers within the enclosure.

Coca. Northwest of Madrid. A brick castle built by Muslim workmen for the archbishop of Seville, Alfonso de Fonseca, in the fifteenth century; massive square double curtain walls are surrounded by a moat; the keep is an enlarged square tower of the inner enclosure guarding the entrance; the crenelations are decorated with distinctive rounded furrows; there are embrasures for cannon, square cross-and-orb gun loops, hexagonal projecting turrets from corner towers of external wall.

GERMANY AND AUSTRIA

An early German or Austrian castle was characterized by its inaccessible site, usually on top of a rocky height, and by its square central Bergfried, or tower; later many castles were built on level ground surrounded by moats. The greatest period of medieval castle-building in Germany was the era of the Hohenstaufens (1138–1254). Most of the famous "Castles on the Rhine" now exist either in ruins or in restorations.

Marksburg. On the Rhine. Built originally in the tenth century to collect tolls on the Rhine, enlarged in the thirteenth to fifteenth centuries, restored by Kaiser Wilhelm II; square central tower, residential quarters, series of gatehouses guarding approach to the upper castle.

Trifels. Rhenish Palatinate. Castle of the German emperors built in the eleventh century on top of a high eminence, expanded in the twelfth and thirteenth centuries by the Hohenstaufens; here Richard the Lionhearted was kept prisoner in 1193 by Emperor Henry VI; 70-foot-high rectangular keep, chapel; castle almost wholly reconstructed. Ruins of two other castles, Anebos and Scharfenberg, are on nearby peaks.

Munzenberg. Hesse. Built 1174; elliptical enclosure on top of a mountain, with two round towers and a forward tower guarding the west approach; living quarters, chapel and kitchen along the inside of the curtain.

Wildenberg. Bavaria. Late twelfth century, rectangular enclosure on top of a mountain; square towers guarding the line of approach.

Eltz. On the Moselle. Begun by the counts of Eltz in 1157, mostly dating from the thirteenth to the sixteenth centuries; the oldest surviving structure is the Platteltz Tower (twelfth or thirteenth century), partly restored after a fire in the 1920s; nearby are the ruins of Trutzeltz, the castle of the archbishop of Trier who carried on a protracted feud with the counts of Eltz and finally compelled them to surrender.

Heidenreichstein. Austria. Built in the twelfth century; a square tower was added in the thirteenth century, a round tower later.

Rapottenstein. Austria. Built in the twelfth century on a rock outcropping; there are a round tower defending the approaches, a square tower higher up, and residential buildings.

Ortenberg. Bavaria. Early thirteenth century; three baileys, the inner and middle in a line, the outer bailey in front of both, with a rising approach; the enemy had to pass the length of the outer bailey under attack from the inner and middle ones, then up a flight of steps and through a barbican and three other gateways before the inner bailey was reached; a trapezoidal keep at the highest point is surrounded closely by the wall of the inner bailey.

Falkenberg. Bavaria. Built about 1290 on a huge natural pile of boulders overlooking the Waldnaab River; the curtain follows the contour of the rocks; the buildings of the castle are between the curtain and a small internal courtyard containing a square keep.

Hohensalzburg. Austria. Residence of the archbishop of Salzburg, built in the twelfth century on a rock 400 feet above the Salzach River; modeled after the Crusader castles, later enlarged and remodeled; massive curtain walls, round towers.

OTHER EUROPEAN CASTLES

Pfeffengen and Dornach. Switzerland. Two shell keeps of the twelfth and early thirteenth centuries built within a few miles of each other; in both cases, the shell wall, instead of being built on top of the mound, is built against its vertical sides, containing the mound and rising high above it.

Chillon. Switzerland. Castle made famous by Byron's poem; built in the thirteenth century on the site of a ninth-century castle, on a rocky island in a lake, reached by a bridge leading to a gatehouse; the curtain wall follows the contours of the rock, and the buildings of the castle are constructed around the inner court, with a square keep at the end farthest from the bridge.

Castle of the Counts of Flanders. Ghent. Built in 1180, on the site of an eleventh-century fortress, by Philip of Alsace on his return from Crusade, and modeled on the Crusader castles; on level ground, surrounded by a moat and high curtain walls with round towers; a rectangular keep has a lesser hall on the first floor, the great hall above.

Carrickfergus. Northern Ireland. Built on the shores of Belfast Loch, c. 1180–1205; square Norman keep joined to curtain walls.

Trim. Ireland. Built c. 1190–1200, the largest Anglo-Norman castle in Ireland; square keep with projecting wings, thirteenth-century curtain walls with round towers.

CRUSADER CASTLES

From a strictly military point of view, the castles built by the Templars, Hospitallers, and other Crusaders are incomparable. Drawing on European, Byzantine, and Muslim models and on their own experience, the Crusaders built strongholds of immense size and ingeniously related defenses in which small garrisons, supplied for as much as five years, could defy large armies.

Saone (Sahyun). Syria. The best-preserved Crusader castle, with a half mile of fortification in the shape of a rough isosceles triangle atop a mountain spur, the two long sides fronting on precipitous cliffs, the base on a 60-foot-wide, 90-foot-deep moat hewn out of the rock, a "needle" of the rock left to act as a bridge pier, with a drawspan to the postern; the square keep built against the curtain wall on the moat side.

Krak des Chevaliers. Syria. The giant "Citadel [Krak] of the Knights," the most powerful and famous of the Crusader castles, almost as well preserved as Saone; begun early in the twelfth century and strengthened by the Hospitallers in 1142; two concentric walls enclose two baileys, an outer and an inner, the latter high on the spur of Gebel Alawi. Besieged at least twelve times, this castle "stuck like a bone in the throat of the Saracens," in the words of a Muslim writer; in one siege, that of 1163, the Hospitallers not only held off the army of Nur-ed-Din but sallied out to surprise and defeat it; even in 1271, a lone outpost in a Muslim sea, its garrison down to 300 knights, the Krak held out until the Muslim general Baibars tricked the defenders with a forged order, after which he chivalrously gave the knights safe conduct to the coast.

Anamur. A seacoast castle in Turkey, with a huge fourteen-sided tower dominating the beach, and three baileys, one facing the land, one the sea, and a third on high ground between the two.

Chastel Pélérin ("Pilgrim Castle"). Israel. Built by the Templars in 1218 and well supplied with artillery and heavily garrisoned when the Muslims besieged it unsuccessfully in 1220, it was never taken, but was abandoned in 1291 after the fall of nearby Acre, and afterward badly damaged by Muslim engineers quarrying it to rebuild the city.

SECTION II
LIFE IN A MEDIEVAL VILLAGE

PROLOGUE
ELTON

"In the district of Huntingdon, there is a certain village to which far-distant antiquity gave the name of Aethelintone," wrote the twelfth-century monk who chronicled the history of Ramsey Abbey, "on a most beautiful site, provided with a course of waters, in a pleasant plain of meadows with abundant grazing for cattle, and rich in fertile fields."[1]

The village that the Anglo-Saxons called Aethelintone (or Aethelington, or Adelintune), known in the thirteenth century, with further spelling variations, as Aylington, and today as Elton, was one of the thousands of peasant communities scattered over the face of Europe and the British Isles in the high Middle Ages, sheltering more than 90 percent of the total population,

the ancestors of most Europeans and North Americans alive today.

Many of these peasant settlements were mere hamlets or scattered homesteads, but in certain large areas of England and Continental Europe people lived in true villages, where they practiced a distinctive system of agriculture. Because England has preserved the earliest and most complete documentation of the medieval village, in the form of surveys, accounts, and the rolls of manorial courts, this book will focus on an English village.

Medieval villages varied in population, area, configuration, and social and economic details. But Elton, a dependency of wealthy Ramsey Abbey, located in the

Anglo-Saxon map of Great Britain "Comes Litoris Saxon Per Britaniam" (c.950).

East Midlands, in the region of England where villages abounded and the "open field" agriculture associated with them flourished, illustrates many of the characteristics common to villages at the high point of their development.

Elton stands today, a village of about six hundred people, in northwest Cambridgeshire,† seventy miles north of London, where it has stood for more than a thousand years. Its present-day gray stone houses cluster along two axes: one the main road from Peterborough to the old market town of Oundle; the other at right angles to it, a street that ends in a triangular village green, beyond which stands an eighteenth-century mill on the banks of the River Nene. Smaller streets and lanes intersect these two thoroughfares. The two sections have long been known as Overend and Nether End. Nether End contains the green, with a Methodist chapel adjoining. Near the river here the construction of a floodbank in 1977 uncovered the foundations of the medieval manor house. Overend centers around the church, with its school and rectory nearby. At the southern limit of Overend stands the village's tourist attraction, Elton Hall, a new home whose gatehouse and chapel alone date as far back as the fifteenth century, the rest from much later.

Two pubs, a post office/general store, and a garage comprise Elton's business center. Buses and cars speed along the Peterborough-Oundle road. Some of the cottages, nestling in their neat gardens, are picturesquely thatched. Off beyond the streets, sheep graze in the meadows. Yet Elton, like many other English villages, is no longer a farming community. Most of its inhabitants work in nearby Peterborough, or commute to London. The family that owns Elton Hall operates an agricultural enterprise, and one independent farmer lives in the village; two have farms outside, in the parish. A few descendants of farm laborers live in subsidized housing on a Council estate.

Except perhaps for the sheep, almost nothing medieval survives in twentieth-century Elton. In the northwest corner of the churchyard, inconspicuous in the shadow of the great square tower, stand the oldest

identifiable objects in Elton, a pair of Anglo-Saxon crosses found during a nineteenth-century restoration of the church.** The present building is mainly the product of the fourteenth and fifteenth centuries; only the stones of the chancel arch date from the thirteenth.

The oldest house surviving in Elton today was built in 1690. Medieval Elton, its houses, yards, sheds, and gardens, the smithy, the community ovens, the cultivated fields, even the meadows, marsh, and woods have vanished. Not only were medieval villages constantly rebuilt, but as forms of agriculture changed and new kinds of landholding were adopted, the very fields and meadows were transformed. We know how villages like Elton looked in the Middle Ages not so much from modern survivals as from the recent investigation of England's extraordinary archeological trove of deserted villages, victims of dwindling population, agricultural depression, and the historic enclosure movement that turned them from busy crop-raising communities to nearly empty sheep pastures. More than two thousand such sites have been identified. Their investigation, based on a technique introduced into England during World War II by German refugee Gerhard Bersu, was pioneered in the 1950s by archeologist John Hurst and historian Maurice Beresford in the now famous Yorkshire deserted village of Wharram Percy. Excavation and aerial photography have since recovered the medieval shape of many villages, the sites of their houses and enclosures, and the disposition of fields, streets, paths, and embankments.[2]

The deserted villages, however, left few written records. These are rich, on the other hand, for many of the surviving villages. They document not merely details of the houses and holdings, but the names of the villagers themselves, their work arrangements, and their diet, recreation, quarrels, and transgressions. Much can be learned from the records of the Ramsey Abbey villages, of which Elton was one, and those of contemporary estates, lay as well as ecclesiastical. The documents are often tantalizing, sometimes frustrating, but supplemented by the archeological record, they afford an illuminating picture of the open field village, a community that originated in the central Middle Ages, achieved its highest stage in the late thirteenth century, and left its mark on the European landscape and on Western and world civilization.

†Formerly Huntingdonshire, until the redrawing of county lines in 1974.

**One expert dates them later, c. 1100.

I

THE VILLAGE EMERGES

n the modern world, a village is merely a very small town, often a metropolitan suburb, always very much a part of the world outside. The "old-fashioned village" of the American nineteenth century was more distinctive in function, supplying services of merchants and craftsmen to a circle of farm homesteads surrounding it.

The medieval village was something different from either. Only incidentally was it the dwelling place of merchants or craftsmen. Rather, its population consisted of the farmers themselves, the people who tilled the soil and herded the animals. Their houses, barns, and sheds clustered at its center, while their plowed fields and grazing pastures and meadows surrounded it. Socially, economically, and politically, it was a community.

World map showing Britain in the lower left hand section and Jerusalem in the center, from a volume of world knowledge, Winchester or Canterbury (11th c.).

In modern Europe and America the village is home to only a fraction of the population. In medieval Europe, as in most Third World countries today, the village sheltered the overwhelming majority of people. The modern village is a place where its inhabitants live, but not necessarily or even probably where they work. The medieval village, in contrast, was the primary community to which its people belonged for all life's purposes. There they lived, there they labored, there they socialized, loved, married, brewed and drank ale, sinned, went to church, paid fines, had children in and out of wedlock, borrowed and lent money, tools, and grain, quarreled and fought, and got sick and died. Together they formed an integrated whole, a permanent community organized for agricultural production. Their sense of common enterprise was expressed in their records by special terms: *communitas villae,* the community of the vill or village, or *tota villata,* the body of all the villagers. The terminology was new. The English words "vill" and "village" derive from the Roman *villa,* the estate that was often the center of settlement in early medieval Europe. The closest Latin equivalent to "village" is *vicus,* used to designate a rural district or area.

Prehistoric, Megalithic tomb of Keriaval with lateral chambers (3rd/4th millennium BC) Carnac, Brittany, France.

A distinctive and in its time an advanced form of community, the medieval village represented a new stage of the world's oldest civilized society, the peasant economy. The first Neolithic agriculturists formed a peasant economy, as did their successors of the Bronze and Iron Ages and of the classical civilizations, but none of their societies was based so uniquely on the village. Individual homesteads, temporary camps, slave-manned plantations, hamlets of a few (probably related) families, fortresses, walled cities—people lived in all of these, but rarely in what might be defined as a village.

True, the village has not proved easy to define.

Historians, archeologists, and sociologists have had trouble separating it satisfactorily from hamlet or settlement. Edward Miller and John Hatcher *(Medieval England: Rural Society and Economic Change, 1086–1343)* acknowledge that "as soon as we ask what a village is we run into difficulties." They conclude by asserting that the village differs from the mere hamlet in that "hamlets were often simply pioneering settlements established in the course of agricultural expansion," their organization "simpler and more embryonic" than that of the true village.[1] Trevor Rowley and John Wood *(Deserted Villages)* offer a "broad definition" of the village as "a group of families living in a collection of houses and having a sense of community."[2] Jean Chapelot and Robert Fossier *(The Village and House in the Middle Ages)* identify the "characteristics that define village settlement" as "concentration of population, organization of land settlement within a confined area, communal buildings such as the church and the castle, permanent settlement based on buildings that continue in use, and . . . the presence of craftsmens."[3] Permanence, diversification, organization, and community—these are key words and ideas that distinguish the village from more fleeting and less purposeful agricultural settlements.

Archeology has uncovered the sites of many prehistoric settlements in Northern Europe and the British Isles. Relics of the Bronze Age (roughly 3000 B.C. to 600 B.C.) include the remains of stonewalled enclosures surrounding clusters of huts. From the Iron Age (600 B.C. to the first century A.D.), circles of postholes mark the places where stood houses and sheds. Stones and ditches define the fields. Here we can first detect the presence of a "field system," a historic advance over the old "slash and burn" agriculture that cleared, cultivated, then abandoned and moved on. The fields, delineated by their borders or barriers, were cultivated in a recognized pattern of crops and possibly fallow.[4] The so-called Celtic fields, irregular squares of often less than an acre, were cultivated with the ard, a sharpened bough of wood with an iron tip, drawn by one or two oxen, which scratched the surface of light soil enough to allow sowing. Other Iron Age tools included hoes, small sickles, and spades. The rotary quern or hand mill (a disklike upper stone turning around a central spindle over a stationary lower stone) was used to grind grain. Crops

Stonehenge Megalithic monument (c.1680 BC) Wiltshire, Great Britain.

included different kinds of wheat (spelt, emmer), barley, rye, oats, vetch, hay, flax, and dye-stuffs. Livestock were cattle, pigs, sheep, horses, domestic fowl, and honey-bees.[5]

A rare glimpse of Iron Age agriculture comes from the Roman historian Tacitus, who in his *Germania* (A.D. 98) describes a farming society primitive by Roman standards:

> Land [is divided] among them according to rank; the division is facilitated by the wide tracts of fields available. These plowlands are changed yearly and still there is more than enough.... Although their land is fertile and extensive, they fail to take full advantage of it by planting orchards, fencing off meadows, or irrigating gardens; the only demand they make upon the soil is to produce a grain crop. Hence even the year itself is not divided by them into as many seasons as with us: winter, spring, and summer they understand and have names for; the name of autumn is as completely unknown to them as are the good things that it can bring.

Tacitus seems to be describing a kind of field system with communal control by a tribe or clan. The context, however, makes it clear that he is not talking about a system centered on a permanent village:

> The peoples of Germany never live in cities and will not even have their houses adjoining. They dwell apart, scattered here and there, wherever a spring, field, or grove takes their fancy. Their settlements *(vici)* are not laid out in our style, with buildings adjacent and connected.... They do not ... make use of masonry or tiles; for all purposes they employ rough-hewn timber.... Some parts, however, they carefully smear over with clay.... They also dig underground caves, which they cover with piles of manure and use both as refuges from the winter and as storehouses for produce.[6]

Tacitus here is referring to the two main house types that dominated

the landscape into the early Middle Ages. The first was the timber-framed building, which might, as in his account, be covered with clay, usually smeared over a framework of branches (wattle and daub), its most frequent design type the longhouse or byre-house, with animals at one end and people at the other, often with no separation but a manure trench. The second was the sunken hut or *grubenhaus,* dug into the soil to the depth of half a yard to a yard, with an area of five to ten square yards, and used alternatively for people, animals, storage, or workshop.

The Roman occupation of Gaul, beginning in the first century B.C., and of Britain, starting a century later, introduced two types of rural community to northwest Europe. The first was the slave-manned villa, a plantation of 450 to 600 acres centered on a lord's residence built in stone. The second was similar, but worked by peasants, or serfs, who cultivated their own plots of land and also that of their lord.[7] To the native Iron Age crops of wheat, barley, flax, and vetch, the Romans added peas, turnips, parsnips, cabbages, and other vegetables, along with fruits and the grape.[8] Plows were improved by the addition of iron coulters (vertical knife-blades in front of the plowshare), and wooden mould-boards, which turned the soil and made superfluous the

Ancient Roman Baths, Bath, Great Britain.

cross-plowing (crisscrossing at right angles) formerly practiced. Large sickles and scythes were added to the Iron Age stock of tools.[9]

The Romans introduced not only a craftsman's but an engineer's approach to farming: wells, irrigation systems, the scientific application of fertilizer, even consideration of the effect of prevailing winds on structures. The number of sheep and horses increased significantly.[10] The Romans did not, however, work any revolution in basic agricultural methods, and the true village remained conspicuous by its absence. In Britain, in Gaul, and indeed throughout the Empire, the population dwelt in cities, on plantations, or dispersed in tiny hamlets and isolated homesteads.

Sometimes small pioneering groups of settlers entered an area, exploited it for a time, then moved on, whether because of deficient farming techniques, a fall in population, military insecurity, or a combination of the three. Archeology has explored a settlement at Wijster, in the Netherlands, dating from about A.D. 150, the site of four isolated farmsteads, with seven buildings, four large houses and three smaller ones. In another century, it grew to nineteen large and seven small buildings; by the middle of the fifth century, to thirty-five large and fourteen small buildings in an organized plan defined by a network of roads. Wijster had, in fact, many of the qualifications of a true village, but not permanence. At the end of the fifth century, it was abandoned. Another site was Feddersen Wierde, on the North Sea, in the first century B.C., the setting of a small group of farms. In the first century A.D. the inhabitants built an artificial mound to protect themselves against a rise in water; by the third century there were thirty-nine houses, one of them possibly that of a lord. In the fifth century it was abandoned. Similar proto-villages have been unearthed in England and on the Continent dating on into the ninth century.[11]

The countryside of Western Europe remained, in the words of Chapelot and Fossier, "ill-defined, full of shadows and contrasts, isolated and unorganized islands of cultivation, patches of uncertain authority, scattered family groupings around a patriarch, a chieftain, or a rich man . . . a landscape still in a state of anarchy, in short, the picture of a world that man seemed unable to control or dominate."[12] Population density was only two to five persons per square kilometer in Britain, as in Germany, somewhat higher in France.[13] Land was plentiful, people scarce.

In the tenth century the first villages destined to endure appeared in Europe. They were "nucleated"—that is, they were clusters of dwellings surrounded by areas of cultivation. Their appearance coincided with the developing seigneurial system, the establishment of estates held by powerful local lords.

In the Mediterranean area the village typically clustered around a castle, on a hilltop, surrounded by its own wall, with fields, vineyards, and animal enclosures in the plain below. In contrast, the prototype of the village of northwest Europe and England centered around the church and the manor house, and was sited where water was available from springs or streams.[14] The houses, straggling in all directions, were dominated by the two ancient types described by Tacitus, the longhouse and the sunken hut. Each occupied a small plot bounded by hedges, fences, or ditches. Most of the village land lay outside, however, including not only the cultivated fields but the meadow, marsh, and forest. In the organization of cropping and grazing of these surrounding fields, and in the relations that consequently developed among the villagers and between the villagers and their lord, lay a major historical development.

Crop rotation and the use of fallow were well known to the Romans, but how the application of these techniques evolved into the complex open field village is far from clear. The theory that the mature system developed in Germany in the early Middle Ages, diffused to France, and was brought to England by the Anglo-Saxons has been exploded without a satisfactory new interpretation gaining consensus. In Anglo-Saxon England a law of King Ine of Wessex (late seventh century) refers to "common meadow and other land divided into strips," and words associated with open-field agriculture turn up in many other laws and charters of the Saxon period. Recent research has revealed common pasturing on the post-harvest stubble as early as the tenth century. Possible contributory factors in the evolution can be discerned. The custom of partible inheritance—dividing the family lands among children, or among male children—may have fragmented tenements into numerous small holdings that made pasturing difficult without a cooperative arrangement. A rising population may have promoted cooperation. The increasing need for land encouraged "assarting," in which a number of peasant neighbors banded together to fell trees, haul out stumps, and cut brush to create new arable land, which was then divided among its cre-

Man plowing with oxen from the *Latin/Luttrell Psalter*
(14th c.).

ators. An assart, cultivated in strips, usually became a new "furlong" in the village field system. A strong and enlightened lord may often have contributed leadership in the enterprises.[15]

What is clear is that a unique form of agrarian organization gradually developed in certain large regions. "On most of the plain of Northern Europe, and in England in a band running southwest from the North Sea through the Midlands to the English Channel, the land lay in great open stretches of field broken here and there by stands of trees and the clustered houses of villages."[16] This was the "champion" country of open field cultivation and the nucleated village, in contrast to the "woodland" country of west and southeast England and of Brittany and Normandy. In woodland country, farming was typically carried on in compact fields by families living on individual homesteads or in small hamlets. Neither kind of landscape was exclusive; hamlets and isolated farmsteads were

found in champion country, and some nucleated villages in woodland country.

In champion (from *champagne,* meaning "open field") country an intricate system evolved whose distinctive feature was the combination of individual landholding with a strictly enforced, unanimous-consent cooperation in decisions respecting plowing, planting, weeding, harvesting, and pasturing.[17]

Scholarly controversy over the beginnings of the system has a little of the chicken-and-egg futility about it. Somehow, through the operation of such natural forces as population growth and inheritance customs on traditional farming methods, the community organized its arable land into two (later often three) great fields, one of which was left fallow every year. Within each field the individual villager held several plots lying in long strips, which he plowed and planted in concert with his fellow villagers.

Common agreement was needed on which large field to leave fallow, which to plant in fall, which in spring. To pasture animals on the stubble after the harvest, an agreed-on harvest procedure was needed. Exploitation of the scarce meadow available to grazing was at least smoothed by cooperative agreement, while fencing and hedging were minimized.

By the year 1200, the open field system had achieved a state of advanced if still incomplete development. Some degree of cooperation in cultivation and pasturage governed farming in thousands of villages, in England and on the Continent.

The broad surge, economic and demographic, that marked the eleventh century continued fairly steadily through the twelfth and thirteenth. Settlements—homesteads, hamlets, villages—were planted everywhere. The peasant villagers who formed the vast majority of the population cultivated wheat above all other crops, followed by rye, barley, oats, beans, peas, and a few other vegetables. Low and precarious crop yields meant that most available land had to be consigned to cereal, the indispensable staff-of-life crop. The value of manure as fertilizer was well understood, but so few animals could be maintained on the available pasture that a vicious circle of reciprocal scarcity plagued agriculture.

Yet there were notable improvements in technology. The heavy, often wet soils of Northern Europe demanded a heavier plow and more traction than the sandier soils of the Mediterranean region. The large plow that evolved, fitted with coulter and mouldboard and requiring several plow animals, represented "one of the most important agricultural developments in preindustrial Europe."[18] It favored the open field system by strengthening the bias toward long strips.

The Romans had never solved the problem of harnessing the horse for traction. The padded horse collar, invented in Asia and diffusing slowly westward, was joined to other improvements—horseshoes, whippletrees, and traces—to convert the horse into a farm animal. Faster-gaited and longer-working, the horse challenged the strong, docile, but ponderous ox as a plow beast and surpassed it as a cart animal. One of the earliest representations of a working horse is in the Bayeux Tapestry (c. 1087). The ox also profited from technical innovation in the form of an improved yoke,[19] and refused to disappear from agriculture; his slow, steady pull offered advantages in heavy going. Indeed, the debate over the merits of the two traction animals enlivened rustic conversation in the England of Queen Victoria, though the horse slowly won

ascendancy. The horse's needs for fodder stimulated cultivation of oats, a spring crop that together with barley, peas, beans, and vetches fitted ideally into open field rotation. Stall-feeding became more prevalent, permitting more use of fertilizer, while the leguminous fodder crops restored nitrogen content to the soil.[20]

The cooperative relationships of the peasants belonged to what might be called the village aspect of their existence; that existence also had a manorial aspect. In Northern Europe and in England following the Norman Conquest, the countryside came to be organized into land-management units called manors. The manor is usually defined as an estate held by a lord, comprising a demesne directly exploited by the lord, and peasant holdings from which he collected rents and fees. The village might coincide with the manor, or it might not. It might be divided into two or more manors, or it might form only part of a manor.

The combination of demesne and tenants, a version of which dates back to the late Roman Empire, is first specifically mentioned in documents of the ninth century in northern France, and in the tenth century in central Italy and England. By the eleventh century it was well established everywhere.[21]

It fitted comfortably into the contemporary political-military order known as feudalism. Evolving in medieval Europe over a lengthy period and imported to England by the Normans, feudalism united the European elite in a mutual-aid society. A lord granted land to a vassal in return for military and other services; lord and vassal swore reciprocal oaths, of protection by the lord, loyalty by the vassal; the vassal received as fief or fee a conditional gift of land, to "hold" and draw revenue from. Older historians, including Marx, used the term feudalism for the whole medieval social order, a peasant society dominated by a military, land-owning aristocracy. Modern usage generally restricts the word to the network of vassal-lord relations among the aristocracy. The system governing the peasant's relation to the lord, the economic foundation of medieval society, is usually designated the "manorial system." Feudalism meant much to the lord, little to the peasant.

The relationships embodied in the feudal and manorial systems were simple enough in theory: In the manorial system, peasant labored for lord in return for land of his own; in the feudal system, lord held lands from king or overlord in return for supplying soldiers on demand. In practice the relationships were never so simple and grew more complicated over time. All kinds of local variations developed, and both peasant labor service and knightly military service were increasingly converted into money payments.

Whatever the effects of the two overlapping systems, they did not prevent villages from flourishing, until everywhere villages began to crowd up against each other. Where once the silent European wilderness had belonged to the wolf and the deer, villagers now ranged—with their lord's permission—in search of firewood, nuts, and berries, while their pigs rooted and their cattle and sheep grazed. Villages all over Europe parleyed with their neighbors to fix boundaries, which they spelled out in charters and committed to memory with a picturesque annual ceremony. Every spring, in what were known in England as the "gang-days," the whole population went "a-ganging" around the village perimeter. Small boys were ducked in boundary brooks and bumped against boundary trees and rocks by way of helping them learn this important lore.[22]

A thirteenth-century European might be hazy about the boundaries of his country, but he was well aware of those of his village.

Region of Elton and
Ramsey Abbey

THE WASH

LINCOLNSHIRE

• Stamford

NORTHAMPTONSHIRE

Peterborough

RIVER NENE

NORFOLK

• Elton

CAMBRIDGESHIRE

RIVER OUSE

HUNTINGDONSHIRE

• Barnwell

• Ramsey

Upwood •

• Wistow

SUFFOLK

Abbot's Ripton •

• Warboys

• Brington

King's Ripton •

• Broughton

Huntingdon •

St. Ives

Houghton •

Hemmingford
Abbot's

Holywell

• Cambridge

OUSE

BEDFORDSHIRE

Peterborough •

Cambridge •

London •

II

THE ENGLISH
VILLAGE: ELTON

By the thirteenth century, the valleys of Huntingdonshire, along with most of the best farm-lands of England, had been continuously inhabited for at least five thousand years. The story of their occupation over these five millennia is the story of a series of incursions of migrating or invading peoples, in varying numbers, affecting the population at different levels and in different degrees.[1]

Native Paleolithic hunting communities were displaced in about 2000 B.C. by newcomers from the Continent who planted crops, founding the first British agricultural communities. Immigrants in the Bronze and Iron Ages expanded the area of settlement, making inroads into the poorer soils of the uplands and forested areas.

By the first century AD a modest agricultural sur-

plus created a trickle of export trade with Roman Gaul, possibly contributing to the somewhat undermotivated Roman decision (AD 43) to send an army across the Channel to annex Britain. The network of symmetrical, square-cornered fortifications built by the legionaries provided local security and stimulated economic life, which was further assisted by newly built Roman roads, canals, and towns.

One road, later named Ermine Street, ran north from London to York. At the point where it crossed the River Nene a city called Durobrivae was built. Many kilns from the Roman period found in the area indicate a flourishing pottery industry. Villas dotting the neighboring countryside marketed their produce in the city. At one time it was thought that such villas belonged to Roman officials; now it is established that most belonged to a native class of Romanized nobles. Far more numerous were the farmsteads, mostly isolated, some huddled in small, probably kinship, groupings.[2]

Further traces of Roman agriculture have been found in Huntingdonshire along the edge of the fens as well as on the River Ouse. Across the border in Bedfordshire, on the River Ivel, aerial photographs show patterns of Roman field systems. The rich farmlands that bordered the fens became chief providers of grain

The region of Elton and Ramsey Abbey.

131

Portrait of Alfred the Great (849–99), King of Wessex. Engraving by George Vertue (1684–1756).

for the legions in the north of England, transported through the fenland rivers and Roman-built canals.[3]

As multiple problems began to overwhelm the Roman Empire, the legions were withdrawn from Britain (AD 410). Trade and the towns fostered by it declined, the roads fell into disuse, and the new cities shrank or, like Durobrivae, disappeared.

Later in the fifth century a new set of uninvited foreigners came to stay. In the violent early phase of the invasion, in the south of England, the Anglo-Saxons wiped out native populations and replaced them with their own settlements, creating a complete break with the past, and leaving the old Romano-British sites, as in Wessex and Sussex, "a maze of grass-covered mounds."[4] In the later stages, as the Anglo-Saxons advanced to the north and west, the occupation was more peaceful, with the newcomers tilling the soil alongside their British neighbors.[5] Scholars believe that some of the Romano-British agricultural patterns survived into the Middle Ages, particularly in the north of England, where groups of estates administered as a single unit, the "multiple estate," flourished.[6]

In the seventh century the newly melded "English" population converted to Christianity. In what historians have entitled England's "Saxon" period, little other change occurred except perhaps a partial loss of Roman technology. The English agriculturalists cultivated the cereal grains and herded the animals that their Roman, Iron Age, and Neolithic forebears had known. Pigs, which could largely support themselves by foraging in the woods, were the most numerous livestock. Cows were kept mainly to breed oxen for the plow team; sheep and goats were the milk and cheese producers. Barley was the favored crop, ground up for baking or boiling or converted to malt—"the Anglo-Saxons consumed beer on an oceanic scale," notes H. P. R. Finberg.[7]

A new wave of invasion was heralded by a piratical Danish raid in 793. In the following century the Danes came to stay. The contemporary Anglo-Saxon Chronicle recorded the landing in East Anglia in 865 of a "great heathen army" which the following year advanced north and west, to Nottingham and York. In 876, Viking leader Healdene "shared out the land of the Northumbrians, and [the Danes] proceeded to plow land to support themselves." In 877, "the Danish army

went away into Mercia, and shared out some of it, and gave some to Ceowulf," a native thegn, or lord.[8] The territory the Danes occupied included the future Huntingdonshire. At first few in numbers, the Danish warriors were supplemented by relatives from Denmark and also by contingents from Norway and Frisia.

Late in the tenth century Alfred the Great of Wessex (849–899) organized a successful resistance to the Danes but was forced to conclude a peace which left them in possession of most of eastern England.

The Danes having converted to Christianity, a number of monasteries were founded in Danish England. In about 970, St. Oswald, archbishop of York, and Aethelwin, ealdorman (royal official) of East Anglia, donated the land on which Ramsey Abbey was built, a wooded island in Ramsey Mere on which Aethelwin had a hunting lodge.

Between the founding and their deaths in 992,

Oswald and Aethelwin donated their own hereditary holdings to the abbey, added land obtained by purchase and exchange, and solicited donations from others, until the abbey held a large block of territory fanning out from the island of Ramsey through Huntingdonshire and three adjacent counties.[9]

A property that was given to the abbey a few years after the death of the founders was the manor and village of Elton. The origin of the name of the settlement that had grown up near the site of vanished Durobrivae is conjectural. The suffix *tun* or *ton* (fence or enclosure in Anglo-Saxon) had broadened its meaning to become "homestead" and finally "collection of homesteads," or "village"; the suffix *inga*, combined with a personal name, indicated the followers or kinsmen of a leader. Originally spelled "Aethelington" or "Ailington," Elton's name has been explained as either "Ella's village," or "the village of the Aethelings," or "the village of Aethelheah's people."[10]

The benefactor who donated Elton to the abbey was a prelate named Aetheric, who was among the first students educated at Ramsey. During his school days, Aetheric and three other boys as a prank tried to ring the great bell in the west tower and broke its rim. The monks angrily urged punishment, but the abbot declared that since the boys were well-born, they would probably repay the abbey a hundred times when they "arrived at the age of maturity."[11]

The Ramsey Abbey chronicler then relates Aetheric's fulfillment of the prophecy. Elton was by now (early eleventh century) a flourishing village with an Anglo-Saxon lord; when he died, his widow married a Danish noble named Dacus. In 1017 Aetheric, now bishop of Dorchester, joined an escort traveling with King Cnut "to the ends of the kingdom." When the party stopped to spend the night in Nassington, a few miles northwest of Elton, Aetheric and four of the king's secretaries were lodged at Elton in Dacus's manor house.

In the course of a festive evening, Dacus talked expansively of the cattle and sheep that grazed his meadows, the plows that cultivated his fields, and the rents the village paid him. Aetheric remarked that he would like to buy such a manor. Dacus had no intention of selling, but told his guest, "If tomorrow at dawn you give me fifty golden marks, I will turn the village over to you." The bishop called on the king's secretaries to witness the offer and asked if Dacus's wife agreed to it. The wife gave her assent. Host and guests retired, but Aetheric mounted a horse and rode to Nassington,

where he found the king playing chess "to relieve the tedium of the long night." Cnut listened sympathetically and ordered a quantity of gold to be sent to Elton. At dawn Aetheric wakened Dacus and triumphantly presented him with the money. Dacus tried to renege, on the grounds that a contract damaging to an heir—his wife—was invalid. But the witnesses swore that the woman had ratified the pact, and when the dispute was submitted to the king, Cnut pronounced in favor of Aetheric. The wife made a last protest, that the village's two mills were not included in the sale and merited another two golden marks, but her claim was rejected. Packing their furniture and belongings, the outwitted couple departed with their household and their animals, leaving "bare walls" to the new lord.

What Aetheric had initially intended to do with his acquisition we are not told, but he soon found a use for it. Obtaining the king's permission, he left the retinue and visited Ramsey. There, to his dismay, he found the monastery in a turmoil. The current abbot had neglected the discipline of the monks and allowed them to fall into "error" (the chronicler gives no details). Aetheric entered the chapter "threatening and roaring and brandishing anathema unless they amended their ways." The monks "threw themselves at his feet with tearful prayers." In reward for their repentance, Aetheric assigned them the village of Elton "in perpetuity for their sustenance."[12] Thus Elton came to belong to Ramsey Abbey as one of its "conventual" or "home" manors, designed for the monks' support.

Danish political power ceased in England in 1042, but the Danish presence survived in many details of language and custom. Danish suffixes—*thorpe* (hamlet), *toft* (homestead), *holm* (water meadow)—were common in the Elton neighborhood, including the names of Elton's own meadows and field divisions. The local administrative area was Norman (Northman) Cross Hundred, after a cross that stood on Ermine Street in the center of the hundred (district), probably marking the site where the hundred court met in the open air. The hundred was a division of the shire or county, part of a system of administration that had developed in the ninth and tenth centuries. Theoretically containing 100 hides, tax units each of about 120 acres, the hundreds were made up of "vills"—villages or townships. The village represented a physical reality alongside the institutional reality of the manor, the lord's estate. The two did not necessarily coincide, as they did in Elton. Throughout Huntingdonshire only 29 of 56 villages were identical with manors.[13] The village remained a permanent political entity, a territorial unit of the kingdom, subject to the royal government for military and police purposes.

The Anglo-Saxon and Scandinavian invasions had involved mass movements of peoples. The Norman Conquest of 1066 was more like the Roman conquest, the intrusion of a small power group. Where the Anglo-Saxons and Danes had displaced whole regional populations, the Normans at first scarcely disturbed the life of the peasants. Ultimately, however, they wrought an alteration in the social and political system that affected nearly everybody.

Both the feudal and manorial systems were present in some degree and in some regions of England at the time of the Conquest; what the Normans did amounted to performing a shotgun marriage of the two and imposing them on all parts of the country. William the Conqueror appointed himself landlord of England and deputized a number of his principal followers as tenants-in-chief to hold most of it for him, supplanting the Anglo-Saxon nobles who formed the pre-Conquest elite.

The great ecclesiastical estates, such as Ramsey Abbey, remained relatively untouched unless they had aided the Anglo-Saxon resistance, as in the case of the neighboring abbeys of Ely and Peterborough. Ramsey was explicitly confirmed in its holdings:

> William, King of the English, to Archbishop Lanfranc and his bishops, and Abbot Baldwin, and the sheriffs, and certain of his faithful, French and English, greeting. Know that I concede to Herbert, Abbot of Ramsey, his sac, and tol and team, and infangenetheof [rights to tolls, fees, and certain judicial profits], in the town and outside, and all his customs, which his antecessor had in the time of King Edward. Witnesses: Robert, Count of Mortain, per Roger Bigod.[14]

William's tenants-in-chief in turn deputized followers of their own. Finding the manorial unit a convenient instrument, they used it where it was already at hand, imposed it where it was not, and effected whatever Procrustean alterations were needed with an unceremonious disregard for the affected locals. "Many a Norman newcomer did not find a manor equipped with a demesne [the lord's own arable land]," says Barbara Dodwell, or with "villein tenements owing week-work [a tenant's year-round labor obligation] . . . but rather a large number of petty tenants and cottagers, some free, some semi-free, some servile."[15] In such a case, the new lord arbitrarily appropriated land for a demesne and conscripted the needed labor. A fundamental Norman legal principle, "No land without a lord," was enunciated and given substance via the manorial system.

As William equipped his tenants-in-chief with collections of manors, and they in turn bestowed them on their vassals, a variety of lordships resulted, with a pyramid of military obligations. Ramsey Abbey's knight services were for unknown reasons light: although Ramsey was the fourth wealthiest ecclesiastical landholder in England, it owed only four knights. The burden of supporting the four, or of hiring substitutes, was shared among certain of the manors.[16]

As it turned out, the abbey might have done better immediately to endow knights with estates in return for military service—to create "knights' fees." The lack of clear-cut military tenures encouraged knights to settle illegally on abbey lands. Two sister villages of Elton, also bestowed on Ramsey Abbey by Bishop Aetheric, were seized by a knight named Pagan Peverel, a veteran of the First Crusade. The abbey protested and the suit

Portrait of William I, The Conqueror (1027–87), King of England, Duke of Normandy, on a penny coin.

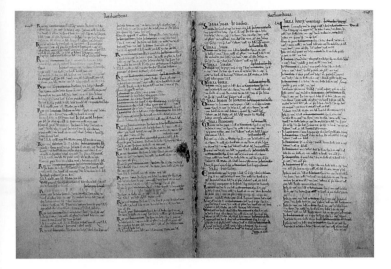

The *Domesday Book* (1085–86), a page of the Northamptonshire Folios.

was heard in Slepe, the village where St. Ives was buried and which soon after took his name. The biographer of St. Ives recorded with satisfaction that not only was justice rendered and the property returned to Ramsey Abbey, but that Pagan Peverel was further punished on his way home:

> On that same day, before Pagan arrived at his lodging, the horse on which he was riding had its feet slip from under it and fell three times to the ground...and a hawk which he was holding was shaken from his hand and made for the wood in swift flight, never to return. The horse of the priest who was traveling with him slipped and fell as well, and its neck being broken—although the priest was unharmed—it breathed its last. There was also Pagan's steward, called Robert, who came in for a more deserved punishment, because...most faithful to his master, he had given approval and assistance to the man's wickedness.

Robert succumbed to a serious illness but was cured after praying at St. Ives's shrine.[17]

Twenty years after the Conquest, to the inestimable profit of historians, was compiled the survey known as the Domesday Book, which one historian has called "probably the most remarkable statistical document in the history of Europe."[18] Executed at the orders of William the Conqueror, the Domesday survey undertook to inventory all the wealth of England, to assure efficient tax collection. Consequently, after a long age of informational darkness, a floodlight of valuable data illuminates the English scene. After Domesday, the light dims once more, until almost as suddenly in the late twelfth century written manorial surveys make

their appearance, and in the middle of the thirteenth manorial court records.

The Domesday Book records about 275,000 heads of households, indicating a total English population of some one and a half to two million, much above early medieval times (though some scholars think that population was higher in late Roman times). Settlements—homesteads, hamlets, villages—already dotted the landscape. In Yorkshire, five out of six of all hamlets and villages had been founded by the time of Domesday.

The Domesday surveyors, proceeding from village to village and calling on lords and peasants to furnish them with information, confronted the difficulty that manor and village (*manerium* and *villa,* in Domesday's Latin) did not necessarily coincide. From the village's point of view, how it was listed in the survey made little difference, and the surveyors simply overrode the problem, focusing their data on the manor. Enough villages are named—some 13,000—to make clear their importance as population centers, however. Churches were given erratic notice, much in some counties, little in others, but enough to indicate that they were now common, if not yet universal, village features.

Under the abbot of Ramsey's holdings in Norman Cross Hundred, Elton was listed with a new spelling:

> M. [Manor] In Adelintune the abbot of Ramsey had ten hides [assessed] to the geld [a tax]. There is land for four plows in the demesne apart from the aforesaid hides. There are now four plows on the demesne, and twenty-eight villeins having twenty plows. There is a church and a priest, and two mills [rendering] forty shillings, and 170 acres of meadow. T.R.E. [in the time of King Edward, 1042–1066] it was worth fourteen *li.* [pounds] now sixteen *li.*[19]

The "ten hides" credited to Elton tell us little about actual acreage. Entries in Domesday were assessed in round numbers, usually five, ten, or fifteen hides. Evidently each shire was assessed for a round number, the hides apportioned among the villages, without strict attention to measurement. Furthermore, though the hide usually comprised 120 acres, the acre varied.

No further information about Elton appears until a manorial survey of about 1160; after that a gap follows until the middle of the thirteenth century, when documentation begins to proliferate.

Drawing on the collection of documents known as the Ramsey Abbey cartulary, on a royal survey done in 1279, on the accounts and court records of the manor, and on what archeology has ascertained from deserted villages, we can sketch a reasonably probable picture of Elton as it was in the last quarter of the thirteenth century.

The royal survey of 1279 credited the "manor and vill" of Elton with a total of 13 hides of arable land of 6 virgates each. Originally designed as the amount of land needed to support a family, the virgate had come to vary considerably. In Elton it consisted of 24 acres; thus the total of village arable was 1,872 acres. The abbot's demesne share amounted to three hides of arable, besides which he had 16 acres of meadow and three of pasture. Two water mills and a fulling mill, for finishing cloth, successors of the two mills that Dacus's wife had

claimed in 1017, also belonged to the abbot.[20]

The village scarcely presented the tidy appearance of a modern English village. Houses did not necessarily face the street, but might stand at odd angles, with a fence or embankment fronting on the street.[21] The nexus of a working agricultural system, the village was a place of bustle, clutter, smells, disrepair, and dust, or in much of the year mud. It was far from silent. Sermons mention many village sounds: the squeal of cartwheels, the crying of babies, the bawling of hogs being butchered, the shouts of peddler and tinker, ringing of church bells, the hissing of geese, the thwack of the flail in threshing time. To these one might add the voices of the villagers, the rooster's crow, the dog's bark, and other animal sounds, the clop of cart horses, the ring of the smith's hammer; and the splash of the miller's great waterwheel.[22]

Stone construction was still rare in England, except in areas like the Cotswolds where stone was plentiful and timber scarce. Elton's houses in the thirteenth century were in all likelihood timber-framed with walls of wattle and daub (oak, willow, or hazel wands coated with clay). Timber-framing had been improved by the importation from the Continent of "cruck" construction, a system of roof support that added space to interiors. The cruck consisted of the split half of the trunk and main branch of a tree. Two or three such pairs, sprung from the ground or from a foundation, could support a ridgepole, their curvature providing enough elevation to save the need for a sunken floor and to put an end to the long, murky history of the sunken hut. Progress in carpentry permitted the framing of walls with squared uprights planted in postholes or foundation trenches, making houses more weathertight.[23]

Roofs were thatched, as from ancient times, with straw, broom or heather, or in marsh country reeds or rushes (as at Elton). Thatched roofs had formidable drawbacks; they rotted from alternations of wet and dry, and harbored a menagerie of mice, rats, hornets, wasps, spiders, and birds; and above all they caught fire. Yet even in London they prevailed. Simon de Montfort, rebelling against the king, is said to have meditated setting fire to the city by releasing an air force of chickens with flaming brands attached.[24] Irresistibly cheap and easy to make, the thatched roof overwhelmingly predominated century after century atop the houses and

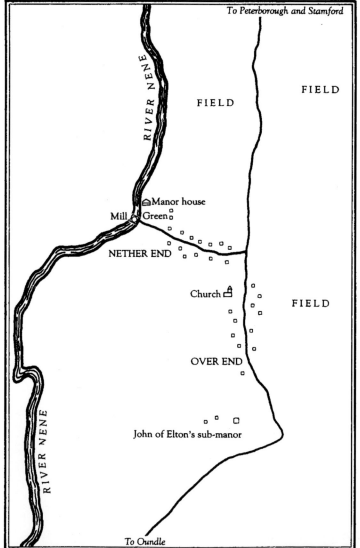

Conjectural map of Elton, c. 1300.

cottages of medieval peasants and townsmen everywhere.[25]

Some village houses were fairly large, forty to fifty feet long by ten to fifteen wide, others were tiny cottages.[26] All were insubstantial. "House breaking" by burglars was literal. Coroners' records speak of intruders smashing their way through the walls of houses "with a plowshare" or "with a coulter."[27] In the Elton manorial court, a villager was accused of carrying away "the doorposts of the house" of a neighbor;[28] an angry heir, still a minor, "tore up and carried away" a house on his deceased father's property and was "commanded to restore it."[29]

Most village houses had a yard and a garden: a smaller "toft" fronting on the street and occupied by the house and its outbuildings, and a larger "croft" in the rear. The toft was usually surrounded by a fence or a ditch to keep in the animals whose pens it contained, along with barns or storage sheds for grain and fodder.[30] Missing was a privy. Sanitary arrangements seem to have consisted of a latrine trench or merely the tradition later recorded as retiring to "a bowshot from the house."[31]

Drainage was assisted by ditches running through the yards. Private wells existed in some villages, but a communal village well was more usual. That Elton had one is indicated by a family named "atte Well." Livestock grazed in the tofts—a cow or an ox, pigs, and chickens. Many villagers owned sheep, but they were not kept in the toft. In summer and fall, they were driven out into the marsh to graze, and in winter they were penned in the manor fold so that the lord could profit from their valuable manure. The richer villagers had manure piles, accumulated from their other animals; two villagers were fined when their dung heaps impinged "on the common highway, to the common harm," and another paid threepence for license to place his on the common next to his house. The croft, stretching back from the toft, was a large garden of half an acre or so, cultivated by spade—"by foot," as the villagers termed it.[32]

Clustered at the end of the street in Nether End, near the river, were the small village green, the manor house, and the mill complex. An eighteenth-century mill today stands on the spot where in the thirteenth century "the dam mill," the "middle mill", and the "small mill" probably stood over the Nene, apparently under a single roof: "the house between the two mills" was repaired in 1296.[33] The foundations were of gone,

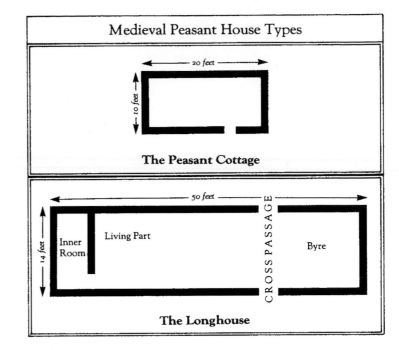

the buildings themselves of timber, with a thatched roof, a courtyard, and a vegetable garden.[34] A millpond furnished power to the three oaken waterwheels.[35] Grass and willows grew all around the pond, the grass sold for fodder, the willow wands for building material.[36]

Back from the river stood the manor house and its "curia" (court), with outbuildings and installations. The curia occupied an acre and a half of land,[37] enclosed with a wall or possibly a fence of stakes and woven rods. Some manor houses had moats to keep livestock in and wild animals out; the excavations of 1977 at Elton revealed traces of such a moat on the side toward the river. An entry gate led to the house or hall (aula), built of stone, with a slate roof.[38] Manor houses were sometimes constructed over a ground-level undercroft, used for storage. The Elton manorial accounts also mention a sleeping chamber, which had to be "pointed and mended" at the same time as the wooden, slate-roofed chapel adjacent to the hall.[39]

Kitchen and bakehouse were in separate buildings nearby, and a granary was built up against the hall.[40] The manorial accounts mention repairs to a "communal privy," probably restricted to the manorial personnels.[41] Elsewhere on the grounds, which accommodated a garden and an apple orchard, stood a stone dairy, equipped with cheese presses, settling pans, strainers, earthenware jars, and churns.[42] The "little barn" and the "big barn" were of timber, with thatched roofs; here

A man sitting by a fire, in an illustration for February, from a calendar of an English psalter (c.1250–75).

mows of grain were stored. The big barn had a slate-roofed porch on one side protecting a great door that locked with a key, and a small door opposite. The door of the little barn was secured by a bolt.[43]

Under a thatched roof, the stone stable housed horses, oxen, and cows, as well as carts, tools, and harness.[44] A wooden sheepfold, also thatched, large enough to accommodate the lord's sheep and those of the villagers, was lighted with candles and an oil lamp every spring at lambing time.[45] Still other buildings included a kiln for drying malt[46] and a pound—a "punfold" or "pinfold"—for stray animals.[47] Two large wooden thatched dovecotes sheltered several hundred doves, sold at market or forwarded to the abbot's table.[48] Among other resident poultry were chickens and geese, and, at least in one year's accounts, peacocks and swans.[49] On its waterfront, the manor possessed several boats, whose repairs were recorded at intervals.[50]

Across the street from the curia stood one of a pair of communal ovens to which the villagers were obliged to bring their bread; the other stood in Overend. The ovens were leased from the lord by a baker. A forge was leased by a smith who worked for both the lord and the tenants.[51] The green, whose presence is attested by the name of a village family, "atte Grene," could not have been large enough to serve as a pasture. Its only known use was as a location for the stocks, where village wrongdoers were sometimes held.

At the opposite end of the village, in Overend, stood the parish church, on the site of earlier structures dating at least to the tenth century. The records make no mention of the rectory, which the enclosure map of 1784 locates in Nether End.

South of the church in Overend lay the tract of land on which two hundred years later Elton Hall was built. In the thirteenth century, this was a sub-manor of Elton, a hide of land held by a wealthy free man, John of Elton, who had tenants of his own.

A medieval village did not consist merely of its buildings. It included the plowed fields, the meadows, and even the surrounding woods, moor, and marsh. Aerial photographs of deserted medieval villages show open fields with their characteristic pattern of ridge and furrow produced by the plowman. Elton's fields, under continuous and changing use, show few traces. A survey of Elton at the beginning of the seventeenth century listed three fields—Ogerston, Middlefield, and Earnestfield—but whether they existed in the thirteenth century remains unknown.[52] None of the dozens of place names in the manorial records can be identified with an entire field. Many are names of furlongs, the subdivisions of fields (Holywellfurlong, Knolfurlong, Michelgrove), others of meadows (Gooseholm, Michelholm, Le Inmede, Butterflymead, Abbotsholm), or Marsh (Oldmoor, Smallmoor, Newtonmoor, Broadmoor, Oldwychslade). Some are recorded as being leased on a regular basis—to the rector, a furlong called Le Brach, to others Milnespightle (Mill Close), and Clack. The village also had a vineyard, possibly connected with the curia.

Brian K. Roberts *(The Making of the English Village)* divides the elements of villages into three overlapping categories: public space, where everyone, including outsiders, has rights; communal space, where all inhabitants have rights, even when the lord holds the land; and private space, where access and use are open only to the proper individuals. The public elements are the church and churchyard, and the highways, streets, and lanes. The communal are the green, the punfold or pound, the oven, the pond, the wells, the stocks, and, most important, the open fields. The private are the manor house and its appurtenances, and the tofts and crofts of the peasants. Some elements are ambiguous: the entries and exits to the fields are both communal and public; the church is not only both public and communal but private, since it belongs to the lord; the smithy, the houses of the demesne servants (cowherd, shepherd), and the rector's house are both communal and private.[53]

Archeologists have classified village plans on the basis of major design elements: "green" villages, clustered around a green or common; street or row villages, built along a street or highway; polyfocal villages, with more than one hub; and composite villages combining several of these types. Elton would seem to be all of these, one of its two sections built around a central green, the other along a highway, each with a separate focus (the manor house, the church). The classification does not really seem very meaningful, and considering the difficulty in tracing the chronology of village plans, not very exact. R. H. Hilton comments that the main physical characteristic shared by medieval villages was their shapelessness. Village streets appear to have come into existence after the tofts and crofts were established, as the paths between the houses became worn down and sunken by the traffic of people, animals, and carts. The village network was in fact more paths than streets.[54]

Elton in the late thirteenth century was a large village, capable of summoning 327 residents to a harvest in 1287.[55] The royal survey of 1279 lists 113 tenants, heads of families.[56] Allowing for wives, children, and landless laborers, a figure of five to six hundred for the total population might be reasonable. This accords with Hilton's estimate that 45 percent of the villages of the West Midlands had a population of between 400 and 600, with 10 percent larger, the rest smaller.[57]

Villages like Elton were not cut off from the world around them. Many Elton surnames indicate family ori-gins elsewhere, and the records sometimes explicitly speak of immigration: Richard Trune, a cotter (cottager), came to Elton from Fotheringhay, in Northamptonshire.[58] Many villagers paid an annual fee for license to live outside the manor (or were cited for failing to pay it). Elton village officials traveled to the fairs and markets to make purchases; so did ordinary villagers to sell their produce. Carrying services owed by villeins took them to Ramsey and "any market where the lord wishes inside the county [of Huntingdonshire]."[59] Other Ramsey Abbey villagers journeyed as far London. Free tenants of Elton attended the abbot's honor (estate) court at Broughton twice a year, as well as the royal courts at Huntingdon and Norman Cross. The world came to Elton, too, in the guise of monks, churchmen, nobles, craftsmen, day laborers, and royal officials.

Thus the village of Elton, Norman Cross Hundred, Huntingdonshire, England, belonging to Ramsey Abbey, occupying some 1,800 acres of farmland, cultivated crops and herded its animals in much the same fashion as thousands of other villages in England and on the Continent. By the standards of a later age, it was neither rich nor prepossessing. But in comparison with earlier times, it was a thriving social organism, and an important innovation in social and economic history.

III
THE LORD

Every village had a lord, but only rarely was he in residence. A resident lord was usually a petty knight who held only one manor, like Henry de Bray, lord of Harlestone (Northampton-shire), whose account book has survived. Henry had twenty-four tenants sharing five hundred acres, contributing annually twelve pounds in cash rents, a pound of pepper, eight fowls, and performing harvest services.[1] At the other end of the spectrum was the earl, count, abbot, or bishop, whose "honor" was composed of manors scattered over a quarter of England.

On the Continent such a magnate—a count of Champagne or Flanders—might rival kings in exercising political authority. In Norman England, where William the Conqueror and his successors monopolized political power, the great lords began as generals in an army of occupation, their military role softening over time into an economic one. A "tenant-in-chief" like the earl of Warenne, lord of scores of villages in a dozen counties, collected all kinds of rents and services

Illustration for March from *Le Breviare d'Amour* (13th c.).

at first- and second-hand without ever setting eyes on most of his sixty-five knight-tenants, hundreds of free-holders, and thousands of bondmen.[2] Between the two extremes of Henry de Bray and the earl of Warenne were middling lords who had several manors and some-times traveled around among them.

Besides great and small, lords divided more defin-ably into lay and ecclesiastical. The abbot of Ramsey, whose twenty-three villages included Elton and who held parts of many others, is a good example of the ecclesiastical lord, whose numbers had steadily increased since the Conquest. The old feudal theory of lordship as a link in the legal chain of authority running from serf to monarch had lost much of its substance. The original basis of the feudal hierarchy—military service owed to the crown—had dissipated, owing partly to the objec-tions of knights and barons to service abroad, and partly to the complexity wrought by the accidents of inheri-tance. It was easier to extract a money payment than to induce an unwilling knight to serve, and money fees, with which soldiers could be hired and equipped, were easier to divide into fractions when a property owed a third or half of a knight's service.

To the village, such legal complications hardly mattered, any more than whether the lord was great or small, lay or ecclesiastical (or male or female, since abbesses, prioresses, widows, and heiresses held many manors). A village might be comfortably shared by two or more lords. Tysoe (Warwickshire) was divided among five different manors, belonging to Baron Stafford, his son, two priories, and the local Knights Templar.[3] Often, however, as in the case of Elton, a village constituted a manor, and was one of several belonging to a single lord.

Whatever the technicalities, the lord was the lord, the consumer of the village surplus. The thirteenth-century manor was not a political or military enterprise but an economic one, with the lord its exploiter and beneficiary.

It already had a history. In the twelfth century, "farming," or leasing, the demesne or even the whole manor had been popular. An entrepreneur paid a fixed sum, assumed control of the day-to-day operation, and profited from the difference between the fee he paid and the revenues he collected. The farmer might be a local knight or rich peasant, or a businessman from a nearby town. Sometimes the villagers themselves banded together in a consortium to farm their manor.[4] One lord might farm another's land when geography made it more convenient. The abbot of Ramsey farmed King's Ripton, a crown manor lying next to Abbot's Ripton. The farm normally comprised land, animals, implements, personnel, labor services of the villeins, and even the fines levied in the manorial court. The farmer usually held the privilege of making land transfers to maintain production, as when a tenant died without a direct heir.[5]

Beginning about 1200, the farming of manors went out of style. The thirteenth century was an age of population expansion, and as town markets for agricultural products grew, more and more lords decided to exploit their manors directly. Some manors continued to be farmed (as was Elton at intervals), but the trend was toward direct and active estate management. To increase demesne production, villeins were often saddled with new labor services, or resaddled with old ones from which they had bought exemption. But the tenants, including the villeins, also began selling in the market. The pendulum swung back, with the lords accepting higher rents and other money payments and using the cash to hire labor to work the demesne. It was an era of prosperity for all, but especially for the lords, who saw their incomes, especially their cash incomes, rise rapidly.

They had no trouble spending them. By his nature the feudal lord was a dedicated consumer. His social status imposed a life-style of conspicuous consumption, which in the Middle Ages meant mainly consumption of food and drink. The lord was "the man who could always eat as much as he wished," says Georges Duby, and also "the man who provided others with food," and was consequently admired for his openhandedness. The very yardstick of his prestige was the number of people he fed: staff, armed retainers, labor force, guests.[6]

The abbot of Ramsey's requirements from his manors included grain, beef, flour, bread, malt for ale, fodder, lard, beans, butter, bacon, honey, lambs, poultry, eggs, herrings, and cheese. Like other lords he also received cash to make the many purchases outside the estate that were needed to keep his household going: horses, cloth, coverlets, hangings, robes, candlesticks, plates.

Thus as consumer the lord needed revenues both in kind and in cash. As a consumer, he also required services, especially carrying services, to bring the produce from his manors to his castle or monastery. He needed even more services in his other economic capacity, that of producer. Here disparity existed not only among greater and lesser lords, but among their manors. Some were large, some small, some contained much demesne land, some little (a few none). Elton's thirteen hides were probably close to average, as was also its proportion of about one quarter demesne land. The precise size of the demesne was never regarded as of great moment. Extents for the Ramsey manors of Warboys and Holywell state disarmingly, "The demesne of this manor consists of many furlongs, but it is not known how many acres are contained in them."[7] The acre itself varied erratically even among manors of the same estate.* On Ramsey manors the hide ranged from four virgates to seven, the virgate from fifteen to thirty-two acres, and the size of the acre is uncertain.[8]

Demesne land might lie in a compact parcel, separate from the villagers' fields, or it might, as it evidently did in Elton, lie scattered in strips like those of the tenants with which it was intermingled.

Where the demesne was large, a large labor force was needed, usually meaning that a substantial proportion of the tenants were villeins owing week-work. Where the demesne was small, most of the tenants were likely to be free, or if unfree, paying a money rent rather than rendering work services.

To his economic roles as consumer, producer, and landlord, the lord added certain others. He had an important, centuries-old judicial function, his manor courts (hallmotes) dealing in a range of civil and criminal cases that provided him with fines, fees, and confis-

cations. In addition to dues exacted from his tenants on a variety of occasions—death, inheritance, marriage—the lord enjoyed the "ban," a monopoly on certain activities, most notoriously on grinding everybody's grain and baking everybody's bread. The ban was resented and sometimes evaded, though rigorously enforced by the manor court. So were the lord's other privileges such as folding all the village sheep so that their manure could improve his demesne. In Elton in 1306 Richard Hubert and John Wrau were fined because they had "refused to allow [their] sheep to be in the lord's fold."[9] The same offense brought Geoffrey Shoemaker and Ralph Attwych penalties of sixpence each in 1312, and in 1331 nine villagers were fined for the infraction, in addition to Robert le Ward, who was penalized for harboring the flock of one of his neighbors "to the damage of the lord."[10] On the other hand, an animal that roamed too freely risked the lord's privilege of "waif and stray": "One female colt came an estray to the value of 18 pence, and it remains. Therefore let the reeve answer [let the reeve sell the colt and turn over the money]."[11] A villager who recovered his impounded animal without license was fined for "making a rescue," as were Thomas Dyer in 1294 and Isabel, daughter of Allota of Langetoft, in 1312.[12]

One of the lord's most valuable privileges aroused little resentment: his right to license markets and fairs, granted him by the king or sometimes by another overlord. The abbot of Ramsey's fair of St. Ives was internationally famous, patronized by merchants from Flanders, France, Italy, and Scandinavia.[13] Such fairs and markets enriched both lord and tenants, at least the luckier and more enterprising. (In 1279 the abbot of Ramsey contemplated a weekly market at Elton, and successfully negotiated an agreement for it with the abbot of Peterborough, but for some reason the project was never carried out.)[14]

Yet despite all his collections, enforcements, and impingements, perhaps the most arresting aspect of the lord's relations with the villagers is the extent to which he left them alone. The once popular picture of the lord as "an omnipotent village tyrant was, in George Homans's words, an unrealistic assumption."[15] The medieval village actually lived and worked in a state of near autonomy. The open field system exacted a concert of the community at every point of the agricultural cycle: plowing, planting, growing, and harvesting. It is now virtually certain that the village achieved this concert by itself with little help or leadership from outside. To Marc Bloch's observation that there was never any "necessary opposition" between the lord's manor and the peasants' village, Homans added that "the manor could be strong only where the village was strong."[16] More recent scholarship has stressed the primacy of the village over the manor in historical development.

The lord could have little objection to village autonomy. What he wanted was the certainty of rents and dues from his tenants, the efficient operation of his demesne, and good prices for wool and grain. The popularity of treatises on estate management is an indicator of what occupied the minds of the great lords of the late thirteenth century. Walter of Henley's *Husbandry* advised its noble readers to "look into your affairs often, and cause them to be reviewed, for those who serve you will thereby avoid the more to do wrong."[17] It was prudent counsel because there was no way for an absentee lord to supervise his scattered manors except through appointed officials.

These officials, in fact, constituted the lord's material presence in the village. Three of them, the steward, the bailiff, and the reeve, were the key executives of the manorial system.

Originally a household servant or majordomo, the estate steward (sometimes called a seneschal) had in the twelfth and thirteenth centuries accomplished a progression paralleling that of Joseph, the Pharaoh's cupbearer who became chief administrator of Egypt. On estate after estate the steward became the lord's deputy, chief executive officer for the vast complex of lands, rights, and people. Bishop Robert Grosseteste (1175–1253), author of another widely read treatise, *Rules of St.*

Robert, defined the steward's duty as to guard and increase the lord's property and stock "in an honest way," and to defend his rights and franchises.[18] A slightly later writer, the anonymous author of *Seneschaucie,* stipulated legal knowledge as a principal qualification, since the steward now represented the lord in court both on and off the estate. His main function, however, was supervision of all the manors of the estate, which he did primarily by periodic visitation.[19] It was hardly possible for a lord to be too careful in his choice, thought the author of *Seneschaucie:* "The seneschal of lands ought to be prudent and faithful and profitable, and he ought to know the law of the realm, to protect his lord's business and to instruct and give assurance to the bailiffs." It was useless to look for wisdom from "young men full of young blood and ready courage, who know little or nothing of business." Wiser to appoint from among those "ripe in years, who have seen much, and know much, and who . . . never were caught or convicted for treachery or any wrongdoing"[20]—something that often befell officials, according to many sermons and satires.

Typically the steward of a great lay lord was a knight, that of a great ecclesiastical lord was a cleric. In the latter case, he was sometimes known as the cellarer, the traditional title of the person in charge of a monastery's food and drink supply. At least two stewards of Ramsey Abbey in the late thirteenth century were monks.[21] Where a knight-steward received his compensation from his fee (land holding), a clerk-steward usually received his from his living, a parish church whose services were conducted by a vicar. Like most such officials, the steward of Ramsey Abbey, in company with his clerk, made periodic tours of the abbey's manors to review the management of the demesne. He did not, as many stewards did, himself audit the manorial accounts. This function was performed on Ramsey manors by a separate clerk of the account who made his own annual tour and who, in a hand that reflected an excellent education, recorded the details of the year's transactions. This clerk, who received a rather modest stipend of five shillings, thus provided an independent check for the abbot on the management of his estate.[22]

The steward appeared in each village only at intervals, usually no more than two or three times a year, for a stay of seldom more than two days. The lord's deputy on each manor throughout the year was the bailiff. Typically appointed on the steward's recommendation, the bailiff was socially a step nearer the villagers themselves, perhaps a younger son of the gentry or a member of a better-off peasant family. He could read

and write; seigneurial as well as royal officialdom reflected the spread of lay literacy.[23]

The bailiff combined the personae of chief law officer and business manager of the manor. He represented the lord both to the villagers and to strangers, thus acting as a protector of the village against men of another lord. His overriding concern, however, was management of the demesne, seeing that crops and stock were properly looked after and as little as possible stolen. He made sure the manor was supplied with what it needed from outside, at Elton a formidable list of purchases: millstones, iron, building timber and stone, firewood, nails, horseshoes, carts, cartwheels, axles, iron tires, salt, candles, parchment, cloth, utensils for dairy and kitchen, slate, thatch, quicklime, verdigris, quicksilver, tar, baskets, livestock, food. These were bought principally at nearby market towns, Oundle, Peterborough, St. Neots, and at the Stamford and St. Ives fairs. The thirteenth-century manor was anything but self-sufficient.

Walter of Henley, himself a former bailiff, advised lords and stewards against choosing from their circle of kindred and friends, and to make selection strictly on merit.[24] The bailiff was paid an excellent cash salary plus perquisites, at Elton twenty shillings a year plus room and board, a fur coat, fodder for his horse, and twopence to make his Christmas oblation (offering). Two other officials, subordinate to the bailiff, are mentioned in the Elton accounts: the *claviger* or macebearer, and the sergeant, but both offices seem to have disappeared shortly after 1300.[25]

The bailiff's residence was the lord's manor house. Set clearly apart from the village's collection of flimsy wattle-and-daub dwellings, the solid-stone, buttressed manor house contrasted with them in its ample interior space and at least comparative comfort. The main room, the hall, was the setting for the manorial court, but otherwise remained at the bailiff's disposal. There he and his family took their meals along with such members of the manorial household as were entitled to board at the lord's table, either continuously or at certain times, plus occasional visitors. A stone bench at the southern end flanked a large rectangular limestone hearth. The room was furnished with a trestle table, wooden benches, and a "lavatorium," a metal washstand. A garderobe, or privy, adjoined. One end of hall was partitioned off as a buttery and a larder. The sleeping chamber, whose existence is attested by repairs to it, and its door may have been a room with a fireplace uncovered by the excavations of 1977. A chapel stood next to the manor house.[16] For the entertainment of guests "carrying the lord's writ," such as the steward or the clerk of the accounts, the bailiff kept track of his costs and submitted the expenses to Ramsey. Visitors included monks and officials on their way to Stamford Fair, or to be ordained in Stamford; other ecclesiastics, among them the abbot's two brothers and the prior of St. Ives; royal officials—the justice of the forest, the sheriff of Huntingdon, kings' messengers, and once "the twelve regarders," knights who enforced the king's forest law.[27] The guests' horses and dogs had to be lodged and fed, and sometimes their falcons, including "the falcons of the lord abbot."[28] In 1298 when the royal army was on its way to Scotland, a special expense was incurred, a bribe of sixpence to "a certain man of the Exchequer of the lord king . . . for sparing our horses."[29] On several later occasions expenses are noted either for feeding military parties or bribing them to go elsewhere.

Assisting the bailiff was a staff of subordinate officials chosen annually from and usually (as in Elton) by the villagers themselves. Chief of these was the reeve. Always a villein, he was one of the most prosperous—"the best husbandman," according to *Seneschaucie*.[30] Normally the new reeve succeeded at Michaelmas (September 29), the beginning of the agricultural year. His main duty was seeing that the villagers who owed labor service rose promptly and reported for work. He supervised the formation of the plow teams, saw to the penning and folding of the lord's livestock, ordered the mending of the lord's fences, and made sure sufficient forage was saved for the winter.[31] *Seneschaucie* admonished him to make sure no herdsman slipped off to fair, market, wrestling match, or tavern without obtaining leave and finding a substitute.[32] He might, as occasionally at Elton, be entrusted with the sale of demesne produce. On some manors the reeve collected the rents.

But of all his numerous functions, the most remarkable was his rendition of the demesne account. He produced this at the end of the agricultural year for the lord's steward or clerk of the accounts. Surviving reeves' accounts of Elton are divided into four parts: "arrears," or receipts; expenses and liveries (meaning deliveries); issue of the grange (grain and other stores on hand in the barns); and stock. The account of Alexander atte Cross, reeve in 1297, also appends an "account of works" performed by the tenants.

Each part is painstakingly detailed. Under "arrears" are given the rents collected on each of several feast days when they fell due, the rents that remained unpaid for whatever reason, and receipts from sales of grain, stock, poultry, and other products. Under "expenses and liver-

ies" are listed all the bacon, beef, meal, and cheeses consigned to Ramsey Abbey throughout the year, and the mallards, larks, and kids sent to the abbot at Christmas and Easter. Numerous payments to individuals—carpenter, smith, itinerant workmen—are listed, and purchases set down: plows and parts, yokes and harness, hinges, wheels, grease, meat, herring, and many other items. The "issue of the grange" in 1297 lists 486 rings and 1 bushel of wheat totaled from the mows in the barn and elsewhere, and describes its disposal: to Ramsey, in sales, in payment of a debt to the rector, and for boonworks; then it does the same for rye, barley, and the other grains. In the stock account, the reeve lists all the animals—horses, cattle, sheep, pigs—inherited from the previous year, notes the advances in age category (lambs to ewes or wethers, young calves to yearlings), and those sold or dead (with hides accounted for).[33]

With no formal schooling to draw on, the unlettered reeve kept track of all these facts and figures by means of marks on a tally stick, which he read off to the clerk of the accounts. Written out on parchment about eight inches wide and segments varying in length, sewed together end to end, the account makes two things clear: the medieval manor was a well-supervised business operation, and the reeve who played so central a role in it was not the dull-witted clod traditionally evoked by the words "peasant" and "villein."

The accounts often resulted in a small balance one way or the other. Henry Reeve, who served at Elton in 1286–1287, reported revenues of 36 pounds ½ penny, and expenditures of 36 pounds 15½ pence, which he balanced with the conclusion: "Proved, and so the lord owes the reeve 15½ pence."[34] His successor, Philip of Elton, who took over in April 1287, reported on the following Michaelmas receipts of 26 pounds 6 shillings 7 pence, expenditures of 25 pounds 16 shillings ½ penny: "Proved and thus the reeve owes the lord 10 shillings 6½ pence."[35]

For his labors, physical and mental, the reeve received no cash stipend, but nevertheless quite substantial compensation. He was always exempted from his normal villein obligations (at Elton amounting to 117 days' week-work), and at Elton, though not everywhere, received at least some of his meals at the manor house table. He also received a penny for his Christmas oblation.[36] On some less favored manors, candidates for reeve declined the honor and even paid to avoid it, but most accepted readily enough. At Broughton the reeve was given the privilege of grazing eight animals in the lord's pasture.[37] That may have been the formal concession of a privilege already preempted. "It would be surprising," says Nigel Saul, "if the reeve had not folded his sheep on the lord's pastures or used the demesne stock to plow his own lands."[38] There were many other possibilities. Chaucer's reeve is a skillful thief of his lord's produce:

> Well could he keep a garner and a bin,
> There was no auditor could on him win.[39]

Walter of Henley considered it wise to check the reeve's bushel measure after he had rendered his account.[40]

Some business-minded lords assigned quotas to their manors—annual quantities of wheat, barley, and other produce, fixed numbers of calves, lambs, other stock, and eggs. The monkish board of auditors of St. Swithun's Abbey enforced their quotas by exactions from the reeve, forcing him to make up out of his pocket any shortfall. It might be supposed that St. Swithun's would experience difficulty in finding reeves. Not so, however. The monks were strict, but their quotas were moderate and attractively consistent, remaining exactly the same year after year for long stretches—60 piglets, 28 goslings, 60 chicks, and 300 eggs—making it entirely possible, or rather probable, that the reeve profited in most years, adding the surplus goslings and piglets to his own stock.[41]

The reeve in turn had an assistant, known variously as the beadle, hayward, or messor, who served partly as the reeve's deputy, partly in an independent role. As the reeve was traditionally a villein virgater, his deputy was traditionally a villein half-virgater, one of the middle-level villagers.

The beadle or hayward usually had primary responsibility for the seed saved from last year's crop, its preservation and sowing, including the performances of the plowmen in their plowing and harrowing, and later, in cooperation with the reeve, for those of the villeins doing mowing and reaping. Walter of Henley warned that villeins owing week-work were prone to shirk: "If they do not [work] well, let them be reproved."[42] The hayward's job also included impounding cattle or sheep that strayed into the demesne crop and seeing that their owners were fined.[43]

Many manors also had a woodward to see that no one took from the lord's wood anything except what he was allowed by custom or payment; some also had a cart-reeve with specialized functions. One set of officials no village was ever without was the ale tasters, who assessed the quality and monitored the price of ale brewed for sale to the public. This last was the only village office ever filled by women, who did most of the brewing.

At Elton the titles "beadle" and "hayward" were both in use. Both offices may have existed simultaneously, with the beadle primarily responsible for collecting rents and the fines levied in court. The beadle's compensation consisted of partial board at the manor house plus exemption from his labor obligation (half the reeve's, or 58½ days a year, since he owed for a half rather than a full virgate). At Elton a reap-reeve was sometimes appointed in late summer to help police the harvest work, a function otherwise assigned to two "wardens of the autumn."[44]

The primary aim of estate management was to provide for the lord's needs, which were always twofold: food for himself and his household, and cash to supply needs that could not be met from the manors. Many lay barons collected their manorial product in person by touring their estates annually manor by manor. Bishop Grosseteste advised careful planning of the tour. It should begin after the post-Michaelmas "view of account," when it would be possible to calculate how lengthy a visit each manor could support. "Do not in any wise burden by debt or long residence the places where you sojourn," he cautioned, lest the manorial economy be so weakened that it could not supply from

Killing a pig, illustration for November from a Cistercian psalter (French School, early 13th c.).

the sale of its products cash for "your wines, robes, wax, and all your wardrobe."[45]

For Ramsey Abbey and other monasteries, such peripatetic victualing was not practical. Instead, several manors, of which Elton was one, were earmarked for the abbey food supply and assigned a quota, or "farm," meaning sufficient food and drink to answer the needs of the monks and their guests for a certain period.[46]

Whatever the arrangement for exploitation of the manors, the thirteenth-century lord nearly always received his income in both produce and cash. The demesne furnished the great bulk of the produce, plus a growing sum in cash from sales at fair or market. The tenants furnished the bulk of the cash by their rents, plus some payments in kind (not only bread, ale, eggs, and cheese, but in many cases linen, wool cloth, and handicraft products). Cash also flowed in from the manorial court fines. Only a few lords, such as the bishop of Worcester, enjoyed the convenience of a revenue paid exclusively in cash.[47]

Cultivation of the demesne was accomplished by a combination of the villein tenants' contribution of week-work and the daily labor of the demesne staff, the *famuli*. In England the tenants generally contributed about a fourth of the demesne plowing, leaving three fourths to the *famuli*.[48] At Elton these consisted of eight plowmen and drivers, a carter, a cowherd, a swineherd, and a shepherd, all paid two to four shillings a year in cash plus "livery," an allowance of grain, flour, and salt, plus a pair of gloves and money for their Christmas oblation.[49] Smaller emoluments were paid to a cook, a dairyman or dairymaid, extra shepherds, seasonal helpers for the cowherd and swineherd, a keeper of bullocks, a woman who milked ewes, and a few other seasonal or temporary hands.[50] On some manors the *famuli* were settled on holdings, one version of which was the "sown acre," a piece of demesne land sown with grain. Ramsey Abbey used the sown acre to compensate its own huge *familia* of eighty persons.[51] Another arrangement was the "Saturday plow," by which the lord's plow cohort was lent one day a week to plow the holdings of *famuli*.[52]

The manorial plowman was responsible for the well-being of his plow animals and the maintenance of his plows and harness. *Seneschaucie* stressed the need for intelligence in a plowman, who was also expected to be versed in digging drainage ditches. As for plow animals, Walter of Henley judiciously recommended both horses and oxen, horses for their superior work virtues, oxen for their economy. An old ox was edible and, fattened up, could be sold for as much as he had cost, according

A man and woman removing weeds or thistles. Detail from the *Latin/Luttrell Psalter* (14th c.).

to Walter (actually, for 90 percent of his cost, according to a modern scholar; in the 1290s, about 12 shillings). Pope Gregory III had proscribed horsemeat in 732, and though most of Europe ignored the ban, in the Middle Ages and long after, in England horsemeat was never eaten. Consequently an old plow horse fetched less than half his original cost of ten to eleven shillings.[53]

Elton's bailiff or the Ramsey steward may have studied Walter of Henley, because eight Elton demesne plowmen and drivers used ten stots (work horses) and eighteen oxen in their four plow teams. Horses and oxen were commonly harnessed together, a practice also recommended by Walter. In the Elton region (East Midlands) a popular combination was two horses and six oxen.[54]

On every manor the tenants' labor was urgently required in one critical stretch of the annual cycle, the boon-works of autumn and post-autumn. To get the demesne harvest cut, stacked, carted, threshed, and stored, and the winter wheat planted before frost, called for mass conscription of villeins, free tenants, their families, and often for recruitment of extra labor from the floating population of landless peasants. At Elton, two *meiatores,* professional grain handlers, and a professional winnower were taken on at harvest time.[55]

Threshing, done in the barn, was a time-consuming job, winnowing an easy one. Hired labor was paid a penny per ring of threshed wheat, a penny per eight rings winnowed.[56]

The staple crops at Elton were those of most English manors: barley, wheat, oats, peas, and beans, and, beginning in the late thirteenth century, rye. The proportions in the demesne harvest of 1286 were about two thousand bushels of barley, half as much wheat, and lesser proportions of oats, drage (mixed grain), and peas and beans.[57] Yields were four to one for barley, four to one for wheat, a bit over two to one for oats, and four to one for beans and peas. The overall yield was about three and two-thirds to one, better than the three and one-third stipulated in the *Rules of St. Robert*.[58] In 1297 the Elton wheat yield reached fivefold, but overall the ratio remained about the same, a third to half modern figures.[59] Prices fluctuated considerably over the half-century from 1270 to 1320, varying from five to eight shillings a quarter (eight bushels) for wheat.[60] Half a ring (two bushels) planted an acre. Even without drought or flood, labor costs and price uncertainty could make a lord's profit on crops precarious.

The treatises offered extensive advice on animal husbandry—standards for butter and cheese production, advice on milk versus cheese, on suspension of the milking of cows and ewes to encourage early breeding, on feeding work animals (best for the reeve or hayward to look to, since the oxherd might steal the provender), and on branding the lord's sheep so that they could be distinguished from those of the tenants. The cowherd should sleep with his animals in the barn, and the shepherd should do the same, with his dog next to him.[61]

In the realm of veterinary medicine, the best that can be said is that it was no worse than medieval human medicine. Without giving specific instructions, Walter of Henley advocated making an effort to save animals: "If there be any beast which begins to fall ill, lay out money to better it, for it is said in the proverb, 'Blessed is the penny that saves two.'"[62] Probably more practical was Walter's advice to sell off animals quickly when disease threatened the herd. Verdigris (copper sulfate), mercury, and tar, all items that appear frequently in the Elton manorial accounts, were applied for a variety of animal afflictions, with little effect on the prevailing rate of mortality, averaging 18 percent among sheep.[63] Sheep pox, "Red Death," and murrain were usually blamed, the word "murrain" covering so many diseases that it occurs more often in medieval stock accounts than any other.[64]

The Elton dairy produced some two hundred cheeses a year, most if not all from ewes' milk, with the bulk of the product going to the cellarer of the abbey, some to the famuli and boon-workers.[65] Most of the butter was sold, some of the milk used to nurse lambs. The medieval practice of treating ewes as dairy animals may have hindered development of size and stamina. But though notoriously susceptible to disease, sheep were never a total loss since their woolly skins (fells) brought a good price. The relative importance of their fleece caused medieval flocks to have a composition which would seem odd to modern sheep farmers. Where modern sheep are raised mainly for meat and the wethers (males) are slaughtered early, in the Middle Ages the wethers' superior fleece kept them alive for four to five years.[66]

Poultry at Elton, as on most manors, was the province of a dairymaid, who, according to *Seneschaucie*, ought to be "faithful and of good repute, and keep herself clean, and . . . know her business." She should be adept at making and salting cheese, should help with the winnowing, take good care of the geese and hens, and keep and cover the fire in the manor house.[67]

The only other agricultural products at Elton were flax, apples and wax, all cultivated on a modest or insignificant scale.[68] The wax was a scanty return on a beekeeping enterprise that failed through a bee disease. On other English manors a variety of garden vegetables, cider, timber, and brushwood were market products. Wine, a major product on the Continent, was a minor one in England.

In the old days of subsistence agriculture, when the manor's produce went to feed the manor and the clink of a coin was seldom heard in the countryside, the surplus of an exceptional season, beyond what everyone could eat, went to waste. But for some time now a momentous change had been under way. The growth of town markets "put most men within the reach of opportunities of buying and selling."[69] The man most affected was the lord, if he awoke to his opportunity. Robert Grosseteste, the practical-minded bishop of Lincoln, urged his readers to ask "how profitable your plow and stock are."[70] Generally the answer was satis-

A person threshing corn, in an illustration for August from the calendar of an English psalter (c.1250–75).

factory. Not only that, but revenue from cash rents was increasing rapidly as the tenants took advantage of the market. One study of central England in 1279 indicates that even the villeins were now paying more than half their dues in money.[71] Besides rents, these included a long list of servile fees and the fines of the manorial court. The very number and variety of the lord's revenues probably helped blind everyone to the inefficiency of the system that supplied them. Like slavery, serfdom required continuous year-round maintenance of a labor force whose labor was needed only in varying degrees in different seasons.

Hired labor and cash rents were the wave of the future. So was the application of technical improvements. Some lords made an effort. Henry de Brays account book records a number of improvements added to his single manor, including building cottages for tenants, widening a stream to provide fish ponds, and constructing a mill and a bridge.[72] At Wharram Percy a wholesale reconstruction of the village was executed, evidently a rare seizure of the opportunity afforded a lord by his legal ownership of the village houses and land.[73] In the towns such a large-scale project was impossible; over centuries changes were restricted to individual building sites.

Naïve but intelligent Walter of Henley has been credited with pioneering scientific agriculture for his recommendations, admittedly general, for improving seed ("Seed grown on other ground will bring more profit than that which is grown on your own")[74] and breed ("Do not have boars and sows unless of a good breed").[75] The Elton records show evidence of attempts to improve the demesne seed by trading among manors. In 1286–1287, thirty rings of wheat were sent to the reeve of Abbot's Ripton and twenty received from the reeve of Weston.[76] *Seneschaucie* was more specific than Walter in respect to improving breeds, assigning the cowherd responsibility for choosing large bulls of good pedigree to pasture and mate with the cows.[77] Robert Trow-Smith believes the experts were heeded to some extent. Progressive lords such as the Hungerfords of Wiltshire imported rams from Lincolnshire and other regions of England, and Trow-Smith ventures a surmise that "the owners of the great ecclesiastical estates in particular" imported breeding stock from the Continent.[78]

Yet the only really widely used device for increasing agricultural production remained the old one of assarting, of enlarging the area of land by cutting down forest or draining marsh. In earlier centuries, when forest and marsh covered the countryside of northwest Europe,

a pioneering effort with axe and spade was natural and obvious. Now, in the late thirteenth century, as villages filled the landscape, scope for assarting was disappearing.

At the same time an opportunity was opening in the booming wool market. Exceeding in volume the demand for grain, meat, leather, and everything else were the purchases by the great merchant-manufacturers of the cloth cities of Flanders, France, and Italy. English wool was especially prized for its fineness, the most sought-after single characteristic of a fiber. Agents of the great wool firms often contracted with a monastic house like Ramsey Abbey for an entire year's clip, or even several years' clip, in advance. Prices remained very steady at four to five shillings a stone (1270–1320). The Elton demesne, which delivered 118 fleeces to Ramsey in 1287, in 1314 carted 521 to the abbey.[79] Clumsy, fragile, and vulnerable, but easy to feed, easy to handle, and producing its fleece reliably every year, the sheep was on its way to becoming England's national treasure.

Appreciative though they were of the wonderful wool market, most lords remained conservative in respect to change, "reluctant to spend heavily from current revenue upon improvements."[80] The most profitable part of the lord's land was the meadow, and the most valuable crop he could raise was hay for winter feed, but on most manors grain remained the top priority. Cereal agriculture retained a mystic prestige among the landholding class as it did, for sounder material reasons, among the peasants.[81]

When foreign wool buyers, their eye on long-term investments, insisted that the sheds where fleeces were shorn and stored be given boarded floors, as did a consortium of merchants from Cahors in dealing with the Cistercian abbey of Pipewell, the abbey gave in and boarded the floors, but that was as far as the lord cared to go in welcoming improvements.[82] The historic shift in British agriculture marked by the enclosure movement got under way, very slowly, only in the fifteenth century.

Content to see their revenues rise and their luxuries multiply, most lords preferred to assure themselves of all that was coming to them under the system rather than striving to improve the system. Manorial custom still ruled the countryside, its authority fortified by the new commitment to the written record, and neither lord nor peasant was sufficiently dissatisfied to press for change. The lord counted on custom to bring laborers to his fields, coins to his coffers, and poultry, cheese, meat, and ale to table. The villager relied on custom to limit services and payments, and to guarantee him his house, his croft, his strips of arable, and his grazing rights.

IV

THE VILLAGERS:
WHO THEY WERE

hree considerations governed the condition of the Elton villager: his legal status (free versus unfree), his wealth in land and animals, and (related to the first two criteria but independent of them) his social standing. How the villagers interacted has only recently drawn attention from historians. Earlier, the peasant's relationship with his lord dominated scholarly investigation. This "manorial aspect" of the peasant's life overshadowed the "village aspect," which, however, is older and more fundamental, the village being older than the manor. The fact that information about the village is harder to come by than information about the manor in no way alters this conclusion. The manor has been described historically as "a landowning and land management grid superimposed on the settlement patterns of villages and hamlets."[1]

Both village and manor played their part in the peasant's life. The importance of the manor's role depended on the peasant's status as a free man or villein, a distinction for which the lawyers strove to find a clear-cut criterion. Henry de Bracton, leading jurist of the thirteenth century, laid down the principle, *"Omnes homines aut liberi sunt aut servi"* (All men are either free or servile).[2] Bracton and his colleagues sought to fit the villein into Roman law, and in doing so virtually identified him as a slave. Neat though that correspondence might be in legal theory, it did not work in practice. Despite their *de jure* unfree status, many villeins succeeded *de facto* in appropriating the privileges of freedom. They bought, sold, bequeathed, and inherited property, including land. Practical need created custom, and custom overrode Roman legal theory.

Back at the time of the Domesday survey, the English villein was actually catalogued among the free men, "the meanest of the free," according to Frederic Maitland, ranking third among the five tiers of peasantry: *liberi homines* (free men); sokemen; villeins; cotters or bordars, equivalent to the serfs of the Continent; and slaves, employed on the lord's land as laborers and servants.[3] In the century after Domesday, slaves disappeared in England, by a process that remains obscure, apparently evolving into either manorial servants or villein tenants. But meanwhile by an equally obscure

Sowing winter grain, illustration for October, by the Limbourg Brothers from the *Très Riches Heures du Duc de Berry* (early 15th c.).

151

process the villein slipped down into the category of the unfree. Historians picture a series of pendulum swings in peasant status reflecting large external economic shifts, especially the growth of the towns as markets for agricultural produce. R. H. Hilton believes that the new obligations were imposed on the English villein mainly in the 1180s and 1190s.[4]

The unfreedom of the villein or serf was never a generalized condition, like slavery, but always consisted of specific disabilities: he owed the lord substantial labor services; he was subject to a number of fines or fees, in cash or in kind; and he was under the jurisdiction of the lord's courts. In Maitland's words, the serf, or villein, remained "a free man in relation to all men other than his lord."[5]

The very concepts of "free" and "unfree" involved a tangle of legal subtleties. On the Continent, nuances of freedom and servility developed early, and with them an array of Latin terms for the unfree: *mancipium, servus, colonus, lidus, collibertus, nativus.*[6] In England, terminology became even more complicated. The variety of nomenclature in Domesday Book, which derived in part from regional patterns of settlement, multiplied in the two subsequent centuries to a point where in Cambridgeshire in 1279 villagers were described by twenty different terms, some meaning essentially the same thing, some indicating slight differences. A few miles north, in southern Lincolnshire, eight more designations appeared. To what Edward Miller and John Hatcher call a "positive jungle of rules governing social relationships" was added the fact that land itself was classified as free or villein, meaning that it owed money rents or labor services. Originally villein tenants had held villein land, but by the thirteenth century many villeins held some free land and many free men some villein land.[7]

But if legal status was clouded by complexity, economic status tended to be quite clear, visible, and tangible: one held a certain number of acres and owned a certain number of cattle and sheep. Georges Duby, speaking of the Continent, observes, "Formerly class distinctions had been drawn according to hereditary and juridical lines separating free men from unfree, but by 1300 it was a man's economic condition which counted most."[8] In England the shift was perhaps a little slower, but unmistakably in the same direction. A rich villein was a bigger man in the village than a poor free man.

In the relations among villagers, what might be called the sociology of the village, much remains obscure, but much can be learned through analysis of the rolls of the manorial courts, which recorded not only enforcement of manorial obligations but interaction among the villagers, their quarrels, litigation, marriages, inheritance, sale and purchase of land, economic activities, and crimes.

Just at this moment a major aid in identification of individuals and families of villagers made its historic appearance: the introduction of surnames. A survey of Elton of about 1160 included in the Ramsey Abbey cartulary and listing current tenants, their fathers, and their grandfathers, gives only a handful of surnames. Where these occur they are taken from place of origin (Ralph of Asekirche, Ralph of Walsoken, Gilbert of Newton); from occupation (Thurold Priest [Presbyter], Thomas Clerk [Clericus], Gilbert Reeve [Praepositus], Ralph Shoemaker [Sutor]); or from paternity (Richard son of Reginald). But most of the villagers are listed only by their first names: Walter, Thomas, Ralph, Roger, Robert, Edward.[9]

A century later, manorial court rolls and a royal survey attach surnames to nearly all the Elton tenants. Some are in Latin, like the given names, some simply in English: Robertus ad Crucem (Robert at the Cross) and Henricus Messor (Henry Hayward), but Iohannes Page (John Page), Henricus Wollemonger (Henry Woolmonger), and Robertus Chapman (whose Old English name, meaning merchant, is cited in Latin elsewhere in the records as Robertus Mercator). Often it is difficult to tell whether the Latin represents a true surname or merely a trade or office: thus "Henricus Faber" may be Henry Smith; or he may be Henry the smith, and may be mentioned elsewhere in the records as Henry son of Gilbert, or Henry atte Water, or Henry of Barnwell. John Dunning's son who left the village and became a tanner at Hayham is always referred to as "John Tanner."

Nearly all surnames derived from the same three sources: parental (or grandparental) Christian names; occupations, offices, or occasionally legal status; and places, either of origin or in the village. In the first category are the Frounceys family, possibly deriving from a "Franceis" in the twelfth-century survey who held a virgate and six acres; the Goscelins; the Blundels (in the twelfth century a Blundel held three virgates); the Benyts (Benedicts); the Huberts; and numerous names prefaced by "son of" (Alexander son of Gilbert, Nicholas son of Henry, Robert son of John). In a few cases villagers are identified by their mothers' first names: William son of Letitia, Agnes daughter of Beatrice. J. A. Raftis in his study of the village of Warboys observed that surnames derived from parental Christian names gradually dropped the "son of" and

Boar Hunt at Vincennes, from the *Très Riches Heures du Duc de Berry* **(early 15th c.).**

became simply Alexander Gilbert, Nicholas Henry, Robert John. Finally, in the latter half of the fourteenth century, the "son" sometimes reappeared as a suffix: Johnson, Jameson, Williamson.[10]

In the category of occupations and offices, Elton names included Miller, Smith, Shoemaker, Carter, Carpenter, Chapelyn, Comber, Cooper, Dyer, Webster (weaver), Chapman (merchant), Shepherd, Tanner, Walker, Woolmonger, Baxter (baker), Tailor, Painter, Freeman, Hayward, and Beadle. No fewer than eight men in the court rolls in the last two decades of the thirteenth century bear the name Reeve, three in one court roll, and one man is given the name (in English) of Reeveson.

The category of names indicating origin usually derived from villages in the immediate vicinity of Elton:

Warmington, Morburn, Water Newton, Stanground, and Alwalton; Barnwell, Keyston, and Brington to the south; Barton in Bedfordshire; Clipsham in Lincolnshire; and Marholm, northwest of Peterborough. Surnames that derived from the part of the village where the family lived mix Latin and English, and occasionally French: Abovebrook, Ad Portam (at the gate), Ad Pontem (at the bridge), Ad Furnam (at the oven), atte (at the) Brook, atte Water, atte Well, Ordevill (hors de ville or Extra Villam, outside the village), In Venella (in the lane), In Angulo (in the nook or corner), Ad Ripam (at the riverbank). In time these were smoothed and simplified into plain Brooks, Gates, Bridges, Lane, Banks, Atwater, or Atwell.

A few Elton surnames seem to have come from personal characteristics or obscurely derived nicknames: L'Hermite (the hermit), Prudhomme (wise man), le Wyse, Child, Hering, Saladin, Blaccalf, Le Long, Le Rus. One family was named Peppercorn, one Mustard.★

Evidence suggests that village society everywhere was stratified into three classes. The lowest held either no land at all or too little to support a family. The middle group worked holdings of a half virgate to a full virgate. A half virgate (12 to 16 acres) sufficed to feed father, mother, and children in a good season; a full virgate supplied a surplus to redeem a villein obligation or even purchase more land. At the top of the hierarchy was a small class of comparatively large peasant landholders, families whose 40, 50, or even 100 acres might in a few generations raise them to the gentry, though at present they might be villeins.

A statistical picture of the pattern was compiled by Soviet economic historian E. A. Kosminsky, who analyzed the landholding information supplied by the Hundred Rolls survey of 1279 of seven Midland counties, including Huntingdonshire. He found that 32 percent of all the arable land formed the lord's demesne, 40 percent was held by villeins, and 28 percent by freeholders. About a fifth of the peasantry held approximately a virgate and more than a third held half-

---

★Surnames are spelled in a variety of ways in the records—for example, Prudhomme, Prodhomme, Prudomme, Prodom, Produmie, Prodome, Produme, Prodomme; Saladin, Saladyn, Saldy, Saldyn, Saldin, Salyn, Saln; Blaccalf, Blacchalf, Blacchelf, Blacchal, Blakchalf. We have chosen one spelling and used it throughout.

virgates. A few highly successful families had accumulated 100 acres or more. In general, the size of holdings was diminishing as the population grew. Out of 13,500 holdings in 1279, 46 percent amounted to 10 acres or less, probably near the minimum for subsistence.[11]

The Hundred Rolls data for Elton are in rough accord with the overall figures. The survey lists first the abbot's holdings; then the tenants, their holdings and legal status, and their obligations to abbot and king.[12]

The abbot's demesne contained the curia's acre and a half, his three hides of arable land, his sixteen acres of meadow and three of pasture, his three mills, and the fishing rights he held on the river.

The list of tenants was headed by "John, son of John of Elton," a major free tenant who held a hide (6 virgates, or 144 acres) of the abbot's land, amounting to a small estate within the manor, with its own tenants: one free virgater and nine cotters (men holding a cottage and a small amount of land).

Next were listed the abbot's other tenants, twenty-two free men, forty-eight villeins, and twenty-eight cotters; and finally the rector and four cotters who were his tenants.

These 114 names of heads of families by no means accounted for all the inhabitants of the village, or even the male inhabitants; at least 150 other identifiable names appear in the court rolls of 1279–1300, representing other family members, day laborers, manorial workers, and craftsmen.

John of Elton—or "John le Lord," as he is referred to in one court record—was the village's aristocrat, though devoid of any title of nobility. His miniature estate had been assembled by twelfth-century ancestors by one means or another.** Of his hide of land, thirty-six acres formed the demesne. He owed suit (attendance) to the abbot's honor court at Broughton, the court for the entire estate, as well as "the third part of a suit" (attendance at every third session) to the royal shire and hundred courts. His one free tenant, John of Langetoft,

**He apparently traced his family back to a "Richard son of Reginald," a free tenant in the survey of 1160, to whom Abbot Walter had granted two virgates of land formerly held by Thuri Priest. Richard may have inherited another virgate from his father, and the family seems to have acquired three virgates belonging to another landholder in the survey, one Reiner son of Ednoth.[13] In a survey of 1218, "John son of John of Elton" is listed as holding a hide of land "of the lord abbot of Ramsey."

held a virgate "by charter" (deed), and paid a token yearly rent of one penny. Half a virgate of the hide belonged to the abbot "freely in perpetual alms." The rest was divided among nine cotters (averaging out to eight acres apiece).

The abbot's twenty-two other tenants listed as free in the Hundred Rolls survey held varying amounts of land for which they owed minor labor services and money rent ranging from four shillings one penny a year to six shillings. Among them were three whose claim to freedom was later rejected by the manorial court, an indication of the uncertainty often surrounding the question of freedom.

The size of the holdings of these twenty-two tenants and the duties with which the holdings were burdened suggest a history that illustrates the changeable nature of manorial landholding. A given piece of land did not necessarily pass intact from father to son through several generations. Divided inheritance, gifts to younger sons, dowries to daughters, purchase and sale, all produced a shifting pattern which over time subdivided and multiplied holdings. In 1160 the twenty-two free tenants had been only nine, and in 1279 nine principal tenants still held the land from the lord abbot. But five of the nine had given (as dowry or inheritance) or sold parcels of their land to thirteen lesser tenants, who paid the principal tenants an annual rent.

One of these lesser tenants was Robert Chapman, listed in the rolls as a cotter on John of Elton's land, but whose name, meaning merchant, suggests his status as a rising parvenu. Evidently a newcomer to Elton, Robert in 1279 held in addition to his cottage three parcels of land totaling eighteen acres which he had undoubtedly purchased. On the other side of the social ledger was Geoffrey Blundel, whose ancestor in 1160 had held three virgates (seventy-two acres), but who in 1279 retained only a virgate and a half, and that divided among five lesser tenants. In the fluctuations of peasant landholding, as in that of their betters, some rose, some sank.

The forty-eight villeins of Elton—"customary tenants," subject to the "custom of the manor," meaning its labor services and dues—included thirty-nine virgaters and nine half-virgaters. Growth of population had turned some family virgates into half-virgates, a process that had advanced much farther elsewhere, often leaving no full virgaters at all. No Elton villein held more than a virgate, though land-rich villeins were a well-known phenomenon elsewhere.[14]

Elton's villeins performed substantial labor services, which were spelled out detail in the survey, the half-virgaters owing half the work obligations of the virgaters. This work had a monetary value, and exemption could be purchased by the tenant, with the price paid going to pay hired labor.

Every "work," meaning day's work, owed by the villein was defined. One day's harrowing counted as one work; so did winnowing thirty sheaves of barley or twenty-four sheaves of wheat; collecting a bag of nuts "well cleaned"; or working in the vineyard; or making a hedge in the fields of a certain length; or carrying hay in the peasant's cart; or if he did not have a cart, hens, geese, cheese, and eggs "on his back."[15]

The time of year affected the price of the work. Works done between August 1 and Michaelmas (September 29), the season of intensive labor, were more expensive. One Elton account records the price of a single work at a halfpenny for most of the year (September 29 to August 1), 2½ pence from August 1 to September 8, and a penny from then to September 29.[16] Later, works were simply priced at a halfpenny from Michaelmas to August 1 and a penny from August 1 to Michaelmas.[17]

In 1286, sixteen of the forty-eight customary tenants had all their year-round works commuted to money payments, and owed only the special works at harvest time.[18] From the annual fee paid by these tenants, called the *censum* (quit-rent), they were said to be tenants ad *censum,* or *censuarii.* The other customary tenants were *ad opus* (at work [services]) and were *operarii.* Though such substitution of money payments for labor services was convenient for the villein in many ways, in other ways it was a disadvantage. Much, obviously, depended on the size of the payment. J. A. Raftis has calculated that the amount of the *censum* paid by a Ramsey Abbey villein was substantially larger than the total sum of the prices of his individual works.[19] The Elton court rolls imply that it was not desirable to be placed *ad censum,* and in fact that tenants were so classed arbitrarily. In 1279 two villagers accused the reeve of "taking the rich off the *censum* and putting the poor on it," apparently in exchange for bribes.[20]

In addition to work services or the *censum,* the customary tenants were subject to a long list of special exactions not imposed on the free tenants. These fell into four categories: charges paid only by the villeins *ad opus;* those paid only by the *censuarii;* those paid by both groups; and the monopolies held by the lord.

The first category included several fines or fees that seem to be relics of services or of contributions in kind: "woolsilver," probably a substitute for a shearing service; "wardpenny" for serving as public watchman; "maltsilver" for making malt for the abbot's ale; "fishsilver" for supplying fish for his Lenten meals; and "vineyard silver" for work in the vineyard. "Foddercorn" was a payment in kind of a ring of oats from each virgate. "Filstingpound" seems to have been an insurance premium paid by the villeins to protect themselves against corporal punishment or against excessive fines in the manorial court. If a villein's daughter had sex out of wedlock, she or her father paid *leirwite* or *legerwite.*

The second category consisted of a special charge owed only by the *censuarii:* 120 eggs from each virgater, 60 at Christmas and 60 at Easter.[21]

In the third category were "heushire," or "house hire," rent for the house on the holding, and several charges whose French names indicate importation to England by the Conquest. Tallage was a yearly tax at Elton, set at eight pence,[22] but on some manors it was levied "at the lord's will"—whenever and however much he chose. When the villein succeeded to a holding, he paid an entry fine or *gersum,* in effect a tax on land. On most manors, when the villein died his family paid heriot, usually his "best beast," the "second best beast" commonly going to the rector of the church; this was a tax on chattels. If the villein's daughter married, she or her father paid merchet.

If the villein wished to leave the manor, he could do so with the payment of a yearly fee, at Elton usually two chickens or capons. This payment, known as *chevage,* was not always easy to collect. Some villagers paid regularly—Henry atte Water, Richard in the Lane, Richard Benyt who had left "to dwell on a free tenement," Simon son of Henry Marshal. Others balked, such as Henry Marshal's son Adam, dwelling at Alwalton with his three sisters in 1300. They were "to be distrained if they come upon the fee," but in 1308 they were still living outside the manor.[23] Another Marshal brother, Walter, refused to pay and in 1308 Robert Gamel and John Dunning, who had stood surety for him, were fined twelve pence and twelve capons "because the same Walter has not yet paid to the lord two capons which he is bound to pay him each year Easter while he dwells with his chattels outside the fee of the said lord, and because they are in arrears during the four years past."[24]

Even more intractable was John Nolly, who was recorded as living "outside the lord's fee" in 1307. John was arrested in 1312 "in the custody of the reeve and beadle, until he finds security to make corporeal residence upon the lord's fee with his chattels, and to make satisfaction to the lord for five capons which are in arrears." The record added: "And because the bailiff witnesses that he is excessively disobedient and refuses to pay the said capons, and that he owes five capons in arrears for the space of five years, it is commanded that he be arrested until he pays the aforesaid capons, and henceforth he is to make corporeal residence upon lord's fee." In 1322, however, the court was still calling for the arrest of John, "a bondman of the lord, who withdraws himself with his chattels from the lord's fee without license." The chattels—in legal theory the lord's property—were usually mentioned along with the villein himself; he "withdrew himself with his chattels" and was ordered to return and bring them back, or to pay the annual fee.[25]

The fourth class of villein obligation, deriving from the lord's monopolies, included the common mill, the common oven, his sheepfold, and his manorial court.

Next in the Hundred Rolls' list of tenants were the abbot's twenty-eight cotters, who in Elton were also villeins in legal status (though on other manors cotters might be free), but who held little or no land and consequently owed little labor. Each held a cottage and yard theoretically "containing one rod" in return for which they helped with the haying, harvesting, sheepshearing, and threshing but not the plowing (they lacked plows and plow beasts), and paid tallage, merchet, and a small rent. Four had besides their cottage and farmyard a croft of half an acre, but eight had only half a rod of yard, two had a sixth of a rod, and one, paying a minimum rent of sixpence a year, only a "messuage," a house and yard with no specification of its size. Like most cotters, they scraped a precarious livelihood by turning their hand to any kind of labor they could find. Most worked as day laborers, but some had craft skills. Among their suggestive names are Comber, Shepherd, Smith, Miller, Carter, and Dyer.

Last on the Hundred Rolls' list came the rector, who held as a free tenant a virgate of land pertaining to the church and another ten acres for which he paid the abbot a yearly rent of half a mark. Four cotters were settled on his land. One was Roger Clerk (Clericus), probably the curate. The other three were all from the same family, and may have been the rector's servants.

Not mentioned in the Hundred Rolls survey, though present in the twelfth-century Ramsey Abbey extent, was a special category of tenant in Elton and some of the other abbey villages, the *akermen* or *bovarii,* descendants of manorial plowmen of a century earlier who were endowed with land of their own, for which they paid a yearly rent. Very little can be gathered about them from the records, except that their combined rent for five virgates of land, 7 pounds 10 shillings, was high (30 shillings per virgate).[26]

Servants of the villagers are omitted from the Hundred Rolls, but are mentioned occasionally in the rolls of the manorial court: Edith Comber, maidservant *(ancilla)* to William son of Letitia, "carried away some of the lord's peas";[27] Alice, servant of Nicholas Miller, was fined for stealing hay and stubble;[28] John Wagge's male servant was fined for careless planting of beans in the lord's field;[29] Matilda Prudhomme's servant Hugh was attacked and wounded by John Blaccalf.[30]

Among the tenants listed in the Hundred Rolls

were many of the village's principal craftsmen. In Elton, the two gristmills were kept under the management of the manorial officials and the profits paid to the abbot. The miller was probably recompensed by a share of the "multure," the portion of flour kept as payment. In most villages the miller "farmed" the mill, paying a fixed sum to the lord and profiting from the difference between that and the multure. The popular reputation of the miller was notorious; Chaucer's miller

> . . . was a master-hand at stealing grain.
> He felt it with his thumb and thus he knew
> Its quality and took three times his clue—
> A thumb of gold, by God, to gauge an oat![31]

At Elton, the miller collected the toll from persons using the mill as a bridge to cross the Nene. One was relieved of his office in 1300 for "letting strangers cross without paying toll," in exchange for "a gift."

Two others, Matefrid and Stephen Miller, success-fully sued William of Barnwell in 1294 for slander in saying that they had taken two bushels of his malt "in a wrongful manner."[32] At the same court, however, the jurors found that another miller and his wife, Robert and Athelina Stekedec, had "unjustly detained" one whole ring of barley (four bushels). They were fined sixpence and ordered to make restitutions.[33]

Two bakers farmed Elton's communal ovens in 1286, Adam Brid paying an annual rent of 13 shillings 4 pence for one and Henry Smith 33 shillings 4 pence for the other.[34] The smithy was not nearly as valuable. Robert son of Henry Smith was recorded as paying an annual rent of two shillings in 1308.[35]

Other tradesmen appear in the court rolls: Thomas Dyer was accused by Agnes daughter of Beatrice of "unjust detention of cloth of linen weave," for the dyeing of which she had promised him a bushel of barley. The jurors decided that Thomas had "only acted justly," since Agnes had not paid him grain, and that he was entitled to hold on to the cloth until she did so.[36]

Baker and butcher shops (15th c.).

Several villagers were part-time butchers and paid, "for exercising the office," an annual fee of two capons: Ralph Hubert, Geoffrey Abbot, William of Bumstead, Robert Godswein, William of Barnwell, Thomas Godswein, Robert Stekedec (who was also a miller), and Richard Tidewell.

Robert Chapman cultivated land while at the same time practicing the trade of merchant. Robert is recorded as selling a bushel of wheat to Emma Prudhomme in 1294,[37] and later of suing her for a hood which she agreed to deliver to John son of John of Elton, but Emma "did not undertake to pay" for it.[38] Other villagers whose names suggest that they practiced trades were Ralph and Geoffrey Shoemaker, Elias and Stephen Carpenter, Roger and Robert Taylor (who may have made shoes, built houses, or made clothing), and William and Henry Woolmonger.

Dwelling uneasily on the fringes of the village, outside its organization, were a shifting set of "strangers." Several times villagers were fined for "harboring" them. They are characterized as "outside the assize": day laborers, itinerant craftsmen, and vagabonds, the latter a class who turn up frequently in the royal coroners' rolls. In 1312 six villagers were fined and commanded to desist from harboring strangers. Richard le Wyse harbored Henry the Cooper and his wife "to the harm of the village"; Robert Gamel harbored Gilbert from Lancashire; Margery daughter of Beatrice harbored Youn the Beggar; John Ballard, Geoffrey atte Cross, and Richard le Wyse commonly entertained strangers "to the terror of the villagers."[39]

In addition to these suspect outsiders, the village had its eccentrics and mentally ill. In 1306 John Chapman was admonished by the court to see that his son Thomas "who is partly a lunatic" (in parte lunaticus) should "henceforth behave himself among his neighbors."[40] The coroners' rolls record other cases involving mental aberration. In 1316 a peasant woman at Yelden, Bedfordshire, afflicted with "an illness called frenzy," got out of bed, seized an axe, slew her son and three daughters, and "hanged herself in her house on a beam with two cords of hemp."[41]

The peasants of a medieval village were once pictured as coexisting in a state of what might be called mediocre equality. Actually wide differences in wealth existed. Land was the most important kind of wealth, and the distribution of land was far from equal. Furthermore, some tenants, both villein and free, were increasing their holdings by buying or leasing from the others.

In theory, all land needed to be preserved and transmitted intact to heirs, both to protect the integrity of the holding for the family and to assure the lord of his rents and services. Alienation—sale—was therefore theoretically forbidden. In reality, sale and lease of land were prominent features of the court rolls of the late thirteenth century, and not new phenomena. The lord's acquiescence reflected the profits to be made from the transaction—the opportunity of raising rents and collecting license fees.

In Elton, where a substantial number of the tenants were free, many of the sales recorded were by free men, some of whom sold consistently, some of whom bought, some of whom both bought and sold. Transactions were nearly all small. John Hering appears in the court rolls in 1292 selling two and a half rods to Alice daughter of Bateman of Clipsham,[42] and again in 1300 selling an acre to Joan wife of Gilbert Engayne of Wansford and also half an acre to Richard of Thorpe Waterville.[43] In 1312 Thomas Chausey sold half an acre to Reginald of Yarwell and two rods to Richard Carpenter.[44] In 1322 Richard Fraunceys sold half an acre to John Smith and half an acre to Richard Eliot;[45] Richard Eliot, meanwhile, acquired another two acres from John Ketel, who also sold a rod of land to Richard Chapleyn of Wansford;[46] John Ketel at the same time bought half an acre of meadow from Clement Crane.[47] Among the villeins, Muriel atte Gate and William Harpe each sold an acre to Nicholas Miller "without the license of the lord" and were fined sixpence each.[48] The only sizable transaction before 1350 was that of Reginald Child and John son of Henry Reeve, who in 1325 divided between them a virgate of land that had belonged to John Wagge. Apparently because they had done so without license, they were fined two shillings "for having the judgment of the court," though the transaction seems to have stood.[49]

Anne De Windt, analyzing land transfers in the Ramsey Abbey village of King's Ripton, where only one of the tenants was free, found 292 transfers among the unfree tenants between 1280 and 1397, the majority dealing with plots of between one-half and two and a half acres in the open fields, the others houses, auxiliary buildings, houseplots, and closes. Approximately one-third of the population participated at one time or another in the real-estate market. Thirty-six percent of the deals involved less than an acre of land, 57 percent from one to ten acres, 7 percent from ten to twenty acres. Some of the buyers were evidently newcomers to the village, purchasing holdings. Others apparently bought to satisfy the needs of daughters and younger

The July wheat harvest, *Hours of Margaret de Foix*, salting manuscript (late 15th c.).

sons. Still others leased the land they had acquired to subtenants, becoming peasant landlords. By the last half of the fourteenth century, a few families in nearly every English village had accumulated enough land to constitute an elite peasant class.[50]

Land was not the only form of wealth. Few areas in the thirteenth century as yet put sheep- or cattle-raising ahead of crop farming, but many villagers owned animals. Information about village stock is scanty, but some has been gleaned from the records of royal taxes levied at intervals to finance war. Villagers were assessed on the basis of their livestock, grain, and other products. M. M. Postan has extracted valuable information from the assessment record of 1291, including data on five Ramsey Abbey villages. Elton was not among the five, but the figures may be taken as broadly typical of the region. They show the average taxpaying villager owning 6.2 sheep, 4.5 cows and calves, 3.1 pigs, and 2.35 horses and oxen. These figures do not mean that each villager owned approximately 16 animals. Exempt were the poor cotters who owned property worth less than 6 shillings 8 pence, about the value of one ox or cow. Furthermore, as Postan demonstrates, many taxpaying villagers owned no sheep, while a few rich peasants held a large fraction of the total village flock. Plow animals, cows, and pigs appear to have been distributed more evenly,[51] though another scholar, speaking of England in general, asserts that "the bulk of the people owned no more working animals, cows, and sheep, than were necessary for their own subsistence."[52]

The Elton manorial court rolls of the early 1300s list numbers of villagers, mostly customary tenants with virgates, but also a few cotters, whose "beasts" or "draught beasts" had committed trespasses "in the lord's meadow" or "in the lord's grain." In 1312 the beasts of twelve villagers grazed in the fields at a time prohibited by the village bylaws, or "trod the grain" of fellow villagers.[53] A number of villagers are mentioned as having horses, many as having sheep or pigs.

The village poor are specifically identified many times in the court rolls when they are forgiven their fines for offenses. Most are cotters. The coroners' rolls record the small tragedies of destitute villagers who "went from door to door to seek bread." Beatrice Bone, "a poor woman," was begging in Turvey, Bedfordshire, in 1273 when she "fell down because she was weak and infirm and died there . . . between prime and tierce," to

be found two days later by a kinswoman.[54] Joan, "a poor child aged five," walked through Risely begging for bread, fell from a bridge, and drowned."[55]

Perhaps as important as either legal status or wealth to most villagers was their standing among their neighbors, their place in the community. As in two other Ramsey Abbey villages studied by Edward Britton (Broughton)[56] and Edwin De Windt (Holywell-cum-Needingworth),[57] Elton shows evidence of a village hierarchy, signaled by the repeated service of certain families in village office, as reeve, beadle, jurors, ale tasters, and heads of tithings. All these officials were chosen by the villagers themselves. All the offices were positions of responsibility, served under oath, and subject to fines for dereliction. A total of over two hundred Elton families can be identified by name in the records between 1279 and 1346.★★★ Of these two hundred families, only forty-nine are recorded as providing village officials. The service of these elite families, moreover, was unevenly distributed:

  8 families had four or more members who served in a total of 101 offices
 14 families had two members who served in a total of 39 offices
 27 families had one member who served in a total of 41 offices

Thus eight families, 3.5 percent of the total village households, filled well over half the terms of office. The number of terms per individual officeholder varied from one to six.

Most of Elton's families who were active in pub-

★★★The Hundred Rolls of 1279, seventeen manorial court rolls (1279–1342), and ten manorial accounts (1286–1346).

lic service, including all eight very active families, were villein virgaters. Four members of the In Angulo family (literal translation: in the nook or corner, English equivalent unknown), accounted for a total of fourteen offices: Geoffrey, listed in the Hundred Rolls of 1279 as a villein and a virgater, served as juror in 1279; Michael as Juror in 1294, 1300, 1306, 1307, and 1312; Hugh as juror in 1300, 1307, 1312, and 1331, as reeve in 1323–1324 and again in 1324–1325; and William as juror in 1318 and 1322. Five members of the Gamel family served: Roger as juror in 1279 and 1294, ale taster in 1279; Robert as juror in 1292 and 1308; Philip as juror in 1300, ale taster in 1312; John as juror in 1308 and 1312 and ale taster in 1331; and Edmund as juror in 1342 and ale taster the same year. Four members of the Brington family served as jurors, Reginald three times. Four of the Child family served in eight offices, three as jurors, William Child three times as reeve. Four Abovebrooks were jurors, and one was also an ale taster. Four atte Crosses served, Alexander four times as juror and once as reeve. The Goscelins contributed jurors, two reeves, and a beadle. The Reeves were jurors, ale tasters, and, naturally, reeves.

That these same families also figure prominently in the court rolls for quarrels, suits, infractions, and acts of violence is a striking fact, corroborating Edward Britton's observations to the same effect about Broughton. Members of three of the most active families were fined and assessed damages in 1279 when Alexander atte Cross, Gilbert son of Richard Reeve, and Henry son of Henry Abovebrook "badly beat" the son of another virgater, Reginald le Wyse.[58] In 1294 Roger Goscelin "drew blood from Richer Chapeleyn," while the wives of two of the Angulo men quarreled and Michael's wife, Alice, "did hamsoken" on Geoffrey's wife, also named Alice — that is, assaulted her in own house; Michael's wife paid a fine and also gave sixpence for "license to agree" with her sister-in-law. Richard Benyt, twice a juror, "badly beat Thomas Clerk and did hamsoken upon him in his own house." John son of John Abovebrook, both father and son officeholders, "took the beasts of Maud wife of John Abovebrook," apparently his stepmother, "and drove them out of her close."[59]

In 1306 what sounds like a free-for-all involving the members of several of the elite families occurred. John Ketel, twice juror and twice ale taster, "broke the head" of Nicholas son of Richard Smith and badly beat Richard Benyt, "and moreover did hamsoken upon

him"; John son of Henry Smith, four times juror, "struck Robert Stekedec and drew blood from him," while his brother Henry Smith "pursued John [Smith] . . . with a knife in order that he might strike and wound him."[60]

Members of the elite families sued each other for debt, accused each other of libel, and committed infractions such as coming late to the reaping in the fall or not sending all of their household or "not binding the lord's wheat in the autumn as [their] neighbors did." Their daughters were convicted of "fornication": in 1303, Matilda daughter of John Abovebrook;[61] in 1307, Athelina Blakeman;[62] in 1312, Alice daughter of Robert atte Cross;[63] in 1316, two women of the In Angulo family, Muriel and Alice.[64]

In short, a handful of village families were active leaders in village affairs, on both sides of the law. Their official posts may have helped them maintain and improve their status, which in turn perhaps lent them a truculence reminiscent of the Tybalts and Mercutios of the Italian cities, with somewhat similar results.

From the terse wording of the court records, a few village personalities emerge. One is that of Henry Godswein, virgater, ale taster, and juror, who in 1279 was fined "because he refused to work at the second boon-work of the autumn and because he impeded said boon-work by ordering that everyone should go home early and without the permission of the bailiffs, to the lord's damage of half a mark."[65] Another is that of John of Elton the younger, whose troubles with his neighbors recur with regularity: a quarrel with his free tenant, John of Langetoft in 1292;[66] one with Emma Prudhomme in 1294;[67] a conviction of adultery in 1292 with Alice wife of Reginald le Wyse;[68] then an accusation of trespass by John Hering in 1306;[69] and finally an episode in 1306 in which John attacked one of his own tenants, John Chapman, "drove him out of his own house," and carried off the hay of Joan wife of Robert Chapman.[70]

Not all the troublemakers were from the elite families. One family that never appeared in the lists of officials but often in the court rolls was the Prudhommes, of whom William was one of Elton's cotters and Walter a free virgater. Walter's wife Emma and Matilda, possibly William's wife, appear a number of times, quarreling with their neighbors, suing or being sued, or as brewers. The family produced the only murderer among the Elton villagers to be named in the court rolls (homicides were judged in royal courts): Richard Prudhomme, who in 1300 was convicted of killing Goscelyna Crane.[71] The Sabbes, also, were prominent mainly for their participation in quarrels and violence, and one of their members, Emma, was fined for being a *"fornicatrix"* and "as it were a common woman," a whore.[72]

Through the formulas and the abbreviated Latin of the court rolls, the villagers' speech echoes only remotely. Prudence Andrew, in *The Constant Star,* a novel about the Peasants' Rebellion of 1381, follows a popular tradition by recording her hero's speech as on an intellectual level above just that of the donkey with whom he sometimes sleeps. No reliable real-life source exists for the everyday speech of the English peasantry (though Chaucer yields hints), but the Inquisition records for the village of Montaillou, in the Pyrenees, roughly contemporary with the court records of Elton, cast valuable light.[73] The Montaillou peasants talk freely, even glibly, about politics, religion, and morality, philosophizing and displaying lively intelligence, imagination, humor, and wisdom. The Elton court records give us a single glimpse of peasants in an informal dialogue. The villagers were gathered in the churchyard on the Sunday before All Saints, when three people belonging to the elite families, Richer son of Goscelin and Richard Reeve and his wife, confronted Michael Reeve "with most base words in front of the whole parish." They accused Michael of a number of corrupt practices often imputed to reeves: "that he reaped his grain in the autumn by boon-works performed by the abbot's customary tenants, and plowed his land in Eversholmfield with the boon plows of the village; that he excused customary tenants from works and carrying services on condition that they leased their lands to him at a low price"; and finally "that he had taken bribes from the rich so that they should not be *censuarii,* and [instead] put the poor *ad censum.*"

Michael sued for libel, and the jurors pronounced him "in no article guilty," fined Richard Reeve and Richer Goscelin two shillings and 12 pence respectively, and ordered Richard Reeve to pay Michael the substantial sum of ten shillings in damages. Michael later forgave all but two shillings of the award.[74]

V

THE VILLAGERS: HOW THEY LIVED

All the villagers of Elton, free, villein and of indeterminate status, virgaters, half-virgaters, cotters, servants, and craftsmen, lived in houses that shared the common characteristic of impermanence. Poorly built, of fragile materials, they had to be completely renewed nearly every generation. At Wharram Percy, nine successive transformations of one house can be traced over a span of little more than three centuries. The heir's succession to a holding probably often supplied an occasion for rebuilding. For reasons not very clear, the new house was often erected adjacent to the old site, with the alignment changed and new foundations planted either in postholes or in continuous foundation trenches.[1]

Renewal was not always left to the tenant's discretion. The peasant taking over a holding might be bound by a contract to build a new house, of a certain size, to

The main Hall (14th c.) with open fireplace at Bunratty Castle, Ireland.

be completed within a certain time span. Sometimes the lord agreed to supply timber or other assistance.[2] The lord's interest in the proper maintenance of the houses and outbuildings of his village was sustained by the manorial court. In Elton in 1306, Aldusa Chapleyn had to find pledges to guarantee that she would "before the next court repair her dwelling house in as good a condition as she received it."[3] Two years later, William Rouvehed was similarly enjoined to "repair and rebuild his dwelling house in as good a condition as that in which he received it for a gersum [entry fee],"[4] and in 1331 three villagers were fined 12 pence each because they did not "maintain [their] buildings."[5]

All the village houses belonged to the basic type of medieval building, the "hall," as did the manor house, the barns, and even the church: a single high-ceilinged room, varying in size depending on the number of bays or framed sections. In peasants' houses, bays were usually about fifteen feet square.[6]

The house of a rich villager such as John of Elton might consist of four or even five bays, with entry in the middle of a long side. Small service rooms were probably partitioned off at one end: a buttery, where drink was kept, and a pantry, for bread, dishes, and utensils, with a passage between leading to a kitchen outside. A

Stewing, chopping vegetables and pounding with a pestle and mortar from the *Latin/Luttrell Psalter* (14th c.).

"solar," a second story either above the service rooms or at the other end, may have housed a sleeping chamber. A large hall might retain the ancient central hearth, or be heated by a fireplace with a chimney fitted into the wall. Early halls were aisled like churches, with the floor space obstructed by two rows of posts supporting the roof. Cruck construction had partially solved the problem, and by the end of the thirteenth century, carpenters had rediscovered the roof truss, known to the Greeks and Romans. Based on the inherent strength of the triangle, which resists distortion, the truss can support substantial weight.[7]

A middle-level peasant, a virgater such as Alexander atte Cross, probably lived in a three-bay house, the commonest type. A cotter like Richard Trune might have a small one- or two-bay house. Dwellings commonly still lodged animals as well as human beings, but the byre was more often partitioned off and sometimes positioned at right angles to the living quarters, a configuration that pointed to the European farm complex of the future, with house and outbuildings ringing a central court.[8]

Interiors were lighted by a few windows, shuttered but unglazed, and by doors, often open during the daytime, through which children and animals wandered freely. Floors were of beaten earth covered with straw or rushes. In the center, a fire of wood, or of peat, commonly used in Elton,[9] burned on a raised stone hearth, vented through a hole in the roof. Some hearths were crowned by hoods or funnels to channel the smoke to the makeshift chimney, which might be capped by a barrel with its ends knocked out. The atmosphere of the house was perpetually smoky from the fire burning all day as water, milk, or porridge simmered in pots on a trivet or in footed brass or iron kettles. At night a fire-cover, a large round ceramic lid with holes, could be put over the blaze.[10]

A thirteenth-century writer, contrasting the joys of a nun's life with the trials of marriage, pictured the domestic crisis of a wife who hears her child scream and hastens into the house to find "the cat at the bacon and the dog at the hide. Her cake is burning on the [hearth] stone, and her calf is licking up the milk. The pot is boiling over into the fire, and the churl her husband is scolding."[11]

Medieval sermons, too, yield a glimpse of peasant interiors: the hall "black with smoke," the cat sitting by the fire and often singeing her fur, the floor strewn with green rushes and sweet flowers at Easter, or straw in winter. They picture the housewife at her cleaning: "She takes a broom and drives all the dirt of the house together; and, lest the dust rise . . . she casts it with great violence out of the door." But the work is never done: "For, on Saturday afternoon, the servants shall sweep the house and cast all the dung and the filth behind the door in a heap. But what then? Come the capons and the hens and scrape it around and make it as ill as it was before." We see the woman doing laundry, soaking the clothes in lye (homemade with ashes and water), beating and scrubbing them, and hanging them up to dry. The dog, driven out of the kitchen with a basinful of hot water, fights over a bone, lies stretched in the sun with flies settling on him, or eagerly watches people eating until they throw him a morsel, "whereupon he turns his back."[12]

The family ate seated on benches or stools at a trestle table, disassembled at night. Chairs were rarities. A cupboard or hutch held wooden and earthenware bowls, jugs, and wooden spoons. Hams, bags, and baskets hung from the rafters, away from rats and mice. Clothing, bedding, towels, and table linen were stored in chests. A well-to-do peasant might own silver spoons, brass pots, and pewter dishes.[13]

When they bathed, which was not often, medieval villagers used a barrel with the top removed. To lighten the task of carrying and heating water, a family probably bathed serially in the same water.[14]

At night, the family slept on straw pallets, either on the floor of the hall or in a loft at one end, gained by a ladder. Husband and wife shared a bed, sometimes with the baby, who alternatively might sleep in a cradle by the fire.

Manorial accounts yield ample information about

what the abbot of Ranney ate, especially his feast-day diet, which included larks, ducks, salmon, kid, chickens at Easter, a boar at Christmas, and capons and geese on other occasions.[15] The monks ate less luxuriously. For their table, Elton (and other manors) supplied the cellarer at Ramsey with bacon, beef, lambs, herring, butter, cheese, beans, geese, hens, and eggs, as well as flour and meal. The inhabitants of the curia, including the reeve, the beadle, some of the servants, and "divers workmen and visitors from time to time," also ate comparatively well, consuming large quantities of grain in various forms as well as peas, beans, bacon, chickens, ducks, cheese, and butter. Food was no small part of the remuneration of servants and staff of a manor. Georges Duby cites the carters of Battle Abbey, who demanded rye bread, ale, and cheese in the morning, and meat or fish at midday.[16]

Less evidence exists for the diet of the average peasant. The thirteenth-century villager was a cultivator rather than a herdsman because his basic need was sub-

sistence, which meant food and drink produced from grain. His aim was not exactly self-sufficiency, but self-supply of the main necessities of life.[17] These were bread, pottage or porridge, and ale. Because his wheat went almost exclusively to the market, his food and drink crops were barley and oats. Most peasant bread was made from "maslin," a mixture of wheat and rye or barley and rye, baked into a coarse dark loaf weighing four pounds or more, and consumed in great quantities by men, women, and children.[18]

For the poorer peasant families, such as the Trunes or the Saladins of Elton, pottage was favored over bread as more economical, since it required no milling and therefore escaped both the miller's exaction and the natural loss of quantity in the process. Barley grains destined for pottage were allowed to sprout in a damp, warm place, then were boiled in the pot. Water could be drawn off, sweetened with honey, and drunk as barley water, or allowed to ferment into beer. Peas and beans supplied scarce protein and amino acids to both pottage and bread. A little fat bacon or salt pork might be added to the pottage along with onion and garlic from the garden. In spring and summer a variety of vegetables was available: cabbage, lettuce, leeks, spinach, and parsley. Some crofts grew fruit trees, supplying apples, pears, or cherries. Nuts, berries, and roots were gathered in the woods. Fruit was usually cooked; raw fruit was thought unhealthy. Except for poisonous or very bitter plants, "anything that grew went into the pot, even primrose and strawberry leaves."[19] The pinch came in the winter and early spring, when the grain supply ran low and wild supplements were not available.

Stronger or weaker, more flavorful or blander, the pottage kettle supplied many village families with their chief sustenance. If possible, every meal including breakfast was washed down with weak ale, home-brewed or purchased from a neighbor, but water often had to serve. The most serious shortage was protein. Some supplement for the incomplete protein of beans and peas was available from eggs, little from meat or cheese, though the wealthier villagers fared better than the poor or middling. E. A. Kosminsky believed that the virgater and half-virgater could have "made ends meet without great difficulty, had it not been for the weight of feudal exploitation"—that is, the labor services and other

Family before fireplace hearth, in an illustration from the January Sign of Capricorn (Fresco, 15th c.).

villein obligations—but that a quarter virgate (five to eight acres) did not suffice even in the absence of servile dues.[20] H. S. Bennett calculated the subsistence level as lying between five and ten acres, "probably nearer ten than five." The most recent scholarly estimate, by H. E. Hallam (1988), is that twelve acres was needed for a statistical family of 4.75. J. Z. Titow pointed out that more acreage was needed per family in a two-field system than a three-field system, since more of each holding was lying fallow. Cicely Howell, studying data from the Midland village of Kibworth Harcourt, concluded that not until the mid-sixteenth century could the half-virgater provide his family with more than eight bushels of grain a year per person from his own land. Poor families survived only by their varied activities as day laborers.[21]

Besides the shortage of protein, medieval diets were often lacking in lipids, calcium, and vitamins A, C, and D.[22] They were also often low in calories, making the inclusion of ale a benefit on grounds of health as well as recreation. Two positive aspects of the villagers' austere regimen—its low protein and low fat content—gave it some of the virtues of the modern "heart-smart" diet, and its high fiber was a cancer preventative.

A middling family like that of Alexander atte Cross or Henry Abovebrook probably owned a cow or two or a few ewes, to provide an intermittent supply of milk, cheese, and butter. Most households kept chickens and pigs to furnish eggs and occasional meat, but animals, like wheat, were often needed for cash sales to pay the rent or other charges. Salted and dried fish were available for a price, as were eels, which also might be fished from the Nene or poached from the millpond.

Medieval literature voiced the popular hunger for protein and fat. A twelfth-century Irish poet describes a dream in which a coracle "built of lard/ Swam a sweet milk sea," and out of a lake rose a castle reached by a bridge of butter and surrounded by a palisade of bacon, with doorposts of whey curds, columns of aged cheese, and pillars of pork. Across a moat of spicy broth covered with fat, guards welcomed the dreamer to the castle with coils of fat sausages.[23]

It was a hungry world, made hungrier by intermittent crop failures, one series of which in the early fourteenth century brought widespread famine in England and northwest Europe. The later, even more devastating cataclysm of the Black Death so reduced the European population that food became comparatively plentiful and the peasants took to eating wheat. The poet John Gower (d. 1408) looked back on the earlier, hungrier period not in sorrow but rather with an indignant nostalgia that reflected the attitude of the elite toward the lower classes:

> Laborers of olden times were not wont to eat wheaten bread; their bread was of common grain or of beans, and their drink was of the spring. Then cheese and milk were a feast to them; rarely had they any other feast than this. Their garment was of sober gray; then was the world of such folk well ordered in its estate.[24]

The peasant's "garment" has often been pictured in the illuminations of manuscripts, but only occasionally in "sober gray"; the colors shown are more often bright blues, reds, and greens. Whether Gower's memory was accurate is uncertain. Peasants did have access to dyestuffs, and Elton had a dyer.

Over the period of the high Middle Ages, styles of clothing of nobles and townspeople changed from long, loose garments for both men and women to short, tight, full-skirted jackets and close-fitting hose for men and trailing gowns with voluminous sleeves, elaborate headdresses, and pointed shoes for women. Peasant dress, however, progressed little. For the men, it consisted of a short tunic, belted at the waist, and either short stockings that ended just below the knee or long hose fastened at

Woman throwing corn to hens and chickens from the *Latin/Luttrell Psalter* **(14th c.).**

Christmas Nativity scene in an illuminated capital initial from a French Book of Hours (c.1490).

the waist to a cloth belt. A hood or cloth cap, thick gloves or mittens, and leather shoes with heavy wooden soles completed the costume. The women wore long loose gowns belted at the waist, sometimes sleeveless tunics with a sleeved undergarment, their heads and necks covered by wimples. Underclothing, when it was worn, was usually of linen; outer garments were woolen.

The tunic of a prosperous peasant might be trimmed with fur, like the green one edged with squirrel found by three Elton boys in 1279 and turned over to the reeve.[25] A poor peasant's garb, on the other hand, might resemble that of the poor man in Langland's fourteenth-century allegory, *Piers Plowman,* whose "coat was of a [coarse] cloth called cary," whose hair stuck through the holes in his hood and whose toes stuck through those in his heavy shoes, whose hose hung loose, whose rough mittens had worn-out fingers covered with mud, and who was himself "all smeared with mud as he followed the plow," while beside him walked his wife carrying the goad, in a tunic tucked up to her knees, wrapped in a winnowing sheet to keep out the cold, her bare feet bleeding from the icy furrows.[26]

The village world was a world of work, but villagers nevertheless found time for play. Every season was brightened by holiday intervals that punctuated the Christian calendar. Many of these were ancient pagan celebrations, appropriated by the Church, often with little alteration of their character. Each of the seasons of the long working year, from harvest to harvest, offered at least one holiday when work was suspended, games were played, and meat, cakes, and ale were served.

On November 1, bonfires marked All Hallows, an old pagan rite at which the spirits of the dead were propitiated, now renamed All Saints. Martinmas (St. Martin's Day, November 11) was the feast of the plowman, in some places celebrated with seed cake, pasties, and a frumenty of boiled wheat grains with milk, currants, raisins, and spices.

The fortnight from Christmas Eve to Twelfth Day (Epiphany, January 6) was the longest holiday of the year, when, as in a description of twelfth-century London, "every man's house, as also their parish churches, was decked with holly, ivy, bay, and whatsoever the season of the year afforded to be green."[27] Villagers owed extra rents, in the form of bread, eggs, and hens for the lord's table, but were excused from work obligations for the

fortnight and on some manors were treated to a Christmas dinner in the hall.

This Christmas bonus often reflected status. A manor of Wells Cathedral had the tradition of extending invitations to two peasants, one a large landholder, the other a small one. The first was treated to dinner for himself and two friends and served "as much beer as they will drink in the day," beef and bacon with mustard, a chicken stew, and a cheese, and provided with two candles to burn one after the other "while they sit and drink." The poorer peasant had to bring his own cloth, cup, and trencher, but could take away "all that is left on his cloth, and he shall have for himself and his neighbors one wastel [loaf] cut in three for the ancient Christmas game to be played with the said wastel."[28] The game was evidently a version of "king of the bean," in which a bean was hidden in a cake or loaf, and the person who found it became king of the feast. On some Glastonbury Abbey manors, tenants brought firewood and their own dishes, mugs, and napkins; received bread, soup, beer, and two kinds of meat; and could sit drinking in the manor house after dinner.[29] In Elton the manorial servants had special rations, which in 1311 amounted to four geese and three hens.[30]

In some villages, the first Monday after Epiphany was celebrated by the women as Rock (distaff) Monday and by the men as Plow Monday, sometimes featuring a plow race. In 1291 in the Nottinghamshire village of Carlton, a jury testified that it was an ancient custom for the lord and the rector and every free man of the village

The Crucifixion from the *Evesham Psalter* (c.1246).

Celebrated with games, Easter week ended with Hocktide, marked in a later day, and perhaps in the thirteenth century, by the young women of the village holding the young men prisoner until they paid a fine, and the men retaliating on the second day.[32]

On May Day the young people "brought in the May," scouring the woods for boughs from flowering trees to decorate their houses. Sometimes they spent the night in the woods.

Summertime Rogation Days, when the peasants walked the boundaries of the village, were followed by Whitsunday (Pentecost), bringing another week's vacation for most villeins. St. John's Day (June 24) saw bonfires lit on the hilltops and boys flourishing brands to drive away dragons. A fiery wheel was rolled downhill, symbolizing the sun's attaining the solstice.[33]

Lammas (August 1) marked the end of the hay harvest and the beginning of grain harvest, with its "boons" or precarias, when all the villagers came to reap the lord's grain and were treated to a feast that in Elton in 1286 included an ox and a bullock, a calf, eighteen doves, seven cheeses, and a quantity of grain made into bread and pottage.[34] On one Oxfordshire manor it was customary for the villagers to gather at the hall for a songfest—"to sing harvest home."[35] Elton records mention an occasional "repegos," a celebration at which the harvesters feasted on roast goose.[36]

One holiday, Wake Day, the feast of the local parish saint, varied from place to place. Probably in the thirteenth century, as later, the villagers kept vigil all night, in the morning heard Mass in honor of their patron saint, then spent the day in sports. Often the churchyard was turned into a sports arena, a usage deplored by the clergy. Robert Manning wrote in his *Handlyng Synne* (1303), a verse translation of a thirteenth-century French *Manuel des Pechiez* (Manual of Sins):

> Carols, wrestling, or summer games
> Whosoever haunteth any such shames
> In church, or in churchyard
> Of sacrilege he may be afraid;
> Or interludes, or singing,
> Or tambour beat, or other piping,
> All such thing forbidden is
> While the priest standeth at Mass.★[37]

★Like all other excerpts in Middle English in this book, this is translated into modern English.

to report with his plow to a certain field that was common to "the whole community of the said village" after sunrise on "the morrow of Epiphany" and "as many ridges as he can cut with one furrow in each ridge, so many may he sow in the year, if he pleases, without asking for license."[31]

Candlemas (February 2), commemorating Mary's "churching," the ceremony of purification after childbirth, was celebrated with a procession carrying candles. It was followed by Shrove Tuesday, the last day before Lent, an occasion for games and sports.

At Easter, the villagers gave the lord eggs, and he gave the manorial servants and sometimes some of the tenants dinner. Like Christmas, Easter provided villeins a respite—one week—from work on the demesne.

A preacher condemned the common people's enjoyment of "idle plays and japes, carolings, making of fool countenances . . . [giving] gifts to jongleurs to hear idle tales . . . smiting . . . wrestling, in other doing deeds of strength."[38]

Many of the games enjoyed by the villagers were played alike by children, adolescents, and adults, and endured into modern times: blind man's buff, prisoner's base, bowling. Young and old played checkers, chess, backgammon, and most popular of all, dice. Sports included football, wrestling, swimming, fishing, archery, and a form of tennis played with hand coverings instead of rackets. The Luttrell Psalter (c. 1340) portrays a num-

Sir Geoffrey Luttrell (1276–1345) on horseback with his wife and daughter-in-law. He commissioned the psalter from which this is taken—the *Latin/Luttrell Psalter* (14th c.).

ber of mysterious games involving sticks and balls and apparatus of various kinds, remote ancestors of modern team sports. Bullbaiting and cockfighting were popular spectator sports.

Yet the favorite adult recreation of the villagers was undoubtedly drinking. Both men and women gathered in the "tavern," usually meaning the house of a neighbor who had recently brewed a batch of ale, cheap at the established price of three gallons for a penny. There they passed the evening like modern villagers visiting the local pub. Accidents, quarrels, and acts of violence sometimes followed a session of drinking, in the thirteenth century as in subsequent ones. Some misadventures may be deduced from the terse manorial court records. The rolls of the royal coroners, reporting fatal accidents, spell many out in graphic detail: In 1276 in Elstow, Osbert le Wuayl, son of William Cristmasse, coming home at about midnight "drunk and disgustingly over-fed," after an evening in Bedford, fell and

The right to brew ale/beer was one of the royal privileges bestowed upon the bishopric of Tournai. Stained glass, by Arnold van Nijmegen (1470–1530?) (c.1490). Cathedral of Notre Dame, Paris.

the Bedfordshire coroners' rolls attest. In 1266, "about bedtime," three men who had been drinking in a Bedford tavern fell to quarreling on the king's highway, two attacking the third and stabbing him in the heart with a sickle.[41] In 1272 in Bromham, four men who had been drinking in a tavern accosted a passerby, Ralph, son of the vicar of Bromham, and demanded to know who he was. Ralph replied defiantly, "A man, who are you?" Whereupon one of the men, Robert Barnard of Wooton, "because he was drunk," struck Ralph over the head with an axe. Ralph's widow testified that all four men had assaulted her husband with axes and staves, and accused the tavern keeper and his wife of having instigated the attack.[42] In another case, an innocent bystander was killed. Four villagers of Wooton who had been drinking in Bedford were returning home when one of them suddenly "and with no ulterior motive" turned, drew his bow, and took aim at a man who was following them. The only woman in the party, Margery le Wyte, threw herself between the two men and received the arrow in her throat "so that she immediately died."[43]

Not all village violence was drink-related. The subject of the numerous altercations recorded in the Elton court records is not usually given, but the coroners' rolls report quarrels about debt, in one case a halfpenny one brother lent another, thefts (a bushel of flour, a basket, a hen), trespass, and once simply "an old hatred." Occasionally the subject was a woman: two brothers in Radwell, Bedfordshire, found their sister Juliana "lying under a haystack" with a young man who "immediately arose and struck [one of the brothers] on the top of the head, to the brain, apparently with an axe, so that he immediately died." The lovers fled.[44] Domestic quarrels got out of hand, as when Robert Haring of Aston, Bedfordshire, and his wife Sybil fell to quarreling, and a friend eating lunch with them tried to intervene as peacemaker and was slain by an axe blow.[45]

Occasionally violence came on a larger scale. The Bedfordshire coroner reported homicides resulting from a melee between the men of a knight's household and those of the prior of Lanthony; from the siege of a church in a dispute over the right to a piece of land, involving large numbers of attackers and besiegers; and

struck his head fatally on a stone "breaking the whole of his head."[39] One man tumbled off his horse riding home from the tavern; another fell into a well in the marketplace and drowned; a third, relieving himself in a pond, fell in; still another, carrying a pot of ale down the village street, was bitten by a dog, tripped while picking up a stone to throw, and struck his head against a wall; a child slipped from her drunken mother's lap into a pan of hot milk on the hearth.[40]

Many violent quarrels followed drinking bouts, as

from a pitched battle between the villages of St. Neots and Little Barford.[46]

Besides such amateur lawbreakers, bands of professional criminals roamed the countryside. Bedfordshire coroners recorded the depredations of one gang of thieves who in 1267 came to the village of Honeydon at about vespers, armed with swords and axes, seized a boy named Philip "who was coming from his father's fold," "beat, ill-treated, and wounded him," and forced him to accompany them to the house of Ralph son of Geoffrey. Recognizing the boy's voice, Ralph opened the door, the thieves fell upon him, wounded him, and tied him up, killed his mother and a servant, and ransacked the house. They then broke into and burglarized seven more houses, killing and wounding several more people. The boy Philip at last managed to escape and give the alarm, but the gang fled and apparently was never apprehended.[47]

Another band of "felons and thieves" committed a similar assault on the village of Roxton in 1269, breaking through the wall of a house and carrying away "all the goods," breaking into the house next door and murdering a woman in her bed, finally invading the house of John the Cobbler by breaking a door and windows, dragging John out and killing him, and wounding his wife, daughter, and a servant. A second daughter hid "between a basket and a chest" and escaped to give the alarm. In this case the thieves were identified by the dying wife of John the Cobbler, one as a former servant of the prior of Newnham, the others as men who had collected the tithes for the prior of Cauldwell and as "glovers of Bedford." They were arrested and brought to justice.[48]

One thief became a victim of his own crime when he entered a house by a ladder to purloin a ham hanging from a roof beam. When the householder, Matilda Bolle, saw him leaving and gave the alarm, he panicked, tumbled from the ladder, and died of a broken neck.[49]

E dieu damour de larc tedu
my auoit toute iour actedu
A moy pourfuiure et efpier
Si farrefta foubz vng figuier
Et quant il eut len en...

VI

MARRIAGE AND THE FAMILY

ithin the village community, the basic social and economic unit was the family household. The number of its members fluctuated through the generational cycle: young couple, couple with children, with grandparents, with brother or sister (or aunt or uncle), solitary widow or widower. Information about the composition of the average household is scarce and unreliable, but the consensus among scholars is that it was small, with no more than five members, and most commonly nuclear—that is, husband and wife with or without children. Size of household tended to reflect economic status, rich households supporting more children, other relatives, and a servant or two.[1]

One important characteristic of the thirteenth-century peasant household was its autonomy. The larger kinship groupings (clan, sippe, kindred) that had played an important role in Anglo-Saxon England and early

medieval France and Germany had lost their powers of protection and supervision, along with the need for such powers. Their functions had been taken over by new police and judicial agencies of the community and state.

The two great fundamentals of family history are marriage and inheritance, always closely linked. In open field country, impartible (undivided) inheritance was the general rule, holdings passing to a single heir, usually the eldest son. A study of seventy-five cases of succession in the Midland village of Wakefield showed that a single son inherited from a father in forty-seven cases; in nine, in the absence of a son, a daughter or daughters did so. In the remaining nineteen cases, a son or daughter succeeded a mother, a brother or sisters succeeded a brother, an uncle succeeded a nephew or niece, a cousin succeeded a cousin, and in one case a (presumably second) husband succeeded a wife. If there was no son but two or more daughters, land was divided among the daughters.[2]

Widows had inferior but definite rights that varied from place to place. Under common (feudal) law, a widow's portion of an estate was from one third to one half, but a widow often automatically succeeded a husband in a peasant holding, not as the heiress, but as the surviving co-tenant. This arrangement allowed her to

God of Love Aiming at Lovers, illuminated by the Master of the Prayer Books, from the *Roman de la Rose* (c. 1487–95).

173

support the family and hold it together. A widow might be pressured by the lord to remarry, to insure that the holding had a man to perform its labor services, but she might preserve her freedom by hiring workers. Most widows eventually married, or turned over the holding to an adult son, but some, like Cecilia Benyt of Cuxham (Oxfordshire), remained in possession of the family holding, never remarrying, although her son was an adult and in fact reeve.[3] Widows' rights, says Rosamond Faith, "seem to have been by far the most durable and firmly established of all inheritance customs."[4] Widows' rights, and inheritance customs in general, were influenced by the longterm fluctuations in availability of land. The scarcer land became, the more attractive a widow became.

A grand principle of inheritance had come to be very widely accepted: "An established holding ought to descend in the blood of the men who . . . held it of old," sometimes expressed as "keeping the name on the land."[5] No one yet disputed the lord's title to his entry fee and even his heriot [death duty], but by now, legal doctrine notwithstanding, the land was felt to belong to the tenant, villein or free, who plowed, harrowed, and planted it. Tradition was even strong enough to inhibit the ford from raising the rent on a holding when a normal succession took place (alert lords and stewards made sure to raise it when a tenant died without heir and a new tenant was found).

The entry fee was substantial, arbitrary, and proportional to the size of the holding: in Elton in 1313, "four shillings from Henry Reed to have one cottage formerly his father's"; "13 shillings 4 pence from Ralph son of Gilbert Shepherd to have one cottage and eight acres of land formerly his father's"; and "60 shillings from John son of Henry Reeve to have one virgate of land formerly his father's." Sometimes the connection between heir and dead tenant is not clear; while Gilbert Shepherd's son Ralph inherited his father's holding, another son, John, paid an entry fee of 2 shillings "to have one cottage formerly belonging to Margery Carter."[6]

Manorial courts sometimes had to rule on complicated inheritance questions. In the Bedfordshire village of Chalgrave in 1279, Richard son of Thomas Ballard presented himself and "demanded the land which was his father's." Investigation showed that Richard had had an elder brother named Walter, who had died, leaving sons. These sons "would have been the next heirs if Walter had held the land while he lived, but he did not have possession of the land, therefore [the

jurors] say that Richard himself is the next heir." The custom of the manor, however, was that "no customary tenant can enter such land after the death of his father while his mother is alive, unless the mother shall agree, and . . . his mother will hold the land all her life if she shall wish." Richard therefore agreed to pay his mother, Avice, a yearly ration of winter wheat (frumentum), beans, and spring wheat (tramesium). Richard paid 12 pence entry fee and promised to do the services "due and accustomed" for the holding, as well as to "maintain the houses of the same tenement."[7]

If the inheriting son was a minor and an orphan and no other relative could be found, the lord might exercise his right of "wardship." Thus at Elton in 1297 John Ketel was "in the custody of the lord," slept and ate in the manor house, and was apparently clothed; at least he was bought a pair of shoes which had to be repaired at the manor's expense.[8] John Daye, who "tore up and carried away" the house on his father's holding "which had come into the hand of the lord through the minority of John son and heir of . . . Richard Daye," was undoubtedly also in wardship.[9]

Where no heir could be found, the lord provided a tenant. "One cottage which John Stabler formerly held in bondage for 12 pence a year is in the hand of the lord," reported the Elton court record in 1342. "Therefore it is commanded to make provision of one tenant. Afterward, they say, Alexander Cook came and paid entry fee."[10]

The Elton accounts also record several cases in which the land of a deceased tenant was rented out by the lord, sometimes to several villagers, in small parcels: "three rods," "an acre," "four acres of land and an acre of meadow." Usually the rent was substantially raked, and the lease made "for the term of life."[11]

Heriot passes unmentioned in Elton documents except for the comment that a widow succeeding to a holding did not pay it (implying that a son succeeding did).[12] Most manors exacted heriot from the widow. A custumal of Brancaster, a Norfolk manor belonging to Ramsey Abbey, states: "If [the villein] virgater dies, the lord has his best beast of the house, if he has a beast. If there is no beast, she gives 32 pence and she holds her husband's land for the service which pertains to it."[13] Usually a person inheriting a virgate gave a cow or horse, one inheriting a half-virgate a sheep. On some Ramsey Abbey manors, the village rector rather than the lord received the best beast, under the name of "mortuary."[14] Sometimes the fine was simply levied in money: at Abbot's Ripton, Hemmingford, and Wistow

Parents carrying struggling children from the *England/
Queen Mary Psalter* **(c.1310–20).**

the widow of a virgater gave five shillings as heriot, half the price of a horse, ox, or cow.[15]

At Chalgrave in 1279, a jury weighed the question of the rival claims of lord and church on the estate of a man who had no animal. The jury decided that the lord "should have the best cloth or grain whichever shall please him the more, before holy church may have anything of the dead person." They cited the precedent of "a certain Ascelina who was the wife of Roger the reeve," and who had held eight acres of land in the time of the grandfather of the present lord, "and had no animal." The lord took in heriot "the best cloth which she had, to wit, one tunic of blanket [cloth], before holy Church took away anything. Afterwards a certain Nigel the Knight, holding the same land, died as tenant, and had no animal. Therefore the lord by custom took one tabard [tunic] of gray in the name of heriot, and he can rightly do so from all his customary tenants in the manor of Chalgrave."[16] One study shows that of eighty-six heriots exacted at Langley, St. Albans, Hertfordshire, in 1348, twenty-two were horses, seventeen cows, eight bulls, five sheep, and remaining thirty-two insignificant chattels such as a mattock or a pitcher, or "nothing because they are poor."[17]

Among the villagers as among the nobility, primogeniture created some problems while solving others. It kept holdings intact, but as land grew scarce, older sons of both nobility and peasantry had to wait until their fathers died or retired before marrying. Younger sons of the nobility traditionally had to leave the family estate to seek their fortunes in war, or embark on careers in the Church. Younger sons of the peasantry might enlist as common soldiers, or (on payment of a fee to the lord) undertake training for lower ranks of the clergy. Among the better-off peasants, many fathers gave younger sons small grants of land, often purchased in the growing peasant land market. Edward Britton found that in Broughton 44 percent of the elite families had two or more sons established simultaneously in the village. Younger sons of the poor peasants were not so lucky, generally having to choose between staying home, celibate, and taking their chances as day laborers, perhaps slipping into vagabondage and crime.[18]

A few peasants made wills, an increasingly popular measure in the fourteenth century, often recorded in the manorial court rolls. In King's Ripton in 1309, Nicholas Newman bequeathed a rod of land to his daughter Agnes, and Roger Dike an acre to his sister Margaret; in 1322 Nicholas son of Hugh left his sister a house and yard "lying next to the manor of the lord abbot," to be held by her for life and then to pass to Joan daughter of Thomas Cooper, and half an acre of land on the Ramsey road to Ivo son of Henry. Alternatively, land might be transferred to a daughter or sister or younger son on the deathbed, evading the inheritance custom. In the period before the Black Death, such transfers were usually not of land handed down in the family, but of acquisitions that the peasant had made during his own lifetime. In the fifteenth century, peasant wills became common.[19]

The land market also facilitated acquisition of dowries for daughters of the richer villagers, who might seek alliance with another village family of their own class or even with the lesser gentry without sacrificing any of the family holding. The dowry of a middling peasant's daughter might also include an acre or two of land, but more often would consist of money, chattels, or both. A poor peasant's daughter might marry with nothing at all. Substantial dowries came into play mainly in the increasing negotiations for upwardly mobile marriages.[20]

Dowries aside, peasant women inherited, held, bought, sold, and leased land. The Elton records disclose many land transactions carried out by women: "And they say that the wife of Geoffrey in Angulo let one acre of land to Richard of Thorpe Waterville, chaplain."[21] "And they say that Muriel atte Gate demised [sold] one acre of her land to Nicholas Miller."[22]

In all transfers of property held by villeins, the lord had an interest. The tangible sign of his interest in peasant marriage was merchet, the fee or fine usually paid by the bride or her father. The origin of merchet (along with its etymology) is lost in the earlier Middle Ages, but by the late thirteenth century it was so long established that it had become a legal test for villein status. In the Elton manorial court of 1279, Reginald son of Benedict tried to escape jury service by claiming that he was free, but lost his case because his sisters had paid merchet. Elias Freeman also was adjudged unfree (in spite of his name) because his ancestor John Freeman had paid merchet for his daughters.[23]

Merchets were regarded as taxes on persons, but Eleanor Searle has argued persuasively that the dowry granted to a daughter was a form of inheritance, and that merchet may better be seen as an inheritance tax on property: "Girls were given land, chattels, or coin . . . as their part of the inheritance." Searle observes that merchet was paid only where a substantial dowry was being given the bride. "A foolish girl or a poor one might marry as she liked." Only if she received part of the family inheritance was she obligated.

Significantly, the size of the merchet evidently related to the value of the dowry. A St. Albans formulary for holding a manorial court included the instruction to inquire "whether any bondman's daughter has married without leave, and what her father has given her by way of goods." When the dowry was in the form of land, it was often transferred at the same time that the merchet was paid. Searle sees an analogue to merchet in the fine paid by a villein for having his sons licensed to be educated for the clergy.[24]

Whatever the relationship of merchet to dowry, the Elton records supply evidence of its close relationship to landholding. When Margery daughter of John atte Gate paid two shillings for "giving herself in marriage," the transaction was recorded by the clerk in the accounts of 1286–1287 as an entry fee (gersum),[25] and in the 1307 accounts, entry fees and merchets are mixed together as if they were interchangeable terms.[26] The Ramsey Abbey register known as the *Liber Gersumarum* includes not only gersums but 426 merchets.[27]

Merchet has traditionally been thought of as paid by the bride's father, yet in many cases the daughter paid the fee, and sometimes the prospective bridegroom, or occasionally the mother, or a collateral relative. In the surviving Elton records between 1279 and 1342, eight fathers, eight daughters, and one mother are recorded as paying. A recent study of the *Liber Gersumarum* showed that payments were made as frequently by daughters as by fathers—each in 33 percent of the cases. The bridegroom paid in 26 percent, and some other relative in the remaining 8 percent.[28] Who paid seems to have depended on circumstance. A bride who paid her own merchet was probably marrying late, and may well have earned the money herself, working as a servant or dairymaid, or even at such masculine-sounding tasks as road repair, manuring, thatching, weeding, mowing, sheep-shearing, carrying, and plowing.[29]

When a widow remarried, on the other hand, the merchet was usually paid by the prospective husband, who would benefit from taking possession of her first husband's lands. An unfree woman marrying a free man, however, was the one who benefited, and she or her father paid the fee, never the bridegroom.[30]

In short, the decision as to who paid merchet was part of the marriage negotiations, usually depending on who gained the most from the marriage. The amount was subject to haggling with the lord's steward—the villein must "make the best bargain he can," in the words of a Ramsey Abbey custumal.[31] Several circumstances influenced the price: whether the woman was marrying a villein in the same village, or a freeman, or a man from outside the village, or "whomever she wished." It was more expensive to marry a freeman or an outsider, or to marry at will, since the lord risked losing the woman's services, chattels, and future children.[32]

Another important factor was the family's ability to pay. Merchet was highest when the bride was an heiress or a widow, generally ranging from five shillings to four pounds. Where no land was involved but only chattels, the range was far lower, sometimes as little as six pence. Muriel daughter of Richard Smith, an Elton cotter, paid three shillings, while Alexander atte Cross and Hugh in Angulo, both virgaters from the elite families, gave five for their daughters, and Emma wife of Richard Reeve six shillings eight pence for hers.[33]

A Medieval couple at their wedding feast. Engraving by Scherr (19th c.).

Many daughters of Elton villeins too poor to be taxed evidently married without paying merchet.

The actual ceremony of rural marriage, or more precisely the lack of ceremony, was a long-standing problem for the Church. Many village couples saw no need for more than a kiss and a promise, which left room for debate over the nature of the alleged promise. The great twelfth-century legal authorities, Gratian and Peter Lombard, had wrestled with the question of what constituted a legal marriage, and Pope Alexander III (1159–1181) had laid down rules: a valid marriage could be accomplished either by "words of the present" (I take thee, John . . .) or by "words of the future," a more indefinite promise, if it was followed by consummation. Consent of the two parties alone was indispensable. The Fourth Lateran Council (1215) stipulated that the wedding must be public and the bride must receive a dowry, but made no provision for witnesses, and did not even insist on Church participations.[34]

Most marriages were arranged between families, and sometimes property considerations resulted in mismatches, such as those described by William Langland:

> It is an uncomely couple . by Christ, so me thinketh
> To give a young wench . to an old feeble,
> Or wed any widow . for wealth of her goods,
> That never shall bairn bear . but if it be in [her] arms.[35]

Robert Manning's *Handlyng Synne* had much to say about the evils of such marriages. When couples were married for property and not love, it was "no right wedding." A man who married a woman "for love of her cattle" would have regrets:

> When it is gone and is all bare
> Then is the wedding sorrow and care.
> Love and cattle then are away,
> And "wellaway," they cry and say.[36]

Even worse was for a man to "wed any woman against her will,"[37] strictly forbidden by the Church, and improbable in the village, where, unlike the castle, most marriages involved some courtship and even sexual contact.

Peasant couples usually spoke their vows at the church door, the most public place in the village. Here the priest inquired whether there were any impediments, meaning kinship in a degree forbidden by the Church. The bridegroom named the dower which he would provide for his wife, giving her as a token a ring

and a small sum of money to be distributed to the poor. The ring, according to a fourteenth-century preacher, must be "put and set by the husband upon the fourth finger of the woman, to show that a true love and cordial affection be between them, because, as doctors say, there is a vein coming from the heart of a woman to the fourth finger, and therefore the ring is put on the same finger, so that she should keep unity and love with him, and he with her."[38]

Vows were then exchanged, and the bridal party might proceed into the church, where a nuptial Mass was celebrated. At one such Mass a fourteenth-century priest addressed the wedding party: "Most worshipful friends, we are come here at this time in the name of the Father, Son, and Holy Ghost, . . . to join, unite, and combine these two persons by the holy sacrament of matrimony, granted to the holy dignity and order of priesthood. Which sacrament of matrimony is of this virtue and strength that these two persons who now are two bodies and two souls, during their lives together shall be . . . one flesh and two souls."[39]

The ceremony was usually followed by a feast, a "bride ale," in a private house or a tavern. In Warboys and some other villages, the groom was obligated to treat the manorial servants to a dinner with "bread, beer meat or fish" on "the day on which he takes a wife."[40]

Enough couples in the village, however, continued to speak their vows elsewhere—in the woods, in a tavern, in bed—to make "clandestine marriage" a universal vexation for the Church courts. Typically, a girl sued a man who disclaimed his promise, though sometimes the shoe was on the other foot. Not until the Protestant Reformation and the Catholic Church's Council of Trent in the sixteenth century was clandestine marriage effectively abolished by requiring witnesses.[41]

"Clandestine marriage" obviously shaded off into seduction. Robert Manning condemned men who

> . . . beguile a woman with words;
> To give her troth but lightly
> For nothing but to lie by her;
> With that guile thou makest her assent,
> And bringest you both to cumberment.[42]

Court records contain numerous instances of women leaving their villages in company of men without any mention of marriage. They contain even more frequent instances of "leirwite" or "legerwite" (lecherwite), a fine for premarital sex, literally for lying down. On some manors a separate fine called "childwite" was

The birth of Louis, son of Elizabeth, Queen of France in 1148. Miniature from the *Histoire de Noble,* by Jacques de Guise. Bibliotheque Municipale, Boulogne-sur-Mer, France.

a leirwite of twelve pence; in the same year's accounts her father paid two shillings merchet "for giving his daughter Athelina in marriage."[44] Premarital sex was thus followed by marriage. The village community seems to have taken a liberal attitude toward young people's sexual activities; in 1316 an Elton jury was fined "because they had concealed all these [five] leirwites."[45]

A more serious matter was adultery, a threat to the family. It lay in the province of the Church courts, but the lord exacted a fine too, usually under a curious legal rationale: the parties had "wasted the lord's chattels in chapter." G. G. Coulton once interpreted this recurring phrase as reflecting the lord's control over the marriage of peasant women.[46] The lord, however, had little to do with arranging peasant marriages. The same words are used in regard to men convicted of adultery, and a reasonable explanation is that the lord used the pretext of loss of village resources as an opportunity to collect a fine of his own in a province that was normally the Church's. The Church court identified the guilty parties in a way that neighbors might be reluctant to do in the manorial court.[47] In the Elton records between 1279 and 1342, six cases of adultery are cited, in three of which only the women are mentioned, in two only the men, in one both parties. Edward Britton, studying the Broughton court rolls between 1294 and 1323, found twenty-four adultery cases, ten citing both the guilty parties, eight only the man, six only the woman.[48]

Divorce (*divortium*—synonymous with annulment) was a recurring problem for the Church among the aristocracy, who searched for ways to dissolve a barren or disappointing marriage, but among the peasants it was a rarity. When it did occur among villagers, the commonest ground was bigamy. Couples sometimes separated, however, either informally or under terms arranged by a Church court, though the latter expedient was expensive and therefore not normally undertaken by villagers.

In the village as in castle and city, babies were born at home, their birth attended by midwives. Men were excluded from the lying-in chamber. Literary evidence suggests that the woman in labor assumed a sitting or crouching position.[49] Childbirth was dangerous for both mother and child. The newborn infant was

levied for bearing a child out of wedlock, but in Elton premarital sex and pregnancy were lumped together. Twenty-two cases of leirwite are listed in surviving Elton records between 1279 and 1342, with fines of either sixpence or twelve pence, in a single case three pence. In all but one, only the woman is named, and she paid the fine; in the single exception, in 1286, Maggie Carter and Richard Miller were fined sixpence each.[43]

Daughters of the elite families figure prominently among those convicted. Despite the fine, little social stigma seems to have been attached to premarital sex. One theory is that peasant women may have become pregnant as a prelude to marriage in order to prove their fertility. In Elton in 1307, Athelina Blakeman paid immediately prepared for baptism, lest it die in a state of original sin. If a priest could not be located in time, someone else must perform the ceremony, a contingency for which water must be kept ready. If the baptizer did not know the formula in Latin, he must say it in English or French: "I christen thee in the name of the Father and the Son and the Holy Ghost. Amen."[50]

The words must be said in the right order. If the baptizer said, "In the name of the Son and the Father and the Holy Ghost," the sacrament was invalid. Robert Manning told the story of a midwife who said the wrong words:

> She held it on her lap before,
> And when she saw that it would die,
> She began loud for to cry,
> And said, "God and Saint John,
> Christen the child both flesh and bone."

When the priest heard the formula she had used, he cried, "God and Saint John give thee both sorrow and shame . . . for in default a soul is lost," and he commanded her no longer to deliver babies. Robert Manning concluded,

> Being a midwife is a perilous thing
> Unless she knows the points of christening.[51]

John Myrc in his *Instructions for Parish Priests* (early fifteenth century) advised that if the baby seemed likely to die, "though the child but half be born/ Head and neck and no more," the midwife should "christen it and cast on water." If the mother died before the child could be born, the midwife must free the child with a knife, to save its life, or at least to assure baptism.[52]

Under normal circumstances the child was washed and sometimes (though not universally) swaddled, the godparents were summoned, and godmother or midwife carried the baby to the church, where the font was kept ever ready. The mother was not present, and in fact was not permitted to enter the church until several weeks later, when she had undergone the ritual of "churching," purification after childbirth.

Preliminary baptismal rites were performed, as in marriage, at the church door. The priest blessed the child, put salt in its mouth to symbolize wisdom and exorcise demons, read a Bible text, and ascertained the child's name and the godparents' qualifications. The party then moved into the church to the baptismal font. The child was immersed, the godmother dried it and dressed it in a christening garment, and the priest anointed it with holy oil. The ceremony was completed at the altar with the godparents making the profession of faith for the child. The christening party then repaired to the parents' house for feasting and gift-giving.[53]

Children were usually named for their principal godparents. Variety of Christian names was limited in the thirteenth and fourteenth centuries, usually Norman rather than Anglo-Saxon, the most popular in Elton being John, Robert, Henry, Richard, William, Geoffrey, Thomas, Reginald, Gilbert, Margaret, Matilda, Alice, Agnes, and Emma. Less common were Nicholas, Philip, Roger, Ralph, Stephen, Alexander, Michael, Adam, and Andrew, Sarah, Letitia, Edith, and Beatrice. There were as yet no Josephs or Marys.

Unlike the lady of the castle or many city women, the peasant mother normally nursed her own children. Only if the mother had no milk, or if she died, was a wet nurse employed. The evidence of the coroners' rolls indicates that during the first year of life, infants were frequently left alone in the house while their parents worked in the fields, looked after the animals, or did other chores. Older children were more likely to be left with a sitter, usually a neighbor or a young girl. Although neglect on the part of busy parents might lead to tragedy, little evidence exists of infanticide, a commonplace of the ancient world.[54]

Medieval parents have been accused by certain modern writers of a want of feeling toward their children, but even in the comparative poverty of the kind of literary expressions—correspondence and memoirs—that have recorded such sentiments for more recent times, the charge scarcely stands up. Between the lines in the accounts of the coroners may be read again and again the anguish of parents over a lost child: one father searching for his son, drowned in a ditch, "found him, lifted him from the water, could not save him, and he died";[55] another, whose son was struck by lightning in a field, came running toward him, found him lying there, took him in his arms to the house . . . thinking to save him";[56] a mother dragged her son out of a ditch "because she believed she could save him";[57] a father whose son fell into the millpond "tried to save [him] and entered the water but could do nothing."[58] Sometimes peasants gave their lives for their children, as in one case when a father was killed defending his young daughter from rape.[59]

A fourteenth-century sermon pictures a mother and her child: "In winter, when the child's hands are cold, the mother takes him a straw or a rush bids him warm it, not for love of the straw, to warm it, but to

Distribution of Alms to the Poor and Lame. English stained glass (15th c.).

warm the child's hands [by pressing them together]." When the child falls ill, "the mother for her sick child takes a candle, and makes a vow in prayers."[60]

The coroners' rolls yield rare glimpses of children at work and play: the baby in the cradle by the fire; little girls following their mothers around, helping stir the pot, draw water, gather fruit; little boys following their fathers to the fields, to the mill, or fishing, or playing with bows and arrows. A sermon pictures a child using his imagination, playing "with flowers . . . with sticks, and with small bits of wood, to build a chamber, buttery, and hall, to make a white home of a wand, a sailing ship of broken bread, a burly spear from a ragwort stalk, and of a sedge a sword of war, a comely lady of a cloth, and be right busy to deck it elegantly with flowers."[61]

A child, said one preacher, did not bear malice, nor rancor nor wrath toward those that beat him ever so sorely, as it happened for a child to have due chastising. But after thou hast beaten him, show him a fair flower or else a fair red apple; then hath he forgotten all that was done to him before, and then he will come to thee, running, with his embracing arms, to please thee and to kiss thee."[62]

Small children played; older ones did chores. In their teens, both boys and girls moved into the adult work world, the girls in and around the house, the boys in the fields. Contrary to what was formerly believed, in this period village children were not ordinarily sent away to become servants in other people's households or to be apprenticed at a craft. Most remained at home.[63]

The Middle Ages produced the world's first hospitals and medical schools, but these important advances hardly affected life in the village. Doctors practiced in city and in court. Villagers were left to their own medical devices. Even the barbers who combined shaving with bloodletting (a principal form of therapy) and tooth-pulling (the sole form of dentistry) were rarely seen in villages. Most manorial custumals provided for a period of sick leave, commonly up to a year and a day. "If [the villein] is ill, so that he cannot leave his house," states a Holywell custumal, "he is quit of all work and heusire before the autumn, except plowing [which presumably he would have to pay someone else to do]. In the autumn he is quit of half his work if he is ill, and he will have relaxation for the whole time he is ill, up to a year and a day. And if his illness lasts more than a year

and a day, or if he falls ill again, from that time he will do all works which pertain to his land."[64]

Life was short. Even if a peasant survived infancy and childhood to reach the age of twenty, he could not expect to live much beyond forty-five, when old age *(senectus)* began.[65] The manorial records make no mention of diseases, though to the well-known afflictions of tuberculosis, pneumonia, typhoid, violence, and accident may probably be added circulatory disorders: stroke and heart attack. The coroners' rolls list several cases of fatal accidents from "falling sickness"—epilepsy. Invalids flocked on pilgrimage to Canterbury and other shrines: spastics, cripples, paralytics, the mentally ill, and the scrofulous (skin disease was especially prevalent in a not very well-washed society).

The most pathetic of the medieval sick, however, were excluded from the benefits of the shrine. Leprosy, mysteriously widespread, inspired a vague terror that outlasted the Middle Ages. Its victims were isolated, either singly or in colonies, and were permitted to emerge in public only when clothed in a shroud and clacking a pair of castanets in warning. The isolation of lepers represented a remarkable advance in medical theory, the recognition of contagion, but at the same time a sad irony, since leprosy (Hansen's disease) is only slightly contagious. The Elton court rolls record a single possible mention of the disease in the fine in 1342 of "Hugh le Lepere" for carrying away the lord's stubble.

As in all societies, the *old and infirm* depended on

the younger generation for help when they were no longer able to work their land. The commonest form such help took in the thirteenth century was an arrangement between tenant and heir, in essence an exchange of the older person's land for the younger person's work. The holding was transferred to the heir, who promised in return to maintain the parents, widowed father or mother or other aged relative, either in a separate dwelling or as free boarders. Typically the son accepted the holding's obligations of work service, rent, and fees, and pledged himself to support his parent or parents, stipulating that he would provide them with a separate house or "a room at the end of the house" that had been theirs, food, fuel, clothing, and again and again "a place by the fire." Most such arrangements must have been informal, leaving no trace in the records, but they were also spelled out in written contracts, entered in the manorial court rolls.[67]

Both sermons and moral treatises warned parents against handing over their land to their sons without such safeguards. Men gave their children land, said Robert Manning, to provide sustenance in their old age; better for them to keep it "than beg it at another's hand." In illustration he told a version of the already old story of the "Divided Horsecloth": a man gave his son "all his land and house and all his cattle in village and field, so that he should keep him well in his old age." The young man married and at first bade his wife "to serve his father well at his will." But soon he had a change of heart, and began to be "tenderer of his wife and child than of his father," and it seemed to him that his father had lived too long. As time passed, the son served him worse and worse, and the father began to rue the day he "gave so much to his son." One day the old man was so cold that he begged his son to give him a blanket. The son called his little boy and told him to take a sack and fold it double and put it over his grandfather. The child took the sack and tore it in two. "Why have you torn the sack?" asked the father. The child replied:

> This deed have I done for thee.
> Good example givest thou me
> How I shall serve thee in thine age.
> . . . This half sack shall lie above thy father,
> And keep the other part to thy behalf.[68]

Most peasants were more careful. In Upwood in 1311 Nicholas son of Adam turned over his virgate to his son John, stipulating that he should have "a reasonable maintenance in that land until the end of his life,"

and that John should give him "every year for the rest of his life" specified amounts of grain.[69] At Cranfield in 1294, Elias de Bretendon made a more complicated agreement with his son John; John was to take over his house, yard, and half virgate for the services and money rent owed the lord. "And . . . the above John will provide suitable food and drink for Elias and his wife Christine while they are alive, and they will have residence with John [in his house]." The contract left nothing to chance:

> And if it should happen, though may it not, that trouble and discord should in the future arise between the parties so that they are unable to live together, the above John will provide for Elias and Christine, or whichever of them should outlive the other, a house and curtilage [yard] where they can decently reside. And he will give each year to the same Elias and Christine or whichever of them is alive, six quarters of hard grain at Michaelmas, namely three quarters of wheat, one and one-half quarters of barley, one and one-half quarters of peas and beans, and one quarter of oats. [The addition evidently gave trouble, since the total is not six but seven quarters.][70]

If the retiring tenant was childless, the pension was contracted for outside the family, an arrangement that became frequent after the Black Death. In 1332 John in the Hale of Barnet, Hertfordshire, agreed with another peasant, John atte Barre, to turn over his house and land in return for a yearly contribution of "one new garment with a hood, worth 3 shillings 4 pence, two pairs of linen sheets, three pairs of new shoes, one pair of new hose, worth 12 pence, and victuals in food and drink decently as is proper." An unusual feature of the contract was that the retiring tenant agreed to work for his replacement "to the best of his ability," and that the new tenant not only paid an entry fee, as was customary, but "satisfied the lord for the heriot of the said John in the Hale by [the payment of] one mare," although the retiree was not yet dead.[71]

Pension contracts were enforceable in the manor court, a sign of one of their most striking aspects: the community's interest in enforcement. "Dereliction of duty to the old [was] a matter of public concern," observes Elaine Clark.[72] A son undertaking to support his aged parents commonly requested the manorial court to witness his oath, or enlisted as guarantors pledges whose names he reported to the steward. For the court's participation the pensioners paid a fee.[73]

In Ellington in 1278, William Koc acknowledged that he was in arrears for the contributions he owed his father, in wheat, barley, beans, and peas, and promised to make amends.[74] The jurors in Warboys in 1334 reported: "And since Stephen the Smith did not keep his mother according to their agreement he is [fined] sixpence. And afterwards the above jurors ordered that the said land be given back to his mother and that she should hold it for the rest of her life. And the above Stephen may not have anything of that land while his mother is alive."[75]

Pensions were sometimes negotiated between the parties, sometimes mandated as deathbed settlements—mainly by husbands in favor of their widows—and sometimes ordered by the manorial court. When a tenant's disability rendered him unfit to discharge the obligations of his holding, it was in the interest of the lord to make a change, but the change served the interest of the elderly tenant as well.[76]

A pension contract that dated back to the early Middle Ages was originally developed in the monasteries to provide for the retirement of monks. The corrody consisted of a daily ration of bread and ale, usually two loaves and two gallons, plus one or two "cooked dishes" from the monastic kitchen. In the later Middle Ages, corrodies became available to lay pensioners, who purchased them like life insurance annuities. The purchaser might stipulate for a certain amount of firewood every year, a room in the monastery, sometimes with a servant, clothing, candles, and fodder for horses. A wealthy peasant might buy a corrody that even included a house and garden, pasture, and cash; a poor one might buy only a ration of dark bread, ale, and pottage.[77]

Still other arrangements might be made. A widow and her young son leased their holding at Stoke Pryor to a fellow villager for twelve years in return for an annual supply of mixed grain; presumably in twelve years the son would be old enough to take over the holding.[78]

The pension agreement implied bargaining power on the part of the aging tenant, nearly always meaning landholding. In its absence, an old man or woman might end like those whose deaths are recorded in the coroners' rolls: Sabinia, who in January of 1267 went into Colmworth, Bedfordshire, to beg bread and "fell into a stream and drowned,"[79] or Arnulf Argent of Ravensden, "poor, weak, and infirm," who was going "from door to door to seek bread," when he fell down in a field and "died of weakness."[80]

When death was imminent, the priest was sent for, and arrived wearing surplice and stole, carrying the blessed sacrament, preceded by a server carrying a lantern and ringing a hand bell. If the case was urgent and no server could be found, the priest might hang the lamp and bill on his arm, or around the neck of his horse. According to Robert Manning, sick men were often reluctant to accept the sacrament because of a belief that if they recovered they must abstain from sex:

> Many a one thus hopes and says,
> "Anoint them not save they should die,
> For if he turns again to life
> He should lie no more by his wife."

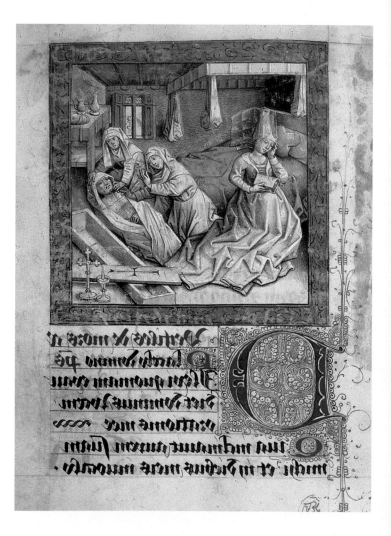

Death, Internment and Burial from the *Hours of the Duke of Burgundy* (1454–55).

Manning counseled against the superstition and recommended more trust in God:

In every sickness ask for [the sacrament] always; God almighty is right courteous.[81]

John Myrc advised that if death was imminent, the priest should not make the sick man confess all his sins, but only counsel him to ask God's mercy with a humble heart. If the dying man could not speak but indicated by signs that he wished the sacraments, the priest should administer them. If, however, the dying man was able to speak, Myrc advised that he should be asked "the seven interrogations": if he believed in the articles of the faith and the Holy Scriptures; if he recognized that he had offended God; if he was sorry for his sins; if he wished to amend and would do so if God gave him more time; if he forgave his enemies; if he would atone for his sins if he lived; and finally, "Do you believe fully that Christ died for you and that you may never be saved but by the merit of Christ's passion, and do you think of God with your heart as much as you may?" The sick man should answer yes and be instructed to say, "with a good steadfast mind, if he can...'Into thy hands I commend my soul.'" If he could not, the priest should say it for him, anoint him, and administer Communion.[82]

Wakes commonly turned into occasions of drink-ing and merriment, condemned by the Church. Robert Grosseteste warned that a dead man's house should be one of "sorrow and remembrance," and should not be made a house of "laughter and play," and a fourteenth-century preacher complained that people "finally like madmen make...merry at our death, and take our burying for a bride ale."[83] In the Ramsey Abbey village of Great Raveley in 1301, ten Wistow men were fined after coming "to watch the body of Simon of Sutbyr through the night," because returning home they "threw stones at the neighbors' doors and behaved themselves badly."[84]

Village funerals were usually starkly simple. The body, sewed in a shroud, was carried into the church on a bier, draped with a black pall. Mass was said, and occasionally a funeral sermon was delivered. One in John Myrc's collection, *Festiall,* ends: "Good men, as ye all see, here is a mirror to us all: a corpse brought to the church. God have mercy on him, and bring him into his bliss that shall last for ever.... Wherefore each man and woman that is wise, make him ready thereto; for we all shall die, and we know not how soon."[85]

A villager was buried in a plain wooden casket or none at all, in the churchyard, called the "cemetery," from *coemeterium* (dormitory), the sleeping place of the Christian dead. Here men and women could slumber peacefully, their toil finished, until the day of resurrection.

VII

THE VILLAGE
AT WORK

For the medieval villager, work was the ruling fact of life. By sunup animals were harnessed and plows hitched, forming a cavalcade that to the modern eye would appear to be leaving the village to work outside it. Medieval people felt otherwise. They were as much in their village tramping the furrowed strips as they were on the dusty streets and sunken lanes of the village center. If anything, the land which literally provided their daily bread was more truly the village. The geography was a sort of reverse analogue of the modern city with its downtown office towers where people work and its suburban bedroom communities where they eat and sleep.

Whether Elton had two or three fields in the late thirteenth century is unknown. Whatever the number, they were twice subdivided, first into furlongs (more or less rectangular plots "a furrow long"), then into selions,

The Working Class by Jean Bourdichon from *The Four Estates of Society* (15th c.).

or strips, long and narrow sets of furrows. Depending on the terrain, a village's strips might be several hundred yards long; the fewer turns with a large plow team the better. The strip as a unit of cultivation went far back, probably antedating the open field system itself. Representing the amount of land that could conveniently be plowed in a day—roughly half a modern acre—it probably originated in the parcellation of land forced by a growing population. By the late thirteenth century the distribution of a village's strips was haphazard, some villagers holding many, some few, and all scattered and intermingled. The one certainty was that everyone who held land held strips in both or all three fields, in order to guarantee a crop every year regardless of which field lay fallow.

The furlong, or bundle of strips, was the sowing unit, all the strips in a given furlong being planted to the same crop. Many furlongs appear by name in the Elton court records: "Henry in the Lane [is fined] for bad plowing in Hollewell furlong, six-pence," indicating, incidentally, that the lord's demesne land was scattered, like the peasants'.[1] Within each furlong the strips ran parallel, but the furlongs themselves, plotted to follow the ambient pattern of drainage, lay at odd angles to each other, with patches of rough scattered throughout.

Threshing, an illustration for August from the *Virgo/Bedford Hours* **(French, c.1423).**

A double furrow or a balk of unplowed turf might separate strips, while between some furlongs headlands were left for turning the plow. Wedges of land (gores) created by the asymmetry of the furlongs and the character of the terrain were sometimes cultivated by hoe.[2] The total appearance of an open field village, visible in aerial photographs of many surviving sites, is a striking combination of the geometric and the anarchic.

Beyond the crazy-quilt pattern of arable land stretched meadow, waste, and woodland, hundreds of acres that were also part of the village and were exploited for the villagers' two fundamental purposes: to support themselves and to supply their lord. But the most significant component of the open field village was always its two or three great fields of cultivated land. The difference between a two- and a three-field system was slighter than might appear at first glance. Where three fields were used, one lay fallow all year, a second was planted in the fall to winter wheat or other grain, the third was planted in the spring to barley, oats, peas, beans, and other spring crops. The next year the plantings were rotated.

In the two-field system one field was left fallow and the other divided in two, one half devoted to autumn and the other to spring crops. In effect, the two-field system was a three-field system with more fallow, and offered no apparent disadvantage as long as enough total arable was available. If, however, a growing village population pressed on the food supply, or if market demand created an opportunity hard to resist, a two-field system could be convened to three-field. Many

two-field systems were so converted in the twelfth and especially the thirteenth century, with a gain of one-third in arable.[3]

Multifield systems, which could accommodate crop rotation, were also common, especially in the north of England. In some places, the ancient infield-outfield system survived, the small infield being worked steadily with the aid of fertilizer, and the large outfield treated as a land reserve, part of which could be cultivated for several successive years (making plowing easier) and then left fallow for several.[4]

But in the English Midlands, and much of northwest Europe, the classic two- or three-field system of open field husbandry prevailed. It involved three essentials: unfenced arable divided into furlongs and strips; concerted agreement about crops and cultivation; and common use of meadow, fallow, waste, and stubble.

Implied was a fourth essential: a set of rules governing details, and a means of enforcing them. Such rules were developed independently in thousands of villages in Britain and on the Continent, at first orally, but by the late thirteenth century in written form as village bylaws. The means of enforcement was provided by the manorial court. Surviving court records include many bylaw enactments and show the existence of many more by citation. For stewards, bailiffs, reeves, free tenants, and villeins, they spelled out a set of restrictions and constraints on plowing, planting, harvesting, gleaning, and carrying. They gave emphatic attention to theft and chicanery, from stealing a neighbor's grain to "stealing his furrow" by edging one's plow into his strip, "a major sin in rural society"[5] (Maurice Beresford). "Reginald Benyt appropriated to himself three furrows under Westereston to his one rod from all the strips abutting upon that rod and elsewhere at Arnewassebroc three furrows to his one headland from all the strips abutting upon that headland," for which Reginald was fined 12 pence by the Elton manorial court of 1279.[6]

Bylaws stipulated the time the harvested crop could be taken from the fields (in daylight hours only), who was allowed to carry it (strangers not welcome), and who was allowed to glean. All able-bodied adults were conscripted for reaping. "And [the jurors] say that Parnel was a gleaner in the autumn contrary to the statutes. Therefore she is in mercy [fined] sixpence."[7] "The wife of Peter Wrau gleaned . . . contrary to the prohibition of autumn."[8] Bylaws ruled the period when the harvest stubble should be opened to grazing, and for which kind of animals, when sheep were barred from the meadows, and when tenants must repair ditches and erect, remove, and mend fences. (Only the lord's land could be permanently fenced, and only if it lay in a compact plot.) Repeatedly, through the year, the village animals were herded into or driven off the open fields as crop, stubble, and fallow succeeded each other.

The regulation of grazing rights was fundamental to the operation of open field farming. The lord's land was especially inviolate to beastly trespass: "Robert atte Cross for his draft-beasts doing damage in the lord's furlong sown with barley, [fined] sixpence."[9] On some manors grazing rights were related to the size of the holding. A Glastonbury survey of 1243 found the holder of a virgate endowed with pasture enough for four oxen, two cows, one horse, three pigs, and twelve sheep, calculated as the amount of stock required to keep a virgate of land fertile.[10]

The open field system was thus not one of free enterprise. Its practitioners were strictly governed in their actions and made to conform to a rigid pattern agreed on by the community, acting collectively.

Neither was it socialism. The strips of plowed land were held individually, and unequally. A few villagers held many strips, most held a few, some held none. Animals, tools, and other movable property were likewise divided unequally. The poor cotters eked out a living by working for the lord and for their better-off neighbors who had more land than their families could cultivate, whereas these latter, by marketing their surplus produce, were able to turn a profit and perhaps use it to buy more land.

How much of his time a villager could devote to cultivating his own tenement depended partly on his status as free or unfree, partly on the size of his holding (the larger the villein holding, the larger the obligation), and partly on his geographical location. In England "the area of heavy villein labor dues—say two or more days each week—was relatively small," consisting mostly of several counties and parts of counties in the east.[11] In the rest of the country, though, rules varied from manor to manor, the level of villein obligations tended to be lower. In several counties in the north and northwest they were very light or nonexistent.

Huntingdonshire, containing Ramsey Abbey and

Elton, was in the very heart of the heavy-labor region, where the obligation was basically two days' work a week. In Elton, the dozen free tenants owed very modest, virtually token service. The cotters owed little service because they held little or no land. Only the two score villein virgaters owed heavy week-work, amounting to 117 days a year (the nine half-virgaters owed fifty-eight and a half days).[12] In addition, the Elton virgater owed a special service, the cultivation of half an acre of demesne land summer and winter, including sowing it with his own wheat seed, reaping, binding, and carrying to the lord's barn.[13]

Some question exists about the length of the work day required of tenants. A Ramsey custumal for the manor of Abbot's Ripton stipulates "the whole day" in summer "from Hokeday until after harvest," and "the

Peasants at work in the fields of a feudal estate, by the Limbourg Brothers from the *Très Riches Heures du Duc de Berry* (early 15th c.).

whole day in winter," but during Lent only "until after none (mid-afternoon)."[14] In some places a work day lasted until none if no food was supplied, and if the lord wanted a longer day, he was obliged to provide dinner. Another determinant of the length of the working day may have been the endurance of the ox (less than that of the horse).[15]

The annual schedule of week-work at Elton divided the year into three parts:

> From September 29 (Michaelmas) of one year to August 1 (Gules of August) of the following year, two days' work per week (for a virgater). From August 1 to September 8 (the Nativity of the Blessed Mary), three days' work per week, with a day and a half of work for the odd three days. This stretch of increased labor on the demesne was the "autumn works." From September 8 to September 29, five days' work a week, known as the "after autumn works."[16]

Thus the autumn and post-autumn works for the Elton virgater totaled thirty-one and a half days, half of the two critical months of August and September, when he had to harvest, thresh, and winnow his own crop.

The principal form of week-work was plowing. Despite employment of eight full-time plowmen and drivers on the Elton demesne, the customary tenants, with their own plows and animals, were needed to complete the fall and spring plowing and the summer fallowing to keep the weeds down. Default of the plowing obligation brought punishment in the manor court: "Geoffrey of Brington withheld from the lord the plow work of half an acre of land. [Fined] sixpence."[17] "John Page withholds a plowing work of the lord between Easter and Whitsuntide for seven days, to wit each Friday half an acre. Mercy [fine] pardoned because afterwards he paid the plowing work."[18]

By the same token, the main kind of work the villein did on his own land was plowing. Stage by stage through the agricultural year he worked alternately for the lord and for himself.

His plow (not every villein owned one) was iron-shared, equipped with coulter and mouldboard, and probably wheeled, an improvement that allowed the plowman to control the depth of furrow by adjusting the wheels, saving much labor. He might own an all-wooden harrow, made by himself from unfinished tree branches, or possibly a better one fashioned by the carpenter. Only the demesne was likely to own a harrow with iron teeth, jointly fabricated by the smith and the carpenter. The villein's collection of tools might include a spade, a hoe, a fork, a sickle, a scythe, a flail, a knife, and a whetstone. Most virgaters probably owned a few other implements, drawn from a secondary array scattered through the village's toolsheds: mallets, weeding hooks, sieves, querns, mortars and pestles, billhooks, buckets, augers, saws, hammers, chisels, ladders, and wheelbarrows. A number of villagers had two-wheeled carts. Those who owned sheep had broad, flat shears, which were also used for cutting cloth.[19]

Plows and plow animals were shared to make up plow teams. Agreements for such joint plowing appear in court records. At one time scholars debated the discrepancy between Domesday Book's repeated references to the eight-ox plow team and iconographic evidence insistently showing smaller teams, but a modern consensus agrees that teams varied in size, up to eight animals and occasionally more. The largest teams were required to break new ground, the next largest for first plowing after Michaelmas or in spring. Medieval cattle were smaller than their modern descendants and by the time of spring plowing were probably weakened by poor winter diet.[20] Domesday Book refers to smaller teams in non-demesne plowing: "three freemen" plowing with two oxen; freemen plowing with three oxen; "two freewomen" plowing with two oxen. "The Domesday plow team . . . was quite certainly not always an eight-ox team on the villein lands," says R. Trow-Smith; neither was the post-Domesday team.[21]

Horses and oxen were often harnessed together for village as for demesne plowing, not because Walter of Henley recommended it but because availability dictated. Cows were even pressed into service, though modern experiments indicate a lack of enthusiasm on the part of the cows. Cows were kept mainly to breed oxen. An ox took two years to train to the plow, and averaged only four years in service. Thus a four-ox team required complete replacement every four years without allowing for sickness or accident.[22] When horses and oxen were harnessed jointly, it was done in pairs, the horses together, the oxen together, to accommodate the two quite different styles of harness, horse collar and ox yoke. Such teaming, common in England up to modern times, in itself implies large teams.

The first plowing in spring, to turn under the residue of crop and the weeds and grasses, was done early enough to allow time for decomposition of the organic material.[23] A second, shallower plowing aerated the soil, preparing it for seeding. The plowman began just to one side of the center line of the strip to be plowed, effected the laborious turn at the end, and returned on the other side of the center.[24] Peas and beans were planted in the furrow, grain on the ridge. Spring, or Lenten, sowing was done as soon as the soil was warm and frost no longer a danger.[25] Patterns of ridge-and-furrow from the Middle Ages are still visible in aerial photographs, sometimes with the boundaries between neighboring selions indicated by balks or rows of stones.

Demesne plowing might cease at none or at vespers, but a man working his own land might keep his hand to the plow longer, under pressure of time or weather. The first winter wheat plowing, in April after the spring crops were sown in other fields, was shallow. A second, in June, went deeper, as did a third in midsummer. The field was then harrowed and the last clods crumbled with a mattock or long-handled clodding beetle.[26] Grain seed was sown from straw basket, two bushels (or more) to the acre.[27] Seed was not sown casually. In 1320 four Elton villagers were fined threepence apiece for carelessness in planting, in one case on the part of a servant who allowed "four or five beans" to fall into a single hole "to the damage of the lord."[28] Besides scarce manure, the peasant cultivator might supply equally scarce marl, a clay containing carbonate of lime.[29]

Walter of Henley warned that spring plowing done too deep too early might make fields muddy at sowing time.[30] Spring crops—barley, oats, peas, beans, vetch—were usually planted more thickly than winter, about four bushels to the acre.[31] For autumn sowing, Walter recommended small furrows with narrow ridges, and planting early enough to allow the seed to take root before the frost.[32] Heavy rain within a week after sowing, followed by a sharp frost, could destroy a winter wheat crop.

It is probable that Elton villagers had their own meadowland. If so, it was doubtless allocated, in accordance with an ancient tradition, by a lottery among all the holders of arable, both free and unfree.[33] Hay was always in short supply because of the lack of artificial meadow, for want of suitable irrigation, and was precious because it was by far the best winter feed available.

Mowing required care and skill. The grass had to be thoroughly dried (tedded) for storage, and if rained on had to be retedded.[34] Demesne mowing at Elton was assigned entirely to the villeins, among whom it was not notably popular; many fines are recorded for failing to do the job properly. They may well have resented being kept from their own mowing. Some lords sweetened

Feeding Pigs from the *England/Queen Mary Psalter* **(c.1310–20).**

the mowing chore with a bonus in the form of a sheep for the mowers to roast, or as on some Ramsey manors, by the game of "sporting chance." At the end of the haymaking, each man was permitted to carry off as large a bundle of hay as he could lift and keep on his scythe; if the scythe broke or touched the ground, he lost his hay and had to buy an obol's worth of ale for his comrades. In Elton, at least by 1311, mowers were being paid a cash bonus.[35]

After haying, the meadow had to be left alone for three or four weeks to allow the grass to grow; consequently another communal agreement was needed about reopening the meadow for grazing. A good hay crop could take the animals through the winter; a good grain crop could do the same for the human beings. The tension of June, relieved by the drudgery of weeding in July, was redoubled in August and September as the fields reached maturity. First in order of priority came the lord's harvest boon. Not only villeins *ad opus* but free tenants, *censuarii*, cotters, and craftsmen, women and children as well as men, turned out—all save those "so old or so weak [that they] could not work"—reaping, gathering, binding, stacking, carrying, and gleaning.[36] Even a villein rich enough to employ labor was not exempt, though he was usually not asked to wield the scythe himself, only to "hold the rod over his workers," as the custumals phrased it.[37]

The word "boon" or "bene" in "harvest boon" or "boon works" literally meant gift, something freely bestowed, but the usage savored of irony, as the court records indicate: "Geoffrey Garnel . . . made default at the boon works of the autumn. Sixpence."[38] "Richard in Angulo, late in his carrying boon works. Sixpence."[39]

Sowing grain, October, from a series of the labors of the months. English stained glass roundel (15th c.).

On the other hand, a dinner of rare abundance was served in the field to the harvest army. For the 329 persons who turned out for the Elton harvest boon of 1298, the reeve, Alexander atte Crown, listed the victuals consumed: eight rings (thirty-two bushels) of wheat, an almost equal quantity of other grains, a bull, a cow, a calf, eighteen doves, and seven cheeses. The second day's work required only 250 hands, who however ate bread made from eleven rings, along with eight hundred herrings, seven pence worth of salt cod, and five cheeses. A partial third day's boon was exacted from sixty villeins, who were fed on three cheeses and "the residue from the expenses of the [manor] house."[40] Of nineteen recorded harvest boons at Elton, this was the only one to last three days. Seven others lasted two days, eleven only one.

The food supplied at boon-works was an important article of the ancient compact between lord and tenants. Size and composition of the loaves of bread made from the grain were commonly stipulated in writing. At Holywell boons, two men were to share three loaves "such that the quantity of one loaf would suffice for a meal for two men," and the bread was to be of wheat and rye, but mainly wheat.[41] At the Ramsey manor of Broughton in 1291 the tenants actually struck over what they deemed an insufficient quantity of bread supplied them, and only returned to work when appeal to the abbey cartulary proved them mistaken. Reapers

liked to wash down their wheat bread with plenty of ale, typically a gallon a day per man, according to one calculation, and "some harvesters consumed twice as much."[42]

Wheat was cut with a sickle, halfway or more up the stalk, and laid on the ground. Binders followed to tie the spears in sheaves and set them in shocks to dry. In demesne harvesting, one binder followed every four reapers, advancing in echelon at a rate of two acres a day.[43] That similar teamwork was applied in village harvesting is a reasonable supposition. Oats and barley were mown with scythes, close to the ground.[44] Harvesting of all three crops left much residue, making gleaning an important function. It was too important, according to Warren Ault, to support a famous assertion by Blackstone in the eighteenth century that "by the common law and custom of England the poor are allowed to enter and glean upon another's ground after the harvest without being guilty of trespass."[45] In the medieval village, gleaning was strictly limited to the old, the infirm, and the very young, less out of charity than to conserve labor, all able-bodied adults of both sexes being needed for the heavier harvest work. Bylaws generally forbade gleaning by anyone offered a fair wage for harvesting, usually meaning "a penny a day and food" or twopence without food (Walter of Henley recommended paying twopence for a man, one penny for a woman).[46] Bylaws welcomed strangers to the village as harvesters while barring them as gleaners.

After cutting, gathering, binding, and stacking their sheaves, the villagers carted them to their barns and sheds to be threshed with the ancient jointed flail and winnowed by tossing in the air from the winnowing cloth or basket, and if necessary supplying a breeze with the winnowing fan.

Besides the grain crops, harvest included "pulling the peas," the vegetable crops that matured in late September and whose harvest also required careful policing against theft.

Yields for the villagers could scarcely have exceeded those of the demesne, which enjoyed so many advantages. Three and a half to one was generally a very acceptable figure for wheat, with barley a bit higher and oats lower, and bad crops always threatening. R. H. Hilton has calculated that an average peasant on a manor of the bishop of Worcester might feed a family of three, pay a tithe to the church, and have enough grain left to sell for twelve or thirteen shillings, out of which his rent and other cash obligations would have to come.[47] If he was required to pay cash in place of his labor obligation, he would need to make up the difference by sale of poultry or wool, or through earnings of wife or sons. As Fernand Braudel observes, "The peasants were slaves to the crops as much as to the nobility."[48]

Harvest time was subject to more bylaws than all the rest of the year together. "The rolls of the manor courts are peppered with fines levied for sheaf stealing in the field, and a close watch had to be kept in the barn as well," says Ault.[49] The small size of the medieval sheaf, twenty to a bushel, contributed to temptation, *Seneschaucie* mentioning as familiar places of secreting stolen grain "bosom, tunic, or boots, or pockets or sacklets hidden near the grange."[50]

Another communal agreement was needed for post-harvest grazing of the stubble. Sometimes a common date was set, such as Michaelmas, for having everybody's harvest in. Bylaws might specify that a man could pasture his animals on his own land as soon as his neighbors' lands were harvested to the depth of an acre. This was easy to do with cows, which could be restrained within a limited space. Sheep and hogs, on the other hand, had to wait until the end of autumn.[51]

The lord's threshing and winnowing were followed by the villagers', with whole families again joining in. Winter was the slack season, at least in a relative sense. Animals still had to be looked after, and harness, plows, and tools mended. Fences, hurdles, hedges, and ditches, both the lord's and those of the villagers, had to be repaired to provide barriers wherever arable land abutted on a road or animal droveway. Houses, byres, pens, and sheds needed maintenance. So did equipment: "The good husbandman made some at least of his own tools and implements."[52]

The true odd-job men of the village were the cotters. They rarely took part in plowing, having neither plows nor plow beasts, but turned to "hand-work" with spade or fork, sheep-shearing, wattle-weaving, bean-planting, ditch-digging, thatching, brewing, even guarding prisoners held for trial. They were commonly hired by wealthier villagers at harvest time, getting paid with an eleventh, a fifteenth, or a twentieth sheaf. Cotters' wives and daughters were in demand for weeding and other chores.[53]

Yet though they occupied the lowest rung on the village ladder, even cotters were capable of asserting their rights, as a remarkable entry in the Elton court rolls of 1300 testifies. Among the few service obligations of the Elton cotters was that of assisting in the demesne hay-making. A score of cotters, including three women, were prosecuted because they did not come to load the carts

of the lord with hay to be carried from the meadow into the manor as formerly they were wont to do in past times, as is testified by Hugh the Claviger.

> They come and allege that they ought not to perform such a custom save only out of love *(amor)*, at the request of the sergeant or reeve. And they pray that this be inquired into by the free tenants and others. And the inquest [a special panel of the court] comes and says that the abovesaid cotters ought to make the lord's hay into cocks in the meadows and similarly in courtyard of the lord abbot, but they are not bound to load the carts in the meadows unless it be out of special love at the request of the lord.

That left the lord's hay sitting in haycocks in his meadow and the cotters in the manor courtyard waiting for it to be brought to them. The steward confessed himself unable to resolve the dispute without reference to the rule and precedent given in the register at Ramsey, and so ordered "that the said cotters should have parley and treaty with the lord abbot upon the said demand." The ultimate issue is not recorded.[54]

The pathetic picture in *Piers Plowman* of the peasant husband and wife plowing together, his hand guiding the plow, hers goading the team, their baby and small children nearby, illustrates the fact that the wife of a poor peasant had to turn her hand to every kind of labor in sight.[55] For most of the time, however, in most peasant households, the tasks of men and women were differentiated along the traditional lines of "outside" and "inside" work. The woman's "inside" jobs were by no means always performed indoors. Besides spinning, weaving, sewing, cheese-making, cooking, and cleaning, women did foraging, gardening, weeding, haymaking, carrying, and animal-tending. They joined in the lord's harvest boon unless excused, and helped bring in the family's own harvest. Often women served as paid labor, receiving at least some of the time wages equal to men's.[56] R. H. Hilton believes that peasant women in general enjoyed more freedom and "a better situation in their own class than was enjoyed by women of the aristocracy, or the bourgeoisie, a better situation perhaps than that of the women of early modern capitalist England."[57] The statement does not mean that peasant women were better off than wealthier women, only that they were less constricted within the confines of their class. "The most important general feature of their existence to bear in mind," Hilton adds, "[is] that they belonged to a working class and participated in manual agricultural labor."[58]

For many village women one of the most important parts of the daily labor was the care of livestock. Poultry was virtually the woman's domain, but feeding, milking, washing, and shearing the larger livestock often fell to her also.

The biggest problem with livestock was winter feed, the shortage of which was once thought to have provoked an annual "Michaelmas slaughter." Given the high rate of loss to natural causes, an annual slaughter would have threatened the survival of a small flock or herd.[59] The feed shortage certainly played a role in keeping numbers of animals down, but some successful peasants just as certainly overcame the problem. At Bowerchalk in Wiltshire, twenty-three tenants are known to have owned 885 sheep, or 41 per owner; at Merton, eighty-five tenants owned 2,563 sheep, and one is known to have owned 158.[60] Individual ownership within a combined flock was kept straight by branding or by marking with reddle (red ochre), many purchases of which are recorded.[61]

Among peasants as among lords, sheep were esteemed as the "cash crop" animals. Though worth at best only one or two shillings, compared with two and a half shillings for a pig, they had unique fivefold value: fleece, meat, milk, manure, and skin (whose special character made it a writing material of incomparable durability). Lambing time was in early spring, between winter and spring sowing, so that the lambs, weaned at twelve weeks, could accompany their mothers to graze the harvest stubble of last year's wheatfield.[62] The sheep were sheared in mid-June and the fleeces carted to market, probably, in the case of Elton, to Peterborough, about eight miles away. Medieval fleeces weighed from a pound to two and a half pounds, much below the modern average of four and a half pounds.[63]

Pigs were the best candidates for a Michaelmas slaughter, since their principal value was as food and since their meat preserved well. A sow farrowed twice a year, and according to *Hosbonderie* was expected to produce seven piglets per litter.[64] Records at Stevenage, Hertfordshire, for the late thirteenth century show sows producing up to nineteen offspring a year, "a good enough figure even by modern standards."[65] They could be eaten "profitably" in their second year, and supplied scarce fat to the medieval diet.[66] Pigs for-

aged for themselves on the acorns, beechnuts, crab apples, hazelnuts, and leaves of the forest floor. For the privilege, exercised mainly in the autumn, their owners paid the lord pannage, in Elton on a sliding scale of a quarter penny to twopence, depending on the pig's size.[67] Probably pannage was originally a fine for overuse of the limited forest mast, which might deprive the wild boar, favored lordly taunting quarry. Feed for pigs was more of a problem in winter, but might be supplemented by whey, a by-product of the cheese-making process.[68]

Unlike sheep, pigs could take care of themselves against predators and so could be allowed to run free. This led to the problem of their rooting in somebody's garden, especially in winter, leading turn to numerous bylaws requiring rings—bits of curved wire—in their noses beginning at Michaelmas or another autumn date.[69]

Cattle were the most expensive animals to keep through the winter but were rarely slaughtered. Cows gave about 120 to 150 gallons of milk a year, far below modern yields, but at a half penny per gallon not a neg-

Workman hammering a nail into a ship's hull. Stone relief sculpture (13th c.). Upper Porch, Sainte Chapelle, Paris.

ligible contribution to a peasant income. Calving percentages were high, somewhat contradicting the theory that cows were seriously underfed in winter.[70] Such better-off Elton villagers as John of Elton, Nicholas Blundel, Richard of Barton, and Richer Chapelyn bought grass from the demesne pasture or from the millpond. Other resources included mistletoe and ivy from the forest.[71]

Goats, from the point of view of husbandry a sort of inferior sheep, were seldom kept in the lowlands (though the Ramsey manor of Abbot's Ripton kept a herd), but in mountainous regions could thrive better than any other stock.[72] Nearly all the villagers kept poultry. Geese were a favorite, producing, according to *Hosbonderie,* five goslings apiece per year.[73]

The marketing of animals was done mainly before Christmas, before Lent, and at Whitsuntide.

Villeins, cotters, and free tenants alike, nearly all the villagers spent their days in the fields, manhandling the plow, swinging the scythe or sickle, loading the cart. Not quite all, however. There were also the two bakers at either end of the village, the smith, the carpenter, and the millers and fullers who operated the three mills astride the Nene. Using water power to grind grain was an old story, using it to finish cloth a new one. For centuries

fullers, or walkers (whence both English surnames), had done their job with their feet, trampling the rough wool fabric in a trough of water after rubbing it with fuller's earth, an absorbent clay that helped get rid of the grease. The water wheel now drove a set of beaters that took the place of the fullers' feet. After the cloth had been partially dried, it was finished by teasing the nap and shearing it with huge flat shears, preparing it for the final step in the process, dyeing.[74]

For the gristmill, either the same or another mill wheel was geared to rotate the upper of a pair of millstones, which was pierced to allow the grain to be fed in. Millstones were expensive, sometimes imported from abroad. When a mill was farmed, the steward might cause millstones to be measured before and after the farm, and the farmer charged for the wear.

All three mills were under the supervision of the bailiff, who rendered an annual accounting (in 1297 he recorded the fullers as finishing 22 ells of wool blanket cloth for the abbot).[75] He sold the multure, the flour taken in payment from the grist mills' captive customers, who were kept ever in line by the manor court: "Andrew Saladin [fined] because he keeps a handmill to the lord's damage" and Andrew's handmill confiscated (1331).[76] The customary tenants were permitted to grind their own grain only if the mill was flooded, in which case they were obligated to come and repair it.[77] The millers were responsible for incidental income from the tolls paid by those using the mill as a bridge, from the sale of eels from the millpond, from flax grown on its shores, and from the rental of boats and the sale of grass.[78]

The bakers' monopoly was also guarded by the court. Three villagers were fined in 1300 for "withdrawing themselves from the lord's common oven," and in 1306 eight, one of whom was excused "because she is poor."[79] Later three villagers were fined for going into the baking business: Walter Abbot, Robert son of the chaplain, and Athelina of Nassington were found to be "common bakers" and had to pay twelve pence apiece.[80]

The smith and the carpenter turn up in the Elton accounts in connection with repairs to the mills as well as work on the demesne plows and carts. The smith made horseshoes either from "the lord's iron" or from "his own iron," and also ox shoes, since oxen were often shod (but neither horses nor oxen necessarily on all four

Canterbury Tales: The Cook from the *Ellesmere Manuscript* **(facsimile ed., 1911).**

The Blacksmith, illustration for the Sign of Scorpio. (Fresco, 15th c.).

feet). The smith fabricated blades, tanged or socketed, to be fitted with wooden knife handles; and also cauldrons, kettles, cups, sickles, billhooks, saws, and fasteners.[81] His shop in the middle of the village was equipped with tools that dated from prehistory: anvil, hammer, and the tongs with which he endlessly returned the workpiece to the fire. He probably also had the more recently invented bellows. Recorded payments to him from the manor ran from a few pence for shoeing horses of the abbot to four shillings sixpence for repairing the demesne plows.[82] Often he collaborated on a job with the carpenter, fashioning a wood-and-iron plow or harrow, wheelbarrow, fork, or spade. The carpenter also appears in the manorial accounts, building a dovecote for the manor house, and repairing the manor's chapel and granary, the porch of the barn, the mill machinery, and the abbey's boats used to transport produce on the Nene.[83]

Other craftsmen probably served the village on a part-time basis. The cotters, jacks-of-all-trades, doubtless developed specializations. The important trade of tanning was apparently not practiced in Elton, at least not on a full-time basis, but an Elton man, son of Richard Dunning, is known to have gone to Hayham to become "a man John Tanner, man of means [who] has many goods."[84] Elton villagers probably did some of their own tanning and harnessmaking at home, along with other craft functions. Among the stream of itinerant tradespeople who passed through the village were slaters, tilers, and thatchers, a tinker ("a man to repair brass jars and brass pans"), carters ("two men with dung carts at mowing time" and "two carters carrying stone"),

men to "brand animals" and to "geld suckling pigs," "a woman milking sheep," "three grooms driving animals into the marsh," "a girl drying malt," "a certain excommunicated clerk helping the swineherd in the wood," and "divers other workmen."[85] Plying trades in the abbey village of Ramsey and in Peterborough, Stamford, and other nearby towns were shoemakers, saddlers, chandlers, coopers, glaziers, tanners, tailors, and other merchant craftsmen.

The countryside profited in quality of life from the growth of city crafts. As Henri Pirenne observed, the old manorial workshops, with their serf labor, turned out tools and textiles "not half as well as they were now made by the artisan of the neighboring town."[86] At the same time, the flight of craftsmen tended to restrict the village to the uninspiring toil of plow and sickle. To the variety of life of the town was added the lure of freedom. On the Continent the rule had long been accepted that "free air makes free men" and residence in a town for a year and a day erased serfdom. In England servile disabilities were canceled by similar residence in a borough with a royal charter or on royal demesne land. What a man needed in order to take advantage of the opportunity was a skill, not easy but not impossible to obtain in the village. According to J. A. Raftis, emigration of villeins from the Ramsey estate "was a regular feature of manorial life from the time of the earliest extant court rolls."[87] One village craft was so widely practiced that it hardly belonged to craftsmen. Every village not only had its brewers, but had them all up and down the street. Many if not most of them were craftswomen (virtually all in Elton). Ale was as necessary to life in an English medieval village as bread, but where flour-grinding and bread-baking were strictly guarded seigneurial monopolies, brewing was everywhere freely permitted and freely practiced. How the lords came to overlook this active branch of industry is a mystery (though they found a way to profit from it by fining the brewers for weak ale or faulty measure). Not only barley (etymologically related to beer) but oats and wheat were used, along with malt, as principal ingredients. The procedure was to make a batch of ale, display a sign, and turn one's house into a temporary tavern. Some equipment was needed, principally a large cauldron, but this did not prevent poor women from brewing. All twenty-three persons indicted by the Elton ale tasters in 1279 were women. Seven were pardoned because they were poor.[88]

Life in a village in the late thirteenth century was

not one of abundance for anybody. "Given the productive powers of their soil, their technical knowledge, their capital resources and the burden of their rents and taxes, the numbers of peasants on the land were greater than its produce could support," conclude M. M. Postan and J. Z. Titow, perhaps pessimistically.[89] Certainly ordinary men and women, whether free or unfree, could not escape occasions or degrees of want. What the village offered, at least to its landed tenants, free or unfree, was a measure of relative security in return for a life of unremitting labor. Not surprisingly, many longed for something a little easier and a little better. The fabled land of Cockaigne of popular literature was a place "where the more you sleep the more you earn," and where people "can eat and drink/ All they want without danger."[90]

From the perspective of modern times, the daily drudgery and scant returns of the medieval village appear less the product of the social system than of the state of technology. And even though, like all the social structures that had preceded it, the manorial system was heavily weighted in favor of the ruling class, it was not wholly one-sided. "The manor does not exist for the exclusive use of the lord any more than it exists for the exclusive benefit of the peasantry," concluded Paul Vinogradoff, one of the earliest of its modern historians.[91]

Yet dissatisfaction was inevitable. Protests and minor riots are recorded at numerous places, over labor service, tallage, merchet, the right to buy and sell mowing service, and other villein burdens.[92] Similar incidents occurred on the Continent throughout the thirteenth century. For the time being, no large-scale movements developed, but the smoldering potential was there. *Piers Plowman* endorsed the existing order but insisted that it should be based on justice on the part of the lord, a philosophical solution with only limited practical merit. The villein was bound to resent not only his obligations but his status, and the lord could not forever hold him to either.

Page from *Piers Plowman* depicting the Dreamer in the first initial (15th c.).

VIII
THE PARISH

esides being a manor, Elton was one other thing: a parish, a church district. Like village and manor, village and parish did not always coincide. Some villages had more than one church, usually because they included more than one manor. Some parishes, especially in the north of England, included more than one village, indicating that a large estate, with its church, had been fractioned into several villages and hamlets. By the thirteenth century, however, most villages were geographically coterminous with their parishes, so that the village formed a religious as well as a secular community.[1]

The parish church, like the village, was a medieval invention, the ancient Romans having worshiped at private altars in their own homes. The thousands of

Christian churches built in the villages across Europe in the Middle Ages were the product of two different kinds of foundation. Some were planted by the city cathedrals and their subordinate baptisteries, and formed an integral part of the Church establishment. Others were private or "proprietary" churches, built by landowners on their own property, to serve their households and tenants. The landowner might be a wealthy layman, or a monastery, or a bishop. The church was the owner's personal property, to be sold or bequeathed as he pleased. Its revenues went into his pocket. He appointed the priest, had him ordained, and paid him a salary. With the settlement of Northern Europe, these private-enterprise churches spread. In England they followed a similar development, and given the sanction of Saxon and Danish kings, acquired the important right to perform the sacraments of baptism and burial. The church tower became a village landmark, and the parish priest, who usually had enough Latin to witness and guarantee legal documents, became a valued member of village society.[2]

It is likely that when Dacus reluctantly sold Elton to Aetheric in 1017 and it came into the possession of Ramsey Abbey, the property included a church. Seventy years later, Domesday Book states that Elton had "a

Monks Taking Prayers by the Parement Master and his workshop from the *Très Belles Heures du Duc de Berry* **(begun c. 1382).**

The Building of a Chapel from the *Roll of St. Guthlac* (13th c.)

church and a priest," and in 1178 Pope Alexander III confirmed that "Elton with its church and all pertaining to it" belonged to Ramsey Abbey.[3]

Of the medieval rectors of Elton, only a few scattered names survive. Thuri Priest was rector in 1160, at the time of the earliest manorial survey; Robert of Dunholm in 1209; Henry of Wingham in mid-thirteenth century; and after 1262 Robert of Hale, a member of a local family whose names occur in the manorial court records.

Meanwhile, the arrangement had undergone a change. The lord still appointed the rector (*persona* in the extents, hence "parson"), but now he bestowed the parish on him as a "living," from which the appointee received all or most of the revenues. Although he was always a cleric, the rector did not necessarily serve in person, but might live elsewhere, hiring a deputy, usually a vicar, and profiting from the difference between the revenues he collected and the stipend he paid his substitute.[4]

In general, a class difference existed between the rectors who served in person and those who merely collected the revenues. The former were typically local men, sons of free peasants or craftsmen, sometimes of villeins who had paid a fine to license their training and ordination. The absentee was more apt to be a member of the nobility or gentry, a younger son who had been ordained and drew his income from parish churches rather than tenants' rents.

Certain absentee rectors held several livings simul-

taneously. Some of these "pluralists" held only a few parishes and supervised them conscientiously; others held many and neglected them. A notorious example was Bogo de Clare, younger son of an earl, who in 1291 held twenty-four parishes or parts of parishes plus other church sinecures, netting him a princely income of £2,200 a year. Bogo spent more in a year on ginger than he paid a substitute to serve one of his parishes, in which he took little interest. A monk visiting one of Bogo's livings on Easter Sunday found that in place of the retable (the decorative structure above the high altar), there were only "some dirty old sticks spattered with cow-dung."[5]

The Church did not condone such excesses as that of Bogo, whom Archbishop John Pecham called "a robber rather than a rector."[6] Efforts were made to limit the number of benefices a man could hold, and bishops visited their parishes to check on conditions. In 1172 Pope Alexander III decreed that vicars must have adequate job security and must receive a third of their church's revenues. The Fourth Lateran Council (1215) further denounced the custom whereby "patrons of parish churches, and certain other persons who claim the profits for themselves, leave to the priests

Canterbury Tales: The Parson from the *Ellesmere Manuscript* (facsimile ed., 1911).

deputed to the service of them so small a portion that they cannot be rightly sustained," and pronounced that the rector when not himself residing must see that a vicar was installed, with a guaranteed portion of the revenues.[7]

By the end of the thirteenth century there were about nine thousand parishes in England, perhaps a quarter of them vicarages. Rich parishes tended to attract men in search of income, leading to vicars in many market towns and large villages, and rectors in small ones.[8]

The "poor parson" of the Canterbury Tales was the brother of a plowman who had carted "many a load of dung . . . through the morning dew." This parson "did not set his benefice to hire/ and leave his sheep encumbered in the mire . . . / He was a shepherd and no mercenary." Despite his peasant background, Chaucer's parson was "a learned man, a clerk/ who truly knew Christ's gospel."[9] His colleagues in the country parishes were not all so well versed. Archbishop Pecham charged priests in general with an "ignorance which casts the people into a ditch of error." Roger Bacon (c. 1214– c. 1294) accused them of reciting "the words of others without knowing in the least what they mean, like parrots and magpies which utter human sounds without understanding what they are saying." The chronicler Gerald of Wales amused his readers with stories about the ignorance of parish priests: one who could not distinguish between Barnabas and Barabbas; another who, confusing St. Jude with Judas Iscariot, advised his congregation to honor only St. Simon at the feast of St. Simon and St. Jude. Still another could not distinguish between the Latin for the obligations of the two debtors in the parable (Luke 7:41–43), one of whom owed five hundred pence and the other fifty. When his examiner pointed out that if the sums were the same, the story had no meaning, the priest replied that the money must be from different mints, in one case Angevin pennies, in the other sterling.[10]

Bishops ordaining candidates for the priesthood, or visiting parishes, often found both candidates and ordained clergy *illiteratus*—unlettered, meaning lacking in Latin and thus ignorant of the Scriptures and the rituals. Laymen were less severe. The dean of Exeter, touring parishes in Devon in 1301, found the parishioners almost universally satisfied with their priests as preachers and teachers.[11]

Facilities for the education of priests were scarce, and many aspiring novices could only apply to another parish priest for a smattering of Latin, the Mass, and the principal rites. The lucky few who were able to attend cathedral schools, monastic schools, and the universities were more likely to become teachers, Church officials, or secretaries in noble households than parish priests. A priest might, however, occasionally obtain a leave of absence to study theology, canon law, and the Bible.[12]

The appearance in the thirteenth century of manuals and treatises for the guidance of parish priests marked a new stage of clerical professionalism. One of the most widely circulated was the *Oculus Sacerdotis* (Eye of the Priest), written by William of Pagula, vicar of Winkfield, Berkshire, in 1314. John Myrc's vernacular, versified *Instructions for Parish Priests,* was a free translation of a portion of William of Pagula's book, intended to inform the reader

How thou shalt thy parish preach
And what thou needest them to teach,
And what thou must thyself be.[13]

Whether the income of the parish church was collected by a resident or an absentee rector, it came from the same sources. Three kinds of revenue were very ancient in England: plow-alms, soul-scot, and church-scot. The first was a charge on each plow-team, payable at Easter; the second was a mortuary gift to the priest, and the third a charge on all free men, paid at Martinmas, always in kind, usually in grain. These were all relatively small charges. The chief support of the church was the tithe or tenth, familiar in the Old Testament, but only becoming obligatory in the Christian Church in the Middle Ages. Gerald of Wales told a story about a peasant who owed ten stone of wool to a creditor in Pembroke at the time of shearing, and when he found that he had only that amount, sent a tithe of it, one stone, to his church, over the protest of his wife, and the remaining nine to his creditor, asking for extra time to make good the deficiency. But when the creditor weighed the wool, it weighed the full ten stone. By this example, Gerald said, "the wool having been miraculously multiplied like the oil of Elisha, many persons . . . are either converted to paying those tithes or encouraged in their readiness to pay."[14]

Tithes were spelled out in detail in a number of the Ramsey Abbey extents: in Holywell, the rector received from the abbot's demesne tithes of sheaves from six acres of a field called Bladdicas, including two acres of wheat, one of rye, one of barley, and two of oats; and tithes of sheaves from the peasants in Southfield and "in

Exterior view of Beauvais Cathedral (begun 1225). Beauvais, France.

the field west of the barns at Needingworth"; and "in the name of tithes" from the peasants, a penny per year for each chicken, an obol for a calf or a sheep, a quarter-penny for a kid, "and if they have seven sheep or kids, the rector will have one of them and [make up the difference] in silver, according to the value of a tenth part." He received a tenth of the milk every day in the year.[15] At Warboys the rector was also entitled to a tenth of the wool, linen, pigs, geese, and garden products. [16]

Tithes were collected as a kind of income tax from the rector's living. From his spiritual jurisdiction over the villagers he collected voluntary offerings, or oblations, at Mass, on the anniversaries of a parishioner's death, at weddings and funerals, and from penitents after confession. Offerings might be in kind: the bread for Communion, wax and candles, eggs at Easter, cheese at Whitsuntide, fowls at Christmas. At Broughton, at the Feast of the Nativity of the Blessed Mary, all the parishioners, free as well as villein, gave as many loaves of bread as they had plow animals, one-third of which went to the church, two-thirds to the paupers of the parish.[17]

Finally, the rector had the income of his "glebe," the land pertaining to the church which he held as a free man, owing no labor services or servile dues, and which he cultivated as a husbandman. Traditionally, the glebe was twice the normal holding of a villein, though in practice it varied. In 1279 the rector of the Elton church held a virgate, probably distributed in the fields, and, adjacent to the church, ten more acres and a farmstead.[8] Surveys of other Ramsey Abbey villages list the rector's lands in more detail. At Warboys, he held two virgates of land, a house and a yard, and common pasture "in the wood, the marsh, and other places."[19] The rector of Holywell held a virgate, "half a meadow which is called Priestsholm," three acres of meadow distributed in "many pieces," a tenth of the villagers' meadow, and shares of a pasture and a marsh.[20] In Abbot's Ripton, the rector had a virgate, a parsonage, three houses with tenants, and "common pasture in Westwood.[21]

The rector of Elton also rented a piece of land called le Brach. The manorial court took unfavorable notice of certain of his activities, the jurors complaining that he "made pits on the common at Broadmoor,"[22]

Bishop educating Priests by Writing the Greek Alphabet on the Floor of the Church from the *Metz Pontifical* (early 14th c.).

and again that he "dug and made a pit and took away the clay at Gooseholm to the general nuisance."[23] He may have been digging marl for fertilizer or clay to mend his walls. Medieval moralists were occasionally concerned lest the priest's role as husbandman crowd out his spiritual life, and that "all his study [become] granges, sheep, cattle, and rents, and to gather together gold and silver."[24] Perhaps for this reason the glebe was sometimes farmed out to a layman, who paid rent to the rector and made a profit on the sale of the crops.

Nothing is known about the rectory at Elton in the thirteenth century, but some information has survived about rectories, a handful of which, built in stone, still stand, though usually much altered. In size and characteristics the medieval parsonage evidently fell roughly between a manor house and a decent peasant house. That at Hale, Lincolnshire, was described as a hall house with two small bedchambers, one for residents and one for visitors, and a separate kitchen, bakehouse, and brewhouse.[25] When the monks of Eynsham Abbey built a vicarage in 1268 for a church they had appropriated, they specified construction of oak timbers and a hall twenty-six feet by twenty with a buttery at one end and at the other a chamber and a privy.[26] Like any other farmhouse, the rectory or vicarage included barns, pens, and sheds.

Records mention several persons assisting the rector or vicar in his professional work and daily life—chaplain, curate, clerk, page—without disclosing whether these were full- or part-time aides, or how they were compensated. Not infrequently there was also a wife or concubine. Clerical celibacy was a medieval ideal more often expressed than honored. Although two Lateran councils in the twelfth century prescribed it, a modern canon-law authority comments that in the thirteenth century "everyone who entered the clergy made a vow of chastity but almost none observed it."[27] Gerald of Wales states that "nearly all" English priests were married, though other sources indicate that only a minority were.[28] Concubinage, usually entirely open, was more common. Robert Manning tells the tale of a woman who lived with a "right amorous priest" for many years and bore him four sons, three of whom became priests, the fourth a scholar. After their father died, the four sons urged the mother to repent her "deadly sin." The mother, however, declared that she would never repent "while I have you three priests to pray and chant for me and to bring me to bliss." The mother died "sooner than she willed." For three nights her sons sat by her body at the wake. On the first, at midnight, to their ter-

A Theology Course from *Postilles sur le Pentateuque* **by Nicolas de Lyre (15th c.).**

ror, "the bier began to quake." On the second night it quaked again and suddenly a devil appeared, seized the corpse, and dragged it toward the door. The sons sprang up, carried it back, and tied it to the bier. On the third night at midnight a whole host of fiends invaded the house and:

> Took the body and the bier
> With loathly cry that all might hear
> And bore it forth none knows where,
> Without end forevermore.

The scholar son then roamed the world advising women not to become "priests' mares," lest they suffer his mother's fate.[29]

The Lanercost Chronicle relates a less cautionary story: a vicar's concubine, learning that the bishop was coming to order her lover to give her up, set out with a basket of cakes, chickens, and eggs, and intercepted the bishop, who asked her where she was going. She replied, "I am taking these gifts to the bishop's mistress who has lately been brought to bed." The bishop, properly mortified, continued on his way to call on the vicar, but never mentioned mistresses or concubines.[30]

The importance of the parish church in the village scheme was permanently underlined by the rebuilding of nearly all of them in stone, a process that began in the late Anglo-Saxon period and was largely completed by the thirteenth century. Many medieval village churches survive today, in whole or, as in the case of Elton's chancel arch, in part. In the smaller villages, the church often remained a single-cell building with

Silver-gilt chalice, French (c.1325).

one large room. In larger parishes, as at Elton, the church was often two-cell, the nave, where the congregation gathered, linked by an arched doorway to the chancel, where the altar stood and the liturgy was performed. Sometimes lateral chapels flanked the chancel, and side aisles were added to the nave.[31]

In 1287 Bishop Quinel of Exeter listed the minimum furnishing of a church: a silver or silver-gilt chalice; a silver or pewter vessel (ciborium) to hold the bread used in Communion; a little box of silver or ivory (pyx) to hold the remainder of the consecrated bread, and another vessel for unconsecrated bread; a pewter chrismatory for the holy oils; a censer and an incense boat (thurible); an osculatorium (an ornament by which the kiss of peace was given); three cruets; and a holy-water vessel. The church must have at least one stone altar, with cloths, canopy, and frontal (front hanging); a stone font that could be locked to prevent the use of baptismal water for witchcraft; and images of the church's patron saint and of the Virgin Mary. Special candlesticks were provided for Holy Week and Easter, and two great portable crosses served, one for processions and one for visitation of the sick, for which the church also kept a lantern and a hand bell.[32] To these requirements a list dictated by Archbishop Winchelsey in 1305 added the Lenten veil, to hang before the high altar, Rogation Day

banners for gang week, "the bells with their cords," and a bier to carry the dead.[33] Conspicuously missing were benches, chairs, or pews; the congregation stood, sat on the floor, or brought stools.

The church was supposed to have a set of vestments for festivals and another for regular use. Bishop Quinel recommended a number of books to help the priest: a manual for baptism, marriage, and burial; an ordinal listing the offices to be recited through the church year; a missal with the words and order of the Mass; a collect book containing prayers; a "legend" with lessons from the Scriptures and passages from the lives of the saints; and music books, including a gradual for Mass, a troper for special services, a venitary for the psalms at matins, an antiphoner for the canonical hours, a psalter, and a hymnal. Books and vestments were stored in a church chest.[34]

The churchyard with its consecrated burial ground was a source of village controversy. In the name of those who lay "awaiting the robe of glory," priests decried its use for such sacrilegious purposes as "dances and vile and dishonorable games which lead to indecency," and court trials, "especially those involving bloodshed." An often-repeated injunction demanded that the churchyard be walled and the walls kept in repair, to ensure that the graves "are not befouled by brute beasts."[35] Robert Manning told the story of a

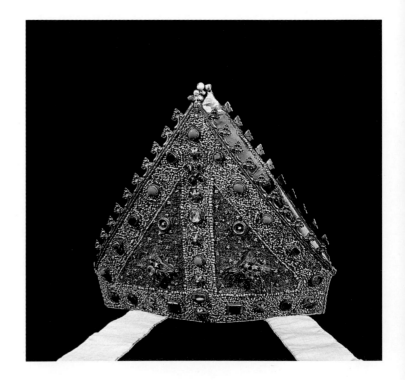

Mitre belonging to William of Wykeham (1324–1414) Bishop of Winchester. Cloth-of-gold on modern backing, embroidered with pearls, imitation turquoises and pastes.

villein of Norfolk who rebuked a knight whose manor "was not far from the church," for allowing his animals to enter the churchyard, since "as oft befalls,/ Broken were the churchyard walls." The peasant addressed the knight:

> "Lord," he said, "your beasts go amiss.
> Your herd does wrong and your knaves
> That let your beasts defile these graves.
> Where men's bones should lie
> Beasts should do no villainy."

The knight's reply was "somewhat vile": Why should one respect "such churls' bones"?
The villein replied:

> "The lord that made of earth earls,
> Of that same earth made he churls . . .
> Earls, churls, all at one,
> Shall none know your from our bones."

The knight, abashed, repaired the churchyard walls "so that no beast might come thereto to eat or defile."[36]

Three services were normally celebrated in the parish church on Sunday: matins, Mass, and evensong. Mass was also said daily, and the priests were supposed to say the canonical hours at three-hour intervals for their own benefit.[37] Sunday Mass was the best-attended service. Robert Manning pictured a man lying abed on Sunday morning and hearing the church bells ring, "to holy church men calling," and preferring to

> . . . lie and sweat
> And take the merry morning sleep;
> Of matins rich men take no keep.

A devil whispers in his ear, urging him to ignore matins:

> "Betimes may you rise
> When they do the Mass service.
> A Mass is enough for you."[38]

Vanity sometimes caused women to be late for Mass, like the lady of Eynsham described by a fourteenth-century preacher, "who took so long over adornment of her hair that she barely arrived at church

A page from the Latin Mass with illuminated letter A.

before the end of Mass." One day the devil in the form of a giant spider descended on her coiffure. Nothing would dislodge it, neither prayer, exorcism, nor holy water, until it was confronted with the Eucharist. The spider then decamped, and presumably the lady thenceforth arrived at church on time.[39]

William of Pagula declared that it was hard to get people to church at all: "Anon he will make his excuse and say, 'I am old or sickly, or the weather is cold and I am feeble.' Or else he will excuse himself and say thus, 'I have a great household,' or else he has some other occupation to do, but for all these excuses, if a man would come and hear him and say, 'I will give good wages [for going to church],' then will they take all manner of excuses back and come to the divine service according to their duty."[40]

The Mass was said in Latin, with little participation by the congregation, and Communion was usually administered only at Easter. Moralists complained that the people chattered, gossiped, and flirted at Mass. John Myrc inveighed against casual worshipers who leaned against a pillar or wall instead of kneeling. When the

Gospel was read, they should stand; when it was finished, they should kneel again. When the bell rang at the consecration, they should raise their hands and pray.[41]

Sermons were infrequent in the thirteenth century. Instead, the priest might devote time to a lesson, instructing the congregation about the Articles of the Faith, the seven deadly sins, or the sacraments, or he might read from a collection of sermons in English, though such books were not yet widely distributed.

The art of preaching, however, was undergoing a revival, led by the mendicant friars, the Dominicans and Franciscans. Arriving in England in the 1220s, these roving brothers preached in the parish church with the permission of the rector, or failing that, in the open air, where their sermons offered a lively alternative to the routine of Sunday services. Illustrated with personal experiences, fables, and entertaining stories, they encouraged the participation of the congregation. A

preacher might call out, "Stop that babbling," to a woman, who did not hesitate to reply, "What about you? You've been babbling for the last half hour." Such exchanges brought laughter, applause, and more friendly heckling.[42]

When sermons were delivered, either by parish priest or friar, they followed an elaborate formula. The preacher announced his Scriptural text *(thema),* then commenced with the *antethema,* usually a prayer and invocation, or "bidding prayer," like the following (for the day of the Assumption of the Blessed Virgin):

> Almighty God, to whose power and goodness infinite all creatures are subject, at the beseeching of thy glorious Mother, gracious lady, and of all thy saints, help our feebleness with thy power, our ignorance with thy wisdom, our frailty with thine sufficient goodness, that we may receive here thine help and grace continual, and finally everlasting bliss. To which bliss thou took this blessed Lady this day as to her eternal felicity. Amen.[43]

The theme was then repeated, followed by an introduction which might begin with an "authority," quoted from the Bible or from a Church Father, or a message for the particular occasion or audience, or an attention-getting "exemplum," an illustrative story ("Examples move men more than precepts," advised St. Gregory). The story might be merely "something strange, subtle and curious," or a terrifying tale about devils, death-bed scenes, and the torments of hell. Sources abounded fable, chronicle, epic, romance. One story that must have had a particular appeal to peasant women began, "I find in the chronicles that there was once a worthy woman who had hated a poor woman more than seven years." When the "worthy woman" went to church on Easter Day, the priest refused to give her Communion unless she forgave her enemy. The woman reluctantly gave lip service to the act of forgiveness, "for the shame of the world more than for awe of God," and so that she could have her Communion.

Then, when service was done...the neighbors came unto this worthy woman's house with presents to cheer her, and thanked God highly that they were accorded. But then this wretched woman said, "Do you

The Last Judgment from a Book of Hours (c.1500).

think I forgave this woman her trespass with my heart as I did with my mouth? Nay! Then I pray God that I never take up this rush at my foot." Then she stooped down to take it up, and the devil strangled her even there. Wherefore ye that make any love-days [peace agreements] look that they be made without any feigning, and let heart and the tongue accord in them.[44]

The body of the sermon was usually divided into three sections: an exposition on three vices or symbolic meanings of the Trinity, or symbolic features of some familiar object—a castle, a chess game, a flower, the human face.

The sermon ended with a flourish, sometimes a smooth peroration, merely summing up the text and discourse, sometimes, especially if the congregation had dozed, a rousing hellfire diatribe. The priest might compare the agony of a sinner in hell with being rolled a mile in a barrel lined with red-hot nails. Devils were favorite descriptive subjects, with their faces "burned and black." One devil was so horrible that "a man would not for all the world look on him once." Hell rang with the "horrible roaring of devils, and weeping, and gnashing of teeth, and wailing of damned men, crying, 'Woe, woe, woe, how great is this darkness!'" If one of them longed for sweetmeats and drink, he got "no sweetness, nor delicacy, but fire and brimstone . . . If one of them would give a thousand pounds for one drop of water, he gets none. . . . There shall be flies that bite their flesh, and their clothing shall be worms . . . and in short, there are all manner of torments in all the five senses, and above all there is the pain of damnation: pain of privation of the bliss of heaven, which is a pain of all pains. . . . Think on these pains; and I trust to God that they shall steer thee to renounce thy drunken living!"[45]

Sometimes the closing peroration pictured the Last Judgment and the doom that preceded it: fifteen days of terrible portents, tidal waves and the sea turning to blood, earthquakes, fires, tempests, fading stars, yawning graves, men driven mad by fear, followed by the accounting from which no man could escape, by brides, or influence, or worldly power, "for if thou shall be found in any deadly sin, though Our Lady and all the saints of heaven pray for thee, they shall not be heard."[46]

Or the preacher might close by reminding his congregation of their mortality. "These young people think," cried one preacher, "that they shall never die, especially before they are old! . . . They say, 'I am young yet. When I grow old I will amend.'" Such persons were reminded to "Go to the burials of thy father and mother; and such shalt thou be, be ye ever so fair, ever so wise, ever so strong, ever so gay, ever so light." Death was the inevitable end, and none too far off. Man's earthly being was in fact insignificant and not very comely: "What is man but a stinking slime, and after that a sack full of dung, and at the last, meat for worms?"[47]

Even without sermons, the medieval parishioner was reminded of his fate by the paintings decorating the church walls, only a few of which have survived.★ In these murals often over the chancel arch, a symbolic

★Such as the Last Judgment discovered in the church at Broughton, currently being restored.

gateway between this world and the next, Christ sat in stern judgment, graves sprang open, and naked sinners tumbled into the gaping mouth of a beast with great pointed fangs, or, chained together, into the claws of demons.

A major function of the parish priest was that of instructing his parishioners. It was up to him to teach the children the Creed, the Lord's Prayer, the Ave, and the Ten Commandments. William of Pagula recommended that the priest give not only religious instruction but practical advice: telling mothers to nurse their own children, not to let them smother in bed or tie them in their cradles or leave them unattended; advising against usury and magic arts; giving counsel on sexual morality and marriage. Marriage was a topic well worth discussion, William pointed out: a horse, an ass, an ox, or a dog could be tried out before it was bought, but a wife had to be taken on trust. A poor wife was difficult to support; living with a rich one was misery. Was it better to marry a beautiful wife or an ugly one? On the one hand, it was hard to keep a wife that other men were pursuing, on the other it was irksome to have one that no one else wanted; but on balance an ugly wife brought less misery.[48]

The priest's instruction of adults came largely through confession, in which he not only examined the penitent's morals but his religious knowledge:

Believest thou in Father and Son and Holy Ghost . . .
Three persons in Trinity,
And in God (swear thou to me)?
That God's son mankind took
In maid Mary (as saith the Book),
And of that maid was born:
Believest thou this? . . .
And in Christ's passion
And in His resurrection. . . ?
That He shall come with wounds red
To judge the quick and the dead,
And that we each one . . .
Shall rise at the day of Doom
And be ready when he come. . . ?[49]

The manuals coached the priest to interrogate the penitent about his behavior: "Have you done any sorcery to get women to lie with you?" "Have you ever plighted your troth and broken it?" "Have you spent Sunday in shooting, wrestling, and other play, or gong to the ale house?" "Have you stolen anything or been at any robbing?" "Have you found anything and kept it?" "Have you borrowed anything and not returned it?" "Have you ever claimed any good deed of charity that was another man's doing?" "Have you been slow to teach your godchildren Pater Noster and Creed?" "Have you come late to church?" "Have you without devotion heard any sermon?" "Have you been glad in your heart when your neighbor came to harm, and grieved when he had good fortune?" "Have you eaten with such greed that you cast it up again?" "Have you sinned in lechery?" "If your children are shrews, have you taught them good manners?"

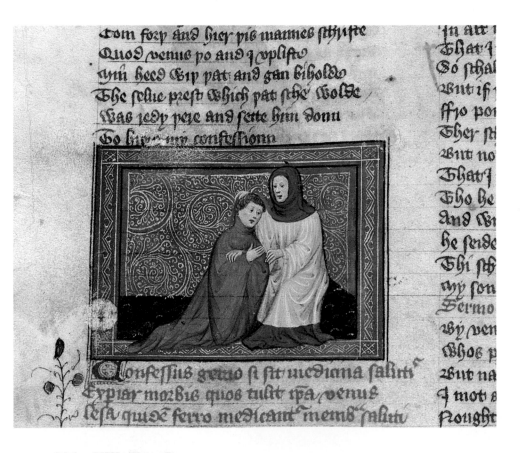

The Lover Confides his Sins to a Confessor, illumination in the style of Hermann Scheerre, written by John Gower (c.1325–1408) made in London from the *Confessio Amantis* (15th c.).

"Have you destroyed grain or grass or other things that are sown? Are you wont to ride through grain when you could go to one side?"[50]

The penitent must confess his sins completely and without reservation. If he killed a man, he must say who it was, where, and why. If he "sinned in lechery," he must not give the name of his partner, but he should tell whether she was married or single, or a nun, where the sin was committed, and how often, and whether it was on a holy day. The penance should fit the sin, light for a light sin, heavy for a heavy, but never too heavy for the penitent to perform, lest he ignore it and be worse off than if he had not gone to confession. "Better a light penance to send a man to purgatory," wrote John Myrc, "than a too heavy penance to send him to hell." Even more sagely, a woman's penance must be such that her husband would not know about it, lest it cause friction between them.[51]

Above all, the priest must teach by example. His preaching was worth little if he lived an evil life. The sins he was especially warned against indicate those he was most likely to fall into. He should be chaste; he should be true; he should be mild in word and deed. "Drunkenness and gluttony, pride and sloth and envy, all these thou must put away." The priest must forsake taverns, trading, wrestling and shooting, hawking, hunting, and dancing. "Markets and fairs I thee forbid." He must wear "honest clothes," and not knightly "basinet and baldric." His beard and crown must be shaven. He must be hospitable to rich and poor. And finally,

Turn thine eye that thou not see
The cursed world's vanity.
Thus this world thou must despise
And holy virtues have in vise [view].[52]

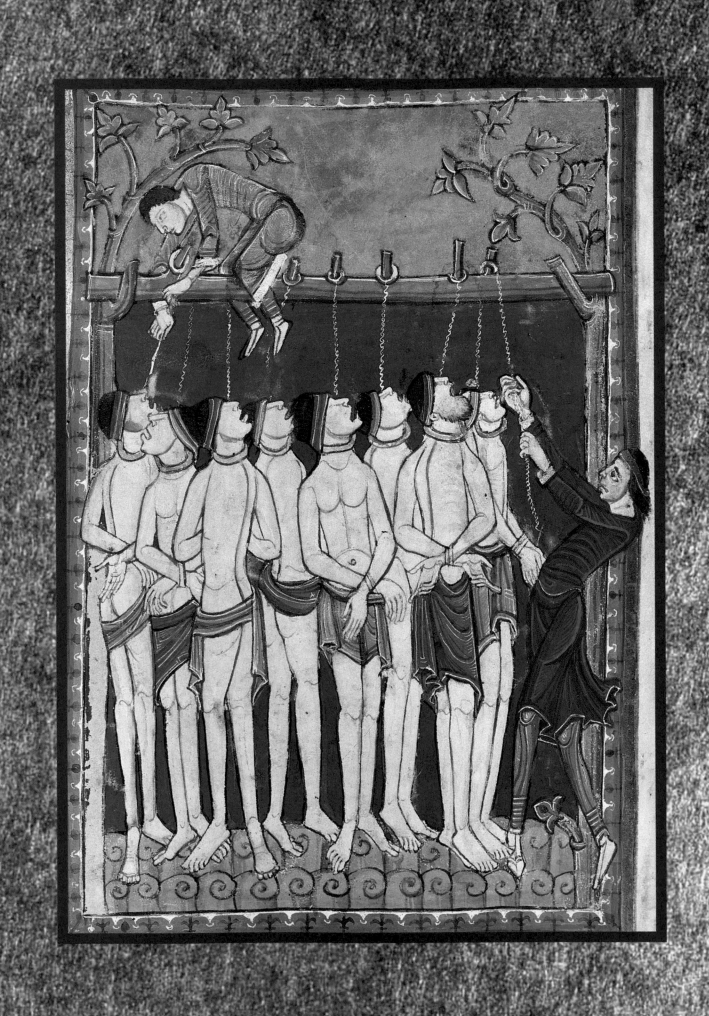

IX
VILLAGE JUSTICE

wice or more each year, the villagers gathered for the hallmote: hall, meaning manor house, and mote, meeting. The records of this legal body provide unique insights into the relationship between lord and village community, and at the same time demonstrate the frictions and stresses of everyday village life.

The hallmote was the lord's manorial court, presided over by his steward, and transacting primarily the lord's business: collecting merchet, heriot, entry fees, and other manorial dues, enforcing labor services, electing manorial officers, granting seisin (legal possession) to heirs and receiving fealty from them, and providing the lord with substantial profits from its fines and confiscations.

Yet the principal actors in the hallmote were villagers, who in effect served as prosecutor, legal authority, witnesses, and judge. Much of the court's business had nothing to do with the lord, but was concerned with

Hanging of Thieves from the *Life, Passion, and Miracles of St. Edmund, King and Martyr,* **(c.1130).**

interaction among the villagers. Finally, the hallmote's proceedings were ruled not by the lord's will but by the ancient and powerful body of tradition known as the custom of the manor.

The hallmote, furthermore, was a legislative as well as a judicial body, promulgating the bylaws that governed field, meadow, pasture, and woods from Michaelmas to Michaelmas, sending the men to work and the animals to graze in strict concert, stipulating who should harvest, who should glean, when, and for how long. Surviving Elton court rolls record no bylaw enactments, only references to infractions of existing bylaws, but elsewhere they are recorded as enacted by the "community," the "homage," the "tenants," or the "neighbors." The lord is rarely mentioned in their framing, though the security of his demesne cultivation was a primary object.[1]

A fragmentary document records the itinerary of the Ramsey Abbey steward for the twenty-three manorial courts of early 1294. Holding court first at Ramsey itself on Thursday, January 7, he rode to the nearest manors—Broughton, Wistow, Ripton, Stukeley, and Gidding—reaching Elton on January 16, a Saturday. Thence he proceeded to Weston on Monday the eighteenth, finished off the Huntingdonshire manors, rode south to Therfield in Hertfordshire, then turned back northeast and held court in the Ramsey manors of Cambridgeshire and Bedfordshire, the last session falling on February 19. Nine of the courts required a second day's sitting, the others were all concluded in a day.[2]

A hallmote held in January pretty surely met inside the manor house. In warmer seasons courts often met in the open air, that of St. Albans assembling under an ancient ash tree.[3] The hall must have been crowded and noisy, with all the villeins gathered, reinforced by a few freeholders whose charters stipulated suit, or whose grandfathers had owed it. Though the steward presided, he did not act as judge. Rather, he lent the authority of the abbot to the judgment rendered by the jury. These twelve (sometimes six or nine) jurati, sworn men, whose oath extended to periods between court sessions, could be fined substantial sums for "concealment," not bringing cases to court, and for "bad answering and false presentment," as happened to Elton jurors on several occasions.[4] They collected and presented evidence, along with the appropriate law, the custom of the manor and the village bylaws. In modern parlance, it was a grand jury, and in fact was sometimes so called, but the commoner term was jury of presentment. The jury's verdict was recorded as, "It is found by the jurors that...", "The jurors say that...", or "And they say that...", followed by the facts of the case and concluding, "Therefore..." and the assessment of fine and damages. The jury's findings received the backing not only of the lord's steward but of the assembled villagers. Their concurrence was usually expressed tacitly, but on certain occasions actively, when plaintiff or defendant or both "put themselves upon the consideration of the whole court." In such a case, the village's assent was inscribed in the court record as *villata dicit* (the village says), or *coram toto halimoto* (in the presence of the whole hallmote), or *per totum halimotum* (by the whole hallmote). In either case, the endorsement of the jury's findings by the assembly at large was of utmost importance.[5]

Sometimes either a plaintiff or a defendant or both asked for an inquest by a special panel, paying for the privilege. Whatever nuances of favor or knowledgeability a litigant hoped to get from one group or the other of his fellow villagers, his fate was nearly always, for better or for worse, in the hands of people who knew him, knew his adversary, knew the circumstances of the case, knew the relevant law and custom, and had talked it over among themselves.

The court's record was kept by the steward's clerk, on a long strip of parchment about eight inches wide, its segments stitched end to end. At its top he inscribed the place and date: "Ayling-tone, on the day of St. Clement the Pope in the 12th year of W[illiam] the Abbot"—in other words, Elton, November 23, 1279. Less accomplished than the clerk of the accounts, he left a record in not very elegant Latin, with many errors in syntax and employing numerous abbreviations. In the left margin he noted the category of case, the judgment, and the amount of the fine. At the end of the record of each court he totaled the fines, exactly as the clerk of the amounts did at the end of the reeve's demesne account. Whatever else the court was, it was part of the lord's business enterprise. By the late thirteenth century, the court records were carefully preserved and often consulted for precedents.[6]

The court's appearance, whether indoors or out, was informal, the crowd of villagers standing before the seated steward and clerk, but court procedure was formal and order strictly enforced. At St. Albans in 1253 a man was fined for cursing the twelve jurors, and many cases are recorded of punishment meted out for false accusations against officials and jurors, for abuse of opposing litigants, and for making a disturbance: *"Fecerunt strepitum, in curia garrulando"* ("they made a racket, talking much in court").[7] In Elton in 1307, John son of John Abovebrook, haled into court for a debt of 32 pence owed to Robert of Teyngton, failed to make good his promise to pay, and the following year was again cited, but "immediately in contempt of the court withdrew without finding pledges." The court ordered that the 32 pence be levied from him, and that he be fined a stiff 40 pence for his behavior. "And afterwards he came and made fine for 40 pence ... and ... he will be obedient henceforth to the lord and to his neighbors."[8]

A fourteenth-century manual for the instruction of novice stewards called *The Court Baron* (another name for the manorial court) prescribes a formality of procedure amounting to ritual. It pictures the clerk commencing by reading aloud a model presentment, a charge of battery done by a villager against an outsider

> Sir steward, Henry of Combe, who is here [pointing], complains of Stephen Carpenter, who is there [pointing], that as he was going his way in the peace of God and in the peace of the lord through this vill which is within the surety of your franchise, at such an hour on such a day in the last year, there came this Stephen Carpenter and encountered him in such a place [naming it], and assailed him with evil words which were undeserved, insomuch that he called him thief and lawless man and whatever other names seemed good to him except only his right name, and told him that he was spying from house to

house the secrets of the good folk of the vill in order that he might come another time by night with his fellows to break [into] their houses and carry off their goods larcenously as a felon; whereupon this Henry answered him civilly and said that he was good and lawful in all things and that [Stephen] was talking at random; whereupon the said Stephen was enraged and snatched his staff of holly out of his hand and gave it to him about his head and across his shoulders and his loins and elsewhere all over his body as he thought fit and then went off. This trespass did the said Stephen wrongfully and against reason and against the peace of the lord and of you, who are charged to guard and maintain the peace, to his damage 20 shillings and shame a half-mark.[9]

The accused then answered the charge with as nice a regard for the proper formula as the clerk had shown, taking each accusation in order:

Tort and force and all that is against the peace of God and the peace of the lord and of you, who are charged to guard and maintain peace, and his [Henry's] damages of 20 shillings and shame of a half-mark and every penny of it, Stephen defends, who is here, and all manner of evil words against Henry of Combe, who is there, and against his suit and all that he surmises against him, that never he called him thief nor gave him evil word, nor surmised evil slander against him, nor with staff of holly nor other staff beat him across the head or shoulders or loins or any part of his body as he surmises; and that this is true, he is ready to acquit himself in all such wise as this court shall award that acquit himself he ought.[10]

It may be doubted that hallmotes insisted on such exquisite perfection of jargon, but it is known that defendants and litigants in serious cases were often alert to slips of language by which technical flaws could be imputed and judgment perhaps evaded.[11]

The steward in *The Court Baron* next addresses the accused: "Fair friend Stephen, this court awards that you be at your law six-handed at the next court to acquit yourself," to which the defendant replies, "Willingly, sir."[12] "Be at your law six-handed" meant that Stephen was to bring with him five men who would join him in swearing either that his account of the case was true or that he was himself a trustworthy person. In cases of more serious character or when there was reason to doubt the accused, he might be called on to "be at your law twelve-handed," requiring him to find eleven "oath helpers." Oath helping, or compurgation, was by 1300 a basic element of medieval jurisprudence. The sense of it

was that several men who attested the truth of their statements on the holy relics would be unlikely to swear their souls away simultaneously.[13]

At this point a uniquely medieval step in the court's procedure took place: both plaintiff and defendant were ordered to "find pledges," persons to act as sureties to guarantee their appearance in court. Such personal pledging was also used to guarantee fulfillment of a promised obligation, or even that the pledge's subject would behave himself. Pledges were held accountable by the court and were liable to fine: "John Page and John Fraunceys were pledges of Henry Smith for the payment of two shillings to John son of Alexander in the Lane . . . and nothing is paid. Therefore both of them in mercy [fined] . . . Better pledges are William of Barnwell and Reginald son of Benedict."[14] Those needing pledges sought them among the better class of fellow villagers, those with substantial holdings, who served in village offices. Reeves and beadles were especially in demand. Pledges' fines were usually three pence, half the standard fine for most offenses. Husbands commonly acted as pledges for wives, but otherwise most pledging was extra-familial.[15]

The Court Baron stipulated a particular order in which cases should be heard. In real life the hallmote heard cases by category, but the categories followed no discernible order. The invariably lengthy list of fines for the ale brewers sometimes led off the Elton calendar, sometimes concluded it, and sometimes came in the middle. In 1279, twenty-three violations of the assize of ale were recorded at the end of the court record, just before the selection of new ale tasters. Prior to the brewing violations, thirty-four cases were presented. Ten dealt with defaults of harvest or plow work, three with chevage, the rest with a variety of offenses, from the diversion of a watercourse by a neighboring village to a theft of furrows by a villager.[16] The dispatch with which cases were handled compared with that of a modern traffic court. Yet "the law's delay" was already an established judicial feature. Most defendants were permitted three summonses, three distraints (for failing to appear), and three essoins (excuses for non-appearance), making nine successive postponements.[17]

Litigations between villagers began with a complaint: "John Juvet complains of John Hering." "Robert Maynard complains of Gilbert de Raundes." "Thomas Clerk complains of Nicholas son of Richard Smith." The complainant brought suit—in other words, he brought men with him to vouch for the truth of his complaint. Both he and the defendant were then ordered to find pledges.

Once the suit was initiated, if the complainant did not carry it through, he and his pledge were fined. "From Ralph Hert and Isolda his wife and their pledge, namely Reginald Child, for their non-suit against Richard Reeve and John Abovebrook, six pence."[18] The defendant might wage his law, as John of Elton did "sufficiently" in 1294 against Emma Prudhomme, who had made accusations against him, and who was herself consequently fined.[19] Or the case might be postponed. The delay might result in settlement, either through the defendant's offering to pay a fine or through the two litigants reaching an out-of-court agreement. Such compacts were encouraged by the judicial device of the "love-day" *(dies amoris),* on which the parties to a dispute were directed to try to reconcile their differences.[20] An out-of-court settlement, however, could not be allowed to become an out-of-pocket settlement for the lord. The parties still owed a fee, in this case recorded under the title of "license to agree": "From John son of John of Elton for license to agree with John of Langetoft and Alice his wife sixpence." "From Nicholas le Rous for license to agree with Henry Daysterre and Emma his wife four pence."[21] Part of the agreement was the determination of which of the two parties would pay the fine.

Yet the court was lenient toward the destitute, or realistic about the difficulty of getting blood out of turnips. "In mercy, but [fined] nothing because [he or she is] poor," recurs many times in the records.

At least once a year, usually in late winter or spring, a form of manorial court known as the view (review) of frankpledge was held. A uniquely English institution, frankpledge antedates the Conquest.[22] All the village's male residents under the age of twelve belonged to units of ten or a dozen called frankpledges or tithings, each of which was collectively responsible for the behavior of its members, and whose interests it defended. If a man was accused by a neighbor, the members of his tithing were responsible for his appearance in court. At the head of each tithing was a leader called a chief pledge, an important man in the village: "It was commanded to Hugh Achard and his tithing at the last view to have [a certain man] at this court and he had him not. Therefore he and his tithing in mercy."[23]

The tithing was not kinship-based, though in some ways it served the purpose of the old clan or supra-family group. Originally it was a cell in the royal administration, and its review in some places was still performed by the king's sheriff (shire-reeve, chief officer of the shire), but usually the local lord had acquired frankpledge along with manorial justice. Carried out by the steward, the view of frankpledge assured the integrity of the village's tithings, making certain that every boy turning twelve years of age and every male newcomer to the village acquired membership. By the end of the thirteenth century, the tithing system and personal pledging were showing signs of decadence as the royal courts developed more modern juridical techniques, such as prison and bail.[24]

In theory, and perhaps at one time in fact, there was some distinction in procedure and type of case between the regular hallmote and the view of frankpledge, but by the late thirteenth century it had virtually disappeared. *The Court Baron's* list of offenses typically heard by the view of frankpledge—shedding of blood, rape, theft of grain or poultry, placing a dung-heap in the high street, building a fence on a neighbor's land or on the king's highway—are very much the same things heard in ordinary hallmotes.[25] However, where the hallmote, usually held in the autumn, elected the reeve, beadle, and wardens of autumn, the view of frankpledge chose the village ale tasters.[26]

Killers, professional robbers, and other hardened felons, regular defendants in the royal courts, were rarely seen in the hallmote, which was nevertheless no stranger to violent crime. It was reported in several different forms: "Agnes daughter of Philip Saladin raised the hue-and-cry upon Thomas of Morburn who wanted to have sex with her."[27] "Matilda Prudhomme justly raised the hue-and-cry against John Blaccalf because he drew blood from Hugh the man of the said Matilda."[28] "The wife of Matfrid and her daughter justly raised the hue-and-cry upon Henry Marshal because he beat them."[29] "It was found by neighboring jurors that John ate Lane maliciously assaulted Alice his stepmother in her own house . . . and beat, ill-treated, and maimed the said Alice with a stick, breaking her right hand."[30]

The last category of assault, in the victim's own home, was considered a graver offense than similar violence on neutral ground, and was usually designated hamsoken: "Matilda Saladin justly raised the hue-and-cry upon five men of Sir Gilbert de Lyndsey who were committing hamsoken upon Philip Saladin and beat and badly treated him."[31] Similarly, drawing blood was regarded as especially serious.

The hue-and-cry raised by the victim, or by a relative, neighbor, friend, or passerby, obligated everyone within earshot to drop what he was doing and come to the rescue. Failure to do so brought a collective penalty: "And they say that Alexander Prudhomme badly beat Henry son of Henry Smith [who] justly raised the hue-and-cry upon him. Not prosecuted, *villata* fined two shillings [and] commanded to distrain Alexander to answer."[32]

Blood did not have to be actually shed, or even a blow struck, to justify the hue-and-cry. Richard son of Richard Reeve gave clear indication of a desire to beat Richard Blakeman, who "by reason of terror and fear" was justified in the jurors' eyes in raising the hue-and-cry.[33]

On the other hand, the hue was not to be raised lightly or wrongfully: "The jurors say that Adam Fot committed hamsoken upon Andrew son of Alkusa and nonetheless the wife of the said Adam unjustly raised the hue-and-cry upon the same Andrew. Fine sixpence."[34] Anyone raising the hue was obliged immediately to find a personal pledge to support his claim of raising it justly.

Sometimes two parties to an altercation raked the hue against each other, in which case the court decided which was justified: "Henry Abovebrook justly raised the hue-and-cry upon Richard Sabyn. Richard fined sixpence. . . . And they say that Richard Sabyn unjustly raised the hue-and-cry upon Henry Abovebrook. Richard fined [an additional] sixpence."[35]

When the hue-and-cry posse collared its quarry, he was turned over to the bailiff, the reeve, or the beadle. In Elton in 1312 the beadle was fined three pence "because he did not arrest John son of Matfrid, a bondman, to answer concerning the hue-and-cry."[36]

Serious injury in an assault case brought damages along with the fine: "It is found by the jurors that Robert Sabyn assaulted Nicholas Miller and beat him to his damage of sixpence. Fine sixpence."[37] The three men who assaulted Gilbert son of Reginald le Wyse in 1279 were directed to "satisfy him for damages" as well as pay a sixpence fine.[38] Similarly in cases of property damage: for the malicious injury to the house of Richard son of Elias done by Thomas of Chausey in 1308, Thomas was directed to pay sixpence damages along with the usual sixpence fine.[39]

Only rarely do the Elton records reveal a punishment imposed other than a fine. In the case in 1292 in which John atte Lane was convicted of maliciously assaulting his stepmother and breaking her hand, the account concludes, "Therefore the said ohn is put in the stocks."[40]

Moral transgression was a precinct of the law in

Judgment scene, Fondazione Cini, Venice, Italy.

which the superior competence of the Church courts was conceded, and in which canon law had developed an extensive literature. Adultery was the most conspicuous of moral offenses, and drew the Church's most severe penalties, typically a whipping for peasants, a heavy fine for their betters. The Church also ruled on the validity of marriage contracts (an active legal issue in the absence of state licensing or requirement of witnesses), separations, prescribed penances for such delinquencies as departing from the traditional posture in intercourse.[41]

Nevertheless, the lord took an interest in sex mores, at least a financial interest, focusing on men and women previously haled into Church court for adultery, and young women detected indulging in premarital sex. The jurors were relied on to report cases of leirwite, or of matrimony without the lord's license, and were fined for failing to do so.

A village woman, however, ran a much greater risk of being fined for her brewing than for her dallying. "[Allota] is a common brewer at a penny and sometimes at a halfpenny, and sold before the tasting [by the village ale tasters] and sometimes made [the ale] weak. Therefore [she is] in mercy two shillings."[42] "Alice wife of Blythe [sold] three times at a halfpenny and at a penny and sold before the tasting, did not bring her measures [to be checked]. Twelve pence." "Matilda Abovebrook at a halfpenny and a penny, sometimes weak ale, she sells before the tasting, did not bring her measures. Sixpence."[43] Sometimes the lengthy list of women (only six men ever appear among Elton brewers) is simply put down in the court record with the fine noted. The unfailing frequency of the ale fines has led to a conjecture that the assize of ale was a sort of back-door license fee collected by the lord in lieu of the monopoly he had failed to obtain in this important branch of village business.[44] At the same time, the very number of home brewers makes credible a need for government regulation, while the fines varied and the charges differed: the ale is "weak," "not of full value," "not worth the money," the measures are not sealed, the price is too high. Enforcement of standards for price and quality was of value to consumers, and the insistence on checking brewers' measures indicates serious purpose.

In Elton as everywhere that open field agriculture prevailed, a large proportion of the manor court's business consisted of enforcement of the bylaws and customs governing crops and pasture. Reeve and bailiff were mainly responsible for bringing to book defaulters on work obligations, but for surveillance of the army of harvest workers they had the help of the two "wardens of autumn." "The wardens of autumn present that Master Stephen made default at one boon-work.... Therefore let him be distrained to answer [be arrested and brought to court]." "Of Reginald Child for the same at another boon-work of the autumn of one man [as] above. Pledge Richard the beadle." "Of John Heryng for the same of one man three pence. Pledge Roger Gamel." "Of Robert Chapman for the same of one man sixpence. Pledge John Page."[45] Failure to appear, tardiness, or simply performing the service badly brought sure, if moderate, penalties.

"I do not advise you to plead against your lord," warned a satiric poem ascribed to a canon of Leicester Abbey. "Peasant, you will be vanquished.... You must endure what the custom of the earth has given you."[46] Modern scholar George C. Homans, however, has written: "The striking fact is that many such disputes [between lord and tenant] were settled in the hallmote just as they would have been if the parties had both been simple villagers." Homans cites a case involving tenants of the Bishop of Chichester in 1315, in which an inquest of three hallmotes backed the tenants in their refusal to cart dung for the lord. "The lord's arbitrary will was bounded, or rather he allowed it to be bounded, by custom as found by the tenants."[47]

A number of cases in Elton pitted villagers against the lord, his steward, or his lesser officials. In 1312 "John Troune entered a plea contrary to the lord's statutes" and was fined sixpence for contempt.[48] Two men who pleaded "in opposition to the steward" in the court of 1331 were fined three pence and sixpence, respectively.[49] Thus an individual peasant, as the canon of Leicester warned, appears to have been at a substantial disadvantage in pleading against his betters. But in three other cases, though no final outcome is recorded, the villagers' side of the argument is unmistakably accorded a respectful hearing. One difference in these cases is that the other party was not the lord or his steward, but a lesser official or officials. Another difference, highly significant in the light of later history, is that the village viewpoint was maintained not by an individual tenant but by a large group of villagers, or even the whole village united.

All three cases were heard in 1300. In the first the villagers accused the bailiff and his assistants of having dug a ditch to enclose "a certain place which is called Gooseholm where they planted willows, which place is a common pasture for all the men of the whole village." In the second case, they accused the bailiffs of encroaching on a furlong called Michelgrove by taking away from all the lands abutting on it "to the breadth of four feet."[50] Presumably the officials were doing their encroaching in the interests of the lord's demesne, though there is no indication that they were acting under instructions.

The third case involved an exchange of complaints between the villagers and Hugh Prest, the claviger. First the jurors reported that "the bailiffs of the lord unjustly hinder the community of the vill of Elton from driving by the way which is called the Greenway all their draught-beasts and other animals, whereas they ought to have it for the common of their pasture." In turn, Hugh Prest cited nine villagers, most of them virgaters, "because they drove their beasts by the way which is called Greenway when the furlongs of the lord abbot abutting thereupon were sown." The jurors protested strongly: "And they say that they and all men of the vill of Elton ought by right to have the said droveway at all times of the year, inasmuch as all strangers passing by the same way can have a free droveway with their animals of all kinds without challenge or hindrance."

Hugh Prest replied that although strangers were permitted to use the droveway, in the past "the said customary tenants and their partners have sometimes contributed four shillings to the use of the lord for having their droveway when the furlongs of the lord there had been sown." The anger and indignation of the villagers is unmistakable in the reply recorded in the court rolls:

"And the aforesaid customary tenants and all others of the vill, free tenants as well as others, and also the twelve jurors whose names are contained at the beginning of the roll, say and swear that if any money has been contributed by the customary tenants of the vill to have their droveway there, the said claviger has taken that money at his will by distraint and extortion and has levied it from them unjustly." The steward, clearly embarrassed at "seeing the dissension and discord between the claviger demanding and the said men gainsaying him, was unwilling to pronounce judgment against the claviger"—as the united villagers clearly insisted. Instead he "left this judgment wholly to the disposition of the lord abbot, that the same lord, having scrutinized the register concerning the custom in the matter of this demand, should do and ordain as he should see ought to be done according to the will of God."[51]

Although no further record of the case has survived, it seems unlikely that the abbot provoked further resentment by the villagers over a problem that touched his interests only lightly and vexed them so much. Homans perhaps exaggerates in claiming that "The lord, in his own court and in a case in which his interest was involved, was treated much like any other villager.[52] Nevertheless, the steward's conciliatory attitude toward angry Elton tenants is noteworthy. One peasant breaking a rule was easy to deal with; a whole village up in arms over what it deemed an infringement of village rights was something else.

The fact that few decisions in the hallmote went against the lord was less owing to pressure on the court exerted by his officials than to the basic relationship between lord and village. His rights, privileges, and monopolies made it unlikely for him to infringe legally on the villagers while making it easy for them to infringe on him.

In the endless small fines levied for default of work obligations, it may even be possible to discern the same rationale as that suggested for the fines for violation of the ale regulations. Edward Britton, reviewing the evidence from Broughton, suggests that the moderation of the fines makes them amount to a standard fee which a villager could pay if he wished to skip a day's work on the demesne.[53]

Not all the infractions by villagers were against the lord. Villagers also infringed on each other: "It is found that Robert of Teygnton carried away the fittings of the plow of John Abovebrook, in consequence whereof the same John lost his plowing during one day to his damage of one halfpenny, which he will pay him," plus a three-penny fine.[54] John Allot was convicted of carrying away the hay of Reginald of Brington "to the value of four pence which he will pay to the same Reginald before the next court, fine pardoned."[55]

Nor did all the cases originate in the fields: "John Ivet has not repaired the house of Richard Crane satisfactorily, as agreed between them, to the damage of Richard sixpence, which John will pay. For trespass, fine three pence."[56] Some court cases were family matters, as when Robert Smith "unjustly detained in his smithy the horse of Sarah his mother against her will," and was fined sixpence.[57]

Debts were a frequent subject of villager-versus-villager suits: "Richard Blythe acknowledges himself to be bound to Andrew Noppe for one ring of barley, which he will pay him. Unjust detention, fine three pence."[58] "John Roger unjustly detains from Richard Baxter one quarter of barley to his damage of two pence, which he will pay him. Sixpence fine."[59] In one case the debt was between two men, both of whom had died: "Sarah widow of Henry Smith, and John and

Hexagonal relief depicting law from Florence's Campanile.

Robert her sons, executors of the testament of Henry, bound to John Hering and Joan widow of Robert Hering for one quarter of barley which Henry borrowed from Robert in their lifetime. Will satisfy them concerning the grain, sixpence fine."[60] The creditor was sometimes an outsider: in 1294 two Elton villagers, Geoffrey in Angulo and Philip Noppe, owed grain to Richard Abraham of Haddon, and were instructed to pay but were excused the court's fine because they were poor.[61]

The Elton records contain no outright references to money-lending, though some of the cases of debt may have been loans disguised as purchases. Other sources show it to have been a common feature of rural life, often leading to court judgment and seizure of property. The loan was often in the form of a pawn. Interest rates were always high and frequently condemned by the Church as usurious, without stemming the flow of loans, in which churchmen themselves engaged. Debtors often took refuge in flight, leading down the path of vagabondage to crime.[62]

One frequently heard suit of villager against villager was for slander. In 1279 Andrew Reeve accused Gilbert Gamel of malingering and working in his own barn and yard instead of performing his labor services. The accusation was public enough so that it "came to the ears of the bailiffs." The jurors cleared Gilbert and fined Andrew twelve pence.[63] Slander could also bring damages. John Page was fined sixpence, and paid Richard Benyt twelve pence damages for "defaming" him.[64] Sarah Wagge "unjustly defamed" Nicholas son of Elias, accusing him of having stolen two of her hens and "eating them to her damage of sixpence"; Sarah was fined sixpence and had to pay Nicholas damages of sixpence, the price of the hens she claimed he had stolen.[65] Another villager "defamed Adam son of Hubert by calling him false and faithless," and was fined three pence.[66] In one case in 1300, Allota of Langetoft accused Robert Harpe of defaming her "by calling her a thief"; the jury found Robert innocent and fined Allota sixpence for false claim.[67]

In the hallmote, a decision might be appealed to the documents, especially the "register of customs" (meaning in all probability the Ramsey Abbey cartulary), as in the case of the Greenway dispute of 1300. The cartulary contained information about tenure, customary obligations, and servile status. When it failed to resolve a question, an appeal could be made to the lord, who might be an impartial arbiter if his own interest was not involved, or perhaps a fair or reasonable one if it was.

There is also evidence of a more modern system of appeal. This was one made from the hallmote to the honor court, the court of the whole estate (honor), which for Ramsey Abbey met at Broughton, with suit owed by the free tenants of Elton and the other manors. A case of 1259 involved a dispute among the villagers about repairs to the millpond after flooding. The twelve jurors of the Elton hallmote, all villeins, accused five free tenants—Reginald Benyt, Ralph Blaccalf, Andrew L'Hermite, Henry Miller, and Henry Fraunceys—of refusing to help, the accused claiming that they were not obligated because of their free status.[68] The case may have been referred to the court at Broughton because of the defendants' allegiance to that court, but in other instances Broughton seems to have acted as a true court of appeal, with villeins summoned thither from their hallmotes. The principal function of the Broughton honor court, however, was not judicial but administrative, the arrangement of the military service owed by the abbey.[69] Elsewhere, the central court of an estate is known to have acted at times as an appeals court. The court of St. Albans, assembled under its famous ash tree, regularly heard cases forwarded to it by the other St. Albans manors, returning its interpretation to the local courts.[70]

For the typical villein tenant, nearly any offense he might commit, from default of his work obligations to hamsoken against his neighbor, brought him to the hallmote, attended by his fellow villagers acting as his judges. Members of his tithing supported his appearance in court. Twelve villagers examined and discussed his case, made accusation against him, and found him guilty or not guilty. If he was required to corroborate his defense or his claim, he called on friends and neighbors to give him oath-help so that he could "be at his law six-handed." When he was fined he appealed to a fellow villager to act as his pledge and guarantee his payment. Rarely was he subjected to either imprisonment or corporal punishment, though aggravated assault might land him in the stocks on the village green.

Fundamental to the system of justice was the inequality between lord and villager. If the villager missed an autumn boon-work, neglected his demesne plowing, or defaulted on any of his other obligations, he was certain of being fined. The system was onerous and exploitative, yet it apparently felt less oppressive to those who lived under it than it appears to modern eyes. The villager knew the rules and could rely on them. If they were not equal for everybody, they were the same for all villeins, a fact which doubtless contributed to the success with which they were applied—"neighbors" who turned out for the harvest boon would feel little sympathy for one who did not.

The hallmote's emphasis on the united voice of the community in judgment reflected the need of a weakly policed society for acceptance of its judicial decisions by all parties. No single individual or small group could be blamed by a losing party in court when his fate had been pronounced *per totum halimotum*.

The apparatus of the law was certainly the more readily accepted because it was operated by the villagers themselves. As Paul Vinogradoff says, in the hallmote, "customs are declared by [the villagers] and not [by the lord]; inquests and juries are empaneled from among them; the agrarian business of the customary court is entirely of their making."[71]

The hallmote was the sole court with which most villeins ever had contact. It belonged to one of the three great medieval systems of justice, the manorial, or seigneurial, courts, the other two systems being the Church courts and the royal courts. Though the three overlapped in some degree, each had its own clientele and its own law. Church courts dispensed canon law in cases either involving clergy or dealing with moral and marital problems of the laity. In England the royal courts dispensed the "common law," created by William the Conqueror out of Saxon, Danish, and Norman precedents and made common to the whole kingdom. Royal courts sat in the shires and hundreds, the political divisions of the kingdom, and royal *eyres* (circuit courts) visited the districts at intervals.

As the clergy formed the main clientele of the Church courts, the free men of the kingdom formed that of the royal courts, and the villeins, subject to the "customary law" of their own manors, that of the manorial courts. But the royal courts also held a monopoly on felony, sometimes known as "high justice," and defined as homicide, rape, larceny, burglary, arson, and petty treason (a crime by a servant or apprentice against a master).[72] Trespass, the other major category of crime, which included assault, breaking and entering, theft of goods worth less than twelve pence, issuing threats, abduction, extortion, false weights and measures, and other petty offenses, was left to the manorial courts in cases involving villeins, and was awarded to the royal courts in those involving free men.[73] Rape was also sometimes dealt with in the manorial court.

The division of function was never as neat as theory suggested. Many lords enjoyed "high justice" as a result of some past concession by the monarch. The abbot of Ramsey held what amounted to exclusive judicial power within his banlieu, a radius of one league (three miles) from the high altar of the abbey church. Lords often held rights to special kinds of crimes, such as "infangenethef," the thief caught in the act within the manor, whose belongings could be confiscated when he was hanged.

Thus any villager who committed homicide or any other felony and was apprehended by the hue-and-cry was subject to the jurisdiction of the royal courts. The case was likely to be given a preliminary investigation by the coroner's court, which held an inquest whenever a death was either accidental, sudden, or in suspicious circumstances. The coroner was a knight or a substantial freeholder, elected in the county court by other knights and freeholders. His jury was made up of twelve freeholders of the hundred where the death had occurred.[74] The coroner examined the body for signs of violence, and questioned neighbors and witnesses, with particular attention to the person or persons who discovered the body. In cases of accidental death, the object that had caused the accident was adjudged the "deodand" (gift to God) and was sold and the price given to the king—a Norman adaptation of an old Anglo-Saxon custom of selling the deodand to buy prayers for the soul of the victim. The deodand might be a horse that threw its rider, the timber of a wall that collapsed, a cart that ran over a man, or a vat of boiling water that overturned.[75]

In cases of murder, the coroner's jury appraised the chattels of the accused, with a view to later confiscation by the king. Sometimes it reported that "nothing could be discovered about his chattels," or that "he had no chattels," but often they were listed in detail: animals, household goods, grain, and tools, with their monetary value. Sometimes only the value was recorded. One such list turns up in the Elton records because the hanged man's forfeited property had disappeared. The villagers *(villata)* were "commanded to answer for the chattels of Richard son of Thomas Frelond of Pappele who was hanged at Peterborough," said chattels consisting of boots, harness, knife, belt, dog collar with silver fittings, gloves, wooden chest, and slippers—total 18 pence 2 farthings.[76]

The prisoner was turned over either to the itinerant justices of the royal eyre, or to the shire or hundred courts, where trial was usually by jury. Jury trial was not, however, perceived as especially protective. Early in the thirteenth century, a prisoner could be tried by jury only with his consent, but the principle was annulled by Edward I in the First Statute of Westminster (1275) mandating jury trial in criminal cases in the interest of more reliable prosecution.

Trial by combat was by now archaic, as was trial by ordeal (immersion in water or exposure to fire), condemned by the Church in 1215. The sense of participation by Providence in the judicial process which combat and ordeal had invoked was retained in the more civilized method of compurgation, or joint oath-swearing on the sacred relics.

In 1285 Edward I issued the Second Statute of Westminster, holding the men of the village and hundred collectively responsible for arresting and holding malefactors—in effect, making the hue-and-cry royal as well as manorial law. Not very surprisingly, large numbers of wrongdoers continued to escape capture. Bands of thieves flourished, terrorizing whole districts. Sometimes they were abetted by wealthy sponsors known as "receivers" or "maintainers." As John Bellamy observes, "There was ... less of a gulf between honest men and criminals than in modern society," a situation that also made corruption of officials easier.[77]

Of those tried by royal justice sitting in cases where the accused was actually detained, only some 10 to 30 percent of the defendants were convicted. One popular technique for evading punishment was the claim of "benefit of clergy," meaning that the accused was a cleric and could only be tried in Church court where capital punishment was not used. Felons not only took the tonsure (clerical haircut) in prison but even learned to read. Benefit of clergy was of limited value to habitual criminals, however, since it could only be claimed once.[78]

The same limitation applied to another Church-related evasion of justice, the sanctuary. All consecrated buildings and land, including every parish church and churchyard, were sanctuary, on a one-time basis, but not for everyone. Excluded were notorious offenders, traitors, heretics, sorcerers, clerics, perpetrators of felonies in church, criminals caught red-handed, and minor offenders in no danger of loss of life or limb. The fugitive had to confess his misdeeds, surrender his weapons, attend Mass, and ring the church bells. In a parish church, where he could remain for forty days, he had to beg food from the priest. The royal coroner came, heard his oath to abjure the realm forever, assigned him a port or border town by which to depart, and saw him branded on the thumb with an A (for abjuror). He was obliged to keep to the highway, to avoid footpaths, to take the first ship available, and until one appeared, to walk into the sea up to his knees each day in sign of his renewed

intention. Very often, however, the abjuror never reached his assigned port, but went into hiding as an outlaw.[79]

Prison as punishment was virtually unknown to the Middle Ages. The Church courts dealt in penances and pilgrimages, the manor court in fines, and the royal court in death penalties, abjuration, and outlawry. The outlaw could be captured or slain by anyone, and his goods appropriated. Outlaws, however, often had powerful protectors and sometimes popular sympathy. The prototype of Robin Hood probably flourished in late thirteenth or early fourteenth century rather than in the twelfth century of Richard Lionheart favored by Walter Scott.[80]

Capital punishment was generally by hanging, with the chief alternative, reserved for better-class offenders, the headsman's axe. Since hanging was by strangulation, the axe was normally less cruel. By a custom that was a relic of ancient Germanic law, the felon's

Execution of Prisoners from the *Chronicles of Enguerrand de Monstrelet* **(1415).**

principal accuser, usually the victim or a relative, was often obliged to find a hangman or perform the office himself. Lack of professionalism may account for recorded cases of the hanged man's surviving.

Deliberately cruel executions were limited to extraordinary crimes: heresy, treason, witchcraft. Mutilation, a common form of punishment in the earlier Middle Ages, was rare by the thirteenth century, but a thief might still lose an ear or thumb, a rapist be castrated, or a vicious assailant blinded. The stocks sometimes caused loss of limb. Torture was a rarity, except when the defendant stood mute, or on the part of some or coroners practicing extortion.[81]

A condemned prisoner in a royal court had a single avenue of appeal, that of royal pardon. His hope of getting one depended on one of two aids: a powerful protector with influence at court, or an ongoing war. In the late thirteenth and early fourteenth centuries, the king's expeditions against the Scots saved many English felons from the scaffold.[82]

Historically, medieval justice stood somewhere between the ancient system of family-and-clan justice by which an offender was punished or protected by his kin, and the modern system of state-organized police and prosecution. Perhaps it resembled other systems in the discrepancy in outcomes between serious felonies, so often unpunished, and minor offenses against the custom of the manor, so frequently pursued and penalized, though rarely beyond a fine of sixpence.

Hen. Secundus

Johes Rex

Henricus III

X

THE PASSING OF THE

MEDIEVAL VILLAGE

arly in the fourteenth century the population of England probably surpassed four million, as compared with the Domesday figure of a million and a half to two million.[1] By far the greater part of the increase came from the villages, "the primary seedbeds of population."[2] The Europewide demographic surge was halted by a series of calamities that began with the floods and famine of 1315–1317. Two catastrophic harvests in succession, possibly related to a long-term climatic change, sent grain prices to levels "unparalleled in English history," and, accompanied by typhoid, hit poor families especially hard.[3] The lords added to the misery by cutting down their alms-giving, reducing staff, and halting livery of grain to their *famuli,* like latter-day governments and business firms responding to business depression by laying off workers and reducing purchases. Severe mur-

Kings of England: Henry II, Richard I, John and Henry III from *The Kings of England from Brutus to Henry III.*

rain and cattle disease added to the calamity. Thefts of food and livestock rose sharply, and bodies of paupers were found in the streets. Dogs and cats disappeared, and cannibalism was rumored.[4]

By the time the next even worse disaster struck, three long-term changes in agriculture and rural life were already evident: a discernible shift from crop farming toward sheep grazing; a general return by lords to farming out their demesnes; and a growth in the proportion of peasant cultivation as opposed to demesne cultivation.[5] The lord was slipping from his role as producer-consumer to being merely a consumer, a "rentier," albeit one with a large appetite.

In Elton in the agricultural year of 1349–1350, three different villeins held the office of reeve, for which there was suddenly little enthusiasm.[6] The Black Death, sweeping through England in the summer of 1349 via the rats that infested houses, barns, and sheds, left so many holdings vacant that it was impossible to collect rents or enforce services. The manorial accounts read like a dirge: "Twenty-three virgates in the hand of the lord [vacant]."[7] "Rent lacking from eleven cottages . . . by reason of the mortality in the preceding year." "Of the rent of . . .

The Black Death, 1348. Engraving by English School (14th c.).

Robert Amys . . . nothing here for the cause above-said. Of the rent of John Suteer . . . and William Abbot . . . nothing here for the cause aforesaid. And [the reeve answers for] two shillings sixpence from Robert Beadle for twelve acres of demesne land formerly of Hugh Prest lately deceased."[8] "From the fulling mill nothing because it is broken and useless."[9] "Of divers rents of tenements which are in the hand of the lord owing to the death of the tenants . . ."[10] "Three capons and no more this year because those liable to chevage are dead."[11]

The following year things were no better: "Of the farm of one common oven . . . nothing this year because it is ruinous. Second common oven . . . nothing for the same cause." "And for sixpence from the smithy this year because it fell down after All Saints and from then on was empty."[12] "Of chevage nothing because all the chevagers are dead."[13]

Expenses were up because of the shortage of villeins doing labor service: "In divers workmen hired by the day to mow and lift the lord's hay, seventeen shillings five pence by tally."[14] The harvest was costly: "Expenses of forty workmen coming at the bailiff's request to one repast and of divers other workmen hired by the day. . . . And in the expenses of forty workmen coming . . . to reap and bind the lord's grain during one day . . . one

young bullock. And in the expenses of two boon-works of the autumn, on each occasion of ninety workmen, each of whom take three loaves whereof eight are made from one bushel . . . and in divers workmen hired to reap and bind the lord's grain for lack of customary tenants . . ."[15]

Grain production on Ramsey manors was reduced by one half.[16] In desperation, stewards and bailiffs strictly enforced work services on the surviving tenants, and sought to hold down the cost of hired labor with the help of a royal Statute of Laborers (1351), backed by a threat of the stocks. The main result they achieved was to stir resentment among both tenants and hired laborers. With depopulation, land inevitably fell in value and labor inevitably rose in price.

The Hundred Years War added heavy taxation to peasant burdens. For many years, "lay subsidies" (to distinguish them from taxes on the clergy) had been occasionally levied at the rate of a tenth or a twentieth on all movable goods above a certain figure. In the long reign of Henry III (1216–1272), the lay subsidy was collected only five times. In those of Edward I (1272–1307) and Edward II (1307–1327), marked by wars with Scotland, the royal tax collectors appeared in the villages a total of sixteen times.

Edward III imposed the tax three times in the first seven years of his lengthy reign, then as the war in France escalated, needed it no fewer than twenty-four times (1334–1377).[17] To facilitate collection, he changed the mechanics of taxation, putting the burden of it on the villagers themselves and charging the royal administration with the task of seeing that every village met its quota. The new method made it possible for the better-off peasants who filled the village offices to arrange distribution of the tax in their favor.[18] Besides the lay subsidy, the village was afflicted with conscription, which itself was apparently a light burden—volunteers were found, and a village might perceive the army a good place to get rid of its bad characters—but each community had to pay for its own recruits' equipment. Finally, in 1377, amid a succession of defeats in France, a poll tax was introduced: four pence per head on everyone over fourteen years of age, with only gen-

Building of Strasbourg Cathedral (c.1400). Principal architect: Erwin de Steinbach. Engraving by Schuler, reproduced in *Magasin Pittoresque* in 1848.

uine beggars exempt. In 1379 a second poll tax was piled on top of a double subsidy, and in 1381 a third on top of a subsidy and a half. Wealthy taxpayers were rather piously requested to help pay the share of poor taxpayers.[19]

The accumulation of tax levies, the Statute of Laborers, and the other burdens, afflictions, and irritants resulted in the Peasant Rebellion of 1381. Sometimes known as Wat Tyler's Rebellion, from the name of one of its several leaders, the English revolt was part of a larger pattern. "A chain of peasant uprisings clearly directed against taxation exploded all over Europe," says Georges Duby.[20] If they were discernibly triggered by taxation, the risings had a broader content, both substantive and ideological. Another leader of the English rebels, the Kentish priest John Ball, preached

that "things cannot go right in England . . . until goods are held in common and there are no more villeins and gentlefolk, but we are all one and the same." Unsympathetic Froissart, chronicler of the nobility, may not be recording Ball's words with reportorial exactness, but there is little doubt that the gist is accurate: "[The lords] are clad in velvet and camlet lined with squirrel and ermine, while we go dressed in coarse cloth. They have the wines, the spices, and the good bread: we have the rye, the husks, and the straw, and we drink water. They have shelter and ease in their fine manors, and we have hardship and toil, the wind and the rain in the fields. And from us must come, from our labour, the things which keep them in luxury." And the fiery preacher's auditors, "out in the fields, or walking together from one village to another, or in their homes,

whispered and repeated among themselves, 'That's what John Ball says, and he's right!'"[21] One chronicler credits Ball with the phrase, "All men are created equal," and with a declaration that villein servitude is "against the will of God."[22] One of several priests who took part in the uprising, Ball was certainly on the far Left of his age, but there is no doubt that the aims of the mainstream of rebellion included the abolition of villeinage. The demand was part forward in the rebels' negotiations dramatized by destruction of manorial records "from Norfolk to Kent," not to mention the number of lawyers killed.[23] The Continental revolts showed the same revolutionary tendencies.

A feature especially noted by modern historians is the participation, even domination, by the better-off peasants. "Peasant revolts...were wont to spring up, not in regions where the serf was in deepest oppression, but in those in which he was comparatively well off, where he was strong enough to aspire to greater liberty and to dream of getting it force," says Sir Charles Oman.[24]

All the risings were suppressed, naturally, by the united upper class—monarchy, nobility, upper clergy, wealthy townsmen—but all nevertheless left their mark. In England the poll tax was abandoned, and the Statute of Laborers left unenforced. Everywhere, the process by which serfdom was withering was accelerated. In England the villein class rid itself of its disabilities mainly through "copyhold tenure," which amounted to a reversal of the law's point of view: instead of the manorial records' proving the legality of a villein's obligations, they were now taken to prove the sanctity of his claim to his holding, since the succession within the family was registered (copied down) in the court rolls. Over the course of the fifteenth century, the villeins bought their way free of, or simply refused to pay, merchet, heriot, gersum, chevage, wardpenny, woolsilver, and all the rest of the vicious or petty exactions of the long past. On Ramsey manors, customary payments and labor services were "relaxed" in 1413. The last fines for default on boon-works were recorded at Elton in 1429. Quietly and unobtrusively, an era in social relations was closed.[25]

Closed, but not altogether forgotten. A century after the Peasant Rebellion, it was still possible to pour scorn on a family of the gentry, such as the Pastons of Norfolk, by pointing triumphantly to their alleged bondman ancestor, while to this day the English language retains the word *villein,* slightly altered, as a pejorative,

and its synonyms *boor* and *churl,* now mainly in adjective form, to convey a connotation of base manners.

The fifteenth century witnessed a return of prosperity—uneven, checkered, with plenty of setbacks and slowdowns, but nevertheless a recovery for Europe and its villages. In the wake of depopulation, individual holdings grew, the shrinkage of arable provided more pasture and stimulated increase of livestock, and the manure probably helped improve crop yields. Wealthy townsmen joined with the newly freed villagers in sharecropping arrangements. "The conduct of village economy passed decisively into the hands of peasants backed by townsmen's money," says Georges Duby.[26]

The era was one of extensive rebuilding. Peasant houses began to be constructed with masonry foundations and stronger frames, and many added rooms or even a second floor, with fireplace and chimney. Manor houses were enlarged. Parish churches were rebuilt in the new Perpendicular style, the vertical lines of the building emphasized with elaborate tracery and fan vaulting. The Elton church was extensively remodeled, the great square tower built, the aisles extended on either side, a south porch added, and the nave lighted by a clerestory.[27]

Not all villages shared in the prosperity, or even survived it. From about 1450, as grass became the favored land use in England, some villages, such as Wharram Percy, saw fields that had grown cereal crops for centuries turned exclusively into pastures for sheep. The smaller and less prosperous villages were especially vulnerable, as were those with few free tenants, who were much harder to displace than villeins. Vulnerable also were villages whose landlords, whether old feudatories or new men of wealth, had connections in the wool trade, or merely intelligently acquisitive appetites.[28] Where enclosure struck, families packed up their belongings, drove their animals ahead of them, and departed the village. Behind them their wattle-and-daub houses tumbled into ruins, the ditches that marked their crofts were filled in by erosion, the fences tottered, and the lanes and footpaths tramped by the feet of so many men and animals disappeared in weeds. The manor house often survived, with the shepherds sleeping in the bailiff's old quarters.

In maps showing the two phenomena, a clear correlation between the belt of open field agriculture and the distribution of the deserted villages can be seen, and a further correlation becomes apparent in comparing the two with a map showing enclosures of the fifteenth and sixteenth centuries.[29]

"Within a century and a half of the Black Death, ten percent of the settlements of rural England had been erased from the landscape," says one historian, possibly with exaggeration.[30] By the year 1600 over thirty villages in Huntingdonshire had been deserted, leaving behind sometimes the ruin of a church, sometimes the site of a manor house, sometimes nothing but plow marks discernible from the air.[31]

The old feudal landlord class was dealt a devastating blow from an unexpected source with Henry VIII's famous "Dissolution" of the monastic orders beginning in 1536. The king, embroiled with the Church over his divorce problems—and, like so many kings, needing money—violently suppressed all the great monasteries and seized their manors, which he then sold off at an ultimate profit of a million and a half pounds. Among the suppressed monasteries was Ramsey Abbey. A Huntingdonshire chronicler, Edmund Gibson, observed, "Most of the County being Abbey-land . . . many new purchasers planted themselves therein."[32] The new purchasers were entrepreneurs out to make money, and not surprisingly many of them saw the merits of sheep farming.

The enclosure movement appeared on the Continent too, but nowhere on the same scale as in England, where petty incidents of resistance multiplied without slowing the progress of the sheep, who, it was said, now devoured men instead of the men devouring sheep. The process "produced much controversy, many pamphlets, a number of government inquiries, some ineffective acts of Parliament, and a revolt in the Midlands in 1607," summarizes Alan R. H. Baker.[33] Yet many of the old villages survived, some even gaining new population and character as numbers of craftsmen quit the cities, in part to escape guild regulation, and took their weaving, dyeing, tanning, and other skills to the now freer village environment. Some villages became primarily industrial. The village of Birmingham in the sixteenth century became a burgeoning town of 1,500, specializing in tanning and clothmaking.[34]

At the same time cereal crop agriculture made belated progress. Yields improved, if slowly, in the seventeenth century, reaching a general average in England of seven to one.[35] Famine became largely a threat of the past. "Starvation . . . cannot be shown to have been an omnipresent menace to the poor in Stuart times," says Peter Laslett.[36]

In 1610 a Herefordshire husbandman named Rowland Vaughan solved the problem of meadow and hay shortage that had vexed medieval lord and villager by devising an irrigation technique.[37] This and other improvements in agricultural technology made possible the servicing of a rapidly expanding market for English produce in Britain, on the Continent, and in English colonies overseas. The market gave scope for the ambitious, the industrious, the competent, and the fortunate, creating new, deeper divisions of rich and poor among the villagers. Individual enterprise moved to the center of the economic stage, as those who could afford it took advantage of the land market to buy up and consolidate holdings, forming compact plots that could be enclosed by fences or hedges and set free from communal regulation. At the other end of the scale, the number of landless laborers multiplied. In some places the old open field arrangements, with their cooperative plowing, common grazing, and bylaws, hung on amid a changing world. In 1545 the hallmote of Newton Longville, Buckinghamshire, ordained "that no one shall pasture his beasts in the sown fields except on his own lands from the Feast of Pentecost next-to-come until the rye and wheat have been taken away under penalty of four pence . . ."[38] But the future of individualism was already assured. "The undermining of the common fields, the declining effectiveness of the village's internal government, and the development of a distinct group of wealthy tenants [spelled the] triumph of individualism over the interests of the community," in the words of Christopher Dyer.[39]

Among the last guardians of the old communal tradition were the English colonists who settled in New England, laid out their villages with churchyard and green (but no manor house), divided their fields into strips apportioned in accordance with wealth, plowed them cooperatively with large ox teams, and in their town meetings elected officials and enacted bylaws on cropping, pasturing, and fencing.[40] But in land-rich North America the open field village was out of place, and it soon became apparent that the American continent was destined for exploitation by the individual homestead farm. (It may be worth noting, however, that even technology-oriented American agriculture proved resistant to radical change; until the introduction of the tractor, one to two acres was considered an ample day's work for two men and a plow team.)

The village of Elton survived famine, Black Death, the Dissolution, and the enclosure movement. It even gained an architectural ornament with the building of Elton Hall, an imposing structure surrounded by a moat, begun by Sir Richard Sapcote about 1470 and expanded in the following centuries along with many other new peasant houses and old manor houses that reflected the general prosperity. Richard Cromwell, a nephew by marriage of Henry VIII's minister Thomas Cromwell, acquired Ramsey Abbey and became landlord of the dependent manors. Elton, however, went to another proprietor, through whom it gained a little guidebook distinction. The king bestowed it on his latest queen, Katherine Howard, as part of her jointure, the property settlement made on noble wives. On Katherine's execution for adultery Henry took back the jointure and presently bestowed Elton in 1546 on his last wife, Katherine Parr, under whose regime Elton Hall was given extensive repairs. On her death in 1548 Elton reverted to the crown, now held by the infant Edward VI, from whom it passed to Queen Elizabeth and James I, who disposed of it to Sir James Fullerton and Francis Maxwell, from whom it passed through still other hands to Sir Thomas Cotton, who held what must have been one of the last views of frankpledge in the manor court in 1633. Sir Thomas's daughter Frances and her husband Sir Thomas Proby inherited Elton; from them it passed to a collateral branch, raised to the peerage as earls of Carysfort, and in 1909 went to a nephew who took the name of Proby, and whose descendants remain in residence in Elton Hall.[41]

Enclosures, slow to penetrate Huntingdonshire, finally replaced the old arable strips and furlongs with rectangular hedged fields; one drives down a long straight road to arrive in a village whose irregular lanes and closes still carry a hint of the Middle Ages.

Though it had many ancestors in the form of hamlets, encampments, and other tiny, temporary, or semipermanent settlements, and though its modern descendants range from market towns to metropolitan suburbs, the open field village of the Middle Ages was a distinctive community, something new under the sun and not repeated since. Its intricate combination of social, economic, and legal arrangements, invented over a long period of time to meet a succession of pressing needs, imparted to its completed form an image, a personality, and a character. The traces of its open fields that aerial photographs reveal, with their faded parallel furrows clustered in plots oddly angled to each other, contain elements of both discipline and freedom.

Simultaneously haphazard and systematic, the medieval village is unthinkable without its lord. So much of its endless round of toil went to cultivate his crops, while its rents, court fines, and all the other charges with the curious archaic names went to supply his personal wants and the needs of his monastic or baronial household. Yet at the same time the village enjoyed a high degree of autonomy, regulating its own cultivation, settling its own quarrels, and living its life with little interference.

The legal division of the villagers into "free" and "unfree" had genuine meaning, but went much less deep than the words imply. The unfree villeins had to work for the lord and pay many fees that the free tenants escaped, yet the division into prosperous and poor was more meaningful. Looking at the men of the Middle Ages, Marc Soch asked, "In social life, is there any more elusive notion than the free will of a small man?"[42]

Village life for men and women alike was busy, strenuous, unrelenting, much of it lived outdoors, with an element of danger that especially threatened children. Diet was poor, dress simple, housing primitive, sanitary arrangements derisory. Yet there were love, sex, courtship, and marriage, holidays, games and sports, and plenty of ale. Neighbors quarreled and fought, sued and countersued, suspected and slandered, but also knew each other thoroughly and depended on each other to help with the plowing and harvesting, to act as pledges, to bear witness, to respond when danger threatened.

The most arresting characteristic of the medieval open field village is certainly its system of cooperation: cultivation in concert of individually held land, and pasturing in common of individually owned animals. It was a system that suited an age of low productivity and scarcity of markets, and one that hardly fostered the spirit of innovation. The lords were content to leave things as they were, the villeins had little power to change them. When change came, it came largely from outside, from the pressure of the market and the enterprise of new landlords. Yet change builds on an existing structure. The open field village helped create the populous—and in comparison with the past, prosperous—Europe of the high Middle Ages, the Europe from which so much of the modern world emerged.

In the shift toward that world, many villagers lost their homes, many of their villages disappeared. Argument, protest, and violence accompanied change, which only historical perspective makes clearly inevitable.

Was something larger lost? A sense of community, of closeness, of mutual solidarity? Perhaps it was, but the clearest message about the people of Elton and other villages of the late thirteenth century that their records give us seems to be that they were people much like ourselves. Not brutes or dolts, but men and women, living out their lives in a more difficult world, one under-equipped with technology, devoid of science, nearly devoid of medicine, and saddled with an exploitative social system. Sometimes they protested, sometimes they even rose in rebellion, mostly they adapted to circumstance. In making their system work, they helped lay the foundation of the future.

SECTION III
LIFE IN A MEDIEVAL CITY

PROLOGUE

The western European city, with all its implications for the future, was born in the Middle Ages. By 1250 it was alive and flourishing, not only on the ancient Mediterranean coast but in northwest Europe. The narrative that follows is an attempt to depict life at the midpoint of the thirteenth century in one of the newly revived cities: Troyes, capital of the rich county of Champagne, seat of a bishop, and, above all, site of two of the famous Fairs of Champagne.

Back in the days when Julius Caesar camped in Gaul and bivouacked in Britain, there were few places in northwest Europe that could be called cities. Lutetia (Paris) was sufficiently important for Caesar's Commentaries to record its destruction by fire. But in most of the region political organization was too undeveloped, commerce too scanty, and religion too primitive to permit the creation of communities larger than villages. Vast areas remained wilderness.

The Roman legions built roads, provided a market for local farm produce, and offered shelter to traders in their fortified camps. One place they fortified was a hamlet at the confluence of the Seine and an important military road, the Via Agrippa. Marcus Aurelius built a tower there, and later emperors, notably Aurelian, employed it as a base. Along with other camp towns, "Tricasses" took on the appearance of a permanent settlement as garrisoned soldiers married local girls, raised families, and stayed on after their discharges to farm outside the walls or perform craftsmen's jobs inside. Graduating from army base to administrative center, the town acquired masonry walls and attracted new inhabitants: tax collectors, bureaucrats, army purveyors, and skilled and unskilled laborers, including prisoners of war brought back from the wilds of Germany and Friesland. Troyes hardly rivaled the opulent cities of southern Europe or even Paris, which by the third cen-

Merchant emblem (1356) depicting a griffin standing on a ball of wool.

tury boasted three baths, a theater, and a racetrack. Troyes may have had one bath, which would have made it the equal in amenity of most of the other northern towns.

The Christian Church furnished a powerful new impetus to the development of many backwoods towns in the north, although the first apostles were not always appreciated by the pagan civil and religious authorities. At Troyes, as elsewhere, a number of martyrs were created by governors and emperors who held with the faith of their fathers. But once the Church had made a believer out of the Emperor Constantine, it had clear sailing. In the fourth and fifth centuries bishoprics sprang up all over the map. The natural place for a bishop to establish himself was in a Roman administrative center, usually a former legionary camp. The new clerical establishments required the services of a secular population of farmers and craftsmen. A new word described these episcopal towns—*cité* (city)—a derivation of the Latin *civitas* that usually took on the meaning of a populated place inside walls.

As the power of the Roman Empire faltered, local Roman officials lost their authority, creating a vacuum that was filled by Christian bishops. By the middle of the fifth century the prestige of the bishop of Troyes was such that when the Huns appeared in the neighborhood everyone turned to him for protection.

The town had just been sacked once by the Vandals, and Attila's Huns were reputed to be even less amicable. Bishop Lupus first sent a deacon and seven clerks to propitiate the enemy, but an unlucky accident caused the mission to miscarry. The clerics' white vestments made Attila's horse rear. Concluding that his visitors were magicians, the Hun chieftain had them slain on the spot, one young clerk escaping to tell the tale. Attila then went off to fight the Romans, Goths, Burgundians, and Franks, who momentarily stopped fighting among themselves to take him on. Beaten, though not badly, Attila returned eastward, with Troyes directly in his path. It was an ominous moment, and once more everyone turned to Bishop Lupus. This time Lupus negotiated in person, and he scored a surprising success. Attila spared Troyes, and, taking the bishop with him as far as the Rhine, sent him home laden with honors. For this diplomatic feat Lupus was first denounced as a collaborator and exiled, but later, on sober second thought, restored to his See, to be eventually canonized as St.-Loup.

By the end of the fifth century the western half of

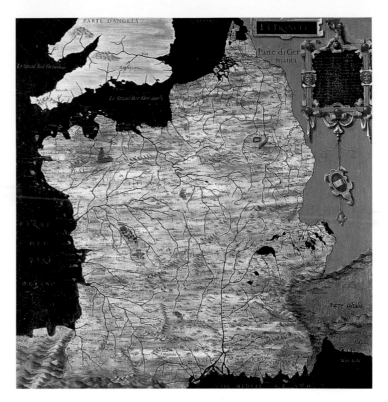

Geographical map of France.

the Roman Empire had slid into chaos. Nearly all the cities, old and new, large and small, declined catastrophically. People borrowed stones and bricks from public monuments to patch up their houses and strengthen walls against hordes of unwelcome immigrants. Commerce, already slowed down by a long-drawn-out, deeply rooted agricultural crisis, was nearly brought to a halt by the turmoil of the great migrations, or invasions, from the north and east. Towns like Troyes remained stunted, half military, half rural. Apart from crude ecclesiastical buildings—bishop's palace, basilica-cathedral, the abbey and a couple of priories—the walls of Troyes enclosed only a few score hovels. Most of the town's forty-acre area was given over to vineyards, vegetable gardens, and pasturage.

Yet the marauding barbarians did contribute something to the growth of such settlements. After pillaging a Roman province, they set up a headquarters that generally metamorphosed into a petty capital. Reims, north of Troyes, became the capital of the Franks, and Troyes a Frankish sub-capital of Champagne. The Franks' chief, Clovis, hardly less truculent a fellow than Attila, was more completely vanquished by St.-Rémi, bishop of Reims, than Attila had been by St.-Loup of Troyes. As St.-Rémi eloquently narrated the story of Jesus' martyrdom, Clovis exclaimed, "If only I'd been there at the head of my valiant Franks!" Clovis received Baptism, and all his valiant Franks promptly did likewise.

In the sixth and seventh centuries a new ecclesiastical source of cities appeared—the Benedictine monastery. The institution spread rapidly, establishing itself sometimes in towns, sometimes in open country, and immediately attracting craftsmen, farmers, and traders. In the Bavarian forest appeared "Monks' Town" —Munich. In Flanders a Benedictine abbey built at the point where the river Aa becomes navigable formed the nucleus of the future manufacturing city of St-Omer.

On the Mediterranean littoral many of the old Roman cities did business in the Dark Ages much as they had done under the Empire. Marseilles, Toulon, Arles, Avignon, and other Provençal ports continued active commerce with the eastern Mediterranean. They imported papyrus and spices, for which the Benedictine monasteries helped provide a market. As a return cargo, the Provençal ships often carried slaves.

This state of affairs came to an end in the seventh century. The electrifying military successes of the followers of Mohammed in the Near East and North Africa were accompanied by a major dislocation of Mediterranean trade. Modern scholars have modified Henri Pirenne's thesis on the causal connection between Mohammed and the Dark Ages, pointing out other influences at work. But it is a fact that as Moslem fleets appeared in the western and central Mediterranean, the old Roman-Christian trading cities were thrown on the defensive and were frequently raided and pillaged. Genoa, once a busy port, declined to a fishing village. New cities, flying the banner of the Prophet, blossomed along the shores of North Africa—Cairo, Mahdia, Tunis. Ancient Greek and Roman ports took on new life under the conqueror's administration. In the harbor of Alexandria, guarded by the lighthouse that had been a wonder of the world for a thousand years, new shipyards furnished the vessels for Moslem commerce and piracy, the products of which, in turn, made Alexandria's markets the largest in the Mediterranean. One Christian— if not exactly European—port was even busier: Constantinople, capital of the eastern Roman Empire, strategically seated astride major trade routes from east, west, north and south. But except for Greek Constantinople the Moslem merchants and raiders virtually took over the maritime world. In the eighth century their advance enveloped Spain and the Balearic Islands, and even a piece of Provence, from which foothold they raided all the ancient cities of the Rhône valley. One party roamed far enough north to sack Troyes.

Sacking was something to which citizens of an early medieval city had to be resigned. Not only pagan invaders, but Christian lords, and even bishops, did their share—Troyes was sacked by the bishop of Auxerre. But the champion raiders, who appeared in the late ninth century, were the Vikings.

By the time they reached Troyes these red-bearded roughnecks from the far north had taken apart nearly every other town on the map—Paris, London, Utrecht, Rouen, Bordeaux, Seville, York, Nottingham, Orléans, Tours, Poitiers; the list is an atlas of ninth-century western Europe. In Champagne the invaders were led by a local freebooter named Hasting, who was noted for his prodigious strength. Reversing the custom by which Vikings

Monk playing the lute.

sometimes settled in southern Europe, Hasting had traveled to Scandinavia and lived as a Northman, returning to lead his adopted countrymen on devastating forays into Normandy, Picardy, Champagne, and the Loire valley.

Troyes was plundered at least twice, perhaps three times. Here, as elsewhere, repeated aggression bred resistance. Bishop Anségise played the role of King Alfred and Count Odo, rallying the local knights and peasants, joining forces with other nearby bishops and lords, and fighting heroically in the pitched battle in which the Vikings were routed. The renegade Hasting, who had carved out a handsome fief for himself, bought peace by ceding Chartres to one of the coalition of his foes, the count of Vermandois,[1] who thereby acquired the basis of a powerful dynasty.

Paradoxically, the Vikings sometimes contributed to the development of cities. Often their plunder came to more than they could carry home, and they sold the surplus. A town strong enough to resist attack might thereby profit from the misfortune of its less prepared neighbors. The Vikings even founded cities. Where the looting was good, they built base camps to use as depots for trading. One such was Dublin. And they gave a helpful stimulus to York by making it their headquarters, though the original inhabitants may not have appreciated the favor.

This aspect of Viking activity notwithstanding, the ninth century was the nadir of city life. Besides the Vikings, the Moslems were still on the prowl, cleaning out St.-Peter's Church outside Rome in 846. Toward the end of this century of calamity the Hungarians—named for an affinity in appearance and manners with the unforgettable Huns—went on a rampage through Germany, northern Italy, and eastern France.

After vast losses of life and property while makeshift solutions were tried—hiding, bargaining, fighting—Europe hit on the answer to invasion: wall-building. Existing towns built walls and prospered by offering security. The lords of the countryside built walls to strengthen their crude castles, thereby enhancing their own importance. Monasteries built walls. Sometimes walls built to protect castle or monastery had the unexpected effect of attracting coopers, blacksmiths, trappers, and peddlers, and so becoming the nuclei of new towns.

A few places even built their walls before they were attacked. The citizens of Saint-Omer dug a wide, deep moat, filled it with water, and erected a rampart with the excavated material, topping it with pointed stakes. Inside was a second, stronger fortification. The Vikings were repelled in 891 and did not venture a second attack. Invigorated by success, the Saint-Omer burghers turned their monastery-village into a real town, with three principal streets. Much the same thing happened at other towns in this low-lying, vulnerable corner of Europe. Arras, Ghent, Bruges, Lille, Tournai, Courtrai, all began to emerge from obscurity. More was going on than defense against raiders. Some towns, notably Ypres, grew up without benefit of any lord, bishop, or fort. They were simply well-situated for the manufacture of wool cloth.

The new walls built from scratch in the tenth century were nearly all of the earthwork-palisade variety, like the walls of Saint-Omer. Adequately manned, they sufficed against enemies armed only with the hand-missile weapons of the Vikings. The old Roman cities, like Troyes, had let their masonry ramparts fall into disrepair and so had come to grief in the violent ninth century. By the middle of the tenth, Troyes had repaired its walls, which served the city well, not against the Vikings, but against its former defender, Bishop Anségise himself. Battling his rival, the count of Vermandois, Anségise borrowed a Saxon army from Emperor Otto the Great and besieged Troyes until another doughty prelate, the archbishop of Sens, relieved the city. Otto interceded for Anségise and got him restored to his See, where he lived peacefully until his death ten years later, but never again did a bishop of Troyes try to contest the primacy of the secular counts. Six hundred years after inheriting authority from the Roman governors, the bishops had to take a back seat.

The newly fortified towns were usually called "bourgs" or "burghs" (later, boroughs) in the Germanic dialects that were evolving into new languages. People who dwelt in the bourgs were known as bourgeois, or burghers, or burgesses. By the middle of the tenth century town-fortresses dotted western and northern Europe as far as the newly fortified bishopric of Hamburg, at the mouth of the Elbe, and Danzig, at the mouth of the Vistula. They were not worthy of comparison with the populous and wealthy centers of Islam—Baghdad, Nishapur, Alexandria, Granada, Cordova—where rich merchants patronized poets and architects. The cities of Europe were full of cattle barns and pigsties, with hovels and workshops clustered around church, castle, and bishop's palace. But growth was unmistakable. By the tenth century the crumbling Roman villas outside the walls of Troyes were interspersed with abbeys and houses.

It was certainly a beginning, and in Italy there was a little more than a beginning. Certain towns, nonexistent or insignificant in Roman times, were suddenly emerging. Venice appeared on the mud flats of the Adige at the head of the Adriatic, and Amalfi, south of Naples, thrust up into the space between the Sorrentine cliffs and the sea. The fact that their locations were inhospitable was no coincidence. A set of immigrants called the Lombards, somewhere between the Franks and the Huns in coarseness of manners, had taken over the Italian interior. The Lombards were strictly landlubbers, so the ideal place for a merchant was a sheltered bit of coastline easy to get at from the water, hard to get at from the land. By the late tenth century Venetian and Amalfitan sails were part of the seascape in the Golden Horn of Constantinople. And though it was considered scandalous, not to mention dangerous, to do business directly with the Moslems, a number of Venetian, Amalfitan, and other Italian businessmen found the necessary hardihood.

Over a lengthy interval in the tenth and eleventh centuries two major developments stimulated city growth. One was land clearance, in which the new Cluniac and Cistercian monastic establishments took a leading role. Behind land clearance lay a number of improvements in agricultural technology that taken as a whole amounted to a revolution. The heavy wheeled plow, capable of breaking up the rich, deep north European bottomlands, came into wide use. At first drawn by the slow-gaited ox, the plow was eventually harnessed, with the aid of the new padded but rigid collar, to the swifter horse. This change was in turn related to changes in crops and crop rotation, as oats and legumes were introduced and in many areas the more productive three-field system supplanted the old Roman two-field method.

The new cities played a considerable role in the agricultural revolution. The old manorial workshops tended to be usurped by better, more efficient forges, smithies, mills, and workshops in the towns. The peasants of northwest Europe harvested their crops with iron-bladed sickles and scythes and plowed them with iron plowshares and coulters that would have been the envy of prosperous Roman farmers. The increased food supply was both a cause and an effect of unmistakable population growth.

The second major influence on urban development was the beginning of medieval mining. The Romans and Greeks had dug mines, but the technique had to be reinvented when silver was discovered in the mountains of Saxony. Saxon miners carried their know-how abroad, mining iron in the Carpathians and

October ploughing, from the workshop of Gerart Horenbout and Simon Bening (c. 1520).

Balkans, and teaching the men of Cornwall how to mine their native tin. Saxon silver flowed in especial abundance to Milan, which outgrew old walls built by the Emperor Maximilian. Milan boasted a hundred towers in the tenth century. Its prosperity had derived originally from its fertile countryside and the road and river network of which it was the hub. But during the tenth and eleventh centuries it became the chief workshop of Europe. Its smiths and armorers turned out swords, helmets, and chain mail for the knights of Italy, Provence, Germany, and even more distant lands, while its mint struck over twenty thousand silver pennies a year.

Improved agriculture and more money brought a boom in business outside Italy also. In Flanders, Ghent burst through the ancient walls of the Vieux Bourg, which had enclosed only twenty-five acres. The new merchants' and weavers' quarter, the Portus, more than tripled the town's size.

In many places the growth of towns involved a special symbiosis with the neighboring countryside. In regions that were well suited to a particular form of agriculture, such as wine growing, cities both marketed the local product and procured imports. At the same time twelfth-century towns continued to take over the old manorial functions. In Troyes eleven mills were established between 1157 and 1191. The wheels in city streams began to provide the power not only for milling grain but for oil presses, working hammers and the forges that manufactured iron for farm implements.

Inside city walls there was less room for orchards, vineyards, and gardens. Towns were losing some of their rural look. Wealthy merchants built large houses. Luxury shops, goldsmiths, and silversmiths appeared side by side with the basic crafts. Horse and donkey traffic made the narrow streets as foul as they were congested. The more closely houses and shops were crowded together, the greater the danger of fire. The water supply was limited. In many towns servants and housewives had to stand in line at the wells with their buckets and jars. By the end of the twelfth century urbanization with all its problems had arrived in the cities of Flanders, not to mention Cologne and Hamburg, London and Paris, Provins and Troyes.

The last two were the scene of a significant new development. In Roman times certain dates and seasons had been set aside for markets and fairs. Throughout the following centuries, even when trade had dwindled to a trickle, the idea had stayed alive; in fact, the less buying and selling there was, the more important it became to have fixed times and places for merchants to meet customers.

But merchants also had to meet merchants. This was not an important problem in the Dark Ages, but when the manufacture of woolen cloth in western Europe began to find an outlet in the Mediterranean, via the Italian cities, and when, reciprocally, Mediterranean luxury products began to sell in western Europe, a pressing need arose for a wholesale market. Venetian and Genoese merchants carried spices over the Alps by pack train to trade for Flemish woolen cloth. In the latter half of the eleventh century the Flemings took to meeting them partway. They did not, however, meet them halfway, which would have been in Burgundy. Instead the rendezvous was in Champagne,

nearer to Flanders than Italy. The reason for this probably lies in the realm of politics.

The adventures of the embattled Bishop Anségise left Troyes in the hands of the counts of Vermandois, who ran out of direct heirs in the eleventh century. A combative cousin named Count Eudes seized Troyes, announced that he was henceforth the count of Champagne, and dared anybody to contradict him. After a turbulent career, Count Eudes died as he had lived, by the sword, or perhaps by the battle ax—his widow had to identify his body by a birthmark. Eudes' two sons divided up his domain and started a war with the king of France, after which one son died and the other, Thibaut the Trickster, duly tricked his nephew out of his share of the inheritance.

Thibaut the Trickster did something else—he gave organization and impetus to the trade fairs that were attracting foreign merchants to Troyes and some of his other towns. His sons, Hugo of Troyes and Etienne, and his grandson, Thibaut II, continued to encourage them. The twelfth century brought boom times, and the Champagne Fairs became the permanent year-round commodity market and money exchange for western Europe. They were so successful that Thibaut II won the sobriquet "Great," along with a reputation for hospitality and charity. An admiring chronicler hailed him as "father of orphans, advocate of widows, eye of the blind, foot of the lame." Approved for his philanthropy, Thibaut the Great was respected even more for his wealth, the source of which was easy to identify. A surviving letter of Thibaut attests the value he attached to the fairs. A rude young baron whose father was a vassal of the king of France waylaid a party of moneychangers from Vézelay on their way to Champagne. Thibaut wrote a strong protest to Suger, the minister of Louis VII: "This insult cannot go unpunished, because it tends toward nothing less than the destruction of my fairs."

Eventually, discussion of the problem led to a remarkable treaty by which the kings of France pledged themselves to take under their protection all merchants passing through royal territory on the roads to and from the Champagne Fairs.

Diplomatic relations between count and king were not uniformly cordial. Thibaut the Great had a misunderstanding with Louis VII and a royal army invaded Champagne. The countryside suffered, but Troyes closed the gates of its well-maintained ancient walls and waited till St.-Bernard mediated peace.

Troyes' walls were in good shape, but they were too confining. By the middle of the twelfth century new districts had to be protected. Two large abbeys to the east and south had attracted settlements, but the main thrust of the town's growth was toward the west and southwest, the quarters of St.-Rémi and St.-Jean, two new churches after which the two fairs held in Troyes each year were named. This large district, twice the size of the ancient *cité,* was thinly populated for half the year, but during July and August (the Fair of St.-Jean) and again during November and December (the Fair of St.-Rémi) it was bursting with men, wagons, animals, and merchandise.

Apart from its seasonal fluctuations of population, Troyes in the twelfth century was much like a score of other growing cities of western Europe. All had strong walls. All had abbeys and monasteries, as well as many churches—most of timber, a few of stone with timber roofs. A feature of many cities, including Troyes, was the palace of a secular prince. There were still empty spaces in these municipalities—swampy land along a river, or an unexploited meadow. Most cities ranged in area from a hundred acres to half a square mile, in population from two or three thousand to between ten and twenty thousand. Some, like Troyes, had excavated canals or canalized rivers. Many had built timber bridges on stone piers, and in London a stone-arch bridge had actually been constructed. London Bridge fell short of Roman quality in design and workmanship, but its nineteen arches, mounted on massive piers of varying sizes, and loaded with shops and houses, formed a monument that tourists admired for the next six hundred years. The houses on the roadways of bridges did nothing to improve traffic conditions but they were in great demand because of their unusual access to both water supply and sewage disposal.

But despite their advances the western cities continued to lag behind those of Italy. Twelfth-century Venice, Genoa, Pisa, and the other Italian maritime towns were sending out fleets of oared galleys that hauled the priceless spices of the Indies across the eastern Mediterranean; they were planting colonies on the shores of the Black Sea, fighting and bartering with the Moslems of Egypt and North Africa, giving powerful support to the Crusaders and taking valuable privileges in return, attacking the "Saracens" in their own backyards, and wresting from them islands and ports. Plunder helped build many of the truculent towers that sprouted in the Italian cities, from which wealthy and quarrelsome burghers defended themselves against their neighbors. In

Pisa, plunder contributed to the construction of a large tower designed to house the bells of a new cathedral; unfortunately this edifice did not settle properly. Venice crowned its Basilica of St. Mark with a huge dome, and built many other churches and public buildings. One public work of no aesthetic value had enormous practical significance. The Arsenal of Venice comprised eight acres of waterfront filled with lumberyards, docks, shipyards, workshops, and warehouses, where twenty-four war galleys could be built or repaired at one time.

While Venice wielded a naval power that kings envied, inland Milan put on a convincing demonstration of a city's ground-force prowess. At the head of a "Lombard League," the Milanese had the effrontery to face up to their lord, the Holy Roman Emperor Frederick Barbarossa, and to give his German army a good beating at the Battle of Legnano, assuring their city's freedom. By that date (1176) Venice, once a dependency of Greek Constantinople, was as sovereign an entity as a pope or emperor. For all intents and purposes, so was Genoa, so was Pisa, so were Florence, Piacenza, Siena, and many other Italian cities. Dominated by wealthy merchants, and frequently embroiled in civil strife ranging from family feuding to class warfare, the Italian cities launched a movement that the cities of the northwest sought to follow.

The essence of the new movement was the "commune," a sworn association of all the businessmen of a town. In Italy, where the nobility lived in towns, many nobles had gone into business, and some of them helped found communes. But the commune, even in Italy, was a burgher organization; in northwest Europe nobles, along with the clergy, were specifically excluded. Cloth merchants, hay merchants, helmet makers, wine sellers—all the merchants and craftsmen of a town—joined together to defend their rights against their secular and ecclesiastical lords. Enlightened princes like Thibaut the Great and Louis VII favored communes as beneficial to town development and therefore to princely revenues. A tithe from a busy merchant was better than every possession of a starving serf. Nevertheless, the communes came in for considerable disapproval, mostly from clerical critics who saw in them a threat to the social order—which indeed they were. A cardinal[2] accused the communes of abetting heresy, of declaring war on the clergy, and of encouraging skepticism. An abbot[2] wrote bitterly: "Commune! New and detestable name! By it people are freed from all bondage in return for a simple annual tax payment; they are not

Knight and attendants (15th c.).

commune formed by the burghers living inside the old Roman *cité*. Burghers living outside the *cité*, on the bishop's land, also joined. The bishop objected strenuously because he wanted to keep collecting feudal dues. Eventually he had to yield, in return for an annual money payment from his burghers. Bishops and abbots did not scruple any more than secular lords to employ dungeon and rack in their quarrels with their subjects, and they usually could count on the support of the Pope. In strong language Innocent II commanded the king of France to suppress "the guilty association of the people of Reims, which they call a commune." Innocent III excommunicated the burghers of Saint-Omer for their conflict with the local abbey.

In Troyes conflict between burgher and church did not develop, probably because by the twelfth century the counts of Champagne had completely eroded the bishop's authority, as the history of the local coinage attests. In Carolingian times the bishop of Troyes had minted coins. In the early twelfth century the monogram of Count Thibaut—TEBO—appeared on one face of the coins of Troyes, the bishop's inscription in the name of St. Peter (BEATUS PETRUS) on the other. On the coins of the later twelfth century the name of Thibaut's successor, Henry the Generous, appeared alone.

condemned for infraction of the laws except to a legally determined fine, and they no longer submit to the other charges levied on serfs."

Mere settlement in a town automatically provided escape from such feudal duties as bringing in the lord's harvest, repairing his castle, presenting him with sheep's dung. By the annual tax payment to which the abbot alluded, town people won freedom from a variety of other payments.

Bishops, living cheek-by-jowl with burghers, and seeing these once-servile fellows growing saucy, often had materialistic as well as ideological reasons for disapproving. At Reims the king of France recognized the

Pope and bishops notwithstanding, the commune swept western Europe. Even villages formed communes, buying their collective freedoms from old feudal charges. Usually the freedoms they received were written down in "charters," which were carefully guarded. Louis VII and other progressive rulers founded "new cities"—with such names as Villeneuve, Villanova, Neustadt—and accorded them charters of freedom to attract settlers. The charter of the town of Lorris, in the Loire Valley, became a model for a hundred other towns of France, while that of Breteuil, in Normandy, became the model for many in England. In Flanders, as early as the eleventh century, towns copied the charter of Saint-Omer. "Charter" joined "commune" as a fighting word to reactionaries.

Interestingly, Troyes and its sister Champagne Fair cities were late in getting charters. This was because of, rather than in spite of, the progressive views of the counts of Champagne. The counts' zeal in protecting and promoting the fairs undercut much of the need for a commune. The businessmen of Troyes enjoyed advantages beyond those that other towns obtained by charter. Nevertheless, in 1230, Troyes received a charter, which was afterward accorded to several other Champagne towns that did not already possess their own.

The sovereign who granted Troyes its charter was Thibaut IV, whose talent as a poet won him the dashing sobriquet of *Thibaut le Chansonnier* ("Songwriter"). Even before he inherited the kingdom of Navarre (after which he signed himself Thibaut, king of Navarre and Champagne), his territories were extensive, though held from seven different lords—the king of France, the emperor of Germany, the archbishops of Sens and Reims, the bishops of Paris and Langres, and the duke of Burgundy. For administrative purposes, the complex territory of Champagne was divided into twenty-seven castellanies, each of which included several barons and a number of knights who owed military service— altogether more than two thousand. (There were also a few hundred knights in Champagne who owed military service to somebody else.)

Throughout the territory Thibaut profited from high justice—the fines and forfeits for major crimes not involving clergy—and a number of imposts, varying from place to place, such as the monopoly of flour mills and baking ovens or fees from noble widows seeking permission to remarry. But far more important were his revenues from the towns, especially Troyes and Provins. Some years after Thibaut's death in 1253 a catalogue of the count's properties and prerogatives was drawn up by committees of citizens *(prud'hommes)* from the towns: the *Extenta terre comitatus Campanie et Brie.* A few citations from the section on Troyes give an illuminating insight into the nature of the count's revenues:

> The Count has the market of St.-Jean . . . estimated to be worth 1,000 pounds (livres), besides the fiefs of the holders of the market, worth 13 pounds.
> He also has the markets of St.-Rémi, called the Cold Fair . . . estimated to be worth 700 pounds . . .
> The Count also has the house of the German merchants in the Rue de Pons . . . worth 400 pounds a year, deducting expenses . . .
> The Count also has the stalls of the butchers in the Rue du Temple and the Rue Moyenne . . . paid half on the day of St. Rémi, and half on the day of the Purification of the Blessed Virgin. The Count

> also has jurisdiction in cases arising in regard to the stalls of the butchers.
> He also has the hall of the cordwainers . . .
> The Count and Nicolas of Bar-le-Duc have undivided shares air a house back of the dwelling of the provost, which contains 18 rooms, large and small . . . rented for 125 shillings, of which half goes to the said Nicolas . . .
> The Count and the said Nicolas have undivided shares in seventeen stalls for sale of bread and fish . . . now rented for 18 pounds and 18 shillings.
> He has the halls of Châlons . . . worth 25 s. in St.-Jean and 25 s. in St.-Rémi . . .

The fact that Thibaut the Songwriter was chronically in debt and at one point even had to mortgage Troyes merely underlines a truth about princes: the more money they have, the more they spend. Whatever his foibles, Thibaut carried on his family's tradition of supporting the fairs. During his reign revenues achieved record heights.

While the Hot Fair (St.-Jean) or the Cold Fair (St.-Rémi) was on, Troyes was one of the biggest and certainly one of the richest cities in Europe. In the off-seasons its population decreased, but remained at a very respectable level. Its permanent population[3] was about ten thousand, a figure exceeded by only a handful of cities in northern Europe: Paris with (about) 50,000; Ghent, 40,000; London, Lille, and Rouen, 25,000. Among many northern European cities of about Troyes' size were Saint-Omer, Strasbourg, Cologne, and York. In populous southern Europe the largest cities were Venice, 100,000; Genoa and Milan, 50,000 to 100,000; Bologna and Palermo, 50,000; Florence, Naples, Marseille, and Toulouse, 25,000. Barcelona, Seville, Montpellier, and many Italian cities were about the size of Troyes.

To pursue demography a little further, it should be noted that the population of western Europe in the mid-thirteenth century was only about sixty million. The pattern of distribution was radically different from that of later times. France, including royal domain and feudal principalities, but excluding eastern areas that became French later on, accounted for more than a third of the total, probably some twenty-two million. Germany, which included much of modern France and Poland, had perhaps twelve million people. Italy had about ten million, Spain and Portugal seven million. The Low Countries supported about four million, as did England and Wales; Ireland had less than a million, Scotland and Switzerland no more than half a million each.

These figures, though far below those produced by the Industrial Revolution, represented an enormous upsurge from Roman and Dark Age times. Practically all the increase was in northwest Europe. There the future lay.

In 1250, when our narrative takes place, Louis IX, St.-Louis, was king of the broad and disparate realm of France. The royal domain, where the king made laws and collected taxes, comprised about a quarter of the whole country; the remainder was parceled out among a score of princes and prelates and hundreds of minor lords and barons, whose relationships with each other were hopelessly intricate. Scientific-minded Frederick II, "the Wonder of the World," was in the last year of his reign as Holy Roman emperor and king of Sicily. Henry III occupied the throne of England, enjoying an uneventful reign, though the loss of the old Plantagenet lands in France had left him less wealthy and powerful than his predecessors. Innocent IV wore the papal tiara in a Rome which had recovered a little of the prestige of its pagan days. In Spain the Moors were hard-pressed by the Christian kingdoms, while on the opposite side of Europe the Mongols, having lately taken over Russia, were raiding Hungary and Bohemia.

For much of Europe, 1250 was a relatively peaceful time. As such, it may not have suited the fierce barons of the countryside, but it was congenial to the city burghers whose lives and activities constituted the real history of the period.

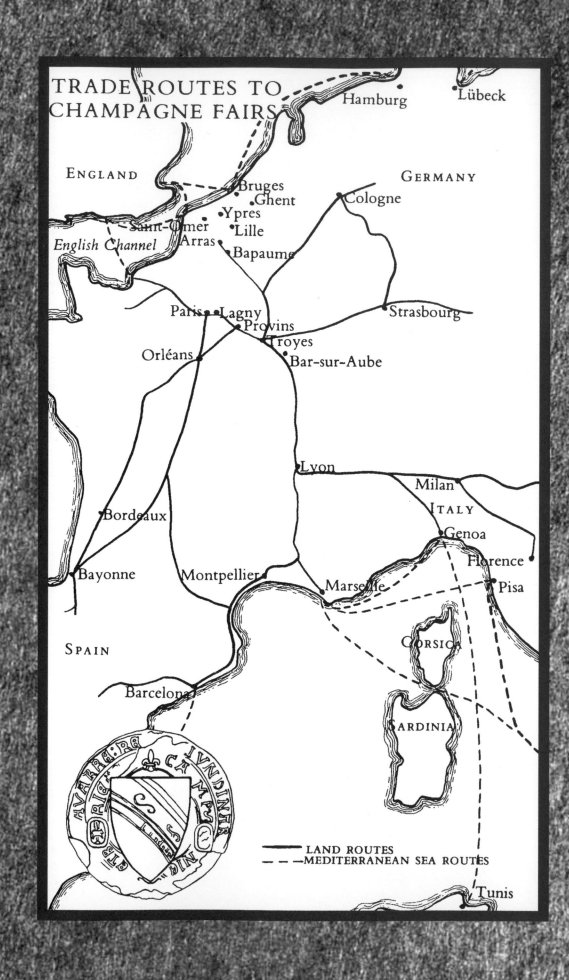

TRADE ROUTES TO
CHAMPAGNE FAIRS

ENGLAND

GERMANY

Hamburg

Lübeck

Bruges
Ghent
Ypres
Lille
Saint-Omer
English Channel
Arras
Bapaume

Cologne

Paris
Lagny
Provins
Troyes
Bar-sur-Aube

Strasbourg

Orléans

Lyon

Milan

ITALY

Bordeaux

Genoa

Florence

Bayonne

Montpellier

Marseille

Pisa

SPAIN

CORSICA

Barcelona

SARDINIA

————LAND ROUTES
- - - - MEDITERRANEAN SEA ROUTES

Tunis

I
TROYES: 1250

A Bar, à Provins, ou à Troies
Ne peut estre, riches ne soies.
[At Bar, at Provins or at Troyes
You can't help getting rich.]
—CHRÉTIEN DE TROYES *(Guillaume d'Angleterre)*

In the first week of July, dust clouds rise along the roads that crisscross the broad plain of Champagne. From every direction—Paris and the west, Châlons and the north, Verdun and the northeast, Dijon and the southeast, Auxerre and Sens, and the south—long trains of pack animals plod to their common destination—the Hot Fair of Troyes.

Some have already covered hundreds of miles by the time they reach the borders of Champagne. The cloth caravans from Flanders move south along the old Roman road from Bapaume. Merchants of the German Hanse follow the Seine in their oceangoing boats as far as Rouen, where they transship to shallow-draft vessels or hire animals. Italians sail from Pisa or Genoa to Marseilles, or take the "Strada Francesca" from Florence to Milan. If they go by the latter route, they climb the Little St.-Bernard Pass in the Savoy Alps, led along precipices, through drifts, and around crevasses by guides in woolen caps, mittens, and spiked boots. Descending the western slopes, they follow the valley of the Isère to Viennea and Lyon. Here they are joined by merchants from Spain and

Languedoc for the last leg of their trip, following the Saône valley north, or cutting northwest by way of Autun, or hiring boats and ascending the Saône.

In level country pack animals can make fifteen to twenty-five miles a day, carrying three to four hundred pounds. Couriers travel faster; the Flemish cloth merchants operate a service between the Champagne Fairs and Ghent which covers two hundred miles in four days. But it takes a company of merchants traveling from Florence to Champagne three weeks, even barring accidents. Because carts mire down in rainy weather, pack animals—horses, asses, and mules—make up the merchant trains.

Among the worst nuisances to merchants are the tolls. River crossings that range from the magnificent Pont d'Avignon to bad ferries and worse fords all charge tolls. So do many roads, even though built by the Romans.

Most of the fair traffic in convoy, sometimes preceded by a standard-bearer, and with crossbowmen and pikemen guarding the flanks—a martial display which serves to advertise the value of the goods. Roads are actually safe enough, at least in the daytime. Besides, merchants en route to the fair enjoy extraordinary guarantees as the result of the treaties made by the counts of Champagne with neighboring princes. This very year, 1250, a merchant was robbed of a stock of cloth and squirrel skins while passing through the territory of the duke of Lorraine. Honoring his treaty obligation, the duke indemnified the merchant.

The countryside through which the merchants approach Troyes is heavily wooded, but the past two centuries have witnessed considerable clearing and cultivating. Castles, villages, and monasteries have multiplied, surrounded by tilled fields and pastures where sheep and cattle graze. Immediately outside the city walls lie fields and gardens belonging to the inhabitants of Troyes itself.

An incoming visitor to the fair enters the city by one of the gates of the commercial quarter—from the west, the Porte de Paris or the Porte d'Auxerre; from the north, the Porte de la Madeleine or the Porte de Preize; from the south, the Porte de Cronciaus. The sand-colored city wall[1] is twenty feet high and eight feet thick, faced with rough-cut limestone blocks of varying sizes, around a core of rock rubble. Above it rise the roofs, chimneys, and church spires of the city. One crosses the dry moat by a drawbridge, passing through a double-leaf iron door flanked by a pair of watchtowers, powerful little forts connected by three passageways, one under the road, one directly above it and one on the level of the wall. Spiraling flights of stone steps lead from the towers to the vaulted interiors.

A party entering the Porte de Paris finds itself in the newest part of the city, the business quarter west of the Rû Cordé, a canal created by a diversion of the Seine. A hundred yards to the right rises the Viscount's Tower,[2] originally the stronghold of the count's chief deputy. The Viscount's post has gradually evolved into a hereditary sinecure, at present shared by three families. The tower is a mere anachronism. Nearby, in a triangular open space, is the grain market, with a hospital named after St.-Bernard on its northern side.

Two main thoroughfares run east and west in the commercial section—the Rue de l'Epicerie, which changes its name several times before it reaches the canal, and to the north the Grande Rue, leading from the Porte de Paris to the bridge that crosses into the old city. It is thirty feet wide and paved with stone.[3] The Grande Rue is appreciably broader and straighter than the side streets, where riders and even pedestrians sometimes must squeeze past each other. The Ruelle des Chats—"Cats' Alley"—is seven feet wide. Even on the Grande Rue one has a sense of buildings crowding in, the three- and four-story frame houses and shops shouldering into the street, their corbelled upper stories looming irregularly above. Façades are painted red and blue, or faced with tile, often ornamented with paneling, moldings, and sawtooth.

Colorful signboards hang over the doors of taverns, and tradesmen's symbols identify the shops. The shops open to the street, the lowered fronts of their stalls serving as display counters for merchandise—boots, belts, purses, knives, spoons, pots and pans, paternosters (rosaries). Inside, shopkeepers and apprentices are visible at work.

Most traffic is on foot—artisans in bright-colored tunics and hose, housewives in gowns and mantles, their hair covered by white wimples, merchants in fur-trimmed coats, here and there the black or brown habit of a priest or monk. Honking geese flutter from under the hooves of horses. Dogs and cats lurk in the doorways or forage for food with the pigeons.

The streets have been freshly cleaned for the fair, but the smells of the city are still present. Odors of animal dung and garbage mingle with pleasanter aromas from cookshops and houses. The most pungent districts are those of the fish merchants, the linen makers, the butchers and, worst of all, the tanners. In the previous century the expanding business of the tanners and butchers resulted in a typical urban problem. The bed of the Vienne became choked with refuse. Count Henry the Generous had a canal dug from the upper Seine, increasing the flow into the Vienne and flushing out the pollution. But the butchers' and tanners' district remains the most undesirable neighborhood in town. Cities such as Troyes legislate to make householders and shopkeepers clean the streets in front of their houses, and to forbid emptying waste water into the streets. But such ordinances are only half effective. Rain compounds the problem by turning the unpaved streets to mud.

The heart of the fair district surrounds the church of St.-Jean-au-Marché, a warren of little streets where the moneychangers have their headquarters, and where the public scales and the guards' quarters are located. This area, half asleep all spring, is now humming. Horses clomp, hammers bang, and bales thud. Commands and curses resound in several languages, as sacks and bales from the ends of the earth are unloaded—savory spices, shimmering silks, pearls from the bottom of the sea, and wagonload after wagonload of rich wool cloth.

Fair merchants can lodge where they wish, but fellow-countrymen tend to flock together—businessmen from Montpellier on the Rue de Montpellier, near the Porte de Paris; those from Valencia, Barcelona, and Larida in the Rue Clef-du-Bois; Venetians in the Rue du Petit Credo, where the count's provost has his lodge; Lombards in the Rue de la Trinité.

Tents and stalls are used only for the sale of secondary merchandise. The main transactions, in wool, cloth and spices, take place in large permanent halls scattered throughout the fair quarter, whose limits are carefully marked to insure collection of tolls from merchants. Several of the great cloth manufacturing cities have their halls in the Rue de l'Epicerie—Arras, Lucca, Ypres, Douai, Montauban. The hall of Rouen is in the Rue du Chaperon, that of Provins between the Rue de la Tannerie and the Commandery of the Knights Templar.

Near the canal, the Rue de l'Epicerie passes the ancient and powerful convent of Notre-Dame-aux-Nonnains and becomes the Rue Notre-Dame. Here, in stalls maintained by the convent, the Great Fire of 1188 began. To the south is the twenty-year-old Dominican friary (the Franciscans are outside the town, near the Porte de Preize). A little to the north, at the end of the Grand Rue, the Pont des Bains crosses the canal into the ancient Gallo-Roman citadel. On the right bank, above the bridge, are the public baths, where the traveler can scrub off the dust of the roads.

Across the canal lies the old city, still enclosed within its dilapidated Roman walls. Wealthy families live there, along with numerous clergy, officials serving the count, Jews in the old ghetto, some of the working class, and the poor. In the southwest corner of the square enclosure, its back to the canal, stands a large stone building, the count's palace. The great hall rises over an undercroft, with the living quarters in the rear. In front of the palace stands the pillory, a wooden structure resembling a short ladder, which often pinions a petty thief or crooked tradesman. The count's own church of St.-Etienne forms an "L" with the palace, so that he can hear masses from a platform at the end of his hall. Immediately to the north is the hospital founded by Count Henry the Generous, and at the northwest extremity of the old city rises the castle, a grim rectangular tower surrounded by a court-

yard with a forbidding wall. The ancient donjon of the counts, the tower is today used as a ceremonial hall for knightings, feasts, and tourneys.

Near the center of the old city is the Augustinian abbey of St.-Loup, named after the bishop who parleyed with Attila. Originally it lay outside the walls, but following the Viking attack in 891, Abbot Adelerin moved the establishment into the city, St.-Loup's remains included. The Rue de la Cité, principal street of the old town, separates the abbey from the cathedral, which is at the southeast corner of the enclosure. Workmen are busy on the scaffolding that sheathes the mass of masonry. A huge crane, standing inside the masonry shell, drops its line over the wall. Masons' lodges and workshops crowd the space between the cathedral and the bishop's palace.

Near the old donjon is the ghetto. Well-to-do Jewish families live in the Rue de Vieille Rome, just south of the castle wall; farther south, others inhabit the Broce-aux-Juifs, an area enclosed by lanes on four sides.

This is Troyes, an old town but a new city, a feudal and ecclesiastical capital, and major center of the Commercial Revolution of the Middle Ages.

ſos cum iuxta moꝛem heoꝛ
eciam in ſeptuaginta edicio
at ꝓ ſtaͦo. Incipit liber heſter

diuicias gloꝛie regni ſui acuͦ
iactanciam potencie ſue multa
delicet et ſeptuaginta dielͥuͦ

II

A Burgher's Home

They live very nobly, they wear a king's clothes, have fine palfreys and horses.
When squires go to the east, the burghers remain in their beds; when the squires go get
themselves massacred, the burghers go on swimming parties.

—Renard le Contrefait
a fourteenth-century clerk of Troyes

In a thirteenth-century city the houses of rich and poor look more or less alike from the outside. Except for a few of stone, they are all tall timber post-and-beam structures, with a tendency to sag and lean as they get older. In the poor quarters several families inhabit one house. A weaver's family may be crowded into a single room, where they huddle around a fireplace, hardly better off than the peasants and serfs of the countryside.

A well-to-do burgher family, on the other hand, occupies all four stories of its house, with business premises on the ground floor, living quarters on the second and third, servants' quarters in the attic, stables and storehouses in the rear. From cellar to attic, the emphasis is on comfort, but it is thirteenth-century comfort, which leaves something to be desired even for the master and mistress.

Illuminated initial illustrating a banquet scene. Private collection.

Entering the door of such a house, a visitor finds himself in an anteroom. One door leads to a workshop or counting room, a second to a steep flight of stairs. The greater part of the second floor is occupied by the hall, or solar, which serves as both living and dining room. A hearth fire blazes under the hood of a huge chimney. Even in daytime the fire supplies much of the house's illumination, because the narrow windows are fitted with oiled parchment.[1] Suspended by a chain from the wall is an oil lamp, usually not lighted until full darkness. A housewife also economizes on candles, saving fat for the chandler to convert into a smoky, pungent but serviceable product. Beeswax candles are limited to church and ceremonial use.

The large low-ceilinged room is bare and chilly. Walls are hung with panels of linen cloth, which may be dyed or decorated with embroidery; the day of tapestry will come in another fifty years. Carpets are extremely rare in thirteenth-century Europe; floors are covered with rushes. Furniture consists of benches, a long trestle table which is dismantled after meals, a big wooden cupboard displaying plates and silver, and a low buffet for the pottery and tinware used every day. Cupboards

Roasting pigs on a spit, from the *Latin/Luttrell Psalter* **(14th c.).**

and chests are built on posts, with planks nailed lengthwise to form the sides. In spite of iron bindings, and linen and leather glued inside or out, the planks crack, split and warp. It will be two centuries before someone thinks of joining panels by tongue and groove, or mortise and tenon, so that the wood can expand and contract.

If furniture is drab, costume is not. A burgher and his wife wear linen and wool in bright reds, greens, blues, and yellows, trimmed and lined with fur. Though their garments are similar, differentiation is taking place. A century ago both sexes wore long, loose-fitting tunics and robes that were almost identical. Now men's clothes are shorter and tighter than women's, and a man wears an invention of the Middle Ages that has already become a byword for masculinity: trousers, in the form of hose, a tight-fitting combination of breeches and stockings. Over them he wears a long-sleeved tunic, which may be lined with fur, then a sleeveless belted surcoat of fine wool, sometimes with a hood. For outdoors, he wears a mantle fastened at the shoulder with a clasp or chain; although buttons are sometimes used for decoration, the buttonhole has not been invented. (It will be by the end of the century.) His clothes have no pockets, and he must carry money and other belongings in a pouch or purse slung from his belt, or in his sleeves. On his feet are boots with high tops of soft leather.

A woman may wear a tunic with sleeves laced from wrist to elbow, topped by a surcoat caught in at the waist by a belt, with full sleeves that reveal those of the tunic underneath. Her shoes are soft leather, with thin soles. Both sexes wear underclothes—women long linen chemises, men linen undershirts and underdrawers with a cloth belt.

Hair is invariably parted in the middle, a woman's in two long plaits, which she covers with a white linen wimple, a man's worn jaw-long, sometimes with bangs, and often topped with a soft cap. Men's faces are stubbly. Only a rough shave can be achieved with available instruments, and a burgher may visit the barber only once a week.

At mealtime a very broad cloth is laid on the trestle table in the solar. To facilitate service, places are set along one side only. On that side the cloth falls to the floor, doubling as a communal napkin. At a festive dinner it sometimes gets changed between courses. Places are set with knives, spoons, and thick slices of day-old bread, which serve as plates for meat. There are several kinds of knives—for cutting meat, slicing bread, opening oysters and nuts—but no forks. Between each two places stands a two-handled bowl, or *écuelle,* which is filled with soup or stew. Two neighbors share the *écuelle,* as well as a winecup and spoon. A large pottery receptacle is used for waste liquids, and a thick chunk of bread with a hole in the middle serves as a salt shaker.

When supper is prepared, a servant blows a horn.

Napkins, basins, and pitchers are ready; everyone washes their hands without the aid of soap. Courtesy requires sharing a basin with one's neighbor.

If there is no clergyman present, the youngest member of the family says grace. The guests join in the responses and the amen.

Supper may begin with a capon brewet, half soup, half stew, with the meat served in the bottom of the *écuelle,* broth poured over, and spices dusted on top. The second course is perhaps a porray, a soup of leeks, onions, chitterlings, and ham, cooked in milk, with stock and bread crumbs added. A civet of hare may follow—the meat grilled, then cut up and cooked with onions, vinegar, wine, and spices, again thickened with bread crumbs. Each course is washed down with wine from an earthenware jug. At a really elaborate meal roast meats and other stews and fish dishes follow. The meal may conclude with frumenty (a kind of custard), figs and nuts, wafers and spiced wine.

On a fast day a single meal is served after Vespers. Ordinarily it is sparse, no more than bread, water, and vegetables. However, the faithful are not uniformly austere, and in fact the clergy often find loopholes in the law. In the last century St.-Bernard testily described a fast day at a Cluniac monastery:

Dish after dish is served. It is a fast day for meat, so there are two portions of fish... Everything is so artfully con-

Woman writing at her desk (self-portrait) from the *Works of Christine de Pisan* (c.1364–1430).

trived that after four or five courses one still has an appetite . . . For (to mention nothing else) who can count in how many ways eggs alone are prepared and dressed, how diligently they are broken, beaten to froth, hard-boiled, minced; they come to the table now fried, now roasted, now mixed with other things, now alone . . . What shall I say of water-drinking, when not even watered wine is admitted? Being monks, we all suffer from poor digestions, and are therefore justified in following the Apostle's counsel [Use a little wine for thy stomach's sake]: only the word "little," which he puts first, we leave out.

Though everything except soup and sauce is finger food, table manners are important.[2] Gentlefolk eat slowly, take small bites, do not talk while eating, do not drink with their mouths full. Knives are never put in the mouth. Soup must be eaten silently, and the spoon not left in the dish. One does not belch, lean on the table, hang over his dish, or pick his nose, teeth, or nails. Food is not dipped into the salt cellar. Bread is broken, not bitten. Blowing on food to cool it is commonly practiced but frowned upon. Because the wine cup is shared, one must wipe the grease from one's lips before putting them to the cup.

When the family has eaten, servants and apprentices take their turn at the table. They are permitted to eat their fill but not to linger. Then the table is cleared; bowls, knives and spoons washed; and pots and kettles cleaned. One servant takes a pair of buckets and heads for the well down the street. Another collects the leftovers from the meal and takes them to the door, where a pauper or two generally waits; in bad times there will be a crowd. In the last century, beggars were permitted to enter great houses and solicit directly from the table, but now they are restricted to the doorstep.

After the solar, the principal room on the second floor is the large kitchen. Its focus is the fireplace, back to back and sharing the chimney with the main hearth in the solar. Tall enough for a man to walk into, the fireplace burns logs that are three and a half feet long. The fire is rarely allowed to die. If it does, the servants must start it again with a fire-iron, a three-inch piece of metal shaped like a flatiron, which is struck against a piece of flint to produce sparks.

On the hearth, a toothed rack supports an iron kettle where water is kept heating. Other kettles and cauldrons stand on trivets. Skimmers, spoons, shovels and scoops, pokers, pincers, spits and skewers, and a long-handled fork hang in front of the chimney. Nearby is the kitchen garbage pit, emptied periodically, and a vat which holds the water supply. Live fish swim in a leather tank, next to a wooden pickling tub. On a long table against the wall are casseroles of varying sizes. Small utensils are stored on a shelf above: sieves, colanders, mortars and pestles, graters. Hand towels hang out of the reach of mice.

Next to the table stands a spice cupboard—locked, because some of its contents are fabulously expensive. Saffron, of which a rich man's wife may hoard a minute quantity, is worth a good deal more than its weight in gold. Ginger, nutmeg, cinnamon, and several other seasonings imported from the distant East are nearly as dear. Less prohibitive are clove, cannel, mace, cumin. Pepper is just costly enough to be a rich man's table seasoning, as is mustard. Apart from these condiments, the housewife relies on the herbs from her own garden, which hang drying in bunches from the kitchen beams: basil, sage, savory, marjoram, rosemary, and thyme.

On the floor above the solar and kitchen are the family bedrooms. Master and mistress sleep on a great canopied bed as much as eight feet long and seven feet wide, the straw-filled mattress hung on rope suspenders, and covered with linen sheets, blankets of wool and fur, and feather pillows. Children's beds are smaller, with serge and linsey-woolsey covers. Bedrooms are sparsely furnished—a washbasin on a stand, a table, a few chairs, a chest. Perhaps once a week a wooden tub for bathing is set up, and servants lug up buckets that have been heated over the kitchen fire. In the interval between baths members of the household may take shampoos.

Along the wall above the head of the bed runs a horizontal pole, or perch, for hanging up clothes at night. Modesty dictates that husband and wife get in bed in their undergarments, removing them after snuffing the candle and tucking them under the pillows. People sleep naked.

The toilet is usually a privy in the stable yard. A few city houses have a "garderobe" off the sleeping room, over a chute to a pit in the cellar that is emptied at intervals. Ideally such a convenience is built out over the water, an arrangement enjoyed by the count's palace on the canal. Next best is a drainpipe to a neighboring ditch or stream.

Ceaseless war is carried on against fleas, bedbugs, and other insects. Strategies vary. One practice is to fold coverlets, furs, and clothes so tightly in a chest that the fleas will suffocate. A housewife may spread birdlime or turpentine on trenchers of bread, with a lighted candle in the middle. More simply, she may cover a straw mattress with a white sheepskin so that the enemy can be seen and crushed. Netting is used in summer against flies and mosquitoes, and insect traps have been devised, of which the simplest is a rag dipped in honey.

Even for a well-to-do city family, making life comfortable is a problem. But arriving at a point where comfort becomes a problem for a fair number of people is a sign of advancing civilization.

III

A MEDIEVAL HOUSEWIFE

He is upheld by the hope of his wife's care . . . to have his shoes removed before a good fire, his feet washed and to have fresh shoes and stockings, to be given good food and drink, to be well served and well looked after, well bedded in white sheets . . . well covered with good furs, and assuaged with other joys and amusements . . . concerning which I am silent; and on the next day fresh shirts and garments.
—THE GOODMAN OF PARIS

At daybreak cathedral bells sound the first note in a clangorous dialogue that keeps time all day for the citizens of Troyes. The cathedral, as the bishop's church, has the right to speak first—before the count's chapel or Notre-Dame-aux-Nonnains—a precedence conceded to Bishop Hervée after an acrimonious dispute. Troyes has so many bells that a verse runs:

Where are you from? I'm from Troyes.
What do you do there? We ring.

The bells do not ring the hours, but at three-hour intervals,[1] marking the offices of the Church. People do not care exactly what time it is; they want to know how much daylight is left. The bells are their only time-keepers. Monasteries, churches, and public buildings may have sundials or clepsydras (water clocks). The weight-driven clock has yet to be invented.

The dawn bells—"Prime"—launch the day's activity. The men of the guard go off duty as thieves slink to their cellars and honest men begin work. Blacksmiths and butchers are among the first. Shutters rattle and shops open. Cows, sheep, and pigs, mooing and squealing their way out of stable yards to pastures outside the walls, meet sleepy maidservants going to the wells with buckets and basins.

In the tall houses, people crawl out of bed, grope for their underclothes beneath the pillow and their outer garments on the perch, and splash their faces and hands with cold water. An honest housewife completes her morning grooming by combing and plaiting her hair. She has heard more than one sermon censuring women who indulge in cosmetics. The preachers like to remind their lady parishioners that wigs are made of the hair of persons who are now likely to be found in hell or purgatory, and that "Jesus Christ and his blessed mother, of royal blood though they were, never thought of wearing" the belts of silk, gold, and silver that are fashionable among wealthy women. The bandeaux which some ladies employ to bind their bosoms are also frowned on; in the next world, the preachers say, these will be transformed into bands of fire.

The feminine ideal is a slender figure, blond hair, and fair skin—"white as snow on ice," says a poet. To achieve this ideal some women use ointments that are guaranteed to tighten complexions, but sometimes take the skin off along with the pigment.

A couple being married by a cleric (13c).

Street trading at the gate of a city from the David Aubert manuscript by Jean Le Tavernier from *Les Conquetes de Charlemagne* (1460).

One of the housewife's first chores in the morning is shopping for food, which must be done daily. In Troyes most of the food purveyors are clustered in the narrow streets that surround St.-Jean—the Rue du Domino, the Rue des Croisettes (Little Crosses), the Cour de la Rencontre (Meeting Court). Many street names designate the trade practiced there—the Rue de la Corderie (Ropemakers), Rue de la Grande Tannerie and Rue de la Petite Tannerie, Rue de l'Orfàvrerie (Goldsmiths), Rue de l'Epicerie (Grocers). The Rue du Temple runs past the commandery of the Knights Templar.

Signs furnish a colorful punctuation to the rows of wooden houses—a bush for the vintner, three gilded pills for the apothecary, a white arm with stripes of red for the surgeon-barber, a unicorn for the goldsmith, a horse's head for the harness maker.

Shoppers must watch their step in the streets, which are full of unpleasant surprises. In the butchers' quarter slaughtering is performed on the spot, and

blood dries in the sun amid piles of offal and swarms of flies. Outside the poulterers' shops geese, tied to the aprons of the stalls, honk and gabble. Chickens and ducks, their legs trussed, flounder on the ground, along with rabbits and hares.

The housewives pinching the fowl carry in their purses three kinds of coins. Two are of copper—oboles and half-oboles, the small change of the Middle Ages. The only coin of value is the silver penny, or denier. A fat capon costs six deniers,[2] an ordinary chicken four, a rabbit five, a large hare twelve.

Near the butchers' and poulterers' stalls are other food speciality shops. A pastry shop offers wafers at three deniers a pound. The spice-grocer displays a variety of wares. Vinegar comes in big jars at from two to five deniers. Most edible oils cost seven to nine deniers, although olive oil is double that price. Salt is cheap (five pounds for two deniers), pepper dear (four deniers an ounce), sugar even dearer. Even honey is expensive. Sweeteners appear on few medieval tables.

At the bakery, where an apprentice may be seen removing loaves from the oven with a long-handled wooden shovel, the prices of the different loaves are legally fixed. So are the weights, with variations permitted from year to year depending on the wheat crop. Bread is rather expensive this year. Some bakers cheat on quality or weight, and for this reason each baker must mark his bread with his own seal. A detected cheater ends up in the pillory with one of his fraudulent loaves hung around his neck.

The housewife is always on the lookout for poor quality or doubtful quantity—watered wine, milk or oil, bread with too much yeast, blown-out meat, stale fish reddened with pig's blood, cheese made to look richer by soaking it in broth. Dishonest tradesmen are the butt of numerous stories. A favorite: A man asked the sausage butcher for a discount because he had been a faithful customer for seven years. "Seven years!" exclaimed the butcher. "And you're still alive?"

Besides the food shops, there are the peddlers. About terce (nine o'clock) their cries augment the din of the streets. They sell fish, chicken, fresh and salt meat, garlic, honey, onions, fruit, eggs, leeks, and pasties filled with fruit, chopped ham, chicken or eel, seasoned with pepper, soft cheese and egg. "Good Champagne cheese! Good cheese of Brie!" cry the street vendors in Paris, and probably in Troyes as well. Wine and milk are also peddled in the street.

Marketing is only the first step in the preparation of food. All cooking is done over the open fire; there are

Denier coin obverse showing a portrait of Charlemagne, Quentovic Mint (768–814).

no ovens in private houses. Food must be prepared and mixed by hand. Utensils are of iron, copper, pewter, earthenware—no steel or glass. There are no paper or paper products, no chocolate, coffee, tea, potatoes, rice, spaghetti, noodles, tomatoes, squash, corn, baking powder, baking soda, or gelatin. Citrus fruit is a rare delicacy.

Techniques for preserving food are limited. Fish are kept live or in pickling tanks, or salted and smoked; meat may be salted; winter vegetables can be stored in a cool cellar; some fruits, vegetables, and herbs are dried in the sun.

The dinner hour depends on the season and the trade of the household; one may dine as early as ten. Kitchen preparations begin early. Servants clean, mince, blanch, parboil, crush herbs in the mortar, fry and grill meat. To thicken sauces, bread crumbs ground with the pestle are used instead of flour. Recipes are characterized by a staggering complexity, except for roasts, which are turned on a spit over the fire. Vegetables must be blanched, rinsed and cooked for long periods in several changes of water; the mortar and strainer are in constant use; the lists of ingredients are endless. Menus in a prosperous household consist of a series of broths or brewets, thick soups, stews, roasts and fish dishes, followed by savories, fruit or pastries, spiced wine, and wafers. At feasts the last course is preceded by glazed and decorated entremets (eaten "between courses"). These are no trifles, but boars' heads, or swans roasted in their feathers, carried around on platters for all to admire.

Many tasks besides those of the kitchen occupy the housewife and her servants, of which even modest households have a few. City women in any case are better off than the peasant wives of the countryside, who must spin their own thread with the distaff and make their own cloth.

Among the daily tasks are making the beds, accomplished with the aid of a long stick to reach across the vast breadth of the master's bed. Covers and cushions must be shaken out and chamber pots emptied. Servants make up the kitchen fire in the morning, fill the water vat and the big iron kettle in the kitchen, sweep out the entrance and the hall, and occasionally lay fresh rushes.

There are laundresses in Troyes, but most households do their own laundry. From time to time, shirts, tablecloths, and bed linen are put in a wooden trough and soaked in a mixture of wood ashes and caustic soda, then pounded, rinsed and dried in the sun. Soft soap is also used, and is made at home by boiling caustic soda with animal fat. A much better hard soap is made in Spain from olive oil, but is too expensive for everyday use.

Furs and woolen clothes are periodically beaten, shaken, and scrutinized. A special cleaning fluid for furs and wool is made of wine, lye, fuller's earth (hydrous silicate of ammonia), and verjuice (pressed from green grapes). Grease stains are soaked in warm wine, or rubbed with fuller's earth, or with chicken feathers rinsed in hot water. Faded colors can be restored with a sponge soaked in diluted lye or verjuice. Furs hardened from dampness are sprinkled with wine and flour and allowed to dry, then rubbed back to their original softness.

Both city and country women cultivate gardens,[3] growing lettuce, sorrel, shallots, beets, scallions, and herbs. The herbs serve medicinal as well as cooking purposes—sage, parsley, fennel, dittany, basil, hyssop, rue, savory, coriander, mint, marjoram, mallow, agrimony, nightshade, borage. Flowers are planted indiscriminately with vegetables and herbs, and their blossoms are often used in cooking. Petals of lilies, lavender, peonies, and marigolds decorate stews; violets are minced with onions and lettuce as a salad, or cooked in broth; roses and primroses are stewed for dessert. Currant and raspberry bushes, pear, apple and medlar trees, and grapevines are also city garden favorites.

In the larger cities garden space has been crowded

A walled town garden from *Livre des Prouffits Champetres.* (15th c.).

Provins, will eventually help provide a romantic name for the bloody English dynastic war.

Monasteries, too, make their contributions to gardening, perpetuating strains of fruits and vegetables that might otherwise have been lost, or spreading new varieties and horticultural information when the monks go on pilgrimages.

To be a woman in the thirteenth century is much like being a woman in any age. Women are somewhat oppressed and exploited, as always, but as in any age, social status is the really important thing, and a burgher's

out by housing. Now cities like Paris are clearing slum areas for use as city parks, like the Pré aux Clercs and the garden that Louis IX has created on one of the islands in the Seine.

Crusades and pilgrimages have introduced new plants, such as the oleander and the pomegranate. Legend will claim that St.-Louis brought the ranunculus to France from the Holy Land, and Thibaut the Songwriter the red rose of Provins, the town's emblem—although the rose that Thibaut brought was probably the pink Rose of Damascus, unusual in the Middle Ages in that it flowered more than once a season. Edmund of Lancaster, after marrying the widow of Thibaut's nephew, will adopt the rose of Provins as the emblem of his own house, so that the red rose of Lancaster, ex-

Coronation of Louis VIII and Blanche de Castile at Reims from the *Chronicle of France or of St. Denis* (14th c.).

wife is no serf. She is a person of dignity and worth, important in her family and respected in the community.

Unmarried women can own property, and in the absence of male heirs they can also inherit. Women of all classes have rights in property by law and customs. Women can sue and be sued, make wills, make contracts, even plead their own cases in court. Women have been known to appear as their husbands' attorneys. A "Portia" character is the heroine of a contemporary romance, The Hard Creditor.

Well-to-do women know how to read and write and figure; some know a little Latin, or boast such lady-

like accomplishments as embroidering and playing the lute. Girls receive instruction from private teachers, or board at convents. The convent of Notre-Dame-aux-Nonnains has a school for girls dating back to the sixth century. Universities are closed to women, but they are equally closed to men except those who are being trained for the clergy, law, or medicine. Among the landed gentry, women are better educated than men. In the romance Galeran a boy and girl brought up together are given typically different schooling—the girl learning to embroider, read, write, speak Latin, play the harp, and sing; the boy, to hawk, hunt, shoot, ride, and play chess.

Women work outside the home at an astonishing variety of crafts and professions. They may be teachers, midwives, laundresses, lacemakers, seamstresses, and even members of normally male trades and occupations[4]—weavers, fullers, barbers, carpenters, saddlers, tilers, and many

Abelard (1079–1142) and his pupil Heloise (1101–63). Painting (1882) by Edmund Blair Leighton (1853–1922).

others. Wives commonly work at their husbands' crafts, and when a man dies his widow carries on the trade. Daughters not infrequently learn their father's craft along with their brothers. In the countryside girls hire out as farm workers. The lady of the manor takes charge of the estate while her husband is off to war, Crusade, or pilgrimage, and wives run businesses while their husbands are away.

Women do suffer from an inequity in respect to wages, which are lower than men's for the same work. An English treatise on husbandry says, "If this is a manor where there is no dairy, it is always good to have a woman there at much less cost than a man."

Politically, women have no voice. They do not sit on the Town Council or in the courts, or serve as provosts or officials. Basically, this is because they do not bear arms. Yet women play political roles, often with distinction—Empress Matilda of England, Eleanor of Aquitaine, Queen Blanche of France, Countess Jeanne of Flanders, Blanche of Champagne, and many more. Countess Marie, wife of Henry the Generous, was asked to arbitrate claims between the churches of St.-Etienne and St.-Loup, and with her brother-in-law, William of the White Hands, archbishop of Reims, to decide important cases, including the seigneury of Vertus. In war, or at least sieges, women often play the heroine.

Women occupy positions of power and influence in the Church. The abbess of a convent such as Notre-Dame-aux-Nonnains[5] is invested with important executive responsibilities. Usually such posts are accorded to ladies of high rank, like Alix de Villehardouin, daughter of the marshal of Champagne. Abbesses are not afraid to assert their rights. A few years hence an abbey of Notre-Dame, Odette de Pougy, will defy the Pope's excommunication and lead a party of armed men to defend what she regards as the rights of her abbey. This establishment owes its extraordinary prestige to its ancient origins, which are believed to date from the third century. The abbess actually enjoys rights over the bishop of Troyes. When a new bishop is installed, he must lead a procession to the abbey, mounted on a palfrey that is handed over, saddle included, to the abbess's stable. Inside the convent, the bishop kneels and receives cross, mitre, and prayer book from the abbess's hands. He recites an oath: "I . . . bishop of Troyes, swear to observe the rights, franchises, liberties, and privileges of this convent of Notre-Dame-aux-Nonnains, with the help of God and his holy saints." The bishop spends the night in the convent and is given as a gift the bed in which he has slept, with all its furnishings. Only the next day does his installation as bishop take place in the cathedral.

Women achieve distinction outside the cloister, too. Marie de France is the most gifted woman poet of the Middle Ages, and "wise Héloïse" the most noteworthy bluestocking, but there are many more. The contemporary scholar Albert the Great, debating whether the Virgin Mary knew the seven liberal arts, resolves the question affirmatively.

The cult of Mary serves to elevate the image of women and to counterbalance the misogyny of ascetic preachers who bestow such epithets as "man's confounder," "mad beast," "stinking rose," "sad paradise," "sweet venom," "luscious sin," and "bitter sweet," while lingering over the attractions of the temptresses. The chivalric ideal also glorifies women. The Church recognizes the wife to be subject to her husband, as Paul recommended, but as his companion, not as mere mistress or servant. Married people are expected to treat each other with respect, and many husbands and wives never call each other anything but Sir and Madam.

Wife-beating is common in an age when corporal punishment is the norm. But wives do not necessarily get the worst of it. A contemporary observer remarks that men rarely have the mastery of their wives, that nearly everywhere women dominate their husbands. One preacher complains that formerly wives were faithful to their husbands and peaceful as ewe lambs; now they are lionesses. Another tells the story of a storm at sea, when the sailors wished to throw into the sea anything that might overload the ship, and a certain husband handed over his wife, saying that there was no object of such intolerable weight. The expression "wearing the pants in the family" is already current, and henpecked husbands are a favorite theme of the fabliaux.

Perhaps the most important point to note about the medieval housewife, in contrast to women of earlier times, is that she has a purse. She goes shopping, she gives alms, she pays fees, she hires labor; she may, if the occasion arises, buy privileges and pay bribes.

She may do many other things with her money. Women make large gifts of land, money, and chattels to church institutions; found convents, monasteries, hospitals, orphanages, and asylums; buy benefices for their sons and places in convents for their daughters; engage in trading operations. They are denounced by priests for usury, pawnbroking, and price manipulations, and for their reckless expenditures for luxury goods. They may travel extensively, sometimes as far as the Holy Land.

A woman of means is always a person to reckon with.

Daughters of burghers, like daughters of knights,

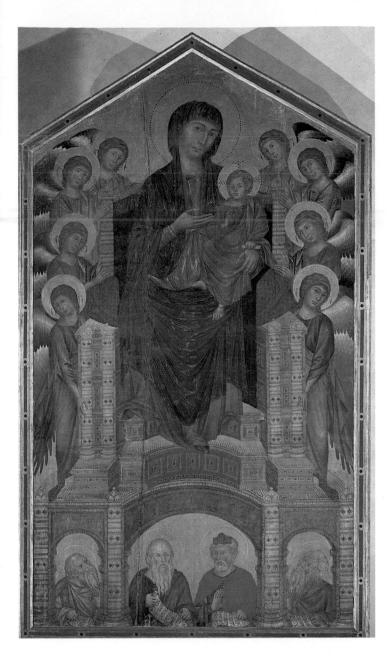

Madonna Enthroned by Cimabue (1240–1302).

learn definite rules of conduct. A poet, Robert of Blois, has codified the behavior of women of the gentle class:

En route to church or elsewhere, a lady must walk straight and not trot or run, or idle either. She must salute even the poor.

She must let no one touch her on the breast except her husband. For that reason, she must not let anyone put a pin or a brooch on her bosom.

No one should kiss her on the mouth except her husband. If she disobeys this injunction, neither loyalty, faith nor noble birth will avert the consequences.

Women are criticized for the way they look at people, like a sparrowhawk ready to pounce on a swallow. Take care: glances are messengers of love; men are prompt to deceive themselves by them.

If a man courts a lady, she must not boast of it. It is base to boast, and besides, if she takes a fancy later to love this person, the secret will be more difficult to keep.

A lady shuns the fashionable décolletage, a sign of shamelessness.

A lady does not accept gifts. For gifts which are given you in secret cost dear; one buys them with one's honor. There are, however, honest gifts which it is proper to thank people for.

Above all, a lady does not scold. Anger and high words are enough to distinguish a low woman from a lady. The man who injures you shames himself and not you; if it is a woman who scolds you, you will break her heart by refusing to answer her.

Women must not swear, drink too much or eat too much.

The lady who, when a great lord salutes her, remains silent with bowed head is badly brought up. A lady removes her hood before those whom she would honor. One may only remain with head beat when one has something to hide—if one has a yellow complexion, or is ugly. If you have an unattractive smile, however, hide it with your hand.

Ladies with pale complexions should dine early. Good wine colors the face. If your breath is bad, hold it in church when you receive the blessing.

Especially in church one must watch one's countenance, for one is in the public eye, which notes evil and good. One must kneel courteously, pray and not laugh or talk too much.

Rise at the moment of the Scripture, cross yourself at beginning and end. At the offering, hold yourself straight. Rise also, hands joined, at the elevation, then pray on your knees for all Christians. If you are ill or pregnant, you may read your psalter seated.

If you have a good voice, sing boldly. In the company of people who ask you, and by yourself for your own pleasure, sing; but do not abuse their patience, so that people will say, as they sometimes do, "Good singers are often a bore."

Cut your fingernails frequently, down to the quick, for cleanliness' sake. Cleanliness is better than beauty.

In passing other people's houses, refrain from glancing inside. To enter without knocking is indiscreet.

One must know how to eat—not to talk or laugh too much at table, not to pick out the best pieces, not to eat too much as a guest, not to criticize the food, to wipe one's mouth but not one's nose on the cloth.[6]

IV
CHILDBIRTH AND CHILDREN

When they are washed of filth, they soon defile themselves again. When their mother washes and combs them, they kick and sprawl, and push with feet and hands, and resist with all their might. They always want to drink, unless they are out of bed, when they cry for meat. Always they cry, jangle and jape, except when they are asleep.

—BARTHOLOMEW ANGLICUS

The greatest hazard in the life of a woman of the thirteenth century is childbirth. If she survives the childbearing period, she stands a good chance of outliving her husband. There are no obstetrical instruments and no techniques for dealing with a breach presentation. Caesarian section is performed only when mother or child is dead, and then without antiseptics or anesthesia. If the pelvic opening is too small for the child's head, nothing can be done.

The baby's chances of survival are poorer than the mother's. Many die at birth, more during infancy. Birth defects are common, and generally attributed to supernatural causes. An eleventh-century king, Robert the

Mother receiving her newly born baby in bed by Guido Bonatti de Forlivio from *Liber Introductorium ad i Udicio Stellarum* (1490).

Pious, was excommunicated for marrying a widow for whose child he had stood godfather. According to a chronicler, the pair was punished when their own child was born "with the head of a goose." Chastened Robert hastily put his queen away in a convent.

An old superstition holds that when twins are born the mother has had intercourse with two different men. In a popular romance, *Galeran,* the wife of a knight insults one of her husband's vassals by telling him that everyone knows twins are the product of two fathers. Two years later the lady has cause to repent her words when she herself gives birth to twin girls. Michael Scot, astrologer to Frederick II, asserts that multiple births are entirely normal and may run as high as seven: three boys, three girls, and the "middle cell"— a hermaphrodite.

Contemporary scientists agree that for a month each planet exerts its influence over the development of the child in the womb. Saturn bestows the virtue of discerning and reasoning, Jupiter magnanimity, Mars animosity and irascibility, the sun the power of learning, and so forth. When the influence of the stars is too strong, the child talks early, has discretion beyond his age, and dies young. Some say that if the hour of conception is known, the entire life of the child can be predicted. Michael Scot urges every woman to note the exact moment, to facilitate astrological forecasting. When his patron Frederick II married a third wife, sister of Henry III of England, he delayed consummation until the morning after the wedding, the moment astrology deemed favorable. Afterwards Frederick handed over his wife to the care of Saracen eunuchs and assured her that she was pregnant with a son, which information he also conveyed in a letter to the English king. Frederick's confidence was justified. The next year a son was born.

It is widely believed that the sex of a child can be foretold and even influenced. A drop of the mother's milk or blood may be dropped into pure spring water; if it sinks, the child will be a boy, if it floats, a girl. Or if a pregnant woman, asked to hold out her hand, extends the right, the child will be a boy; if the left, a girl. A woman who wants to have a boy is supposed to sleep on her right side.

When labor is imminent, the lying-in chamber is prepared for visiting and display—the best coverlets, fresh rushes on the floor, chairs and cushions. A cupboard exhibits the family's finest possessions—gold and silver cups, enamelware, ivory, richly bound books. Dishes of sugared almonds and candied fruits are set out for the guests.

Doctors do not attend women in childbirth. Men are excluded from the lying-in chamber. Midwives are therefore indispensable, so much so that when Louis IX decided to take his queen along on a Crusade, he also took a midwife, who assisted at two royal childbirths in the Orient.

During labor the midwife rubs her patient's belly with ointment to ease her travail and bring it to a quicker conclusion. She encourages the patient with comforting words. If the labor is difficult, sympathetic magic is invoked. The patient's hair is loosened and all the pins are removed. Servants open all the doors, drawers, and cupboards in the house and untie all the knots. Jasper is a gemstone credited with childbirth-assisting powers, as well as the powers of preventing conception, checking menstrual flow, and reducing sexual desire. The dried blood of a crane and its right foot are also useful in labor, and one authority recommends water in which a murderer has washed his hands. In extreme cases there are incantations of magical words, whispered in the patient's ear, but priests frown on this practice.

When the baby is born, the midwife ties the umbilical cord and cuts it at four fingers' length. She washes the baby and rubs him all over with salt, then gently cleanses his palate and gums with honey, to give him an appetite. She dries him with fine linen and wraps him so tightly in swaddling bands that he is almost completely immobilized and looks not unlike a little corpse in a winding sheet.

He is shown to his father and the rest of the family, then placed in the wooden cradle next to his mother's bed, in a dark corner where the light cannot injure his eyes. A servant rocks him, so that the fumes from the hot, moist humors of his body will mount to his brain and make him sleep. He remains securely bundled until he is old enough to sit up, lest his tender limbs be twisted out of shape. He is nursed, bathed, and changed every three hours, and rubbed with rose oil.

Well-to-do women rarely nurse their own children. The wet nurse is chosen with care, for all manner of qualities may be imbibed with her milk. She must be of good character, have no physical defects, and be neither too fat nor too thin. Above all, she must be healthy, for corrupt milk is blamed for many of the maladies that afflict infants. She must watch her diet—eat white bread, good meat, rice, lettuce, almonds and hazelnuts, and drink good wine. She must rest and sleep well and use moderation in bathing and in working. If her milk fails, she eats peas and beans and gruel boiled in milk. She avoids onions, garlic, vinegar and highly seasoned foods. If the doctor prescribes medicine for the baby, it is administered to the nurse. As the baby grows bigger, she will chew his meat for him. She is often the recipient of presents to sweeten her disposition and milk.

The baby is usually baptized the day he is born. Covered with a robe of silk and gold cloth, the little bundle is borne to church by one of his female relatives, while another holds the train of his mantle. The midwife carries the christening bonnet. Nurse, relatives, godparents, and friends follow. If the child is a boy, two godfathers and a godmother are chosen; if a girl, two godmothers and one godfather. The temptation to enlist as many important people as possible in the child's behalf led to naming so many godparents that the Church has now restricted the allotment to three, who are expected to give handsome presents.

The church door is decorated for the occasion, fresh straw spread on the floor, and the baptismal font covered with velvet and linen. The baby is undressed on

Children catching butterflies and playing with a whip-top and walker by Jacobus from *Omne Bonum*.

a silk-cushioned table. The priest traces the sign of the cross on his forehead with holy oil, reciting the baptismal service. The godfather lifts him to the basin, and the priest plunges him into the water. The nurse dries and swaddles him, and the midwife ties on the christening cap to protect the holy oil on his forehead.

Birth records[1] are purely private—records kept by the parish are three hundred years in the future. In a well-to-do family the father may write the baby's name and birth date in the Book of Hours, the family prayer book. If it is ever necessary to establish age or family origin in a court of law, the oral testimony of the midwife, godparents, and priest will be taken down and recorded by a notary.

When the mother recovers from her confinement, she is "churched." Until this ceremony has taken place she is considered impure and may not make

bread, serve food, or have contact with holy water. If a mother is churched on Friday, she will become barren. A day when a wedding has taken place in the church also threatens bad luck.

On an appropriate day for the ceremony the mother puts on her wedding gown and, accompanied by family and friends, enters the church carrying a lighted candle. The priest meets her at the door, makes the sign of the cross, sprinkles her with holy water, and recites a psalm. Holding one end of his stole, she follows him into the nave, while he says, "Enter the temple of God, adore the Son of the holy Virgin Mary, who has given you the blessing of motherhood." If a mother dies in childbirth, this same ceremony takes place, with the midwife or a friend acting as proxy.

Leaving the church, the mother keeps her eyes straight in front of her, for if she sees someone known for his evil character, or with a defect, the baby will be similarly afflicted. But if her glance lights on a little boy, it is a happy omen—her next child will be a boy.

The celebration is topped off with a feast for god-parents, relatives, and friends.

From swaddling bands, the infant graduates directly to adult dress. He is subject to fairly strict discipline, often physical, but is indulged in games and play. His mother may hide and watch while he searches for her, then, just as he begins to cry, leap out and hug him. If he bumps himself on a bench, she beats the bench until the child feels avenged.

Children play with tops, horseshoes, and mar-bles. They stagger about on stilts. Girls have dolls of baked clay or wood. Adults and children alike engage in outdoor games such as prisoner's base, bowling, blindman's buff. Sports are popular too—swimming, wrestling, and early forms of football and tennis; the latter is played without a racket but with a covering for the hand. All classes enjoy cock fighting. In winter, people tie on their feet skates made of horses' shin-bones, and propel themselves on the ice with a pole shod with iron. Boys joust with the pole as they shoot past each other.

Young and old play dice, chess, and checkers. Chess is in great vogue. Some people own magnificent boards, mounted on trestles, with heavy pieces carved out of ivory—the bishop with his mitre, the knight fighting a dragon, king and queen in ceremonial robes and crowns. The game has recently evolved into its permanent form; until the twelfth century the two principal pieces on either side were two kings, or a king and his minister, who followed him step by step. But the minister was turned into a "dame" without at first changing his obedient course of play. Then the dame became queen and was left free to maneuver in all directions.

The Church condemns games of all forms—par-lor games, playacting, dancing, cards, dice, and even physical sports, particularly at the universities. Games flourish, nevertheless, even at the court of pious St.-Louis, as the Troyen knight-chronicler Joinville observes. On shipboard during his Crusade, the king, in mourning for his brother Robert of Artois, lost his tem-per when he found his other brother, the count of Anjou, playing backgammon with Gautier de Nemours. The king seized dice and boards and flung them into the sea, scolding his brother for gambling at such a moment. "My lord Gautier," observes Joinville,

"came off best, for he tipped all the money on the table into his lap."

Parlor games are played, too, such as those described in Adam de la Halle's *Jeu de Robin et de Marion*. In "St.-Cosme" one player represents the saint and the others bring him offerings, which they must present without laughing. Whoever falls victim to his grimaces must pay a forfeit, and become St.-Cosme himself. In another game, "The King Who Does Not Lie," a king or queen chosen by lot and crowned with straw asks questions of each player, being required in return to answer a question from each. The questions and replies of the peasant characters in *Robin* are ingenuous: "Tell me, Gautier, were you ever jealous?" "Yes, sire, the other day when a dog scratched at my sweetheart's door; I thought it was a man." "Tell us, Huart, what do you like to eat most?" "Sire, a good rump of pork, heavy and fat, with a strong sauce of garlic and nuts."

There is no children's literature in the sense of stories written solely for children. But folk tales, passed down through the centuries in many versions, are the greatest single source of popular entertainment for adults and children alike. One that cannot fail to delight is the story of the shepherd and the king's daughter:

> Once there was a king who always told the truth, and who was angry when he heard the people at his court going about calling each other liars. One day he said that no one was to say, "You're a liar," any-more, and to set the example, if anyone heard him say, "You're a liar," he would give him the hand of his daughter.
>
> A young shepherd decided to try his luck. One night after supper, as he sometimes liked to do, the king came to the kitchen and listened to the songs and tales of the servants. When his turn came, the shepherd began this story: "I used to be an appren-tice at my father's mill, and I carried the flour on an ass. One day I loaded him too heavily, and he broke right in two."
>
> "Poor creature," the king said.
>
> "So I cut a hazelnut stick from a tree, and I joined the two pieces of the donkey and stuck the piece of wood from front to rear to hold it together. The donkey set out again and carried the flour to my clients. What do you think of that, sire?"
>
> "That's a pretty tall tale," the king said. "But continue."
>
> "The next morning I was surprised to see that the stick had grown, and there were leaves, and even hazelnuts on it, and the branches went on growing and grew until they reached the sky. I climbed up the hazelnut tree, and I climbed and I climbed and

pretty soon I reached the moon."

"That's pretty steep, but go on."

"There were some old women winnowing oats. When I wanted to go back to earth, the donkey had gone off with the hazelnut tree, so I had to tie the oat beards together to make a rope to go back down."

"That's very steep," the king said. "But go on."

"Unluckily my rope was short, so that I fell on a cliff so hard that my head was driven into the stone up to my shoulders. I tried to get loose, but my body got separated from my head, which was still stuck in the stone. I ran to the miller and got an iron bar to get it out."

"Steeper and steeper," said the king. "But continue."

"When I came back an enormous wolf wanted to get my head out of the rock to eat it, but I gave him a blow with the iron bar so that a letter was forced out of his behind!"

"Very steep indeed!" cried the king. "But what did the letter say?"

"The letter said, sire, that your father was a miller's apprentice at my grandfather's house."

"You're a liar!" cried the king indignantly.

"Well, king, I have won," said the shepherd. And that's how the shepherd got the king's daughter!

V

WEDDINGS AND

FUNERALS

In the great hall there was much merry-making, each one contributing what he could to the entertainment: one jumps, another tumbles, another does magic; there is story-telling, singing, whistling, playing on the harp, the rote, the fiddle, the flute and pipe, singing and dancing. At the wedding that day everything was done which can give joy. Not a wicket or a gate was left closed; but the exits and entrances all stood ajar, so that no one, poor or rich, was turned away.

—CHRÉTIEN DE TROYES *in Eric et Enide*

Marriage in the thirteenth century normally unites people of the same class. But social mobility is present here as in all times. Marriages joining prosperous burgher families with the petty nobility are not uncommon. Marriage is also an avenue for an artisan to make his fortune; an alliance with a rich widow may mean a house in town, a stock of clothing belonging to the late husband, furniture, silver, and real estate.

Arranged marriages are the rule, but the Church emphasizes consent. Its preachers heap scorn on marriages based exclusively on financial considerations. "One might as well publish the banns of Lord Such-and-Such with the purse of Madame So-and-So, and on the day of the wedding lead to the church not the

fiancée but her money or her cows," says the sharp-tongued Paris preacher Jacques de Vitry. By Church law, a bride must be at least twelve, a bridegroom fourteen. Consanguinity is taboo; bride and groom cannot be related in the fourth degree (until the Fourth Lateran Council in 1215 it was the seventh). The expression of the free accord of the two parties is the most important feature of the marriage ritual.

Marriages are recognized between slaves, between freemen and serfs, between Catholics and heretics, or Catholics and excommunicants, but not between Christians and heathens, since the latter have not been baptized. Until the Fourth Lateran Council, marriage between an adulterer who became free to marry and his fellow-sinner was prohibited, as was marriage between an abductor and a victim he later set free; now both are permitted.

Divorce (annulment) is rare. It is only permitted on the grounds that the union has broken one of the Church's three laws on marriage—age, consent, and consanguinity. The intricacies of consanguinity some-

A marriage scene. Spanish School (12th c.).

times provide a loophole toward annulment for the rich and powerful, but even they cannot easily get away with fraudulent claims. King Philip Augustus ran afoul of the Church when he sought to get rid of his Danish wife, and finally had to take her back.

Marriages, at least those of the wealthy classes, have a legal as well as religious basis, with a contract drawn up by the notary specifying the bride's dowry. The son and daughter of wealthy burghers may start life with a house, one or two small farm properties, some cash, and the rent from a house in town. The contract may also specify what property will be the bride's after her husband's death; if it does not, she automatically inherits one-third of his worldly goods.

After the contract is drawn up, the next step is the betrothal, a religious ceremony of a solemnity approach-

ing that of marriage itself. In fact, the similarity of the vows exchanged to those of the marriage ceremony gives rise to an awkward difficulty that results in many suits in the ecclesiastical courts. The Church emphasizes the distinction between these "words of the future" spoken at the betrothal and the "words of the present" that will be said at the wedding, but sometimes couples consider themselves married when they are no more than betrothed, converting an engagement into a clandestine marriage, which one party may later find easy to dissolve.

The priest asks the prospective groom, "Do you promise that you will take this woman to wife, if the Holy Church consents?" He addresses the girl similarly. The couple exchange rings, and the banns are published on three successive Sundays. Weddings cannot take place during Advent and the twelve days of Christmas, or during Lent, or between Ascension Sunday and the week of Pentecost.

On the day of the wedding, the bride's mother and sisters and some of her friends help her to dress. There is no special bridal costume. She simply wears her best clothes: her finest linen chemise; her best silk tunic, trimmed with fur, perhaps with a velvet surcoat over it, embroidered with gold thread; and a mantle edged with gold lace. On her head a small veil is held by a narrow gold band; on her feet are shoes of fine leather, worked with gold.

The groom is also dressed in his best. As they ride to church, a little troop of *jongleurs* precedes them, playing on flute, viol, harp, and bagpipe. Behind ride parents and relatives and the other wedding guests. All along the way crowds gather to watch. In the square in front of the church everyone dismounts, and the priest steps out under the portico, carrying an open book and also the wedding ring.

He interrogates the couple: Are they of age? Do they swear that they are not within the forbidden degree of consanguinity? Do their parents consent? Have the banns been published? Finally, do they themselves both freely consent? Taking each other's right hand they repeat their vows.

The priest delivers a short homily. A typical example, by Henri of Provins, dwells on religious education of children, domestic peace, and mutual fidelity. Henri

bserves that at the moment of the Flood, the Lord by preference saved married creatures; that if the blessed Virgin, the Queen of Paradise, had not been married God would not have been born from her womb; and that conjugal life represents a model of felicity in this world.

The priest blesses the ring; the groom takes it and slips it in turn on each of three fingers of the bride's left hand, saying, "In the Name of the Father, and of the Son, and of the Holy Ghost." Finally he fits it onto her third finger, saying, "With this ring I thee wed."

Alms are distributed by the bride and groom to the poor who have collected outside the portico, and the wedding party enters the church. At this point, some ten years before in Dijon, a moneylender met with disaster at his wedding when one of the sculptures on the portico—a stone figure of a usurer in a Last Judgment scene—fell and struck him a fatal blow on the head with its purse. His relatives and friends obtained permission to demolish the other sculptures on the portico.[1]

By their exchange of promises, the young couple are married. After the nuptial mass, the groom receives the Kiss of Peace from the priest and transmits it to his bride. They leave the church, remount their horses, and the procession returns to the bride's home, again led by the little troop of minstrels.

A wedding feast in a wealthy burgher's household is gargantuan, with wine by the barrel, legs of beef, mutton, veal and venison, capons, ducklings, chicken, rabbits, wafers from the wafer maker, spices, confections, oranges, apples, cheese, dozens of eggs, perhaps a boar's head or a swan in its plumage. An array of extra servants is hired for the day—porters, cooks, waiters, carvers, stewards, a sergeant to guard the door, a chaplet maker to prepare garlands.

Jongleurs[2] accompany the successive courses with music, and as soon as the spiced wine, wafers, and fruit are served the entertainment begins. It starts off with handsprings, tumbles, and other acrobatics. Imitations of bird calls, sleight-of-hand tricks, and a juggling act are likely to be on the program. Interspersed are singers who accompany themselves on two musical inventions of the Middle Ages: the six-stringed, pear-shaped lute, which is plucked, or the five-stringed viol, the first bowed instrument. Both are tuned in fourths and fifths,

A bethrothal banquet from *Les Cantiques de Sainte Marie* **(Spanish, 13th c.).**

the accompaniment following the tune either in unison or at intervals of an octave or a fifth, sometimes with a drone note (a repeated tone with unchanging pitch) in the bass.

The professional entertainment over, tables are dismantled and guests join hands to dance and sing carols, accompanied by lute and viol, or perhaps by a tabor-pipe and tabor—a small flute played with the left hand and a light tambourine-like drum played with the right; sometimes the tabor is fastened to the player's shoulder and he uses his own head as a drumstick.

At suppertime the tables are set up again, for more food, more wine, more music. At Vespers the priest arrives, and the guests accompany the young couple to their house. The priest blesses the new hearth, the chamber, and the nuptial bed, and gives his blessing again to bride and groom. The bride's mother has taken care to search the bed to make sure that no ill-wisher has secreted anything there that may impede conjugal relations, such as two halves of an acorn or granulated beans.

The celebration is usually over in the morning, but a really big wedding can go on for days. One such wedding, described in a romance called *Flamenca,* lasted "several weeks." The streets were decorated with tapestries, spices burned in all the squares of the town; "five hundred sets of clothes, of purple decorated with gold leaf, a thousand lances, a thousand shields, a thousand swords, a thousand hauberks and a thousand chargers" were prepared as gifts for the wedding guests. The wedding cortege was "several leagues long." "Two hundred jongleurs" fiddled while the guests danced, and story tellers recounted the tales of "Priam, Helen, Ulysses, Hector, Achilles, Dido and Aeneas, Lavinia, Polynices, Tydee and Eteocles, Alexander, Cadmus, Jason, Daedalus and Icarus, Narcissus, Pluto and Orpheus, Hero and Leander, David and Goliath, Samson and Delilah, Julius Caesar, the Round Table, Charlemagne and Oliver of Verdun." The festivities were "as delightful as Paradise."

Like marriage, death has its ritual. For a well-to-do burgher the most important task in preparation for departure from this world is the disposition of his property. The Church strongly advises not only making a will in plenty of time, but giving in advance the endowments that will speed the donor through purgatory. The preacher Henri of Provins tells the story of a man dining at the house of a friend, who sends a servant to light his way home so that he will not stumble and fall in the mud. If the servant carries the lantern behind the guest's back, says Henri, it will not prevent him from stumbling or falling. Thus it is with alms: If you keep them to distribute after your death, your lantern will be carried behind your back. Henri to the contrary notwithstanding, many burghers like to hang on to their wealth till the last possible moment.

That moment is extreme unction, after which the Church considers a man as good as dead. A sick man who recovers after receiving it must fast perpetually, go barefoot, and never again have intercourse with his wife. In some places he cannot even amend his will.

A dying man in particular fear of hell, because he is pious or guilty, may express his penitence by having himself laid on the ground on a hair cloth sprinkled with ashes. Louis IX, given up by the doctors, adopted this practice and discoursed so eloquently on the insubstantiality of this world's wealth and power that he drew tears from his audience—and then recovered to go on a Crusade. Prince Henry of England, son of Henry II, after tying a rope around his neck and having himself dragged to his bed of ashes, where gravestones were placed at his head and feet, also recovered.

When a burgher dies, a public crier is hired to announce his death and the hour and place of burial. The doors of the house and of the death chamber are draped with black serge. Two monks from the abbey wash the body with perfumed water, anoint it with balsam and ointment, and encase it in a linen shroud; then they sew it in a deerskin and deposit it in a wooden coffin. Draped in a black pall, the coffin is placed on a bier consisting of two poles with wooden crosspieces and taken to the church, attended by a cortege of clergy and black-clad mourners, the widow and family making loud and visible lament. The bier halts outside the chancel gates (if the dead man is a priest, the body is laid out within the chancel), and the Mourning Office is said—the "Dirge," from *Dirige,* the first word of the first antiphon. When the mass is over, the priest removes his chasuble, censes the body and sprinkles it with holy water, says the Lord's Prayer, in which all join; then he pronounces the Absolutions, a series of prayers and antiphons of forgiveness and deliverance from judgment.

As the cortege proceeds to the church burial grounds, monks from the abbey lead the way with crosses, sacred books and thuribles, and mourners follow with candles. The latter are numerous, for the poor can earn alms by carrying candles in a rich man's funeral procession. When the place of burial is reached, the priest makes the sign of the cross over the grave, sprinkles it with holy water, and digs a shallow trench in the shape of the cross. The real gravedigging is then done to the accompaniment of psalms. The wooden coffin is lowered, the final collect for forgiveness said, the grave filled in, and a flat tombstone laid. (Those who cannot afford coffins rent one, and the remains are buried without the coffin.)

The procession returns to the church, singing the Seven Penitential Psalms. For a time the tomb will be lighted with candles and a funeral lamp. In a few years the bones may be lifted out of the grave and stacked, so that the space can be used again.

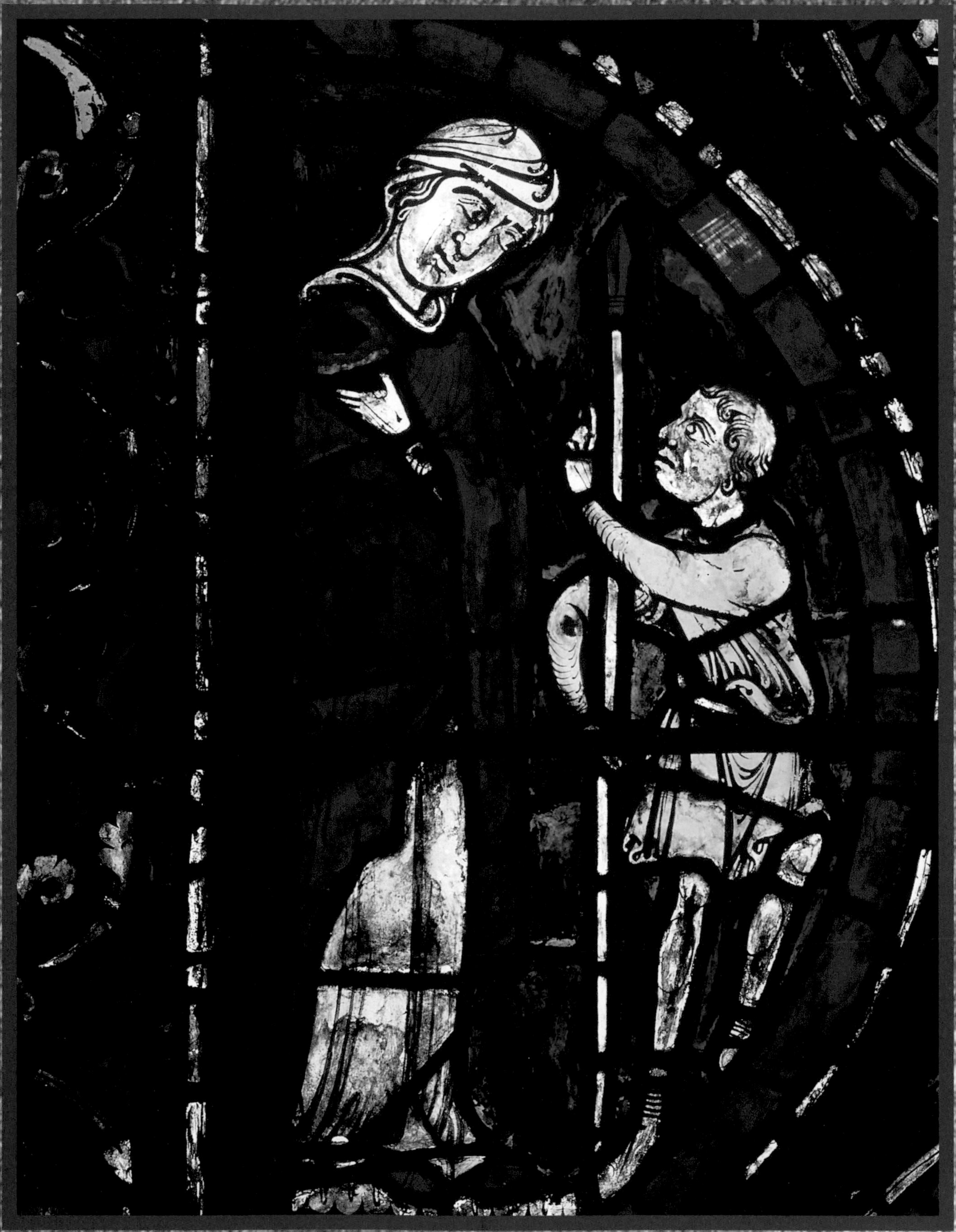

VI
SMALL BUSINESS

And he looks at the whole town
Filled with many fair people;
The moneychangers' tables covered with gold and silver
And with coins;
He sees the squares and the streets
Filled with good workmen
Plying their various trades:
One making helmets, one hauberks,
Another saddles, another shields,
Another bridles, and another spurs,
Still another furbishes swords,
Some full cloth, others dye it,
Others comb it, others shear it;
Others melt gold and silver,
Making rich and beautiful things,
Cups, goblets, écuelles,
And jewels with enamel inlay,
Rings, belts, clasps;
One might well believe
That the city held a fair all year round,
It was full of so many fine things,
Of pepper, wax and scarlet dye,
Of black and gray velvet
And of all kinds of merchandise.

—CHRÉTIEN DE TROYES I
in *Perceval, le Conte du Graal*

Detail showing The Donors: Wheelwrights, coopers, and carpenters from the stained glass Noah Window, Chartres Cathedral, France.

Almost every craftsman in Troyes is simultaneously a merchant. The typical master craftsman alternately manufactures a product and waits on trade in his small shop, which is also his house. Sometimes he belongs to a guild, although in Troyes only a fraction of the hundred and twenty guilds of Paris[1] are represented. Many crafts stand in no need of protective federation or have too few members to form a guild.

Each shop on the city street is essentially a stall, with a pair of horizontal shutters that open upward and downward, top and bottom. The upper shutter, opening upward, is supported by two posts that convert it into an awning; the lower shutter drops to rest on two short legs and acts as a display counter. At night the shutters are closed and bolted from within. Inside, the shop master and apprentice and a male relative or two, or the master's wife, work at the craft.

In a tailor's shop, the tailor sits inside, cutting and sewing in clear view of the public, an arrangement that simultaneously permits the customer to inspect the work and the tailor to display his skill. When the buying public arrives—even if it is only a single housewife—tailors, hatmakers, shoemakers and the rest desert their benches and hurry outside, metamorphosing into salesmen who are so aggressive that they must be restrained by guild rules—for example, from addressing a customer who has stopped at a neighbor's still.

Related crafts tend to congregate, often giving their name to a street. Crafts also give their names to craftsmen—Thomas le Potier ("Potter"), Richarte le Barbier ("Barber"), Benoît le Peletier ("Skinner"), Henri Taillebois ("Woodman"), Jehan Taille-Fer ("Smith"). With the rise of the towns, surnames are becoming important; the tax collector must be able to draw up a list. But neither in the case of the man nor the street is the name a reliable guide to the occupation. Just as a grocer's son may be a chandler, so the Street of the Grocers may be populated by leather merchants and shoemakers.

Not far from the helmetmakers, armorers, and swordmakers one may be sure to find the smiths, who not only produce horseshoes and other finished hardware for retail sale, but supply the armorers with their wrought iron and steel. Iron ore is obtained almost entirely from alluvial deposits—"bog iron"—and only rarely by digging. Though coal is mined in England, Scotland, the Saar, Liège, Aix-la-Chapelle, Anjou, and other districts, iron ore is smelted almost exclusively by charcoal. A pit is dug on a windy hilltop, drains inserted to allow the molten iron to be drawn off, and charcoal and ore layered in the hole, which is sealed at the top with earth. The advantage of this method is that the iron drawn off has some carbon in it; in other words, it is steel of a sort. Medieval metallurgists do not really understand how this happens. This "mild steel" is taken in lumps to the smithy.

The blacksmith's furnace is table-high, with a back and a hood, and like those of the smelters, burns charcoal. The smith's apprentice plies a pair of leather bellows while the smith turns the glowing bloom with a long pair of tongs. When it is sufficiently heated, the two men drag it out of the furnace to the floor, where they break off a chunk and take it to the anvil, which is

Another panel of the donors, Chartres Cathedral.

mounted on an oak stump. They pound, then return the chunk to the fire, then back to the anvil for more pounding, then back to the fire. Hour after hour the two swing their heavy hammers in rhythmic alternation, their energy slowly converting the intractable metal mass. This metal may vary considerably in character, depending on the accident of carbon-mixing at the smelter.

If the smith is fabricating wire, the next step will be to draw a piece of the hot metal through a hole with pincers. Several such drawings, each time through a smaller hole in a plate, accomplished with patience and much labor, produce a wire of the correct diameter, which is re-tempered and cut into short lengths. These are sold to the armorer up the street, who pounds them around a bar into links, the basis of chain mail.

The sages believe iron is a derivative of quicksilver (mercury) and brimstone (sulfur). The smith and the armorer know only that the material they get from the smelter sometimes is too soft to make good weapons or good chain mail, in which case they consign it to peaceful uses—plowshares, nails, bolts, wheel rims, cooking utensils. Other craftsmen who use the products of the forge include cutlers, nail makers, pin makers, tinkers, and needle makers. But the great use of iron, the one that ennobles the crafts of smith and armorer, is for war, either real or tournament-style.

There are also metalworkers on a more refined plane: goldsmiths and silversmiths. Since the twelfth century those of Troyes have enjoyed a wide reputation. The beautifully worked decoration of the tomb of Henry the Generous and the silver statue of the same count are justly famous. Goldsmiths are the aristocrats of handicraft, though not all are rich. Some goldsmiths scrape along working alone, making and selling silver ornaments, with hardly a thread of gold to their name. But most have an apprentice and a small store of gold, and fabricate an occasional gold paternoster or silver cup. The most prosperous have well equipped shops with two workbenches, a small furnace, an array of little anvils of varying sizes, a supply of gold, and two or three apprentices. One holds the workpiece on the anvil while the master hammers it to the desired shape and thickness, wielding his small hammer with incredible speed. Gold's value lies not merely in its rarity and its glitter but in its wonderful malleability. It is said that a goldsmith can reduce gold leaf by hammering to a thickness of one ten-thousandth of an inch. Thin gold leaf embellishes the pages of the illuminated manuscripts over which monks and copyists labor.

Hours of labor, tens of thousands of blows, with the final passage of the hammer effacing the hammer marks themselves—these are the ingredients of goldsmithing, a craft of infinite patience and considerable artistry.

But the bulk of even a prosperous goldsmith's work is in silver, the second softest metal. Sometimes a smith makes a whole series of identical paternosters or ornaments. To do this he first creates a mold or die of hardwood or copper and transfers the shape and design to successive pieces of silver by hammering. For repair jobs he keeps on hand a quantity of gold and silver wire, made in the same way the blacksmith makes his iron wire.

As the armorer depends on the smith, the shoemaker depends on the tanner, though he prefers to have his shop at a distance from his supplier's operation. The numerous tanners of Troyes occupy two streets southeast of the church of St.-Jean. Hide-curing, either by tanning or the ancient alternative method of tawing, creates a pungent atmosphere. Masters and apprentices may be seen outdoors, scraping away hair and epidermis from the skins over a "beam" (a horizontal section of treetrunk) with a blunt-edged concave tool. The flesh adhering to the underside is scraped off with a sharp concave blade. Next the hide is softened by rubbing it with cold poultry or pigeon dung, or warm dog dung, then soaked in mildly acid liquid produced by fermenting bran, to wash off the traces of lime left by the dung.

For extra soft leather—shoe uppers, coverings of coffers, scabbards, bagpipes, bellows—the leather is returned to the beam to be shaved down with a two-handled currier's knife. Then it goes to the pit, which is filled and drained with a succession of liquid baths. The first is old and mellow, the last fresh and green, their flavor imparted by oak bark, oak galls, acacia pods, and other sources of tannin. In the final stages the hides lie flat in the pit of liquid for several weeks, with crushed bark between the layers. The whole process of tanning takes months—usually, in fact, over a year. A new, quicker process, employing hot water, will appear later in the century, taking as little as ten days.

Tanning in oxhide is a laborious process, but it multiplies the skin's value. Whitened oxhide and horse-hide are even more expensive.

Footwear is insubstantial—little better than slippers. Ladies of fashion wear goatskin leather, or cordwain (from "cordovan," a fine leather originally made by the Moors of Cordova), even less sturdy than ordinary cowhide.

The shoemaker is not only a skilled craftsman, but a merchant of sonic status, capable of acquiring modest wealth. A shoemaker of Troyes named Pantaléon has given his son Jacques an education in the Church. Jacques is today a canon at Lyons, soon will be bishop of Verdun, and will eventually become Pope Urban IV.

Besides shoemakers, hatmakers, candlestick makers, and other craftsmen, there are the practitioners of the service trades: food purveyors, oil merchants, pastry cooks, wine sellers, and beer sellers. In addition there is the wine crier, who is also an inspector. Each morning

he goes into the first tavern he can find that has not yet hired a crier for the day; the tavern keeper must accept him. He oversees the drawing of the wine, or draws it himself, and tastes. Then, furnished with a cup and a leather flagon stoppered with a bit of hemp, he goes out to cry the wine and offer samples of it to the public. Before setting out he may ask those in the tavern how much the tavern keeper charged them, in order to check on the prices. Customers are served directly from the barrel; glass bottles are almost nonexistent.

There are some fifty vintages in thirteenth-century France. Among the favorites are Marly, Beaune, Epernay, Montpellier, Narbonne, Sancerre, Carcassonne, Auxerre, Soissons, Orléans, and, most highly regarded, Pierrefitte. Burgundy is already famous and northern Champagne produces excellent wine, though not the sparkling variety with which the province will centuries later become identified. Cider is unknown except in Normandy, and outsiders who have tasted it consider it to be a curse God has visited on the Normans. One observant chronicler reports that the French prefer white wine, the Burgundians red, the Germans "aromatic wines," and the English beer.

Another trade closely associated with the taverns is prostitution. The girls of the Champagne Fair cities are famous throughout Europe. When the fair is on, servant girls, laundresses, tradeswomen, and many others find a profitable sideline. Child labor being the rule, prostitution begins at an early age.

Taverns are the chief setting for another vice—gaming. The dicemakers' guild has strict laws against making fraudulent dice, which nevertheless find their way into the hands of professional sharpers. The fine for making such dice is heavy, so the sharpers pay a high price for them. Poor light in the taverns facilitates trickery.

Others engaged in service trades include the coal sellers, hay merchants, barbers, furniture menders, dish menders, and clothes menders—these latter three being the leading itinerants, whose peculiar rhymed gibberish echoes daily through the streets.

An ancient trade of the countryside, recently urbanized, is that of the miller. The numerous mills of Troyes are owned by the count, the bishop, the abbeys, the hospital, and various other proprietors. Most are situated on canals, with a few on the Seine

A Watermill from *L'Instruction Dung Josne Prince* **(15th c.).**

below the city, mounted on floating hulls, the wheel over the side and the millstones seated on a cupola-shaped platform amidships. Sacks of grain are brought by boat to the miller, who pours the grain into the funnel over an opening in the upper stone. The current turns the wheel, which activates the stone, and the milled flour trickles into a sack beneath the platform.

Both millers and mills have other functions besides grinding grain. In slack periods the millers fish or spear eels. Mill wheels furnish power for a growing variety of businesses, notably tanning and fulling. The old undershot wheel, pushed lazily around by the current flowing against the lower paddles, is being supplanted by the overshot wheel, which is turned by water flowing over the top. Either type of wheel can be used when a weir or dam is constructed that creates a narrow, rapid current. The power of this current can be multiplied by guiding it to the midpoint of a waterwheel, so that the wheel's turn starts underneath, or by guiding it to the top of the wheel, so that the wheel's turn starts at the top. Although water mills are important, old-fashioned mills worked by horses and cattle still hold their own, because animals can work in all weather, whereas river and millrace currents may freeze in winter or dry up in summer.

From time to time the horse market is held in the Corterie-aux-Chevaux, near the Porte de la Madeleine. Nervous colts, sedate palfreys, powerful chargers, mares with foals trotting at their heels, broad-shouldered oxen, pack-asses and pack-mules, pigs, hogs, cows, chickens, ducks, and geese noisily crowd the market place. Knights, ladies, burghers and peasants bargain, argue, examine animals, turn back horses' lips, feel coats and muscles, and now and then mount a palfrey or a charger.

Only nobles and rich burghers ride horses; everyone else rides donkeys or walks. A pregnant lady or wounded knight may be carried in a litter (carriages are far in the future). The knights who come to the horse mart sometimes take prospective mounts outside the city walls to try out. Often there are races, with the noisy assistance of the boys and young men.

The saddlemakers display their work at the market, and it is worthy of display. Bows of saddles are wooden, often ornamented with plates of ivory, hammered metal, or elaborately painted leather, with semiprecious stones soldered into the surface of the pommel and cantle. The saddlecloth is richly embroidered.

Sidesaddles are manufactured for ladies, but not all ladies use them.

Farm implements, fashioned by the city's blacksmiths, are on display too. These include sickles for harvesting grain, long-handled scythes with lateral grips added for efficient haymaking, sharp-bladed felling axes. Wooden spades have iron cutting edges. There are also farm machines—many-toothed harrows and wheeled plows, with coulter, plowshare and mouldboard for turning the earth to left or right.

The development of heavier breeds of horses has greatly augmented their value. They bring much higher prices than a mule or an ordinary draft horse. If Julius Caesar could wander through the horse market of Troyes, he would be startled far less by the wheeled plow and the new, heavily padded, rigid horse collar than by the size of the horses. Neither the Romans nor their foes ever rode anything like these. The Parthians and Byzantine Greeks began the development of the big warhorse, now completed in this area of northern France and Flanders. It is no accident that this is *par excellence* the region of feudal chivalry.

Guilds have two kinds of regulations. One has to do with external affairs, with what might be called the commercial side of the guild; the other deals with internal matters, such as wages, duration and conditions of apprenticeship, welfare, and obligations to the guild.

Every guild recognizes its stake in protecting the public, for since the guild restricts competition, it has an obligation to guarantee standards of quality. On being invested, the officers of the bakers' guild solemnly swear that they will "guard the guild" carefully and loyally, and that in appraising bread they will spare neither relatives nor friends, nor condemn anyone wrongly through hatred or ill-feeling. Officers of other guilds swear similar oaths. Guild legislation on the quality of merchandise is painstakingly detailed. Precise quantities and types of raw materials are specified and supervision follows through all the stages of manufacture and sale. Ale must have no constituents except grain, hops, and water. The beadmaker must discard beads less than perfectly round. Butchers are not to mix tallow with lard or sell the flesh of dogs, cats, or horses. Makers of bone handles are forbidden to trim them with silver lest they pass them for ivory. Knife handles may not be covered with silk, brass, or pewter for the same reason. If a tailor spoils a piece of cloth by

The Baker and the Drinking Brawl from a fresco depicting the Sign of Scorpio.

faulty cutting, he has to make restitution to the customer and pay a fine besides. Chandlers must use four pounds of tallow for each quarter-pound of wick, and wax tapers are not to be adulterated with lard. A tailor may not mend old clothes, for that function belongs solely to the old-clothes mender, who in turn must not make new clothes. Sometimes the old-clothes mender does such a good job that the result looks like new; therefore, to keep the distinction visible, the mender is enjoined from pressing, folding, and hanging his products like new garments.

In most guilds inspection is no sham formality. Visits are made unexpectedly, scales checked, substandard goods confiscated on the spot, either to be destroyed or to be given to the poor, while the culprit pays a fine commensurate with the value of the merchandise. The jeweler found using colored glass and the spice dealer guilty of purveying false merchandise pay the highest fines.

Combinations to fix prices or to seek a monopoly on materials are forbidden. Retailers cannot buy eggs, cheese, and other produce from farmers except at the Friday and Saturday markets, and even here they cannot buy until the farmer is actually, in the marketplace with his wagon or pack animal. They cannot buy from him on consignment, or arrange in advance to take his produce. These restrictions are all designed to prevent monopoly of food in time of famine, a threat never far distant. Unhappily, guild regulations and town ordinances alike frequently go unobserved.

The second kind of guild regulation, governing its internal affairs, often merely codifies ancient customs, such as observance of holidays, early closing on Saturdays during Lent and during the "short days" of the year.

The membership of most guilds is divided simply into masters and apprentices. A middle grade, the valet or journeyman, has been introduced in a few crafts where business demands more labor but masters do not want more competition. In most guilds a master is permitted only a single apprentice, or perhaps two. Grain merchants, ale brewers, goldsmiths, greengrocers, shoemakers, and some others are allowed more, and all masters are given great freedom in hiring relatives—as many sons, brothers, even nephews as they wish. Guild regulations reflect the nature of industry, which is small scale and familial.

Guilds often provide members with baptismal gifts when their children are born, help ill and destitute members, pay something toward hospital and funeral expenses, and do a little charitable work. This mutual-aid aspect of the craft guild goes far back. A guild that does not provide benevolent services usually has a "brotherhood," an auxiliary that may be the original form of the association. Weavers, furriers, bakers, and many other crafts have brotherhoods, each under an appropriate patron saint: St. Catherine for the wheelwrights, because she was broken on the wheel; St. Sebastian for the needlemakers, because he was martyred by arrows; St Mary Magdalen for the perfumers, because she poured oil on Jesus' feet; St.-Barbe ("beard") for the brushmakers; St.-Cloud ("nail") for the nailmakers; St. Clare ("clear") for the mirrormakers.

The contract between master and apprentice (regardless of whether they belong to a guild) is sometimes written, sometimes simply "sworn on the relics"—all medieval oaths are taken on sacred relics. The master undertakes to feed, lodge, clothe, and shoe his apprentice and "to treat him honorably as the son of a goodman." Sometimes the apprentice receives a stipend—a small one. Sometimes the master also undertakes to educate the apprentice. Often he needs employees who can read and write and add and subtract. Twice a week the apprentice may go to the notary to learn his letters.

An apprentice's day is long and hard. His situation depends very largely on the personality and condition of his master. A kind master is a blessing; perhaps an even greater blessing is a prosperous master. A kind mistress may be important too. Since the apprentice's labor is not restricted to the trade and he may be called on to do any kind of household chore, many apprentices find themselves more tyrannized by mistresses than by masters. Guilds often specify in their regulations that an apprentice should not be beaten by the master's wife.

Apprenticeship varies in duration, usually from four years to twelve; five years is common. The length of service is often related to the size of the initiation fee, as in the case of weavers, whose craft can be quickly learned and yet is remunerative. A weaver's apprentice may become a master in four years by paying four pounds (livres), in five years by paying three pounds, in six years by paying one pound, in seven years without any payment. Brasswire makers require twelve years, or ten years plus a fee of twenty shillings (sous). Goldsmiths undertake a ten-year apprenticeship.

An apprentice has five obligations to fulfill. First, he must supply a certificate to the officers of the guild, stating that he is "prudent and loyal." Second, he must demonstrate that he knows the craft. In some guilds the emerging apprentice must produce a "masterpiece." An apprentice hatmaker fashions a hat, a cake baker bakes cakes. Third, the apprentice must show that he has enough capital to go into business. Sometimes his capital is his tools, sometimes he needs cash. Fourth, he must swear on the saints' relics to uphold the guild's law and customs, which the officers read aloud to him, explaining and clarifying as they go. Finally, he pays a fee, which goes not to the guild but to the prince—in Troyes the count of Champagne—for guilds "belong" to the sovereign. In 1160 Louis VII sold five of his Paris guilds (the leatherworkers, pursemakers, baldric makers, shoe repairmen and dockworkers) to the widow of a wealthy burgher, who thereafter collected the dues formerly owed the king.

On paying his fee, the apprentice becomes a member of the corporation, the inner body of the guild, that consists of the masters alone, or the masters and journeymen. His rise in status calls for a celebration—a round of drinks at the tavern, or possibly a dinner. Or he may merely pay five or ten sous to the corporation treasury.

Synagogue with St. Paul preaching to the Jews from a 12th century mosaic in the Duomo, Monreale, Italy.

An apprentice's ambition may even soar beyond acquiring the status of a master. He may dream of some day being an officer of the corporation. Officers are elected by the masters, or by the masters and journeymen, and the election is ratified by the count's provost.

Married apprentices are not unknown, and occasionally a master may even provide his apprentice with an allowance for taking his meals outside the master's house. But such cases are the exception.

A craft may make a man modestly rich. Of course it may also make him stoop-shouldered, but this is a hazard of any trade. A man repeats the same motion with hammer, with maul, with saw, with shears, with needle, with loom, ten, twelve, fourteen hours at a stretch, day in and day out, transmitting the energy of his hand, arm and shoulder into chalice, statue, vestment or article of furniture. Forty years of such effort can leave him bent and crooked. His servile forefathers, however, ended their days not only crippled and deformed by their labors but with nothing to show for it.

In the old *cité* near the Abbey of St.-Loup is one of the crowded town's most crowded districts. This is the Broce-aux-Juifs, the old ghetto of Troyes. Its streets are hardly distinguishable from the rest of the old quarter, except for the Mezuzah (a small parchment scroll inscribed with Old Testament writings) on every doorpost. The men, women and children on the streets do not look very different from their Christian neighbors, except that on the breast of each is sewn a yellow circle, or wheel. They speak perfectly good French, though they use Hebrew characters in writing. Jews make their living, like Christians, by manufacture and trade—as goldsmiths and leatherworkers, tanners and glassblowers, weavers and dyers. In the south of France they practice viticulture, though agriculture generally is closed to them, as are many avenues of commerce. Some enlightened princes, like Louis IX of France and Edward I of England, favor abolishing the Jewish disabilities, even while Louis' zeal for the Christian religion causes him to burn copies of the Talmud.

Many Jews lend money, mostly on a small scale, against pledges. A dozen are wealthy and even own land outside town. Some devote their lives to scholarship. The ghetto of Troyes, which had one of the earliest Jewish schools in northwest Europe, has been the home of several of the most famous Jewish scholars of the Middle Ages, such as Salomon ben Isaac (Rashi) and his grandson Jacob ben Meir, who presided over a major synod in Troyes in the previous century. The most important member of the community in the thirteenth century is the wealthy Jacob of Troyes, who holds the title "Master of the Jews." He is in effect mayor of the ghetto, which is a separate, privileged community, a foreign colony not unlike the Christian merchants' colonies in the Levant, or the colonies of Italians and other nationalities in London. Jews do not belong to the commune and do not participate in the town government. A legal case involving a Christian and a Jew must be taken to the count's court, where the testimony of a Christian against a Jew, or of a Jew against a Christian, must be corroborated by a coreligionist. A Jewish merchant receives full protection against thieves. If he is robbed in another principality, on the road to Troyes, the count demands restitution as forcefully as for a Christian merchant.

The same is true of other sovereigns. The Pope has threatened excommunication in defense of Roman Jewish bankers. When a Jewish merchant from Aragon was robbed by Castilian bandits, the king of Aragon promised to repay him at the expense of Castilian merchants unless the king of Castile made good the loss.

Princely punctilio about the rights of Jewish merchants and bankers is securely anchored in self-interest. But princely self-interest is a capricious force. The chief threat to Jewish life comes not from popular outbursts, which are rare, but from official edicts. A prince who needs money is tempted to lose his tolerance, listen to a charge (or cause one to be made), and order expulsion of all Jews from his territory. Expulsion automatically involves confiscation of goods.[2] It also, almost as automatically, involves an increment to the sovereign at some later date when the Jews are graciously permitted to reenter the territory. Seventy years ago, at the time of the Third Crusade, the Jews of Troyes suffered expulsion, as did Jews in many other places. The synagogue in the old ghetto was taken over by Christians and converted to a church, St.-Frobert. A second synagogue in the new commercial quarter west of the *cité* suffered a similar fate, and became St.-Pantaléon. The street next to it remains, and will remain through the centuries, the Rue de la Synagogue.

Even the emotionally charged accusation of ritual murder is usually a pretext for a fine rather than capital punishment. An alleged ritual murder in London in 1244 resulted in an exorbitant fine—60,000 marks, levied against the Jewish community. Frederick II, king of Sicily and emperor of Germany, recently heard an indictment against the Jews of the town of Fulda. The scientific-minded emperor ordered an investigation, interrogating converted Jews from England. Concluding that there was no basis for the ancient charge, Frederick forbade further accusations. However, he did not neglect to collect a fine from the Jews of Fulda for breach of the peace. The Pope (Innocent IV) has also discredited the ritual murder superstition, which nonetheless persists among the ignorant masses.

Jewish conversion to Christianity is rare, but not unknown. Sometimes special protection is extended to converts not only against reprisals by Jews and insults by Christians, but against loss of property. More often, however, a converting Jew faces a considerable bill from his Christian prince, who does not wish to sacrifice the Jewish taxes without compensation. There are many other ways a prince may make money from his Jews. Henry III, present king of England, has recently mortgaged his Jews to his brother, Richard of Cornwall.

Forcible conversion is forbidden, as is interference with celebration of Jewish rites. However, the terms in which the prohibition is couched indicate that Christians are less tolerant than one could wish. "During the celebration of their festivals," Pope Innocent III ruled, "no one shall disturb them by beating them with clubs or by throwing stones at them." It is also expressly forbidden to extort money from the Jews by threatening to exhume the bodies of their dead from the Jewish cemetery.

Yet despite the suspicion and hostility with which the Broce-aux-Juifs is hedged around, contacts between Christians and Jews are numerous and not necessarily uncongenial. Jews have often served as bankers to the counts and have farmed tolls and taxes. The erudite Count Henry the Generous, the present count's grandfather, is said to have consulted Jewish scholars on textual problems of the Old Testament. Jewish and Christian merchants and moneymen often embark on joint ventures. That many Jews of Troyes prosper is demonstrated by the fine houses along the Rue de Vieille Rome, south of the ancient donjon.

If the thirteenth century is not the best time to be a European Jew, neither is it the worst.

VII
BIG BUSINESS

Feudal dues, guild regulations, princely prerogatives and ecclesiastical dicta notwithstanding, the western European businessman of the thirteenth century makes money—often a great deal. There are two main avenues to fortune, the cloth trade and banking. Very commonly the two are combined by a single entrepreneur.

The typical capitalist of Troyes conducts his typically many-sided business from the ground floor of his house in one of the better streets on the outskirts of the fair quarter. There are two rooms on this floor. In front is the workroom where the apprentice puts in his long hours. It is likely to be piled with a variety of merchandise—skins, furs, silks, utensils, copper wire, iron tools, paper, parchment—whatever the merchant happens to be dealing in. But the most important item is fairly certain to be wool, which is raw, semi-finished or finished.

Sheep in Pen being Milked with Women Walking Away from the *Latin/Luttrell Psalter* (14th c.).

In the rear is the counting room, where the merchant and perhaps his eldest son do their office work. Light is poor. A prominent piece of office equipment is the calculating board, a table marked out with horizontal lines on which bone counters are manipulated. The bottom line represents units, the next not tens but twenties—because in the universal money of account, twenty shillings (sous) equals one pound (livre). Vertical lines assist in positioning the counters.

Records are kept on wax tablets. Parchment, a seal, half a dozen quills, ink, and ribbon or cord supply the tools for correspondence. When a merchant writes a letter, he closes it with his seal affixed to a ribbon or cord. Most business letters are written in French, but sometimes correspondence is in Latin, and occasionally in Italian, or even a more exotic tongue, in which case the assistance of a professional scribe may be required. A couple of tables, three or four hard chairs or stools, a chest or two, and a few candles nearly complete the inventory of office furnishings.

But there is one more piece of furniture, the most important. The merchant's strongbox is bound with iron and fastened with a large iron lock. In it he keeps his working capital. Though cash is less important in business life than it was a hundred years ago, a prosperous

279

merchant still has a tidy hoard of silver-copper-zinc deniers (pennies),[1] along with a stack of parchment pledges. The livre (pound) and sou (shilling), though used to count with throughout Europe, do not yet actually exist as coins. The only important coin circulating in any volume is the penny, which comes in a remarkable variety of sizes and alloys. About five-eighths of an inch in diameter, and at its best about one-third fine silver, it will suffice to hire a workman for three or four hours. It varies capriciously because a large number of princes and bishops enjoy the right of coinage. Mints being expensive to operate, they require profit margins, and the temptation is strong to widen this margin by increasing the copper content of the coins. The *denier de Provins* (Provins penny), minted at Troyes' sister city, is universally respected for its reliable content of thirty per cent fine silver. But some lords take a shortsighted view and profit from debasements. However, even those who debase the currency are very jealous of the privilege, and tampering with coinage by subjects is attended everywhere by the most ferocious legal penalties.

Though the pounds-shillings-pence ratio (one to twenty to twelve) may seem clumsy, merchants have no difficulty with it. Lately a big new silver coin has been minted in Italy. Called a *grosso* (groat),[2] it has the value of twelve pennies, thereby converting the imaginary shilling for the first time into a reality. But the grosso circulates very little outside Italy, where business is bigger than in the West.

Troyen merchants invest their pennies in many things, but above all in wool. Some wool is grown locally, but the best comes from abroad, especially from England. A poet uses the metaphor "carrying wool to England" in the sense of "carrying coals to Newcastle." Long-wooled flocks roam the grasslands and fens of the Cotswolds and Lincolnshire; short-wooled animals, the hills and moors of the Welsh and Scottish borders and the downlands of Shropshire and Herefordshire. The flocks belonging to monasteries, such as those of Tintern Abbey, are especially famous. Most of the English wool feeds the looms of Flanders, but some finds its way to France and Champagne. Merchants of Troyes also buy Burgundian wool, nearly as good as English. Buying in quantity, a merchant gets a much better price than could an individual weaver. He then in turn supplies weavers, specifying the kind of weave he wants. In theory he sells raw wool to individual weavers and buys finished wool back, but since he usually buys from the same weavers, a wool merchant actually operates a factory scattered through town.

If the wool market is strong, as it usually is, the weavers are able to buy bread to feed the wives and children who crowd their upper-story tenement dwellings and who help spin and weave. But if the cloth market drops, as a result perhaps of a war which severs trade routes, merchants naturally turn their attention and capital elsewhere, and weavers' families beg in front of the church doors.

The weavers' guild is the first to include a number of "valets" or "journeymen." By 1250 the towns of Flanders have many of these. Finished with their apprenticeship, the journeymen are not yet permitted to become masters, yet their labor is needed by cloth merchants. Even in good times they are subject to the caprices of the market and their employers. Every Monday morning they gather in the squares and before the churches, where the masters hire labor for the week. On Saturday night, after a week's dawn-to-dusk work, the journeyman is paid off and must again look for work on Monday morning.

Five years ago something incredible happened in Douai, one of the richest Flemish cloth towns. The weavers got together and refused to work. The outraged cloth merchants crushed this insurrectionary movement, and every burgher trusts that workingmen will never do anything of the kind again.

A merchant may enter into a long-term contract with one of the great English abbeys to take all the shearings of the abbey for a period of years, often seven. He pays a cash sum in advance, and agrees to a fixed annual payment for the duration of the contract. The contract is drawn by a notary, first in rough draft, then with care on parchment in three copies, one for each of the parties and one for his own files, which acquire the force of legal records.

When a wool consignment from England is delivered to a merchant of Troyes, it is first given preliminary treatment at his house. An apprentice removes damaged wool and sorts the good wool into three grades—fine, medium, and coarse. Next it must be washed in lye to remove grease, and spread on boards in the sun to dry. Forceps in hand, the hardworking apprentice gets on his hands and knees to remove bits of soil and other particles. If they cannot be picked out, he clips them with small shears. The wool of carcass sheep is kept separate; it is an offense to mix with live shearings.

When the wool has been washed and dried, it must be laboriously beaten, combed, and carded. Then the merchant consigns it to the weaver, whose wife spins it into yarn with a distaff and spindle. The warp thread, stronger than the woof, must be sized and wound and sorted into the required number of threads of a certain length, and the woof thread must be wound onto the bobbin to be inserted in the shuttle. Although spinning

Peasants tending sheep (c. 1050).

is still done in ancient fashion, looms have advanced well beyond Roman models. The weaver sits in a high-backed chair with his feet on the treadles, tossing his shuttle of wool back and forth between the rising and falling heddles, which raise and lower the warp threads.

The material that comes from the weaver's loom is not finished cloth. It must be taken to the fuller, who soaks and shrinks the fabric, and rubs it with fuller's earth, not only to clean it but to give it body and help it take dye. The soaking is done in a trough, the fuller and his assistants trampling the mixture in their bare feet (whence another word for fuller—"walker"—the English surnames Fuller and Walker denoting the same trade). This process also hardens the material. When the cloth has been soaked, it is hung to dry on an upright wooden frame called a tenter, fastened by tenterhooks placed along parallel bars which can be adjusted so that the cloth is stretched to the right length and breadth. This task is often undertaken by women. Then the cloth is finished by raising the nap with teasels while it is still damp and by shearing it when dry with great flat shears, three or four feet long. The finest cloth is shorn and reshorn a number of times. Finally it is brushed, pressed, and folded.

Dyeing may take place at any stage in the manufacture. Sometimes the cloth is already dyed in the yarn stage, or even in its original raw form, whence the expression "dyed in the wool." Sometimes it is sold as undyed cloth, especially to the *Arte di Calimala,* the clothfinishing industry of Florence. Sometimes dyeing is the last step in the process. The dyer heats his tub over a fire and, turning the cloth with long poles, soaks it in water colored with woad (blue), madder (red), or other dyes, tempered by wood ashes. One can tell a dyer anywhere by the color under his nails. He dyes not only cloth, but sometimes other products, such as wooden crucifixes and ornaments.

Besides wool, the merchant may deal occasionally in three other textiles. One is linen, woven from flax, a vegetable fiber grown widely throughout Europe. Another is silk, imported from the East for hundreds of years, but now a major industry in Italy, Sicily, and Spain. The third is cotton, originally imported from India, but introduced into Spain by the Moors and manufactured in France, Italy, and Flanders.

Wool is the beginning, rather than the end, of a Troyen wool merchant's business. When he sells cloth at the fair to the Italians, he may buy spices from the Far East, wines from Burgundy or metal from Germany. Some merchandise he can resell immediately to customers pledged in advance. Some he must break down into small lots. Some he may warehouse and hold for a rising market. Some, such as wood and metal, he sends out for finishing.

He is likely to invest part of his profits in real estate. He can rent houses in the city, perhaps to his own weaver families, and outside the city he may buy forest land, which cannot fail to rise in value, and in the meantime can be farmed for timber. He may acquire fishing rights in a stream or pond, operating as a fishing landlord and dividing the catch with his fisherman tenants.

Almost inevitably, whether he wants to or not, the successful merchant turns moneylender. People who want to borrow money go where the money is. In mid-thirteenth century the ancient monopoly of the Jews has become a large-scale business from which most of the Jewish lenders have been elbowed aside. The Italians are the biggest bankers today, but businessmen of northwest Europe give them increasing competition. Moneychangers tend naturally to become moneylenders. The men of Cahors, in southern France, who have long made a specialty of moneychanging, are among the most prominent pawnbrokers. Their knowledgeability in coinage makes them also expert at evaluating silver plate and jewelry. The word "Cahorsin" has joined "Jew" and "Lombard" as a synonym for moneylender.

All moneylenders are resented—even Christian knights. The Templars, originally a band of Crusaders from Champagne who swore an oath at Solomon's Temple to devote their lives to defending Jerusalem, are celebrated as much for their financial as for their military prowess. Their commanderies, which stand in most of the important towns of northwest Europe, including Troyes, are usually square stone buildings looking like a cross between a blockhouse and a bank.

But if moneylenders are resented, they are also respected. So prestigious is the profession of moneychanger that instead of the master paying his apprentice or even supporting him, he demands and gets a payment from the apprentice's father for the lad's education. The following clause appears in a contract between a moneychanger and an apprentice's father in Marseilles in 1248: ". . . and if it should happen, which God forbid, that the said William should cause you any loss I promise to reimburse you by this agreement, believing in your unsupported word . . ."

Moneylenders run risks, so interest rates are high. The Church officially condemns all interest as usurious, but churchmen nevertheless borrow, and lend, too.

The highest rates are charged by the Jews, who

run the greatest risks, partly because their political position leaves them vulnerable to the connivance of their debtors with the authorities, and partly because they draw the worst borrowers—those who have trouble borrowing anywhere else. Like the Cahorsin, the Jewish moneylending business is largely pawnbroking. To become a pawnbroker in Troyes one must purchase a "table," a license from the count.

Nevertheless a moneylender, Christian or Jewish, has a growing power behind him, and it is much easier to collect a debt in 1250 than it was a hundred years earlier. Generally a debtor who fails to meet his obligations may expect to have his goods seized and handed over to the creditor. If they are insufficient to meet the debt he will be imprisoned or banished from the city, the latter punishment being more effective from the creditor's point of view, since it gives the debtor a chance to raise money. By an old custom a defaulted debt is an obligation of the debtor's commune. It is to the advantage of both sovereign and citizens to have their town enjoy a reputation of security for businessmen.

Noblemen are the greatest borrowers. Count Henry II of Champagne borrowed from ten bankers to equip himself for the Third Crusade, and ultimately he left the debt to be paid by his successor. The present count, Thibaut IV, borrowed large sums in his youth and refused to pay up. The bankers, some of whom were Italian and one a Jew, appealed to the Pope, who excommunicated the count and placed the whole of Champagne under interdict; no church services could be celebrated till the debt was paid. Not long after, spendthrift Thibaut got himself into another such jam. This time he went even further; he seized one of his creditors, an Italian banker named Ilperni, threw him into prison, frightened him, and extracted twelve hundred livres from him. The Pope, furious, threatened fresh excommunication and interdict, and rash Thibaut only escaped by promising to go on Crusade. At this very moment Thibaut owes two thousand livres to the monks of St.-Denis in Paris, who hold the gold cross from his chapel of St.-Etienne-de-Troyes as a pledge.

Lending and credit are intimately connected with the Champagne Fairs. Promises to pay are often dated from one fair to the next, or extended in installments over the next several fairs. Discounting is often done on such promises to pay; that is, a merchant may sell such a promise at something less than its face value if he needs immediate cash.

House "rent" is a form of interest. The householder borrows money to build or buy his house, agreeing to pay a certain rate of interest, usually eight to ten per cent. He may never pay anything on the principal of the loan, for which the lender always has the security of the house. The house may pass through several generations of such "rent paying".

Besides feudal lords, businessmen, and ordinary citizens, towns themselves often borrow, offering "life rents" in the term of annual or quarterly payments during the life of the lender. Sometimes the obligation is made for two lives, the lender's and his heir's. To combat fraud, towns offer prizes for news of the death of a rent holder.

The successful bourgeois entrepreneur stirs considerable envy. He is reputed to have acquired his wealth, the amount of which is generally exaggerated, by sharp practice rather than by hard work. The mystery by which capital grows is not understood by those who do not possess it. Neither are the worries of the businessman whose capital is committed to the hazards of a baron's whim, a flock's health, the stormy seas, or the chance of war.

The silver of commerce has in everyone's eyes, even in those of the merchants themselves, something of the diabolical. "He owes a fine candle to God, one may believe, who has remained honest in commerce without scorning the poor and without hating religion," says a popular proverb. And a writer describes a character: "After having passed most of his life in innocence, he became a merchant."

Nevertheless, the poets do not accord the merchants the kind of contempt they heap on peasants. Even the trouvères, spokesmen of chivalry, show a grudging respect for these townsmen, who not infrequently cross the line dividing their class from the nobility. A wealthy burgher may be knighted for his financial services to a great lord. Renier Accore, for example, a Florentine merchant who became a citizen of Provins, did business with the great nobles of Champagne, and became a knight and the Seigneur de Gouaix. Many burghers have seen their sons knighted. Some of the trouvères themselves are burghers, such as Adam de la Halle, whose graceful verses to his equally non-noble wife are widely quoted, and Gilbert de Barneville, who compares his mistress to the Northern Star.

Patents of nobility are hardly necessary. Universally accorded the title of "Sire," the wealthy merchants may be said to possess their own rank of nobility. Such officials of the count's service as Sire Doré ("Golden"), who married a noble Genoese lady and was Keeper of the Fair in 1225, and Sire Herbert Putemonnaie ("Badmoney"), financial agent of the count, need not genuflect to knights or petty barons. A son of a fishmonger, Sire Girard Meletaire, served as provost of Troyes in 1219, chamberlain to the count in 1230, and was its first mayor in 1231. Another burgher, Pierre Legendre, was bailiff of Provins in 1228, mayor of Troyes in 1232, and Keeper of the Fair in 1225 and 1228. His daughter married a wealthy Italian, Nicholas of Cremona, whose family handled transalpine affairs for the count.

If the breach between wealthy townsmen and the poor is indisputably widening, that between wealthy townsmen and the lordly aristocracy of the countryside is narrowing.

VIII
THE DOCTOR

Requesting a urinal, Renard had Noble the Lion fill it, then held it up to the light and examined it to distinguish the effect of the divers humors in the King's body. Then he pronounced, "Sire, you have an ague fever, but I have the remedy for it . . ."

—ROMAN DE RENARD

I n a city the size of Troyes there are fewer than half a dozen licensed doctors,[1] not counting the numerous midwives, barbers, monks, and outright quacks who practice medicine or some branch of it. The trained physician is an aristocrat of professionals, enjoying high status and excellent fees. His practice is naturally confined to the better class, as the medical texts and treatises make clear.

One such treatise recommends interrogating the servant who has come to fetch the doctor, so that "if you can learn nothing from examining the patient, you still may astonish him with your knowledge of the case." At the patient's house the well advised doctor conducts himself with a certain ceremony. In the sick room he bows, seats himself, and drawing a sand-glass from his bag takes the patient's pulse. He requests a sample of urine, which he sniffs and tastes for sugar. In case of a gross infection he examines the urine for sediment. He inquires about the patient's diet and stool, and then delivers a discourse on the disease. The stomach, he may explain, is a cauldron in which food is cooked. If it is filled too full, it will boil over and the food remain uncooked. The liver supplies the heat for this interior furnace. The humors must be kept in balance—phlegm, blood, bile and black bile, which are respectively cold and moist, hot and moist, hot and dry, and cold and dry. Fevers are tertian, quartan, daily, hectic, and pestilential. Which kind is present can be determined by the pattern of recurrence, whether every third day, or every fourth, and whether it grows more severe. Recovery depends on many things, including the phases of the moon and the position of the constellations.

On quitting the sick chamber, the doctor may assure the patient that recovery will soon come with God's help; but with the family, he cannily adopts a graver tone, implying that he did not wish to alarm the sufferer, but that it is a lucky thing that science was called in. He may leave a prescription of herbs and drugs, and recommend diet—perhaps chicken broth, the milk of pulverized almonds, or barley water mixed with figs, honey, and licorice.

Physicians performing eye and nose operations from a medical treatise in Latin. (12th c.).

An old man lies sick in a bedroom while his wife reads a devotional book and a servant waits on them (1470).

Often the doctor is invited to dine with the family. He accepts, without seeming too eager. During the course of the meal he may entertain the table with accounts of illnesses and wounds he has cured, but he makes sure to send a servant two or three times to ask the patient how he fares, thus reassuring him that he has not been forgotten.

If the thirteenth-century doctor's science is questionable by the standards of a later age, it is nevertheless an advance over the past. In the earlier Middle Ages abbeys and monasteries were the repositories of medical knowledge. The principal effect of their regime was to repeal Hippocrates' law that illness is a natural phenomenon and to make it appear to be a punishment from on high. This view is not dead in the thirteenth century, and even doctors pay it lip service, but the secular practitioner represents a distinct move toward the rational understanding of illness.

He also represents a move toward commercialization. The same medical text that tells him how to treat a patient gives precise instructions on bill collecting: "When the patient is nearly well, address the head of

the family, or the sick man's nearest relative, thus: God Almighty having deigned by our aid to restore him whom you asked us to visit, we pray that He will maintain his health, and that you will now give us an honorable dismissal. Should any other member of your family desire our aid, we should, in grateful remembrance of our former dealings with you, leave all else and hurry to serve him." This formula, devised at the world's first and most famous medical school, that of Salerno, is hard to improve on. The fees which doctors charge are scaled to the patient's wealth and status. A rich man's illness may be valued at ten livres or more; kings have been charged a hundred. Setting a broken or dislocated limb is a matter of several sous or even a livre. Popular spite attributes a proverb to the medical profession: "Take while the patient is in pain."

A second text offers more hints for the general practitioner. "When you go to a patient, always try to do something new every day, lest they say you are good at nothing but books." And even more cogently: "If you unfortunately visit a patient and find him dead, and they ask you why you came, say you knew he would die that night, but want to know at what hour he died."

One acerbic writer asserts that the wily physician tells one person that the patient will recover, another that he will succumb, thus assuring his reputation in at least one quarter. "If the patient has the good fortune to survive," he concludes, "he does so in spite of the bungling doctor, but if he is fated to perish, he is killed with full rites."

Skeptical barbs notwithstanding, the profession attracts many of the ablest young men of the age. Besides Salerno, there is an almost equally respected school at Montpellier, where Arab and Jewish scholars from Spain mix with Provençals, Frenchmen, Italians, and others. Paris and Montpellier have the only two medical schools in northwest Europe, though there are now several in Italy. After a preliminary three-year course, the prospective physician takes a five-year course, followed by a year's internship with an experienced practitioner. He is then allowed to take a formal examination, upon successfully completing which he receives from the faculty a license to practice. Since the universities are highly ecclesiastical in makeup, the license is given in the name of the Pope, and is conferred by the bishop in a ceremony in church.

But the Church's control is nominal. The real shortcoming in medical education is its subservience not to the saints but to astrology and numerology. Constellations and planets are believed to preside over different parts of the body. Numerology provides complicated guides for the course of an illness. The body is believed to have four "humors" and three "spirits," all of which must be checked by examination of the urine and stool and by feeling the pulse, then adjusted by bloodletting, from the side of the body opposite the site of the disease.

All these ideas are derived from the Greeks, and they go to make up an anatomy and physiology as simple and logical as an arithmetic problem.

Medical textbooks[2] are few and precious. Most of the Greek writings have arrived in the West by a circuitous route, first translated into Arabic, then from Arabic into Latin. The translators who undertake the latter task are often teams of Jewish and Christian scribes working in Spain; the Jewish scholars render the Arabic roughly into Latin, and the Christians polish this version into scholarly language. How many errata and variations creep into a Greek work on its journey to Montpellier and Paris may be imagined.

Their knowledge of Arabic has placed Jewish physicians in the forefront of medicine, and their services are frequently called for by princes and great lords. One of their principal specialties is diseases of the eye. Even a rigorous enforcer of restrictions on Jews like Alphonse de Poitiers, brother of St.-Louis, will consult a Jewish specialist about all eye malady. Like the Arab physicians, Jewish doctors are moving toward a fully rational therapy, yet all medicine—Christian, Arab, and Jewish—is still bound up with astrology, numerology, and magic.

With these aids and his own common sense, the medieval doctor battles valiantly against a variety of ailments. Skin diseases are very widespread in an age when rough wool is often worn next to the skin; when bathing, at least among the masses, is infrequent; and laundry hard to do. Defects of diet—the scarcity of fresh fruit and vegetables—create a dangerous scorbutic tendency in the whole population, and, in the cities especially, insufficient sanitary arrangements facilitate the spread of infection and contagion. In winter, dwellings are cold and drafty. Pneumonia is a great killer. Typhoid is common, as are many types of heart and circulatory disease.

But the most frequent demand for medical aid is

for treatment of wounds and injuries. Here the medieval surgeon achieves his best success, even showing some understanding of the problem of infection. He applies such medicaments as sterile white of egg to piercing and cutting wounds. A contemporary Italian, Friar Theodoric of Lucca, son of a Crusading surgeon, recommends wine, which of course contains alcohol, and cautions against the complicated salves and nostrums in fashion with some doctors. Surgical instruments include scissors, speculum, razor, scalpel, needle and lancet.

A variety of surgical operations are performed for such disorders as cataracts and hernias; lithotomy (removal of stones from the kidney or gall bladder) and trepanning are also practiced. None of these operations promises well for the subject.

Occasionally the agony of the surgical patient may be relieved by some form of narcosis. Theodoric of Lucca speaks of sponges drenched with opium, and mandrake, dried, then soaked in hot water and inhaled. Bartholomew Anglicus expatiates on the value of mandrake as an anesthetic: "Those who take a portion of it will sleep for four hours and feel neither iron nor fire." However, he adds: "A good leech [physician] does not

A Pharmacy, miniature from the *Canon maior* by Avicenna.

Bloodletting using leeches by Aldebrande de Florence from *Medecine Treatise* (French, 1356).

desist from cutting or burning because of the weeping of the patient."

Bloodletting, that long-popular health measure, is commonly done by barbers, some of whom have recently abandoned the shave and haircut to devote themselves exclusively to surgery. Many also specialize in pulling teeth. Owing to poor diet, teeth are a chronic health problem, more because of bad gums than cavities. Wealthy patients have been known to pay as much as five livres for an extraction, while barbers get as much as fifteen sous for a bleeding. The lower classes are spared these luxuries.

Mental illness is widespread. Birth injuries often leave brain damage. Collective mental disorders, such as St. Vitus' Dance, are notorious, though the most famous outbreak of this "dancing mania" will not appear until the fourteenth century. Joining hands, the victims dance in wild delirium until they fall exhausted, foaming at the mouth. This communal fit is treated either by swaddling the victims like babies, to prevent them from injuring themselves and others, or by exorcism.

The mentally ill are rarely confined, though they are sometimes tied to the rood screen in church, so that they may be improved by attending mass. Or the sign of the cross is shaved into the hair of their heads. They are invariably numbered among the armies of pilgrims at the shrines—along with the spastics, the paralytics, the scrofulous, and the very numerous cripples—at Rome, Mont-Saint-Michel, Roc Armadour, Compostela, and on the road to Jerusalem.

In this pathetic troop one never sees the most pitiful of all the medieval sick—the victims of leprosy. This very widespread disease, attended by its frightful disfigurement, has inspired terror in the clergy as well as the laity.

There are two thousand leper colonies in France, including several in the neighborhood of Troyes. A famous one, the Leproserie des Deux Eaux, was founded in the eleventh century by Count Hugo on the eve of his departure for the First Crusade. Before the leper is committed to the enclosure, his isolation is sanctified by a special church ritual. The unfortunate victim is brought to the tribunal of the diocesan official and examined by surgeons. The "separation" is pronounced the following Sunday. The unhappy man, dressed in a shroud, is carried to the church on a litter by four priests singing the psalm, "Libera me." Inside the church the litter is set down at a safe distance from the congregation. The service of the dead is read. Then, again singing the psalm, the clergy carry the leper out of the church, through the streets, out of town, to the leper colony. He is given a pair of castanets, a pair of gloves, and a bread basket. After the singing of the "De profundis" the priest intones, "Sis mortuus mundo, vivens iterum Deo" (Be thou dead to this world, living again to God), concluding, "I forbid you ever to enter a church or a monastery, a mill, a bakery, a market or any place where there is an assemblage of people. I forbid you to quit your house without your leper's costume and castanets. I forbid you to bathe yourself or your possessions in stream or fountain or spring. I forbid you to have commerce with any woman except her whom you have married in the Holy Church. I forbid you if anyone speaks to you on the road to answer till you have placed yourself below the wind." Then everyone leaves the poor victim condemned to a living death.

The disease is believed to be transmitted not only by touch but by breath. With all the care taken to isolate lepers, from time to time rumors lead to panic and lynching.

Cruel though medieval treatment of leprosy is, it represents a step forward in the history of medicine: recognition of the problem of contagion. Ironically, leprosy (Hansen's disease) is only slightly contagious, and the frightening disfigurement results not from the disease itself but from loss of sensation in nerve endings and consequent wearing away of tissue. But medieval medicine accurately guesses that diseases are transmitted by contact or through the air.

A still more important contribution of medieval medicine is the hospital, a wholly new idea. Hospitals, like monasteries and abbeys, are favorite recipients of Christian charity. The Hôtel-Dieu-le-Comte in Troyes was founded by Count Henry the Generous some seventy-five years ago, and has continued to profit by gifts not only from the count's successors but from others as well. One lady bequeathed the revenue of seven chambers of a house facing the public baths. Another gave a carpenter and his family, who were her serfs. A burgher gave a stall in Moneychanger's Place at the fair. Another gave a fisherman, his family and all his possessions, and his fishing rights in the Seine. Still another endowed the hospital with three garments, worth thirteen sous apiece, and six pairs of shoes a year. A vintner gave income from his vineyards to buy earthenware bowls and cups for the sick and wine to celebrate mass. Other rents, revenues, fees, and taxes from fairs, mills, vineyards, bakeries, farms, and fisheries have poured in.

Counts and popes have accorded this hospital, like many others, their blessing and protection. Eight priests, of whom one is prior and master of the house, staff the hospital, assisted by as many nuns as are needed. When a patient is admitted, he confesses and takes communion, his feet and body are washed, and he is given hospital clothes and food. If his disease is considered contagious, he is isolated—an advance in medicine in itself. The critically ill are also isolated, for intensive care. Upon recovery, indigent patients are furnished with clothes. The hospital does not receive women in childbirth, because their cries may disturb other patients; nor does

it take foundlings, the blind, the crippled, and victims of plague (or leprosy), who would swamp the hospital. Responsibility for the care of these unfortunates falls on the parish churches.

The regimen of the hospital is strict and simple, with emphasis on common sense. In fact, there remains a considerable fund of common sense in medieval man's attitude toward health. Many sound health rules are contained in aphorisms and verses, one of the most famous compendiums of which is known as the Health Rule of Salerno. It is said to have been inspired by Robert of Normandy, wounded in the First Crusade, during his stay at the famous medical center. Written in Latin verse, it contained these recommendations, given here in the Elizabethan translation of Sir John Harington:

> A King that cannot rule him his diet
> Will hardly rule his realm in peace and quiet.
> For healthy men may cheese be wholesome food,
> But for the weak and sickly 'tis not good.
> Use three doctors still, first Dr. Quiet,
> Next Dr. Merry-man and Dr. Diet . . .
> Wine, Women, Baths, by art of nature warme,
> Us'd or abus'd do men much good or harme.
> Some live to drinke new wine not fully fin'd,
> But for your health we wish that you drink none,
> For such to dangerous fluxes are inclin'd,
> Besides the lees of wine doe breed the stone.
> But such by our consent shall drink alone.
> For water and small biere we make no question
> Are enemies to health and good digestion;
> And Horace in a verse of his rehearses,
> That water-drinkers never make good verses.

IX

THE CHURCH

*I know you need a short sermon and
a long table. May it please God not to make
the time of the mass last too long for you.*

—AN EASTER SERMON BY ROBERT DE SORBON

Churches in the thirteenth century are places where people go not only to pray or visit the shrines of Saints, but for secular purposes, because churches are often the only large public buildings in town. Business life often centers around a town's principal church. In Troyes the fairs crowd the precincts of St.-Jean and St.-Rémi. In Provins the stalls of the moneychangers are set up in front of St.-Ayoul. In many towns churches are used for town meetings, guild meetings, and town council sessions.

Everywhere the church is a familiar, friendly place. It is not, however, particularly comfortable. There are no benches or pews.[1] Some worshippers bring stools and cushions, some kneel on the straw-covered floor. The building is chilly, even in mild weather, and in the winter many of the congregation come armed

Stained glass and cross, Chartres Cathedral.

with handwarmers—hollow metal spheres holding hot coals.

A bell signals the start of service. The congregation stands as the procession of priests, choir, and clerks enters singing a hymn. The melody of Gregorian chant, seeming to wander at will, actually follows strict rules in mode, rhythmic pattern, phrasing, accent, and relationship of words to music. The group sings in unison, or sometimes in an antiphon between choir and cantor or between two halves of the choir. A momentous change is just taking place, however—the birth of polyphonic music. Out of a part of the chant in which the melody is accompanied by a sustained note in the tenor, music for more than one voice part is developing. First the tenor, from a single note of indefinite length, becomes a separate melody with its own rhythm; then another voice is added; and out of this grows a "motet," a sort of little fugue. Another important innovation is the beginning of modern notation, with rhythm indicated as well as pitch.

The singers may be accompanied by a "portative organ," which looks like the fruit of a union between an accordion and a full-sized organ. It is suspended from the player's neck; he operates the bellows on the back of the instrument with his left hand and the keyboard with his right. Some churches have standard organs, powerful, clumsy, and generally out of tune. The one constructed at Winchester in 980, with four hundred pipes and two manuals, produced a noise so great that everyone "stopped with his hand his gaping ears, being in no wise able to draw near and hear the sound." Instrumental keys, introduced in the twelfth century, are so heavy and stiff that they must be played with the clenched fist. Organs have a range of three octaves, and are the first instruments to become entirely chromatic.

The Gregorian liturgy, having triumphed over several rivals, is in use throughout western Europe. In almost any church in France, England, Germany, Italy, or

Spain the service is celebrated exactly as it is in Troyes. The congregation stands, kneels, and sits in accordance with the ritual; otherwise, however, it takes little active part in the service.

Few present understand Latin, but sermons are delivered in the vernacular, except when the audience is clerical. The sermon usually lasts half an hour, measured by the water clock on the altar. The priest mounts the pulpit and begins by making the sign of the cross, then gives his *thema* or text in a short Latin passage from the Gospels, which he translates for the benefit of the congregation. This he follows with a rhetorical introduction explaining his unfitness to discuss the subject (the sentiments are humble but the language is flowery) and with an invocation to the divine spirit. Then he develops his text.

Frequently he runs over the time limit in order to get in his "example." This indispensable part of the program consists of a story, illustrative of the sermon's text, told with dramatic flair. For a sermon on the Christian virtues, a popular example goes like this:[2]

A merchant is returning from the fair, where he has sold all his merchandise and gained a large sum of money. Pausing in a city—such as Amiens or Troyes—he finds himself before a church, and goes into the chapel to pray to the Mother of God, Holy Mary, putting his purse beside him on the ground. When he rises, he forgets the purse and goes away without it.

A burgher of the city is also accustomed to visit the chapel and pray before the blessed Mother of God Our Lord, Holy Mary. He finds the purse and sees that it is scaled and locked. What is he to do? If he lets it be known that he has found it, people will cry that they have lost it. He decides to keep the purse and advertise for its owner, and he writes out a notice in big letters, saying that whoever has lost anything should come to him, and posts it on the door of his house.

When the merchant has gone a good distance, he realizes that his purse is missing. Alas, all is lost! He returns to the chapel, but the purse is gone. The priest, questioned, knows nothing about it. Coming out of the chapel, the merchant finds the notice, enters the house, sees the burgher who found the purse and says to him, "Tell me who wrote those words on your door." And the burgher pretends he knows nothing but says, "Good friend, many people

View of the medieval pipe organ at Chartres Cathedral, France.

Construction of a temple in the presence of St. Augustine from a 14th century fresco in the Choir of the St. Mary of Lluca Church, Bishopric of Vic, Catalonia, Spain.

come here and put up signs. What do you want? Have you lost anything?" "Lost anything!" cries the merchant. "I have lost a treasure so great that it cannot be counted." "What have you lost, good friend?" "I lost a purse full of money, sealed with such and such a seal and such and such a lock." Then the burgher sees that the merchant is telling the truth, so he shows him the purse and returns it to him. And when the merchant finds the burgher so honest, he thinks, "Good sir God, I am not worthy of such a treasure as I have amassed. This burgher is far worthier than I." "Sir," he says to the burgher, "surely the money belongs to you rather than to me, and I will give it to you, and commend you to God." "Ah, my friend," says the burgher, "take your money; I haven't earned it." "Certainly not," says the merchant, "I will not take it." And he leaves.

The burgher runs after him crying, "Stop thief! Stop thief!" The neighbors take up the hue and cry and catch the merchant, and ask, "What has this man done?" "He has stolen my poverty and my honesty, which I have carefully preserved up to this moment."

The congregation thoroughly enjoys the performance, with its moral, which the priest takes care to point out.

Besides homely anecdotes, the preachers find their examples in extracts from history or legend, lives of the saints, Bible stories, contemporary events, personal memories, fables from Aesop or other fabulists, morals drawn from bestiaries or from accounts of plants, the human body, or the stars.

Oratorical devices[3] are not beneath a priest. If attention lags during the sermons, he may suddenly exclaim, "That person who is sleeping in the corner will never know the secret that I'm going to tell you!" Or when the ladies become restive during a sermon on the wickedness of women, he may address them: "Shall I speak of the good woman? I will tell you about that old lady there who has fallen asleep. For Heaven's sake if someone has a pin, wake her up; people who sleep during the sermon somehow manage to stay awake at table."

The sermon is followed by the Creed, the Offertory, and the celebration of Communion, which has been preceded by the Kiss of Peace. The priest kisses the Gospel, which is kissed in turn by every member of the congregation. Those who receive the sacrament come forward and stand before the altar with hands outstretched, palms touching, one knee bent slightly forward; they do not kneel. The priest celebrates Communion in front of the altar with his back to the people—a recent innovation.

Communion over, the service nears its end, and the priest asks prayers for certain persons: for the Church, for Count Thibaut, his peace and prosperity, for the bishop and other priests, for the Holy Land and its defenders, for the dead, some of whom he mentions by name. He may even lower his voice and ask a blessing for an unlucky priest who has been disciplined. Everyone kneels and the prayers are recited together, with several Paters and Aves. Then the priest pronounces his final blessing, and the service is over.

Like the Christian service, worship in the synagogue retains an age-old universal form. The Almemar (the platform from which the Scriptures are read), and the ark containing the sacred scrolls stand in the center of the paved floor. Wax candles illuminate the interior. Tallow, though permitted for private use, is forbidden in the synagogue.

Services are read twice daily, in late afternoon and again in the evening. Behavior is casual, compared with that of a Christian congregation. Children are noisy, adults wander in and out. A Takkanah (edict) imposes a heavy fine for striking one's neighbor in the synagogue. Jewish services are well attended, though workers who must rise at sunup are excused except on the Sabbath. The form of service is identical throughout northern France. The ancient custom by which men of the congregation read successive portions of the Scriptures has been modified, and the Reader performs this task, either alone or with various individuals who are called up. Sermons are delivered only on festivals, when the whole congregation sings the Hallel (Psalms 113–118), which is possibly what provoked a famous complaint by Pope Innocent III against excessive noise emanating from synagogues.

One of the features of the Christian religion which has given worship a distinctive character is the taste for intercessory saints. Though prayers to a saint may be said at home as well as in church, their effect is believed to be greatly enhanced by the presence of part of the saint's mortal remains. This conviction dates from the martyrdom of the early Christians. Bones and other physical fragments of men stoned, burned, and tortured were reverently rescued and preserved.

Saints and martyrs multiplied, and their relics multiplied even more rapidly. Churches were built on the tombs of martyrs. Princes and bishops went to extraordinary lengths to acquire relics. Constantinople became the center of a vast commerce, owing to its favorable position near the scenes of the Old and New Testaments. St. Helena, mother of Constantine, is said to have found the three crosses of Calvary and identified the True Cross by touching a dead man with it and bringing him to life. So precious was this relic that it was cut into bin and bestowed, traded, and sold all over Europe (to such effect that Calvin later counted enough pieces of it "to make a full load for a good ship").

The capture of Jerusalem in 1099 brought a flood of relics—Judas' pieces of silver, one of the Biblical sower's wheat seeds, two heads of St. John the Baptist

The Holy Trinity with scenes of Saints, Evangelists and Angels attributed to the Maitre aux Boquetaux, from *Guyart des Moulins/Bible Historiale*, Vol. I (1357).

Reliquary chest of Pepin of Aquitaine (c.1100).

"authentic relic" of the Lord's circumcision, claimed by a number of churches.

Despite cavils, the cult of relics is at its zenith in the middle of the thirteenth century. Every church has its treasures. Besides the relics brought back by Garnier de Traînel, the cathedral treasury of Troyes displays the basin in which Christ washed the disciples' feet; the surplice of St. Thomas of Canterbury, on which traces of his brains are visible, and a foot of St. Margaret. The treasury of Sens contains a drop of blood and a bit of the garment of St. Clement and one of Judas' thirty pieces of silver. The church of Ste.-Croix at Provins has an arm of St. Lawrence and a fragment of the True Cross, given by Count Thibaut on his return from a Crusade in 1241. Sometimes relics are preserved in gold and enamel boxes, ornamented with jewels; sometimes they are fitted into a more artfully contrived reliquary—an arm-bone encased in a sculptured arm of brass, enamel and gold, or a piece of skull fitted neatly into a lifelike representation of a saint's head in silver and brass.

The number of saints is large and indeterminate. In early Christian times cults were local, and inquiries into qualifications for sainthood were usually instituted by the bishop of the diocese in which the candidate lived. Not until the tenth century did the Pope come to play an important part in canonization, and in the twelfth, Alexander III established once and for all the principle that no person, however holy his reputation, could be venerated as a saint without direct papal authorization. In the thirteenth century the process of canonization is undergoing its final development.[4] Petition must be made to the Pope, who appoints two or more commissioners as his representatives. They set up a court of inquiry, examine witnesses, and fill the role of

("Was this saint then bicephalous?" acidly demanded Guibert of Nogent), and hundreds of other items. But this was a trickle compared to the torrent loosed by the capture of Constantinople in 1204. Bishop Garnier de Traînel, who served as chaplain of the Latin army, brought back many treasures to Troyes, among them a silver arm encompassing a relic of St. James the Greater; the skull of St. Philip the Apostle, incased in a reliquary decorated with a gold crown studded with precious stones; and several pieces of the True Cross, enclosed in a Byzantine cross of gilded silver set with five fine emeralds. The Crown of Thorns, pawned by the new Latin emperor to the Venetians, was eventually purchased by St.-Louis, who built the Sainte-Chapelle to receive it, apparently regarding it as superior in authenticity to the two other Crowns of Thorns that Paris already possessed. Other relics aroused skepticism even in a religious age: one of Christ's baby teeth ("How did anyone think to save it?" wondered Guibert of Nogent), pieces of stone tablets on which God was said to have written the Ten Commandments, and the devil's advocate as well as of defendant and judge. The petitioners choose a proctor who marshals witnesses and expedites the suit if there is a delay. A record of the proceedings is kept, put into "public form" by a notary, and presented to the papal Curia, where canonization is finally granted or denied. The successful candidate is placed in the martyrology, but in 1250 church calendars still present wide local variations.

Despite the popularity of such regional patrons as St.-Loup, one saint stands far above all others in appeal. The prayers of Christians are directed more often to the Virgin Mary than to all the rest together. Virgin worship goes back to the fourth century, when controversies over the nature of Christ brought the need for a new intercessor between God and man. In the thirteenth century this worship is at its height. The monastic orders find in the Virgin an ascetic ideal. The Carmelites celebrate Our Lady of Carmel, the Franciscans have instituted the Feast of the Presentation, the Dominicans have popularized the Hail Mary. Works of Marian theology and devotion by St.-Bernard and St.-Bonaventure have been translated into the popular tongue and are widely read.

Many a burgher seeks the intercession of saints by visiting their relics, either to effect a cure or to do penance for a sin. One may make a pilgrimage to the new cathedral at Chartres and follow the "Chartres mile" on one's knees—a labyrinth of concentric circles in the middle of the nave. Or the pilgrim may journey to Roc Amadour, where he strips to his shirt, binds himself in chains, and climbs the hundred and twenty-six steps to the Chapel of Our Lady on his knees. There a priest recites prayers of purification and removes the chains, presenting him with a certificate and a lead medallion with the image of the Virgin. Henry II, St. Dominic, St.-Louis, Blanche of Castille and thousands of others, famous and obscure, have climbed those steps.

Some burghers possess lead medallions from half a dozen pilgrimages, either the result of persistent attempts to cure an affliction, or exceptional piety—or perhaps a fondness for travel. Chaucer's pilgrims were not the first to enjoy their trip.

If there are saints to pray to, there are also devils to fear. Every corner of hell is minutely described by the priests and depicted on church portals. People are often possessed by devils, which must be exorcised by the priest. Belief in demons is older than the Church, which has certified their existence (Thomas Aquinas cites the authority of the saints and of the Christian faith) Thoughts of hell and purgatory give Christians mo-

ments of apprehension and even terror, and influence some decisions, especially in the realm of charity. But though merchants are aware that the Bible does not recommend laying up riches as a means of gaining the kingdom of Heaven, they go right on laying them up.

In the cosmos of the thirteenth century many mysteries are unsolved and, failing other hypotheses, must be explained by supernatural means. Yet the outlook of the burghers of Troyes is not devoid of skepticism and common sense. Though the Roman Church is at the pinnacle of its prestige, there is a strong current of resistance to its authority. The weapons of excommunication and interdict are not as effective as they used to be, partly through overuse. The late Bishop Hervée, quarreling with Thibaut the Songwriter over prerogatives, threatened the count with excommunication so frequently that the Pope felt constrained to caution the embattled prelate. And even the Pope's own edict did not prevent Dandolo, the elderly Doge of Venice, and his fellow Crusaders from capturing the Christian city of Zara and dividing the spoils.

The cities, with their notorious worldliness, are widely blamed by the Church for the spread of skepticism and something worse—heresy. A powerful, subversive religious underground has stirred upheaval throughout Europe. Several heretical movements varying from moderate to lunatic-fringe have been suppressed, but one, the most dangerous of all, continues to alarm all right-thinking people. Albigensianism, or Catharism, originally brought to the West from Bulgaria by weavers and cloth merchants and fostered, as the Church complains, by the new independence and skepticism of the cities, has been the object of a vigorous crusade, lasting thirty-four years, with a ten-year interval of truce. Many of its practitioners have gone into hiding, and the Inquisition, placed in the hands of the new mendicant orders, is busy ferreting out suspects everywhere.

The orthodox majority hates and fears the heretics, whose doctrines are shocking enough without being exaggerated, as they naturally are. Cathars deny the Redemption and the Incarnation. Some claim that Christ's entry into the world was made by way of Mary's ear. They scoff at the Old Testament and take stock in neither hell nor purgatory, maintaining that this world is hell enough. They reject the Cross, which they consider as a merely material object. Their conviction that marriage is evil, because procreation embeds souls deeper in the material world, has given an especially dubious reputation to the Cathars, who are believed to have originated in Bulgaria—hence the latter-day connotation in French and English of the word *bougre,* originally meaning Bulgar.

Parties of Dominican and Franciscan inquisitors journey from town to town inviting heretics to reform and Christians to inform. Heretics who confess and repent may get off with a penance, which sometimes takes the form of a saffron-colored cross sewed on breast and back. Whipping and imprisonment may be employed, though not torture—as yet. A guilty and unrepentant heretic may be "delivered to the secular arm" to be burned. Verdict is pronounced and sentence executed in the town square, and the ashes are cast into the nearest river.

The heresy hunters visited Champagne in the 1230s, their activities reaching a frightful climax in 1239, on the eve of Count Thibaut's departure for the Holy Land. An old woman of Provins, Gille, called "the Abbess," who had been in prison since 1234 awaiting sentence for heresy, bought her own release by disclosing the names of other heretics to the notorious inquisitor Robert le Bougre, an ex-Cathar turned Dominican. At Mont-Aimé, some fifty miles north of Troyes, one hundred and eighty-three men and women were burned in the presence of a huge throng of spectators. When the fires were lit, the Cathar leader raised his voice and gave his fellow martyrs absolution, nobly explaining that he alone would be damned because there was no one to absolve him.

X

THE CATHEDRAL

Nothing doing in the workyard,
for the moment I'm out of money.

—FROM THE ACCOUNTS OF
A FOURTEENTH-CENTURY CATHEDRAL

The Cathedral of St.-Pierre and St.-Paul has experienced many vicissitudes through the centuries that it has been the church of the bishop of Troyes. From small beginnings as a chapel, occupying the site of the present choir, it grew slowly into a ninth-century basilica of sufficient size and dignity to serve as the scene for a council of Pope John VIII.

Fourteen years later the Vikings burned St.-Pierre to the ground; Bishop Milon restored it in the following century. In the new cathedral St.-Bernard preached to a capacity crowd in 1147 and cured many sick, including a servant of the bishop, an artisan, and an epileptic girl. Milon's work was destroyed by the Great Fire of 1188, after which Bishop Hervée undertook to rebuild the church, using the new engineering technique which a

later day will call Gothic. At the time of Hervée's death, in 1223, the sanctuary and the seven chapels of the apse were nearly finished. His successor, Bishop Robert, continued the work; it is proceeding today under Bishop Nicholas de Brie and will go on for the next three centuries, stopping and starting as money comes in.

In Italy churches and cathedrals are often projects of communes; in northwest Europe the lead is more frequently taken by the bishop or abbot. Abbot Suger of St.-Denis led his carpenters into the forest to choose timber for his beams and personally ascertained "with geometric and arithmetical instruments" that the new choir aligned with the old nave. At Troyes the bishop is invariably the moving force in the endless task of construction and reconstruction.

Cathedrals are usually built on the crypts of their predecessors. The new cathedral of St.-Pierre is being constructed on the site of the old, but the larger apse, with its radiating chapels, requires more room, so Hervée negotiated a trade with a fisherman who owned the strip between the crumbling Roman wall and the branch of the Seine that marks the eastern limits of the old city. The wall was dismantled, and the chevet of the new cathedral now extends beyond it.

Constructing a cathedral with scale model, details of stonework, architect's tools and plans. Painting by Ferdinand Knab (1877).

As work on a cathedral halts, resumes, progresses, halts again, several master builders may be in charge at different periods, which among other things leads to stylistic alterations and inconsistencies. Also, during these changes, the names of the masters[1] tend to get lost. None of St.-Pierre's early builders are known by name, though they were without doubt prominent men in their own lifetimes. The cathedral builder, in fact, is one of the outstanding figures of the Middle Ages. If vanished records swallow the names of many, enough information survives to supply evidence of the kind of men they were. Many insured the durability of their fame by inscribing their signatures on their works. Carved into the soffit of the topmost window facing the New Tower of Chartres is the name "Harman" and the date "1164." On the roof of St. Mary's, Beverley, can be read the message: "Hal Carpenter made this rowfe." Names are signed in the labyrinth on the floor of the nave at Amiens: Robert de Luzarches, Thomas de Cormont, and Renard de Cormont; and at Reims: Jean d'Orbais, Jean le Loup, Gaucher de Reims, and Bernard de Soissons. Tombs bear the names of many builders. One at Reims is dedicated to Master Hugues Libergier, "who began this church in the year of the Incarnation 12..."—the precise date obscured by the footsteps of seven hundred years. Documents record the names of many others, such as Pierre de Montreuil, one of the best-known men of his time, who in 1248 completed the Sainte-Chapelle in Paris in the amazing time of thirty-three months—showing what a Gothic engineer could do when the money did not run out. The brilliant Villard de Honnecourt perpetuated his name and fame by leaving a large parchment sketchbook filled with drawings, plans, and elevations which is one of the priceless documents of the thirteenth century.

The names of builders are well known to prospective employers. William of Sens was hired in 1174 to rebuild Canterbury Cathedral on the strength of his reputation as the builder of the Cathedral of Sens. Builders are well paid, with a liberal daily stipend supplemented by a clothing allowance, a food allowance, fodder for their horses, a fur-trimmed robe, and often special privileges, such as freedom from taxes for life. Typically rising from the ranks of the masons, they are remarkably versatile. Not only do they habitually combine the functions of engineer and architect, but some are adept sculptors and painters, or even poets. They are expert at every kind of construction—castles, walls, bridges, secular buildings. One architect, John of Gloucester, not only supervised the works at Westminster Abbey, but

undertook at Westminster Palace to repair a chimney and a conduit supplying water to the king's lavatory, and to build a drain to carry off refuse of the kitchen to the Thames, "which conduit the king ordered to be made on account of the stink of the dirty water which was carried through his halls which was wont to affect the health of the people frequenting them."

The builders' plans[2] are skillfully drafted on parchment, to explain their intentions to bishop and chapter: ground plans for each part of the nave, choir and transepts, sketches of portals with sculpture indicated, scale drawings of bays and ambulatories, variant possibilities for roofing and drainage. Accomplished mathematicians, especially strong in geometry, they determine proportions by supplementing measurements in feet and inches with modules, based on squares, equilateral triangles, and other regular polygons. This knowledge is so esoteric that it remains a professional secret.

The master builder is not only well paid but highly respected, as are the master masons. A preacher cannot restrain his indignation in describing the lordly status of these elite commoners: "In great buildings the master-in-chief orders his men about but rarely or never lends his own hand to the work; and yet he is paid much more than all the others . . . The master masons, with walking sticks and gloves, say, 'Cut here,' and 'Cut there,' but they do no work themselves."

The master builder is the general of a skilled, and consequently expensive, army of workers. Pilgrims and other faithful sometimes contribute voluntary labor, usually in the transport department. Occasionally a long line of penitents hitch themselves to a wagonload of stone, doing the work of oxen. On the whole, oxen do the work better. A more efficacious form of volunteer labor is the peasant with ox and wagon who receives an indulgence from the bishop in return for his help. Even so, moving a large quantity of stone a long distance overland is a serious problem. Troyes imports some of its stone from Tonnerre, only twenty-five miles south, but without a connection by water. The stone quintuples in cost on the journey. Water transport is much cheaper. The marble for the columns of the great abbey church at Cluny was moved ten times as far, down the Durance from the Alps and up the Rhône. When they can, bishops cannibalize pagan monuments, as at Reims, where an early archbishop obtained permission from Louis the Pious to dismantle the Roman ramparts so that he could build the old Romanesque cathedral.

But a convenient quarry is even better than an old Roman wall. Suger's discovery of the quarry at Pontoise

The flying buttress, a revolutionary support innovation of the Gothic system of construction. Notre-Dame, Paris.

was regarded as miraculous. The bishops of Troyes have a quarry which is worked by masons from the cathedral work gang.

Never do volunteers figure as an important element of the labor force. They cannot dress stone, or set it in courses, or make mortar and tile, or lay lead roofs and gutters, or construct arch ribs, or sculpture stone, or carve wood, or fabricate stained glass, or assemble it into windows. Cathedral labor is necessarily professional.

In the terminology of construction workers of a later day, the masons are "boomers." They go where the job is, living in barracks in the cathedral yard, collecting their pay, saving it if they are prudent, spending it on drink and girls if they are not. Many own their own valuable tools, which are passed from father to son. Others depend on tools supplied by the employer, who is normally responsible for repair and maintenance. Keeping soft iron points and edges sharp is a problem. Besides picks, hammers, wedges and points, basic to stone dressing, masons need hatchets, trowels, spades, hoes, buckets and sieves for mortar, and lines for laying out walls.

Masons are free men, skilled at their profession, capable of rising in the world. There are several categories with varying wage rates: plasterers and mortarers, stonecutters, master masons, and unskilled laborers. They usually spend their first years in the quarry, learning to cut stone. A mason in the quarry may be paid twenty-four deniers a week plus his meals and lodging, though in winter his wage is automatically cut to match the shorter working day. A summer wage may reach thirty deniers. There is plenty of work for an expert mason; from eight to ten churches a year are going up in France alone.

On a summer day, the workyard before a cathedral hums with activity. Masons are clustered in twos and threes. One man hammers while a comrade holds the point to the stone, cutting a voussoir, one of the wedge-shaped stones that form the ribs of an arch. Most difficult to fashion is the keystone, whose projections must fit into cuts made in the four rib stones that meet it, to pin the vault securely at the top. Some workers are dressing stone blocks for the exterior masonry. The Master of the Works, or one of his aides, may construct wooden "molds" against which the stone blocks are measured to insure uniformity and accuracy. A master mason marks each finished block with a number, to facilitate assembly of the great jigsaw puzzle. Some men are at work on more delicate pieces, sections of pier capitals or portal frieze borders. Some are busy making mortar with buckets, sieves, hoes, and trowels. They have the valuable assistance of a recent invention—the wheelbarrow. Two blacksmiths are sharpening tools, one turning the grindstone as the other hones the cutting edge of a hatchet. One shed shelters a forge where the iron clamps[3] and dowels are wrought. Another is the carpenters' shack, near which is the pit where the heavy beams for the timbering are sawed by the big two-handed pit saw. The plumbers also have their shed, where they fashion lead fittings for eaves and gutters.

An exceptionally skilled craftsman at work in the yard may be the bell founder, really a brass founder, who makes brass pots, washbasins, and mortars when there are no bells to be cast. He has a large pit dug, and in it he constructs a mold with a clay core which supports a wax model of the bell, in turn encased in a clay "cope." The mold will be dried by kindling a fire in the brickwork of the core, which will at the same time melt the wax, leaving a space to be filled in with bell metal. This is a mixture of copper and tin. Experience has shown that the best proportion is thirteen parts copper to four of tin; a higher percentage of tin improves the tone of the bell but makes the metal brittle. The bell is "long-waisted"[4] (longer in proportion to its diameter than bells in later centuries). It will be rung with a simple lever; later bells will be operated with a half wheel, three-quarter wheel, and finally a complete wheel. The founder casts his bells so that they will have a "virgin ring" and will need no further tuning. Tuning is a laborious and noisy process of chipping around the inside of a bell.

When the metal is poured and the bell mounted, the bishop baptizes it as if it were a child, with salt,

The Gothic cathedral of Notre-Dame, Paris. Note the flying buttresses and large windows (completed c.1330).

water, and holy oil. He prays that when it is sounded faith and charity may abound among men, that all the devices of the devil—hail, lightning, winds—may be rendered vain by its ringing, and all unseasonable weather be softened.

The bell founder signs his work with the mark of a shield with three bells, a pot and a mortar, and sometimes with an inscription such as "Iohannes Sleyt Me Fecit" or "Iohannes De Stafforde Fecit Me in Honore Beate Marie," or a bit of bell ringer's verse: "I to the church the living call, and to the grave do summon all," or "Sometimes joy and sometimes sorrow, marriage today and death tomorrow."

Dominating the scene is the great incomplete shell of the cathedral itself. The rising wall is covered with scaffolding fashioned of rough-hewn poles lashed together in trusses, with the diagonals cinched by tourniquets. Inside the walls a giant crane stands on a platform, its long arm reaching over the wall, dangling a line to the ground. When the line is secured around a building stone, word is passed from the ground outside via the men on the scaffold to the crane operator inside. The "engine" is started—a yoke of oxen harnessed to walk in a circle around the crane platform, winding the line on a windlass. The driver commands, the whip snaps, the oxen shove, the windlass turns, the line moves, the block rises, till it reaches the scaffold where the men are waiting. Cries go back and forth over the wall, the "engine" is halted, the men on the scaffold grasp the block, maneuver it in, call for another lift of a foot or so, then for a back-off to lower the stone in place, and amid shouts, commands and perhaps a few curses, the block is securely bedded in the prepared mortar course. Smaller stones are lifted by a higher windlass, which is turned by a crank—another invention of the Middle Ages.

Most of the masonry work consists of old, long-practiced technique. The Romans maneuvered bigger blocks into position than any that medieval masons tackle. On the Pont du Gard there are stones eleven feet in length. But medieval masons are steadily improving their ability to handle large masses of stone. In the bases of piers, monoliths weighing as much as two tons are sometimes used. The Romans habitually built without mortar, dressing their stones accurately enough so that walls and arches stood simply by their own weight. Some builders are beginning to assay this, but by and large medieval masonry relies on mortar.

Thirteenth-century timbering is also less daring than Roman. The entrance to the choir at present is a veritable maze of heavy crisscrossing timbers supporting the work in progress on the first bay of the choir vault.[5] The rough-hewn timbers stand in a network of Xs and Vs, supporting a rude ogival arch of timber on which the stone ribs are laid. The timber arch does not meet the stone accurately at all points, and where it fails to do so, chips or blocks are driven into the interstice.

In the early Middle Ages, the problem of fire-proofing a church was reduced to the question of how to support a masonry vault with something less expensive than a thick wall. Roman engineers actually had a solution, the groined vault, contrived by making two of their ordinary semi-circular "barrel vaults" intersect. The weight of the resulting structure was distributed to the corners, permitting it to be supported by piers, and so providing architectural advantages. But the groined vault, though used by the Romans in the Baths of Caracalla and by some builders since, presents a difficulty. The variously-shaped stone blocks must be meticulously cut; in other words, they are expensive.

When medieval engineers found another way to mount a vault on piers they opened the door to Gothic architecture.[6] The Romans, acquainted with the pointed arch, found as little use for it as had the Greeks or Persians. It was French engineers of the twelfth century who made the discovery that two pointed arches, inter-secting overhead at right angles, created an exception-ally strong stone skeleton, which could rest solidly on four piers. The stones were easy to cut and the spaces between could be filled with no exceptional skill on the part of the mason. And once mounted on its piers, the new vault could be raised to astonishing heights at moderate cost. The higher the vault, the more room for windows, and the better illuminated the church. A problem remained. As the vault rose, the piers required reinforcement to contain the thrust from the ribs, which threatened to topple them outward.

At first this difficulty was met by buttressing, that is, by giving an extra thickness to the exterior wall at the point where the rib connected. But this made it impossible to put side aisles in the church. The spectac-ular answer to the problem was the flying buttress, a beam of masonry that arched airily over the low roof of the side aisle to meet the point where the rib support-ing the main vault connected with the top of the pier.

By 1250 the intricate combination of piers, ribs, and flying buttresses has become an established, func-tioning system, one which would have opened the eyes of Roman engineers.

Medieval builders have a better theoretical grasp of structural relationships than had their Roman prede-cessors, who often used unnecessarily heavy underpin-nings. But there is still no such thing as theoretical cal-culation of stress, or even accurate measurement. Gothic churches are full of small errors of alignment, and some-times a vault crashes. But with or without a grounding in theory, the new technology usually works, and works so well that though originally conceived in a spirit of economy, it has had a history similar to that of many other engineering advances. It has opened such social and aesthetic possibilities that in the end it has raised the cost of church construction. A hundred years ago the nave of one of the first Gothic cathedrals, at Noyon, soared to a height of eighty-five feet. Notre-Dame-de-Paris then rose to a hundred and fifteen feet, Reims to a hundred and twenty-five, Amiens to a hundred and forty, and Beauvais, just started, is aiming at over a hun-dred and fifty. Spires above the bell towers reach much higher, that of Rouen ultimately holding the champi-onship at four hundred and ninety-five feet, higher than the Great Pyramid.

It is no accident that the development of Gothic architecture coincides with growing affluence. The bishop of Troyes could not have undertaken the new Cathedral of St.-Pierre two hundred years ago, not merely for want of engineering technique but for want of cash.

Money to pay for a cathedral comes from a num-ber of sources. Added to the steadily growing revenues of the chapter and its dependencies are the profits from indulgences, which are the bishop's monopoly. Many an avaricious baron has made peace with God by a hand-some gift to a cathedral building fund. Deathbed be-quests[7] are an especially fruitful source. The Church has campaigned long and shrewdly in favor of wills. Relics, which are part of the reason for building a cathedral, help raise money long before its completion. They attract pilgrims to the site, and since they are portable, they can be sent on mission to the surrounding coun-tryside. Those of Laon journeyed as far south as Tours

A stained glass window detail showing a shoemaker (13th c.), Chartres Cathedral, France.

and north and west to England, where they visited Canterbury, Winchester, Christchurch, Salisbury, Wilton, Exeter, Bristol, Barnstable, and Taunton, performing miracles all along the way.

Even with all the resources of guilty consciences and psychological cures, few cathedrals would be completed without the assistance of an entirely different factor: civic pride. The cathedral belongs to the town as well as to the bishop and is often used for secular purposes, such as town meetings. The burghers can be counted on to give it financial support, not merely through private contributions by the wealthy, but through corporate contributions by the guilds. Proud, devout, and affluent, the guilds compete with each other and with the great lords and prelates in endowing the pictures in glass of Bible stories and lives of the saints which are the chief glory of the cathedral, and which represent no less than half its total cost. For at least one cathedral, Chartres, we have precise figures: of one hundred and two windows, forty-four were donated by princes and other secular lords, sixteen by bishops and other ecclesiastics, and forty-two by the town guilds, who signed their identities with panels representing their crafts.

Windows are not all installed at once. A cathedral's glass may be incomplete a hundred or two hundred years after the masonry is begun. The installation of a window in the clerestory of the choir is an event. The mosaic of colored glass is passed up from hand to hand and eased onto the projecting dowels of a horizontal iron saddle bar, the ends of which are buried in the masonry. A second narrow bar with openings that match

the dowels fits parallel to the first bar and is fastened to it with pins. Together these bars, and the vertical stanchions, hold the glass in place and brace it against wind pressure.

Glass is not manufactured at the site of the cathedral, nor indeed even inside the city. The glassmakers locate their hut in a nearby forest, which supplies fuel and raw materials. Glassmaking is a very ancient art, and "stained" (colored) glass is at least several centuries old, but not until recently has it been in great demand. The new technology and the new affluence have created this major industry.

The glassmaking process, brought to the West by the Venetians, has changed little through the ages—two parts ash (beechwood for best results) to one part sand in the mixture, a hot fire in a stone furnace, blowing and cutting. Blowing is done with a six-foot-long tube, creating a bubble of glass in the form of a long cylinder closed at one end and nearly closed at the other. The cylinder is cut along its length with a white-hot iron, reheated, and opened along the seam into a sheet. The result is a piece of glass of uneven thickness, full of irregularities—bubbles, waves, lines—not very clear, of a pale greenish color. Medieval glassmakers, like their predecessors, cannot turn out a good transparent, colorless pane. One consequence has been that glass never had much appeal as material for the small windows of the Romanesque buildings.

The vast Gothic window spaces have changed the situation. Imperfections in the glass are unimportant, as coloring becomes not only acceptable but desirable. Colors, apart from the indeterminate green of "natural" glass, have always been readily obtainable by adding something to the basic mixture—cobalt for blue, manganese for purple, copper for red. As the big new church windows came into fashion the glaziers took to cutting up sheets of colored glass and leading bits together to make a design. Almost at once the idea occurred of making the designs not merely geometric but pictorial, and the art of stained glass was born. Art begets artists, and the function of assembling the pieces of glass into pictures that the sun turned into miracles of radiant color devolved on those who were skilled at it.

The cathedral windows are made from glass manufactured in the hut in the forest, but are designed and assembled in a studio near the cathedral, under the direction of the master glazier. His craft demands special knowledge (often transmitted from father to son), exceptional skill, and long experience. Like the master builder and the masons, the window maker and the workmen he commands are itinerants, moving from town to town and church to church.

The master glazier oversees every part of the operations of his shop, but one function that he reserves for himself alone is that of drawing the picture. First he produces a small scale-drawing of the whole window on parchment, coloring in the segments. Then he draws a cartoon the size of the panel on which he is working, not on parchment, but on the wooden surface of an enormous bench or table of white ash. A panel is sketched on the table in the form of a diagram in black and white, indicating by numbers and letters which colors are to be used in each tiny section. As the big panes made by the glaziers are cut roughly to size with a hot iron under the master's eye, each piece is laid in its correct position on the table. It does not quite fit. Using a notched tool called a grozing iron, a workman dextrously nibbles the piece's edges to precision.

A visitor watching the workmen fashion the legend of St. Nicholas, or the story of the Wise and Foolish Virgins, for St.-Pierre's windows would scarcely be able to make out any picture at all. The work table is a jigsaw confusion of oddly-shaped segments, with only here and there a recognizable fragment: a purple demon, or the white and yellow robes of the virgins.

Variations in the thickness of the glass produce colors that vary in intensity. In windows of the twelfth century this accident was used to artistic effect in the alternation of light and dark segments. But the men working on St.-Pierre's glass do not take time to sort it out; the thirteenth century's booming market has eliminated this subtlety of workmanship. Even so, the effects achieved are astounding, and will in centuries to come be attributed by legend to a secret process known only to medieval glaziers. In reality the master glazier has no secrets.[8] He carefully paints the lines in the drapery of the garments, the features of the faces, and decorative details; then he supervises the firing of the segments in the kiln and sees that they are assembled properly. The assembly is accomplished by means of doubly-grooved lead cames bent to follow the shape of the glass segments. The cames are soldered to each other at their intersections and sealed with putty, to keep out the rain. Lead is the source of another aesthetic accident: it keeps the colors from radiating into each other when the sunlight strikes.

The finished panel is wrapped in cloth and carried to the cathedral. Measurements do not always prove exact. If the panel turns out to be too large, it is cut down. If it is too small, it is built up with a border. As it is fastened into place, the glazier sees it against the light for the first time. Until that moment of truth he must rely on past experience and observation of other windows for his effects.

Once the panel is made, the design is rubbed off the table and vanishes forever. Occasionally a design may be copied on parchment and used elsewhere, but this is rare. The master glazier is not aiming at immortality or even fame, though he is agreeably aware that his name is well known among glassmakers, masons, prelates, and even the general public. Yet he puts something into his work that is not merely talent and knowledge. Neither is it religious zeal. It is pride, and he can find ample justification for it in religion, for the priests say that God was a craftsman who looked on his work and found it good.

Although he is aware of the dazzling brilliance of his windows when they are in place, as the builder is of the soaring majesty of his completed masonry, neither of them regards his work as art, or himself as an artist. They are not necessary geniuses, but all of them are intelligent men with expert skill, standing historically at the end of a remarkable series of accidents—the cross-rib vault, which led to the flying buttress and the expansion of window space, and the imperfect glazing techniques that dictated colored glass.

Thirteenth-century bishops are delighted with the technology that gives them their incomparable cathedrals. Interestingly enough, clerical opinion in the past was not always so favorable. St.-Bernard[9] wrote angrily to William, abbot of St.-Thierry, about the great Cluniac churches: "Why this excessive height, this enormous length, this unnecessary width, these sumptuous ornaments and curious paintings that draw the eyes and distract the attention from meditation?...We, the monks, who have forsaken ordinary life and who have renounced the riches and ostentation of the world . . . in whom do we hope to awaken devotion with these ornaments?...One could spend a whole day gaping instead of meditating on God. What ineptitude, and what expense!"

But St.-Bernard is dead, and even his Cistercians have grown less puritanical. Few object today to the new style. Besides, St.-Bernard notwithstanding, the cathedrals' success in creating an atmosphere of mystery and awe is of incontestable value to religion. No man, burgher or baron, can enter a Gothic cathedral without experiencing a sense of human insignificance in the presence of such majesty.

XI

SCHOOL AND
SCHOLARS

He would dispense his instructions to his hearers gradually, in a manner commensurate with their powers of assimilation. . . . In view of the fact that exercise both strengthens and sharpens the mind, Bernard would bend every effort to bring his students to imitate what they were hearing. In some cases he would rely on exhortation, in others he would resort to punishments, such as flogging. . . .

—JOHN OF SALISBURY, DESCRIBING THE TEACHING METHODS OF
BERNARD OF CHARTRES, TWELFTH CENTURY

Along with workmen, housewives, priests, cows, horses, and pigs, the stream of morning traffic includes a scattering of boys with close-cropped hair, carrying hand-copied Latin grammars under their arms. They are on their way to school. As they trudge along, kicking stones and horse manure and calling greetings to each other, they are only faintly conscious of the novelty of their position.

There are no public schools in Troyes. But having taken primary instruction from a parish priest, these boys are now enrolled in the cathedral school. They are the elite of the city's youth—mostly the sons of the well-to-do. To their inherited station in life they are adding the advantage of education, and they are placing themselves permanently above the level of weavers, peasants, and ignorant tradesmen.

Schoolmaster teaching students anatomy from *Le Livre des Proprietes des Choses* by Jean Cordichon.

The cathedral school was not originally conceived as a secondary school. Founded in the seventh century by Bishop Ragnegisile, it remained for centuries merely a training school, turning out clerks for the diocese. The bishop himself did the teaching. Today's boys still wear the tonsure, as a sign of what is called "a disposition toward an order." The chancellor of the cathedral teaches theology and confers teaching licenses, but most of the instruction is in the hands of the schoolmaster and his assistant canons, who teach a distinctly secular course.

In the schoolroom the pupils sit on the floor, all ages together. Instruction is predominantly oral and in Latin, though beginners are allowed to lapse into the vernacular. The schoolmaster lectures, and students take notes on oblong wooden tablets coated with black or green wax, using a stylus of bone, ivory, or metal. The whitish scratches it makes can be erased by rubbing with its rounded end. The scholars soon acquire a Latin shorthand: *Sic hic e faI sm qd ad smilr a e pducible a do, g a e et silr hic, a n e g a n e pducible a do* means *Sictit bic est fallacia secundum quid ad simpliciter, A est producible a Deo, ergo A est. Et similiter hic, A non est, ergo A non est producibile a Deo* ("Thus here is the second fallacy, which is simply, A is created by

307

The Seven Liberal Arts by Giovanni dal Ponte (c.1435).

God, therefore A exists; and similarly this, A does not exist, therefore A is not created by God"). In drill, pupils repeat in chorus after the teacher and go on repeating an exercise until they have learned it by heart. Since books have to be copied by hand and writing materials are expensive, memory and oral exercises are indispensable.

The schoolmaster reads aloud, explaining and underlining as he goes, pointing out figures of speech, rhetorical devices, well-chosen words, adjectives that suit the nouns they modify, metaphors that give speech a beyond-the-ordinary meaning. Though discipline may be mild, the attention of the students does not wander, for each of them must recite tomorrow part of what he has heard today.

The lecture, the main teaching session of the day, takes place in the early afternoon. Following it, there is a period of free discussion, then drill, and finally a lesson chosen for moral and religious edification, closing with the Sixth Penitential Psalm and the Lord's Prayer. The next morning is devoted to the "repetition," recalling and committing to writing things learned the previous day. At this time the pupils are also required to imitate the Latin masters they are studying by writing compositions of their own, in verse and prose. They are expected to commit to memory every day a selection from Ovid or Virgil, or another Latin author. These will be helpful in writing letters or compositions, which are traditionally crammed with quotations.

A letter from Gerald of Wales to the archbishop of Canterbury quotes in five pages three times from the Book of Wisdom, twice from St. Jerome, once each from Proverbs, Psalms, Virgil, and Ovid, and seven times from Horace. A letter written by Nicolas of Clairvaux[1] to the bishop of Auxerre, whose See was renowned for its wines, runs:

In the words of the Gospel, *they have no more wine.* (John 2:3). Do not send me the wine of sorrow (Psalms 59:5), *but the wine which rejoices the heart of man* (Psalms 103:15), whose color is excellent, the savor very fine, and whose *agreeable odor* (Exodus 29:18) testifies to its quality. It is in these three elements that it manifests its perfection, and *the cord with three strands does not easily break* (Eccl. 4:12).

The wines of our region are turbid and do not come from those plants which grow in your region in a state of blessedness; their juice has not passed from one nation to another, and from one kingdom to another people *(Psalms 104:13). . . . Send separately to the abbot and to me;* the Jews do not deal with the Samaritans *(John 4:9).*

Theoretically, the curriculum consists of the "seven liberal arts."[2] But schools rarely teach all seven of the arts, and the emphasis is very unequal. These "arts" are "liberal" because their purpose is not moneymaking and because they are worthy of a free man. There are seven mainly because people are fond of the number seven, one of the keys to a numerologically ordered universe. In the sixth century Boethius divided the liberal arts into the *trivium* and *quadrivium* ("three roads"' and "four roads"). The trivium comprises the literary subjects: grammar, rhetoric, and logic; the quadrivium the scientific: arithmetic, geometry, astronomy, and music.

The bishops' schools of the sixth to ninth centuries offered little more than what was indispensable for clerks—Latin, enough arithmetic and astronomy for the computation of Easter and other moveable feasts, and music for the chant. Monastic schools taught a similar curriculum. Like the episcopal schools, they were internal—that is, they trained their own personnel. When they occasionally received children of princes and nobles, it was rather as pages than as regular pupils. Parish priests, too, trained their own successors.

After Charlemagne's time the bishops' schools began to expand and to take outside pupils, boys from the town and boarding scholars. Gradually they came to eclipse the monastic schools. This urbanization and secularization created an educational revolution during the eleventh century. In the hundred years that followed, the cathedral schools became international centers of adult scholarship as well as training schools for the diocesan clergy. The emphasis was on grammar and rhetoric, with theology, philosophy, and canon law, as added disciplines. The most famous school was at Chartres, where, under the direction of the great schoolmaster Bernard (not to be confused with St.-Bernard of Clairvaux) there was a revival of classical literary humanism.

Now, in the thirteenth century, the function of higher education has been largely absorbed by the universities. Where universities are within easy reach, the cathedral schools restrict themselves chiefly to grammar, rhetoric and the rudiments of logic. In remote districts, cathedral schools teach a curriculum similar to that of the universities.

The grammar of the cathedral school embraces not only linguistics but writing, spelling, composition, speech, and general literature, including poetry and history. Pupils must master the elements of Latin by memorizing the *Ars Minor* of Donatus, a fourth-century authority. Ten pages of question-and-answer supply a knowledge of the eight parts of speech. From this the student proceeds to the same author's *Ars Grammatica,* and then to Priscian's *Grammatical Commentary,* a sixth-century work. Donatus and Priscian wrote for pupils to whom Latin was a native language, and are not ideally suited for northwest Europe in 1250. Two new manuals in verse are beginning to replace them, Alexander of Villedieu's *Doctrinale*[3] and the *Grecismus* of Eberhard of Bethune (so-called because it includes some Greek etymology).

Twelfth- and thirteenth-century writers have developed an extraordinary fondness for versifying, and almost every species of literary production appears at one time or another in verse. Historical chronicles are often written in verse. There are verse formularies for letter writing. Sermons sometimes lapse into poetry or rhythmic prose. There is a versified Bible (the *Aurora* of Peter Riga). Even legal documents are sometimes rhymed.

In grammar, the student is exposed to a series of authors, pagan and Christian, with little critical evaluation or regard for chronological order. Anything written in a book has a certain sacredness, all the established authors are authorities, and all are timeless, from Aesop to Horace. Some, like the late Roman elegiac poet Maximianus, are surprisingly profane and even erotic, but they are nevertheless studied for their rhetorical artifices. Sometimes the pagan spirit of Roman poetry arouses qualms. Guibert of Nogent confesses in his autobiography that early in his monastic life he took up verse making and even fell into "certain obscene words and composed brief writings, worthless and immodest, in fact bereft of all decency," before abandoning this shocking practice in favor of commentaries on the Scriptures. St.-Bernard himself wrote verse in his youth at Cîteaux, and was guilty of great proficiency. By the end of the twelfth century, verse writing was forbidden to members of the austere

The Liberal Arts: Grammar, Dialectic and Rhetoric from the *Satyricon* by Martianus Capella (c.1200).

Cistercian order, but many abbots and bishops continue to write love poetry.

All the scholars observe that grammar helps in understanding the Holy Scriptures. The Bible, they point out, is rich in figures of speech, and a study of the literary art assists in appreciating it. Like St. Jerome, they compare secular learning to a heathen slave girl; the Hebrew who wishes to marry her must cut her hair and nails; similarly, the Christian who loves secular learning must purify it from all errors so that it will be worthy to serve God.

The authors who are so revered fulfill many needs. They dispense information about everything from medicine to history. Ovid is prized for his moral sayings. Collections of "sentences," or apothegms containing wise saws from the writings of antique and medieval authors, are popular.

After grammar comes rhetoric, the second of the arts in the trivium, literally the "craft of speech." In democratic Athens and Rome speechmaking was a major element in public life. In the Middle Ages political oratory has little place, and judicial rhetoric is only beginning to reappear with the revival of Roman law. Yet students practice both these forms of eloquence as school exercises. Of more practical use is the course in letter writing.

Logic, or dialectic, the third subject of the trivium, teaches clear thinking. It leans heavily on Aristotle. Disputation is a teaching method and a pastime. On examination and speech day at a cathedral school, the students may hold competitions in syllogism, fictitious arguments, harangues, and epigrams.

The scientific part of the curriculum, the quadrivium, is not much influenced by the Greek science that scholars and translators are bringing in from the Moslem world. The pupil at the cathedral school absorbs relatively little true scientific knowledge. He may be given a smattering of natural history from the popular encyclopedias of the Dark Ages, based on Pliny and other Roman sources. He may learn, for example, that ostriches eat iron, that elephants fear only dragons and mice, that hyenas change their sex at will, that weasels conceive by the ear and deliver by the mouth.

The most popular subject in the quadrivium is astronomy, a mixture of science and astrology. Arithmetic involves, as earlier, the *computus,* a body of rules for determining the date of moveable feasts. The scholar may also learn the use of the abacus, the computer of the ancient and medieval world. He learns something of the properties of numbers, especially ratio and proportion, and the propositions (without the proofs) of Euclid's first book of geometry. As part of his geometry

course he may acquire some rudiments of geography, studying a map of the world[4] that shows the circular earth composed of three continents equal in size—Asia, Africa, and Europe—separated by narrow bands of water. East is at the top, Jerusalem at the center. In various places on the map one may marvel at dragons, sirens, men with dogs' heads, men with feet turned backward, men with umbrella feet with which they protect themselves from the sun while lying down. It is not a map for finding one's way, but for illustration and edification. More practical and less picturesque maps exist—mariners' charts produced by sailors armed with the newly introduced compass and astrolabe, accurately delineating coastlines, capes, bays, and shallows, and locating ports of call and places for watering and victualing so that a navigator can find them easily. But the schoolboy and his teachers know nothing of such maps.

The science of the thirteenth century, in fact, resides mainly outside the schools. Furriers, trappers, hunters, and poachers could correct much of the natural history in the encyclopedias. The craftsmen who are building the cathedral know geology, engineering, geometry, arithmetic, and mineralogy, and have an intimate acquaintance with nature. The capitals of their piers are decorated with leaves of plantain, ivy and oak, arum, ranunculus, fern, clover, coladine, hepatica, columbine, cress, parsley, strawberry, snapdragon, and broom—all observed with care and recreated with precision. The notebook of the great architect-engineer Villard de Honnecourt is filled not only with columns and vaults, but with animal and even insect life—a lobster, parrots, a snail's shell, a fly, a dragonfly, a grasshopper, not to mention a bear, a lion, a cat, and a swan. Even the gargoyles with which the cathedral workers give an aesthetic justification to their drainspouts reveal a command of animal anatomy.

Many of the businessmen fathers of the cathedral schoolboys are aware of a truly remarkable new piece of learning, a historic advance in the most basic of all sciences, mathematics. Introduced into western Europe from Moslem North Africa, not by a scholar, but by an Italian businessman, it is nothing less than the use of Arabic numbers. Leonard Fibonacci, a Pisan, has written a treatise called *Liber Abaci* popularizing the new system and summarizing the arithmetical knowledge of the Arabs. The numerals (actually Indian in origin) are spreading through the Italian business community. The key to the Hindu-Arabic system is the zero, which permits the position of the digit to indicate its value as unit, ten, hundred, or thousand. Rapid and accurate compu-

The Seasons, *Latinum Codex.*

tation can be done, something difficult with clumsy Roman numbers. The businessmen of Troyes still prefer their calculating boards, but they are familiar with the new notation through their contacts with Italian businessmen and moneychangers at the fairs.

The cathedral school offers no French grammar, composition, or literature, no languages except Latin—not even Greek. It teaches no history, except a bit incidentally in the grammar course, and no science, except a little natural science that emerges from a study of the "authors." Music is taught only as a theoretical science. There are no courses in social science, physical education, or art.

The use of Latin throughout the schools gives a wide currency to ideas and makes sources of culture accessible to everyone, even though students probably never learn to read it as proficiently as their native French, English, or German. Latin is a cultural catalyst, but it is also an impediment to self-expression and communication.

There is no university in Troyes, which is not surprising, since there are only five in northwest Europe,5—at Paris, Orléans, Angers, Oxford, and Cambridge. There are three more in the south of France, eleven in Italy, three in Spain. Of these twenty-two, the two oldest, at Bologna and Paris, are by far the most important. Their precise origins are lost in the twelfth century, but they are true archetypes, for the Greeks and Romans had no universities.

A bright alumnus of the cathedral school at Troyes who wishes to continue his education may journey to Paris, only a hundred miles away. If he does, he will join some two or three thousand young men in the Latin Quarter, who every morning grope their way out of their lodgings to join the crowd of clerical gowns and tonsured heads hurrying to the Street of the Straw, so-named from the floor covering on which students sit all morning. At noon the scholars break for dinner, meeting again in the afternoon for another lecture or a disputation. When the day is over they may turn to studying or copying by candlelight, or, since all forms of athletics, and even chess, are prohibited, to gaming, drinking, and whoring. Although scholars usually enter the university at fourteen or fifteen, their private lives are almost entirely unsupervised. There are no university buildings.6 Classes are held in the masters' houses. Student lodgings, schools, and brothels are cheek by jowl, and sometimes masters and students conduct disputations on the second floor, whores and pimps on the first.

The favorite sport of university students is fighting—with each other, with the townspeople, with the provost's guard. Some of their riots make history, for the University of Paris is by 1250 an institution of formidable stature. A democratic anomaly in the heart of a feudal monarchy, it enjoys remarkable power and prestige and extraordinary privileges. Though it has a charter from the king of France, it is thoroughly international, with some of its most celebrated scholars from Italy, Germany, and England. Pope Innocent III was a master at Paris; Thomas Aquinas is studying there in 1250.

Though the University of Paris is famous for its faculty of theology,7 the learning it transmits to most of its students is more secular than that of the cathedral schools. Aristotle is the supreme text and master. After six years' study a student may face the examiners, and if he passes receive a license to teach. Ultimately he may take orders and become a church official, or a scholarly luminary at this or another University. He may go on to study medicine or law, both lucrative and prestigious professions. He may become a copyist. Or he may enter the service of some prince or baron. For a young burgher of Troyes, the count of Champagne's service is most attractive. He can rise to become bailiff, or keeper of the Fair, with splendid emoluments, not to mention opportunities for graft. Education pays, in the thirteenth as in other centuries.

XII

BOOKS AND AUTHORS

Sire cuens, j'ai vielé
Devant vous en vostre ostel,
Si ne m'avez rien doné
Ne mes gages aquité:
C'est vilanie!
[Sir count, I have played the
viol before you in your house, and
you have given me nought, nor paid my
expenses: 'Tis villainy!]

—COLIN MUSET

A number of students in the twelfth century followed none of the conventional paths. Instead they undertook the footloose and precarious existence of wandering scholars, drifting from one school or one patron to another, passing their days in taverns, living by their wits. Some of them, the so-called "Goliards," contributed to the world's literature a stock of Latin verse of a new kind—lyric, frankly pagan, satirical, and irreverent.

But many of the poets who have created a literary revival in the past century and a half write in the vernacular, especially in one of two varieties of French—Provençal or northern. An important center for the latter is Troyes. Count Henry the Generous and his bluestocking countess, Marie, daughter of Louis VII of France and Eleanor of Aquitaine, patronized a number of poets, of whom the most famous was Chrétien de Troyes. Chrétien's verse tales of the Round Table not only are of high literary merit, but serve as the chief source of all Arthurian romances.

Another sort of Champenois literary production came out of the Fourth Crusade. Geoffroi de Ville-hardouin, marshal of Champagne and native of the neighborhood of Troyes, helped sack Constantinople and afterwards wrote an account of his adventures whose naive vigor and honesty won him a niche in lit-

The Round Table and the Holy Grail from the Gualtier Map in the *Livre de Messire Lancelot du Lac* **(1470).**

spite against him and invaded Champagne, setting haystacks and hovels ablaze. Stopped by the walls of Troyes, they were forced to turn around and go home when a relieving force arrived, sent by Queen Blanche.

Partly as a result of the war, Thibaut was constrained to sell three of his cities—Blois, Chartres and Sancerre—to the king of France. At the last moment he felt a reluctance to hand over Blois, cradle of his dynasty, and carried stubbornness to the point of courting a royal invasion. But forty-six-year-old Blanche of Castile dissuaded thirty-three-year-old Thibaut in an interview of which the dialogue was recorded, or at least reported, by a chronicler:

> *Blanche:* Pardieu, Count Thibaut, you ought to have remembered the kindness shown you by the king my son, who came to your aid, to save your land from the barons of France when they would have set fire to it all and laid it in ashes.

> *Thibaut* (overcome by the queen's beauty and virtue): By my faith, madame, my heart and my body and all my land is at your command, and there is nothing which to please you I would not readily do; and against you or yours, please God, I will never go.

Thibaut's fancy for Blanche needed sublimation. Sage counselors recommended a study of canzonets for the viol, as a result of which Thibaut soon began turning out "the most beautiful canzonets anyone had ever heard" (a judgment in which a later day concurs). The verses of Thibaut the Songwriter were sung by trouvères and jongleurs throughout Europe. A favorite:

> Las! Si j'avois pouvoir d'oublier
> Sa beauté, sa beauté, son bien dire,
> Et son très-doux, très-doux regarder,
> Finirois mon martyre.

> Mais las! mon couer je n'en puis ôter,
>   Et grand affolage
>   M'est d'espérer:
>   Mais tel servage
>   Donne courage
>   A tout endurer.

> Et puis, comment, comment oublier
> Sa beauté, sa beauté, son bien dire,
> Et son très-doux, très-doux regarder?
>   Mieux aime mon martyre.

erature as well as history. Neither a clerk nor a poet, but a plain soldier, Geoffroi wrote in vernacular prose, and so won the distinction of creating the very first masterpiece in French prose.

The present count of Champagne, Thibaut IV, is a poet. Guarded through his minority by his capable mother, Blanche of Navarre, Thibaut grew up to marry, one after the other, a Hapsburg, a Beaujeu, and a Bourbon princess, by whom he had eight children. To these children he added four more, products of his numerous love affairs. But the enduring passion of his life was a chaste one, owing to the inaccessibility of its object, the queen of France. This lady, Blanche of Castile, wife and widow of Louis VIII and mother of Louis IX (St.-Louis), was a dozen years Thibaut's senior. Nevertheless Thibaut's penchant for Blanche was such that he was suspected of poisoning her husband when the king died suddenly. The injustice of the accusation provoked Thibaut to a couple of baronial troublemakers, Hugo of La Marche and Peter of Brittany, in a sort of antiroyal civil war. When on sober second thought Thibaut changed his mind, Hugo and Peter turned their

Could I forget her gentle grace,
Her glance, her beauty's sum,
Her voice from memory efface,
I'd end my martyrdom.

Her image from my heart I cannot tear;
To hope is vain;
I would despair,
But such a strain
Gives strength the pain
Of servitude to bear.

Then how forget her gentle grace,
Her glance, her beauty's sum,
Her voice from memory's efface?
I'll love my martyrdom.

Thibaut is a prince; Chrétien de Troyes was (probably) a clerk; Geoffroi de Villehardouin was a noble. But there is another native Troyen writer, in 1250 just embarking on his career, who is a plain burgher. "Rutebeuf" (Rough-ox) he calls himself, and his verses have little in common with the polished elegance of Chrétien or the tender passion of Thibaut. Rutebeuf describes real life—mostly his own.

Dieus m'a fait compagnon à Job,
Qu'il m'a tolu à un seul cop
    Quanques j'avoie.
De l'ueil destre, dont mieus veoie,
Ne voi je pas aler la voie
    Ne moi conduire...

Car je n'i voi pas mon gaain.
Or n'ai je pas quanques je ain,
    C'est mes domages.
Ne sai ç'a fait mes outrages;
Or devendrai sobres et sages
    Après le fait,
Et me garderai de forfait
Mais ce que vait? Ce est ja fait;
    Tart sui meüs,
A tart me sui aperceüs
Quant je sui en mes las cheüs.
    C'est premier an
Me gart cil Dieus en mon droit san
Qui pour nous ot paine et ahan,
    Et me gart l'ame.

Or a d'enfant geü ma fame;
Mes chevaus a brisié la jame
    A une lice;
Or veut de l'argent ma norrice
Qui me destraint et me pelice
    Pour l'enfant paistre
Ou il revendra braire en l'estre...

God has made me a companion for Job,
Taking away at a single blow,
All that I had.
With my right eye, once my best,
I can't see the street ahead,
Or find my way...

I can't earn a living,
I enjoy no pleasures,
That's my trouble.
I don't know if my vices are to blame;
Now I'm becoming sober and wise,
After the fact,
And will keep from doing wrong,
But what good is that? It's done now.
I'm too late.
I discovered too late
That I was falling into a trap.
It's the first of the year.
May God who suffered pain for us
Keep me healthy.

Now my wife has had a child;
My horse has broken his leg
On a fence,
Now my nurse is asking for money,
She's taking everything I've got
For the child's keep,
Otherwise he'll come back home to yell...

t qui proit sou
ffire a raconter
la charite fer
uante de la q

la voncloe il ama dieu
dune affection tendre
nonques ne le lessa a
amer. mes touz iours

Louis IX (St. Louis) pronouncing judgment by G. Ge Saint Pathus from *Life and Miracles of St. Louis* (12th c.).

Copyist at his desk comparing two books by Jean de Vignay from the original of Vincent of Beauvais (c.1340).

Thibaut and Rutebeuf are not only widely sung and recited, but published. By 1250 books are multiplying spectacularly, even though every single book must be copied by hand. During the Dark Ages book copying took refuge in the monasteries, but now it is back in town. Schools and universities supply a market for textbooks, and copyists are therefore often located in the neighborhood of the cathedral or university, but they do more than copy texts. They also serve as secretaries, both for the illiterate and for those who want a particularly fine handwriting in their correspondence.

A copyist sits in a chair with extended arms across which his writing board is placed, with the sheets of parchment held in place by a deerskin thong. His implements include a razor or sharp knife for scraping, a pumice, an awl, a long narrow parchment ruler, and a boar's tooth for polishing. He works near the fire, or keeps a basin of coals handy to dry the ink, which is held in an oxhorn into which he dips a well-seasoned quill. The oxhorn fits into a round hole in the writing board, with a cover.

The copyist begins by scraping the parchment clean of scales and incrustations, smoothing it with the pumice, and marking out lines and columns with ruler and awl. Then he sets to work. Some of his productions

may be ornate works of art—Latin psalters or French romances, in gold, silver, and purple ink, with initials overlaid with gold leaf. Bound in ivory and metal covers mounted on wood, these elaborate volumes are fabulously expensive. By far the greater number of books consist of plain, legibly written sheets bound in plain wooden boards, perhaps with untooled leather glued over for extra protection. Students often bind several books together under the same covers. Even these cheaper books are expensive, owing not only to the cost of parchment but to the enormous labor involved in their production. It takes about fifteen months to copy the Bible. Books are valuable pieces of property, often pawned, and rented out as well as sold. Students are the chief renters. When a student rents a book he usually does so in order to copy it. He pays rent by the *pecia*—sixteen columns of sixty-two lines, each with thirty-two letters, renting for a penny or halfpenny. An industrious student can create his own library, but it is a work of long night watches. Across the bottom of the last page of many a book is written *Explicit, Deo Gratias* ("Finished, thank God"). Some students end with a more jocular flourish: "May the writer continue to copy, and drink good wine"; "The book finished, may the master be given a fat goose"; "May the writer be given a good cow and a horse"; "For his pen's labor, may the copyist be given a beautiful girl"; "Let the writer be given a cow and a beautiful girl."

Books are kept not on open shelves but in locked chests. Students who borrow are cautioned not to scratch grooves in the margin with their fingernails or to use straws from the lecture floor as placemarks. A Jewish ethical treatise warns that a man must not express his anger by pounding on a book or by hitting people with it. The angry teacher must not hit the bad student with a book, nor should the student use a book to ward off blows.

Despite the cost, books enjoy a wide circulation. An opponent of Abélard noted that "his books cross the sea, pass the Alps . . . are carried through kingdom and province." Normal, or legitimate, book circulation is reinforced by a black market. Many scholars borrow books and surreptitiously copy them. John of Salisbury lent a book to a friend at Canterbury, and later referred to him as "that thief at Canterbury who got hold of the *Policraticus* and would not let it go until he had made a copy." St.-Bernard wrote a would-be borrower, "As regards the book you ask for . . . there is a certain friend of ours who has kept it a long time now, with the same eagerness you show. You shall have it as soon as possible, but although you may read it, I do not allow you to copy it. I did not give you leave to copy the other one I lent you, although you did so."

Copyists are not always accurate. Authors sometimes conclude their books with the injunction: "I adjure you who shall transcribe this book, by our Lord Jesus Christ and by His Glorious coming, Who will come to judge the quick and the dead, that you compare what you transcribe and diligently correct it by the copy from which you transcribe it, and this adjuration also, and insert it in your copy."

Works are seldom composed on parchment. Authors usually write on wax tablets and have their productions copied by scribes. If the work is written in the vernacular, it may be dictated to a scribe, who writes first on wax and copies over on parchment.

Even the most luxurious of the illuminated manuscripts show minor defects. The illuminator does not always leave space for the picture caption, which must be crowded in somehow, often impinging on the text. Against such a contingency, the captions may be lettered in red. Sometimes the illuminator leaves space for a caption which the copyist overlooks. Blank sections of columns—most books are lettered in double columns—show where a copyist finished his assigned section in less space than had been allowed. Now and then words skipped by a careless copyist are inserted in the margin. Sometimes the artist turns such an error into a joke. A verse omitted from the text is added at the top of the page, and the figure of a scribe in the margin tugs at a rope tied to the first letter of the misplaced line, while a second man leans out from the proper space on the page, ready to receive the rope and pull the line into place.

The style of lettering has undergone an important series of changes through the Middle Ages. At the end of the Roman period, Roman square capitals developed into the more casual "rustic" style, out of which slowly grew a small-letter alphabet. The "Caroline minuscule," evolved during Charlemagne's reign at Alcuin's school at Tours, crowned this achievement with an alphabet that clearly differentiated between capitals and small letters, not only in size but in form. At the present moment a new, more elaborate style is sweeping northern Europe: Gothic or black-letter, with stiff, narrow angular letters executed with heavy lines that look black on the page.

Many kinds of books are available from thirteenth-century booksellers,[1] and wealthy individuals, as well as universities, are acquiring libraries.[2] Among the Latin classics there are the antique poets and the more recent didactic poets, the new scientific writings and translations, books of law, such as Justinian's *Code* and *Digest* and the *Decretum* of Gratian; medical books—Galen and Hippocrates, works of theology and philosophy, "vocabularies" (dictionaries of important terms), books of "sentences" (aphorisms), chronicles, encyclopedias, and compilations.

But these weighty volumes in Latin are getting serious competition in French. More and more people want something to read, or especially something to read aloud—and can afford to pay for it. Saints' lives, biographies, *dits* (poems on such everyday subjects as the cries of Paris street peddlers), paraphrases of the stories of antique writers, moralizing poems—all these are popular. The rather tedious *Roman de la Rose* is in great vogue—an allegory by Guillaume de Lorris in which a Lover strives to win his Lady, encouraged and frustrated by various personifications, such as Welcome, Shame, Danger, Reason, Pity. Many works are written more to amuse than correct—such as the *Bible of*

From the *Roman de la Rose*: **Jealousy erects a Fortress, originally written by Guillaume de Lorris and Jean de Meung (c.1230–80).**

Guiot, by a jongleur from Provins, or the *Lamentations of Matthew.*

A series of verse tales known as the *Roman de Renard* has been popular through the twelfth and thirteenth centuries, not only in France, but in Flanders and Rhenish Germany. They are copied over and over by scribes and clerks, in numerous variations. The main characters are Renard the fox, Ysengrin the wolf, Tybert the cat, and King Noble the lion. In a favorite Renard story the fox, stealing chickens from a monastery farmyard, looks into a well and, seeing his own reflection, takes it for his wife Hermeline. Climbing into one of the two buckets that serve the well, he descends, to find nothing but water and stones at the bottom. He struggles in vain to escape. Meanwhile Ysengrin the wolf happens on the well, looks in, and sees his reflection, which he takes for his own wife, Lady Hersent, with Renard at her side. Renard tells him that he is dead, and the well is Paradise. If Ysengrin will confess his sins and climb into the other bucket, he can also achieve the celestial realm, where there are barns full of cows and sheep and goats, and yards full of fat chickens and geese, and woods abounding in game. When Ysengrin jumps into the bucket at the top, he descends while clever Renard ascends and escapes. In the morning when the monks come to draw water, they pull the wolf out and beat him. There is no moral; in the Renard stories wickedness more often triumphs than justice.

Most popular of all are the *fabliaux,*[3] the humorous short stories in verse, sometimes written, sometimes recited. These stories, the product of authors of various social classes, are enjoyed by all kinds of audiences. Some have folk tale origins, some are drawn directly from life. Their common ingredient is humor, often bawdy. Certain characters recur: the merchant, usually older than his wife, cuckolded, swindled, beaten; the young man, often a student, who outwits the husband; the lecherous priest who is his rival. The women, treacherous, lustful, and faithless, may be beaten by their husbands but always manage to get the better of them.

Finally, there are the romances, normally in verse, but sometimes in a combination of verse and prose, or even entirely in prose. Best known of the composers of these courtly tales, after Chrétien de Troyes, is Marie de France, who composed many of her romances (which she called "lays") on Arthurian themes. The authors of many thirteenth-century romances are unknown, but their work is characterized by a high degree of sophistication and realistic detail. Love stories like *Galeran* or

The Kite deal with star-crossed lovers, united in a happy ending; picaresque tales like *Joufroi* carry a knightly hero through various adventures amorous and military, none of which is treated very seriously.

One of the best is the Provençal romance *Flamenca.* At her wedding feast, Flamenca's husband, Archimbaud of Bourbon, sees the king, as he leads her from a tourney, familiarly embrace her, accidentally touching her breast. Archimbaud misinterprets the gesture and is devoured by jealousy. He tears his hair and beard, bites his lips and grits his teeth, eschews society, can finish nothing he starts, understands nothing that is spoken to him, babbles nonsense, and watches his wife all the time. Word spreads about his affliction, and soon all Auvergne is resounding with songs, satires, and sayings on the subject. He grows worse. He ceases to bathe. His beard resembles a badly mowed wheat field; he tears it out in tufts and puts them in his mouth. In short, he is like a mad dog. A jealous man is not wholly sane.

Flamenca's life becomes cruel. Archimbaud has her shut up in a tower with two young servants, Alis and Marguerite, and spies on them by a peephole in the kitchen wall. They are only allowed to leave this prison to go to church on Sundays and feast days, and then Archimbaud forces them to sit in a dark corner, closed off by a thick screen as high as Flamenca's chin. Only when they stand for the reading of the Scripture can they be seen, and instead of letting them go to the altar for Communion, Archimbaud has the priest come to them. Flamenca is not permitted to take off her veil or gloves. Only the little clerk who brings her the book for the Kiss of Peace can see her face.

Two years pass. As it happens, next door to Archimbaud's house is a bathing establishment[4] where he takes his wife on occasion to distract her, always searching the premises first and then standing guard outside. When Flamenca is ready to leave, she rings a bell and her husband opens the door, as usual overwhelming her with reproaches: "Will you be ready to leave this year or the next? I was going to give you some of the wine the host sent me, but I've changed my mind. I won't let you go to the baths again for a year, I assure you, if you drag it out like today." The servants insist that it is their fault; they bathed after Madame. "You like water better than geese," declares the jealous one, biting his nails.

Enter the hero of this piece, a knight named Guillaume de Nevers, handsome, with curly blond hair, a high and broad white forehead, black arched eyebrows, laughing dark eyes, a nose as straight as an arrow shaft, well-made ears, a fine and amorous mouth, a slightly cleft chin, straight neck, broad shoulders and chest, powerful muscles, straight knees, arched and graceful feet. This fine fellow has studied in Paris and is so learned that he could run a school anywhere. He can read and sing better than any clerk; he can fence; he is so agile that he can put out a candle with his foot when the candle is stuck in the wall over his head. Furthermore, he is rich, and he has the tastes of a gentleman—tourneys, dances, games, dogs, and birds. He is generous, too, and always pays more than the asking-price, gives away his profits from tourneys, is liberal with his men. He is more expert at making songs than the cleverest jongleur.

This paragon has never been in love, but he has read the best authors and knows that he must soon have this experience. Hearing of Flamenca's beauty and her misfortunes, he decides that she shall be his lady, and goes to Bourbon full of delicious hopes.

He puts up at the bathing establishment, so that from his window he can gaze up at the tower where Flamenca is imprisoned. He goes to church and impresses everyone by reciting a prayer in which he says the sixty-two names of God, in Hebrew, Greek, and Latin. Flamenca arrives, and when she uncovers her head to receive the holy water, he has a glimpse of her hair; at the reading of the Gospel, when she rises to cross herself, he sees her bare hand and is seized by emotion. A moment later, when the acolyte brings her the breviary to kiss, he sees her mouth. Asking for the book when the service is over, he kisses the same page.

That night in a dream Guillaume discovers what he must do. The next day he rents the entire bathing establishment, explaining that he needs solitude. Everyone else moves out; then he orders workers to dig a tunnel between his apartments and the room where Flamenca bathes. Next he flatters the priest into sending his clerk to Paris to study, and undertakes to serve in his place. Now, Sunday after Sunday, a dialogue takes place. When Guillaume brings Flamenca the breviary to kiss, he sighs, "Alas!" The following week she replies, "Why do you sigh?" The next week, Guillaume tells her, "I am dying."

During that week the tunnel is finished. On Sunday she answers, "Of what?" On Rogation Day, he

says, "Of love"; the following Sunday she asks, "For whom?" On Pentecost he replies "For you." She replies a week later with an ambiguous, "What can I do about it?"

He admires her cleverness and promises "fair Lord God" that he will give all his income in France to the Church and the bridge-building brotherhood if He will let him have Flamenca—he will even give up his place in Paradise.

The dialogue continues. "Cure me," Guillaume demands; on St.-Jean's Day she riposts, "How?" and, in taking the book, brushes his fingers with hers. On Sunday he answers, "I know a way." Flamenca's servants advise her to reply, "Take it"—though she is not sure it is honorable to give in so quickly.

The next day Guillaume tells the host and hostess that they may move back to their bathing establishment. In church Guillaume and Flamenca regard each other tenderly, and he says, "I have taken it." Another month is occupied by the following exchange: "How then?" "You will go." "Where?" "To the baths." "When?" "Soon." She hesitates, in spite of the urgings of her maidens. At last she announces to them, "I will answer yes, for I see that otherwise I could not go on living." Then she faints. Archimbaud runs in with cold water and throws it in her face, and she persuades him that she is ill and needs to visit the baths. The following Sunday, she says a single word: "Yes."

As usual, Archimbaud conducts the three women to the baths and they bar the door after him. At that moment Guillaume raises the stone at the end of the tunnel and appears, candle in hand. He invites the ladies to pass into his apartments through the tunnel. With characteristic thoughtfulness, he has brought two friends, Ot and Clari, for the maidens Alis and Marguerite. For four whole months the six lovers continue to meet. They live in perfect happiness.

Flamenca is now self-confident. She approaches her husband and demands that he restore her liberty on condition that she promises to behave as well as she has up to the present moment. He agrees, washes his head, forgets his functions as turnkey, and becomes once more the man of the world. As a result Flamenca is soon surrounded by ladies and knights, and finds it impossible to visit the baths without at least seven ladies accompanying her. She sends Guillaume away... [5]

qui non abijt in consilio
impiorum & in uia peca
toz non stetit: & in cathe
dra pestilentie non sedit.
Sed in lege domini uo

XIII

THE NEW THEATER

*Paradise is to be made in a raised spot, with curtains and cloths of silk
hung round it . . . Then must come the Saviour clothed in a dalmatic, and
Adam and Eve be brought before him. Adam is to wear a red tunic and Eve a woman's
robe of white, with a white silk cloak; and they are both to stand before the figure . . .
And the Adam must be well trained to speak composedly, and to fit gesture to
the matter of speech. Nor must they foist in a syllable or clip one of the verse,
but must enounce firmly and repeat what is set down for them in due order.*

—STAGE DIRECTIONS FOR LE MYSTÈRE D'ADAM

City people are enjoying a revival in the theater as well as in books. The theater of Greece and Rome was lost with the Dark Ages, but an entirely new drama is growing up in, of all places, the church. With many of its thirty-odd holidays retaining a festive touch of paganism—the Yule log, the pranks and garlands of May Day, the schoolboy games of Shrove Tuesday—the Church has long tolerated a variety of irreverent customs. On the Feast of the Holy Innocents choirboys change places with bishop, dean and other cathedral officials, conduct services, and lead a torchlight procession. The Feast of the Circumcision sees even more unlikely sights as the minor clergy lead an ass into church, drink wine and munch sausages before the altar, wear their vestments inside out and hold their books upside down, while they punctuate the service with heehaws. They sing and dance in the streets, often choosing songs that shock elderly parishioners.

A celebration of holidays in a different spirit has led to the rebirth of the theater. "Troping"—embroidering parts of the service with added words and melodies—especially at Easter and Christmas, is the source of this development. In the ninth century a trope was added to the opening of the Easter service in the form of a dialogue between the three Marys and the angel at the tomb, sung by two halves of the choir, or a soloist and the choir. Soon this trope, which begins *Quem quaeritis in sepulchro?* ("Whom do you seek in the sepulchre?") was transferred to the end of the Easter matin service, and dramatic action was added, with costumes and properties. Next an older ceremony was incorporated; a cross was wrapped in cloth on Good Friday and laid in a small stone sepulchre constructed near the altar, sometimes over the tomb of a wealthy burgher or a noble who provided for it in his will. A lamp was placed and vigil kept until Easter morning, when the cross was removed during matins and laid upon the altar, symbolizing the Resurrection. The *Quem quaeritis* was used at the end of this ceremony, as a climax. New scenes were added, with the apostles Peter and John and Mary Magdalen.

Beatus Page from the Peterborough Psalter.

In its present form, in the thirteenth century, the play is presented at the end of the Easter matin service. A priest representing the angel at the tomb, dressed in white vestments and holding a palm in his hand, quietly approaches the sepulchre. Then the three Marys, also played by priests, two dressed in white and one (Magdalen) in red, their heads veiled, come bearing thuribles with incense, walking sadly and hesitantly, as if looking for something. A dialogue begins, chanted in Latin:

> *The Angel (gently):* Whom do you seek in the sepulchre, O followers of Christ?
>
> *The Three Marys:* Jesus of Nazareth.
>
> *The Angel:* He is not here, He has risen as He prophesied. Go, announce that He is risen from the dead.
>
> *The Three Marys (turning to the choir):* Hallelujah, the Lord is risen today!
>
> *The Angel (calling them back):* Come and see the place. (*He rises and lifts the veil which hides the sepulchre, showing that the cross that represents Christ's body is gone.*)

Now the apostles Peter and John appear, Peter dressed in red and carrying keys, John in white, holding a palm. In accordance with the Gospel, John reaches the sepulchre before Peter, but Peter enters first. He holds up the gravecloth in which the cross was wrapped during the vigil, and a dialogue ensues between the apostles and the three Marys, ending with the antiphon, "The Lord is risen from the tomb," and the placing of the gravecloth upon the altar.

Two of the Marys depart, leaving Mary Magdalen behind at the tomb. The risen Christ appears to her. At first she mistakes him for a gardener, and approaches him weeping; but he warns her, "Touch me not!" With a cry of recognition, she prostrates herself at his feet—a moment of true theater.

The performance ends with the triumphant hymn *Te Deum Laudamus* ("We praise Thee, God"), at the conclusion of which all the bells ring out together.

A Christmas play has evolved in a similar way, starting with another trope, *Quem quaeritis in praesepe?* ("Whom do you seek in the manger?") First it was merely sung by two parts of the choir; then it was dramatized; an Epiphany play of the visit of the Magi was added; and finally a meeting with Herod, the first individualized role in medieval drama. Herod's is a star role, his violent personality suggesting histrionic potential. Episodes of the Slaughter of the Innocents and the lament of Rachel complete the cycle.

Another play sometimes presented during the

Medieval theater scene (11th c).

Christmas season is *The Prophets.* Its origin is not a chant, like that of the Easter and Christmas plays, but a sermon said to have been delivered by St. Augustine, part of which is often used as a lesson for the Christmas offices. In this sermon the lector calls upon the Jews to bear witness to the Christ out of the mouths of their own prophets. He summons Isaiah, Jeremiah, Daniel, Moses, David, Habakkuk, Simeon, Zacharias, Elizabeth, and John the Baptist, and bids each to speak in turn. The reading of the sermon develops into a dramatic dialogue between the priest and the prophets, to which is added a miniature drama of Balaam and the ass. Balaam addresses the ass, "Why do you loiter, obstinate beast? My spurs are splitting your ribs and your belly." The ass, played by a choirboy in a donkey's skin, replies, "I see an angel with a sword before me, forbidding me to pass, and I fear that I will be lost." Sometimes this play about the prophets is tacked on the end of the basic Christmas play. One version brings St. Augustine himself onto the stage, plus a Boy-Bishop, a devil, and a comic Archsynagogus, satirizing the Jewish faith.

All these playlets, growing out of the liturgy and chanted as part of the service, are done entirely in Latin, and so are only visually comprehensible to most of the lay audience. But during the course of the twelfth century passages in the vernacular occurred in several plays, such as the *Raising of Lazarus,* by a pupil of Abélard's named Hilarius, and the Beauvais *Play of Daniel,* one of the masterpieces of medieval drama. The popularity of this innovation doubtless led to the production, late in the century, of the first play (at least the first to survive) written entirely in French, *Le Mystère d'Adam.* Widely played at Easter throughout the thirteenth century, *Adam* retains Latin only in the stage directions and a few interpolations. As if to symbolize its liberation from the liturgy, the play is performed in the open air, outside the church. A platform built on the church steps serves as stage, an arrangement which allows the church itself to represent the dwelling of God. The verses are no longer chanted, but recited. The first scene is Paradise, strewn with flowers and greenery and trees with fruit hung from their branches. A "Figure" representing an abstraction of God appears, and Adam and Eve are brought before him, Adam wearing a red tunic and Eve a white dress with a white mantle. They stand before God, Adam with calm visage, Eve with a more modest air.

The lesson is read in Latin: "In the beginning God created Heaven and earth, and created man in His own image and after His likeness." The choir then chants, again in Latin: "And the Lord God formed man of the dust of the ground, and breathed into his nostrils the breath of life, and man became a living soul."

Now the dialogue begins, in French. God instructs Adam and Eve in their duties and leads them into Paradise, where He points out the forbidden fruit, then retires into the church, leaving Adam and Eve to walk about Paradise in delight. But a pack of demons run out on the stage with grotesque gestures, approaching Paradise from time to time and slyly pointing out the forbidden fruit to Eve. The Devil himself appears, confronts Adam, and tempts him to pick the fruit, but Adam remains firm. With downcast countenance the Devil retreats to the doors of Hell, where he holds council with the other demons. Then he makes a sally among the audience, stirring a noisy reaction, and returns to Paradise, this time addressing Eve. With smiling face and flattering air, he tells her that she is more intelligent than Adam. Eve replies that Adam is a little hard. "Though he be harder than Hell," the Devil promises, "he shall be made soft." He praises her beauty. "You are a gentle and tender thing, fresh as a rose, white as crystal . . . You are too tender and he is too hard. But nevertheless you are wiser and more courageous . . ."

Eve makes a show of resistance. The Tempter departs. Adam, who has been watching mistrustfully, reproaches her for listening. Now a serpent rises by the trunk of the forbidden tree. Eve puts her ear to his mouth, then takes the fruit and presents it to Adam. He eats, realizes his sin, and throws himself on his knees. Out of sight behind the curtain, he puts off his red tunic and dons a garment of fig-leaves. He rises and begins his lament. When God reappears, Adam and Eve hide in a corner of Paradise, and when called upon they rise but crouch in shame and weep. They confess their sin, Adam blaming his error on Eve, Eve on the serpent.

God pronounces his curse on them and on the serpent, and drives them out of Paradise, barring the gate with an angel dressed in white who bears a shining sword in his hand. God withdraws into the church.

Adam takes up a spade and Eve a hoe, and they begin to cultivate the earth and sow it with wheat. After they have sown, they sit down to rest, gazing at Paradise and weeping. While they are thus occupied, the Devil sneaks in, plants thorns and thistles in their garden, and escapes. When they see the thorns and thistles, they are smitten with grief and throw themselves on the ground, beating their breasts, and once more Adam reproaches Eve. Now the Devil reenters with three or four of his demons, carrying iron chains and fetters, which they place on the necks of Adam and Eve. The luckless pair are hauled off toward Hell (underneath the platform), from which other demons come to meet them, reveling at their perdition. Smoke arises, the devils exclaim in glee, clashing pots and kettles, and caper about the stage.

This is the favorite part of the play for the audience. There are two more brief acts, one the story of Cain and Abel, who are also dragged off to Hell at the end, the demons beating Cain as they go but treating Abel somewhat more gently. Finally, there is a brief version of *The Prophets,* which winds up the entertainment.

A trouvère from Arras named Jean Bodel has gone still further in removing drama from the church. His *Play of St. Nicholas,* written at the beginning of the thirteenth century, is based on one of the legends of that saint in which he is entrusted with the treasure of a rich man (in this case a pagan king, who becomes a Herod-figure of violent speech and gesture); thieves steal the treasure and St. Nicholas restores it. This simple story is developed into a full-length play with colorful and individualized characters. The thieves are given picturesque names—Click, Pinchdice, Razor—and roles to match. Another play believed to be written by Bodel, *Le Courtois d'Arras,* is a version of the story of the Prodigal Son, with Arras as its background. Both plays are set in the streets and taverns of a thirteenth-century town, with innkeepers, thieves, and other real-life figures.

With plays staged outside the church, with dialogue the audience can understand and scenes that are more and more secular, the theater has outgrown its confining cradle.[1] Though for a long time to come it will draw heavily on religion for its themes, it now stands on its own feet as an independent art.

XIV

DISASTERS

Pestilence ravaged the country that year; many were consumed inwardly by the sacred fire;
their bodies rotted; their entrails turned black as coal; they died miserably or had
the even worse misfortune to live after having lost feet and hands to gangrene,
and finally many were cruelly tortured by a contraction of nerves.

—SIGEBERT DE GEMBLOUX

ew Troyens alive in 1250 remember the decade of the 1180s, but everybody has heard tales of it. In a space of eight years three of the five major disasters that commonly befall medieval cities struck Troyes. In 1180 the Seine overflowed its banks in the worst flood recorded in the city's annals, inundating streets and houses and taking a heavy toll of people and animals. Four years later a crop failure in Champagne resulted in one of the worst famines the city has ever experienced. Finally, one night in 1188 fire broke out in the fair quarter near the Abbey of Notre-Dame-aux-Nonnains, crossed the canal to the old *cité,* gutted the cathedral and the new church of St.-Etienne, damaged the count's palace, razed the public baths, destroyed hundreds of houses, and consumed thousands of pounds' worth of fair merchandise.

Famine of 1335 grain distribution in the Orsanmichele in the *Biadiolo Codex* (The Grainmerchant) by Domenico Lenzi (14th c.).

Precautions against these recurring disasters are totally inadequate. Crop surpluses are never enough to make possible a rational system of storage. Even great lords cannot put aside enough grain to carry them through a famine. The Lord of Brienne, scion of a famous Crusading family, was reduced by the famine of 1184 to robbing the Abbey of St.-Loup, something, he confessed later, "which I ought not to have done, but it was to provision my castle."

The first effects of a food shortage are rumors, hoarding, and black-marketing. The prices of both grain and bread are regulated in ordinary times, and even the size and weight of the round loaf. But bakers have many tricks for reducing the actual content of the standard loaf, and when grain is in short supply they are not slow to use them. Worse than the bakers are the speculators, who evade laws limiting the amount of grain a single individual can purchase, and who illegally buy up from farmers before the grain reaches the city market. The council and the provost may take extraordinary measures, and if the shortage is severe and prolonged, speculators dangle from the gallows. During a famine the clergy parade the relics of the cathedral. The knot of beggars at the church door grows into a crowd, and churchgoers must force their way through the whining, hand-stretching throng of men, women and children.

Famine is often accompanied by its sister, pestilence. Even a merely severe winter often leaves a city population prey to mysterious maladies, such as the scurvy that decimated St.-Louis' Crusading army in Egypt. Epidemic afflictions of skin, mouth, lungs, and other organs, such as that chronicled by Sigebert de Gembloux in Champagne and Flanders in 1089, recur unpredictably. The fourteenth century will experience a visitation of the Black Plague beside which all previous contagions will seem mild.

As for floods, inland Troyes is lucky in comparison with cities situated on larger rivers or in exposed coastal regions. The cities of the medieval Netherlands undergo repeated devastation despite their dikes. Once a storm finds a weak or low dike, the reciprocal flow of the tides through the hole swiftly widens the gap. The death toll for one thirteenth-century Dutch flood is over fifty thousand.

Open-flame illumination and heating make fire a year round hazard in every section of town. The cheek-by-jowl timber-frame dwellings and shops, sometimes sharing party walls, form a perfect avenue for the flames. Householders are theoretically forbidden to have straw roofs or wooden chimneys, but even these elementary precautions are hard to enforce. An effective measure, stone party walls, has been thought of, but only the rich can afford to build in stone. Buckets of sand and tubs of water quench many fires in early stages, but once furnishings, floors, and partitions take flame little can be done except to pray, and form a bucket brigade—measures about equally effective. If the season is wet and the wind from the right direction, damage may be limited to a few houses or a single street. If the season is dry and the wind fresh and contrary, a large part of a city may be doomed.

The chronicle that records the fire of 1188 gives few details except for the fact that the Devil made an appearance in Troyes shortly beforehand, and was exorcised by a priest with a vial of holy water. But a vivid account of a fire of the same era is that of Gervaise, a monk of Canterbury, in 1174:

> At about the ninth hour, during an extraordinarily violent south wind, a fire broke out . . . by which three houses were half-destroyed. While the citizens were assembling and bringing the fire under control, cinders and sparks carried aloft by the wind

were deposited upon the church, and being driven between the joints of the lead roof, remained there among the old timber rafters, to which they soon set fire; from these the fire was communicated to the larger beams and braces, no one yet perceiving. . . .

> But beams and braces burning, the flames rose to the top of the roof; and the sheets of lead yielded to the increasing heat and began to melt. Thus the raging wind, finding a freer entrance, increased the fairy of the fire; and the flames beginning to show themselves, a cry arose in the churchyard: "The church is on fire!"

> Then the people and the monks assemble in haste, they draw water, they brandish their hatchets, they run up the stairs, full of eagerness to save the church, already, alas, beyond help. When they reach the roof and perceive the black smoke and scorching flames that pervade it throughout, they abandon the attempt in despair, and thinking only of their own safety, make all haste to descend.

> And now that the fire had loosened the beams from the pegs that bound them together, the half-burnt timbers fell into the choir below upon the seats of the monks; the seats, consisting of a great mass of woodwork, caught fire, and thus the mischief grew worse and worse. . . .

> And now the people ran to the ornaments of the church, and began to tear down the *pallia* and curtains, some that they might save, some to steal them. The reliquary chests were thrown down from the high beam and thus broken, and their contents scattered; but the monks collected them and carefully preserved them against the fire. . . .

> Not only was the choir consumed in the fire, but also the infirmary, with the chapel of St. Mary, and several other offices in the court; moreover many ornaments and goods of the church were reduced to ashes.

Besides these peacetime calamities, there is always the possibility of war. Here at least people in the city enjoy an advantage over the peasants in the villages. When the feudal army rides, it sets fire to everything it cannot carry off, but the walls of a city like Troyes are nearly always proof against such depredations. The besieging army of Hugo of La Marche and Peter of Brittany was easily held at bay outside Troyes in 1230. Even an enemy armed with a formidable array of siege engines and missile weapons has a difficult time break-

Attack on a town from *Li Romans de Godefroi de Buillon et de Salehadin* (14th c.).

ing into a walled city. A feudal army can rarely be kept in the field longer than a month or two. The military obligation of vassals does not extend further, and mercenary troops are too expensive for any but a very wealthy prince bent on a highly important objective, such as a Crusade. Ordinarily, the attacker must within the limits of a short campaign muster either an overwhelming assault force to scale the walls at many points simultaneously, or a powerful enough battery of siege engines to knock down walls or gates. He has a third alternative, if the ground is favorable, and if the defense is insufficiently alert: mining.

The overwhelming assault force may prevail when the stronghold under attack is a castle with a weak garrison. A tightly-packed city of ten thousand citizens, like Troyes, is unlikely to succumb even to a very large storming party, because there are enough men night and day to keep an alert guard at every point of the two-thousand-yard rampart. When the assault force approaches, under cover of a "castle," or moveable wooden platform, to fill in the ditch around the walls and plant scaling ladders, the garrison can quickly concentrate at the threatened point or points. Lofty walls, and especially round towers, give the defenders all the advantage in the contest of arrows, bolts, and missiles. Combustibles can be flung down on the attackers' castle, and even if some of the storming party gain a foothold on the wall, they can be isolated by the fire from the neighboring towers, for the space in front of the wall is always kept clear of any cover. The towers

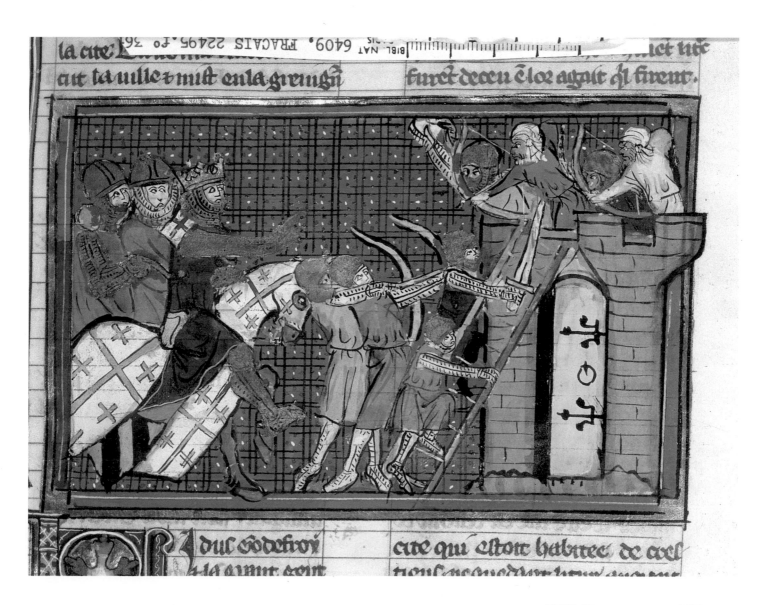

project, so that they can bring flanking fire to bear on attackers scaling the wall.

The old-fashioned Roman siege engines have been much improved. The Romans employed only tension and torsion as motive power. Medieval military engineers have added the counterweight, which provides both more power and greater accuracy. A trebuchet, or counterweight engine consists of a long firing pole balanced on a pivot, or cross-pole, in turn mounted on a pair of uprights. The firing pole is not set on its mid-point, but on a point about a quarter from its butt end, which is faced toward the enemy. The long end is pulled down, the missile placed in a cavity or sling, and secured by a wooden catch worked by a winch, while the butt end is loaded with wedge-shaped weights of iron or stone. When the catch is released, the counterweight drops, sending the missile flying. On more sophisticated models, the counterweight can be moved closer or farther from the pivot, increasing or decreasing the range. A couple of zeroing-in shots permit a good engineer to fire with considerable accuracy. The missile is ordinarily a heavy stone, though variants include combustible materials and occasionally the heads of enemies. Some military experts prefer a simpler model of counterweight engine, worked by ropes pulled down by men. This is inferior in range and accuracy, but it has the advantage of being highly maneuverable, so that several may be quickly brought to bear on a single weak point in the enemy's defenses.

Artillery, however, is no monopoly of the attackers. In the crypts of the towers of Troyes' ramparts, a great number of dismantled engines stand ready for assembly, together with a supply of stone ammunition.

How effective catapult artillery is against a stone wall depends on the wall. Some old walls, made of a thin shell of rough-cut stone covering an earth core, can be battered to pieces. But a good modern wall, laid in even courses locked into a rubble core, can defy all the engines an enemy can bring to bear, as has been repeatedly demonstrated by the redoubtable though weakly garrisoned Crusader forts in Syria.

The attackers' third alternative, mining, is the most promising, provided soft ground can be found. Against a castle it is particularly effective, because the mine can be driven under either a section of the wall or under the main keep. No explosive is involved—the mine is "discharged" simply by setting fire to the tim-

bering which supports the mine roof. As the timbers burn, the ground above collapses. At one siege in Syria the Saracen engineers first undermined and collapsed a tower in the curtain wall. But the garrison, composed of Knights of St. John, successfully fought off the subsequent assault and reestablished the barricade in the rubble of the tower. The Saracens then dug a mine into the interior of the castle, directly under the keep, and invited the Franks to send their own engineers to inspect it. When the Frankish engineers reported back that the discharge of the mine would cause the certain collapse of the keep, the Knights agreed to surrender on terms—marching out and abandoning the castle to the Saracens.

The proper defense against the mine is the countermine. Ten years ago a memorable duel of mine and countermine took place between defending and attacking engineers at Carcassonne. The seneschal of the city, William des Ormes, reported that the Albigensian rebels, under Raymond Trencavel, viscount of Béziers, found their siege artillery of little avail and so switched to mining.

> The rebels began a nine against the barbican [fortified tower] of the gate of Narbonne [wrote the seneschal]. And forthwith we, having heard the noise of their work underground, made a countermine, and constructed in the inside of the barbican a great and strong wall of stones . . . so that we retained full half the barbican when they set fire to the hole so that when the wood burned a portion of the front of the barbican fell.

> They then began to mine against another turret . . . We countermined, and got possession of the hole which they had excavated. They began therefore to run a mine between us and a certain wall and destroyed two embrasures . . . But we set up there a good and strong palisade between us and them.

> They also started a mine at the angle of the town wall, near the bishop's palace, and by dint of digging from a great way off they arrived at a certain wall . . . but when we detected it we made a good and strong palisade between them and us, higher up, and countermined. Thereupon they fired their mine and flung down some ten fathoms of our embrasured front. But we made hastily another good palisade with a brattice and loopholes, so none among them dared to come near us in that quarter.

They began also a mine against the barbican of be Rodez gate, and kept below ground, wishing to arrive at our walls, making marvelous great tunnel. But when we perceived it we forthwith made a palisade on one side and the other of it. We countermined also, and having fallen in with them, carried the chamber of their mine.

Altogether the assailants drove seven different mines, starting from the cellars of houses in the suburb outside. A final attempt to storm the barbican failed, and the approach of a royal relieving army forced Trencavel to raise the siege.

This was an exceptionally determined effort. In the skirmishing warfare more normal in the thirteenth century, a walled city can usually assure its safety merely by closing its gates on the approach of an enemy force.

XV

TOWN GOVERNMENT

*"I am a good lawyer," said Renard. "Often I've made right out of wrong
and wrong out of right, as it suited me."*

—ROMAN DE RENARD

Medieval cities enjoy a great deal of individual liberty, varying degrees of self-government, and little democracy. Their charters, many of which were written in the twelfth century, are principally grants of freedom from feudal obligations—the head tax, the labor service, the tax at will, the marriage tax—in return for payment of a cash impost. Limits are set for their military service, they are allowed to operate their own law courts for lesser crimes ("low justice") and, usually, they are permitted a mayor and council.

The charter is essentially a compact between the burghers and their seigneur, or a contract for which the commune is the collective bargaining agent.

The mayor and council may be elected by the heads of the corporations (masters of the guilds), or they may simply replace themselves at intervals by "co-optation," that is, by naming their own successors. Whatever the method, the result is to place town government in the hands of wealthy burghers closely allied in interest to their prince. Typically a small number of families monopolize political power.

In Venice twenty-seven families supply half the member of the 480-man Grand Council. Some families are represented on the same city council for generations and even centuries. The Lanstiers sat on the town council of Arras for three hundred years. The more sophisticated the town's economic life, the more it participates in international commerce, the more this oligarchic tendency is exaggerated. In Pisa thirty families monopolize the government throughout the thirteenth century.

The commune of Troyes does not include everyone who lives in the city. It is restricted to the "Third Estate"—merchants and craftsmen. Knights who have houses in town may not belong. The clergy too—bishop, abbot, canons, priests and monks—are excluded. But if a knight or a clerk goes into business, not only may he join, he must. On the other hand, members of the commune do not necessarily live in the city; some live in the suburbs but do business in the city.

Members of a commune invariably take an oath,

**The First Lord Mayor of London, Henry Fitzailwin
(d.1216). Aquatint by W. Woodcock.**

331

swearing on the relics that they will faithfully guard the life and possessions of their dear lord, his lady, and his children, and sustain them against all men and women whomsoever, and at the same time be loyal to every member of the commune, not aid foreigners against the burghers, obey the mayor, pay their part of the debts of the city, and be good and loyal burghers.

Under the mayor and the town councillors serve a bureaucracy of officials, treasurers, clerks, and magistrates. The town watch guards the ramparts by day and patrols the streets by night. In case of attack, the watch is supplemented by the whole militia. Often a charter specifies that "all who have sworn the communal oath must join the defense, none may remain at home, except one sick, infirm or so poor that he must himself take care of his sick wife or children."

Nearly all charters promise the seigneur *ost et chevauchée* (military service) but on varying terms. That of Troyes exempts moneychangers and fair merchants while the fair is taking place. Laon, whose charter was one of the earliest in northwest Europe, owes a fixed quota: one hundred and twenty foot sergeants and three wagons. Arras has a more advanced arrangement: the town is obligated to supply either a thousand foot sergeants or three thousand livres, a cash sum sufficient to hire a thousand soldiers for the summer. Many towns have demanded and won geographical and political limits to their military service. The citizens of Brai-sur-Somme are required to march only in case of general war or an expedition for the faith, and for either purpose no farther than Reims and Châlons, Tournai and Paris, at their own expense. Men of Poitiers do not have to cross the Loire, those of Chaumont and Pontoise can stop at the edge of the Seine or the Oise.

Recently a new turn has been given to the question of military service. With the growth of proletarian discontent many towns are taking care to restrict the privilege of arms to the wealthy. In Troyes only those citizens possessing *vingt livres vaillant* ("twenty pounds' worth of property") are authorized to own a crossbow and fifty bolts.

Of the two aspects of the charter, individual liberty and self-government, the former is much the more important. The constitutional history of Troyes is a vivid illustration of this fact of medieval life. Though traces of town government appeared in the late twelfth and early thirteenth century, Troyes apparently did not receive a charter until 1230, when Thibaut the Songwriter, financially embarrassed by his war with Peter of Brittany and Hugo of La Marche, signed a formal guarantee of the citizens' ancient privileges and in addition established a Town Council. The councilmen, thirteen in number, were appointed directly by Thibaut; from their company they elected a mayor. The council's function was, quite baldly, to raise money. Members of the commune of Troyes, freed from all servile imposts, were required to pay a fixed annual cash levy, based on the amount of their property. The *taille* (tax) was assessed at a rate of six deniers per livre on moveable property,

Allegories of Equity and Felony by Frere Laurent, illuminated by the Maitre Honore from *La Somme Le Roy* (13th c.).

significant provisions of the Magna Carta protects the English barons against loss of their lucrative courts to the king. Like most charters, that of Troyes of 1230 reserved for the count "high justice"—jurisdiction over murder, rape, and robbery. He was also awarded two-thirds of the fines for false measure—an important matter in a fair town—and all cases concerning his churches, knights, fiefs, and Jews. For a yearly cash payment he relinquished other kinds of justice to the town.

In Champagne, cases reserved for the count are heard by his provost. This office is usually filled by a burgher, who works on a commission basis, pocketing a share of the fines he levies. A provost is usually not above accepting gifts, though the practice is officially frowned on. For many of the offenses he tries the penalty is death and confiscation of property. A murderer with wealthy relatives stands a better chance of escaping the gallows than a poor man—a situation not confined to the Middle Ages.

Hanging is a painful death, because the drop technique has not yet been invented, and death comes by strangulation. Torture is rarely employed. If the provost feels it is necessary to extort a confession, he may have a prisoner's teeth extracted, or have him toasted over a fire, or given a stretch on the rack. But few provosts are so fastidious as to insist on a confession. They prefer to listen to the evidence and give the word to the hangman. Traitors, witches, and heretics are burned at the stake, executions in the latter two categories being accompanied by numerous prayers. On the other hand, thieves may be let off with a taste of the branding iron, or a lopped-off hand, and youthful first offenders may escape with a flogging. It even happens that a poor man who steals a shirt is freed after a brief imprisonment on the grounds that he is ill and the offense is small. The crypt under the old castle is used for confinement of those awaiting trial. Actual prison sentences are rare.

The town tries cases involving petty theft, fraud, and minor assault. It also hears litigation concerning commercial transactions and property. The mayor and four or five councilmen act as judges, listening to the evidence and delivering their verdict unanimously. A few typical recorded cases[1] give the flavor of thirteenth-century urban court problems:

A burgher has discovered some silver wine cups belonging to him in the possession of another towns-

two deniers per livre on real estate. It was the job of the mayor and council to obtain a sworn statement from each burgher of the precise value of his property. But the richest burghers, among whom the councilmen were doubtless numbered, did not have to make such a statement; they were permitted the option of paying a flat rate of twenty livres.

The tax system specified by the charter of Troyes has been popular for some time, but by mid-century two other kinds of taxation have appeared: the cash poll tax and the sales tax. All three reflect the changing fiscal situation, in which sovereign counts, dukes, and kings are succeeding in touching the rapidly growing liquid wealth of the city burghers. The petty lords of the countryside have no such sources of income, and so are losing ground financially to the heads of incipient national states.

Another major source of revenue is the cause of violent wrangling among the competing authorities. This is justice. Whoever administers justice keeps the fines and forfeits, so kings, counts, barons, bishops, and burghers quarrel jealously, over jurisdiction. One of the

Kneeling crusader with his horse, Westminster Psalter (English, 12th c.).

man, who proves that he purchased them from a tin merchant, who in turn declares that he bought them from a fourth man. Hauled into court, the fourth man swears that he is "pure and innocent," the unvarying formula of the accused, and calls to witness the uprightness and honesty of his life. He is not, however, able to give a convincing account of how he came into possession of the cups, which are ordered returned to the rightful owner. The accused man is sent to the crypt until the judges can hear further witnesses. A woman whose son has been hanged for fatally assaulting another young man in a tavern by bashing his head with a heavy flagon is accused by the victim's relatives of instigating the crime. They want a money payment, but are disappointed. The mayor after due deliberation declares the woman innocent. A knight who owns a house on which the tenant has not paid any rent for a year demands permission to seize the tenement's doors and shutters, which is granted, with a fraction of the sale going to the court. A woman who keeps a lodging house is summoned for creating a "vile nuisance." She has had a wooden pipe built from the privy chamber of her house to the gutter, rendering it evil-smelling and sometimes blocking it up. The neighbors bring her into court where she is fined six deniers and ordered to remove the pipe within forty days.

Civil and criminal law are not yet clearly distinguished. Traces of the old Germanic custom, by which every offense was personal, and murderers paid money ransoms to the relatives of their victims, survive in the mid-thirteenth century. It is difficult to prosecute a felon without the testimony of his victim or his victim's relatives, and sometimes a killer can still buy his freedom by compensating the family (paying *wergild*).

Together with this view of crime as a civil offense, the early Middle Ages also preserved the barbarian customs of duel and ordeal. By 1250 judicial duel is officially forbidden nearly everywhere but is still widely practiced. Even peasants often settle their disputes with cudgels. Legal or not, the loser or his family must pay a heavy fine, and if the quarrel is settled before the combat takes place, fines must still be paid, so that the seigneur does not lose his profit.

But trial by ordeal has fallen into disrepute. Formerly a man was allowed to prove his innocence by thrusting his hand into hot water, or picking up a hot iron, or risking drowning. But in the view of the thirteenth century, sensibly expressed by Frederick II, the ordeal "is not in accord with nature and does not lead to truth... How could a man believe that the natural heat of glowing iron will become cool or cold without an adequate cause... or that because of a seared conscience the element of cold water will refuse to accept the accused?... These judgments of God by ordeal which men call 'truth-revealing' might better be called 'truth-concealing.'"

Roman law is slowly superseding *wergild,* as well as duel and ordeal; court trial, examination of witnesses under oath, and even the use of trained lawyers are becoming more common. Rediscovery of such collections as the *Digest* of Justinian has led to a renaissance of law, coinciding with the more sophisticated needs of reviving commercial life. The markets and fairs, and especially the Fairs of Champagne, have given a powerful impetus to the development of merchants' law.

There is a third law court in most towns—that of the bishop. Here again revenue is of prime importance, and the bishop will fight with every weapon in his spiritual arsenal to defend his court against encroachment from town or provost. Even a clerk in minor orders who has no intention of becoming a priest can insist on being tried in the ecclesiastical court, where he is certain to be more gently treated than by town magistrate or provost. In the bishop's court the law is a composite of Scripture, oral tradition, precedents in Roman and Germanic law, decrees of Church councils, and legislation by the Pope. The celebrated Gratian brought this hodgepodge into an orderly system in the twelfth century, and at the same time founded a whole methodology by posing one text against another and reconciling them.

Roman law is now taught in law schools at Montpellier, Orléans, Angers, Bologna, Reggio, and other places, but Paris teaches only canon law. Lawyers are not particularly popular. Their pretensions are resented, and their pedantic interpretations irritate everyone. They insist on exact forms and formulas. But they are improving the administration of justice and pointing the way to guarantees for the accused that a future age will regard as indispensable.

A jurisdictional dispute among the courts of a town sometimes becomes a bigger legal cause than the case that was originally to be tried. In 1236 the mayor and councillors of Laon imprisoned three men who the canons of the cathedral thought should be tried in the ecclesiastical court. The town officials refused to hand over the prisoners, whereupon the canons issued bans of excommunication against the councillors. But the parish priest to whom the bans were given sided with the town and refused to publish them. The canons excommunicated the priest. Priest and townsmen took the case all the way to Rome and won a favorable judgment, enforced by a papal excommunication against the canons. The same priest savored the revenge of entering the church at Vespers, lighted candle in hand, pronouncing the sentence, and turning the candle upside down.

Many regions are beginning to enjoy a medieval advance in jurisprudence—the court of appeals. The Parlement of Paris and the Parliament of London are two of the most famous. Another is taking shape in Troyes—the Council and Tribunal of the Count of Champagne, meeting from time to time in the *Grands Jours de Troyes*. In its origins no more than the count's court sitting in judicial session, it will develop into a regularly appointed body of chief vassals, leading burghers and prelates, and will serve as trial court for the nobility and appeals court for the lower classes.

The Charter of 1230 may have sufficed for Thibaut's financial needs in 1230, but a little more than a decade later it no longer did. Probably the minor Crusade of 1239, in which Thibaut distinguished himself, plunged him into fresh debts. In any case the mayor and council proved incapable of raising enough money for their sovereign, and so without ceremony he turned them out of office. In their place he installed a group headed by an enterprising Cahorsin financier named Bernard de Montcuc, who had arrived in Troyes some years earlier as a moneychanger. Together with his associates, who included two of his brothers, Bernard undertook to advance Thibaut four thousand three hundred pounds *(livres Tournois)* a year for five years—a thousand at the Hot Fair, two thousand at the Cold Fair, and the remainder at the Fair of Bar-sur-Aube. With these loans Thibaut could pay off his debts and presumably have enough to live on. Bernard and his consortium were repaid by two means: first, a special sales tax over the five-year period levied at four deniers per livre (one-sixtieth) on all merchandise sold in Troyes, and second,

Monzon Castle, a Knights Templars stronghold in Huesca, Spain.

The illuminated manuscript illustration contains the following medieval French text:

nepueu de leuefque le conte de falmes et fon
filz furent pris et plufs autres nobles qui eftoi
ent de la partie de leuefque mais ilz furent af
fes toft deliures de prifon par paiant vne grät
fome dargent. De la mort du maiftre du tem
ple.

Acft an auffi ou mops de mars
ou temps de karefme le general
maiftre du temple et vn autre
grant maiftre apres lui en lordre fi cöme len dit
vifiteur. a paris en lifle deuant les auguftins
furent ars et ramenes en poudre mais cöme
onques fourfaiz noient nulle recognoiffä
ce. Lan de grace mil ccc. xiiii. enfuiuant

Jacques de Molay, last leader of the Knights Templars burned at the stake for heresy (1314) on orders of Phillip IV, the Fair. From *Chronicle of France or of St. Denis* (14th c.).

the farming out of low justice. As a sop to the businessmen of Troyes, those paying the sales tax were exempted from military service. To clear the way for these revenues politically, Thibaut appointed Bernard and his friends to serve in turn as mayors throughout the emergency.

Thus in Thibaut's view the government of Troyes is little more than a money-raising agency. Though the Troyes burghers doubtless grumbled at first, their acceptance of the Montcuc scheme and their generally passive attitude toward the charter indicate a lethargy toward political affairs that differentiates them sharply from most other townsmen. In many cities charters have been won after violence and bloodshed, and once won are jealously guarded. The difference in the Troyen attitude is unquestionably a reflection of the vast advantages accru-

Jacques de Molay, last leader of the Knights Templars burned at the stake for heresy (1314) on orders of Phillip IV, the Fair. From *Chronicle of France or of St. Denis* (14th c.).

ing to the burghers of Troyes from their fairs. Though their political liberties have proved illusory, their individual liberties are genuine. They possess freedom without self-government, and as long as the fairs prosper they will be satisfied.

Troyes is not the only town to suffer from a prince's follies, and at the head of the list of princely follies stands Crusading. Burgher discontent has played a major role in the decline of the Crusading business since Peter the Hermit. In 1095 idealism caused many people to do foolish things, but by the thirteenth century ordinary people have lost their appetite for warfare, while princes and barons have grown more cautious about selling estates to equip armies. Nowadays only princes who can exact large contributions from their towns can think about Crusading. In most of France and Flanders the principal form of such contributions is the feudal "aid," originally a gift to a lord on the occasion of a daughter's marriage or a son's knighting—a ham from one peasant, a sack of grain from another. In the more affluent, urbanized society of the thirteenth century, the aid is a cash payment. When a sovereign requests it, his towns must assess themselves. No town is happy about an aid, and some find it thoroughly objectionable. Douai, in Flanders, paid 32,600 livres over a period of twenty years for a variety of needs and extravagances of its counts and countesses. Noyon went bankrupt, the goods of its burghers being seized to pay creditors.

Two years ago, in 1248, Louis IX, valiant and devout king of France, went on Crusade. The king's idealism about the Holy Land was shared by few of his subjects or peers. Some two thousand eight hundred knights and eight thousand foot sergeants were recruited, nearly all on a mercenary basis. Jean de Joinville, seneschal of Champagne, accompanied the king, who was a personal friend, with reluctance. Later he described his departure from home: "I never once let my eyes turn back towards Joinville, for fear my heart might be filled with longing at the thought of my beautiful castle and the two children I had left behind." The happiest result of the expedition, in fact, is Joinville's own memoir of it, which adds a leaf to Troyes' literary laurels. After a rather brilliant beginning, in a successful amphibious assault on Damietta, the expedition bogged down in the swampy upriver country around the fortress city of Mansourah. Famine and scurvy turned the camp into a hospital and charnel house, and the survivors were easily taken prisoner by the Saracens. The queen ransomed the king by trading Damietta, after which Louis ransomed Joinville and the other knights by paying four hundred thousand livres. Originally the sultan demanded five hundred thousand, but when the king unhesitatingly agreed, the equally chivalrous sultan knocked off a hundred thousand livres, commenting, "By Allah, this Frank does not haggle!"

The money was raised on the spot by a bit of pressure on the wealthy Knights Templar, but is now in the process of being paid by the king's subjects, mainly the burghers of his cities, already touched for sizeable aids, and facing still more bills for Louis' new fortifications in Syria. It is hardly surprising that quite a few burghers identify themselves with the wrong side of the debate between Crusaders and non-Crusaders that is a favorite subject of the trouvères. They feel that after all, "it is also a good and holy thing to live quietly at home, in friendship with neighbors, taking care of children and goods, going to bed early and sleeping well." If the sultan of Egypt should take it into his head to invade France, they will be ready to pay an aid, and take up their pikes and crossbows besides. But they do not see the wisdom of journeying far over the sea to die, and die expensively at that.

XVI

THE CHAMPAGNE FAIR

There are ten fairs in the land of France,
One at Bar, another at Provins,
Another at Troyes and a fourth at Lendit,
And three in Flanders, and the eighth at Senlis,
The ninth at Cesoirs, the tenth at Lagny.

—GARIN DE LOHERAIN

he Hot Fair of Troyes, celebrated in song and story, is the most important of the six Fairs of Champagne, which are divided unequally among four towns stretching across the county from its easternmost to westernmost borders. Geography and season make the first two fairs of the cycle,[1] those of Lagny and Bar–sur-Aube, the smallest. Lagny is close to Paris, Bar on the edge of Burgundy, a hundred miles east. The Lagny Fair is held in January-February, that of Bar next in March-April. Third in the calendar year comes the May Fair of Provins, running through May and June, followed by the Hot Fair, or Fair of St.-Jean, held in Troyes at the height of summer in July and August. The distance from

Provins to Troyes is only forty miles, and many fair clients pack up at Provins to unpack again in Troyes. The next fair, in September-October, is the Fair of St.-Ayoul in Provins, and again there is heavy inter-fair traffic. Finally comes the Fair of St.-Rémi, the Cold Fair of Troyes, in November and December. These four, in the two neighboring cities, lasting through the good traveling weather, form the major loci of this unrivaled marketplace for wholesale merchants and moneymen from Flanders, Italy, England, Germany, Spain, and even more distant places.

The Hot Fair is the climax of weeks of preparation. Apprentices have been up early and late, sewing, cleaning, sorting, finishing, storing, and repairing. The big halls and little stalls of the fair area have been put in order for their guests, as have the hostels and houses used for lodgings. In the taverns the dice are freshly cleaned, a precaution that may prevent a few knife fights. The cadre of regular prostitutes has been reinforced by serving wenches, tradeswomen, and farmers' daughters. Cooks, bakers, and butchers have added extra

A Moor and a Christian playing the lute, in a miniature from the Cantigas of Alfonso X "the Wise" (1221–84).

The Foire du Lendit at Saint-Denis, in a miniature from the *Grandes Chroniques de France* **(late 14th c.).**

help and lengthened their families' working hours.

An army of officials ensures that all goes smoothly. At their head are two Keepers of the Fair, chosen from the ranks of both nobles and burghers. They are appointed by the count at the excellent stipend of 200 pounds (livres) a year, expense allowances of 30 pounds, and exemption from all tolls and taxes for life. Their chief assistants, the keepers of the Seal, receive 100 pounds apiece. A lieutenant of the Fair commands the sergeants, a hundred strong, who guard the roads and patrol the fair. There are tax collectors, clerks, porters, roustabouts, and couriers. Notaries[2] attest all written transactions. Inspectors check the quality of merchandise. Finally, heralds scour the countryside to advertise the fair to the rustics.

The hubbub of the fair is as sweet a sound to the count as to the citizens of Troyes. Notaries, weighers, and other fee collectors divide their earnings with him. Thieves and bandits come under his high justice, their booty confiscated in his name. Sales taxes, the "issue" fee levied on departing merchandise, and other charges go to the count. So do rents on many stalls, booths, halls, stables, and houses. The bishop profits, too, drawing a sizeable income from rents, as do burghers and knights of Troyes. The Knights Templar draw revenues from their monopoly of wool weighing.

In return for all the fees and charges, the visiting merchants get freedom and protection. Fair clients are guaranteed security for themselves and their merchandise from the day of arrival to the day of departure, sunrise to sunset. At the height of the fair the streets are even lighted at night, making them almost safe.

Merchants are not only protected from bandits and robber barons, but from each other, and in fact today this is the more important protection of the two. Crimes committed at the fair are answerable to special courts, under the supervision of the Keepers of the Fair, but both town and provost try cases too, and law enforcement becomes a lively three-way competition. The special courts were actually created because the foreign merchants demanded protection against the other two agencies. Merchants can choose which court they will be tried in, and the most important cases fall to the courts of the fair. Energetic measures are taken to ensure collection of debts. A debtor or a swindler will be pursued far beyond the walls of Troyes and stands little

chance of escaping arrest if he shows his face at another fair. This is not all. He is liable to arrest in any city of Flanders or northern France, and if he is Italian he will be least safe of all in his home town, for the keepers of the Fair will threaten reprisal against his fellow townsmen if they do not assist in bringing him to justice. The extent to which these guarantees are actually enforced was graphically demonstrated eight years ago when a caravan of merchants was set upon by robbers on the highway between Lodi and Pavia. It was ascertained that the bandits were from Piacenza. The aggrieved merchants reported the offense to the keepers of the Champagne Fairs, who promptly and effectively threatened to exclude the merchants of Piacenza unless restitution was made.

These protections, together with a general diminution of lawlessness and improved physical conditions for travel, have brought merchants from all over Europe in steadily increasing numbers. Throughout the yearly cycle the stream of traffic to and from Champagne never ceases.

But merchants can trade at the fair without making the journey in person. A regular contract form known as a "letter of carriage" exists for the purpose: "Odon Bagnasque, carrier, promises to Aubert Bagnaret to transport at his own cost, including tolls, with risks of robbery falling to Aubert, six bales from Marseilles to Troyes, from the day of this act to Christmas, in exchange for a horse given by Aubert." Or they can enter into a form of partnership developed by the Italians, known as the *commenda,* by which a younger man undertakes the risks of a journey in return for a quarter of the profits, while an older merchant puts up the capital. When the young businessman has some capital of his own, he can alter the agreement and put up a third of the capital, taking half the profit. This and other forms of contract are so common in Italy that a Genoese patrician dying in 1240 left no property but his house and a portfolio of *commenda* investments.

The fair, though primarily a wholesale and money market for big business, is also a gala for common folk. Peasants and their wives, knights and their ladies, arrive on foot, on horses, on donkeys, to find a bargain, sell a hen or a cow, or see the sights. Dancers, jugglers, acrobats, bears, and monkeys perform on the street corners; jongleurs sing on the church steps. Taverns are noisily thronged. The whores, amateur and professional, cajole and bargain.

For a farmer or backwoods knight, the fair is an opportunity to gape at such exotic foreigners as Englishmen, Scots, Scandinavians, Icelanders, and Portuguese, not to mention Provençaux, Frenchmen, Brabanters, Germans, Swiss, Burgundians, Spaniards, and Sicilians. Most numerous are the Flemings and the "Lombards," a term which includes not only men from Lombardy, but Florentines, Genoese, Venetians and other north Italians. The rustic visitor hears many languages spoken, but these men of many nations communicate with little difficulty. Some of the more learned know Latin, and there are always plenty of clerks to translate. But the *lingua franca* of the fairs is French; though there is little sense of French nationality, and though French is not universally spoken throughout the narrow realm of the king of France, nearly every merchant and factor at the fair can acquit himself in this tongue. French is already acquiring exotic words which the Italians have picked up from their Arab business contacts. Eventually *douane, gabelle, gondran, jupe, quintal, recif,* and many more will find their way into French. English will acquire *bazaar, jar, magazine, taffeta, tariff, artichoke, tarragon, orange, muslin, gauze, sugar, alum, saffron.*

The first week of the fair is occupied with the merchants' entry—registration, unpacking, setting up displays. Then the fair opens with a ten-day Cloth Market. The Italian merchants pass from one to another of the halls of the famous cloth cities, examining the bolts, which have already been subjected to a rigid inspection at home, for every cloth town guards its reputation like Caesar's wife. It is an offense to sell defective cloth abroad; below-grade or irregular material must be marketed locally. Each kind of wool is folded in a different way, both to make it identifiable and to display its special virtues. An expert can recognize at a glance the cloths of Douai, Arras, Bruges, Tournai or Ypres—towns which, together with a number of others of the Low Countries and northern France, form the "Hanse of the Seventeen Towns," an association of wool producers who have agreed to sell their cloth only at the Champagne Fairs.

Each town has its own standard bolt—those of Provins and Troyes are twenty-eight ells long; those of Ghent thirty, except for the scarlets, which are thirty-six; those of Ypres twenty-nine ells, and so forth. A special official is on hand to explain the different lengths. The ell itself varies in other parts of Europe, but here it is the standard ell of Champagne, two feet six inches. An iron ruler of this length is in the hands of the Keepers of the Fair. Against it all the wooden rulers in use have been measured.

The tables in the cloth halls are a kaleidoscope of colored bolts, ranging from ecru, uncolored and little finished, through gray, brown, vermillion, rose and scarlet. The reds, highly prized and expensive, are a specialty of the famous *Arte di Calimala* of Florence, whose agents at the fair buy undyed cloth and sell dyed. Here and there is cloth heavy with gold and silver thread. Though wool predominates, there are also silks, mostly from Lucca; cotton from Italy, France, and Flanders; flax in the form of linen for sheets, sacks, purses, and clothing, and of hemp for nets, ropes, bowstrings, and measuring lines.

Bargaining finished, deals concluded and notarized, and arrangements made for the transfer of goods, the sergeants close the Cloth Market with the traditional cry of "Hare! Hare!" and attention turns to the next order of business. This is *"avoir de poids,"* goods that must be weighed—sugar, salt, alum, lacquer, dyes, grain, wines. These come from a diversity of places—salt from Salins in Franche-Comté, sugar from Syria, wax from Morocco and Tunisia. But just as the king of textiles is wool, the prince of avoir de poids is spices. They are the fabulous commodities that alone sustain a trade by pack train, galley, camel caravan, and Arab dhow. There are literally hundreds of spices; one medieval list names two hundred and eighty-eight.[3] The Italian merchants themselves do not know where all the spices come from. They load their precious cargoes at Constantinople, or Acre, or Antioch, or Tripoli, and if they question their Arab suppliers, they receive a shrug or a strange answer. Cinnamon, they may be told, comes from the nest of a bird of Arabia who favors this aromatic fruit as building material. Cassia trees grow in glens or lakes watched over by ferocious winged animals. Another opinion holds that the spices are harvested by the Egyptians, who stretch nets across the Nile.

Few of the merchants at the Hot Fair believe these fairy tales. They know the spices come from the distant East, from coasts and islands no European visits, lost in a fog of fourth-hand knowledge. It is not difficult for them to credit the costs involved in the arduous and perilous freightage over thousands of leagues. Tolls must be paid by the dozens, and caravans guarded. Losses must be made up for in the prices. No wonder a pound of mace at the fair is worth as much as three sheep.

The very mystery of the spices adds something to their desirability. Their basic value is twofold: as flavoring for meat whose toughness needs long cooking, and as preservatives. For these two purposes, one spice surpasses all others: pepper. This small black wrinkled berry has become a metaphor—"dear as pepper." It is not the most expensive spice; saffron and cinnamon are much costlier. But at four sous a pound it is expensive enough, and by far the most popular of the spices. Pepper merchants sell it retail by the peppercorn; a housewife may buy just one if she wishes.

Its popularity and costliness cause pepper to be guarded like diamonds. Longshoremen who handle it are closely watched and frequently searched. Crossbows and blades bristle on the galleys that bring it through the Mediterranean, and in the pack trains that carry it through the Alpine passes and across the hills and plains of Burgundy and Champagne.

All these precautions do not protect the pepper from depredations of a different kind—those of grocers, wholesalers and middlemen, any of whom may mix a bit of something with it—perhaps a few peppercorns confected from clay, oil, and mustard, difficult to distinguish from the genuine article. At the fair, experts scrutinize every batch of pepper with eyes, fingers, and nose. The arguments that ensue add to the din around St.-Jean.

When a spice deal is consummated, the merchandise is taken to a weighing station. The weighing, too, is followed by several pairs of alert eyes. Only responsible merchants are permitted inside the spice halls and the weighing station.

Other food products besides spices do a brisk retail business, as celebrated in a contemporary verse:

A Laigny, à Bar, à Provins
Si i a marcheand de vins
De blé, de sel et de harenc...
At Lagny, Bar, and Provins

There are sellers of wine,
Grain, salt and herring.

Among the comestibles are meat and cheese (that of Brie is already celebrated) and, above all, wine. The wines of Champagne—Reims, Epernay and Bar-sur-Aube—are popular, but the principal wine sold at the Champagne Fairs is that of Auxerre, a few miles south of Troyes. (Wine is too bulky a commodity to be shipped far, except by water.)

Dyestuffs are also included in avoir de poids. Some are produced in Flanders and sold to the Italians, some sold by the Italians to the Flemings and Champenois. The greatest demand is for indigo, from India, which the Italians buy in the Syrian ports. Alum, an essential to the dyeing as to the tanning process, is now produced in Spain as well as Egypt and the East. The Italians produce certain other dyes, violets and reds, from lichen and insects—tricks they have learned from their Moslem suppliers, either by observation or espionage.

During this part of the fair, a host of commodities is sold, ranging from raw materials like skins and metals to finely worked handicrafted products. Armorers buy iron from Germany and steel from Spain. Lead, tin, and copper are on hand, from Bohemia, Poland, Hungary, and England. Furs and skins sold by local dealers compete with imports from across the Rhine and even from Scandinavia. Then there are luxury goods from the East, imported by the Italians: camphor, ambergris, musk, rubies, lapis lazuli, diamonds, carpets, pearls, and ivory tusks. The Champagne Fairs are a source of supply for the ivory carvers of Reims, Metz, and Cologne, whose intricate masterpieces, ivory replicas of castles and cathedrals, are on display. So is the art of the Italian and local goldsmiths and silversmiths, and astonishing work in ebony, such as carved chess sets from the Far East. Amid the shoes and leather displayed, the famous Spanish cordovan is in the limelight.

The happy uproar of opening day does not diminish during the weeks that follow. Bargaining is conducted with zest and vehemence. Faults are found with the merchandise: there are complaints that cloth has been stretched, flax left out all night in the damp to increase in weight; that wine has been falsely labeled. The loudest bargaining, the bitterest disputes and the most frequent invocations of the saints are heard in front of the small stalls. Big companies like the Bardi and Guicciardini of Florence, the Bonsignori and Tolomei of Siena, and the Buonconti of Pisa have reputations to

Phillip IV, the Fair, King of France (1268–1314). Tomb at Royal Abbey Church, St. Denis, France.

maintain for quality and probity.

Throughout the month following the Cloth Market, however, the busiest section of the Fair is the moneychangers' area near St.-Jean. The commerce of which the Champagne Fairs are the focus has stimulated a lively flow of foreign exchange, and the fairs themselves are the natural center of this money trade. Travelers who are not fair clients may visit Troyes simply to have their money changed or to buy letters of credit. Essentially private businessmen, the twenty-eight moneychangers are at the same time functionaries of the fair. Half of them are Italians, many from Siena. The other half are Jews and Cahorsins.

The standard coin of the fairs is the *denier de Provins* (Provins penny). A strong currency, of high and stable relative value, it has even inspired an Italian copy, the "Provinois of the Senate," minted in Rome for fair-bound merchants. But dozens of other pennies of widely varying worth also put in an appearance. Money-changing is governed by strict regulations. One ironclad rule directs the changer to remove from circulation all debased or false coins. Exchange rates on all kinds of money are posted, the quotations made in terms of one sou (twelve pennies) of Provins.

But the moneychangers' function at the fair is not limited to providing a standard medium of exchange for the merchants' use. They are also the focus of a very extensive system of credit.[4] This operates in several ways. A certain Florentine house is a regular purchaser of cloth at the fairs. But the company's cargoes of spices and luxury goods, which they sell in Champagne, do not always arrive on time. Therefore they keep a balance to their account with the moneychangers so that their agents are never without funds. Further, they can deposit Florentine money in Florence or Genoa and have the money paid to their agent at Troyes in silver of Provins.

Or an Italian merchant may borrow a sum in Genoa in local currency, pledging as security the goods he is shipping to Champagne, and specify that repayment is to be made in money of Provins at the Fair. If the goods are entrusted to a third party, the contract may specify that they travel at the creditor's risk.

An even more sophisticated method of credit is employed by the big Italian houses. Instead of sending a pack caravan to arrive during the opening week, the firm dispatches a courier with a bill of lading for its agent in Champagne. The agent buys cloth on credit and sends it off to Italy. When his firm's merchandise arrives, in time for the avoir de poids market, the agent turns seller and negotiates credit transactions in reverse, acquiring enough paper for his spices to cover his cloth debts.

Apart from credit transactions and currency exchange, the fair moneychangers do a great deal of business in straight loans. The "Lombards" are notable pawnbrokers. Behind his moneychanging stall a Lombard

Edward III, King of England (1312–77), pictured as founder of the Order of the Garter (15th c.).

An ever more complex financial system is taking shape. A merchant's promise to pay may itself be sold at a discount, and a third party may appear at the subsequent fair to claim the debt. A merchant of Florence may buy a stock of cloth from a merchant of Ghent at the May Fair of Provins, and promise to pay twenty pounds at the Hot Fair of Troyes. The two take their "Letter of the Fair," spelling out the agreement, to the Keeper of the Fair, and have it witnessed and scaled with the fair seal. The Fleming then has in his possession a negotiable piece of paper, which he may use to pay for his own purchases of pepper and cinnamon. The Letter of the Fair makes it possible to execute a considerable proportion of the fair's business without recourse to the moneychangers, and without the need for handling large sums of cash.

Thus in the cheerful clamor of the fair, the jingle of silver is quietly being replaced by the rattle of the abacus and the scratching of the quill, turning bales and bolts into livres and deniers, and recording them in notarial documents.

Here, more than in anything else in this busy, knowledgeable, money-oriented city of shopkeepers, lies a portent of the future.

AFTER 1250

The growing financial sophistication evident at the Hot Fair of Troyes in the year 1250 led in succeeding decades to a paradox not uncommon in history. The Champagne Fairs became so successful that they made themselves obsolescent.

Historians used to blame politics for the fourteenth-century decline of the fairs. The dynasty of Thibaut the Great came to an end with the marriage of Jeanne de Navarre, only surviving grandchild of Thibaut the Songwriter, to King Philip the Fair, whose taxes and wars were once believed to have ruined the fairs. But there was sufficient evidence of trouble before Philip. His predecessor in Champagne was an Englishman, Edmund of Lancaster, who married Jeanne's widowed mother, Blanche of Artois. Edmund and Blanche raised taxes to a point where in Troyes' sis-

may have a back room full of rings, paternosters, and silver plate. Not only businessmen, but all classes use the fairs as banking places. Princes, barons, bishops all borrow at the Hot Fair and promise to repay at the Fair of St.-Ayoul. Not all this lucrative loan business is in the hands of the moneychangers, but they are generally involved, as are the notaries (who are also frequently Italian).

Sometimes a merchant borrows at one fair and promises to repay in installments at the next three or more, as he sells his goods. This sort of arrangement is taken care of in the closing days of the fair, during the debt settlement *(pagamentum)*, a time of general liquidation of the promises to pay that have accumulated on all sides. Among other things, the system of dating loans from one fair to another helps solve the problem of variant calendars.[5] Venetian, Pisan, and Florentine merchants do not agree on when the year begins, or even what year it is.

Black Death (1348–50) at Tournai by Gilles de Muisit.

ter city, Provins, the mayor sought to ease the burden of his fellow burghers by lengthening the weavers' hours of labor. Workmen rioted and killed the mayor and several of his councillors. Repression and reprisal followed.

Social relations were growing complicated. The hallowed formula of three estates—clergy, nobility, and common folk—was never very realistic, even at the height of feudalism. By the late thirteenth century the "third estate" included bankers, engineers, salesmen, doctors, and poets along with peasants and proletarians. The topmost group of this class, the "patricians," played a more and more active social and political role. While in cities like Provins they importuned their feudal lords to help them punish unruly workers, in other places they stoutly contested their lords' rights to military service and aids. The refusal of Bourges to contribute to St.-Louis' quixotic enterprise of 1270, upheld by the Parlement of Paris, gave the crusading business a final push into the grave.

But class war was not more responsible than taxes for the decline of the Champagne Fairs. An unparalleled

school for banking, bookkeeping, and merchandising, the fairs helped kill themselves by nourishing more efficient methods of doing business. The grandson of the Italian businessman who struggled over the Alpine passes, at the head of his pack train, stayed home in his countinghouse and struggled over accounts. Traveling partners were replaced by permanent factors stationed in the principal cities of the north. (The Paris factor of the famous Bardi firm of Florence in the early fourteenth century had a bright son named Giovanni Boccaccio.) Ultimately the old overland route of the spice and cloth trade was itself superseded. As early as 1277 a venturesome Genoese galley rounded Gibraltar and crossed the stormy Bay of Biscay to the English Channel, though it was some time before shipping became safe enough to compete in cost with land transport. For shipments by both land and sea, the business tycoon of the fourteenth century took advantage of another new business technique—cargo insurance.

A variety of calamities, some natural and some manmade, befell Troyes, Champagne, and western Europe generally in the fourteenth century. Philip the Fair's

war with Flanders interrupted the fairs. Agriculture suffered a number of bad harvests, one in 1304 bringing famine in Troyes, and others affecting various regions in the 1320s. Edward III of England prepared for his expedition in quest of the crown of France by borrowing a quarter of a million pounds from Italian, Flemish, German, and English moneymen and then declaring bankruptcy, bringing ruin to the mighty firms of Bardi and Peruzzi. Finally the appalling catastrophe of the Black Death (1348–50) shook the entire agricultural and commercial structure of the West.

But even without war, famine and pestilence, there is reason to believe that the boom had temporarily run its course. Exactly what caused the slowdown of the fourteenth and early fifteenth centuries remains a mystery. Even if increasing taxes did not kill the Champagne Fairs, they may have contributed to the big depression. Some scholars point to the growth of monopolies. An example is the tanners of Troyes, who became rich and powerful by cartel buying and selling. Even more striking is the story of the butchers of Paris, who in 1260 acquired a perpetual lease on the twenty-five municipal butcher stalls of the city. In the course of a hundred years their number shrank to six families, none personally engaged in the trade, but all very wealthy and playing a major political role in the Hundred Years' War.

In the second round of the war, starring Henry V and Joan of Arc, Troyes enjoyed a brief prominence, first in 1420 as the scene of Henry's marriage to Catherine of France, consecrated in St.-Jean, and next in 1429 by

Joan's capture of the city *en route* to crowning the dauphin at Reims. But Troyes was on the downgrade. Though it remained a bishopric and continued to serve as a local center for commerce and manufacture, it had long ceased to be either a political capital or a nucleus of international trade. Paris, capital of a powerful central monarchy, took over as the major economic hub, growing to a metropolis of more than a hundred thousand by the end of the war (1453). London, capital of a rival kingdom and port for England's growing wool-cloth industry, was not much smaller. Across the Channel, Antwerp, the best port on the coast, rode the crest of the new seaborne commerce, leaving behind the old cloth towns of Flanders—Ypres, Saint-Omer, Arras, Douai. In Germany, Hamburg and Lubeck, on either flank of the Danish peninsula, led the cities of the Hanseatic League on a brilliant career of commercial and political supremacy in the Baltic, monopolizing trade and fisheries, fighting wars with kings and collecting tolls.

In southern France some of the old cities (Avignon, Montpellier) declined, while others (Marseilles, Lyon) held their own. In Italy, Florence rose to ever new heights under the leadership of a parvenu banking house, the Medici, as did Milan under the Visconti. Genoa crushed its ancient rival, Pisa, then met with difficulties in its turn and lost most of its far-flung colonial empire, though it remained a major financial center on the strength of its banking *savoir-faire*. With the downfall of its maritime rivals, Venice became the unchallenged queen of the Mediterranean, a position so glamorous that it was some time before Venetians became aware that the Mediterranean itself was losing importance through the opening of a sea route to the East and the discovery of a New World in the west. That the discovery was made by an experienced Genoese sailor, hired by the queen of the Atlantic maritime kingdom of Castile, was not surprising.

America had of course been discovered before, but Leif Ericson, Bjarni Herjulfson, and their companions brought along only the limited technology of the Old World's tenth century. The difference between the Viking explorers and Columbus is the difference between the early and late Middle Ages. The Vikings had no wheeled plows, no felling axes, no iron harrows, no horse collars or horseshoes, no overshot waterwheels, no wealth of handicrafts to conciliate the aborigines, and no firearms (introduced in western Europe in the fourteenth century) to coerce them. Neither did they have the booming market for gold, silver, and furs that provided a lively stimulus for the Spaniards, English and French.

The Commercial Revolution, as modern scholars have named it, supplied the economic and technological basis for exploitation of the New World. At the same time it laid the foundations in mining and metallurgy, banking and merchandising, for the momentous developments in northwest Europe in the sixteenth, seventeenth, and eighteenth centuries. The descendants of the craftsmen, merchants, and moneylenders of thirteenth-century France, England, Germany, and Flanders steadily augmented their power, toppling thrones, overturning churches, burying hallowed customs and taking over the privileges of the privileged classes. Without the Commercial Revolution of the Middle Ages, neither the French Revolution nor the Industrial Revolution is conceivable.

Like a number of other sleepy old towns, Troyes received a stimulus from the Industrial Revolution. It even regained a modicum of its ancient status, develop-ing its own manufacturing specialty, knitwear, and winning the honorable title of leader of the nightcap industry. Its worst fire, in 1524, wiped out the rich and populous commercial quarter, destroying the cloth halls, the Templar commandery, the Belfry (formerly the Viscount's Tower), and seriously damaging the churches of St.-Pantaléon, St.-Jean, and St.-Nicolas. Four and a half centuries of wear and tear, including the invasion of 1940 and the liberation of 1944, have further depleted the town's medieval heritage. A few buildings weathered every rack, among them the Hôtel-Dieu-le-Comte, largely rebuilt, the Abbey of St.-Loup, which now houses a library and museums, and the cathedral with its stained glass. The "old quarter" of Troyes today, which includes the old fair quarter, actually dates from the rebuilding after the fire. Much of the original street lay-out remains: Cats' Alley is still only seven feet wide, with the housetops leaning against each other.

An intangible relic also survives. Among such ancient professions as that of gem cutter, precious-metal worker, and apothecary, "Troy weight," with its medieval ratio of twenty pennyweight to the ounce and twelve ounces to the pound, is still in use—a last souvenir of the great days of the Champagne Fairs.

GENEALOGY OF THE COUNTS OF CHAMPAGNE

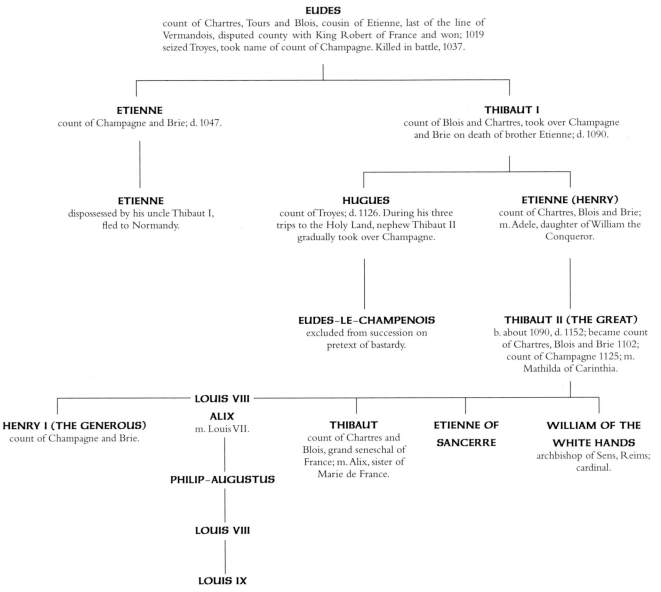

EUDES
count of Chartres, Tours and Blois, cousin of Etienne, last of the line of Vermandois, disputed county with King Robert of France and won; 1019 seized Troyes, took name of count of Champagne. Killed in battle, 1037.

ETIENNE
count of Champagne and Brie; d. 1047.

THIBAUT I
count of Blois and Chartres, took over Champagne and Brie on death of brother Etienne; d. 1090.

ETIENNE
dispossessed by his uncle Thibaut I, fled to Normandy.

HUGUES
count of Troyes; d. 1126. During his three trips to the Holy Land, nephew Thibaut II gradually took over Champagne.

ETIENNE (HENRY)
count of Chartres, Blois and Brie; m. Adele, daughter of William the Conqueror.

EUDES–LE–CHAMPENOIS
excluded from succession on pretext of bastardy.

THIBAUT II (THE GREAT)
b. about 1090, d. 1152; became count of Chartres, Blois and Brie 1102; count of Champagne 1125; m. Mathilda of Carinthia.

LOUIS VIII

HENRY I (THE GENEROUS)
count of Champagne and Brie.

ALIX
m. Louis VII.

THIBAUT
count of Chartres and Blois, grand seneschal of France; m. Alix, sister of Marie de France.

ETIENNE OF SANCERRE

WILLIAM OF THE WHITE HANDS
archbishop of Sens, Reims; cardinal.

PHILIP–AUGUSTUS

LOUIS VIII

LOUIS IX (ST.-LOUIS)

HENRY I

(THE GENEROUS)

b. 1127; count of Champagne 1152–1181; m. Marie, daughter of Louis VII and Eleanor of Aquitaine. Eleanor afterward m. Henry II of England and bore Richard the Lionhearted and John, making Marie half sister to three kings: Philip-Augustus, John and Richard.

HENRY II (THE YOUNG)

b. 1166; count of Champagne 1181–1192; king of Jerusalem 1192–1197; d. 1197 at Acre. His mother Marie was regent until his majority in 1187.

THIBAUT III

b. 1179; count of Champagne 1197–1201; m. Blanche of Navarre; d. 1201 on eve of Fourth Crusade. His mother Marie was regent from 1192 until his majority in 1198.

THIBAUT IV (THE SONGWRITER)

b. 1201; count of Champagne 1201–1253; king of Navarre 1234–1253; m. Gertrude de Habsburg (or de Dabo); annulled, no issue; Agnes de Beajeu, one daughter; Marguerite de Bourbon, four sons, three daughters.

THIBAUT V

count of Champagne, king of Navarre 1253–1271; m. Isabelle, daughter of St.-Louis.

HENRY III (THE FAT)

count of Champagne, king of Navarre 1271–1274; m. Blanche of Artois, niece of St.-Louis, who after his death m. Edmund of Lancaster.

JEANNE DE NAVARRE

m. Philip IV (the Fair), grandson of St.-Louis, king of France, 1285–1314.

LOUIS X (THE BRAWLER)

king of France and Navarre 1314–1316.

EXPLANATORY NOTES
SECTION III

PROLOGUE

1. the count of Vermandois: During the ninth century Troyes was held by a miscellaneous succession of non-hereditary counts, including Adelerin, the abbot of St.-Loup. The first of the Vermandois counts to reign in Troyes was Héribert, who died in 943. His son Robert, who repelled Bishop Anségise's effort to recover power in the city, died without issue and was succeeded by his brother Héribert, with whose son Etienne (d. 1015) the dynasty came to an end.

2. a cardinal . . . an abbot: Jacques de Vitry and Guibert of Nogent.

3. population: All figures are conjectural. Estimates of city populations for the Middle Ages are obtained from a base figure, such as the number of hearths in a tax list, men in a communal army or fleet, signatories to a treaty, members of a key profession (such as notaries), etc., multiplied by a coefficient representing the assumed relation of the base to the total population.

CHAPTER I
TROYES: 1250

1. city wall: The walls of Troyes have long since been replaced by boulevards. The description of the wall given here is based on that of neighboring Provins, built in the same period and still standing, including the handsome Porte-St.-Jean.

2. Viscount's Tower: A mere anachronism in the thirteenth century. But in the next century it regained importance, becoming the "belfry," stronghold of the burghers and hall of municipal government.

3. paved with stone: Probably. A document of 1231 attests that the section of the thoroughfare immediately west of Troyes was paved. City pavements were rare outside Italy, although in Paris Philip Augustus is said to have paved some streets in the early thirteenth century.

CHAPTER II
A BURGHER'S HOME

1. oiled parchment: Glass was seldom used even in the houses of the wealthy. In England, where great nobles possessed scattered estates, they sometimes carried glazed casements from one residence to another. Wooden shutters were also common.

2. table manners: These injunctions are taken from three sources: Roman de la Rose and Robert of Blois's Chatoiement des Dames, both thirteenth century, and Disciplina Clericalis, written in the eleventh century by Petrus Alfonsus, a converted Spanish Jew, translated into French at the end of the twelfth century and popular in the thirteenth.

CHAPTER III
A MEDIEVAL HOUSEWIFE

1. at three-hour intervals: The eight services of canonical office celebrated by the Church were (approximately):

Matins at midnight
Lauds at 3 A.M.
Prime at 6 A.M.
Tierce at 9 A.M.
Sext at midday
None at 3 P.M.
Vespers at 6 P.M.
Compline at 9 P.M.

In its simplest form, the clepsydra was similar to the sand-glass, with hour-levels marked as water dripped through an aperture. Elaborate mechanical clepsydras were also made, which with their trains of cogged wheels were ancestors of modern clocks. A drawing of Villard de Honnecourt shows an escapement, one of the basic mechanisms of clockwork.

The remarkable scientist and scholar Gerbert, who became Pope Sylvester II, is said to have invented the mechanical clock in 996, but the clock he had constructed at Magdeburg was doubtless a water clock, as were other clocks described during the following three centuries. In 1360 the first unquestionably mechanical clock in the modern sense was built by De Vick for Charles V of France.

2. A fat capon costs six deniers: Most of the commodity prices cited here and elsewhere in the text are drawn from the massive compendium of the Vicomte d'Avenel, who gathered price and wage figures in western Europe from 1200 to 1800. Original sources are cited in his work.

3. gardens: These plants are taken from John of Garlande's thirteenth-century dictionary.

4. members of normally male professions: Cf. Villon, "Les Regretz de la belle Héaulmière."

5. abbess of Notre-Dame: When Pope Urban IV wanted to build a church on the site of his father's shoe shop, he found himself embroiled with the abbess on whose seigneury the construction impinged. She led an armed party that attacked and demolished the work in 1266.

6. wipe . . . one's nose: Langlois, who edited Robert of Blois's Chatoiement des Dames for modern readers, suggests that the injunction is intended as humor, and is not a true indication of manners.

CHAPTER IV
CHILDBIRTH AND CHILDREN

1. Birth records: When Jeanne of Champagne was betrothed in 1284 an extensive investigation was necessary to determine her birth date.

CHAPTER V
WEDDINGS AND FUNERALS

1. demolish . . . portico: Evidently the portico was repaired later, because the protecting statues are still a feature of Notre-Dame-de-Dijon.

2. Jongleurs: from instructions written for jongleurs of Provence.

CHAPTER VI
SMALL BUSINESS

1. the hundred and twenty guilds of Paris: In 1268, 120 crafts registered and wrote out their statutes at the invitation of Etienne Boileau, provost of Paris.

Preserved in the taille (tax list) of Paris for the year 1292 are the numbers of practitioners of the regulated crafts, by then totaling 130. The principal ones:

366 shoemakers	42 meat butchers
214 furriers	41 fish merchants
199 maidservants	37 beer sellers
197 tailors	36 buckle makers
151 barbers	36 plasterers
131 jewelers	35 spice merchants
130 restaurateurs	34 blacksmiths
121 old-clothes dealers	33 painters
106 pastrycooks	29 doctors
104 masons	28 roofers
95 carpenters	27 locksmiths
86 weavers	26 bathers
71 chandlers	26 ropemakers
70 mercers	24 innkeepers
70 coopers	24 tanners
62 bakers	24 copyists
58 water carriers	24 sculptors
58 scabbard makers	24 rugmakers
56 wine sellers	24 harness makers
54 hatmakers	23 bleachers
51 saddlers	22 hay merchants
51 chicken butchers	22 cutlers
45 purse makers	21 glovemakers
43 laundresses	21 wood sellers
43 oil merchants	21 woodcarvers
42 porters	

2. confiscation: In 1268 Thibaut V, preparing to go on the last Crusade, again confiscated the goods of Troyen Jews and burned thirteen.

CHAPTER VII
BIG BUSINESS

1. silver-copper-zinc pennies: Though the basic coin of the Middle Ages was called denier in France, penny in England, pfennig in Germany, etc., it was universally written in Latin, denarius, as was the pound (libra) and shilling (solidus), which accounts for the odd abbreviations of modern English coinage, the last relic of the medieval money system.

2. grosso (groat): St.-Louis issued a gros tournois even larger than the grosso in 1266, and Edward I of England a still larger groat in 1270. Simultaneously gold coinage returned for the first time since the Dark Ages, first in Italy, then in France and England. The French gold coin, écu, was valued at 10 gros tournois, or 120 deniers de Provins or one-half livre.

CHAPTER VIII
THE DOCTOR

1. fewer than a half dozen doctors: This is a fairly safe conjecture. In Paris in 1274 there were eight qualified physicians, a number which rose rapidly to 29 in 1292. On the other hand, 38 men and women of Paris in 1274 were identified as practicing medicine without benefit of a diploma. In the fourteenth century, the Faculty of Medicine of the University of Paris launched a vigorous war against the unlicensed practitioner.

2. medical textbooks: Pietro d'Abano, Taddeo Alderotti, Lanfranc, Henri de Mondeville and others added much new work in the later thirteenth century.

CHAPTER IX
THE CHURCH

1. no benches or pews: Lecoy de la Marche, in *La Chaire Française*, insists that there were benches in the churches, on the grounds that otherwise people could not have fallen asleep (they were the butts of many clerical jokes and diatribes). Others feel that the congregation could have slept as soundly on cushions and portable seats.

2. sermon on the Christian virtues: This sermon was preached to pilgrims at Notre-Dame of Amiens.

3. oratorical tricks: These were employed by the famous Paris preacher Jacques de Vitry, cardinal-archbishop of Acre.

4. process of canonization: Details of procedure were fixed in the thirteenth century, and beyond a fourteenth-century refinement have scarcely changed since.

CHAPTER X
THE CATHEDRAL

1. names of the masters: Our earliest source of information about the builders of St.-Pierre is the cathedral accounts from 1293 to 1300. One Master Jacopo Lathomo (the Stone Cutter) is mentioned in a legacy of 1295–6 to the cathedral, and French scholars speculate that he may have been an architect who worked on the cathedral about 1270. The first certain reference to an architect in the records is to Master Henri, whose expenses for a trip with a servant are recorded in 1293–4; the next year he goes to the quarry on Ascension Day with Masters Richer and Gautier; in 1295–6 Renaudin, valet of the masons, presents himself to Henri at Auxerre, so that they may visit the quarry at Dangis; the following year they are at Dangis again. In 1297–8 Geoffroi of Mussy-sur-Seine takes over the job.

In 1920 a French scholar, de Mély, published in the *Revue Archéologique* the then astonishing number of over five hundred architect-engineers in France alone. Many more medieval builders have been identified since. In 1954 John Harvey published a dictionary of English medieval architects.

2. The builder's plans: Very few survive. Parchment was precious and was commonly scraped and reused. An extant plan of Strasbourg Cathedral dates from the thirteenth century.

3. iron clamps: Metallic reinforcement of masonry was common—windows, steeples, and pinnacles made use of wrought iron for clamps, stays, tie-rods and dowels.

4. the bell is long-waisted: When change-ringing became popular at the end of the Middle Ages, shorter-waisted belts were cast because it was easier to raise and ring them.

5. choir vault: The steeply pitched timber roofs of Gothic churches do not touch the vaulting beneath. The sketchbook of Villard de Honnecourt shows timbering built up from the tops of the piers, at the point of the springing of the arches, and secured by wooden ties. The timber roof was apparently then erected and the vaulting finished under cover. Rafters were about fourteen inches apart, often covered with leading.

6. Gothic architecture: Hans Straub, in his History of Civil Engineering, names four structural developments of the Gothic builders: (1) the distinction between bearing pillars and nonbearing walls; (2) the pointed arch, which is "statically efficient," that is, can carry heavy loadings; (3) vault-supporting ribs in place of the Roman solid vaults; (4) buttresses and flying buttresses.

7. Deathbed bequests: Among the legacies to the Troyes cathedral in 1298–9 is that of Pierre, the town hangman.

8. the master glazier has no secrets: Art has its own historical laws, and there is undeniably a charm in twelfth- and thirteenth-century glass which the work of later centuries does not have, probably because in later days the use of the medium to its best advantage, as a mosaic of colored light, was sacrificed to realistic representation.

9. St.-Bernard: The great ascetic's viewpoint was not entirely abandoned by the later Middle Ages, and certainly found an echo in the Protestant movements of the fifteenth and sixteenth centuries. Sale of indulgences to pay for church-building, especially St. Peter's in Rome, was a powerful stimulus to discontent, and the very magnificence of church architecture remained an irritant to some.

CHAPTER XI
SCHOOLS AND SCHOLARS

1. Nicolas of Clairvaux: Translated by John Benton in Annales de Bourgogne.

2. seven liberal arts: A fifth-century writer named Martianus Capella, in a romance called The Wedding of Philology and Mercury, which remained popular throughout the Middle Ages, personifies the seven arts as women, distinguished by their varying clothing, implements and coiffures.

3. Alexandre of Villedieu's Doctrinale: Through the fourteenth and fifteenth centuries the Doctrinale remained the universal grammar of Europe.

4. a map of the world: Several twelfth- and thirteenth-century maps are extant, including the world disk in Hereford Cathedral (late thirteenth century), which depicts imaginary continents and seas with fabulous beasts; the Psalter Map (c. 1230); and the Ebstorf Map (from the same period as the Hereford Map.)

5. five in northwest Europe: No German universities came into existence until the fourteenth century. By the end of the Middle Ages there were some eighty European universities, two-thirds of which were in France and Italy.

6. no university buildings: The movement toward permanent buildings did not get seriously under way until the fifteenth century. At Paris, the only remaining monuments of the thirteenth-century university are the old church of St.-Julien-le-Pauvre, where university meetings were often held, and the cathedral from which the university sprang. Bologna has no university buildings from earlier than the fourteenth century. At Bologna, where classes were some-times very large, popular professors lectured in public buildings or in the open air. At Cambridge, the oldest college, Peterhouse (thirteenth century) has only parts of its earliest buildings; Merton, at Oxford, also preserves some original fragments.

7. theology: Theology did not become prescribed training for the priesthood until the Counter Reformation.

CHAPTER XII
BOOKS AND AUTHORS

1. booksellers: The Paris taille of 1292 lists 8 bookstores, 17 bookbinders, 13 illuminators and 24 clerk-copyists. At least in Paris, most booksellers were also tavernkeepers: Nicholas l'Anglois, librairie et tavernier. By 1323 there were 28 bookstores.

2. libraries: By 1290 the Sorbonne had 1,017 volumes; by 1338 it had 1,722. Other libraries were expanding at a similar rate, suggesting the economic context for the fifteenth-century development of movable type.

3. fabliaux: Because of their well-advertised ribaldry, the fabliaux were once attributed exclusively to the non-noble class, a notion modern scholars have discarded.

4. bathing establishment: Bourbon-l'Archimbault, where the story takes place, remains a spa today.

5. This romance survives in a single mutilated thirteenth-century manuscript at Carcassonne, which terminates abruptly, shortly after this point. It is hard to see how the author could have improved on the ending as it stands.

CHAPTER XIII
THE NEW THEATER

1. the theater has outgrown its confining cradle: Secular and comic elements multiplied in both mysteries (Biblical—like the Adam play) and miracles (saints' lives—like the play of St. Nicholas). Herod developed into a melodramatic villain, the Magdalen's early life was explored, obscure Biblical personages were expanded into comic characters. Finally plays exploited purely secular themes. Adam de la Halle's Jeu de Robin et de Marion, based on the story of Robin Hood and presented at the Court of Naples in 1283, interspersed dialogue with songs and dances. It has been called the first comic opera.

In the fourteenth century guilds and corporations took over the religious drama, usually assigning Biblical scenes to appropriate trades—the story of Jonah to the fishmongers, the Marriage at Cana to the wine merchants, the building of the ark to the plasterers, the Last Supper to the bakers. In the second half of the fourteenth century, the great cycles of mystery plays were founded at Chester, Beverly, London, York and Coventry, unfolding the principal stories of the Bible in sequence. Though amateurs, the actors were paid: account books for the York cycle list such items as "20 d. [pence] to God, 21 d. to the demon, 3d. to Fauston for cock crowing, 17 d. to two worms of conscience." The morality play, whose characters were virtues and vices and other abstractions, as in Everyman, became popular in the fifteenth century.

CHAPTER XV
TOWN GOVERNMENT

1. typical recorded cases: Two are patterned after a court report published by Maurice Prou and Jules d'Auriac in Actes et comptes de la commune de Provins de l'an 1271 à l'an 1330; one is cited by

Paul Vinogradoff in Crump and Jacob's *Legacy of the Middle Ages* (see Bibliography, Chapter 2); the fourth, that involving the lady with the gutter pipe, is from a *Speculum* article by Ernest L. Sabine (see Bibliography, Chapter 2).

CHAPTER XVI
THE CHAMPAGNE FAIR

1. the cycle: Our knowledge of the divisions of the six Fairs of Champagne comes partly from the Extenta of 1276–1278 (see Prologue), partly from an earlier document surviving in six variant texts. The generally agreed-on dates are:

Lagny: January 2 to February 22.

Bar-sur-Aube: Opened between February 24 and March 30, closed between April 15 and May 20.

Mai de Provins: Opened between April 28 and May 30, closed between June 13 and July 16.

St.-Jean de Troyes (Hot Fair): July 9–15 to August 29-September 4.

St.-Ayoul de Provins: September 14 to November 1 (All Saints' Day).

St.-Rémi de Troyes (Cold Fair): November 2 to December 23.

In addition to the great international fairs, there were a number of small trade fairs in Champagne, at Bar-sur-Seine, Châlons-sur-Marne, Château-Thierry, Nogent, Reims and other places. Troyes itself had three small fairs, the Fair of Clos, that of Deux Eaux and that of the Assumption.

2. notaries: "It is certain," says O. Verlinden in the Cambridge Economic History, "that there existed at the Champagne Fairs a real records department." Hardly a fragment survives. A single leaf, from a register of the Hot Fair at Troyes of 1296, drawn up by an Italian notary, contains fifteen deeds mentioning merchants from Piacenza, Genoa, Milan, Asti, Como, Savona, Florence, Montpellier, Narbonne, Avignon, Carpentras and St.-Flour.

3. two hundred and eighty-eight spices: Pegolotti of Florence (1310–1340), whose list may include a few variants or duplications.

4. an extensive system of credit: The Riccardi of Lucca declared that they could borrow up to 200,000 pounds at a single fair.

5. the problem of variant calendars: The calendar was in a state of confusion, principally because of a widespread disagreement over when the new year began. January 1 was the first day of the Roman civil year, and the revival of the study of Roman law led to the use of this reckoning in some places, but it was the rarest of all the modes of dating the beginning of the year. In some places, the month in which the Passion and Resurrection were believed to have occurred, was considered the first month, but not everywhere, which led to some curious situations for a traveler. March 1 was officially celebrated as the beginning of the year in Venice. At Pisa, on the other hand, the year was reckoned from the presumed date of the Annunciation, that is from March 25 preceding A.D. 1. In Florence the years of the Incarnation were dated from March 25 a year later. In other places the year began on Christmas or Easter.

In a treatise on medieval timekeeping Reginald L. Poole (see Bibliography, Chapter 2) imagines a traveler setting out from Venice on March 1, 1245, the first day of the Venetian year; finding himself in 1244 when he reached Florence; and after a short stay going on to Pisa, where he would enter the year 1246. Continuing westward, he would return to 1245 when he entered Provence, and upon arriving in France before Easter (April 16) he would be once more in 1244. However, this confusion would not much discommode him, for he would think not in terms of the year but of the month and day, or the nearest saint's day.

BIBLIOGRAPHICAL NOTES
SECTION II

PROLOGUE
ELTON

1. *Chronicon abbatiae Rameseiensis,* ed. by W. Duncan Macray, London, 1886, p. 135.

2. Maurice Beresford and John G. Hurst, eds. *Deserted Medieval Villages,* London, 1971; Maurice Beresford, *The Lost Villages of the Middle Ages,* London, 1954; John G. Hurst, "The Changing Medieval Village," in J. A. Raftis, ed., *Pathways to Medieval Peasants,* Toronto, 1981; Trevor Rowley and John Wood, *Deserted Villages,* Aylesbury, England, 1982.

CHAPTER I
THE VILLAGE EMERGES

1. Edward Miller and John Hatcher, *Medieval England: Rural Society and Economic Change, 1086–1348,* London, 1978, pp. 85–87.

2. Rowley and Wood, *Deserted Villages,* pp. 6–8.

3. Jean Chapelot and Robert Fossier, *The Village and House in the Middle Ages,* trans. by Henry Cleere, Berkeley, 1985, p. 327.

4. P. J. Fowler, "Later Prehistory," in H. P. R. Finberg, gen. ed., *The Agrarian History of England and Wales,* vol. 1, pt. 1, Prehistory, ed. by Stuart Piggott, Cambridge, 1981, pp. 157–158.

5. Butser Ancient Farm Project Publications: *The Celtic Experience; Celtic Fields; Evolution of Wheat; Bees and Honey; Quern Stones; Hoes, Ards, and Yokes; Natural Dyes.*

6. Tacitus, *De Vita Iulii Agricola and De Germania,* ed. by Alfred Gudeman, Boston, 1928, pp. 36–37, 40–41.

7. Chapelot and Fossier, *Village and House,* pp. 27–30.

8. S. Applebaum, "Roman Britain," in H. P. R. Finberg, ed., *The Agrarian History of England and Wales,* vol. 1, pt. 2, A.D. 43–1042, Cambridge, 1972, p. 117.

9. Ibid., pp. 73–82.

10. Ibid., pp. 186, 208.

11. Chapelot and Fossier, *Village and House,* pp. 61, 100–103.

12. Ibid., p. 26.

13. Ibid., p. 15.

14. Ibid., pp. 144–150.

15. Joan Thirsk, "The Common Fields" and "The Origin of the Common Fields," and J. Z. Titow, "Medieval England and the Open-Field System," in *Peasants, Knights, and Heretics: Studies in Medieval English Social History,* ed. by R. H. Hilton, Cambridge, 1981, pp. 10–56; Bruce Campbell, "Commonfield Origins—the Regional Dimension," in Trevor Rowley, ed., *Origins of Open-Field Agriculture,* London, 1981, p. 127; Trevor Rowley, "Medieval Field Systems," in Leonard Cantor, ed., *The English Medieval Landscape,* Philadelphia, 1982; H. L. Gray, *English Field Systems,* Cambridge, Mass., 1915; C. S. and C. S. Orwin, *The Open Fields,* Oxford, 1954.

16. Joseph and Frances Gies, *Life in a Medieval Castle,* New York, 1974, p. 148.

17. George C. Homans, *English Villagers in the Thirteenth Century,* New York, 1975, pp. 12–28.

18. Grenville Astille and Annie Grant, eds., *The Countryside of Medieval England,* Oxford, 1988, pp. 88, 94.

19. Georges Duby, *Rural Economy and Country Life in the Medieval West,* Columbia, S.C., 1968, pp. 109–111.

20. Joan Thirsk, "Farming Techniques," in *Agrarian History of England and Wales,* vol. 4, 1500–1640, ed. by Joan Thirsk, Cambridge, 1967, p. 164.

21. R. H. Hilton, *The Transition from Feudalism to Capitalism,* London, 1984, pp. 15–16.

22. W. G. Hoskins, *The Midland Peasant: The Economic and Social History of a Leicestershire Village,* London, 1957, p. 79; Homans, *English Villagers,* p. 368.

CHAPTER II
THE ENGLISH VILLAGE: ELTON

1. For Huntingdonshire: Peter Bigmore, *The Bedfordshire and Huntingdonshire Landscape,* London, 1979. For England in general: H. C. Darby, *A New Historical Geography of England Before 1600,* Cambridge, 1976; Cantor, ed., *The English Medieval Landscape;* W. G. Hoskins, *The Making of the English Landscape,* London, 1955.

2. Applebaum, "Roman Britain," in *The Agrarian History of England and Wales,* vol. 1, pt. 2, p. 53.

3. Bigmore, *Bedfordshire and Huntingdonshire Landscape,* pp. 37–42.

4. Frank M. Stenton, *Anglo-Saxon England,* Oxford, 1971, p. 25.

5. H. C. Darby, "The Anglo-Scandinavian Foundations," in Darby, ed., *New Historical Geography,* pp. 13–14.

6. Ibid., p. 15.

7. H. P. R. Finberg, "Anglo-Saxon England to 1042," in *The Agrarian History of England and Wales,* vol. 1, pt. 2, p. 422.

8. *The Anglo-Saxon Chronicles,* trans. by Anne Savage, London, 1983, pp. 90–92, 96.

9. J. A. Raftis, *The Estates of Ramsey Abbey: A Study of Economic Growth and Organization,* Toronto, 1957, pp. 6–9.

10. A. Mawer and F. M. Stenton, *The Place-Names of Bedfordshire and Huntingdonshire,* London, 1926, pp. 183–184; James B. Johnston, *The Place Names of England and Wales,* London, 1915, p. 258; Eilert Ekwall, *The Concise Oxford Dictionary of English Place Names,* Oxford, 1947, p. 158.

11. *Chronicon abbatiae Rameseiensis,* pp. 112–113.

12. Ibid., pp. 135–140.

13. E. A. Kosminsky, *Studies in the Agrarian History of England in the Thirteenth Century,* Oxford, 1956, p. 73.

14. *Cartulariurn monasterii de Rameseia,* ed. by William Hart, London, 1884–1893, vol. 1, p. 234. (Henceforth referred to as *Cart. Rames.*)

15. Barbara Dodwell, "Holdings and Inheritance in East Anglia," in *Economic History Review* 2nd ser. 20 (1967), p. 55.

16. Raftis, *Estates of Ramsey Abbey,* pp. 26–34.

17. Susan B. Edgington, "Ramsey Abbey vs. Pagan Peverel, St. Ives, 1107," *Records of Huntingdonshire 2* (1985), pp. 2–5; Edgington, "Pagan Peverel: An Anglo-Norman Crusader," in *Crusade and Settlement,* ed. by P. Edbury, Cardiff, 1985, pp. 90–93.

18. H. C. Darby, "Domesday England," in Darby, ed., *New Historical Geography,* p. 39.

19. W. Page and G. Proby, eds., *Victoria History of the Counties of England: Huntingdonshire,* vol. 1, London, 1926, p. 344. (Henceforth referred to as *V.C.H. Hunts.*)

20. *Rotuli Hundredorum temp. Hen. III et Edw. I in Turri Lond' et in curia receptae scaccarii Westm. asservati,* London, 1818, vol. 2, p. 656. (Henceforth referred to as *Rot. Hund.*)

21. Beresford, *Lost Villages,* p. 55.

22. G. R. Owst, *Literature and Pulpit in Medieval England,* Oxford, 1961, pp. 27–28, 37.

23. R. H. Hilton, *A Medieval Society: The West Midlands and the End of the Thirteenth Century,* New York, 1966, p. 95; Hoskins, *The Midland Peasant,* p. 284; Chapelot and Fossier, *Village and House,* pp. 253–254, 296–302; Margaret Wood, *The English Mediaeval House,* London, 1965, pp. 215–216; Maurice W. Barley, *The English Farmhouse and Cottage,* London, 1961, pp. 22–25; H. M. Colvin, "Domestic Architecture and Town-Planning," in A. Lane Poole, ed., *Medieval England,* London, 1958, vol. 1, pp. 82–88.

24. Wood, *English Mediaeval House,* p. 293.

25. Chapelot and Fossier, *Village and House,* pp. 313–315; Sarah M. McKinnon, "The Peasant House: The Evidence of Manuscript Illuminations," in Raftis, ed., *Pathways to Medieval Peasants,* p. 304; Colvin, "Domestic Architecture," p. 87.

26. Hurst, "The Changing Medieval Village," pp. 42–43; Beresford and Hurst, *Deserted Medieval Villages,* pp. 104–105; Hilton, *A Medieval Society,* p. 97.

27. *Bedfordshire Coroners' Rolls,* ed. by R. F. Hunnisett, Streatley, England, 1969, pp. 8, 35, 45, 83, 92, 112–113.

28. *Elton Manorial Records, 1279–1351,* ed. by S. C. Ratcliff, trans. by D. M. Gregory, Cambridge, 1946, p. 152. (Henceforth referred to as *E.M.R.*)

29. Ibid., pp. 392, 393.

30. Hilton, *A Medieval Society,* p. 95.

31. Beresford and Hurst, *Deserted Medieval Villages,* p. 116.

32. *E.M.R.,* pp. 196, 300, 316; Grenville Astill, "Rural Settlement, the Toft and the Croft," in Astill and Grant, eds., *Countryside of Medieval England,* pp. 36–61.

33. *E.M.R.,* p. 52.

34. Ibid., pp. 52, 370.

35. Ibid., p. 52.

36. Ibid., pp. 50, 82, 100.

37. *Rot. Hund.,* p. 656; Leslie E. Webster and John Cherry, "Medieval Britain in 1977," *Medieval Archaeology,* pp. 142, 178.

38. *E.M.R.,* pp. 22, 66, 275.

39. Ibid., pp. 13, 79, 214.

40. Ibid., pp. 137, 138, 169, 275, 322, 323, 336.

41. Ibid., p. 213.

42. Ibid., pp. 21, 64, 138, 169, 170, 215, 386.

43. Ibid., pp. 65, 66, 80, 169, 174, 176, 185, 322, 323.

44. Ibid., pp. 14, 22, 137, 386.

45. Ibid., pp. 14, 137, 138, 139, 323.

46. Ibid., pp. 137, 138, 168, 214, 371.

47. Ibid., p. 169.

48. Ibid., pp. 137, 213, 214, 272, 288.

49. Ibid., pp. 52, 77–78.

50. Ibid., p. 112.

51. Ibid., pp. 10, 19, 57, 126, 158, 203, 266–267.

52. Ibid., p. li.

53. Brian K. Roberts, *The Making of the English Village, a Study in Historical Geography,* Harlow, England, 1987, pp. 21–29; Chapelot and Fossier, *Village and House,* p. 184.

54. Hilton, *A Medieval Society,* pp. 93–95.

55. *E.M.R.,* p. 69.

56. *Rot. Hund.,* pp. 656–658.

57. Hilton, *A Medieval Society,* p. 92.

58. *E.M.R.,* p. 97.

59. *Rot. Hund.,* p.657.

CHAPTER III
THE LORD

1. *The Estate Book of Henry de Bray,* Northamptonshire, c. 1289–1340, ed. by D. Willis, Camden Society 3rd ser. 27 (1916).

2. Miller and Hatcher, *Medieval England,* p. 17.

3. R. H. Hilton, *The English Peasantry in the Later Middle Ages,* Oxford, 1975, pp. 132–133.

4. Homans, *English Villagers,* pp. 330–331.

5. Raftis, *Estates of Ramsey Abbey,* p. 77; R. Lennard, *Rural England, 1086–1135, a Study of Society and Agrarian Conditions,* Oxford, 1959, p. 199.

6. Christopher Dyer, *Lords and Peasants in a Changing Society: The Estates of the Bishopric of Worcester, 680–1548,* Cambridge, 1980, p. 55; Duby, *Rural Economy and Country Life,* p. 35.

7. Kosminsky, *Studies in Agrarian History,* Table 3, p. 100; Cart. Rames., vol. 1, pp. 294, 306.

8. Raftis, *Estates of Ramsey Abbey,* pp. 68–69.

9. *E.M.R.,* p. 117.

10. Ibid., pp. 193, 299.

11. Ibid., p. 45.

12. Ibid., p. 46.

13. Ellen W. Moore, *The Fairs of Medieval England: An Introductory Study,* Toronto, 1985.

14. *Cart. Rames.,* vol. 2, p. 342.

15. George Homans, "The Rural Sociology of Medieval England," *Past and Present 4* (1953), p. 39.

16. Ibid., p. 40.

17. *Walter of Henley's Husbandry, Together with an Anonymous Husbandry, Seneschaucie,* etc., ed. by E. Lamond, Oxford, 1890, p. 35.

18. Ibid. *(Rules of St. Robert),* p. 125.

19. Ibid. *(Seneschaucie),* pp. 88–89; Frances Davenport, *The Economic Development of a Norfolk Manor, 1086–1565,* Cambridge, 1906, pp. 22–23.

20. *Walter of Henley (Seneschaucie),* p, 105.

21. *E.M.R.,* p. xviii.

22. *E.M.R.,* p. 173, Davenport, *Economic Development of a Norfolk Manor,* p. 23.

23. Miller and Hatcher, *Medieval England,* pp. 192–193.

24. *Walter of Henley,* p. 11.

25. *E.M.R.,* pp. xxxvii–xxxviii.

26. Ibid., pp. 2, 4, 138, 272, 275, 386.

27. Ibid., pp.67–68, 140–141, 276–277.

28. Ibid., pp. 13, 67.

29. Ibid., p. 63.

30. *Walter of Henley (Seneschaucie),* p. 99.

31. Homans, *English Villagers,* pp. 297–305; Duby, *Rural Economy and Country Life,* p. 233; Raftis, *Estates of Ramsey Abbey,* pp. 125–127; Miller and Hatcher, *Medieval England,* pp. 193–197.

32. *Walter of Henley (Seneschaucie),* p. 100–102.

33. *E.M.R.,* pp.56–85.

34. Ibid., p. 15.

35. Ibid., p. 24.

36. Ibid., p. 68.

37. Raftis, *Estates of Ramsey Abbey,* p. 95.

38. Nigel Saul, *Scenes from Provincial Life, Knightly Families in Sussex, 1280–1400,* Oxford, 1987, p. 127.

39. Geoffrey Chaucer, *The Canterbury Tales,* in *The Complete Works of Geoffrey Chaucer,* ed. by F. N. Robinson, Boston, 1933, p. 25 (lines 593–594).

40. *Walter of Henley,* pp. 17–18.

41. J. S. Drew, "Manorial Accounts of St. Swithun's Priory, Winchester," in *E.M.R.,* Carus-Wilson, ed., *Essays in Economic History,* London, 1962, pp. 27–30.

42. *Walter of Henley,* p. 11.

43. Homans, *English Villagers,* p. 293.

44. *E.M.R.,* pp. 70, 79, 278, 373.

45. *Walter of Henley, (Rules of St. Robert),* p. 145.

46. *Cart. Rames.,* vol. 3, pp. 168–169, 230–232.

47. Paul Vinogradoff, *The Growth of the Manor,* London, 1911; Dyer, *Lords and Peasants,* p. 67.

48. M. M. Postan, "The Famulus: The Estate Labourer in the Twelfth and Thirteenth Centuries," *Economic History Review,* supplement no. 2, Cambridge, 1954, p. 3.

49. *E.M.R.,* pp. 16, 173, 218.

50. Ibid., pp. 24, 48, 172–173, 217–218.

51. Postan, "The Famulus," p. 21; *Cart. Rames.,* vol. 3, pp. 236–241; vol. 1, pp. 319, 330, 340, 351, 363.

52. Postan, "The Famulus," p. 21.

53. *Walter of Henley (Seneschaucie),* p. 110; *Walter of Henley,* pp. 11–13; David L. Farmer, "Prices and Wages," in H. E. Hallam, ed., *The Agrarian History of England and Wales,* vol. 2, 1042–1350, Cambridge, 1988, p. 748; Annie Grant, "Animal Resources," in Astill and Grant, eds., *Countryside of Medieval England,* p. 174.

54. *E.M.R,* pp. 25–26; J. A. Raftis, "Farming Techniques (East Midlands)," in *The Agrarian History of England and Wales,* vol. 2, pp. 336–337.

55. *E.M.R,* p. 173.

56. Raftis, *Estates of Ramsey Abbey,* p. 206.

57. *E.M.R,* pp. lii–liii.

58. Raftis, *Estates of Ramsey Abbey,* p. 167.

59. Warren O. Ault, *Open-Field Farming in Medieval England: A Study of Village By-Laws,* London, 1972, p. 31.

60. Farmer, "Prices and Wages," in *The Agrarian History of England and Wales,* vol. 2, p. 734.

61. *Walter of Henley (Seneschaucie),* p. 113.

62. *Walter of Henley,* p. 25.

63. Robert Trow-Smith, *History of British Livestock Husbandry,* London, 1957–1959, vol. 1, p. 156.

64. Ibid., p. 153.

65. *E.M.R,* pp. liii–liv.

66. Trow-Smith, *British Livestock Husbandry,* vol. 1, p. 149.

67. *Walter of Henley (Seneschaucie),* pp. 117–118.

68. *E.M.R,* p. lv.

69. Miller and Hatcher, *Medieval England,* p. 77.

70. *Walter of Henley (Rules of St. Robert),* p. 141.

71. E. A. Kosminsky, "Services and Money Rents in the Thirteenth Century," in Carus-Wilson, ed., *Essays in Economic History,* pp. 31–48.

72. *The Estate Book of Henry de Bray,* pp. xxiv–xxvii.

73. Beresford and Hurst, *Deserted Medieval Villages,* p. 127.

74. *Walter of Henley,* p. 19.

75. Ibid., p. 29.

76. *E.M.R,* pp. 17, 25.

77. *Walter of Henley (Seneschaucie),* p. 113.

78. Trow-Smith, *British Livestock Husbandry,* p. 112.

79. Ibid., p. 161; Farmer, "Prices and Wages," in *The Agrarian History of England and Wales,* vol. 2, p. 757; *E.M.R,* p. liii.

80. Miller and Hatcher, *Medieval England,* p. 215.

81. Thirsk, "Farming Techniques," in *The Agrarian History of England and Wales,* vol. 4, p. 163.

82. Trow-Smith, *British Livestock Husbandry,* p. 169.

CHAPTER IV
THE VILLAGERS: WHO THEY WERE

1. Miller and Hatcher, *Medieval England,* p. 20.

2. Ibid., p. 113.

3. Frederic William Maitland, *The Domesday Book and Beyond,* New York, 1966 (first pub. in 1897), p. 31.

4. R. H. Hilton, "Freedom and Villeinage in England," in Hilton, ed., *Peasants, Knights, and Heretics,* pp. 174–191.

5. F. Pollock and F.W. Maitland, *The History of English Law Before the Time of Edward I,* Cambridge, 1968, vol. 1, p. 419. On the subject of freedom versus serfdom: R. H. Hilton, *The Decline of Serfdom in Medieval England,* London, 1969; Miller and Hatcher, *Medieval England,* pp. 111–133; M. M. Postan, "Legal Status and Economic Condition in Medieval Villages," in M. M. Postan, *Essays on Medieval Agriculture and General Problems of the Medieval Economy,* Cambridge, 1968, pp. 278–289.

6. Miller and Hatcher, *Medieval England,* pp. 111–112.

7. Ibid., p. 112.

8. Duby, *Rural Economy and Country Life,* p. 282.

9. *Cart. Rames.,* vol. 3, pp. 257–260.

10. J. A. Raftis, *Warboys: Two Hundred Years in the Life of an English Medieval Village,* Toronto, 1974, pp. 67–68.

11. Kosminsky, *Studies in the Agrarian History of England,* pp. 230–237.

12. *Rot. Hund.,* pp. 656–658.

13. *V.C.H. Hunts.,* p. 161.

14. *Rot. Hund.,* pp. 656–658.

15. *Cart. Rames.,* vol. 1, pp. 299–300, 310, 324, 336, 345, 350, 357, 361, 365, 393–394, 460–461, 475, 483; vol. 2, pp. 45–46.

16. *E.M.R,* p. 128.

17. Ibid., p. 268.

18. Ibid., p. 10.

19. Raftis, *Estates of Ramsey Abbey,* pp. 224–227.

20. *E.M.R,* pp. 5–6.

21. Ibid., pp. 28, 78, 181, 227, 287–288, 334.

22. *Rot. Hund.,* p. 657.

23. *E.M.R,* pp. 93, 150.

24. Ibid., pp. 147, 151.

25. Ibid., pp. 147, 201, 255.

26. Ibid., p. 10. See also Postan, "The Famulus," pp. 7–14.

27. *E.M.R,* p. 93.

28. Ibid., p. 261.

29. Ibid., p. 249.

30. Ibid., p. 44.

31. Chaucer, *Canterbury Tales,* p. 32.

32. *E.M.R,* p. 43.

33. Ibid., p. 44.

34. Ibid., p. 10.

35. Ibid., p. 126.

36. Ibid., p. 43.

37. Ibid., p. 43.

38. Ibid., p. 43.

39. Ibid., p. 196.

40. Ibid., p. 115.

41. *Bedfordshire Coroners' Rolls,* p. 114.

42. *E.M.R,* p. 34.

43. Ibid., p. 89.

44. Ibid., p. 190.

45. Ibid., p. 254.

46. Ibid., p. 261.

47. Ibid., p. 257.

48. Ibid., p. 261.

49. Ibid., p. 293.

50. Anne De Windt, "A Peasant Land Market and Its Participants: King's Ripton 1280–1400," *Midland History 4* (1978), pp. 142–149.

51. M. M. Postan, "Village Livestock in the Thirteenth Century," *Economic History Review* 2nd ser. 15 (1962), pp. 219–249.

52. Trow-Smith, *British Livestock Husbandry,* vol. 1, p. 103.

53. *E.M.R,* p. 200.

54. *Bedfordshire Coroners' Rolls,* p. 87.

55. Ibid., p. 82.

56. Edmund Britton, *The Community of the Vill: A Study in the History of the Family and Village Life in Fourteenth-Century England,* Toronto, 1977.

57. Edwin De Windt, *Land and People in Holywell-cum-Needingworth: Structures of Tenure and Patterns of Social Organization in an East Midlands Village, 1253–1453,* Toronto, 1972.

58. *E.M.R,* p. 3.

59. Ibid., p. 44.

60. Ibid., pp. 120–121.

61. Ibid., p. 122.

62. Ibid., p. 146.

63. Ibid., p. 200.

64. Ibid., p. 234.

65. Ibid., p. 2.

66. Ibid., p. 30.

67. Ibid., p. 46.

68. Ibid., p. 34.

69. Ibid., p. 116.

70. Ibid., p. 120.

71. Ibid., p. 95.

72. Ibid., p. 261.

73. Emmanuel Le Roy Ladurie, *Montaillou, The Promised Land of Error,* trans. by Barbara Bray, New York, 1978.

74. *E.M.R,* pp. 5–6.

CHAPTER V
THE VILLAGERS: HOW THEY LIVED

1. Beresford and Hurst, *Deserted Medieval Villages,* p. 122; Cantor, "Villages and Towns," in Cantor, ed., *The English Medieval Landscape,* pp. 173–174; Chapelot and Fossier, *Village and House,* pp. 204–205; Hurst, "The Changing Medieval Village," p. 44.

2. R. K. Field, "Worcestershire Peasant Buildings, Household Goods and Farming Equipment in the Later Middle Ages," *Medieval Archaeology* 9 (1965), pp. 105–145.

3. *E.M.R,* p. 115.

4. Ibid., p. 151.

5. Ibid., p. 300.

6. Beresford and Hurst, *Deserted Medieval Villages*, p. 104; Hilton *A Medieval Society*, pp. 96–97; Trow-Smith, *British Livestock Husbandry*, vol. 1, p. 114.

7. Wood, *English Mediaeval House*, pp. 300–302; Chapelot and Fossier, *Village and House*, pp. 284–314; Colvin, *English Farmhouse*, pp. 21–36.

8. Beresford and Hurst, *Deserted Medieval Villages*, p. 105.

9. *E.M.R*, p. 170.

10. Beresford and Hurst, *Deserted Medieval Villages*, pp. 98, 100; Wood, *English Mediaeval House*, pp. 257–260.

11. *Hali Meidenhod*, ed. by O. Cockayne, London, 1922, p. 53.

12. Owst, *Literature and Pulpit*, pp. 27, 35–36.

13. Barbara Hanawalt, *The Ties That Bound: Peasant Families in Medieval England*, New York, 1986, pp. 45–49; Hoskins, *The Midland Peasant*, pp. 295–296; Hilton, A *Medieval Society*, pp. 100–101; Field, "Worcestershire Peasant Buildings," pp. 121–123.

14. Wood, *Mediaeval English House*, pp. 368–374.

15. *E.M.R*, pp. 12, 62, 78, 133, 209.

16. Duby, *Rural Economy and Country Life*, p. 65.

17. Miller and Hatcher, *Medieval England*, p. 164.

18. H. E. Hallam, "The Life of the People," in *Agrarian History of England and Wales*, vol. 2, pp. 830, 838.

19. Cecily Howell, *Land, Family, and Inheritance in Transition*, Cambridge, 1983, pp. 164–165; Grenville Astill, "Fields," in Astill and Grant, eds., *Countryside of Medieval England*, p. 118.

20. Kosminsky, *Studies in the Agrarian History of England*, p. 240.

21. Miller and Hatcher, *Medieval England*, pp. 147–148; H. S. Bennett, *Life on the English Manor, A Study of Peasant Conditions, 1150–1400*, Cambridge, 1960 (first pub. in 1937), p. 95; Hallam, "Life of the People," in *The Agrarian History of England and Wales*, vol. 2, p. 824; J. Z. Titow, *English Rural Society, 1200–1350*, London, 1969, p. 79; Howell, *Land, Family, and Inheritance*, p. 159.

22. Michel Mollat, *The Poor in the Middle Ages, an Essay in Social History*, trans. by Arthur Goldhammer, New Haven, 1986, pp. 194–195.

23. Anear MacConglinne, "The Vision of Viands," in *The Portable Medieval Reader*, ed. by James Bruce Ross and Mary Martin McLaughlin, New York, 1966, pp. 497–499.

24. John Gower, *Miroir de l'Omme*, II, lines 450–460, in *Complete Works of John Gower*, ed. by G. C. Macaulay, Oxford, 1899–1902, vol. 1, p. 293.

25. *E.M.R*, p. 47.

26. William Langland, *Piers Plowman's Crede*, ed. by W. W. Skeat, London, 1867, pp. 16–17.

27. John Stow, *Survey of London*, London, 1603, p. 92, translating William Fitzstephen's description of twelfth-century London, cited in Bennett, *Life on the English Manor*, p. 261.

28. Homans, *English Villagers*, p. 358.

29. Bennett, *Life on the English Manor*, p. 262.

30. *E.M.R*, p. 172.

31. Homans, *English Villagers*, p. 362.

32. Ibid., p. 365.

33. Ibid., pp. 368, 370.

34. *E.M.R*, p. 69.

35. Homans, *English Villagers*, p. 372.

36. *E.M.R*, p. 172.

37. Robert Manning, *Handlyng Synne*, ed. by Idelle Sullens, Binghamton, New York, 1983, p. 224.

38. Owst, *Literature and Pulpit*, p. 362.

39. *Bedfordshire Coroners' Rolls*, pp. 97–98.

40. Hanawalt, *Ties That Bound*, pp. 44, 60.

41. *Bedfordshire Coroners' Rolls*, pp. 2–3.

42. Ibid., pp. 55–57.

43. Ibid., p. 108.

44. Ibid., p. 51.

45. Ibid., pp. 71–72.

46. Ibid., p. xxiii.

47. Ibid., p. 7.

48. Ibid., pp. 12–13.

49. Ibid., p. 116.

CHAPTER VI
MARRIAGE AND THE FAMILY

1. Frances and Joseph Gies, *Marriage and the Family in the Middle Ages*, New York, 1987, pp. 157–177.

2. Miller and Hatcher, *Medieval England*, p. 138.

3. P. D. A. Harvey, *A Medieval Oxfordshire Village: Cuxham, 1240 to 1400*, Oxford, 1965, p. 124.

4. Rosamond Jane Faith, "Peasant Families and Inheritance Customs in Medieval England," *Agricultural History Review* 4 (1966).

5. Ibid., pp. 86–87.

6. *E.M.R*, p. 208.

7. *Court Roll of Chalgrave Manor*, ed. by Marian K. Dale, Bedfordshire Historical Record Society 28 (1950), p. 10.

8. *E.M.R*, pp. 56, 68, 70.

9. Ibid., p. 392.

10. Ibid., p. 313.

11. Ibid., pp. 84–85, 264, 317.

12. Ibid., p. 313.

13. *Cart. Rames.*, vol. 1, p. 416.

14. Ibid., vol. 1, pp. 294, 306, 320, 330, 352.

15. Ibid., vol. 1, pp. 359, 384.

16. *Court Roll of Chalgrave Manor*, p. 9.

17. Trow-Smith, *British Livestock Husbandry*, pp. 100–101.

18. Britton, *Community of the Vill*, pp. 59–64.

19. Anne De Windt, "Peasant Land Market," pp. 151–153.

20. Duby, *Rural Economy and Country Life*, p. 284.

21. *E.M.R*, p. 96.

22. Ibid., p. 261.

23. Ibid., p. 5.

24. Eleanor Searle, "Seigneurial Control of Women's Marriage: The Antecedents and Function of Merchet in England," *Past and Present 82* (1979), pp. 3–43; also Searle, "Freedom and Marriage in Medieval England: An Alternative Hypothesis," *Economic History Review* 2nd ser. 29 (1976).

25. *E.M.R*, p. 28.

26. Ibid., p. 132.

27. Judith M. Bennett, "Medieval Peasant Marriage: An Examination of the Marriage License Fines in Liber Gersumarum," in Raftis, ed., *Pathways to Medieval Peasants*, p. 195.

28. Ibid., p. 197.

29. Ibid., pp. 205–209, 213–214.

30. Ibid., pp. 208–209.

31. *Cart. Rames.*, vol. 1, p. 432.

32. Bennett, "Medieval Peasant Marriage," pp. 200–204.

33. *E.M.R*, pp. 61, 132, 208–209.

34. Gies, *Marriage and the Family*, pp. 135–141.

35. William Langland, *The Vision of Piers Plowman*, ed. by A. V. C. Schmidt, London, 1984, passus ix, lines 162–165, p. 97.

36. Manning, Handlyng Synne, p. 279.

37. Ibid., p. 277.

38. G. R. Owst, *Preaching in Medieval England*, London, 1926, p. 269.

39. Ibid., p.269.

40. *Cart. Rames.*, vol. 1, p. 312.

41. Gies, *Marriage and the Family*, pp. 242–245, 299–300.

42. Manning, *Handlyng Synne*, p. 211.

41. *E.M.R*, p. 3.

44. Ibid., pp. 132, 146.

45. Ibid., p. 200.

46. G. G. Coulton, *Medieval Village, Manor, and Monastery*, New York, 1960 (first pub. in 1925), pp. 477–478.

47. J. A. Raftis, in correspondence with the authors.

48. Britton, *Community of the Vill*, pp. 34–37.

49. Hanawalt, *Ties That Bound*, p. 216.

50. John Myrc, *Instructions for Parish Priests*, ed. by E. Peacock, London, 1868, pp. 18–19.

51. Manning, *Handlyng Synne*, pp. 240–241.

52. Myrc, *Instructions for Parish Priests*, pp. 4–5.

53. Hanawalt, *Ties That Bound*, pp. 172–173.

54. Ibid., pp, 175–179.

55. *Bedfordshire Coroners' Rolls*, p. 1.

56. Ibid., p. 51.

57. Ibid., pp. 59–60.

58. Ibid., p. 98.

59. Barbara Hanawalt, "Childbearing Among the Lower Classes of Late Medieval England," *Journal of Interdisciplinary History* 8 (1977), pp. 20–21.

60. Owst, *Literature and Pulpit*, pp. 34–35.

61. Ibid., pp. 33–34.

62. Ibid., p. 34.

63. Hanawalt, *Ties That Bound*, pp. 166–167.

64. *Cart. Rames.*, pp. 300–301.

65. M. M. Postan and J. Titow, "Heriots and Prices on Winchester Manors," *Economic History Review* 2nd ser. 11 (1959), pp. 392–410; Hanawalt, *Ties That Bound*, pp. 228–229; Miller and Hatcher, *Medieval England*, pp. viii–ix.

66. *E.M.R*, p. 311.

67. Elaine Clark, "Some Aspects of Social Security in Medieval England," *Journal of Family History* 7 (1982), pp. 307–320.

68. Manning, *Handlyng Synne*, pp. 30–32.

69. J. A. Raftis, *Tenure and Mobility: Studies in the Social History of the Mediaeval English Village*, Toronto, 1964, pp. 43–44.

70. Ibid., pp. 44–45.

71. Homans, *English Villagers*, p. 146.

72. Clark, "Some Aspects of Social Security," p. 313.

73. Ibid., pp. 312–313.

74. Raftis, *Tenure and Mobility*, p. 45.

75. Ibid., p. 44.

76. Clark, "Some Aspects of Social Security," pp. 310–311.

77. Howard Morris Stuckert, *Corrodies in English Monasteries: A Study in English Social History of the Middle Ages*, Philadelphia, 1923; Hilton, A Medieval Society, pp. 111–113.

78. Hilton, *A Medieval Society*, p. 163.

79. *Bedfordshire Coroners' Rolls*, p. 4.

80. Ibid., p. 89.

81. Manning, *Handlyng Synne*, pp. 280–281.

82. Myrc, *Instructions for Parish Priests*, pp. 53–59.

83. *Roberti Grosseteste Epistolae episcopi quondam Lincolniensis*, ed. by H. R. Luard, London, 1861, p. 74, cited in Homans, *English Villagers*, p. 392.

84. Homans, *English Villagers*, p. 392.

85. Cited in Owst, *Preaching in Medieval England*, p. 268.

CHAPTER VII
THE VILLAGE AT WORK

1. *E.M.R*, p. 90; Raftis, "Farming Techniques," in *The Agrarian History of England and Wales*, vol. 2, p. 329.

2. Ault, *Open-Field Farming*, pp. 22–23.

3. Gray, *English Field Systems*, especially pp. 39–49 and 71–82; Gray expresses the change from two-field to three-field as bringing "under tillage one-sixth more of the [total] arable" (p. 76); Homans, *English Villagers*, p. 57; Duby, *Rural Economy and Country Life*, pp. 22–23; 92–96; Miller and Hatcher, *Medieval England*, pp. 88–97.

4. Miller and Hatcher, *Medieval England*, pp. 89–97 for a general discussion of field systems; Homans, *English Villagers*, p. 54; Trevor Rowley, "Medieval Field Systems," in Cantor, ed., *The English Medieval Landscape*, pp. 36–38.

5. Maurice Beresford, *Studies in Leicestershire Agrarian History*, London, 1949, p. 93, cited in Ault, *Open-Field Farming*, p. 52.

6. *E.M.R*, p. 4.

7. Ibid., p. 34.

8. Ibid., p. 30.

9. Ibid., p. 3.

10. Miller and Hatcher, *Medieval England,* p. 99.

11. Ibid., p. 123.

12. *E.M.R,* p.

13. V.C.H. Hunts., vol. 1, p. 75; Rot. Hund., p. 657.

14. *Cart. Rames.,* vol. 1, pp. 323–324.

15. Raftis, *Estates of Ramsey Abbey,* pp. 194–195; Robert R. Reynolds, *Europe Emerges: Transition Toward an Industrial World-Wide Society,* 600–1750, Madison, 1967 p. 132.

16. *E.M.R,* p.

17. Ibid., p. 4.

18. Ibid., p. 5.

19. John Langdon, "Agricultural Equipment," in Astill and Grant, eds., *Countryside of Medieval England,* p. 96; Orwin and Orwin, *The Open Fields,* p. 12; Field, "Worcestershire Peasant Buildings," pp. 123–125.

20. Ault, *Open-Field Farming,* p. 20; Miller and Hatcher, *Medieval England,* pp. 154–155.

21. Trow-Smith, *British Livestock Husbandry,* pp. 69–70.

22. Butser Hill Ancient Farm Project; M. L. Ryder, "Livestock," in *The Agrarian History of England and Wales,* vol. 1, pt. 1, p. 349; *E.M.R,* p. lix; Trow-Smith, *British Livestock Husbandry,* vol. 1, p. 123.

23. Ault, *Open-Field Farming,* p. 20.

24. Ibid., p. 22; Orwin and Orwin, *The Open Fields,* pp. 33–35; Homans, *English Villagers,* pp. 44–45.

25. Ault, *Open-Field Farming,* p. 23.

26. Thirsk, "Farming Techniques," in *The Agrarian History of England and Wales,* vol. 4, p. 166; *Walter of Henley,* p. 19.

27. Ibid., p. 19; J. A. Raftis, "Farming Techniques: the East Midlands," in *The Agrarian History of England and Wales,* vol. 2, p. 327.

28. *E.M.R,* p. 249; Christopher Dyer, "Farming Techniques: the West Midlands," in *The Agrarian History of England and Wales,* vol. 2, p. 378.

29. Homans, *English Villagers,* p. 40.

30. *Walter of Henley,* p. 13; Raftis, "Farming Techniques: the East Midlands," in *The Agrarian History of England and Wales,* vol. 2, p. 327.

31. Dyer, *Lords and Peasants,* p. 69.

32. *Walter of Henley,* p. 15.

33. Maitland, *Domesday Book and Beyond,* p. 348.

34. Ault, *Open-Field Farming,* pp. 26–27.

35. *Cart. Rames.,* vol. 1, p. 311; *E.M.R,* p. 173; Homans, *English Villagers,* pp. 269–270.

36. *Cart. Rames.,* vol. 1, p. 311.

37. Ibid., vol. 1, pp. 311, 336.

38. *E.M.R,* p. 30.

39. Ibid., p. 3.

40. Ibid., p. 69.

41. *Cart. Rames.,* vol. 1, p. 300.

42. Britton, *Community of the Vill,* pp. 170–171; H. E. Hallam, "The Life of the People," in *The Agrarian History of England and Wales,* vol. 2, p. 838.

43. *Walter of Henley (Hosbonderie),* p. 69.

44. Ault, *Open-Field Farming,* p. 28.

45. Cited in Ault, *Open-Field Farming,* p. 31 *(Commentary on the Laws of England,* vol. 3, p. 212, 1772).

46. *Walter of Henley,* p. 69; Homans, *English Villagers,* p. 103.

47. Hilton, *A Medieval Society,* p. 123.

48. Fernand Braudel, *Civilization and Capitalism 15th–18th Century,* vol. 1, *The Structures of Everyday Life: The Limits of the Possible,* New York, 1981, p. 124.

49. Ault, *Open-Field Farming,* p. 29.

50. *Walter of Henley (Seneschaucie),* p. 99.

51. Ault, Open-Field Farming, pp. 42–43.

52. Langdon, "Agricultural Equipment," in Astill and Grant, eds., *Countryside of Medieval England,* p. 103.

53. Duby, *Rural Economy and Country Life,* p. 270; F. R. H. DuBoulay, *The Lordship of Canterbury,* London, 1966, p. 12.

54. *E.M.R,* p. 92.

55. Langland, *Piers Plowman's Crede,* pp. 16–17.

56. Hilton, *The English Peasantry in the Later Middle Ages,* pp. 102–103.

57. Ibid., p. 105.

58. Ibid., p. 97.

59. Trow-Smith, *British Livestock Husbandry,* p. 129.

60. Ibid., p. 147.

61. Ibid., p. 159.

62. Thirsk, "Farming Techniques," in *The Agrarian History of England and Wales,* vol. 4, p. 187.

63. Miller and Hatcher, *Medieval England,* p. 217.

64. *Walter of Henley (Hosbonderie),* pp. 76–77.

65. Trow-Smith, *British Livestock Husbandry,* p. 128.

66. Ault, *Open-Field Farming,* pp. 48–49.

67. *V.C.H. Hunts.,* p. 78.

68. Joan Thirsk, "Farming Techniques," in *The Agrarian History of England and Wales,* vol. 4, pp. 192–193.

69. Ault, *Open-Field Farming,* p. 50.

70. Trow-Smith, *British Livestock Husbandry,* pp. 117, 121; Miller and Hatcher, *Medieval England,* p. 217.

71. James Greig, "Plant Resources," in Astill and Grant, eds., *Countryside of Medieval England,* p. 121; *E.M.R,* p. 60.

72. Raftis, "Farming Techniques," in *The Agrarian History of England and Wales,* vol. 2, p. 338; Thirsk, "Farming Techniques," in *The Agrarian History of England and Wales,* vol. 4, p. 195.

73. *Walter of Henley (Hosbonderie),* p. 77.

74. Joseph and Frances Gies, *Life in a Medieval City,* New York, 1969, pp. 102–103.

75. *E.M.R,* p. 81.

76. Ibid., p. 303.

77. *Cart. Rames.,* vol. 1, pp. 489–490.

78. *E.M.R,* pp. 52.

79. Ibid., pp. 96, 117.

80. Ibid., p. 260.

81. Ibid., pp. 64, 111–112, 211.

82. Ibid., pp. 13, 64.

83. Ibid., p. vii.

84. Ibid., pp. 5, 45.

85. Ibid., pp. 66, 67, 138, 141, 171, 172.

86. Henri Pirenne, *Economic and Social History of Medieval Europe,* New York, 1937, p. 88.

87. Homans, *English Villagers,* p. 236; Raftis, *Tenure and Mobility,* p. 139.

88. *E.M.R,* pp. 6–7.

89. Postan and Titow, "Heriots and Prices on Winchester Manors."

90. Mollat, *The Poor in the Middle Ages,* p. 178.

91. Vinogradoff, *Growth of the Manor,* p. 307.

92. Hallam, "The Life of the People," in *The Agrarian History of England and Wales,* vol. 2, p. 846.

CHAPTER VIII
THE PARISH

1. Miller and Hatcher, *Medieval England,* pp. 106–107.

2. John Godfrey, *The English Parish, 600–1300,* London, 1969; J. R. H. Moorman, *Church Life in England in the Thirteenth Century,* Cambridge, 1945, pp. 2–9.

3. *Cart. Rames.,* vol. 2, p. 136.

4. Moorman, *Church Life in England,* pp. 24–37; A. Hamilton Thompson, *The English Clergy and Their Organization in the Later Middle Ages,* Oxford, 1947, pp. 101–131.

5. Moorman, *Church Life in England,* pp. 26–28.

6. *Chronicon de Lanercost,* Edinburgh, 1839, p. 158, cited in Moorman, *Church Life in England,* p. 27.

7. Moorman, *Church Life in England,* pp. 28–31; Godfrey, *The English Parish,* pp. 74–75.

8. Ibid., pp. 76–77.

9. Chaucer, *Canterbury Tales,* pp. 30–31.

10. Moorman, *Church Life in England,* pp.90–91.

11. Ibid., pp. 92–94.

12. Ibid., pp. 95–98.

13. Myrc, *Instructions for Parish Priests,* p. 1; W. A. Pantin, *The English Church in the Fourteenth Century,* Cambridge, 1955, pp. 195–243.

14. *The Autobiography of Giraldus Cambrensis,* ed. and trans. by H. E. Williams, London, 1937, p. 40.

15. *Cart. Rames.,* vol. 1, pp. 293–294.

16. Ibid., vol. 1, p. 306.

17. Ibid., vol. 1, p. 331

18. *Rot. Hund.,* p. 658.

19. *Cart. Rames.,* vol. 1, pp. 305–306.

20. Ibid., vol. 1, p. 293.

21. Ibid., vol. 1, p. 320.

22. *E.M.R,* p. 196.

23. Ibid., p. 300.

24. Owst, *Preaching in Medieval England,* p. 31.

25. Moorman, *Church Life in Medieval England,* p. 59.

26. Colin Platt, *The Parish Churches of Medieval England,* London, 1981, p. 58.

27. Adhémar Esmein, *Le Mariage en droit canonique,* ed. by R. Génestal, Paris, 1929–35, vol. 1, p. 131.

28. Moorman, *Church Life in England,* pp. 64–65.

29. Manning, *Handlyng Synne,* pp. 201–203.

30. *Chronicon de Lanercost,* pp. 2–3, cited in Moorman, *Church Life in England,* p. 64.

31. Platt, *Parish Churches,* pp. 13–26.

32. Ibid., pp. 27–28.

33. P. H. Ditchfield, *Old Village Life,* London, 1920, pp. 104–105.

34. Platt, *Parish Churches,* pp. 28–29.

35. W. O. Hassall, *How They Lived: An Anthology of Original Accounts Written Before 1485,* New York, 1960, p. 344.

36. Manning, *Handlyng Synne,* pp. 217–218.

37. Moorman, *Church Life in England,* pp. 68–70.

38. Manning, *Handlyng Synne,* pp. 108–109.

39. Owst, *Preaching in Medieval England,* p. 170.

40. Ibid., p. 172.

41. Myrc, *Instructions for Parish Priests,* p. 9.

42. Moorman, *Church Life in England,* pp. 79–80.

43. Owst, *Preaching in Medieval England,* p. 319.

44. Owst, *Literature and Pulpit,* p. 156.

45. Owst, *Preaching in Medieval England,* pp. 336–337.

46. Ibid., p. 339.

47. Ibid., pp. 341–342.

48. Pantin, *English Church in the Fourteenth Century,* pp. 199–200.

49. Myrc, *Instructions for Parish Priests,* p. 26.

50. Ibid., pp. 29–43.

51. Ibid., pp. 43–48.

52. Ibid., pp. 1–3.

CHAPTER IX
VILLAGE JUSTICE

1. Homans, *English Villagers,* pp. 309–327.

2. *E.M.R,* pp. 37–38.

3. A. E. Levett, *Studies in Manorial History,* Oxford, 1938, p. 111.

4. Homans, *English Villagers,* p. 312; *E.M.R,* pp. 7, 34, 47, 105.

5. Levett, *Studies in Manorial History,* p. 149.

6. *E.M.R,* p. 1.

7. Levett, *Studies in Manorial History,* p. 151.

8. *E.M.R,* p. 153.

9. *The Court Baron,* ed. by F. W. Maitland and W. P. Baildon, London, 1891, p. 27.

10. Ibid., p. 28.

11. Homans, *English Villagers,* pp. 315–316.

12. *The Court Baron,* p. 28.

13. Homans, *English Villagers,* pp. 314–315.

14. *E.M.R,* p. 2.

15. Martin Pimsler, "Solidarity in the Medieval Village? The Evidence of Personal Pledging at Elton, Huntingdonshire," *Journal of British Studies* 17 (1977), pp. 1–11; Britton, *Community of the Vill*, p. 104.

16. *E.M.R,* pp. 2–7.

17. Homans, *English Villagers,* p. 315.

18. *E.M.R,* p. 89.

19. Ibid., p. 46.

20. Homans, *English Villagers,* p. 315.

21. *E.M.R,* pp. 30, 89.

22. Marc Bloch, *Feudal Society,* trans. by L. A. Manyon, Chicago, 1964, vol. 1, p. 271.

23. *E.M.R,* p. 5.

24. Homans, *English Villagers,* pp. 324–325; John G. Bellamy, *Crime and Public Order in the Later Middle Ages,* London, 1973, pp. 90–91.

25. *The Court Baron,* pp. 93–94.

26. *V.C.H. Hunts.,* vol. 1, p. 159.

27. *E.M.R,* p. 3.

28. Ibid., p. 44.

29. Ibid., p. 94.

30. Ibid., p. 31.

31. Ibid., p. 94.

32. Ibid., p. 120.

33. Ibid., p. 197.

34. Ibid., p. 102.

35. Ibid., p. 94.

36. Ibid., p. 189.

37. Ibid., p. 152.

38. Ibid., p. 3.

39. Ibid., p. 152.

40. Ibid., p. 31.

41. Gies, *Marriage and the Family,* p. 63; Jean-Louis Flandrin, "Sex in Married Life in the Early Middle Ages," in Philippe Ariés and André Béjin, *Western Sexuality,* London, 1985, pp. 140–157.

42. *E.M.R,* pp. 31–32.

43. Ibid., p. 39.

44. Homans, *English Villagers,* pp. 312–313.

45. E M. R., p. 42.

46. Mollat, *The Poor in the Middle Ages,* p. 172.

47. Homans, *English Villagers,* p. 320.

48. *E.M.R,* p. 200.

49. Ibid., p. 299.

50. Ibid., p. 94.

51. Ibid., p. 98.

52. Homans, *English Villagers,* p. 323.

53. Britton, *Community of the Vill,* pp. 170–171.

54. *E.M.R,* p. 153.

55. Ibid., p. 44.

56. Ibid., p. 191.

57. Ibid., p. 146.

58. Ibid., p. 154.

59. Ibid., p. 257.

60. Ibid., p. 154.

61. Ibid., p. 42.

62. Mollat, *The Poor in the Middle Ages,* p. 171; Duby, *Rural Economy and Country Life,* pp. 253–254.

63. *E.M.R,* p. 3.

64. Ibid, p. 30.

65. Ibid., p. 247.

66. Ibid., p. 247.

67. Ibid., p. 90.

68. W. O. Ault, *The Court Rolls of Ramsey Abbey and the Honour of Clare,* New Haven, 1928, p. xx.

69. Britton, *Community of the Vill,* pp. 174–175.

70. Levett, *Studies in Manorial History,* p. 140.

71. Vinogradoff, *Growth of the Manor,* p. 364.

72. Bellamy, *Crime and Public Order,* pp. 32–33.

73. Ibid., p. 33.

74. *Bedfordshire Coroners' Rolls,* pp. v–ix.

75. Ibid., pp. 58, 74, 76–77, 89–90.

76. Ibid., passim.; *E.M.R,* p. 238.

77. Bellamy, *Crime and Public Order,* p. 30.

78. Ibid., p. 160.

79. Ibid., p. 113.

80. Ibid., p. 87.

81. Ibid., p. 188.

82. *Bedfordshire Coroners' Rolls,* p. 107.

CHAPTER X
THE PASSING OF THE MEDIEVAL VILLAGE

1. H. C. Darby, "Domesday England," and R. E. Glasscock, "England Circa 1334," both in Darby, ed., *A New Historical Geography,* pp. 45–47, 143–145; Hallam, "Population Movements in England, 1086–1350," in *The Agrarian History of England and Wales,* vol. 2, p. 536, gives higher estimates.

2. J. C. Russell, "Late Medieval Population Patterns," *Speculum 20* (1945), p. 164.

3. Ian Kershaw, "The Great Famine and Agrarian Crisis in England, 1315–1322," in Hilton, ed., *Peasants, Knights, and Heretics,* p. 95.

4. Ibid., pp. 93–94, 102–104.

5. Alan H. R. Baker, "Changes in the Later Middle Ages," in Darby, ed., *A New Historical Geography,* pp. 291–318.

6. *E.M.R,* p. 337.

7. Ibid., p. 342.

8. Ibid., p. 351.

9. Ibid., p. 359.

10. Ibid., p. 361.

11. Ibid., p. 342.

12. Ibid., p. 364.

13. Ibid., p. 383.

14. Ibid., p. 373.

15. Ibid., p. 373.

16. Raftis, *Estates of Ramsey Abbey,* p. 253.

17. R. H. Hilton, *Bondmen Made Free: Medieval Peasant Movements and the English Rising of 1381,* New York, 1973, p. 147.

18. Ibid., p. 148.

19. Ibid., pp. 160–162.

20. Duby, *Rural Economy and Country Life,* p. 334.

21. Froissart, *Chronicles,* trans. by Geoffrey Brereton, Harmondsworth, England, 1968, p. 212.

22. Thomas Walsingham, *Historia Anglicana,* cited in R. B. Dobson, *The Peasants' Revolt of 1381,* London, 1970, pp. 373–375.

23. Hilton, *Bondmen Made Free,* p. 227.

24. Cited in Maurice Ashley, *Great Britain to 1688,* Ann Arbor, 1961, p. 147.

25. Hilton, *Transition from Feudalism to Capitalism,* p. 25; Dyer, Lords and Peasants, pp. 285–286; V.C.H. Hunts., vol. 1, p. 84.

26. Duby, *Rural Economy and Country Life,* p. 357.

27. *V.C.H. Hunts.,* p. 162.

28. Beresford, *Lost Villages,* p. 166.

29. R. A. Donkin, "Changes in the Early Middle Ages," and Baker, "Changes in the Later Middle Ages," both in Darby, ed., *A New Historical Geography,* pp. 82, 208, 212.

30. Bigmore, *Bedfordshire and Huntingdonshire Landscape,* p. 132.

31. Ibid., pp. 126–127.

32. Cited in Bigmore, *Bedfordshire and Huntingdonshire Landscape,* p. 136.

33. Baker, "Changes in the Later Middle Ages," in Darby, ed., *A New Historical Geography,* p. 211.

34. Ibid., p. 242.

35. Braudel, *Civilization and Capitalism,* vol. 1, p. 123.

36. Peter Laslett, *The World We Have Lost: England in the Industrial Age,* New York, 1971, p. 35.

37. Joan Thirsk, "Farming Techniques," in *The Agrarian History of England and Wales,* vol. 4, pp. 180–181.

38. Ault, *Open-Field Farming,* p. 143.

39. Dyer, *Lords and Peasants,* p. 372.

40. Ault, *Open-Field Farming,* p. 78.

41. *V.C.H. Hunts.,* p. 160.

42. Marc Bloch in *The Cambridge Economic History of Europe,* vol. 1, *The Agrarian Life of the Middle Ages,* ed. by M. M. Postan, Cambridge, 1966, p. 61.

General Bibliography

A Roll of the Household Expenses of Richard de Swinfield, ed. John Webb. London, 1853.

Adams, Henry, *Mont-St. Michel and Chartres.* Boston, 1913.

Adelson, Howard L., *Medieval Commerce.* Princeton, 1962.

Agrarian History of England and Wales, The. H. P. R. Finberg, general editor. Vol. 1, Pt. 1, Prehistory, edited by Stuart Piggott, Cambridge, 1981. Vol. 1, Pt. 2, a.d. 43–1042, edited by H. P. R. Finberg, Cambridge, 1972. Vol. 2, 1042–1350, edited by H. E. Hallam, Cambridge, 1988. Vol. 4, 1500–1640, edited by Joan Thirsk, Cambridge, 1967.

Albertus Magnus, *Opera Omnia,* vol. XII, *Quaestiones super de Animalibus,* ed. Berhardus Geyer. *Aschendorff,* 1955.

Alcock, N. W. "The Medieval Cottages of Bishops Clyst, Devon." *Medieval Archaeology 9* (1965): 146–153.

Allengry, Charles, *Les foires de Champagne.* Paris, 1915.

Anderson, R., *Examples of the Municipal, Commercial and Street Architecture of France and Italy from the 12th to the 15th century.* Edinburgh, n.d.

Anderson, W. F. D., *Castles of Europe: from Charlemagne to the Renaissance.* London, 1970.

Andreas Capellanus, *The Art of Courtly Love,* trans. J. J. Parry. New York, 1941.

Anglo-Saxon Chronicle, The, trans. James Ingram. London, 1923.

Annales Prioratus de Dunstaplia, ed. H. R. Luard. London, 1886.

Ariès, Philippe, and André Béjin, eds. *Western Sexuality: Practice and Precept in Past and Present Times.* London, 1985. *Centuries of Childhood,* trans. Robert Baldick. London, 1962.

Armitage, Ella, *Early Norman Castles.* London, 1912.

Astill, Grenville, and Annie Grant, eds. *The Countryside of Medieval England.* Oxford, 1988.

Aucassin and Nicolette and Other Medieval Romances and Legends, trans. Eugene Mason. New York, 1958.

Ault, W. O., *The Self-Directing Activities of Village Communities in Medieval England.* Boston, 1952. "Some Early Village By-Laws." *English Historical Review,* 1930.

Ault, Warren O., *Open-Field Farming in Medieval England: A Study of Village By-Laws.* New York, 1972. *Open-Field Husbandry and the Village Community: A Study of Agrarian By-Laws in Medieval England.* Philadelphia, 1965.

Autobiography of Giraldus Cambrensis, The. Edited and translated by H. E. Williams. London, 1937.

Babees' Book, The, trans. E. Richert. London, 1923.

Baldwin, J. F., "The Household Administration of Henry Lacy and Thomas of Lancaster." *English Historical Review,* 1927.

Barber, Richard W., *The Knight and Chivalry.* New York, 1970.

Barley, M. W. *The English Farmhouse and Cottage.* London, 1961.

Baskerville, C. R., "Dramatic Aspects of Medieval Folk-Festivals in England." *Studies in Philology,* 1920. "Mummers' Wooing Plays in England." *Modern Philology,* 1924.

Bateson, Mary, *Medieval England,* 1066–1350. London, 1905.

Bautier, R. H., "Les Foires de Champagne," in *Recueils Jean Bodin,* Vol. V, *La foire.* Brussels, 1953.

Bayet, Marie, *Les Châteaux de France.* Paris, 1927.

Beard, Mary, *Women as a Force in History.* New York, 1946.

Bedfordshire Coroners' Rolls. Translated by R. F. Hunnisett. Bedfordshire Historical Record Society 41 (1961).

Beeler, John, *Warfare in England, 1066–1189.* Ithaca, N.Y., 1966. *Warfare in Feudal Europe, 730–1200.* Ithaca, N.Y., 1966.

Bellamy, John G. *Crime and Public Order in the Later Middle Ages.* London, 1973.

Bemis, Albert, and Burchard, John, *The Evolving House.* Cambridge, 1933.

Bennett, H. S. *Life on the English Manor, A Study of Peasant Conditions, 1150–1400.* Cambridge, 1960 (first published in 1937).

Bennett, H. S., *Life on the English Manor.* Cambridge, England, 1960.

Benton, John F., "The Court of Champagne as a Literary Center," in *Speculum, XXXVI* (1961). "Comital Police Power and the Champagne Fairs," a paper presented before the American Historical Association, December 28, 1965. "Nicolas de Clairvaux à la recherche du vin d'Auxerre, d'après une lettre inédite du XIIe siècle," in *Annales de Bourgogne, XXXIV* (1962).

Benton, John, "Clio and Venus: An Historical View of Medieval Love," in F. X. Newman, ed., *The Meaning of Courtly Love.* Albany, 1968. "The Court of Champagne as a Literary Center." *Speculum,* 1961.

Beresford, Maurice, and John G. Hurst, eds. *Deserted Medieval Villages.* London, 1971.

Beresford, Maurice. *Studies in Leicestershire Agrarian History.* London, 1949.

Berkeley, 1975.

Bibolet, Françoise, "Le role de la guerre de cent ans dans le dévelope-ment des libertés municipales à Troyes," in *Mémoires de la Société académique d'agricultures, des sciences, arts et belles-lettres du département de l'Aube,* Vol. XCIX, 1939–1942. Troyes, 1945.

Bigmore, Peter. *The Bedfordshire and Huntingdonshire Landscape.* London, 1979.

Blair, Peter Hunter. *An Introduction to Anglo-Saxon England.* Cambridge, 1966.

Bloch, Marc, "Champs et villages." *Annales d'histoire économique et sociale,* 1934. "Village et seigneurie," *Annales d'histoire économique et sociale.* 1937. *Feudal Society,* trans. L. A. Manyon, 2 vols. Chicago, 1964. *Segneurie française et manoir anglaise.* Paris, 1960.

Boissonnade, P., *Life and Work in Medieval Europe,* trans. Eileen Power. New York, 1964.

Book of the Knight of La Tour-Landry, Compiled for the Instruction of His Daughters, The, ed. Thomas Wright. London, 1868.

Boserup, Ester, *The Conditions of Agricultural Growth.* London, 1965.

Bourquelot, Felix, "Etudes sur les foires de Champagne au XIIe, XIIIe et XIVe siècles" in Mémoires présentés par divers savants à l'Académie des Inscriptions et Belles-Lettres, Deuxième série. Paris, 1865.

Boutiot, T., *Dictionnaire topographique du département de l'Aube.* Paris, 1874. *Histoire de la ville de Troyes et de la Champagne méridionale.* Troyes, 1870.

Boyer, Marjorie N., "Medieval Pivoted Axles." *Technology and Culture,* 1960.

Brand, John, *Observations on Popular Antiquities.* London, 1900.

Braudel, Fernand. *Civilization and Capitalism 15th–18th Century.* Vol. 1, *The Structures of Everyday Life: The Limits of the Possible.* New York, 1981.

Braun, Hugh, *The English Castle.* London, 1936.

Briggs, Martin S., *The Architect in History.* Oxford, 1927. *A Short History of Building Crafts.* Oxford, 1925.

Brissand, Jean, *A History of French Public Law,* trans. James N. Garner. Boston, 1915.

Britton, Edward. *The Community of the Vill: A Study in the History of the Family and Village Life in Fourteenth-Century England.* Toronto, 1977. "The Peasant Family in Fourteenth-Century England." *Peasant Studies* 5 (1976): 2–7.

Brooke, Christopher, *From Alfred to Henry III, 871–1272.* Edinburgh, 1961.

Brown, R. Allen, *Dover Castle.* London, 1966 (Ministry of Works). *Rochester Castle.* London, 1969 (Ministry of Works).

Burtt, Joseph T., ed., "Account of the Expenses of John of Brabant and Henry and Thomas of Lancaster, 1292," in *Camden Miscellany.* London, 1853.

Cam, Helen. *Liberties and Communities in Medieval England: Collected Studies in Local Administration and Topography.* Cambridge, 1933.

Cambridge Economic History of Europe, Vol. II: Trade and Industry in the Middle Ages, ed. M. Postan and E. E. Rich. Cambridge, 1952. Vol. III: *Economic Organization and Policies in the Middle Ages,* ed. M. Postan, E. E. Rich, and Edward Miller. Cambridge, 1963

Cambridge Economic History of Europe, The, vol. I, *The Agrarian Life of the Middle Ages,* second edition, ed. M. M. Postan. Cambridge, England, 1966.

Cambridge Medieval History, 8 vols. New York, 1936.

Cantor, Leonard, ed. *The English Medieval Landscape.* Philadelphia, 1982.

Cartularium monasterii de Ramesia. Edited by William H. Hart. 3 vols. London, 1884–1893.

Carus-Wilson, E. M. *Essays in Economic History.* London, 1962.

Castiglioni, Arturo, *A History of Medicine,* trans. E. B. Krumbhaar. New York, 1946.

Cave, Roy C., and Coulson, Herbert H., ed., *A Source Book for Medieval Economic History.* New York, 1938.

Chambers, E. K., *The English Folk Play.* Oxford, 1933. *The Medieval Stage.* Oxford, 1903.

Chapelot, Jean, and Robert Fossier. *The Village and House in the Middle Ages.* Translated by Henry Cleere. Berkeley, 1985.

Chapin, Elizabeth, *Les villes de foire de Champagne.* Paris, 1937.

Chaucer, Geoffrey. *The Canterbury Tales.* Translated by Nevill Coghill. Baltimore, 1960.

Chertsey Abbey Court Rolls Abstracts. Edited by E. Toms. Surrey Record Society 38 (1937) and 48 (1954).

Choisy, Auguste, *Histoire de l'architecture,* 2 vols. Paris, 1899.

Chrétien de Troyes, *Perceval le Gallois ou le conte de Graal,* ed. Ch. Potvin. Mons, Belgium, 1866–1871. *Yvain,* trans. André Mary. New York, 1963.

Chronicle of Florence of Worcester, trans. Thomas Forester. London, 1854.

Chronicon abbatiae Rameseiensis. Edited by W. Dunn Macray. London, 1886.

Chronicon de Lanercost. Edited by J. Stevenson. Edinburgh, 1839.

Chronicon de Mailros, ed. J. Stephenson. Edinburgh, 1845.

Cipolla, Carlo M., "Currency Depreciation in Medieval Europe," in *Change in Medieval Society,* ed. Sylvia Thrupp. New York, 1964. *Money, Prices and Civilization in the Mediterranean World, Fifth to Seventeenth Century.* Princeton, 1956.

Clark, Elaine. "Some Aspects of Social Security in Medieval England." *Journal of Family History* 7 (1982): 307–320.

Clarke, W. K., *Liturgy and Worship.* London, 1950.

Cleator, P. E., *Castles and Kings.* London, 1963.

Cohen, Gustave, *Histoire de la chevalerie en France au moyen âge.* Paris, 1949.

Colman, F. S. *A History of the Parish of Barwick-in-Elmet, in the County of York.* Thoresby Society 17 (1908).

Colvin, H. M. "Domestic Architecture and Town Planning," in A. Lane Poole, ed., *Medieval England,* vol. 1: 77–97. London, 1958.

Colvin, H. M., ed., *Building Accounts of Henry III.* Oxford, 1971.

Cottrell, Leonard, *The Roman Forts of the Saxon Shore.* London, 1971 (Department of the Environment).

Coulton, G. G., *Life in the Middle Ages,* vol. III. Cambridge, England. 1928–9. *Medieval Village, Manor and Monastery.* New York, 1960.

Court Baron, The. Edited by F. W. Maitland and W. P. Baildon. London, 1891.

Court Roll of Chalgrave Manor. Edited by Marian K. Dale. Bedfordshire Historical Record Society 28 (1950).

Court Rolls of the Abbey of Ramsey and the Honour of Clare. Edited by Warren O. Ault. New Haven, 1928.

Court Rolls of the Manor of Carshalton from the Reign of Edward III to That of Henry VII. Translated by D. L. Powell. Surrey Record Society 2 (1916).

Court Rolls of the Wiltshire Manors of Adam de Stratton. Edited by R. B. Pugh. Wiltshire Archaeological Society Record Series 24 (1970).

Creekmore, Hubert, *Lyrics of the Middle Ages.* New York, 1959.

Crombie, A. C., *Medieval and Early Modern Science.* New York, 1959.

Cronne, H. A., *The Reign of Stephen, 1135–54, Anarchy in England.* London, 1970.

Crosland, Jessie, *Medieval French Literature.* New York, 1956.

Crozet, René, *Histoire de Champagne.* Paris, 1933.

Crump, C. G., and Jacob, E. F., ed., *The Legacy of the Middle Ages.* Oxford, 1926.

Curtius, Ernst Robert, *European Literature and the Latin Middle Ages.* New York, 1953.

Custumals of the Manors of Laughton, Willingdon, and Goring. Edited by A. E. Wilson. Sussex Record Society 60 (1961).

Custumals of the Sussex Manors of the Archbishop of Canterbury. Edited by B. C. Redwood and A. E. Wilson. Sussex Record Society 57 (1958).

Cutts, E. L. *Parish Priests and Their People in the Middle Ages in England.* London, 1898.

d'Andeli, Henri, *The Battle of the Seven Arts,* ed. L.J. Paetow. Berkeley, 1914.

Daniel-Rops, Henri, *Cathedral and Crusade.* London, 1956.

Darby, H. C. *A New Historical Geography of England Before 1600.* Cambridge, 1973.

d'Arobois de Jubainville, M. H., *Histoire des comtes de Champagne.* Paris, 1865.

d'Avenel, Vicomte G., *Histoire économique de la propriété, des salaires, des denrées et de tous les prix en général depuis l'an 1200 jusqu'en l'an 1800.* 7 vols. Paris, 1898.

Davenport, Frances G. *The Economic Development of a Norfolk Manor, 1086–1565.* Cambridge, 1906.

Davis, H.W.C., *England Under the Normans and Angevins, 1066–1272.* London, 1937.

Dawson, Christopher, *Mediaeval Religion and Other Essays.* London, 1934.

De Windt, Anne. "A Peasant Land Market and Its Participants, King's Ripton (1280–1400)." *Midland History* 4 (1978): 142–159.

De Windt, Edwin. *Land and People in Holywell-cum-Needingworth: Structures of Tenure and Patterns of Social Organization in an East Midlands Village, 1253–1457.* Toronto, 1972.

Delarue, Paul, ed., *The Borzoi Book of French Folk Tales.* New York, 1956.

Denholm-Young, N. *Collected Papers on Medieval Subjects.* Oxford, 1946.

Dion, Roger, *Histoire de la vigne et du vin en France des origines au XIVe siècle.* Paris, 1959.

Disciplina Clericalis. Heidelberg, 1911.

Ditchfield, P. H. *Old Village Life.* London, 1920.

Dix, Gregory, *The Shape of the Liturgy.* Westminster, 1943.

Dobson, R. B., ed. *The Peasants' Revolt of 1381.* London, 1970.

Dodwell, Barbara. "Holdings and Inheritance in East Anglia." *Economic History Review,* 2nd ser., 20 (1967): 53–66.

Douglas, David C., *The Norman Achievement, 1050–1100.* Berkeley, 1969. *William the Conqueror: the Norman Impact upon England.* Berkeley, 1967.

Downs, Norton, ed., *Basic Documents in Medieval History.* Princeton, 1959.

Du Boulay, F. R. H. *The Lordship of Canterbury.* London, 1966.

Du Colombier, Pierre, *Les chantiers des cathédrales.* Paris, 1953.

Duby, Georges, *Rural Economy and Country Life in the Medieval West,* trans. Cynthia Postan. Columbia, S.C., 1968.

Dutton, Ralph, *The Châteaux of France.* London, 1957.

Dyer, Christopher. "Families and Land in the West Midlands," in R. M. Smith, ed., *Land, Kinship, and Life Cycle.* Cambridge, 1986: 305–311. *Lords and Peasants in a Changing Society: The Estates of the Bishopric of Worcester, 680–1540.* Cambridge, 1980.

Echagüe, José Ortiz, *España: castillos y alcazares.* Madrid, 1956.

Edgington, Susan B. "Pagan Peverel: An Anglo-Norman Crusader." In P. Edbury, ed., *Crusade and Settlement.* Cardiff, 1985. "Ramsey Abbey vs. Pagan Peverel, St. Ives, 1107." *Records of Huntingdonshire 2* (1985).

Edward, second duke of York, The Master of Game, ed. W. A. Grohman and F. Baille. London, 1909.

Ekwall, Eilert. *Concise Oxford Dictionary of English Place Names.* Oxford, 1947.

Elton Manorial Records, 1279–1352. Edited by S. C. Ratcliff, translated by D. M. Gregory. Cambridge, 1946 (privately printed for the Roxburghe Club).

Emery, Richard, *The Jews of Perpignan in the Thirteenth Century, and Economic Study Based on Notarial Records.* New York, 1959.

English, Barbara. *A Study in Feudal Society: The Lords of Holderness, 1086–1260.* Oxford, 1979.

Esmein, Adhémar. *Le Mariage en droit canonique.* Edited by R. Génestal. 2 vols. Paris, 1929–1935.

Espinas, Georges, *Deux fondations de villes dans l'Artois et la Flandre française Xe–XVe siècles.* Paris, 1946. *La vie économique et sociale au moyen âge.* Fontenay-le-Comte, 1946. *La vie urbane de Douai au moyen âge.* Paris, 1913. *Les finances de la commune de Douai des orgines au XVe siècle.* Paris, 1902.

Estate Book of Henry de Bray, Northamptonshire c. 1289–1340, The. Edited by D. Willis. Camden Society, 3rd ser., 27 (1916).

Evans, Joan, *Life in Mediaeval France.* Oxford, 1925

Evans, Mary, *Costume Throughout the Ages.* Philadelphia, 1930.

Face, R. D., "Techniques of Business in the Trade Between the Fairs of Champagne and the South of Europe in the Twelfth and Thirteenth Centuries," in *Economic History Review,* 1958.

Fairholt, E. W, *Satirical Songs and Poems on Costume.* London, 1899.

Faith, Rosamond J. "Peasant Families and Inheritance Customs in Medieval England." *Agricultural History Review* 4 (1966): 77–95.

Faral, Edmond, *La vie quotidienne au temps de Saint Louis.* Paris, 1938.

Faral, Edmond, *Les jongleurs en France au moyen âge.* Paris, 1910.

Fedden, Henry R., and Thomson, John, *Crusader Castles.* London, 1957.

Field, John. *English Field-Names, a Dictionary.* Newton Abbot, 1972.

Field, R. K. "Worcestershire Peasant Buildings, Household Goods, and Farming Equipment in the Later Middle Ages." *Medieval Archaeology* 9 (1965): 105–145.

Finberg, H. P. R. *Tavistock Abbey: A Study in the Social and Economic History of Devon.* Cambridge, 1951.

Foix, Gaston de la, *Le Livre de la chasse,* ed. Paul Lacroix. Paris, 1886.

Formilli, C. J. G., *The Castles of Italy.* London, 1933.

Frank, Grace, *The Medieval French Drama*. Oxford, 1954.

Franklin, Alfred, *La vie privée au temps des primiers Capétiens*. Paris, 1911.

Frederick II, emperor of Germany, *The Art of Falconry*, trans. Casey A. Wood and F. Marjorie Fyfe. Stanford, 1961.

Froissart, Jean. *Chronicles*. Translated by Geoffrey Brereton. Harmondsworth, England, 1968.

Fulcher of Chartres, *A History of the Expedition to Jerusalem, 1095–1127*, trans. Frances Rita Ryan, ed. Harold S. Fink. Knoxville, 1969.

Galbert of Bruges, *The Murder of Charles the Good, Count of Flanders*, trans. James Bruce Ross. New York, 1967.

Ganshof, F. L., *Feudalism*, trans. Philip Grierson. New York, 1964.

Gasquet, F. A., *Parish Life in Medieval England*. London, 1929.

Gasquet, F. A., *Parish Life in Medieval England*. London, 1922.

Gautier, Léon, *Chivalry*, trans. D. C. Dunning. London, 1959.

Geiringer, Karl, *Musical Instruments: Their History in Western Culture from the Stone Age to the Present*. New York, 1945.

Gesta Francorum et Aliorum Hierosolimitanorum, The Deeds of the Franks and Other Pilgrims to Jerusalem, ed. Rosalind Hill. London, 1962.

Gesta Stephani, *The Deeds of Stephen*, trans. K. R. Potter. London, 1955.

Gies, Joseph, *Bridges and Men*. New York, 1963.

Girart de Roussillon, *Chanson de geste*, trans. Paul Meyer. Paris, 1884.

Giuseppi, M. S., "The Wardrobe and Household Accounts of Bogo de Clare, 1284–6." *Archaelogica*, 1920.

Godefroy de Paris, *Chronique, suivie de la taille de Paris en 1313*. Paris, 1827.

Godfrey, John. *The English Parish, 600–1300*. London, 1969.

Goodman of Paris, The, trans. Eileen Power. London, 1928.

Gower, John. *Le Miroir de l'Omme*. In *Complete Works of John Gower*. Edited by G. C. Macaulay. 4 vols. Oxford, 1899–1902.

Gras, N. S. B., *The Economic and Social History of an English Village, 909–1928*. Cambridge, Mass., 1930.

Gray, Howard L. *English Field Systems*. Cambridge, Mass., 1915.

Guibert de Nogent, *Autobiography*, trans. C. C. Swinton Bland. London, 1925.

Guilbert, Aristide, *Histoire des villes de France*. Paris, 1845.

Guillaume de Lorris and Jean de Meung, *Le roman de la Rose*, trans. André Mary. Paris, 1949.

Hahn, Hanno, *Hohenstaufenburgen in Süditalien*. Ingelheim, Germany, 1961.

Hali Meidenhod. Edited by Oswald Cockayne. London, 1922.

Hamlin, Talbot, *Architecture through the Ages*. New York, 1940.

Hanawalt, Barbara. "Childrearing Among the Lower Classes of Medieval England." *Journal of Interdisciplinary History 8* (1972): 1–22. "Community, Conflict, and Social Control: Crime in the Ramsey Abbey Villages." *Mediaeval Studies 39* (1977): 402–423. *Crime and Conflict in English Communities, 1300–1348*. Cambridge, Mass., 1979. *The Ties That Bound: Peasant Families in Medieval England*. New York, 1986.

Harvey P. D. A. *A Medieval Oxfordshire Village: Cuxham, 1240 to 1400*, Oxford, 1965.

Harvey, John, *English Mediaeval Architects: a Biographical Dictionary Down to 1550*. London, 1954. *The Gothic World, 1100–1600*. London, 1950. *The Gothic World, 1100–1600*. London, 1950.

Harvey, P. D. A., *A Medieval Oxfordshire Village, Cuxham, 1240 to 1400*. Oxford, 1964.

Haskins, Charles Homer, *The Normans in European History*. New York, 1915. *The Renaissance of the Twelfth Century*. Cambridge (Mass.), 1927. *The Rise of the Universities*. New York, 1923. *Studies in the History of Mediaeval Science*. Cambridge (Mass.), 1927.

Hassall, W. O. *How They Lived: An Anthology of Original Accounts Written Before 1485*. New York, 1962.

Hazeltine, Harold D., "Roman and Canon Law in the Middle Ages," Cambridge Medieval History, Vol. V. New York, 1929.

Hazlitt, W. C., *Faiths and Folklore of the British Isles*, 2 vols. New York, 1965. *Old Cookery Books and Ancient Cuisine*. London, 1902.

Headlam, Cecil, *The Story of Chartres*. London, 1902.

Heaton, Herbert, *Economic History of Europe*. New York, 1936.

Heeren, A. H. L., *Essai sur l'influence des croisades*. Trans. from German to French by Charles Villers. Paris, 1808.

Hellman, Robert, and O'Gorman, Richard, ed. and trans., Fabliaux, *Ribald Tales from the Old French*. New York, 1965.

Hennings, Margaret A., *England Under Henry III, Illustrated from Contemporary Sources*. London, 1924.

Herlihy, David, *Pisa in the Early Renaissance: A Study of Urban Growth*. New Haven, 1958.

Herr, Friedrich, *The Medieval World*, trans. Janet Sondheimer. London, 1961.

Hilton, R. H., *A Medieval Society: the West Midlands at the End of the Thirteenth Century*. London, 1966. *Decline of Serfdom in Medieval England*. London, 1969. *Bond Men Made Free, Medieval Peasant Movements and the English Rising of 1381*. New York, 1973. "The Content and Sources of English Agrarian History Before 1500." *Agricultural History Review 3* (1955): 3–19. *The Decline of Serfdom in Medieval England*. London, 1969. *The English Peasantry in the Later Middle Ages*. Oxford, 1975. "Medieval Agrarian History," in *The Victoria County History of Leicestershire 2* (1954): 145–198. *A Medieval Society: The West Midlands at the End of the Thirteenth Century*. New York, 1966.., ed. *Peasants, Knights, and Heretics: Studies in Medieval English Social History*. Cambridge, 1981. ed. *The Transition from Feudalism to Capitalism*. London, 1984.

Historical Works of Giraldus Cambrensis, trans. Thomas Forester and Sir Richard Colt Hoare, ed. Thomas Wright. London, 1913.

History of Technology, vol. II, ed. Charles Singer, E. J. Holmyard, A. R. Hall, and Trevor Williams. Oxford, 1956.

History of Technology, Vol. II, ed. Charles Singer, E. J. Holmyard, A. R. Hall, and Trevor Williams. Oxford, 1956.

Hollister, C. Warren, *The Military Organization of Norman England*. Oxford, 1965.

Holmes, Urban Tigner, Jr., and Klenke, Sister M. Amelia, O. P., *Chrétien, Troyes and the Grail*. Chapel Hill, N.C., 1959.

Holmes, Urban Tigner, Jr., *Daily living in the Twelfth Century, Based on the Observations of Alexander Neckam in London and Paris*. Madison, Wis., 1952.

Homans, G. C., *English Villagers of the Thirteenth Century*. New York, 1960. "The Rural Sociology of Medieval England," in *Past and Present*, 1953.

Homans, George C. *English Villagers of the Thirteenth Century*. New

York, 1975 (first published in 1941). "The Rural Sociology of Medieval England." *Past and Present 4* (1953): 32–43.

Hoskins, W. G. *The Making of the English Landscape.* London, 1955. *The Midland Peasant: The Economic and Social History of a Leicestershire Village.* London, 1957.

Howard, G. E., *A History of Matrimonial Institutions.* Chicago, 1904.

Howell, Cecily. *Land, Family, and Inheritance in Transition, Kibworth Harcourt 1288–1709.* Cambridge, 1983. "Peasant Inheritance Customs in the Midlands, 1280–1700," in Jack Goody, ed., *Rural Society in Western Europe.* Cambridge, 1976: 112–155.

Huvelin, P., *Essai historique sur le droit des marchés et des foires.* Paris, 1897.

Inglis, Brian, *A History of Medicine.* New York, 1965.

Jervis, W. W., *The World in Maps, a Study in Map Evolution.* New York, 1937.

John of Garland, *Morale Scolarium,* ed. L. J. Paetow. Berkeley, 1927.

John of Salisbury, *Metalogicon,* trans. and ed. Daniel D. McGarry, Berkeley, 1955.

Johnston, James B. *The Place Names of England and Wales.* London, 1915.

Joinville, Jean de, and Villehardouin, Geoffroi, *Chronicles of the Crusades,* trans. M.

Joinville, Jean de, *Life of St. Louis,* trans. M. R. B. Shaw. Baltimore, 1963.

Jones, Andrew. "Harvest Customs and Labourers' Perquisites in Southern England, 1150–1350." *Agricultural History Review 25* (1977): 14–22, 98–107.

Keeton, George W., *The Norman Conquest and the Common Law.* London, 1966.

Kerridge, E. "A Reconsideration of Some Former Husbandry Practices." *Agricultural History Review 3* (1955): 27–38.

Kibre, Pearl, *The Nations in the Medieval Universities.* Cambridge (Mass.), 1948. *Scholarly Privileges in the Middle Ages.* Cambridge (Mass.), 1962.

Knoop, Douglas, and Jones, G. P., "The English Medieval Quarry," in *Economic History Review,* November 1938. *The Medieval Mason.* Manchester, 1933.

Kohler, Carl, *A History of Costume.* London, 1928.

Kosminsky, E. A. *Studies in the Agrarian History of England in the Thirteenth Century.* Oxford, 1956.

L'Histoire de Guillaume Maréchal, comte de Striguil et de Pembroke, régent d'Angleterre de 1216 à 1219, ed. Paul Meyer. Paris, 1891–1901.

La Chace dou Serf, ed. Baron Jerome Pichon. Paris, 1840.

Labarge, Margaret Wade, *A Baronial Household of the Thirteenth Century.* New York, 1966.

Lacroix, Paul, *Costumes Historiques de la France.* Paris, 1860.

Lanel, Luc, *L'Orfèvrerie.* Paris, 1949.

Langland, William, *Piers the Ploughman,* trans. into modern English by J. F. Goodridge. London, 1959. *The Vision and Creed of Piers Plowman.* Edited by Thomas Wright. London, 1887. The Vision of Piers Plowman. Edited by A. V. C. Schmidt. London, 1984.

Langlois, Charles-Victor, *La connaissance de la nature et du monde au moyen âge.* Paris, 1911. *La société au XIII siècle d'après dix romans d'aven-* ture. Paris, 1914. *La Vie en France au moyen âge de la fin du XIIe au milieu du XIVe siècle, d'après des moralistes du temps.* Paris, 1925.

Laslett, Peter. *The World We Have Lost: England Before the Industrial Age.* New York, 197 I.

Latouche, Robert, *The Birth of Western Economy,* trans. E. M. Wilkinson. London, 1961.

Lavedan, Pierre, *French Architecture.* London, 1956.

Le courtois d'Arras, in *Jeux et sapience du moyen-âge,* ed. Albert Pauphilet. Paris, 1941.

Le Goff, Jacques, *La civilisation de l'occident médiéval.* Paris, 1964.

Le Jeu de St. Nicholas, in *Jeux et sapience.*

Le Roman de la rose ou Guillaume de Dole, ed. G. Servois. Paris, 1893.

Le Roman du castelain de Couci et de la dame de Fayel, ed. John E. Matzke and Maurice Delbouille. Paris, 1936.

Le Roy Ladurie, Emmanuel. Montaillou, *The Promised Land of Error.* Translated by Barbara Bray. New York, 1978.

Lea, Henry Charles, *History of the Inquisition in the Middle Ages.* New York, 1888.

Leach, A. F., *The Schools of Medieval England.* London, 1915.

Lecoy de la Marche, A., *La chaire française au moyen âge.* Paris, 1886. *La société au treizième siècle,* Paris, 1888.

Lecoy de la Marche, A., *La Chaire française au moyen âge.* Paris, 1886.

Lefèvre, André, "Les finances de la Champagne au XIIIe et XIV siècles," in *Bibliothèque de l'École des Chartes,* 4th series, IV and V. Paris, 1868–9.

Lennard, R. *Rural England 1086–1135: A Study of Social and Agrarian Conditions.* Oxford, 1959.

Lestocquoy, J., *Les villes de Flandre et d'Italie.*

Levett, A. E. *Studies in Manorial History.* Oxford, 1938.

Lewis, Alun, "Roger Leyburn and the Pacification of England, 1256–7." *English Historical Review,* 1939.

L'Image du Monde de Maître Gossoulin, trans. into Modern French, O. H. Prior. Paris, 1913.

Longlois, Charles-Victor, *La Vie en Grance au moyen âge de la fin du XIIe au milieu du XIVe siècle d'après des moralistes du temps.* Paris, 1925.

Longnon, Auguste, *Documents rélatifs au comté de Champagne et de Brie, 1172–1367.* 3 vols. Paris, 1904.

Lopez, Robert S., "Some Tenth Century Towns," in *Medievalia et Humanistica,* 1955.

Lopez, Robert S., and Raymond, Irving W., *Medieval Trade in the Mediterranean World.* New York, 1955.

Luchaire, Achille, *Les communes françaises à l'époque des Capétiens directs.* Paris, 1911. *Social France at the Time of Philip-Augustus.* New York, 1929.

Maitland, Frederic William. *Domesday Book and Beyond, Three Essays in the Early History of England.* New York, 1966 (first published in 1897).

Mannyng, Robert, *Handlyng Synne,* and William of Wadington's *Manuel des Pechiez,* ed. Frederick Furnival. London, 1901–3.

Marchegay, Paul A., and Salmon, André, eds., *Chroniques des comtes d'Anjou.* Paris, 1856–71.

Marcus, Jacob R., *The Jew in the Medieval World, a Source Book, 315–1791.* Cincinnati, 1938.

Mawer, A., and F. M. Stenton. *The Place-Names of Bedfordshire and Huntingdonshire.* London, 1926.

Mazaros, J. P., *Histoire des corporations françaises d'arts et métiers.* Paris, 1878.

McCulloch, Florence, "The Funeral of Renard the Fox in a Walters Book of Hours," in *Journal of the Walters Art Gallery,* Baltimore, 1962–3.

Medieval Customs of the Manors of Taunton and Bradford-on-Tone. Edited by T. J. Hunt. Somerset Record Society 66 (1962).

Milham, Willis, *Time and Timekeepers.* New York, 1923.

Miller, Edward, and John Hatcher. *Medieval England: Rural Society and Economic Change, 1086–1348.* London, 1978.

Millett, F. B., *Craft Guilds of the Thirteenth Century in Paris.* Kingston (Ont.), 1915.

Mollat, Michel. *The Poor in the Middle Ages, an Essay in Social History.* Translated by Arthur Goldhammer. New Haven, 1986.

Moore, Ellen W. *The Fairs of Medieval England: An Introductory Study.* Toronto, 1985.

Moorman, J. R. H. *Church Life in England in the Thirteenth Century.* Cambridge, 1945.

Morris, William Alfred, *The Medieval English Sheriff to 1300.* Manchester, England, 1927.

Müller-Warner, Wolfgang, *Castles of the Crusades.* New York, 1966.

Mundy, John H., and Riesenberg, Peter, ed., *The Medieval Town.* Princeton, 1958.

Mundy, John H., *Liberty and Political Power in Toulouse, 1050–1230.* New York, 1954.

Myrc, John. *Instructions for Parish Priests.* Edited by E. Peacock. London, 1868.

New Oxford History of Music, vol. II, *Early Medieval Music up to 1300,* ed. Dom Anselm Hughes. London, 1954.

Nichols, J. R., *Bells through the Ages, the Founders' Craft and the Ringers' Art.* London, 1928.

Norgate, Kate, *The Minority of Henry III.* London, 1912.

Norman, A. V. B., *The Medieval Soldier.* New York, 1971.

O'Neil, B. H. St. J., *Castles: an Introduction to the Castles of England and Wales.* London, 1973 (Ministry of Works).

Ochinsky, D., "Medieval Treatises on Estate Management." *Economic History Review,* 1956.

Ogg, Oscar, *The 26 Letters.* New York, 1948.

Oman, C. W. C., *The Art of War in the Middle Ages.* Ithaca, N.Y., 1953.

Oman, Charles, *A History of the Art of War in the Middle Ages.* New York, 1924.

Ordericus Vitalis, Ecclesiastical History of England and Normandy, trans. Thomas Forester, 4 vols. London, 1858.

Orwin, C. S., *The Open Fields.* Oxford, 1967.

Owst, G. R. *Literature and Pulpit in Medieval England.* Oxford, 1961. Preaching in Medieval England. Oxford, 1926. Literature and Pulpit in Medieval England. Oxford, 1961.

Paetow, L. J., *Guide to the Study of Medieval History.* New York, 1931.

The Arts Course at Medieval Universities with Special Reference to Grammar and Rhetoric. Champagne, Ill., 1910.

Page, F. M. *The Estates of Crowland Abbey: A Study in Manorial Organization.* Cambridge, 1934.

Painter, Sidney, *Feudalism and Liberty,* ed. Fred A. Cazel, Jr. Baltimore, 1961. *Studies in the History of the English Feudal Barony.* Baltimore, 1943. *William Marshal, Knight Errant, Baron and Regent of England.* Baltimore, 1933. *French Chivalry.* Ithaca, N.Y., 1962.

Pantin, W. A. *The English Church in the Fourteenth Century.* Cambridge, 1955.

Paris, Gaston, ed., "Le Lai du Lecheoir," *Romania,* 1879.

Paris, Matthew, *English History from the Year 1235 to 1273,* trans. J. A. Giles. London, 1854.

Parker J. H., and Turner, T. H., *Some Account of Domestic Architecture in England.* Oxford, 1877.

Parker, John Henry, *ABC of Gothic Architecture.* Oxford, 1910.

Parrish, Carl, *A Treasury of Early Music.* New York, 1958.

Peckham, W. D., ed. "Thirteen Custumials of the Sussex Manors of the Bishop of Chichester." *Sussex Record Society Publications 31* (1925).

Peers, Charles, *Pevensey Castle.* London, 1953 (Ministry of Works).

Perks, J. C., *Chepstow Castle.* London, 1962 (Ministry of Works).

Pevsner, Nikolaus, *An Outline of European Architecture.* London, 1943.

Pfander, Homer G. *The Popular Sermon of the Medieval Friar in England.* New York, 1937.

Phythian-Adams, C. *Continuity, Fields, and Fission: The Making of a Midland Parish.* Leicester University, Department of English Local History, *Occasional Papers,* 3rd ser., 4 (1978).

Pimsler, Martin. "Solidarity in the Medieval Village? The Evidence of Personal Pledging at Elton, Huntingdonshire." *Journal of British Studies 17* (1977): 1–11.

Piper, Otto, *Abriss der Burgenkunde.* Leipzig, 1914.

Pirenne, Henri. *Economic and Social History of Medieval Europe.* Translated by I. E. Clegg. New York, 1937.

Platt, Colin. *The Parish Churches of Medieval England.* London, 1981.

Platts, Graham. *Land and People in Medieval Lincolnshire.* Lincoln, England, 1985.

Pollock, F. and F. W. Maitland. *The History of English Law Before the Time of Edward I.* Cambridge, 1968.

Poole, Austin L., *Medieval England,* vol. I. Oxford, 1958.

Poole, Reginald L., *Medieval Reckonings of Time.* New York, 1935.

Postan, M. M. *Essays on Medieval Agriculture and General Problems of the Medieval Economy.* Cambridge, 1968. "The Famulus: The Estate Labourer in the Twelfth and Thirteenth Centuries." *Economic History Review* Supplement No. 2. Cambridge, 1954. *The Medieval Economy and Society: An Economic History of Britain, 1100–1500.* Berkeley, 1972. "Village Livestock in the Thirteenth Century." *Economic History Review,* 2nd ser., 15 (1962): 219–249.

Postan, M. M., and J. Z. Titow. "Heriots and Prices on Winchester Manors." *Economic History Review,* 2nd ser., 11 (1959): 392–413.

Postan, M. M., *Essays on Medieval Agriculture and General Problems of the Medieval Economy.* Cambridge, England, 1973. *The Medieval Economy and Society. An Economic History of Britain, 1100–1300.* Berkeley, 1972.

Power, Eileen, "The Position of Women," in C. G. Crump and E. F.

Jacob, eds., *Legacy of the Middle Ages.* Oxford, 1926. *The Wool Trade in English Medieval History.* London, 1941.

Power, Eileen, trans. and ed., *The Goodman of Paris.* London, 1928.

Powicke, F. M., *King Henry III and the Lord Edward,* 2 vols. Oxford, 1947.

Prentice, Sartell, *The Voices of the Cathedral.* New York, 1938.

Prestage, Edgar, ed., *Chivalry, A Series of Studies to Illustrate Its Historical Significance and Civilizing Influence.* London, 1928.

Prou, Maurice, "La Fôret en Angleterre et en France." *Journal des savants,* 1915.

Prou, Maurice, and d'Auriac, Jacques, *Actes et comptes de la commune de Provins de l'an 1271 à l'an 1330.* Provins, 1933.

Rabinowitz, Louis, *The Social Life of the Jews of Northern France in the XII–XIVth Centuries.* London, 1938.

Raftis, J. A. *The Estates of Ramsey Abbey: A Study of Economic Growth and Organization.* Toronto, 1957. ed. *Pathways to Medieval Peasants.* Toronto, 1981. "Social Structures in Five East Midland Villages: A Study of Possibilities in the Use of Court Roll Data." *Economic History Review,* 2nd. ser., 18 (1965): 83–100. *Tenure and Mobility: Studies in the Social History of the Mediaeval English Village.* Toronto, 1964. *Warboys: Two Hundred Years in the Life of an English Mediaeval Village.* Toronto, 1974.

Rashdall, Hastings, *The Universities of Europe in the Middle Ages.* Oxford, 1936.

Razi, Zvi. *Life, Death, and Marriage in a Medieval Parish: Economy, Society, and Demography in Halesowen, 1270–1400.* Cambridge, 1980.

Réau, Louis, *La civilisation française au moyen âge.* Paris, 1958.

Reese, Gustave, *Music in the Middle Ages.* New York, 1940.

Renart, Jean, *L'Escoufle,* ed. Joseph Bédier. Paris, 1913. *Galeran de Bretagne,* ed. Lucien Foulet. Paris, 1925.

Renn, D. F., *Norman Castles.* London and New York, 1968. *Three Shell Keeps.* London, 1969 (Ministry of Works).

Renouard, Yves, "Le Grand Commerce des vins de Gascogne au moyen âge." *Revue historique,* 1959.

Reynolds, Robert L., *Europe Emerges, Transition Toward an Industrial World-Wide Society.* Madison, Wis., 1961.

Richardson, H. G. "The Parish Clergy of the Thirteenth and Fourteenth Centuries." *Transactions of the Royal Historical Society,* 3rd ser., 6 (1912): 89–128. "Business Training in Medieval Oxford." *American Historical Review,* 1941.

Robert, Ulysse, *Les signes d'infamie au moyen âge, Juifs, Sarrasins, hérétiques, lépreux, cagots et filles publiques.* Paris, 1891.

Roberti Grosseteste Epistolae episcopi quondam Lincolniensis. Edited by H. R. Luard. London, 1861.

Roberts, Brian K. *The Making of the English Village, a Study in Historical Geography.* London, 1987. "Village Plans in County Durham: A Preliminary Statement." *Medieval Archaeology 16* (1972): 33–56.

Roger of Wendover, *Flowers of History,* trans. J. A. Giles, 2 vols. London, 1849.

Rogers, James E. Thorold, *Six Centuries of Work and Wages.* New York, 1884.

Roserot, Alphonse, *Troyes, son histoire, ses monuments des origines à 1790.* Troyes, 1948.

Roth, Cecil, "The Jews in the Middle Ages," *Cambridge Medieval History,* Vol. VII. New York, 1932.

Rotuli hundredorum tempore Hen. III & Edw. I in Turr' Lond' et in curia receptae scaccarii Westm. asservati, 2 vols. London, 1812, 1818.

Round, J. H., "Castle Watchmen." *English Historical Review,* 1920. "The Staff of a Castle in the Twelfth Century." English Historical Review, 1920.

Round, J. H., *Feudal England.* London, 1895.

Rowley, Trevor, and John Wood. *Deserted Villages.* Aylesbury, England, 1982.

Rowley, Trevor, ed. *The Origins of Open-Field Agriculture.* London, 1981.

Runciman, Steven, *A History of the Crusades.* Cambridge, 1951. *The Medieval Manichee.* New York, 1961.

Russell, J. C. "Late Medieval Population Patterns." *Speculum 20* (1945). *Late Ancient and Medieval Population.* Philadelphia, 1958.

Rutebeuf, *Oeuvres complètes,* 2 vols., ed. Edmond Faral and Julia Bastin. Paris, 1959–60.

Sabine, Ernest L., "Latrines and Cesspools of Medieval London," in *Speculum,* 1934.

Sachs, Curt, *The History of Musical Instruments.* New York, 1940.

Saige, Gustave, *Les Juifs du Languedoc antérieurement au XIVe siècle.* Paris, 1881.

Salusbury, G. T., *Street Life in Medieval England.* Oxford, 1939.

Salzman, L. F., *English Life in the Middle Ages.* London, 1926.

Sanders, I. J., *English Baronies, a Study of Their Origin and Descent, 1086–1327.* Oxford, 1960.

Sanford, Vera, *A Short History of Mathematics.* Boston, 1930.

Saul, Nigel. *Scenes from Provincial Life, Knightly Families in Sussex, 1280–1400.*

Sawyer, P. H., ed. *Medieval Settlement: Continuity and Change.* London, 1976.

Sayous, Edouard, *La France de St. Louis d'après la poésie nationale.* Paris, 1866.

Scammell, Jean. "Freedom and Marriage in Medieval England." *Economic History Review 27* (1974): 523–537. "Wife-Rents and Merchet." *Economic History Review,* 2nd ser., 29 (1976): 487–490.

Schmidt, Richard, *Burgen des Deutschen Mittelalter.* Munich, 1957.

Schumer, Beryl. *The Evolution of Wychwood to 1400: Pioneers, Frontiers, and Forests.* Leicester University, Department of English Local History, *Occasional Papers,* 3rd ser., 6 (1984).

Searle, Eleanor. "Freedom and Marriage in Medieval England: An Alternative Hypothesis." *Economic History Review,* 2nd ser., 29 (1970): 482–490. *Lordship and Community: Battle Abbey and Its Banlieu.* Toronto, 1974. "Seigneurial Control of Women's Marriage: The Antecedents and Function of Merchet in England." *Past and Present 82* (1979): 3–43.

Sée, Henri, *Histoire économique de la France.* Paris, 1939.

Seebohm, F. *The English Village Community: An Essay on Economic History.* London, 1883.

Select Cases from the Coroners' Rolls. Edited by G. J. Turner. London, 1896.

Select Cases from the Ecclesiastical Courts of the Province of Canterbury, c. 1200–1301. Edited by Norma Adams and Charles Donahue. London, 1981.

Select Civil Pleas, a.d. 1200–1203. Edited by William Paley Baildon. London, 1896.

Select Pleas in Manorial and Other Seignorial Courts, Hen. III–Edw. I. Edited by F. W. Maitland. London, 1889.

Shelby, L. R., "The Role of the Master Mason in Medieval English Building," in Speculum, 1964.

Shirley, W. W., ed., Royal and Other Historical Letters Illustrative of the Reign of Henry III Vol. I, 1216–1235. London, 1862.

Shneidman, J. Lee, The State and Trade in the Thirteenth Century. Madrid, 1958.

Smail, R. C., Crusading Warfare, 1097–1193. Cambridge, 1956.

Société Jean Bodin, Recueils, La Ville. Brussels, 1954.

Southern, R. W., The Making of the Middle Ages. New Haven, 1953.

Spufford, M. A Cambridgeshire Community: Chippenharn from Settlement to Enclosure. Leicester University, Department of English Local History, Occasional Papers 20 (1964).

Stenton, Doris M., English Society in the Early Middle Ages (1066–1307). Harmondsworth, England, 1951. The Englishwoman in History. London, 1957.

Stenton, Sir Frank, The First Century of English Feudalism. Oxford, 1961.

Stephenson, Carl, "The Problem of the Common Man in Early Medieval Europe." American Historical Review, 1946. Borough and Town, a Study of Urban Origins in England. Cambridge (Mass.), 1933. Medieval History. New York, 1935. Also, fourth edition, ed. and rev. Bryce Lyon, New York, 1962. Medieval Institutions. Ithaca, 1954.

Stone, E. N., trans., Three Old French Chronicles of the Crusades. Seattle, 1939.

Stow, John, A Survay of London. London, 1598 (University Microfilms).

Stow, John. Survey of London. Edited by H. B. Wheatley. London, 1956.

Straub, Hans. A History of Civil Engineering, trans. E. Rockwell. London, 1953.

Strayer, Joseph R., Feudalism. Princeton, 1965.

Stuckert, Howard M. Corrodies in the English Monasteries: A Study in English Social History of the Middle Ages. Philadelphia, 1923.

Tacitus. De vita Iulii Agricola and De Germania. Edited by Alfred Gudeman. Boston, 1928.

Tannahill, Reay, Food in History. New York, 1973.

Taylor, C. C. "Polyfocal Settlement and the English Village." Medieval Archaeology 21 (1977): 189–193.

Technology in Western Civilization, ed. Melvin Kranzberg and Caroll W. Pursell, Jr. New York, 1967.

Thatcher, Oliver J., and McNeal, Edgar, A Source Book for Medieval History. New York, 1905.

The Chronicle of Jocelin of Brakelond, trans. L. C. Jane. New York, 1966.

Thirsk, Joan. The Rural Economy of England, Collected Essays. London, 1984.

Thompson, A. Hamilton, Military Architecture in England During the Middle Ages. London, 1912. The English Clergy and Their Organization in the Later Middle Ages. Oxford, 1947.

Thomson, Daniel, The Weavers' Craft, a History of the Weavers' Incorporation of Dunfermline. Paisley, Scotland, 1903.

Thorndike, Lynn, "Elementary and Secondary Education in the Middle Ages," in Speculum, 1940. ed., University Records and Life in the Middle Ages. New York, 1944.

Thorndike, Lynn, "More Copyists' Final Jingles," in Speculum, 1956. A History of Magic and Experimental Science During the First Thirteen Centuries of Our Era. 8 vols. New York, 1964.

Thrupp, Sylvia, The Merchant Class of Medieval London, 1300–1500. Chicago, 1948. A Short History of the Worshipful Company of Bakers of London. London, 1933.

Titow, J. Z. English Rural Society, 1200–1350. London, 1969. Winchester Yields: A Study in Medieval Agricultural Productivity. Cambridge, 1972.

Tomkeieff, O. G., Life in Norman England. New York, 1967.

Tout, T. F., Chapters in the Administrative History of Mediaeval England, vols. I and II. Manchester, England, 1920.

Toy, Sidney, A History of Fortification from 3000 B.C. to A.D. 1700. London, 1955. The Castles of Great Britain. London, 1953.

Toynbee, Margaret, S. Louis of Toulouse and the Process of Canonization in the Fourteenth Century. Manchester, 1929.

Trench, Charles Chenevix, The Poacher and the Squire, a History of Poaching and Game Preservation in England. London, 1967.

Trow-Smith, Robert. History of British Livestock Husbandry. 2 vols. London, 1957–1959.

Turner, G. J., ed., Select Pleas of the Forest. London, 1900.

Turner, H. T., ed., Manners and Household Expenses of England in the Thirteenth and Fifteenth Centures. London, 1841.

Tuulse, A., Castles of the Western World. London, 1958.

Victoria History of the Counties of England: Huntingdonshire. Edited by W. Page and G. Proby. 3 vols. London, 1926, 1932, 1936.

Vinogradoff, Paul. The Growth of the Manor. London, 1911.

Vitry, Jacques de, Exempla, or Illustrative Stories from the Sermones Vulgares, ed. Thomas F. Crane. London, 1890.

Von Simson, Otto, The Gothic Cathedral. New York, 1962.

Walker, Kenneth, Story of Medicine. New York, 1954.

Walker, Williston, A History of the Christian Church. New York, 1959.

Walter of Henley's Husbandry, Together with an Anonymous Husbandry, Seneschaucie, and Robert Grosseteste's Rules, trans. Elizabeth Lamond. London, 1890.

Wenger, O. P., Les Monnaies. Lusanne, n.d.

West, Stanley. "The Anglo-Saxon Village of West Stow: An Interim Report of the Excavations, 1965–1968." Medieval Archaeology 13 (1969): 1–20.

White, Lynn, Medieval Technology and Social Change. Oxford, 1963. "Technology and Invention in the Middle Ages," in Speculum, 1940.

Wilkinson, B., Studies in the Constitutional History of the Thirteenth and Fourteenth Centuries. Manchester, England, 1952.

William of Malmesbury, Historia novella, trans. K.R. Potter. London, 1955.

Willis, R., The Architectural History of Canterbury Cathedral. London, 1845.

Wood, Margaret E., The English Mediaeval House. London, 1965.

Wright, Lawrence, Clean and Decent. London, 1960.

Wright, Richardson, The Story of Gardening. New York, 1934.

Young, Karl, The Drama of the Medieval Church. Oxford, 1933.

COPYRIGHT ACKNOWLEDGMENTS

PHOTOGRAPHY CREDITS

Art Resource, NY : pp. 44, 125, 159, 292.

A.M Rosati/ Art Resource, NY.: 322.

Archive Alinari/ Regione Umbria Venezia/ Art Resorce, NY.: 213.

Biblioteca Nazionale Napoli/ Art Resource, NY : pp. 63.

Giraudon/ Art Resource, NY: pp. 2, 52, 58, 70, 92, 108, 140, 153, 178, 184, 201, 264, 275, 288, 295, 306, 309, 333, 340, 343, 346.

Museo dell'Opera de Duomo, Firenze/ Art Resource, NY.: 215.

The Pierpont Morgan Library/Art Resorce, NY.: 208.

Scala/ Art Resource, NY : pp. 94, 157, 165, 194, 228, 229, 230, 274, 287, 324.

Scala/ Galleria degli Uffizi Firenze/Art Resource, NY.: 255.

Scala/ Biblioteca Statale Lucca/Art Resource, NY.: 311.

Scala/ Archi Rampanti. Paris, Notre- Dame/Art Resource, NY.: 301.

Victoria & Albert Museum, London/ Art Resource, NY: pp. 36, 62, 76, 79, 150, 180, 190.

Visuals Arts Library/ Art Resource, NY.: 320.

Biblioteque Municipale, Besancon, France : pp. 146.

The Bridgeman Art Library International Ltd.: 335.

Alecto Historical Editions, London/ The Bridgeman Art Library International Ltd.: pp. 15 T, 35, 135.

Antony Miles, Ltd., Salisbury, Wiltshire, UK/The Bridgeman Art Library International Ltd.: pp. 124 B.

Archivo de la Corona de Aragon, Barcelona, Spain/The Bridgeman Art Library International Ltd.: pp. 29, 262.

Archivo Catedral de Tarazona, Zaragoza, Aragon, Spain/ The Bridgeman Art Library Ltd.: 248.

Ashmolean Museum, Oxford, UK/The Bridgeman Art Library International Ltd.: pp. 167.

Biblioteque Municipale, Rouen, France/ The Bridgeman Art Library International Ltd.: pp. 120.

Bibliotheque Nationale, Paris, France/The Bridgeman Art Library International Ltd.: pp. 15 B, 25, 32, 40, 68, 89, 110, 143, 196, 218, 252 B, 312, 315, 327.

Bibliotheque Royale de Begique, Brussels, Belgium/ he Bridgeman Art Library International Ltd.: 250, 345.

Bischopric of Vic, Osona, Catalonia, Spain/ The Bridgeman Art Library International Ltd.: 293.

British Library, London, UK/The Bridgeman Art Library International Ltd.: pp. 14 B, 20, 43, 60, 64 T, 64 B, 66, 73, 100, 122, 127, 147, 154, 164, 166, 168, 169, 172, 175, 186, 189, 198 T, 203, 220, 232, 235, 244, 245, 252 T, 256, 259, 278, 280, 284, 294, 316, 334, 336, 344.

British Museum, London/The Bridgeman Art Library International Ltd.: pp. 134.

Carnac, Brittany, France/The Bridgeman Art Library International Ltd.: pp. 124 T.

Corpus Christi College, Oxford, UK/The Bridgeman Art Library International Ltd.: pp. 78, 138, 148, 195, 206.

GLOSSARY

AD CENSUM Status of villeins who pay a cash rent in lieu of labor services.

AD OPUS Status of villeins owing labor services.

AID A special obligation of a vassal to provide money for such occasions as his lord's ransom, the marriage of his daughter, the knighting of his son or for going on Crusade.

ALLURE Wall-walk, passage behind the parapet of a castle wall.

ALMONER Official appointed to distribute alms.

AMERCEMENT A fine.

ASSART Tract of wasteland cleared or drained to be added to village arable.

ASSIZE OF BREAD AND ALE Royal law fixing prices and standards.

BAILEY Courtyard.

BAILIFF The lord's chief official on the manor.

BALK Turf left unplowed to provide separation between strips.

BALLISTA Engine resembling a crossbow, used in hurling missiles or large arrows.

BARBICAN An outwork or forward extension of a castle gateway

BARON Noble of high rank, in England a tenant-in-chief holding his lands directly from the king.

BEADLE Manorial official, usually assistant to reeve.

BENEFICE The grant made by a lord, usually of land.

BONDMAN Serf, q.v., villein.

BOON-WORK Obligation of tenants for special work services, notably the lord's harvest.

BUTTERY Room for the service of beverages.

BYLAWS Rules made by open-field villagers governing cultivation and grazing.

CASTELLAN Governor of a castle

CASTLE-GUARD Feudal obligation to serve in the garrison of a castle, either for a period each year or during war.

CAT Assault tower.

CATAPULT Stone-throwing engine, usually employing torsion.

CELLARER Official of a monastery responsible for food supplies.

CENSUARIUS Tenant ad censum.

CHAMBERLAIN Household official in charge of the lord's chamber

CHAPLAIN OR CHANCELLOR Priest or monk in charge of the chapel and of the secretarial department of the castle

CHARTER Official document, usually deed or grant of privilege.

CHEMISE Inner walled enclosure of a castle.

CHEVAGE Payment, typically in kind, owed annually by villein living outside the manor.

CHEVAUCHÉE (CAVALCADE) Feudal duty to accompany the lord on a minor expedition or as an escort.

COLÉE OR BUFFET Traditional blow administered to the newly made knight at his dubbing.

CORBEL A stone or timber bracket supporting a projection from a wall.

CORRODY Old age pension, usually purchasable from a monastery, consisting of lodging, food, and incidentals.

COTTER Tenant of a cottage, usually holding little or no land.

CRENELATION A notched battlement made up of alternate crenels (openings) and merlons (square sawteeth)

CROFT Garden plot of a village house.

CURIA Courtyard.

CURIA REGIS English royal council and court of justice.

CURTAIN A castle wall enclosing a courtyard.

CUSTUMAL Document listing obligations and rights of tenants.

DEMESNE Part of the manor cultivated directly by the lord.

DISTRAINT Summons or arrest.

DONJON OR KEEP The inner stronghold of a castle.

DRAWBRIDGE A wooden bridge leading to a gateway, capable of being raised or lowered.

EARL Count; highest English title in the Middle Ages.

ENCEINTE An enclosing wall, usually exterior, of a fortified place.

ESCALADE Scaling of a castle wall.

ESSOIN Excuse for non-attendance in court, or delay permitted a defendant.

EXTENT Document enumerating lands, services, and rents of a manor.

EYRE English circuit court.

EYRE Royal circuit court ("justices in eyre").

FARM Lease.

FEE, FIEF Land granted by a lord in return for services.

FEUDALISM Medieval social and political system by which the lord-vassal relationship was defined.

FIEF, FEE OR FEUD Land or revenue-producing property granted by a lord in return for a vassal's service.

FOREBUILDING A projection in front of a keep or donjon, containing the stairs to the main entrance.

FRANKPLEDGE Police system by which every member of a tithing was responsible for the conduct of every other member.

FURLONG Plot of arable land, subdivision of a field.

GARDEROBE Latrine.

GERSUM Entry fee for taking possession of a tenancy.

GLEBE Land assigned to support the parish church.

GORE Wedge of arable land created by irregularity of terrain and plowing in strips.

HALL Principal living quarters of a medieval castle or house.

HALLMOTE Manorial court.

HAMSOKEN Assault in the victim's own house.

HAYWARD OR MESSOR Lesser manorial official; assistant to reeve.

HEADLAND Segment of land left at end of plow strips for turning plow around.

HERIOT A death-duty to the lord; in the case of a villein on a manor, usually the best beast.

HEUSHIRE House rent.

HIDE Tax assessment unit of land area, varying in size, theoretically 120 acres.

HONOR Great estate of a tenant-in-chief.

HOST OR OST Feudal military service in the lord's army.

HUE-AND-CRY Criminal apprehension system by which all within earshot were required to give chase to the malefactor.

HUNDRED Administrative division of English shire (county).

INFANGENETHEF Right to prosecute thieves caught in the act within a territory and to confiscate their goods.

JUSTICIAR Regent in England under William I, chief minister until the 1220s.

KEEP See donjon.

LEIRWITE Fine levied against an unmarried woman for sexual misconduct.

LOVE-DAY (DIES AMORIS) Opportunity given litigants to reconcile differences.

MACHICOLATION A projection in the battlements of a wall with openings through which missiles can be dropped on besiegers

MANGONEL A form of catapult.

MANOR Estate held by a lord and farmed by tenants who owed him rents and services, and whose relations with him were governed by his manorial court.

MANOR Estate consisting of lord's demesne and tenants' holdings.

MARCHER LORD Lord of a border district, such as the boundaries of Wales and Scotland.

MARSHAL Household official in charge of the stables, later a royal officer.

MERCHET Fee paid by villein for a daughter's marriage.

MERLON Part of a battlement, the square "sawtooth" between crenels.

MESNIE Military personnel of a castle household.

MESSUAGE House and yard.

MEURTRIÈRE Arrow loop, slit in battlement or wall to permit firing of arrows, or for observation.

MORTUARY Death duty paid by villein to parish church, usually second-best beast or chattel.

MOTTE An earthwork mound on which a castle was built.

MULTURE Portion of meal or flour kept by the miller in payment for his services.

ORIEL Projecting room on an upper floor (in the medieval sense; later an upper-floor bay window).

PANNAGE Fee to allow pigs to feed on forest mast.

PARAPET Protective wall at the top of a fortification, around the outer side of the wall-walk.

PINFOLD OR PUNFOLD The lord's pound for stray animals.

PLEDGING Legal institution by which one villager served as guaranty for another's court appearance, veracity, good conduct, payment of a debt, etc.

PORTCULLIS Vertical sliding wooden grille shod with iron suspended in front of a gateway, let down to protect the gate.

POSTERN OR SALLY-PORT Secondary gate or door.

PROVOST Feudal or royal magistrate.

QUARTER Unit of volume, eight bushels.

QUINTAIN Dummy with shield mounted on a post, used as a target in tilting.

RAM Battering-ram.

REEVE Manorial overseer, usually a villager elected by tenants of the manor.

REGALIAN Royal.

RELIEF A fine paid by the heir of a vassal to the lord for the privilege of succeeding to an estate.

RING Unit of volume, four bushels.

SAPPING Undermining, as of a castle wall.

SCREENS Wooden partition at the kitchen end of a hall, protecting a passage leading to buttery, pantry and kitchen.

SCUTAGE Shield-tax, a tax paid in lieu of military service.

SEISIN Legal possession of a property.

SELION Plow strip.

SENESCHAL OR STEWARD Manager of an estate or a household.

SERF Peasant burdened with week-work, merchet, tallage and other obligations; bondman, villein.

SHERIFF Royal official in charge of a shire or county.

SOLAR Originally a room above ground level, but commonly applied to the great chamber or a private sitting room off the great hall.

SPRINGALD War engine of the catapult type, employing tension.

SQUIRE Knight-aspirant.

STEWARD OR SENESCHAL Chief official of an estate, supervisor of the lord's manors.

SUIT Attendance.

TALLAGE Annual tax levied by lord on villeins.

TALLY, TALLY-STICK Reeve's method of accounting for manor's production, deliveries, receipts and expenditures; notched stick on which it was kept.

TITHE Payment to church consisting of a tenth of produce.

TITHING Unit of ten or twelve village men mutually responsible for each other's conduct.

TOFT Yard of a village house.

TREBUCHET War engine developed in the Middle Ages employing counterpoise.

VASSAL A person granted the use of land in return for homage, fealty and military service.

VILLEIN A non-free man, owing heavy labor service to a lord, subject to his manorial court, bound to the land and subject to certain feudal dues.

VIRGATE Land unit theoretically sufficient to support a peasant family, varying between 18 and 32 acres (in Elton, 24).

WARD Courtyard or bailey.

WARDENS OF AUTUMN Officials appointed by the villagers to help supervise harvest work.

WARDSHIP Right of guardianship exercised by a lord over a minor.

WEEK-WORK Principal labor obligation of a villein, comprising plowing and other work every week throughout the year.

WOODWARD Manorial official in charge of the lord's woodland.

INDEX

A

G

Galbert of Bruges, 27
Galeran, 253, 257, 318
Gamel, Geoffrey, 189
Gamel, Gilbert, 216
Gamel, Robert, 156, 158, 160
Gamel, Roger, 160, 214
games, see recreation
Gangdays, see Rogation Days
gardens, 37, 233, 240, 251-252
garderobe, see latrine, see also sanitation
Garin de Loherain, 339
Garnier de Traînel, bishop of Troyes, 295
garrison, 12, 19, 38, 51, 97, 98, 101, 102
Gate Fulford, Battle of, 13
Gate, Margery atte, 176
Gate, Muriel atte, 175
gatehouse, 8, 9, 17, 18, 98, 111, 114, 117
gates of Troyes, 240
Gautier de Nemours, 260
geese, 193
Gembloux, Sigebert de, 325, 326
Genoa,, 230, 233, 234, 236, 239, 341, 343, 345, 346
Geoffrey, count of Anjou, 87-88
Geoffrey of Monmouth, 89
geography, 310
geometry, 308, 310
Gerald of Wales (Giraldus Cambrensis), 60, 69, 72, 199, 201, 308
German castles, 118
Gervaise of Canterbury, 326
Gesta Stephani, 45, 99, 102
Ghent, 15, 231, 232, 236, 239, 341, 344
ghetto, 241, 276
Gibraltar, 345
Gibson, Edmund, 225
Gilbert de Barneville, 283
Gioia del Colle, 117
Girant de Roussillon, 87, 91
Gisors, 112, 115
glass, 34, 56
    stained, 304-305
Glastonbury Abbey, 167, 187
gleaning, 82, 186, 190

glebe, 85, 200
goats, 132, 193
godparents, 258, 259
Godswein, Henry, 160
goldsmiths, 233, 271, 274, 275
Goliards, 313
Gonzaga family, 117
Goodman of Paris, 249
gore (wedge of land), 186
Gormaz, 117
Goscelin, Richer son of, 161
Goscelin, Roger, 160
Gothic architecture, 299-305
government, 331-337
Gower, John, 166
grammar, 307, 309-311
Grands Jours de Troyes, 335
Gratian, 177, 317, 335
Gravina, 117
grazing rights, 187, 191
Great Raveley (Huntingdonshire), 183
green, village, 137, 138
Gregory III, Pope, 147
Gregory VII, Pope, 116
Grosseteste, Robert, bishop of Lincoln, 39, 57, 62, 65, 143, 146-147, 148
grosso (groat), 280
Guader, Ralph de, earl of Norfolk, 15
guarantees to merchants, 239, 340
Guardaira, Alcala de, 117
Guibert of Nogent, 295, 309
guilds, 270, 272, 273-275, 281, 303
Guillaume de Lorris, 317
Guiot de Dijon, 63
gunpowder, 111-112

H

Hadrian's Wall, 12
Hale (Lincolnshire), 201
hall, 17, 18, 19, 33-36, 37-39, 51, 59, 103, 112, 114, 115, 116
Hallam, H. E., 166
hallmote, see manorial court

houses, 125, 126, 136–137, 163–164, 224, 227, 240, 243–247, 279
    construction of, 136, 163–164
    hall, 163
    heating of, 164
    interiors of, 164
    of peasants, 78
rebuilding of, 163
    size of, 137
    types of, 125, 126
Howard, Katherine, 226
Howell, Cicely, 166
hue-and-cry, 75, 212–213, 218
Hugo of La Marche, 314, 326, 332
hundred, 26, 133
Hundred Rolls survey of 1279, 136, 139, 149, 152, 154–155, 156–158, 159
Hundred Years' War, 111, 222, 346
Hungarians, 231
Huns, 229, 231, 232
hunting, 24, 42, 67–72
Huntingdon, 139, 145
Huntingdonshire, 120, 121, 131–132, 133–134, 139, 187, 209, 225, 226
huntsman, 67–68, 73
Hurst, John, 121

I

Industrial Revolution, 237, 347
infangenethef, 217
inheritance, 78, 90, 126, 155, 173–174
    ceremony attending on, 83
Innocent II, Pope, 235

Innocent III, Pope, 235, 277, 294, 311
Innocent IV, Pope, 237, 277
Inquisition, 297
insurance, cargo, 345
interest, 282–283
interior decoration, 37
Irish castles, 119
iron and steel, 270–271
irrigation, 126, 225
Isabel of Leicester, countess of Pembroke, 22
Isabella, countess of Arundel, 44
Isabelle of Angoulême, 45
Isère, 239
Italian castles, 116–117
Ivel, River, 131
Ives, Saint, 135
ivory, 342

J

Jacob of Troyes, "Master of the Jews," 276
Jacques de Vitry, 263
James of St. George, 18–19
Jean de Colmieu, 12
Jean of Tours, 87–88
Jeanne de Navarre (Jeanne of Champagne), 344
Jerusalem, 282, 288, 294, 310
jesters, 63
Jeu de Robin et de Marion, 260–261
Jews, 241, 276–177, 282, 283, 286, 287, 343
Joan of Arc, 45, 115, 116, 346
Jocelin of Brakelond, 39, 73, 93
John VIII, Pope, 299
John of Brabant, 54, 64
John of Crakehall, 74
John of Gaunt, 115

John of Gloucester, 300
John of Salisbury, 307, 316
John of Toul, 30
Joinville, Jean, Sieur de, 95, 260, 336
jongleurs, see minstrels
Joufroi, 318
journeymen, 274, 275, 276, 281
jousting, 92, 93–94
judicial combat, 22, 25
judicial duel, see trial by combat
jurors, 159, 210, 213, 216–217
jury system, 25, 28, 83
justice, 25, 26, 28, 52, 77, 80, 82–84, 236, 333–335
justiciar, 26, 99
Justinian, 317, 334

K

keep, 12, 13, 18, 35, 98, 100, 103, 112, 115, 118, 119
    rectangular, 15, 16, 17, 19, 35, 38, 114–115
    round, 17, 18, 115, 116
    shell, see shell keeps
    transitional, 17, 115
Keepers of the Fair, 283, 311, 340, 341, 344
Kemys, Sir Nicholas, 112
Kenilworth, 16, 101–102, 112, 114–115
Ketel, John, 158, 160, 174
Kibworth Harcourt, 166
Kidwelly, 115
King's Ripton (Huntingdonshire), 142, 158–159, 175
kitchen, 26–27, 38, 51, 54–55, 59, 60–61, 78, 246
The Kite, 318